P9-DIW-605

Soho and Trafalgar Square
Pages 100–111

Bloomsbury and Fitzrovia
Pages 122–33

Covent Garden and the Strand
Pages 112–21

Holborn and the Inns of Court
Pages 134–43

Smithfield and Spitalfields
Pages 162–73

The City
Pages 144–61

Bloomsbury
and Fitzrovia

Smithfield
and
Spitalfields

Holborn and the
Inns of Court

Soho and
Trafalgar
Square

Covent
Garden
and the
Strand

The City

R I V E R   T H A M E S

South Bank

Southwark and
Bankside

Whitehall and
Westminster

Whitehall and Westminster
Pages 70–87

Piccadilly and St. James's
Pages 88–99

South Bank
Pages 186–93

Southwark and Bankside
Pages 174–85

LONDON

EYEWITNESS TRAVEL

LONDON

Main Contributor **Michael Leapman**

LONDON, NEW YORK,
MELBOURNE, MUNICH AND DELHI
www.dk.com

Project Editor Jane Shaw
Art Editor Sally Ann Hibbard
Editor Tom Fraser
Designers Pippa Hurst, Robyn Tomlinson
Design Assistant Clare Sullivan

Contributors
Christopher Pick, Lindsay Hunt

Photographers
Max Alexander, Philip Enticknap,
John Heseltine, Stephen Oliver

Illustrators
Brian Delf, Trevor Hill, Robbie Polley

This book was produced with the assistance
of Websters International Publishers.

Printed and bound in China by L. Rex Printing Company Limited

First American Edition, 1993
14 15 16 17 10 9 8 7 6 5 4 3 2 1

Published in the United States by
DK Publishing, 375 Hudson Street,
New York, New York 10014

**Reprinted with revisions 1994, 1995, 1996, 1997, 1999, 2000 (twice),
2001, 2002, 2003, 2004, 2005, 2006, 2007, 2008, 2009, 2010, 2011,
2012, 2013, 2014**

Copyright © 1993, 2014 Dorling Kindersley Limited, London
A Penguin Random House Company

ISSN 1542-1554
ISBN 978-1-46541-050-4

Floors are referred to throughout in accordance with European usage,
i.e. the "first floor" is the floor above ground level.

MIX
Paper from
responsible sources
FSC™ C018179
www.fsc.org

**The information in this
DK Eyewitness Travel Guide is checked annually.**
Every effort has been made to ensure that this book is as up-to-date as possible
at the time of going to press. Some details, however, such as telephone numbers,
opening hours, prices, gallery hanging arrangements, and travel information are
liable to change. The publishers cannot accept responsibility for any consequences
arising from the use of this book, nor for any material on third party websites, and
cannot guarantee that any website address in this book will be a suitable source of
travel information. We value the views and suggestions of our readers very highly.
Please write to: Publisher, DK Eyewitness Travel Guides, Dorling Kindersley,
80 Strand, London, WC2R 0RL, UK, or email: travelguides@dk.com.

Front cover main image: The Houses of Parliament and Lambeth Bridge

◀ View of St. Paul's Cathedral from One New Change

Contents

Portrait of Sir Walter Raleigh (1585)

Introducing
London

Bedford Square doorway (1775)

The Broadwalk at Hampton Court (c.1720)

Beefeater at the Tower of London

Bandstand in St. James's Park

St. Paul's Church: Covent Garden

Travelers' Needs

Houses of Parliament

Survival Guide

HOW TO USE THIS GUIDE

This Eyewitness Travel Guide helps you get the most from your stay in London with the minimum of practical difficulty. The opening section, *Introducing London*, locates the city geographically, sets modern London in its historical context, and describes the regular highlights of the London year. *London at a Glance* is an overview of the city's specialties. *London Area by Area* takes you around the city's areas of interest. It describes all the main sights with maps, photographs, and detailed illustrations. In addition, six planned walking routes take you to parts of London you might otherwise miss.

Well-researched tips on where to stay, eat, shop, and be entertained are in *Travelers' Needs*. *Children's London* lists highlights for young visitors, and *Survival Guide* tells you how to do anything from mailing a letter to using the Underground.

London Area by Area

The city has been divided into 16 sightseeing areas, each with its own section in the guide. Each section opens with a portrait of the area, summing up its character and history and listing all the sights to be covered. Sights are numbered and clearly located on an *Area Map*. After this comes a large-scale *Street-by-Street Map* focusing on the most interesting part of the area.

Finding your way around the area section is made simple by the numbering system. This refers to the order in which sights are described on the pages that complete the section.

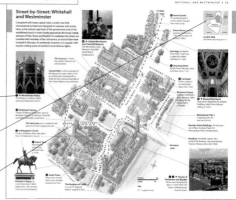

Color-coding on each page makes the area easy to find in the book.

A locator map shows you where you are in relation to surrounding areas. The area of the *Street-by-Street Map* is highlighted.

Numbered circles pinpoint all the listed sights on the area map. St. Margaret's Church, for example, is ❻

Recommended restaurants in the area are listed and marked on the map.

1 Area Map
For easy reference, the sights in each area are numbered and located on an *Area Map*. To help the visitor, the map also shows Underground and train stations.

Stars indicate the sights that no visitor should miss.

A locator map shows you where you are in relation to surrounding areas. The area of the *Street-by-Street Map* is shown in red.

A suggested route for a walk takes in the most attractive and interesting streets in the area.

2 Street-by-Street Map
This gives a bird's-eye view of the heart of each sightseeing area. The numbering of the sights ties in with the area map and the fuller descriptions on the pages that follow.

London at a Glance

Each map in this section concentrates on a specific theme: *Remarkable Londoners, Museums and Galleries, Churches, Parks and Gardens, Ceremonies.* The top sights are shown on the map; other sights are described on the following two pages.

Each sightseeing area is color-coded.

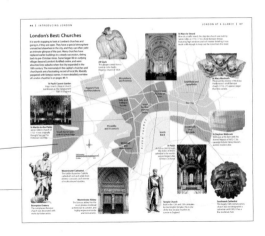

Practical Information lists all the information you need to visit every sight, including a map reference to the *Street Finder* at the back of the book.

Numbers refer to each sight's position on the area map and its place in the chapter.

3 Detailed information on each sight

All important sights in each area are described in depth in this section. They are listed in order, following the numbering on the *Area Map*. Practical information on opening hours, telephone numbers, websites, admission charges, and facilities available is given for each sight. The key to the symbols used can be found on the back flap.

The facade of each major sight is shown to help you spot it quickly.

The Visitors' Checklist provides the practical information you will need to plan your visit.

Stars indicate the most interesting architectural details of the building, and the most important works of art or exhibits on view inside.

Numbered circles point out major features of the sight listed in a key.

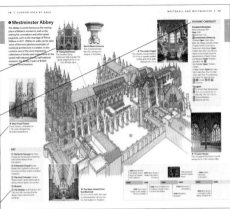

4 London's major sights

These are given two or more full pages in the sightseeing area in which they are found. Historic buildings are dissected to reveal their interiors; museums and galleries have color-coded floor plans to help you find important exhibits.

INTRODUCING LONDON

GREAT DAYS IN LONDON

For things to see and do, visitors to London have endless options. Whether here for several days, or just wanting a flavor of this great city, you need to make the most of your time. Over the following pages, you'll find itineraries for some of the best attractions London has to offer, arranged first by theme and then by length of stay. Price guides on pages 10–11 include travel on public transportation, food, and admission for two adults, while family prices are for two adults and two children.

Café at the National Portrait Gallery with a view of Trafalgar Square

History and Culture

Two adults
allow at least £140

- Art at the National Gallery
- Coffee with a view
- Houses of Parliament
- Buckingham Palace

Morning
Start the day by 10am in **Trafalgar Square** *(see p104)*. This is when the **National Gallery** *(see p106)* opens. Give yourself an hour and a half. The gallery is free, but visitors are encouraged to make a donation. Then go for coffee at the Portrait Restaurant on the top floor of the neighboring **National Portrait Gallery** *(see p104)*, which has a great view over Trafalgar Square and Nelson's column. Set off down Whitehall to Parliament Square, a 15-minute walk that may be extended by the passing distractions of Horse Guard's Parade, **Banqueting House** *(see p82)*, and **Downing Street** *(see p77)*. See the **Houses of Parliament** *(see pp74–5)* before visiting the next highlight, the magnificent **Westminster Abbey** *(see pp78–9)*. There are a number of inexpensive lunch spots around St. James's Park tube station, such as Fuller's Ale and Pie House, 33 Tothill Street. Or go to the more pricy but attractive Inn the Park (reserve ahead; 020 7451 9999) by the lake in **St. James's Park** *(see p95)*.

Afternoon
On the far side of St. James's Park is **Buckingham Palace** *(see p96–7)*. The Queen's Gallery has changing exhibitions, and you can buy regal souvenirs in its shop. For tea, head up past St. James's Palace to Piccadilly. You may not feel you can afford £40 per person for tea at the Palm Court at the **Ritz** *(see p93)*, but there are several cafés and patisseries nearby, such as Richoux at 172 Piccadilly. For the best evening entertainment, get tickets for a West End play or show. These should be bought in advance *(see p335)*, although last-minute tickets are sometimes available at the theater box offices.

Shopping in Style

Two adults
allow at least £55

- St. James's – shopping with history
- Old Bond Street for style
- Browse in trendy Covent Garden and the Piazza

Morning
Start in Piccadilly and **St. James's Street**, *(see pp90–91)*, home of suppliers to royalty and historic fashion leaders: John Lobb, the bootmaker is at No. 9 and Lock the hatter at 6. Turn right into Jermyn Street for high-class men's tailors such as Turnbull & Asser and New Lingwood, outfitters to Eton College. Floris the perfumer at 89 was founded in 1730, and the cheese shop Paxton & Whitfield at 93 has been here since 1740. Walk through Piccadilly Arcade to **Fortnum & Mason** *(see p305)*, where the Fountain Tea Room can provide refreshment before buying souvenirs. Stop in at

Historic shopping mall at the Burlington Arcade, Piccadilly

◀ *The Thames from Somerset House Terrace towards the City (c.1750–51) by Canaletto*

The Queen's House, Greenwich

The Royal Academy *(see p92)* and the **Burlington Arcade** *(see p93)*, before heading up **Old Bond** and **New Bond** streets *(see p315)* for the most chic shopping in town, with art galleries, antiques, and designer shops. Try South Molton Street for women's fashion and Oxford Street for **Selfridges** department store *(see p313)*.

Afternoon
Head to **Covent Garden** *(see p116)*. Take a look around the **London Transport Museum** *(see p116)*, then wander the Piazza and streets to the north; Floral Street is renowned for high fashion. Check out alternative lifestyles in **Neal's Yard** *(see p117)*. Stop for tea in Paul bakery and café at 29 Bedford Street.

The Great Outdoors

Two adults
allow at least £100

- Sail to the Cutty Sark
- Ponds and a memorial in the Palace gardens
- Tea at Kensington Palace

Morning
Take a 1-hour boat trip from Westminster Millennium Pier to **Greenwich** *(see pp240–45)*. A morning is easily passed at this UNESCO World Heritage Site. There's the Maritime Museum, Royal Observatory, Queen's House, and Cutty Sark. Have a snack lunch overlooking the river at the historic **Trafalgar Tavern** *(see p244)*.

Afternoon
Return by boat and head to **Kensington Gardens** *(see p210)*. Admire the boats on the Round Pond, and see what's in the **Serpentine Gallery** *(see p212)*. To the east is the Princess Diana Memorial Fountain. By the Long Water is the delightful statue of Peter Pan. Visit **Kensington Palace** *(see p212)*, Princess Diana's former home. Have tea in the Palace's Orangery Tea Room.

A Family Fun Day

Family of Four
allow at least £250

- Take the kids to the Tower
- Lunch at St. Katharine's Dock
- Enjoy the undersea world
- Explore Chinatown

Morning
Head to the **Tower of London** *(see pp156–9)*, London's top visitor attraction and an established family favorite. Buy tickets ahead of time to avoid the line. The fascinating castle and Crown Jewels will take at least a couple of hours to explore. For lunch, head across the road to **St. Katharine's Dock** *(see p160)* where, among an eclectic collection of yachts and pleasure cruisers, there are several good places to eat.

Predators at the London Aquarium

Afternoon
The **London Eye** is a thrilling trip above the city on the South Bank *(see p191*; online bookings can be made at www.london eye.com).

Vertigo sufferers need not panic – there are plenty of entertainment options at and below ground level, especially in **County Hall** *(see p190)*, which was the seat of London's local government for more than 60 years. This leisure complex is home to the Sea Life London Aquarium and the London Dungeon. Older children will enjoy the video games and simulators, bowling alley, and bumper cars in the Namco Station. Afterward, head to **Chinatown** *(see p110)*, situated in and around Gerrard Street, which has many superb restaurants, colorful shops, and a vibrant street life. Go for an early Chinese supper of *dim sum*, or small dishes. If the kids are still going strong, end the day with a movie at one of the many theaters in **Leicester Square** *(see p105)*.

View of the Houses of Parliament from the London Eye, South Bank

2 days in London

- Enjoy a panoramic spin on the London Eye
- Admire Wren's masterpiece, St. Paul's Cathedral
- Take a Beefeater tour of the Tower of London

Day 1
Morning Start off by examining monuments to England's kings and queens on a self-guided tour of **Westminster Abbey** (pp78–81). Don't miss the intricate Lady Chapel and peaceful cloisters. Next, wander through **Parliament Square** (p76) into idyllic **St. James's Park** (p95), with its pelicans and black swans, reaching **Buckingham Palace** (p96–7) in time for some pomp and circumstance at the 11:30am Changing of the Guard ceremony. If it's fall or winter, try **Horse Guards Parade** (p82) instead. Then walk through stately **Trafalgar Square** (p104) into the West End. Buy theater tickets for the evening at bargain prices from the official discount booth on **Leicester Square** (p105).

Afternoon Head to **Chinatown** (p110) for dim sum, then spend an hour or two admiring works by Van Eyck, Van Gogh, and Constable at the **National Gallery** (pp106–109). If there's time before the show, head to Covent Garden's **Piazza and Central Market** (p116) to watch the street performers.

Day 2
Morning The **Tower of London** (pp156–9) is a must-see. Two hours is enough time to join an entertaining Beefeater tour and inspect the murderous-looking Tudor weaponry in the White Tower. Afterward, head to the **Monument** (p154), Sir Christopher Wren's splendid 17th-century column built to commemorate the Great Fire of London. Climb its spiral staircase for a spectacular view that takes in landmarks old and new. Next, walk to Wren's glorious masterpiece, **St. Paul's Cathedral** (pp150–53). Highlights include the Whispering Gallery, the spectacular dome, and the crypt.

Naval gunship HMS *Belfast* moored in front of Tower Bridge

Afternoon Cross the Millennium Bridge to Bankside, taking in views of **Tower Bridge** (p155). Grab lunch at one of the artisan food stands or cafés at **Borough Market** (p178), then stroll to **Shakespeare's Globe** (p179) for an enthralling auditorium tour. Next door is **Tate Modern** (pp180–83), housing paintings and art installations on a magnificent scale. End the day with a ride on the **London Eye** (p191), timing it as the sun sets over the city.

3 days in London

- Uncover England's history at Westminster Abbey and the Houses of Parliament
- View contemporary art at Tate Modern
- Meet the Old Masters at the National Gallery

Day 1
Morning Spend a few hours at the **Tower of London** (pp156–9): explore the armory, infiltrate the torture chambers, and admire the Crown Jewels. Afterward, have a drink by the colorful quayside at **St Katharine's Dock** (p160), then cross **Tower Bridge** (p155) to Shad Thames: its scrubbed-up dockside warehouses are now pricy penthouses. The white building houses the **Design Museum** (p185), which hosts ever-changing exhibitions on furniture and fashion.

Afternoon Walk along the riverside and stop off to look around **HMS Belfast** (p185), now a floating naval museum, before detouring into **Southwark** (pp176–7) for

one of London's most macabre attractions: the **Old Operating Theatre** (pp178–9). Located in St. Thomas' church, the surgery dates from before anesthetics.

Day 2
Morning Get to **Westminster Abbey** (pp78–81) early to explore its royal memorials. Nearby rise the Neo-Gothic **Houses of Parliament** (pp74–5) and **Big Ben** (p76). Cross the river and head for the **Southbank Centre** (pp188–9), which offers diversions for every taste. As well as the **London Eye** (p191), there's the aquarium at **County Hall** (p190), the **Hayward Gallery** (p190), and the **Royal Festival Hall** (p190).

Afternoon Wander the huge galleries of **Tate Modern** (pp180–83). Then walk over the Millennium Bridge for views of **Shakespeare's Globe** (p179) and **Tower Bridge** (p155), reaching **St. Paul's Cathedral** (pp150–53) in time for Choral Evensong.

A performance in progress at Shakespeare's Globe in Southwark

Day 3
Morning Start the day at Covent Garden's **Piazza and Central Market** (p116), then join a tour of the **Royal Opera House** (p117). If time allows, cross the cobbled piazza and pop into the **London Transport Museum** (p116). Next, browse the quirky and designer shops that line **Neal Street** and colorful **Neal's Yard** (p117).

Afternoon Head to **Leicester Square** (p105) for cheap theater tickets, then walk to **Trafalgar Square** (p104) and spend a few hours at the **National Gallery** (pp106–9) for world-famous art, and the adjacent **National Portrait Gallery** (pp104–5) for paintings of royalty and celebrities. Round off the day with a meander in **St. James's Park** (p95) and a peek at **Buckingham Palace** (p96–7) before the theater.

5 days in London

- Visit Buckingham Palace, the Queen's official home
- Discover ancient treasures at the British Museum
- Explore South Kensington's world-class museums

Day 1
Morning Begin at the **Design Museum** (p185) for avant-garde exhibits. Then walk over **Tower Bridge** (p155), from where you can see one of Britain's great battleships, **HMS Belfast** (p185). Next, spend two hours at the **Tower of London** (pp156–9) and have lunch at **St. Katharine's Dock** (p160).

Afternoon Allow time to see two of Sir Christopher Wren's works of art, **St. Paul's Cathedral** (pp150–53) and the **Monument** (p154), before heading to **Southwark** (pp176–7). Explore the intriguing **Old Operating Theatre** (p178–9) and view contemporary art at **Tate Modern** (p180–83). End the day with a play (Apr–Oct) at **Shakespeare's Globe** (p179).

Day 2
Morning Soak up the ambience of the West End with a visit to its heart, **Leicester Square** (p105).

Take in some culture at the **National Gallery** (pp106–9) and the **National Portrait Gallery** (pp104–5), which showcases a fascinating collection of paintings and photographs, before stopping for lunch in **Chinatown** (p110).

Afternoon Walk to **Covent Garden** (pp114–15) and take a backstage tour of the **Royal Opera House** (p117), then climb aboard old streetcars at the **London Transport Museum** (p116). Afterward, peruse trendy shops along **Neal Street** (p117).

Day 3
Morning Start the day at the **British Museum** (pp126–29), a treasure trove charting 2 million years of human civilization. Don't miss the ancient Egyptian mummies and the Rosetta Stone.

Afternoon Head to **Trafalgar Square** (p104), then stroll along **The Mall** (p95) to **Buckingham Palace** (p96–7), to visit the State Rooms (Jul–Sep). End the day by relaxing in **St. James's Park** (p95).

Day 4
Morning Start with a spin on the **London Eye** (p191), then head to **Westminster Abbey** (pp78–81). This incredible building has witnessed royal weddings and coronations. If it's summer, book a tour of the **Houses of Parliament** (pp74–5), or at other times line up to see the Lords and Commons in action. As you leave, look up at the clock tower of **Big Ben** (p76).

Afternoon Make your way to the **Imperial War Museum** (pp192–3), with its poignant

Al fresco eating and drinking at bohemian Gabriel's Wharf

exhibition on the Holocaust. For something lighter, walk through the vibrant **Southbank Centre** (pp188–9) to the boutiques and cafés of **Gabriel's Wharf** (p193).

Day 5
Morning Start in **Notting Hill** (p221), with a turn around **Portobello Road** (p221). If it's a Saturday, the bric-a-brac market enlivens this desirable neighborhood. From here, wander into **Kensington Gardens** (p210) for a view of the palace and the Peter Pan statue.

Afternoon Exit into South Kensington's museum quarter. With three world-class museums, there's something for everyone. Choose between the **Science Museum** (pp208–9), with its hands-on experiments and aircraft simulators, the **Natural History Museum** (pp204–5) for animatronic dinosaurs and touch-screen creepy-crawlies, or the **Victoria and Albert Museum** (pp212–15), for one of the world's finest collections of decorative art.

Assembled crowds watch a daredevil street performer in Covent Garden's piazza

Putting London on the Map

London, the capital of the United Kingdom, is a city of over seven million people covering 620 sq miles (1,606 sq km) of southeast England. It is built on the Thames River and is at the center of the UK road and rail networks. From London, visitors can easily reach the UK's other main tourist attractions.

Western Europe

NORWAY
SWEDEN
DENMARK
North Sea
UNITED KINGDOM
REP. OF IRELAND
NETHERLANDS
POLAND
London
BELGIUM
GERMANY
CZECH REPUBLIC
SLOVAKIA
Atlantic Ocean
FRANCE
SWITZ.
AUSTRIA
HUNGARY
SLOV.
CROATIA
BOSNIA HERZ.
SERBIA
MONTEN.
KOS.
MAC.
ITALY
ALBANIA
GREECE
PORTUGAL
SPAIN

Chesterfield
Mansfield
Newark-on-Trent
A1
A46
M1
Nottingham
Derby
A52
Loughborough
Coalville
Leicester
A444
Nuneaton
A6
Corb
M6
Coventry
A14
Kettering
Warwick
Wellingborough
A45
M40
A423
Northampton
Stratford-on-Avon
M1
A43
A429
Banbury
Milton Keynes
Evenlode
A44
A34
A41
Gloucester
Cotswolds
Aylesbury
A465
Abergavenny
A48
A40
Oxford
A449
Stroud
Cirencester
Thames
Abingdon
M40
Pontypool
M5
High Wycombe
A420
A429
A419
Henley-on-Thames
Newport
M4
Swindon
A34
M4
Cardiff
M4
Bristol
A350
Chippenham
Kennet
Reading
Barry
A38
Kennet and Avon Canal
Newbury
Camberley
Weston-super-Mare
Bath
M4
A34
A33
A37
A36
Basingstoke
Aldershot
Frome
Salisbury Plain
A303
Andover
Farnham
M5
Test
A31
Bridgwater
A39
Winchester
M3
Taunton
A303
Salisbury
Petersfield
A358
A36
A3
Yeovil
Avon
A31
Waterlooville
M5
Stour
New Forest
Southampton
Havant
A303
A37
North Dorset Downs
A31
Ringwood
M27
Portsmouth
Honiton
A35
A31
Poole
Christchurch
Isle of Wight
Dorchester
Frome
Bournemouth
Weymouth
Purbeck Hills
Poole Bay
Weymouth Bay

Channel Islands, St Malo
Cherbourg
Bilbao, Santander
Le Havre, Caen, St Malo, Cherbourg

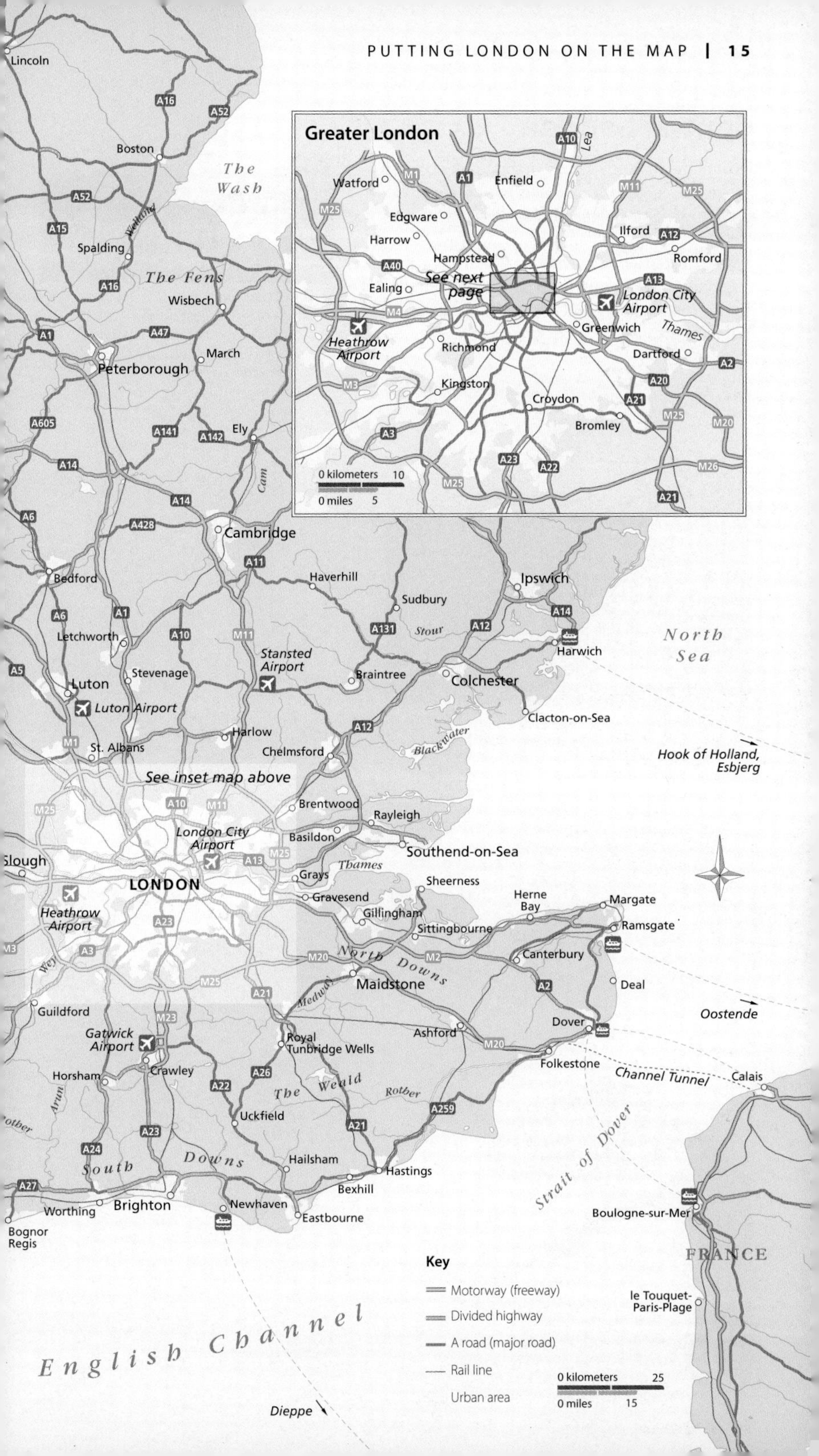

Lincoln

A16

A52

Greater London

A10 Lea

Watford M1 A1 Enfield M11 M25

Boston

The Wash

Edgware

A52 M25

Harrow Ilford A12

A15 Hampstead Romford

Spalding A40 A13

The Fens See next London City
page Airport

A16 Wisbech Ealing A1 Greenwich Thames

A47 Heathrow Richmond Dartford
Airport A2

A1 March A20

Peterborough Kingston A21

A605 Croydon M25 M20

A141 A142 Ely A3 Bromley M26

A23

Cam A22 A21

A14 0 kilometers 10 M25

A14 0 miles 5

A428 Cambridge

A11

Bedford Haverhill Ipswich

A6 Sudbury North

Letchworth A10 M11 Stour A12 A14 Sea

A6 A1 Stansted Braintree Harwich
Airport

A5 Luton Colchester

Luton Airport A12

Stevenage Clacton-on-Sea

M1 Harlow Blackwater

St. Albans Chelmsford Hook of Holland,
See inset map above Esbjerg

M25 A10 M11 Brentwood Rayleigh

London City Basildon Southend-on-Sea
Slough Airport A13 M25 Thames

Grays Sheerness

LONDON Gravesend Margate

Heathrow A23 Gillingham Herne Ramsgate
Airport Sittingbourne Bay

M3 A3 M20 North Downs Canterbury

Wey M2 A2 Deal

M25 A21 Maidstone Oostende

Guildford Medway Dover

Gatwick Royal Ashford M20
Airport Tunbridge Wells Folkestone Channel Tunnel Calais

Horsham Crawley The Weald Rother

A22 A259 Strait of Dover

Rother Arun A21 Uckfield

A24 A23 Hailsham Boulogne-sur-Mer

South Downs Hastings

A27 Bexhill FRANCE

Bognor Worthing Brighton Newhaven Eastbourne
Regis

Key

English Channel

le Touquet-
Paris-Plage

Motorway (freeway)

Divided highway

A road (major road)

Rail line 0 kilometers 25

Urban area 0 miles 15

Dieppe

Central London

Most of the sights described in this book lie within 14 areas of central London, plus two outlying districts of Hampstead and Greenwich. Each area has its own chapter. If time is short, you may decide to restrict yourself to the five areas that contain most of London's famous sights: Whitehall and Westminster, The City, Bloomsbury and Fitzrovia, Soho and Trafalgar Square, and South Kensington.

Tower of London
For much of its 900-year history, the Tower was an object of fear. Its bloody past and the Crown Jewels make it a major attraction *(see pp156–9)*.

National Gallery
This gallery has over 2,300 paintings, and the collection is particularly strong on Dutch, early Renaissance Italian, and 17th-century Spanish painting *(see pp106–9)*.

Natural History Museum
Life on Earth and the Earth itself are vividly explored at the museum, through a combination of interactive techniques and traditional displays *(see pp204–5)*.

For keys to symbols *see back flap*

| 0 kilometers | | 1 |
| 0 miles | 0.5 | |

Buckingham Palace
The office and home of the monarchy, the palace is also used for state occasions. The State Rooms open to the public in the summer *(see pp96–7)*.

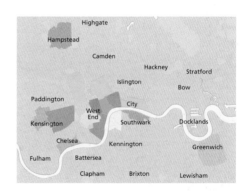

Museum of London
This museum, on the edge of the Barbican complex in the City, provides a lively account of London life from prehistoric times to the present day *(see pp168–9)*.

Houses of Parliament
The Palace of Westminster has been the seat of the two Houses of Parliament, called the Lords and the Commons, since 1512 *(see pp74–5)*.

THE HISTORY OF LONDON

In 55 BC, Julius Caesar's Roman army invaded England, landed in Kent, and marched northwest until it reached the broad Thames River at what is now Southwark. There were a few tribesmen living on the opposite bank, but no major settlement. However, by the time of the second Roman invasion 88 years later, a small port and mercantile community had been established here. The Romans bridged the river and built their administrative headquarters on the north bank, calling it Londinium – a version of its old Celtic name.

London as Capital

London was soon the largest city in England and, by the time of the Norman Conquest in 1066, it was the obvious choice for national capital.

Settlement slowly spread beyond the original walled city, which was virtually wiped out by the Great Fire of 1666. The post-Fire rebuilding formed the basis of the area we know today as the City, but by the 18th century, London enveloped the settlements around it. These included the royal city of Westminster, which had long been London's religious and political center. The explosive growth of commerce and industry during the 18th and 19th centuries made London the biggest and wealthiest city in the world, creating a prosperous middle class who built the fine houses that still grace parts of the capital. The prospect of riches also lured millions of the dispossessed from the countryside and from abroad. They crowded into unsanitary dwellings, many just east of the City, where docks provided employment.

By the end of the 19th century, 4.5 million people lived in inner London and another 4 million in its immediate vicinity. Bombing in World War II devastated many central areas and led to substantial rebuilding in the second half of the 20th century, when the docks and other Victorian industries disappeared.

The following pages illustrate London's history by giving snapshots of significant periods in its evolution.

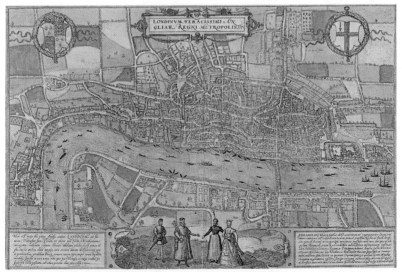

A map of 1580 showing the City of London and, near the lower left corner, the City of Westminster

◀ A 15th-century manuscript showing the Tower of London with London Bridge in the background

Roman London

When the Romans invaded Britain in the 1st century AD, they already controlled vast areas of the Mediterranean, but fierce opposition from local tribes (such as Queen Boudicca's Iceni) made Britain difficult to control. The Romans persevered, however, and had consolidated their power by the end of the century. Londinium, with its port, developed into a capital city; by the 3rd century, there were some 50,000 people living here. But, as the Roman Empire crumbled in the 5th century, the garrison pulled out, leaving the city to the Saxons.

Extent of The City
⬜ 125 AD   ⬛ Today

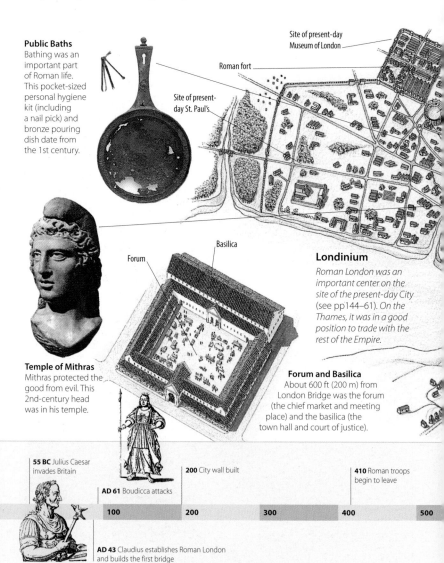

Public Baths
Bathing was an important part of Roman life. This pocket-sized personal hygiene kit (including a nail pick) and bronze pouring dish date from the 1st century.

Roman fort

Site of present-day Museum of London

Site of present-day St. Paul's

Temple of Mithras
Mithras protected the good from evil. This 2nd-century head was in his temple.

Forum

Basilica

Londinium
Roman London was an important center on the site of the present-day City (see pp144–61). On the Thames, it was in a good position to trade with the rest of the Empire.

Forum and Basilica
About 600 ft (200 m) from London Bridge was the forum (the chief market and meeting place) and the basilica (the town hall and court of justice).

55 BC Julius Caesar invades Britain

AD 61 Boudicca attacks

200 City wall built

410 Roman troops begin to leave

| 100 | 200 | 300 | 400 | 500 |

AD 43 Claudius establishes Roman London and builds the first bridge

London Wall
The tombstone of a Roman legionnaire was built into the city wall. The writing tablets in his left hand suggest he did clerical work.

Amphitheater
Entertainment was brutal. A popular spectacle was gladiators, dressed like this figurine, fighting to the death.

Where to see Roman London

Most traces of the Roman occupation are in the City *(see pp144–61)* and Southwark *(pp174–85)*. The Museum of London *(pp168–9)* and the British Museum *(pp126–9)* have extensive collections of Roman finds. There's a Roman pavement in the crypt of All Hallows by the Tower *(p155)*, and in the 1990s an amphitheater was found below the Guildhall *(p161)*. The foundations of the Temple of Mithras are on view near the site on Queen Victoria Street.

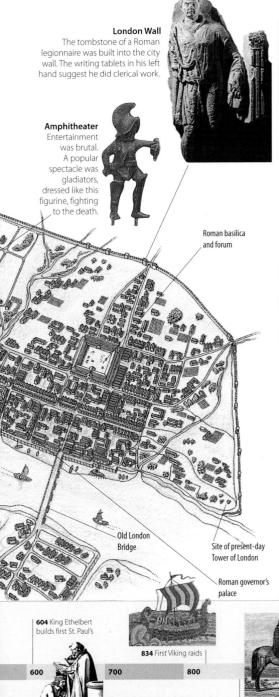

Roman basilica and forum

Old London Bridge

Site of present-day Tower of London

Roman governor's palace

This section of the Roman wall, built in the 3rd century to defend the city, can be seen from the Museum of London.

London's best Roman mosaic is this 2nd-century pavement, found in 1869 in the City, now in the Museum of London.

604 King Ethelbert builds first St. Paul's

834 First Viking raids

1014 Norse invader Olaf pulls down London Bridge to take the city

600　　700　　800　　1000

871 Alfred the Great becomes king of Wessex

Medieval London

The historic division between London's centers of commerce (the City) and government (Westminster) started in the mid-11th century when Edward the Confessor established his court and sited his abbey *(see pp78–81)* at Westminster. Meanwhile, in the City, tradesmen set up their own institutions and guilds, and London appointed its first mayor. Disease was rife and the population never rose much above its Roman peak of 50,000. The Black Death (1348) reduced the population by half.

Extent of The City
☐ 1200   ☐ Today

London Bridge

The first stone bridge was built in 1209 and lasted 600 years. It was the only bridge across the Thames in London until Westminster Bridge (1750).

Houses and shops projected over both sides of the bridge. Shopkeepers made their own merchandise on the premises and lived above their shops. Apprentices did the selling.

The Chapel of St. Thomas, erected the year the bridge was completed, was one of its first buildings.

St Thomas à Becket
As Archbishop of Canterbury he was murdered in 1170, at the prompting of Henry II with whom he was quarrelling. Thomas was made a saint and pilgrims visited his Canterbury shrine.

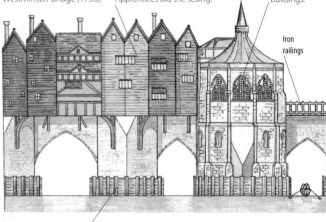

Iron railings

Dick Whittington
The 15th-century trader was mayor of London *(see p41)*.

The piers were made from wooden stakes rammed into the river bed and filled with rubble.

Stag Hunting
Such sports were the chief recreation of wealthy landowners.

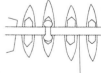

The arches ranged from 15 ft (4.5 m) to 35 ft (10 m) in width.

1042 Edward the Confessor becomes king

1086 Domesday Book, England's first survey, published

1191 Henry Fitzalwin becomes London's first mayor

| 1050 | 1100 | 1150 | 1200 | 1250 |

1066 William I crowned in Abbey

1065 Westminster Abbey completed

1176 Work starts on the first stone London Bridge

1215 King John's Magna Carta gives City more powers

1240 First parliament sits at Westminster

Chivalry
Medieval knights were idealized for their courage and honor. Edward Burne-Jones (1833–98) painted George, patron saint of England, rescuing a maiden from this dragon.

Geoffrey Chaucer
The poet and customs controller (*see p41*) is best remembered for his *Canterbury Tales*, which creates a rich picture of 14th-century England.

Where to see Medieval London

There were only a few survivors of the Great Fire of 1666 (*see pp26–7*) – the Tower (*pp156–9*), Westminster Hall (*p74*) and Westminster Abbey (*pp78–81*), and a few churches (*p48*). The Museum of London (*pp168–9*) has artifacts, while Tate Britain (*pp84–7*) and the National Gallery (*pp106–9*) have paintings. Manuscripts, including the Domesday Book, are found at the British Library (*p127*).

The Tower of London was started in 1078 and became one of the few centers of royal power in the largely self-governing City.

Plan of the Bridge
The bridge had 19 arches to span the river, making it, for many years, the longest stone bridge in England.

A 14th-century rose window is all that remains of Winchester Palace near the Clink on Bankside (*see p184*).

Many 13th-century pilgrims went to Canterbury.

1348 Black Death kills thousands

1394 Westminster Hall remodeled by Henry Yevele

The Great Seal of Richard I, who spent most of his 10-year reign fighting abroad.

1350	1400	1450

1381 Peasants' Revolt defeated

1397 Richard Whittington becomes mayor

1476 William Caxton sets up first printing press at Westminster

Elizabethan London

In the 16th century, the monarchy was stronger than ever before. The Tudors established peace throughout England, allowing art and commerce to flourish. This renaissance reached its zenith under Elizabeth I as explorers opened up the New World, and English theater, the nation's most lasting contribution to world culture, was born.

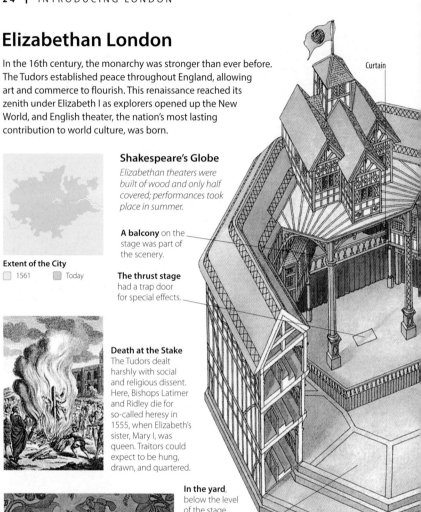

Curtain

Shakespeare's Globe
Elizabethan theaters were built of wood and only half covered; performances took place in summer.

Extent of the City
⬜ 1561 ⬛ Today

A balcony on the stage was part of the scenery.

The thrust stage had a trap door for special effects.

Death at the Stake
The Tudors dealt harshly with social and religious dissent. Here, Bishops Latimer and Ridley die for so-called heresy in 1555, when Elizabeth's sister, Mary I, was queen. Traitors could expect to be hung, drawn, and quartered.

In the yard, below the level of the stage, commoners stood to watch the play.

Hunting and Hawking
Popular 16th-century pastimes are shown on this cushion cover.

1536 Henry VIII's second wife, Anne Boleyn, executed

1535 Sir Thomas More executed for treason

1553 Edward dies, succeeded by his sister Mary I

1530   **1540**   **1550**

Rat catchers and other pest controllers could not prevent epidemics of plague.

1547 Henry dies, succeeded by his son Edward VI

1534 Henry VIII breaks with the Roman Catholic church

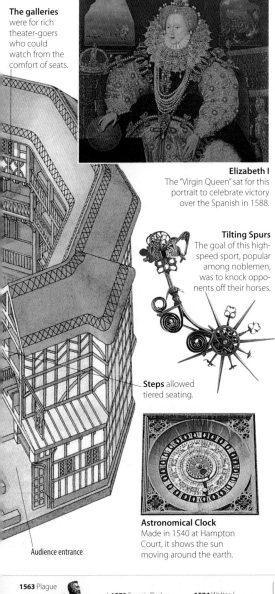

The galleries were for rich theater-goers who could watch from the comfort of seats.

Elizabeth I
The "Virgin Queen" sat for this portrait to celebrate victory over the Spanish in 1588.

Tilting Spurs
The goal of this high-speed sport, popular among noblemen, was to knock opponents off their horses.

Steps allowed tiered seating.

Astronomical Clock
Made in 1540 at Hampton Court, it shows the sun moving around the earth.

Audience entrance

Where to see Elizabethan London

The Great Fire of 1666 wiped out the City. Fortunately, Middle Temple Hall (*see p141*), Staple Inn (*p143*), and the Lady Chapel inside Westminster Abbey (*pp78–81*) were beyond its reach. The Museum of London (*pp168–9*), the Victoria and Albert Museum (*pp212–15*), and the Geffrye Museum (*p250*) have fine furniture and artifacts. Farther afield are Hampton Court (*pp256–9*) and Sutton House (*p250*).

Elizabeth I watched *Twelfth Night* by Shakespeare under the hammerbeam roof of Middle Temple Hall in 1603.

The Parr Pot, now in the Museum of London, was made by Venetian craftsmen in London in 1547.

1563 Plague sweeps Europe

1570 Francis Drake makes first voyage to the West Indies

1584 Walter Raleigh's first attempt to colonize America

1588 Drake defeats Spanish Armada

1591 First play by Shakespeare produced

| 1560 | 1570 | 1580 | 1590 |

1558 Mary I's death makes Elizabeth queen

Gloves made from imported silk and velvet

1603 Elizabeth dies, James I accedes

Restoration London

Civil War had broken out in 1642 when the mercantile class demanded that some of the monarch's power be passed to Parliament. The subsequent Commonwealth was dominated by Puritans under Oliver Cromwell. The Puritans outlawed simple pleasures, such as dancing and theater, so it was no wonder that the restoration of the monarchy under Charles II in 1660 was greeted with rejoicing and the release of pent-up creative energies. The period was, however, also marked with two major tragedies: the Plague (1665) and the Great Fire (1666).

Extent of the City
☐ 1680   ☐ Today

St. Paul's was destroyed in the fire that raged as far west as Fetter Lane (map 14 E1).

London Bridge itself survived, but many of the buildings on it burned down.

Oliver Cromwell
He led the Parliamentarian army and was Lord Protector of the Realm from 1653 until his death in 1658. In the Restoration, his body was dug up and hung from the gallows at Tyburn, near Hyde Park (see p213).

Charles I's Death
The king was beheaded for tyranny on a freezing day (January 30, 1649) outside Banqueting House (see p82).

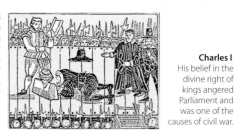

Charles I
His belief in the divine right of kings angered Parliament and was one of the causes of civil war.

1605 Guy Fawkes leads failed attempt to blow up the King and Parliament

1620

1623 Shakespeare's First Folio published

1625 James I dies, succeeded by his son Charles I

1630

Feathered helmet worn by Royalist cavaliers.

1640

1642 Civil war starts when Parliament defies king

1650

1649 Charles I executed, Commonwealth established

Newton's Telescope
Physicist and astronomer
Sir Isaac Newton
(1642–1727)
discovered the
law of gravity.

Samuel Pepys
His exuberant
diaries tell us
much about
courtly life
of the time.

The Tower of London
was just out of the
fire's reach.

Where to see Restoration London

Wren's churches and his St. Paul's Cathedral *(see p49 and pp150–3)* are, with Inigo Jones's Banqueting House *(p82)*, London's most famous 17th-century buildings. Other fine examples are Lincoln's Inn *(p138)* and Cloth Fair *(p167)*. The Museum of London *(pp168–9)* has a period interior. The British Museum *(pp126–9)* and the Victoria and Albert *(pp212–15)* have pottery, silver, and textile collections.

Ham House *(p255)* was built in 1610 but much enlarged later in the century. It has the finest interior of its time in England.

The Great Fire of 1666

An unidentified Dutch artist painted this view of the fire that burned for 5 days, destroying 13,000 houses.

The Plague
During 1665, carts
collected the dead
and took them to
communal graves
outside the city.

Peter Paul Rubens painted the ceiling in 1636 for Inigo Jones's Banqueting House *(p82)*. This is one of its panels.

1664–5 Plague kills 100,000

1666 Great Fire

1685 Charles II dies, Catholic James II becomes king

1692 First insurance market opens at Lloyd's

1660

1670

1680

1690

1660 Monarchy restored under Charles II

A barber's bowl made by London potters in 1681.

1688 James ousted in favor of Protestant William of Orange

1694 First Bank of England set up by William Paterson

Georgian London

The foundation of the Bank of England in 1694 spurred the growth of London, and by the time George I came to the throne in 1714, it had become an important financial and commercial center. Aristocrats with West End estates began laying out elegant squares and terraces to house newly rich merchants. Architects such as the Adam brothers, John Soane, and John Nash developed stylish medium-scale housing. They drew inspiration from the great European capitals, as did English painters, sculptors, composers, and craftsmen.

Extent of the City
◻ 1810 ◼ Today

Great Cumberland Place
Built in 1790, it was named after a royal duke and military commander.

Portman Square
was on the town's outskirts when it was started in 1764.

Manchester Square
was laid out in 1776–8.

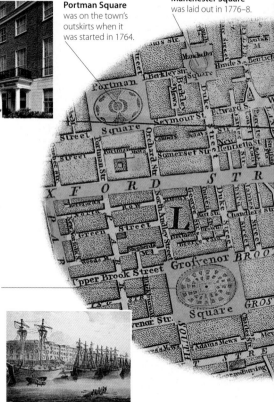

Grosvenor Square
Few of the original houses remain on one of the oldest and largest Mayfair squares (1720).

Docks
Specially built docks handled the growth in world trade.

1714 George I becomes king

1727 George II becomes king

1760 George III becomes king

1768 Royal Academy of Art established

1720

1740

1760

1770

1717 Hanover Square built, start of West End development

1729 John Wesley (1703–91) founds the Methodist Church

1759 Kew Gardens established

John Nash
Stylish Nash shaped 18th-century London with variations on Classical themes, such as this archway in Cumberland Terrace, near Regent's Park.

Where to see Georgian London

The portico of the Theatre Royal Haymarket *(see pp336–7)* gives a taste of the style of fashionable London in the 1820s. In Pall Mall *(p94)*, Charles Barry's Reform and Travellers' Clubs are equally evocative. Most West End squares have some Georgian buildings, while Fournier Street *(p172)* has good small-scale domestic architecture. The Victoria and Albert Museum *(V&A, pp212–15)* has silver, as do the London Silver Vaults *(p143)*, where it is for sale. Hogarth's pictures, at Tate Britain *(pp84–7)* and Sir John Soane's Museum *(pp138–9)*, show the social conditions.

This English grandfather clock (1725), made of oak and pine with Chinese designs, is in the V&A.

Georgian London
The layout of much of London's West End has remained very similar to how it was in 1828, when this map was published.

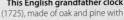

Berkeley Square
Built in the 1730s and 1740s in the grounds of the former Berkeley House, several characteristic original houses remain on its west side.

Ironwork
Crafts flourished. This ornate railing is on Manchester Square.

Captain Cook
This Yorkshire-born explorer discovered Australia during a voyage around the world in 1768–71.

Signatories of the American Declaration of Independence

1802 Stock Exchange formally established

1820 George III dies, Prince Regent becomes George IV

1830 George IV dies, brother William IV is king

| 1790 | 1800 | 1810 | 1820 | 1830 |

1776 Britain loses American colonies with Declaration of Independence

1811 George III goes mad, his son George is made Regent

1829 London's first horse bus

Victorian London

Much of London today is Victorian. Until the early 19th century, the capital had been confined to the original Roman city, plus Westminster and Mayfair to the west, ringed by fields and villages such as Brompton, Islington, and Battersea. From the 1820s, these green spaces quickly filled with row houses for the growing numbers attracted to London by industrialization. Rapid expansion brought challenges to the city. The first cholera epidemic broke out in 1832, and in 1858 came the Great Stink, when the smell from the Thames River was so bad that Parliament had to go into recess. But Joseph Bazalgette's sewer system (1875), involving banking both sides of the Thames, eased the problem.

Extent of the City

⬜ 1900   ⬛ Today

Nearly 14,000 exhibitors came from all over the world, bringing more than 100,000 exhibits.

Pantomime
The traditional family Christmas entertainment – still popular today *(see p326)* – started in the 19th century.

The building was 1,850 ft (560 m) long and 110 ft (33 m) high.

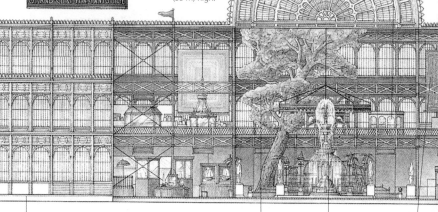

Soldiers marched and jumped on the floor to test its strength before the exhibition opened.

Massive elm trees growing in Hyde Park were left standing and the exhibition was erected around them.

The Crystal Fountain was 27 ft (8 m) high.

Carpets and stained glass were hung from the galleries.

1836 First London rail terminus opens at London Bridge

1837 Victoria becomes queen

1851 Great Exhibition

A Wedgwood plate in typically florid Victorian style

1861 Prince Albert dies

1840

1850

1860

1840 Rowland Hill introduces the Penny Post

Season ticket for Great Exhibition

1863 Metropolitan Railway, world's first subway system, is opened

Railroads
By 1900, fast trains, such as this Scotch *Express*, were crossing the country.

Where to see Victorian London

Grandiose buildings best reflect the spirit of the age, notably the rail termini, the Kensington Museums (*see pp200–15*), and the Royal Albert Hall (*p209*). Leighton House (*p220*) has a well-preserved interior. Pottery and fabrics are in the Victoria and Albert Museum, and London's Transport Museum (*p116*) has buses, trolleys, and trains.

Crystal Palace
Between May and October 1851, 6 million people visited Joseph Paxton's superb feat of engineering. In 1852 it was dismantled and reassembled in south London, where it remained until destroyed by fire in 1936.

Formal Dress Under Victoria, elaborate men's attire was replaced by more restrained evening wear.

The Victorian Gothic style suited buildings like the Public Record Office in Chancery Lane.

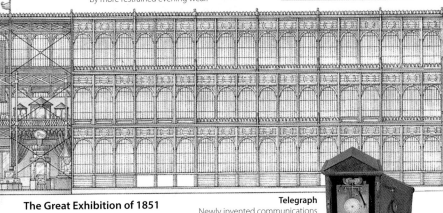

The Great Exhibition of 1851

The exhibition, held in the Crystal Palace in Hyde Park, celebrated industry, technology, and the expanding British Empire.

Telegraph
Newly invented communications technology, like this telegraph from 1840, made business expansion easier.

1870 First Peabody Buildings, to house the poor, built in Blackfriars Road

1890 First electric Underground line, from Bank to Stockwell, opens

1891 First LCC public housing built, in Shoreditch

1901 Queen Victoria dies, Edward VII accedes

1870 | **1880** | **1890** | **1900**

A special box for carrying top hats

1889 London County Council (LCC) established

1899 First motor buses introduced

Commemorative fan for the Boer War, which ended in 1903

London Between the World Wars

The society that emerged from World War I grasped eagerly at the innovations of early 20th-century London – the automobile, the telephone, mass transit. Movie theaters brought transatlantic culture, especially jazz and swing music. Victorian social restraints were discarded as people flocked to dance in restaurants, clubs, and dance halls. Many left the crowded inner city for new suburban subdivisions. Then came the 1930s global Depression, whose effects had barely worn off when World War II began.

Extent of the City
1938   Today

METRO-LAND PRICE TWO-PENCE

Commuting
London's new outer suburbs were made popular by the Underground. In the north was "Metroland," named after the Metropolitan line, which penetrated Hertfordshire.

Communications
The radio provided home entertainment and information. This is a 1933 model.

High Fashion
The sleek flowing new styles contrasted with the fussy elaboration of the Victorians and Edwardians. This tea gown is from the 1920s.

Formal evening wear, including hats for both sexes, was still required when going to stylish West End night spots.

A London Street Scene
Maurice Greiflenhagen's painting (1926) captures the bustle of London after dark.

Medals, like this one from 1914, were struck during the campaign for women's suffrage.

1921 North Circular Road links northern suburbs

1910

1920

1910 George V succeeds Edward VII

Cavalry was still used in the Middle Eastern battles of World War I (1914–18).

1922 First BBC national radio broadcast

Early Cinema
London-born Charlie Chaplin (1889–1977), seen here in *City Lights*, was a popular star of both silent and talking pictures.

George VI
Oswald Birley painted this portrait of the king who became a model for wartime resistance and unity.

Seven new theaters were built in central London from 1924 to 1931.

Early motor buses had open tops, like the old horse-drawn buses.

Throughout the period, newspaper circulations increased massively. In 1930 *The Daily Herald* sold 2 million copies a day.

World War II and the Blitz

World War II saw large-scale civilian bombing for the first time, bringing the horror of war to Londoners' doorsteps. Thousands were killed in their homes. Many people took refuge in Underground stations, and children were evacuated to the safety of the country.

WOMEN OF BRITAIN COME INTO THE FACTORIES

As in World War I, women were recruited for factory work formerly done by men who were away fighting.

Bombing raids in 1940 and 1941 (the Blitz) caused devastation all over the city.

1929 US stock market crash brings world Depression

1939 World War II begins

1925

1930

1927 First talking pictures

1936 Edward VIII abdicates to marry US divorcée Wallis Simpson. George VI accedes

1940 Winston Churchill becomes Prime Minister

Postwar London

Much of London was flattened by World War II bombs. Afterward, the chance for imaginative rebuilding was missed – some badly designed postwar developments are already being razed. But by the 1960s, London was such a dynamic world leader in fashion and popular music that *Time* magazine dubbed it "swinging London." Skyscrapers sprang up, but some stayed empty as 1980s boom gave way to 1990s recession.

Extent of the City
☐ 1959   ▨ Today

The Beatles
The Liverpool pop group, pictured in 1965, had rocketed to stardom two years earlier with songs of appealing freshness and directness. The group symbolized carefree 1960s London.

Margaret Thatcher
Britain's first woman Prime Minister (1979–90) promoted the market-led policies that fueled the 1980s boom.

Festival of Britain
After wartime, the city's morale was lifted by the Festival, marking the 1851 Great Exhibition's centennial (*see pp30–31*).

The Royal Festival Hall (1951) was the Festival's centerpiece and is still a landmark (*see p190*).

Telecom Tower (1964), at 620 ft (189 m) high, dominates the Fitzrovia skyline.

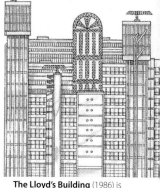

The Lloyd's Building (1986) is Richard Rogers' Postmodernist emblem (*see p161*).

OLYMPIC GAMES
LONDON
OFFICIAL SOUVENIR

1948 Olympic Games held in London

1952 George VI dies; his daughter Elizabeth II accedes

Minis became a symbol of the 1960s; small and maneuverable, they typified the go-as-you-please mood of the decade.

1977 Queen's Silver Jubilee; work starts on Jubilee line Underground

1945	1950	1955	1960	1965	1970	1975	1980

1951 Festival of Britain

1945 End of World War II

1954 Food rationing, introduced during World War II, abolished

RATION BOOK

1963 National Theatre founded at the Old Vic

1971 New London Bridge built

1982 Last of the London docks closes

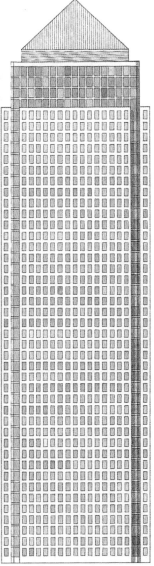

Canada Tower (1991) in Canary Wharf *(see p251)* was designed by César Pelli.

Docklands Light Railway
In the 1980s, new, driverless trains started to transport people to the developing Docklands.

Postmodern Architecture

Since the 1980s, architects have reacted against the stark shapes of the Modernists. Landmarks like the "Gherkin" by Norman Foster and The Shard by Renzo Piano now dominate the skyline. Architect Richard Rogers emphasizes structural features; others, like Terry Farrell, adopt a more playful approach using pastiches of Classical features.

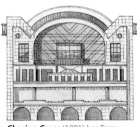

Charing Cross (1991) has Terry Farrell's glass structure on top of the Victorian station *(see p121)*.

Youth Culture

With their new mobility and spending power, young people began to influence the development of British popular culture in the years after World War II. Music, fashion, and design were increasingly geared to their rapidly changing tastes.

Punks were a phenomenon of the 1970s and 1980s. Their clothes, music, hair, and habits were designed to shock.

The Prince of Wales
As heir to the throne, he is outspokenly critical of much of London's modern architecture. He prefers more traditional styles.

1984 Thames Barrier completed

1986 Greater London Council abolished

1992 Canary Wharf development opens

2000 Ken Livingstone becomes London's first directly elected mayor

The observation wheel, the London Eye, was raised during the spring of 2000.

2011 Prince William marries Catherine Middleton at Westminster Abbey

1985	1990	1995	2000	2005	2010	2015	2020

1985 Ethiopian famine leads to Live Aid relief campaign

Vivienne Westwood's clothes won prizes in the 1980s and 1990s.

1997 Princess Diana's funeral procession brings London to a halt

2005 London shaken by bombs on the mass transit system

2013 Birth of Prince George to William and Catherine

2012 London hosts the Olympic games

Kings and Queens in London

London has been the royal capital of England since 1066, when William the Conqueror began a tradition of holding coronations in Westminster Abbey. Since then, successive kings and queens have left their mark on London, and many of the places described in this book have royal associations: Henry VIII hunted at Richmond, Charles I was executed on Whitehall, and the young Queen Victoria rode on Queensway. Royalty is also celebrated in many of London's traditional ceremonies – for more details on these, turn to pages 54–7.

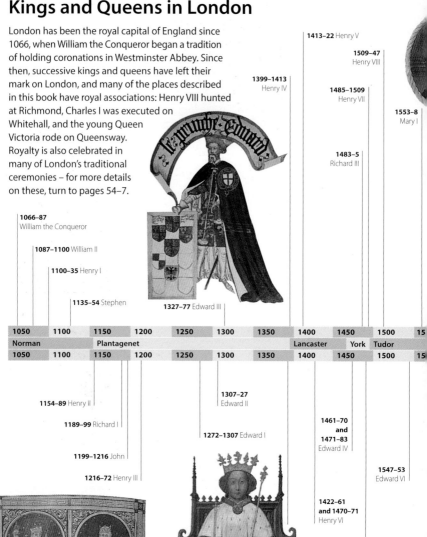

1413–22 Henry V

1509–47 Henry VIII

1399–1413 Henry IV

1485–1509 Henry VII

1553–8 Mary I

1483–5 Richard III

1066–87 William the Conqueror

1087–1100 William II

1100–35 Henry I

1135–54 Stephen

1327–77 Edward III

1050	1100	1150	1200	1250	1300	1350	1400	1450	1500	15
Norman		Plantagenet					Lancaster	York	Tudor	
1050	1100	1150	1200	1250	1300	1350	1400	1450	1500	15

1154–89 Henry II

1189–99 Richard I

1199–1216 John

1216–72 Henry III

1307–27 Edward II

1272–1307 Edward I

1461–70 and 1471–83 Edward IV

1547–53 Edward VI

1422–61 and 1470–71 Henry VI

1377–99 Richard II

Matthew Paris's 13th-century chronicle showing Kings Richard I, Henry II, John, and Henry III.

1483 Edward V

1901–10
Edward VII

1936 Edward VIII

1689–1702
William and Mary

1685–8 James II

1702–14
Anne

1660–85
Charles II

1714–27
George I

1603–25
James I

1837–1901
Victoria

1727–60
George II

1952– Elizabeth II

1600	1650	1700	1750	1800	1850	1900	1950	2000	2050
Stuart		Hanover				Windsor			
1600	1650	1700	1750	1800	1850	1900	1950	2000	2050

1830–37
William IV

1936–52 George VI shown
on the George Medal

1649–60 The Commonwealth,
established by Oliver Cromwell

1820–30
George IV

1910–36
George V

1625–49 Charles I

1558–1603
Elizabeth I

1760–1820 George III

LONDON AT A GLANCE

There are nearly 300 places of interest described in the Area by Area section of this book. These range from the magnificent National Gallery *(see pp106–9)* to the gruesome Old St. Thomas' Operating Theatre *(p178)*, and from ancient Charterhouse *(p162)* to modern Canary Wharf *(p251)*. To help you make the most of your stay, the following 18 pages are a time-saving guide to the best London has to offer. Museums and galleries, churches, and parks and gardens each have a section, and there are guides to remarkable Londoners and ceremonies in London. Each sight mentioned is cross-referenced to its own full entry. Below are the ten top tourist attractions to get you started.

London's Top Ten Tourist Attractions

St. Paul's
See pp150–53.

National Gallery
See pp106–9.

London Eye
See p191.

Changing of the Guard
Buckingham Palace, see pp96–7.

Hampton Court
See pp256–9.

Westminster Abbey
See pp78–81.

British Museum
See pp126–9.

Houses of Parliament
See pp74–5.

Tower of London
See pp156–9.

Victoria and Albert Museum
See pp212–15.

◀ The spectacular Great Court at the British Museum

Remarkable Londoners

London has always been a gathering place for the most prominent and influential people of their times. Some of these figures have come to London from other parts of Britain or from countries farther afield; others have been Londoners, born and bred. All of them have left their mark on London, by designing great and lasting buildings, establishing institutions and traditions, and writing about or painting the city they knew. Most of them have also had an influence on their times that spread out from London to the rest of the world.

Venus Venticordia by Dante Gabriel Rossetti

left his mark with such iconic buildings as 30 St Mary Axe, known as "the Gherkin."

Artists

Painters in London, as elsewhere, often lived in enclaves, for mutual support and because they shared common priorities. During the 18th century, artists clustered around the court at St. James's to be near their patrons. Thus both William Hogarth (1697–1764) and Sir Joshua Reynolds (1723–92) lived and worked in Leicester Square, while Thomas Gainsborough (1727–88) lived on Pall Mall. (Hogarth's Chiswick house was his place in the country.)

Later, Cheyne Walk in Chelsea, with its river views, became popular with artists, including the masters J. M. W. Turner (1775–1851), James McNeill Whistler (1834–1903), Dante Gabriel Rossetti (1828–82), Philip Wilson Steer, (1860–1942), and the sculptor Sir Jacob Epstein (1880–1959). Augustus John (1879–1961) and John

John Nash's Theatre Royal Haymarket (1821)

Architects and Engineers

A number of people who built London still have works standing. London-born Inigo Jones (1573–1652) was the father of English Renaissance architecture. He lived and worked at Great Scotland Yard, Whitehall, then the residence of the royal architect – he was later succeeded by Sir Christopher Wren (1632–1723).

Wren's successors as the prime architects of London were his protégé Nicholas Hawksmoor (1661–1736)

and James Gibbs (1682–1754). Succeeding generations each produced architects who were to stamp their genius on the city: the brothers Robert (1728–92) and James Adam (1730–94), then John Nash (1752–1835), Sir Charles Barry (1795–1860), Decimus Burton (1800–81), Alfred Waterhouse (1830–1905), Norman Shaw (1831–1912), and Sir George Gilbert Scott (1811–78). Sir Joseph Bazalgette (1819–91) built London's sewer system and the Thames Embankment. More recently, Sir Norman Foster (1935–) has

Historic London Homes

Four writers' homes that have been recreated are those of the romantic poet **John Keats** (1795–1821); the historian **Thomas Carlyle** (1795–1881); the lexicographer **Dr. Samuel Johnson** (1709–84); and the prolific and popular novelist **Charles Dickens** (1812–70). The house that the architect **Sir John Soane** (1753–1837) designed for himself remains largely as it was when he died, as does the house where the psychiatrist **Sigmund Freud** (1856–1939) settled after fleeing from the Nazis before World War II.

Apsley House, on Hyde Park Corner, was the residence of the **Duke of Wellington** (1769–1852), hero of the Battle of Waterloo. The life and music of Baroque composer **George Frideric Handel** (1685–1759) are on display at his former home in Mayfair. Finally, the rooms of Sir Arthur Conan Doyle's fictional detective **Sherlock Holmes** have been created in Baker Street.

Carlyle's House

Plaques

All over London, the former homes of well-known figures are marked by plaques. Look for these, especially in Chelsea, Kensington, and Mayfair, and see how many names you recognize.

No. 3 Sussex Square, Kensington

No. 27b Canonbury Square, Islington

No. 56 Oakley Street, Chelsea

Singer Sargent (1856–1925) had studios on Tite Street. John Constable (1776–1837) is best known as a Suffolk painter but lived for a while in Hampstead, from where he painted many fine views of the heath.

Writers

Geoffrey Chaucer (c.1345–1400), author of *The Canterbury Tales*, was born on Upper Thames Street, the son of an innkeeper. William Shakespeare (1564–1616) and Christopher Marlowe (1564–93) were both associated with the theaters in Southwark, and may have lived nearby.

The poets John Donne (1572–1631) and John Milton (1608–74) were both born on Bread Street in the City. Donne, after a profligate youth, became Dean of St. Paul's. The diarist Samuel Pepys (1633–1703) was born off Fleet Street.

The young novelist Jane Austen (1775–1817) lived briefly off Sloane Street, near the Cadogan Hotel, where the flamboyant Oscar Wilde (1854–1900) was arrested in 1895 for homosexuality. Playwright George Bernard Shaw (1856–1950) lived at No. 29 Fitzroy Square in Bloomsbury. Later, the same house was home to Virginia Woolf (1882–1941) and became a meeting place for the Bloomsbury Group, which included Vanessa Bell, John Maynard Keynes, E. M. Forster,

Roger Fry, and Duncan Grant. Current authors with works set in London include Monica Ali and Zadie Smith.

Leaders

In legend, a penniless boy named Dick Whittington came to London with his cat seeking streets paved with gold, and later became Lord Mayor. In fact, Richard Whittington (1360?–1423), Lord Mayor three times between 1397 and 1420 and one of London's most celebrated early politicians, was the son of a noble. Sir Thomas More (1478–1535), a Chelsea resident, was Henry VIII's chancellor until they quarreled over the king's break with the Catholic church and Henry ordered More's execution. More was canonized in 1935. Sir Thomas Gresham (1519?–79) founded the Royal Exchange. Sir Robert Peel (1788–1850) started the London police force, who were known as "bobbies" after him.

George Bernard Shaw

Actors

Nell Gwynne (1650–87) won more fame as King Charles II's mistress than as an actress. However, she did appear on stage at Drury Lane Theatre; she also sold oranges there. The Shakespearean actor Edmund Kean (1789–1833) and the great tragic actress

Sarah Siddons (1755–1831) were more distinguished players at Drury Lane. So were Henry Irving (1838–1905) and Ellen Terry (1847–1928), whose stage partnership lasted 24 years. Charlie Chaplin (1889–1977), born in Kennington, had a poverty-stricken childhood in the slums of London.

In the 20th century, a school of fine actors blossomed at the Old Vic, including Sir John Gielgud (1904–2001), Sir Ralph Richardson (1902–83), Dame Peggy Ashcroft (1907–91), and Laurence (later Lord) Olivier (1907–89), who was appointed the first director of the National Theatre.

Laurence Olivier

Where to Find Historic London Homes

Thomas Carlyle *p198*
Charles Dickens *p127*
Sigmund Freud *p248*
George Frideric Handel *p341*
William Hogarth *p261*
Sherlock Holmes *p228*
Dr. Samuel Johnson *p142*
John Keats *p235*
Sir John Soane *p138*
The Duke of Wellington *p99*

London's Best: Museums and Galleries

London's museums are filled with an astonishing diversity of treasures from all over the world. This map highlights 15 of the city's most important galleries and museums, whose exhibits cater to most interests. Some of these collections started from the legacies of 18th- and 19th-century explorers, traders, and collectors. Others specialize in one aspect of art, history, science, or technology. A more detailed overview of London's museums and galleries is on pages 44–5.

British Museum
This Anglo-Saxon helmet is part of a massive collection of antiquities.

Wallace Collection
Frans Hals's *Laughing Cavalier* is a star attraction in this museum of art, furniture, armor, and *objets d'art*.

Royal Academy of Arts
Major international art exhibitions are held here, and the renowned Summer Exhibition, when works are for sale, takes place every year.

Regent's Park and Marylebone

Kensington and Holland Park

South Kensington and Knightsbridge

Piccadill and St James'

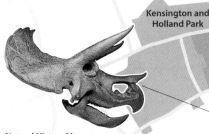

Natural History Museum
All of life is here, with vivid displays on everything from dinosaurs (like this *Triceratops* skull) to butterflies.

Chelsea

Science Museum
Newcomen's steam engine of 1712 is just one of many exhibits that appeal to both novice and expert.

Victoria and Albert
It is the world's largest museum of decorative arts. This Indian vase is from the 18th century.

National Portrait Gallery
Important British figures are documented in paintings and photographs. This is Vivien Leigh, by Angus McBean (1954).

National Gallery
The world-famous paintings in its collection are mainly European and date from the 15th to the 19th centuries.

British Museum

Museum of London
London's history is told through fascinating objects such as this 15th-century reliquary.

Tower of London
The Crown Jewels and a vast collection of arms and armor are here. This armor was worn by a 14th-century Italian knight.

National Portrait Gallery

Bloomsbury and Fitzrovia

Smithfield and Spitalfields

Holborn and the Inns of Court

The City

Design Museum
The changing exhibitions here showcase all aspects of design, from household prototypes to high fashion garments.

Soho and Trafalgar Square

Covent Garden and the Strand

Southwark and Bankside

South Bank

Whitehall and Westminster

RIVER THAMES

0 kilometers   1
0 miles   0.5

Tate Modern
Works of the 20th century, such as Dali's *Lobster Telephone*, are celebrated here.

Tate Britain
Formerly the Tate Gallery, this museum showcases an outstanding collection of British art covering the 16th century to the present.

Imperial War Museum
It uses displays, film, and special effects to recreate 20th-century battles. This is one of the earliest tanks.

Courtauld Gallery
Well-known works, such as Manet's *Bar at the Folies-Bergère*, line its galleries.

Exploring Museums and Galleries

London boasts an astonishingly rich and diverse collection of museums. The city's position for centuries at the hub of world-wide trade has been partly responsible for this extraordinarily rich cultural heritage. Britain's rule of a far-flung empire has also played its part. The world-renowned collections are impressive, but find time for the city's range of smaller museums, which are often more peaceful than their grander counterparts. Brimming with character, they cover every imaginable theme, from buses and toys to electricity and water power.

Geffrye Museum: Art Nouveau Room

Antiquities and Archaeology

Some of the most celebrated artifacts of ancient Asia, Egypt, Greece, and Rome are housed in the **British Museums's** fine collection. Other antiquities, including books, manuscripts, paintings, busts, and gems, are displayed in **Sir John Soane's Museum**, which is one of the most idiosyncratic to be found in London.

The **Museum of London** contains much of archaeological interest from all periods of the city's history.

Eclectic collection at Sir John Soane's Museum

Furniture and Interiors

The Museum of London recreates typical domestic and commercial interiors from the Roman period right up to the present day. The **Victoria and Albert Museum** (or V&A) contains complete rooms rescued from now-vanished buildings, plus a magnificent collection of furniture ranging from the 16th century to work by

Design Museum display of chairs

contemporary designers. On a more modest scale, the **Geffrye Museum** consists of fully-furnished period rooms dating from 1600 to the 1990s. Writers' houses, such as the **Freud Museum**, give insights into the furniture of specific periods, while the **Linley Sambourne House** offers visitors a perfectly preserved example of a late Victorian interior.

Costumes and Jewelry

The **V&A's** vast collections include English and European clothes of the last 400 years, and some stunning jewelry from China, India and Japan. The priceless Crown Jewels, at the **Tower of London**, should not be missed. Here you can also see the world's largest cut diamond, Cullinan I, set in the Sovereign's Sceptre. **Kensington Palace's** Court Dress Collection opens a window on Court uniforms and protocol from about 1750. The **British Museum** displays ancient Aztec, Mayan and African costume.

Crafts and Design

Once again, the **Victoria and Albert Museum (V&A)** is the essential first port of call; its collections in these fields remain unrivaled. The **William Morris Gallery** shows every aspect of the 19th-century designer's work within the Arts and Crafts movement. The **Design Museum** focuses on modern design including products and fashion, while the **Crafts Council Gallery** displays (and sometimes sells) contemporary British craftwork.

Military Artifacts

The **National Army Museum** uses vivid models and displays to narrate the history of the British Army from the reign of Henry VII to the present. The regiments of Foot Guards, who are the elite of the British Army, are the main focus of the **Guards Museum**. The **Tower of London** holds part of the national collection of arms and armor; the **Wallace Collection** also has a large and impressive display. The **Imperial War Museum** has recreations of World War I trenches and the 1940 Blitz. The **Florence Nightingale Museum** illustrates the hardships of 19th-century warfare.

Imperial War Museum

Toys and Childhood

Teddy bears, toy soldiers, and dollhouses are some of the toys that can be seen in **Pollock's Toy Museum**. The collection includes Eric, "the oldest known teddy bear." The **V&A Museum of Childhood** and the **Museum of London** are a little more formal, but still fun, and illustrate aspects of the social history of childhood, with both offering some interesting children's activities.

Science and Natural History

Computers, electricity, space exploration, industrial processes, and transportation can all be studied at the **Science Museum**. Transportation enthusiasts are also catered to at the **London Transport Museum**. There are

other specialized museums, such as the **Faraday Museum,** concerning the development of electricity, and the **Kew Bridge Steam Museum**, focusing on water power. The **National Maritime Museum** and the **Royal Observatory** in Greenwich chart both maritime history and the creation of GMT, by which the world still sets its clocks. The **Natural History Museum** mixes displays of animal and bird life with ecological exhibits. The **Museum of Garden History** is devoted to the favorite British pastime.

Visual Arts

The particular strengths of the **National Gallery** are early Renaissance Italian and 17th-century Spanish painting and a wonderful collection of Dutch masters. **Tate Britain** specializes in British paintings spanning all periods, while **Tate Modern** has displays of international modern art from 1900 to the present day. The **V&A** is strong on European art of 1500–1900 and British art of 1700–1900. The **Royal Academy** and the **Hayward Gallery** specialize in major temporary exhibitions.

The **Courtauld Institute of Art Gallery** contains Impressionist and Post-Impressionist works, while the **Wallace Collection** has 17th-century Dutch and 18th-century French paintings. The **Dulwich Picture Gallery** includes works by Rembrandt, Rubens, Poussin, and Gainsborough, while **Kenwood House** is home to

Samson and Delilah (1620) by Van Dyck at the Dulwich Picture Gallery

paintings by Reynolds, Gainsborough, and Rubens in fine Adam interiors. The **Saatchi Gallery** is devoted to contemporary, mainly British, art.

Where to find the Collections

Ornate Drawing Room at the Wallace Collection

London's Best: Churches

It is worth stopping to look at London's churches and going in, if they are open. They have a special atmosphere unmatched elsewhere in the city, and they can often yield an intimate glimpse of the past. Many churches have replaced earlier buildings in a steady succession, dating back to pre-Christian times. Some began life in outlying villages beyond London's fortified center, and were absorbed into suburbs when the city expanded in the 18th century. The memorials in the capital's churches and churchyards are a fascinating record of local life, liberally peppered with famous names. A more detailed overview of London churches is on pages 48–9.

All Souls
This plaque comes from a tomb in John Nash's Regency church of 1824.

Bloomsbury and Fitzrovia

St. Paul's Covent Garden
Inigo Jones's Classical church was known as "the handsomest barn in England."

Regent's Park and Marylebone

Soho and Trafalgar Square

St. Martin-in-the-Fields
James Gibbs's church of 1722–6 was originally thought "too gay" for Protestant worship.

South Kensington and Knightsbridge

Piccadilly and St. James's

Whitehall and Westminster

0 kilometers   1
0 miles   0.5

Westminster Cathedral
The Italian-Byzantine Catholic cathedral's red-and-white brick exterior conceals a rich interior of multicolored marble.

Westminster Abbey
The famous abbey has the most glorious medieval architecture in London, and highly impressive tombs and monuments.

Brompton Oratory
This sumptuous Baroque church was decorated with works by Italian artists.

St. Mary-le-Strand
Now on a traffic island, this shiplike church was built by James Gibbs in 1714–17 to a lively Baroque design. Featuring high windows and rich interior detailing, it was built solidly enough to keep out the noise from the street.

St. Mary Woolnoth
The jewel-like interior of Nicholas Hawksmoor's small Baroque church (1716–27) appears larger than the outside.

Smithfield and
Spitalfields

Holborn and
the Inns of
Court

Covent
Garden
and the
Strand

The City

R I V E R   T H A M E S

Southwark
and
Bankside

South
Bank

St. Stephen Walbrook
Wren was at his best with this domed interior of 1672–7. Its carvings include Henry Moore's austere modern altar.

St. Paul's
At 360 ft (110 m) high, the dome of Wren's cathedral is the world's second largest after St. Peter's in Rome.

Temple Church
Built in the 12th and 13th centuries for the Knights Templar, this is one of the few circular churches to survive in England.

Southwark Cathedral
This largely 13th-century priory church was not designated a cathedral until 1905. It has a fine medieval choir.

Exploring Churches

The church spires that puncture London's skyline span nearly a thousand years of the city's history. They form an index to many of the events that have shaped the city – the Norman Conquest (1066); the Great Fire of London (1666); the great restoration, led by Wren, that followed it; the Regency period; the confidence of the Victorian era; and the devastation of World War II. Each has had its effect on the churches, many designed by the most influential architects of their times.

St. Paul's, Covent Garden

Medieval Churches

The most famous old church to survive the Great Fire of 1666 is the superb 13th-century **Westminster Abbey,** the church of the Coronation, with its tombs of British monarchs and heroes. Less well known are the well-hidden Norman church of **St. Bartholomew-the-Great**, London's oldest church (1123); the circular **Temple Church,** founded in 1160 by the Knights Templar; and **Southwark Cathedral**, set amid Victorian railroad tracks and warehouses. **Chelsea Old Church** is a charming village church near the river.

Churches by Jones

Inigo Jones (1573–1652) was Shakespeare's contemporary, and his works were almost as revolutionary as the great dramatist's. Jones's Classical churches of the 1620s and 1630s shocked a public used to conservative Gothic finery. By far the best-known is **St. Paul's Church** of the 1630s, the centerpiece of Jones's Italian-style piazza in Covent Garden. **Queen's Chapel, St. James's** was built in 1623 for Queen Henrietta Maria, the Catholic wife of Charles I. It was the first Classical church in England and has a magnificent interior but is, unfortunately, usually closed to the public.

Churches by Hawksmoor

Nicholas Hawksmoor (1661–1736) was Wren's most talented pupil, and his

Spires

Look for London's richly decorated church steeples. Here are four of the city's most distinctive to get you started.

St. Martin-in-the-Fields, by James Gibbs, is in a prominent position grandly overlooking Trafalgar Square.

Clock dating from 1758

St. Mary-le-Bow, by Christopher Wren, has a copper dragon weathervane on top of its fine steeple.

Graceful bow arches

St. Bride's has Wren's tallest steeple. Originally 234 ft (71m) high, 8 ft (2.5 m) were lost in a thunderstorm in 1764.

Four octagonal tiers

St. George's Bloomsbury, by Nicholas Hawksmoor, is topped by George I in a Roman toga.

Steeple rising in steps

churches are among the finest Baroque buildings to be found in Britain.

St. George's, Bloomsbury (1716–31) has an unusual centralized plan and a pyramid steeple topped by a statue of King George I. **St. Mary Woolnoth** is a tiny jewel of 1716–27, and farther east **Christ Church, Spitalfields** is a Baroque tour-de-force of 1714–29, now being restored.

Among Hawksmoor's East End churches are the stunning **St. Anne's, Limehouse** and **St. Alfege**, of 1714–17, which is across the river in Greenwich. The tower on this temple-like church was added later by John James in 1730.

St. Anne's, Limehouse

Churches by Gibbs

James Gibbs (1682–1754) was more conservative than his Baroque contemporaries such as Hawksmoor, and he also kept his distance from the Neo-Classical trend so popular after 1720. His idiosyncratic London churches were enormously influential. **St. Mary-le-Strand** (1714–17) is an island church that appears to be sailing down the Strand. The radical design of **St. Martin-in-the-Fields** (1722–6) predates its setting, Trafalgar Square, by a hundred years.

Regency Churches

The end of the Napoleonic Wars in 1815 brought a flurry of church-building. The need for

Christopher Wren

Sir Christopher Wren (1632–1723) was leader among the many architects who helped restore London after the Great Fire of London. He devised a new city plan, replacing the narrow streets with wide avenues radiating from piazzas. His plan was rejected, but he was commissioned to build 52 new churches; 31 have survived various threats of demolition and the bombs of World War II, although six are shells. Wren's great masterpiece is the massive **St. Paul's**, while nearby is splendid **St. Stephen Walbrook**, his domed church of 1672–77. Other landmarks are **St. Bride's**, off Fleet Street, said to have inspired the traditional shape of wedding cakes, **St. Mary-le-Bow** in Cheapside and **St. Magnus Martyr** in Lower Thames Street. Wren's own favorite was **St. James's, Piccadilly** (1683–4). Smaller gems are **St. Clement Danes**, Strand (1680–82) and **St. James, Garlickhythe** (1674–87).

churches in London's new suburbs fused with a Greek Revival. The results may lack the exuberance of Hawksmoor, but they have an austere elegance of their own. **All Souls, Langham Place** (1822–4), at the north end of Regent Street, was built by the Prince Regent's favorite, John Nash, who was ridiculed at the time for its unusual combination of design styles. Also worth visiting is **St. Pancras**, a Greek Revival church of 1819–22, which is typical of the period.

Victorian Churches

London has some of the finest 19th-century churches in Europe. Grand and colorful, their riotous decoration is in marked contrast to the chaste Neo-Classicism of the preceding Regency era. Perhaps the best of the capital's late Victorian churches is

Brompton Oratory

Westminster Cathedral, a stunningly rich Italianate Catholic cathedral built in 1895–1903, with architecture by J. F. Bentley and Stations of the Cross reliefs by Eric Gill. **Brompton Oratory** is a grand Baroque revival, based on a church in Rome and filled with magnificent furnishings from all over Catholic Europe.

Where to Find the Churches

London's Best: Parks and Gardens

Since medieval times, London has had large expanses of green. Some of these, such as Hampstead Heath, were originally common land, where farmsteaders could graze their animals. Others, such as Richmond Park and Holland Park, were royal hunting grounds or the gardens of large houses; several still have formal features dating from those times. Today you can cross much of central London by walking from St. James's Park in the east to Kensington Gardens in the west. Planned parks, like Battersea, and botanical gardens, like Kew, appeared later.

Hampstead

Hyde Park
The Serpentine is one of the highlights of a park that also boasts restaurants, an art gallery, and Speakers' Corner.

Hampstead Heath
This breezy, open space is located in the midst of north London. Nearby Parliament Hill offers views of St. Paul's, the City, and the West End.

Kensington Gardens
This plaque is from the Italian Garden, one of the features of this elegant park.

Kensington and Holland Park

South Kensington and Knightsbridge

Kew Gardens
The world's premier botanic garden is a must for anyone with an interest in plants, exotic or mundane.

Holland Park
The former grounds of one of London's grandest homes are now its most romantic park.

0 km   1
0 miles 0.5

Richmond Park
The biggest Royal Park in London remains largely unspoiled, with deer and magnificent river views.

Regent's Park
In this civilized Park, surrounded by fine Regency buildings, you can stroll around the rose garden, visit the open-air theater, or simply sit and admire the view.

Greenwich Park
Its focal point is the National Maritime Museum, well worth a visit for its architecture as well as its exhibits. There are also fine views.

Bloomsbury and Fitzrovia

Regent's Park and Marylebone

Smithfield and Spitalfields

Holborn and the Inns of Court

Soho and Trafalgar Square

THAMES

The City

RIVER

Piccadilly

South Bank

Southwark and Bankside

Whitehall and Westminster

Chelsea

Green Park
Its leafy paths are favored by early-morning joggers from the Mayfair hotels.

Greenwich and Blackheath

Battersea Park
Visitors can rent a rowboat for the best view of the Victorian landscaping around the lake.

St. James's Park
Located in the heart of the city, this park is a popular escape for office workers. It is also a reserve for wildfowl.

Exploring Parks and Gardens

London has one of the the world's greenest downtowns, full of tree-filled squares and grassy parks. From the intimacy of the Chelsea Physic Garden to the wild, open spaces of Hampstead Heath, every London park has its own charm and character. For those looking for a specific outdoor attraction – such as sports, wildlife, or flowers – here are some of the most interesting London parks.

Colorful flower beds at St. James's Park

Flower Gardens

The British are famed for their gardens and love of flowers, and this is reflected in several of London's parks. Really avid gardeners will find all they ever wanted to know at **Kew Gardens** and the **Chelsea Physic Garden**, which is especially strong on herbs. Closer to the center of town, **St. James's Park** boasts some spectacular flower beds, filled with bulbs and bedding plants, which are changed every season. **Hyde Park** sports a magnificent show of daffodils and crocuses in the spring, and London's best rose garden is Queen Mary's in **Regent's Park.**

Kensington Gardens' flower walk has an exemplary English mixed border, and there is also a delightful small 17th-century garden at the **Museum of Garden History**.

Battersea Park also has a charming flower garden, and indoor gardeners should head to the **Barbican Centre**'s well-stocked conservatory.

Formal Gardens

The most spectacular formal garden is at **Hampton Court**, which has a network of gardens from different periods, starting with Tudor. The gardens at **Chiswick House** remain dotted with their

18th-century statuary and pavilions. Other restored gardens include 17th-century **Ham House**, and **Osterley Park**, whose 18th-century layout was retraced through the art of dowsing. **Fenton House** has a really fine walled garden; **Kenwood** is less formal, with its woodland area. **The Hill** is great in summer. The sunken garden at **Kensington Palace** has a formal layout and **Holland Park** has flowers around its statues.

Restful Corners

London's squares are cool, shady retreats but, sadly, many are reserved for keyholders, usually residents of the surrounding houses. Of those open to all, **Russell Square** is the largest and most secluded. **Berkeley Square** is open but barren. **Green Park** offers shady trees and deck chairs, right in central London. The Inns of Court provide some pleasant havens: **Gray's Inn** gardens, **Middle Temple** gardens, and **Lincoln's Inn Fields**. **Grosvenor Square** is one of London's

Sunken garden at Kensington Palace

Green London

In Greater London there are 1,700 parks covering a total of 67 sq miles (174 sq km). This land is home to some 2,000 types of plants and 100 bird species that breed in the trees. Trees help the city to breathe, manufacturing oxygen from the polluted air. Here are some of the species you are most likely to see in London.

The London plane, now the most common tree in London, grows along many streets.

The English oak grows all over Europe. The Royal Navy used to build ships from it.

oldest Georgian squares, while **Soho Square**, surrounded by streets, is more urban.

Music in Summer

Stretching out on the grass or in a deck chair to listen to a band is a British tradition. Military and other bands give regular concerts throughout the summer at **St. James's** and **Regent's Parks** and also at **Parliament Hill Fields**. The concert schedule will usually be found posted close to the bandstand in the park.

Open-air festivals of classical music are held in the summer in several parks *(see p341)*.

Wildlife

There is a large and well-fed collection of ducks and other water birds, even including a few pelicans, in **St. James's Park**. Duck lovers will also appreciate **Regent's, Hyde, and Battersea parks,** as well as **Hampstead Heath**. Deer roam in **Richmond** and **Greenwich Parks**. For a wide variety of captive animals, **London Zoo** is in **Regent's Park**, and there are aviaries or aquariums at several parks and gardens, including **Kew Gardens** and **Syon House**.

Geese in St. James's Park

Historic Cemeteries

In the late 1830s, private cemeteries were established around London to ease the pressure on the overcrowded and unhealthy burial grounds of the inner city. Today, some of these, notably **Highgate Cemetery**, **Kensal Green Cemetery** (Harrow Road, W10), and **Brompton Cemetery** (Fulham Road, SW10), are worth visiting for their Victorian monuments. **Bunhill Fields** is earlier; it was first used during the plague of 1665.

Kensal Green Cemetery

Boating pond at Regent's Park

Sports

Cycling is not universally encouraged in London's parks, and footpaths tend to be too bumpy to allow much roller-skating. However, most parks have tennis courts, which normally have to be reserved in advance with the attendant. Rowboats may be rented at **Hyde**, **Regent's** and **Battersea Parks**, among others. Athletics tracks are at both Battersea Park and **Parliament Hill**. The public may swim at the ponds on **Hampstead Heath** and in the Serpentine in Hyde Park. Hampstead Heath is also ideal kite-flying territory.

Where to Find the Parks

Barbican Centre *p167*
Battersea Park *p343*
Berkeley Square *p273*
Bunhill Fields *p170*
Chelsea Physic Garden *p199*
Chiswick House *pp260–61*
Fenton House *p235*
Gray's Inn *p143*
Green Park *p99*
Greenwich Park *p245*
Ham House *p254*
Hampstead Heath *p236*
Hampton Court *pp256–9*
Highgate Cemetery *p248*
The Hill *p237*
Holland Park *p220*
Hyde Park *p213*
Kensington Gardens *pp212–13*
Kensington Palace *p212*
Kenwood House *pp236–7*
Kew Gardens *pp262–3*
Lincoln's Inn Fields *p139*
London Zoo *p229*
Middle Temple *p141*
Museum of Garden History *p192*
Osterley Park *p255*
Parliament Hill Fields *pp236–7*
Regent's Park *p226*
Richmond Park *p254*
Russell Square *p126*
St. James's Park *p95*
Soho Square *p110*
Syon House *p255*

The common beech has a close relation, the copper beech, with reddish-purple leaves.

The horse chestnut's hard, round fruits are used by children for a game called conkers.

London's Best: Ceremonies

Much of London's rich inheritance of tradition and
ceremony centers on royalty. Faithfully enacted
today, some of these ceremonies date back to
the Middle Ages, when the ruling monarch had
absolute power and had to be protected from
opponents. This map shows the venues for some
of the most important ceremonies in London.
For more details on these and other ceremonies,
please turn to pages 56–7; information on all sorts
of events taking place in London throughout the
year can be found on pages 58–61.

St. James's Palace and Buckingham Palace
Members of the
Queen's Life Guard
stand at the gates
of these two palaces.

Bloomsbury and Fitzrovia

Soho and Trafalgar Square

South Kensington and Knightsbridge

Piccadilly and St. James's

Hyde Park
Royal Salutes are fired by
guns of the King's Troop
Royal Horse Artillery on
royal anniversaries and
ceremonial occasions.

Whitehall and Westminster

Chelsea

Chelsea Hospital
In 1651 Charles II hid from
parliamentary forces in an
oak tree. On Oak Apple
Day, Chelsea Pensioners
decorate his statue with
oak leaves and branches.

Horse Guards
At Trooping the
Colour, the most
elaborate of London's
royal ceremonies, the
Queen salutes as
a battalion of Foot
Guards parades its
colors before her.

The City and Embankment
At the Lord Mayor's Show, pikemen and musketeers escort the newly elected Lord Mayor through the City in a gold state coach.

Smithfield and Spitalfields

Holborn and the Inns of Court

Covent Garden and the Strand

The City

RIVER THAMES

0 kilometers 1
0 miles 0.5

Southwark and Bankside

South Bank

Tower of London
In the nightly Ceremony of the Keys, a Yeoman Warder locks the gates. A military escort ensures that the keys are not stolen.

Houses of Parliament
Each fall, the Queen goes to Parliament in the Irish State Coach to open the new parliamentary session.

The Cenotaph
On Remembrance Sunday the Queen pays homage to the nation's war dead.

Attending London's Ceremonies

Royalty and commerce provide the two principal sources of London's rich calendar of ceremonial events. Quaint and old-fashioned these events may be, but what may seem arcane ritual has real historical meaning – many of the capital's ceremonies originated in the Middle Ages.

A Queen's Guard in winter

Royal Ceremonies

Although the Queen's role is now largely symbolic, the Guard at Buckingham Palace still patrols the palace grounds. The impressive ceremony of the **Changing of the Guard** – dazzling uniforms, shouted commands, military music – consists of the Old Guard, which forms up in the palace forecourt, going off duty and handing over to the New Guard. The Guard consists of three officers and 40 men when the Queen is in residence, but only three officers and 31 men when she is away. The ceremony takes place in front of the palace. In another changeover ceremony, the Queen's Life Guards travel daily from Hyde Park Barracks to Horse Guards Parade.

One of the Queen's Life Guards

The **Ceremony of the Keys** at the Tower of London is one of the capital's most timeless ceremonies. After each of the Tower gates has been locked, the last post is sounded by a trumpeter before the keys are secured in the Queen's House.

The Tower of London and Hyde Park are also the scene of **Royal Salutes** that take place on birthdays and other occasions throughout the year. At such times, 41 rounds are fired in Hyde Park at noon, and 62 rounds at the Tower at 1pm. The spectacle in Hyde Park is a stirring one as 71 horses and six 13-pounder cannons swirl into place and the roar of the guns begins.

The combination of pageantry, color, and music makes the annual **Trooping the Colour** the high point of London's ceremonial year. The Queen takes the Royal Salute, and after her troops have marched past, she leads them to Buckingham Palace, where a second march-past takes place. The best place to watch this spectacle is from the Horse Guards Parade side of St. James's Park. Bands of the Household Cavalry and the Foot Guards stage the ceremony of

Beating the Retreat at Horse Guards Parade. This takes place on two successive evenings a year, in June, leading up to Trooping the Colour. The spectacular **State Opening of Parliament**, when the Queen opens the annual parliamentary session in the House of Lords – usually in November – is not open to the general public, although it is now televised. The huge royal procession, which moves from Buckingham Palace to Westminster, is, however, a magnificent sight, with the Queen traveling in the highly ornate Irish State Coach drawn by four horses.

Military Ceremonies

The Cenotaph in Whitehall is the setting for a ceremony held on **Remembrance Sunday**, to give thanks to those who died fighting in any conflict from World War I onward.

National **Navy Day** is commemorated by a parade down the Mall, followed by a service held at Nelson's Column in Trafalgar Square.

Royal salute, Tower of London

Trooping the Colour

Silent Change ceremony at Guildhall for the new Lord Mayor

Ceremonies in the City

November is the focus of the City of London's ceremonial year. At the **Silent Change** in Guildhall, the outgoing Lord Mayor hands over symbols of office to the new Mayor in a virtually wordless ceremony. The following day sees the rumbustious **Lord Mayor's Show**. Accompanying the Lord Mayor in his gold state coach, a procession of bands, decorated floats, and military detachments makes its way through the City from Guildhall past the Mansion House to the Law Courts, and back again along the Embankment.

Lord Mayor's chain of office

Many of the ceremonies that take place in the City are linked to the activities of the Livery Companies (see p152). These include the Worshipful Companies of **Vintners and Distillers'** annual celebration of the wine harvest and the Stationers' **Cakes and Ale Sermon**, held in St. Paul's. Cakes and ale are provided according to the will of a 17th-century stationer.

Name-Day Ceremonies

Every May 21, **King Henry VI**, who was murdered in the Tower of London in 1471, is still remembered by the members of his two famous foundations, Eton College and King's College, Cambridge, who meet for a ceremony at the Wakefield Tower where he was killed. **Oak Apple Day** commemorates King Charles II's lucky escape from the Parliamentary forces of Oliver Cromwell in 1651. The King managed to conceal himself in a hollow oak tree, and today Chelsea Pensioners honor his memory by decorating his statue at Chelsea Royal Hospital with oak leaves and branches. On December 18, the lexicographer **Dr. Johnson** is commemorated in an annual service held at Westminster Abbey.

Informal Ceremonies

Each July, six guildsmen from the Company of Watermen compete for the prize in **Doggett's Coat and Badge Race**. In fall, the **Pearly Kings and Queens**, representatives of east London's traders, meet at St. Mary-le-Bow. In March, children are given oranges and lemons at the **Oranges and Lemons service** at St. Clement Danes church. In February, clowns take part in a service for **Joseph Grimaldi** (1779–1837) at the Holy Trinity Church in Dalston, E8.

Pearly Queen

LONDON THROUGH THE YEAR

Springtime in London carries an almost tangible air of a city waking up to longer days and outdoor pursuits. The cheerful yellow of daffodils studs the parks, and less hardy Londoners turn out for their first jog of the year to find themselves puffing in the wake of serious runners training for the Marathon. As spring turns into summer, the royal parks reach their full glory, and in Kensington Gardens, nannies gather to chat under venerable chestnut trees. As fall takes hold, these same trees are ablaze with red and gold, and Londoners' thoughts turn to afternoons in museums, followed by tea in a café. The year closes with Guy Fawkes and Christmas shopping. The official visitor organization, Visit London, www.visitlondon.com *(p354)*, and the listings magazines *(p334)* have details of seasonal events.

Spring

The weather during the spring months may be raw, and an umbrella is a necessary precaution. Druids celebrate the spring equinox in a subdued ceremony on Tower Hill. Painters compete to have their works accepted by the Royal Academy. Soccer teams close their season in May with the FA Cup Final, while cricketers don their sweaters to begin theirs. Oxford and Cambridge Universities row their annual boat race along the Thames, and Marathon runners pound the streets.

Runners in the London Marathon passing Tower Bridge

March
Chelsea Antiques Fair *(week varies, also Sep)*, Chelsea Old Town Hall, King's Rd SW3. **Ideal Home Show** *(17 days from mid-Mar)*, Earl's Court, Warwick Rd SW5. It is a long-established show with the latest in domestic gadgetry and state-of-the-art technology. **Oranges and Lemons Service** *(3rd Thu in Mar)*, St. Clement Danes *(p57)*. Service for schoolchildren; each child is given an orange and a lemon. **Oxford and Cambridge boat race** *(late Mar or early Apr)*, Putney to Mortlake *(p347)*. **Spring equinox celebration** *(Mar 21)*, Tower Hill EC3. Historic pagan ceremony with modern-day druids. **London Festival of Railway Modelling** *(late Mar)*, Alexandra Palace. Of real interest to people of all ages, and held in a gorgeous Victorian setting.

Easter
Good Friday and **Easter Monday** are public holidays. **Easter parades**, Battersea Park *(p253)*. **Easter Kite Festival**, Hampstead Heath *(p236)*. **Easter procession and hymns** *(Easter Mon)*, Westminster Abbey *(pp78–81)*. **London Harness Horse Parade** *(Easter Mon)*, Battersea Park *(p253)*.

The Holy Cross being carried through the streets during the Good Friday procession

April
Head of the River Race *(early Apr)*, more than 400 teams row from Mortlake to Putney. **Queen's Birthday gun salutes** *(Apr 21)*, Hyde Park, Tower of London *(p56)*. **London Marathon** *(Sun in Apr or May)*, champions and novices run from Greenwich to Westminster *(p347)*.

May
First and last Mon are public holidays. **FA Cup Final**, soccer season's climax *(p346)*. **Beating the Bounds** *(Ascension Day)*, throughout the City. Young boys from the City parish beat buildings that mark the parish boundaries. **Oak Apple Day** *(May 29)*, Royal Hospital, Chelsea *(p57)*. **Covent Garden May Fayre and Puppet Festival** *(mid-May)*, St. Paul's Church, Covent Garden *(pp113–21)*. **Chelsea Flower Show** *(late May)*, Royal Hospital, Chelsea.

Average Daily Hours of Sunshine

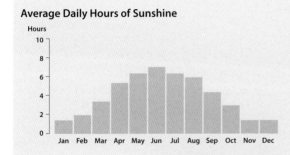

Hours

Jan Feb Mar Apr May Jun Jul Aug Sep Oct Nov Dec

Sunshine Chart
London's longest and hottest days fall between May and August. In the height of summer, daylight hours can extend from well before 5am to after 9pm. Daytime is much shorter in the winter, but London can be stunning in the winter sunshine.

Summer

London's summer season is packed full of indoor and outdoor events. The weather is unreliable, even at the height of summer, but unless you are notably unlucky, there should be enough pleasant days to sample the city's offerings.

The selection includes many traditional events, such as the Wimbledon tennis championships and the cricket test matches at Lord's and the Oval. Well out of view of the general public and prying photographers, the Queen holds garden parties for favored subjects in the splendid grounds of Buckingham Palace. The summer public holiday is also marked with fairs in some of London's parks.

June

Beating the Retreat *(p56)*
Coronation Day gun salutes *(Jun 2)*, Hyde Park and Tower of London *(p56)*. **Art Antiques London** *(mid-Jun)*, Kensington Gardens W8. The world's top dealers gather in a specially built pavilion opposite the Royal Albert Hall *(p209)*
Trooping the Colour, Horse Guards Parade *(p56)*.
Duke of Edinburgh's Birthday gun salutes *(Jun 10)*, Hyde Park and Tower of London *(p56)*.
Wimbledon Lawn Tennis Championships *(two weeks in late Jun)*; *(p346)*. **Cricket test match**, Lord's Cricket Ground *(p346)*. **Open-air theater season** *(throughout the summer)*, stages in Regent's Park and Holland Park. Shakespeare, Shaw, and others

Revelers at Notting Hill Carnival

offer the perfect opportunity for a picnic with a cultural flavor *(p336)*. **Open-air concerts**, Kenwood, Hampstead Heath, Crystal Palace, Marble Hill, St. James's Park *(p341)*. **Summer festivals** *(late Jun)*, Spitalfields and Primrose Hill. Contact Visit London *(p354)* or see the listings magazines *(p334)* for times and venues of all these events and see July, below. **City of London Festival** *(late Jun–mid-July)*, various City venues *(p145)*. Arts and music festival with concerts taking place in some of London's most beautiful historic churches.

July

Summer festivals, Greenwich and Docklands, Regent's Park, Richmond, and Soho. **Sales**, mid-year, price reductions in shops across London' *(p313)*.

Hampton Court Flower Show, Hampton Court Palace *(pp256–9)*. **Henry Wood Promenade Concerts (The Proms)** *(late Jul–Sep)*, Royal Albert Hall *(p209)*. **Royal Academy of Arts Summer Exhibition** *(Jun–Aug)*, Piccadilly *(p92)*. **Doggett's Coat and Badge Race** A historic river-rowing contest between Thames watermen *(p65)*.

August

Last Monday in August is a public holiday. **Notting Hill Carnival** *(late Aug holiday weekend)*. An internationally famous and well attended Caribbean carnival organized by the area's various ethnic communities *(p221)*. **Fairs** *(Aug holiday)*. Throughout London's parks in the summer.

Regimental band, St. James's Park

Average Monthly Rainfall

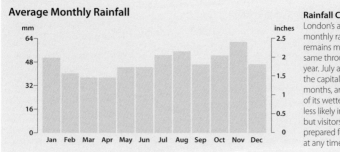

Rainfall Chart
London's average monthly rainfall remains much the same throughout the year. July and August, the capital's warmest months, are also two of its wettest. Rain is less likely in spring, but visitors should be prepared for a shower at any time of year.

Fall

There is a sense of purpose about London in the fall. The buildup to the busiest shopping season, the start of the academic year, and the new parliamentary session, opened by the Queen, inject some life into the colder months. The cricket season ends in mid-September, while food-lovers may be interested in the spectacular displays of fresh fish that are laid out in the vestry of St. Mary-at-Hill, celebrating the harvest of this island nation.

Memories of a more turbulent opening of Parliament are revived on November 5. Bonfires and fireworks across the country commemorate the failed conspiracy, led by Guy Fawkes in 1605, to blow up the Palace of Westminster. A few days later, the dead of any conflict, from World War I onward, are honored at a ceremony held in Whitehall.

Pearly Kings gathering for the harvest festival at St. Mary-le-Bow

London-to-Brighton veteran car run

September
The Mayor's Thames Festival, *(mid-Sep)*. Entertainment by and on the river between Westminster Bridge and Southwark Cathedral. **Great River Race**, Thames. **Last Night of the Proms** *(mid-Sep)*, Royal Albert Hall *(p209)*. Entertaining the masses with rousing classical hits and favorite British patriotic pieces.

October
Pearly Harvest Festival *(first Sun)*. The Festival begins at Guildhall Yard, from where a parade of Pearly Kings and Queens makes its way to St. Mary-le-Bow Church for the Harvest Festival service *(p149)*. **Harvest of the Sea** *(second Sun)*, St. Mary-at-Hill Church *(p154)*. **Vintners' and Distillers' Wine Harvest** *(p57)*. **Navy Day** *(p56)*.

November
State Opening of Parliament *(p56)*. **Guy Fawkes Night** *(Nov 5)*. Listings magazines give details of fireworks displays *(p334)*. **Remembrance Day Service** *(p56)*. **Silent Change** *(p57)*. **Lord Mayor's Show** *(p57)*. **London to Brighton** veteran car rally *(first Sun)*. **Christmas lights** *(late Nov– Jan 6)*. The West End *(p315)*, especially Regent Street, lights up for the festive season.

Fireworks explode during Guy Fawkes Night

Average Monthly Temperature

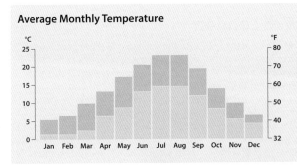

Temperature Chart
The chart shows the average minimum and maximum temperatures for each month. High temperatures averaging 75°F (22°C) belie London's reputation for year-round chilliness, although November through to February can be extremely cold and icy.

Winter

Some of the most striking images of London are drawn from winter: paintings of frost fairs in the 17th and 18th centuries, when the Thames River froze over completely; and Claude Monet's views of the river and its bridges.

For centuries, thick "pea-souper" fogs were an inevitable part of winter, until the Clean Air Act of 1956 banned coal-burning in open grates.

Christmas trees and lights twinkle everywhere – from the West End shopping streets to construction sites. The scent of roasting chestnuts pervades as street vendors sell them from glowing mobile braziers.

Seasonal menus feature roast turkey, mince pies, and Christmas pudding. Traditional fare in theaters includes colorful family pantomimes (where the customary cross-dressing between the sexes baffles many visitors – *p336*) and popular ballets such as *Swan Lake* or *The Nutcracker*.

Skaters use open-air ice rinks at Canada Square, Greenwich, Hyde Park, Hampton Court, and Somerset House (*see p119*). It is rarely safe to use the parks' frozen lakes.

Winter in the picturesque gardens of Kensington Palace

December

Oxford vs. Cambridge rugby union match Twickenham (*p347*). **Spitalfields Music Winter Festival** (*mid-Dec*), Old Spitalfields Market (*p172*). **London International Horse Show** (*late Dec*), Olympia. Equestrian competition.

Christmas, New Year

Dec 25–26 and **Jan 1** are public hols. There is no train service on Christmas Day.

Carol services (*leading up to Christmas*), Trafalgar Square (*p104*), St. Paul's (*pp150–53*), Westminster Abbey (*pp78–81*), and many other churches. **Turkey auction** (*Dec 24*), Smithfield Market (*p166*). **Christmas Day swim** Serpentine, Hyde Park (*p213*). **New Year's Eve celebrations** (*Dec 31*), Trafalgar Square, St. Paul's.

January

Sales (*p313*). **New Year's Day Parade** starts at Parliament Sq (*p76*). **London Boat Show**, ExCel London, Docklands E16. **International Mime Festival** (*mid-Jan–early Feb*), various venues. **Charles I Commemoration** (*last Sun*), procession from St. James's Palace (*p93*) to Banqueting House (*p82*). **Chinese New Year** (*late Jan–mid-Feb*), Chinatown (*p110*) and Soho (*p111*).

February

Queen's Accession gun salutes (*Feb 6*), 41-gun salute Hyde Park; 62-gun salute Tower of London (*p56*). **Pancake races** (*Shrove Tue*), Lincoln's Inn Fields (*p139*) and Covent Garden (*p114*).

Public Holidays

New Year's Day (Jan 1); **Good Friday**; **Easter Monday**; **May Day** (first Monday in May); **Whit Monday** (last Monday in May); **August Bank Holiday** (last Monday in Aug); **Christmas Day and Boxing Day** (Dec 25–26).

Christmas illuminations in Trafalgar Square

A River View of London

Cruising down the Thames is one of the most interesting ways to experience London. As the country's main commercial artery from the Roman invasion to well into the 1950s, the river is packed with historical sites, including the reconstruction of the Elizabethan Globe Theatre, royal palaces and parks, various celebrated bridges, and decommissioned power stations. Now the river is the city's foremost leisure amenity, with the banks accessible via the Thames Path and numerous riverside pubs, and commuters as well as tourists sailing the river.

Passenger boat services cover about 30 miles (50 km) of the Thames, from Hampton Court in the west to the Thames Barrier in the east. The most popular and best served section runs through the heart of the city from Westminster to Tower Bridge. Often accompanied by interesting and witty commentary, a cruise along this fascinating stretch of the Thames should not be missed.

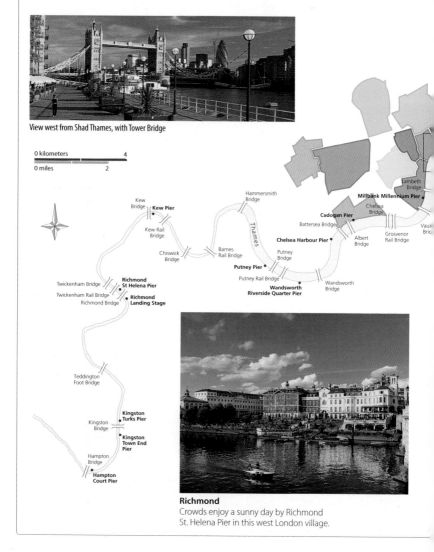

View west from Shad Thames, with Tower Bridge

0 kilometers 4
0 miles 2

Kew Bridge
Kew Pier
Kew Rail Bridge
Chiswick Bridge
Barnes Rail Bridge
Hammersmith Bridge
Thames
Chelsea Harbour Pier
Putney Bridge
Putney Pier
Putney Rail Bridge
Wandsworth Riverside Quarter Pier
Wandsworth Bridge
Battersea Bridge
Cadogan Pier
Albert Bridge
Grosvenor Rail Bridge
Chelsea Bridge
Lambeth Bridge
Millbank Millennium Pier
Vaux Bric

Twickenham Bridge
Richmond St Helena Pier
Twickenham Rail Bridge
Richmond Bridge
Richmond Landing Stage

Teddington Foot Bridge

Kingston Turks Pier
Kingston Bridge
Kingston Town End Pier
Hampton Bridge
Hampton Court Pier

Richmond
Crowds enjoy a sunny day by Richmond St. Helena Pier in this west London village.

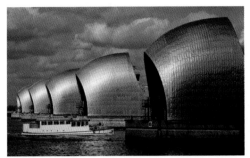

The Thames Barrier
Completed in 1982, the world's second-largest movable flood barrier protects London from rising water levels. The massive steel gates have been raised over 100 times.

Riverside pubs
Beautifully preserved pubs, such as the Prospect of Whitby in Wapping, hug the river's banks.

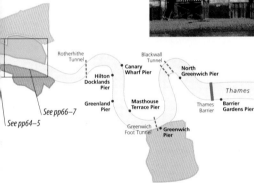

Rotherhithe Tunnel
Blackwall Tunnel
Canary Wharf Pier
North Greenwich Pier
Hilton Docklands Pier
Greenland Pier
Masthouse Terrace Pier
Thames Barrier
Thames Barrier Gardens Pier
Thames
Greenwich Foot Tunnel
Greenwich Pier
See pp66–7
See pp64–5

Cruise Operators

Bateaux London/ Catamaran Cruisers
Tel 020 7695 1800.
bateauxlondon.com

City Cruises
Tel 020 7740 0400.
citycruises.com

Crown River Cruises
Tel 020 7936 2033.
crownriver.com

Thames Clippers
Tel 0870 781 5049.
thamesclippers.com

Thames Executive Charters
Tel 01342 820600.
thamesexecutive charters.com

Thames River Services
Tel 020 7930 4097.
thamesriverservices. co.uk

Turks Launches
Tel 020 8546 2434.
turks.co.uk

Westminster Passenger Service Association (Upriver) Ltd
Tel 020 7930 2062
wpsa.co.uk

Cruise Highlights

Most regular services run from April through September, with some routes having winter schedules. During the summer, sailing times are frequent from Westminster and Embankment to Greenwich, with a boat arriving between every half hour and every hour. Commuter river services link Canary Wharf and Chelsea Harbour with some of the city's main termini. Numerous operators cover a variety of routes, and a River Thames Boat Service Guide is available at tube stations. Most operators give a third off the ticket price to Travelcard holders (see p370).

Greenwich (see pp238–45)
Blessed with frequent service, accessing this area steeped in shipping lore by boat gives a day-trip a fitting nautical spin.
Operators: Bateaux London/ Catamaran Cruisers, City Cruises, Thames River Services.
Piers: Westminster, Waterloo, Embankment, Bankside, Tower.
Duration: 1 hr (Westminster).
Thames Barrier (see p251) Sail between the nine massive piers that raise the steel gates. Cruises to the barrier also pass the O2 Arena, formerly the Millennium Dome.
Operator: Thames River Services.
Piers: Westminster, Greenwich.
Duration: 30 min (Greenwich).

Kew (see pp262–3) A cruise to Kew leaves the city behind after passing the Battersea Power Station and sailing through Hammersmith.
Operator: WPSA (upriver only).
Piers: Westminster.
Duration: 1.5 hr (Westminster).
Hampton Court (see pp256–9) Arrive at Hampton Court in regal style, but be aware that the round trip from Westminster can take up to eight hours. Consider sailing from one of the piers upriver.
Operator: WPSA (upriver only), Turks Launches.
Piers: Kew, all Richmond and Kingston piers.
Duration: 2 hrs (Kew).

Westminster Bridge to Blackfriars Bridge

Until World War II, this stretch of the Thames marked the division between rich and poor London. On the north bank were the offices, shops, luxury hotels, and apartments of Whitehall and the Strand, the Inns of Court, and the newspaper district. To the south were smoky factories and slum dwellings. After the war, the Festival of Britain in 1951 started the revival of the South Bank *(see pp186–93)*, which now has some of the capital's most interesting modern buildings.

Savoy Hotel
This hotel is on the site of a medieval palace *(p118).*

Shell Mex House
Once offices for the oil company, they were built in 1931 on the site of the vast Cecil Hotel.

Somerset House, built in 1786, houses an art gallery *(p119).*

Embankment Gardens is the site of many open-air concerts held in the bandstand during the summer months *(p120).*

Cleopatra's Needle was made in ancient Egypt and given to London in 1819 *(p120).*

Waterloo Bridge

 Temp

🚇 Charing Cross

Charing Cross
The rail terminus is encased in a Post-modernist office complex *(p121).*

🚇 Embankment
🚢 Embankment Pier

Festival Pier 🚢

The South Bank was the site of the 1951 Festival of Britain and is London's most important arts complex. It is dominated by the Royal Festival Hall, the National Theatre, and the Hayward Gallery *(pp186–93).*

London Eye Pier

Hungerford Railway Bridge and Golden Jubilee Footbridges

Jubilee Gardens

The London Eye offers breath-taking views over London *(p191).*

The Banqueting House is one of Inigo Jones's finest works, built as part of Whitehall Palace *(p82).*

The Ministry of Defence is a bulky white fortress completed in the 1950s.

Westminster Pier

Westminster

Westminster Bridge

County Hall
This is home to the state-of-the-art London Aquarium and its 350 species of fish.

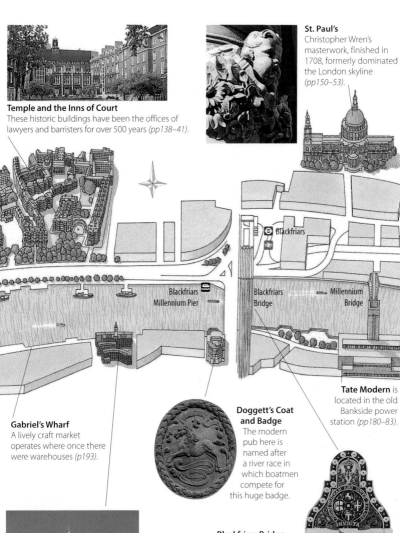

Temple and the Inns of Court
These historic buildings have been the offices of
lawyers and barristers for over 500 years *(pp138–41)*.

St. Paul's
Christopher Wren's
masterwork, finished in
1708, formerly dominated
the London skyline
(pp150–53).

🚇 Blackfriars

Blackfriars
Millennium Pier

Blackfriars
Bridge

Millennium
Bridge

Tate Modern is
located in the old
Bankside power
station *(pp180–83)*.

Gabriel's Wharf
A lively craft market
operates where once there
were warehouses *(p193)*.

**Doggett's Coat
and Badge**
The modern
pub here is
named after
a river race in
which boatmen
compete for
this huge badge.

Blackfriars Bridge
The logo of a former railroad
company adorns the bridge.

OXO Tower
The windows were designed
to spell the brand name of a
popular meat extract.

St. Paul's
The cathedral dominates views from the South Bank.

For key to symbols *see back flap*

Southwark Bridge to St. Katharine's Dock

For centuries, the stretch just east of London Bridge was the busiest part of the Thames, with ships of all sizes jostling for position to unload at the wharves on both banks. Then, in the 19th century, the construction of the docks to the east eased congestion. Today most landmarks on this section hark back to that commercial past.

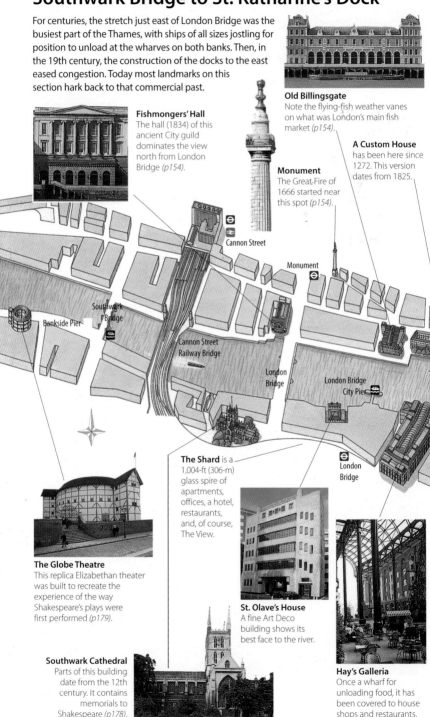

Old Billingsgate
Note the flying-fish weather vanes on what was London's main fish market *(p154)*.

Fishmongers' Hall
The hall (1834) of this ancient City guild dominates the view north from London Bridge *(p154)*.

A Custom House
has been here since 1272. This version dates from 1825.

Monument
The Great Fire of 1666 started near this spot *(p154)*.

Cannon Street

Monument

Southwark Bridge

Bankside Pier

Cannon Street Railway Bridge

London Bridge

London Bridge City Pier

The Shard is a 1,004-ft (306-m) glass spire of apartments, offices, a hotel, restaurants, and, of course, The View.

London Bridge

The Globe Theatre
This replica Elizabethan theater was built to recreate the experience of the way Shakespeare's plays were first performed *(p179)*.

St. Olave's House
A fine Art Deco building shows its best face to the river.

Southwark Cathedral
Parts of this building date from the 12th century. It contains memorials to Shakespeare *(p178)*.

Hay's Galleria
Once a wharf for unloading food, it has been covered to house shops and restaurants.

Southwark Wharves
Now there are walkways with river views where ships used to dock.

Tower of London
Look for Traitors' Gate, where prisoners would be taken into the Tower by boat (pp156–9).

Tower Bridge
It still opens to let tall ships pass, but not as often as it did when cargo vessels came through (p155).

St. Katharine's Dock
The former dock is now a lively attraction for visitors. Its yacht marina is a highlight (p160).

Tower Millennium Pier

Tower Bridge

St Katharine's Pier

The stunning City Hall
houses the Mayor and the governing offices.

Victorian warehouses
on Butlers Wharf have been converted into apartments.

HMS Belfast
This World War II cruiser has been a museum since 1971 (p185).

Design Museum
Opened in 1989, this ship-like building is a shining example of Docklands' renaissance (p185).

Aerial view of the City of London by night ▶

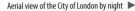

LONDON AREA BY AREA

WHITEHALL AND WESTMINSTER

Whitehall and Westminster have been at the center of political and religious power in England for a thousand years. King Canute, who ruled at the beginning of the 11th century, was the first monarch to have a palace on what was then an island in the swampy meeting point of the Thames and its vanished tributary, the Tyburn. Canute built his palace beside the church that, some 50 years later, Edward the Confessor would enlarge into England's greatest abbey, giving the area its name (a minster is an abbey church). Over the following centuries, the offices of state were established in the vicinity. All this is still reflected in Whitehall's heroic statues and massive government buildings. But to its north, Trafalgar Square marks the start of the West End entertainment district.

Sights at a Glance

Historic Streets and Buildings
1. Houses of Parliament pp74–5
2. Big Ben
3. Jewel Tower
5. Dean's Yard
7. Parliament Square
9. Downing Street
10. Cabinet War Rooms and Churchill Museum
11. Banqueting House
12. Horse Guards Parade
14. Queen Anne's Gate
16. St. James's Park Station
17. Blewcoat School

Churches, Abbeys, and Cathedrals
4. Westminster Abbey pp78–81
6. St. Margaret's Church
18. Westminster Cathedral
19. St. John's, Smith Square

Museums and Galleries
15. Guards' Museum
20. Tate Britain pp84–7

Theatres
13. Trafalgar Studios

Monuments
8. Cenotaph

Street Finder, maps 13, 20, 21

◀ The clock face on the Houses of Parliament

For keys to symbols see back flap

Street by Street: Whitehall and Westminster

Compared with many capital cities, London has little monumental architecture designed to dazzle. Here, at the historic seat both of the government and of the established church, it most closely approaches the broad, stately avenues of Paris, Rome, and Madrid. On weekdays the streets are crowded with members of the civil service, as most of their work is based in this area. On weekends, however, it is popular with tourists visiting some of London's most famous sights.

🔟 ★ Cabinet War Rooms and Churchill Museum
The War Rooms were Winston Churchill's World War II headquarters.

The Treasury is where the nation's finances are administered.

Central Hall is a florid example of the Beaux Arts style, built in 1911 as a Methodist meeting hall. In 1946 the first General Assembly of the United Nations was held here.

❹ ★ Westminster Abbey
The Abbey is London's oldest and most important church.

❼ Parliament Square
Statues of famous statesmen, such as Benjamin Disraeli, Sir Winston Churchill and Nelson Mandela, stand here.

The Sanctuary was a medieval safe place for those escaping the law.

❻ St. Margaret's Church
Society weddings often take place here, in Parliament's church.

❺ Dean's Yard
Westminster School was founded here in 1540.

Richard I's Statue, by Carlo Marochetti (1860), depicts the 12th-century *Coeur de Lion* (Lionheart).

❸ Jewel Tower
Kings once stored their most valuable possessions here.

The Burghers of Calais is a cast of Auguste Rodin's original in Paris.

STOREY'S GATE

KING CHARLES

GREAT GEORGE STREET

BROAD

SANCTUARY

PARLIAMENT

ST MARGARET STREET SO

GREAT COLLEGE STREET

ABINGDON STREET

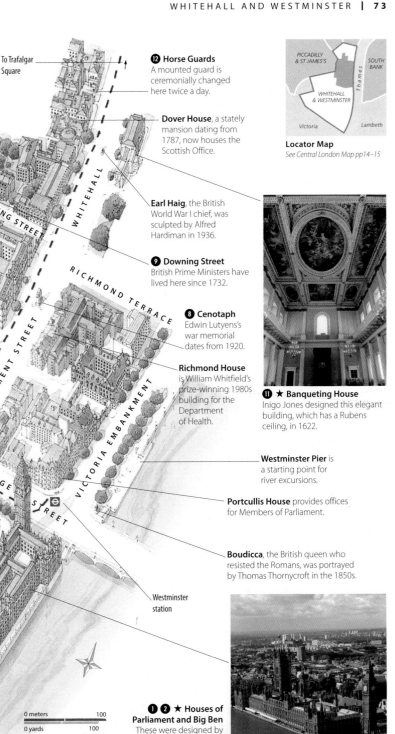

To Trafalgar Square

⑫ **Horse Guards**
A mounted guard is ceremonially changed here twice a day.

WHITEHALL

Dover House, a stately mansion dating from 1787, now houses the Scottish Office.

OWNING STREET

Earl Haig, the British World War I chief, was sculpted by Alfred Hardiman in 1936.

RICHMOND TERRACE

❾ **Downing Street**
British Prime Ministers have lived here since 1732.

❽ **Cenotaph**
Edwin Lutyens's war memorial dates from 1920.

PARLIAMENT STREET

Richmond House is William Whitfield's prize-winning 1980s building for the Department of Health.

VICTORIA EMBANKMENT

BRIDGE STREET

Westminster station

Locator Map
See Central London Map pp14–15

PICCADILLY & ST JAMES'S
SOUTH BANK
Thames
WHITEHALL & WESTMINSTER
Victoria
Lambeth

⑪ ★ **Banqueting House**
Inigo Jones designed this elegant building, which has a Rubens ceiling, in 1622.

Westminster Pier is a starting point for river excursions.

Portcullis House provides offices for Members of Parliament.

Boudicca, the British queen who resisted the Romans, was portrayed by Thomas Thornycroft in the 1850s.

❶ ❷ ★ **Houses of Parliament and Big Ben**
These were designed by Barry in 1834 when the Palace of Westminster burned down.

0 meters 100
0 yards 100

Key

— Suggested route

❶ Houses of Parliament

For over 500 years the Palace of Westminster has been the seat of the two Houses of Parliament, called the Lords and the Commons. The Commons is made up of elected Members of Parliament (MPs) of different political parties; the party – or coalition of parties – with the most MPs forms the government, and its leader becomes Prime Minister. MPs from other parties make up the Opposition. Commons debates can become heated and are impartially chaired by an MP designated as Speaker. The Government formulates legislation, which must be agreed to in both Houses before becoming law.

★ Commons Chamber
The room is upholstered in green. The Government sits on the left, the Opposition on the right, and the Speaker presides from a chair between them.

The mock-Gothic building was designed by Victorian architect Sir Charles Barry. Victoria Tower, on the left, contains over 3 million parliamentary records, including every Act of Parliament passed since 1497.

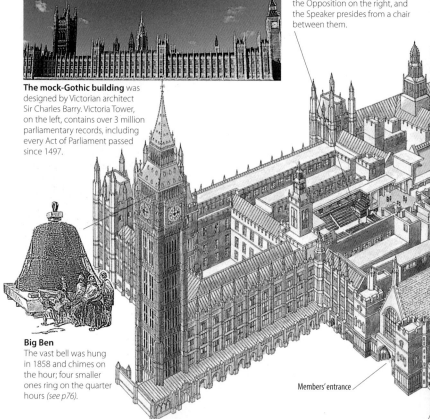

Big Ben
The vast bell was hung in 1858 and chimes on the hour; four smaller ones ring on the quarter hours (see p76).

Members' entrance

KEY

① **Peers** are members of the House of Lords. They come from many walks of life and bring experience and knowledge from a wide range of professions. This is their lobby.

② **Royal Gallery** is used for quiet work by members of the Lords, and occasional special events.

★ Westminster Hall
The only surviving part of the original Palace of Westminster, it dates from 1097; its hammerbeam roof is 14th-century.

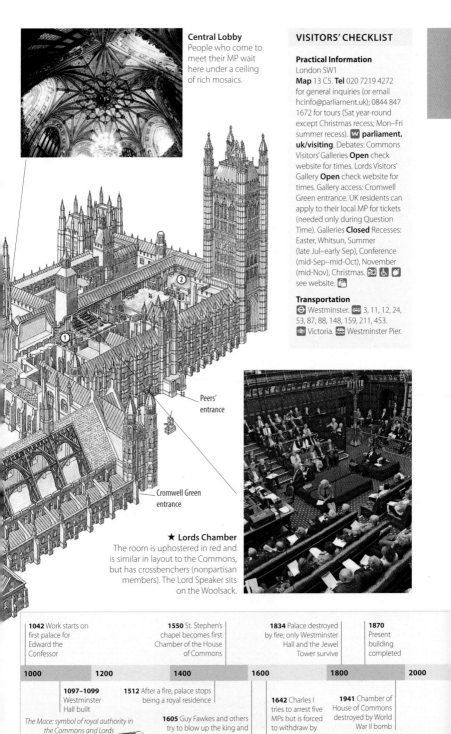

Central Lobby
People who come to meet their MP wait here under a ceiling of rich mosaics.

Peers' entrance

Cromwell Green entrance

★ **Lords Chamber**
The room is uphostered in red and is similar in layout to the Commons, but has crossbenchers (nonpartisan members). The Lord Speaker sits on the Woolsack.

1042 Work starts on first palace for Edward the Confessor	**1550** St. Stephen's chapel becomes first Chamber of the House of Commons	**1834** Palace destroyed by fire; only Westminster Hall and the Jewel Tower survive	**1870** Present building completed	
1000	**1200**	**1400**	**1600**	**1800**	**2000**

1097–1099 Westminster Hall built

1512 After a fire, palace stops being a royal residence

The Mace: symbol of royal authority in the Commons and Lords

1605 Guy Fawkes and others try to blow up the king and Houses of Parliament

1642 Charles I tries to arrest five MPs but is forced to withdraw by the Speaker

1941 Chamber of House of Commons destroyed by World War II bomb

The world's most famous clock tower, which houses Big Ben

❷ Big Ben

Bridge St SW1. **Map** 13 C5. 🔵 Westminster. 🎥 for UK residents only; 9:15am, 11:15am & 2:15pm Mon–Fri.

Big Ben is not the name of the world-famous four-faced clock in the 315-ft (96-m) tower that rises above the Houses of Parliament, but of the resonant 14-ton bell on which the hours are struck, thought to have been named after the Chief Commissioner of Works Sir Benjamin Hall in 1858. Cast in Whitechapel, it was the second giant bell made for the clock, the first having been cracked during a test ringing. The clock is the largest in Britain, its four dials 23 ft (7.5 m) in diameter and the minute hand 14 ft (4.25 m) long, made of hollow copper for lightness. It has kept exact time for the nation more or less continuously since it was first set in motion in May 1859, and has become a symbol of Britain the world over. The tower itself was renamed the Elizabeth Tower in 2012 in honor of Queen Elizabeth II in her Diamond Jubilee Year.

❸ Jewel Tower

Abingdon St SW1. **Map** 13 B5. **Tel** 020 7222 2219. 🔵 Westminster. **Open** Apr–Oct: 10am–5pm daily; Nov–Mar: 10am–4pm Sat & Sun. **Closed** Jan 1, Dec 24–26. 🎫 🔖 ground floor only. 📷
w english-heritage.org.uk

This and Westminster Hall *(see p74)* are the only vestiges of the old Palace of Westminster. The tower was built in 1365 as a stronghold for Edward III's treasure and today houses a fascinating exhibition, *Parliament Past and Present,* that relates the history of Parliament. It includes a display devoted to the history of the Jewel Tower itself.

The tower served as the weights and measures office from 1869 until 1938, and another small display relates to that era. Alongside are the remains of the moat and a medieval quay.

❹ Westminster Abbey

See pp78–81.

❺ Dean's Yard

Broad Sanctuary SW1. **Map** 13 B5. 🔵 Westminster. Buildings **Closed** to the public.

An arch near the west door of the Abbey leads into this secluded grassy square, surrounded by a jumble of buildings from many different periods. A medieval house on the east side has a distinctive dormer window and backs

Entrance to the Abbey and cloisters from Dean's Yard

onto Little Dean's Yard, where the monks' living quarters used to be. Dean's Yard is private property. It belongs to the Dean and Chapter of Westminster and is close to Westminster School, whose famous former pupils include poet John Dryden and playwright Ben Jonson. Scholars are, by tradition, the first to acknowledge a new monarch.

❻ St. Margaret's Church

Parliament Sq SW1. **Map** 13 B5. **Tel** 020 7654 4840. 🔵 Westminster. **Open** 9:30am–3:30pm Mon–Fri, 9:30am–1:30pm Sat, 2–5pm Sun. 🕆 11am Sun. ✉ 🔖 via North Door

Overshadowed by the Abbey, this late-15th-century church has long been a favored venue for political and society weddings, such as Winston and Clementine Churchill's. Although much restored, the church retains some Tudor features, notably a stained-glass window commemorating the marriage of King Henry VIII and his first wife, Catherine of Aragon.

❼ Parliament Square

SW1. **Map** 13 B5. 🔵 Westminster.

Laid out in the 1840s to provide a more open exposure for the new Houses of Parliament, the square became Britain's first official roundabout in 1926. Today it is hemmed in by heavy traffic. Statues of statesmen and soldiers are dominated by Winston Churchill in his greatcoat, glowering at the House of Commons. On the north side, Abraham Lincoln sits in front of the mock-Gothic Middlesex Guildhall, completed in 1913.

❽ Cenotaph

Whitehall SW1. **Map** 13 B4. 🔵 Westminster.

This suitably bleak and pale monument, completed in 1920 by Sir Edwin Lutyens to commemorate the dead of

World War I, stands in the middle of Whitehall. Every year on Remembrance Day (the Sunday closest to November 11), the monarch and other dignitaries place wreaths of red poppies on the Cenotaph. This solemn ceremony, commemorating the 1918 armistice, honors the victims of World War I and World War II *(see pp56–7)*.

The Cenotaph

⑩ Churchill Museum and Cabinet War Rooms

Clive Steps, King Charles St SW1. **Map** 13 B5. **Tel** 020 7930 6961. ⊜ Westminster. **Open** 9:30am–6pm daily (last adm: 5pm). **Closed** Dec 24–26. 🅿🅰🅱🆀🅿 **w iwm.org.uk/cabinet**

This intriguing slice of 20th-century history is a warren of rooms below the Government Office Building north of Parliament Square. It is where the War Cabinet – first under Neville Chamberlain, then Winston Churchill – met during World War II when German bombs were falling on London. The War Rooms include living quarters for key ministers and military leaders

Telephones in the Map Room of the Cabinet War Rooms

and a Cabinet Room, where many strategic decisions were made. They are laid out as they were when the war ended, complete with period furniture, including Churchill's desk, communications equipment, and maps for plotting military strategy. The Churchill Museum is a multimedia exhibit recording Churchill's life and career.

⑨ Downing Street

SW1. **Map** 13 B4. ⊜ Westminster. **Closed** to the public.

Sir George Downing (1623–84) spent part of his youth in the American colonies. He was the second graduate of the nascent Harvard College before returning to fight for the Parliamentarians in the English Civil War. In 1680 he bought

some land near Whitehall Palace and built a street of houses. Four of these survive, though they are much altered. George II gave No. 10 to Sir Robert Walpole in 1732. Since then it has been the official residence of the Prime Minister and contains offices as well as a private apartment. In 1989, for security reasons, iron gates were erected at the Whitehall end.

The famous front door of No. 10

No. 12, the Whips' Office, is where Party campaigns are organized.

Government policy is decided in the Cabinet Room at No. 10.

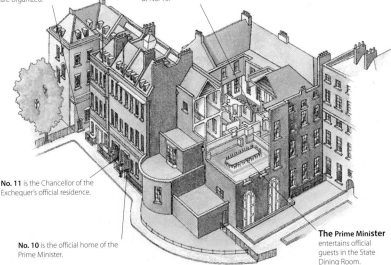

No. 11 is the Chancellor of the Exchequer's official residence.

No. 10 is the official home of the Prime Minister.

The Prime Minister entertains official guests in the State Dining Room.

❹ Westminster Abbey

The Abbey is world-famous as the resting place of Britain's monarchs, and as the setting for coronations and other great pageants, such as the marriage of Prince William in 2011. Within its walls can be seen some of the most glorious examples of medieval architecture in London. It also contains one of the most impressive collections of tombs and monuments in the world. Half national church, half national museum, the Abbey is part of British national consciousness.

★ Flying Buttresses
The massive flying buttresses help transfer the great weight of the 102-ft- (31-m-) high nave.

North/Main Entrance
The stonework here, like this carving of a dragon, is Victorian.

★ West Front Towers
These towers, completed in 1745, were designed by Nicholas Hawksmoor.

KEY

① **The North Transept** has three chapels on the east side containing some of the Abbey's finest monuments.

② **St. Edward's Chapel** houses Edward the Confessor's shrine and the tombs of other English medieval monarchs.

③ **The South Transept** contains "Poets' Corner," where memorials to famous literary figures can be seen.

④ **Museum**

⑤ **The Cloisters**, built mainly in the 13th and 14th centuries, link the Abbey church with the other buildings.

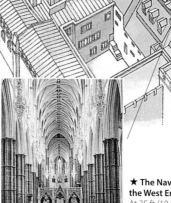

★ The Nave viewed from the West End
At 35 ft (10 m) wide, the nave is comparatively narrow, but it is the highest in England.

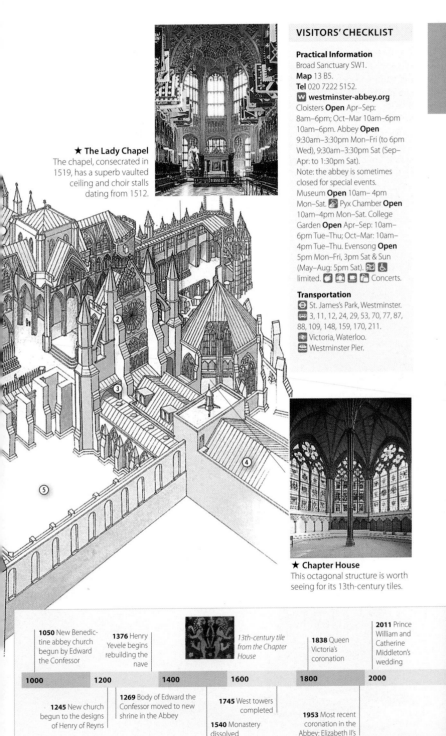

★ **The Lady Chapel**
The chapel, consecrated in 1519, has a superb vaulted ceiling and choir stalls dating from 1512.

VISITORS' CHECKLIST

Practical Information
Broad Sanctuary SW1.
Map 13 B5.
Tel 020 7222 5152.
W **westminster-abbey.org**
Cloisters **Open** Apr–Sep: 8am–6pm; Oct–Mar 10am–6pm 10am–6pm. Abbey **Open** 9:30am–3:30pm Mon–Fri (to 6pm Wed), 9:30am–3:30pm Sat (Sep–Apr: to 1:30pm Sat).
Note: the abbey is sometimes closed for special events.
Museum **Open** 10am– 4pm Mon–Sat. Pyx Chamber **Open** 10am–4pm Mon–Sat. College Garden **Open** Apr–Sep: 10am–6pm Tue–Thu; Oct–Mar: 10am–4pm Tue–Thu. Evensong **Open** 5pm Mon–Fri, 3pm Sat & Sun (May–Aug: 5pm Sat). limited. Concerts.

Transportation
St. James's Park, Westminster. 3, 11, 12, 24, 29, 53, 70, 77, 87, 88, 109, 148, 159, 170, 211.
Victoria, Waterloo.
Westminster Pier.

★ **Chapter House**
This octagonal structure is worth seeing for its 13th-century tiles.

1050 New Benedictine abbey church begun by Edward the Confessor	**1376** Henry Yevele begins rebuilding the nave		*13th-century tile from the Chapter House*	**1838** Queen Victoria's coronation	**2011** Prince William and Catherine Middleton's wedding
1000	**1200**	**1400**	**1600**	**1800**	**2000**
1245 New church begun to the designs of Henry of Reyns	**1269** Body of Edward the Confessor moved to new shrine in the Abbey	**1745** West towers completed **1540** Monastery dissolved		**1953** Most recent coronation in the Abbey: Elizabeth II's	

A Guided Tour of Westminster Abbey

The abbey's interior presents an exceptionally diverse array of architectural and sculptural styles. These range from the austere French Gothic of the nave to the stunning complexity of Henry VII's Tudor chapel and the riotous invention of the later 18th-century monuments. Many British monarchs were buried here; some of their tombs are deliberately plain, while others are lavishly decorated. At the same time, there are monuments to a number of Britain's greatest public figures – ranging from politicians to poets – crowded into the aisles and transepts.

② Grave of the Unknown Warrior
The body of an unknown soldier was brought from the battlefields of World War I and buried here in 1920. His grave commemorates all who have lost their lives in war.

Historical Plan of the Abbey

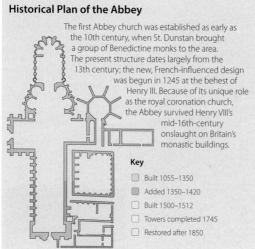

The first Abbey church was established as early as the 10th century, when St. Dunstan brought a group of Benedictine monks to the area. The present structure dates largely from the 13th century; the new, French-influenced design was begun in 1245 at the behest of Henry III. Because of its unique role as the royal coronation church, the Abbey survived Henry VIII's mid-16th-century onslaught on Britain's monastic buildings.

Key

☐ Built 1055–1350
▨ Added 1350–1420
☐ Built 1500–1512
☐ Towers completed 1745
☐ Restored after 1850

Main entrance

The Choir houses a gilded 1840s screen, which contains remnants of the 13th-century original.

The Jericho Parlour, added in the early 16th century, contains some fine paneling. It is closed to the public.

The Jerusalem Chamber has a 17th-century fireplace, fine tapestries, and an interesting painted ceiling. It is closed to the public.

The Deanery, home of the Dean of Westminster, was once the monastic abbot's house. It is closed to the public.

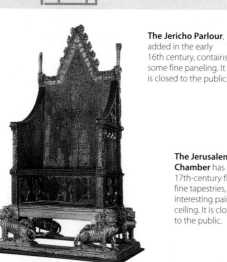

① Coronation Chair
Constructed in 1301, this chair has been used at every coronation since 1308.

Coronation

The abbey has been the fittingly sumptuous setting for all royal coronations since 1066. The last occupant of the Coronation Chair was the present monarch, Elizabeth II. She was crowned in 1953 in the first televised coronation.

The Chapel of St. John the Baptist is full of tombs dating from the 14th to the 19th centuries.

St. Faith Chapel contains works of art that date back to the 13th century.

The Pyx Chamber's gaunt columns date from the 11th century. This is where the coinage was tested in medieval times.

Key

— Tour route

Dean's Yard entrance

③ **The Nave**
The nave is 35 ft (10 m) wide and 102 ft (31 m) high. It took 150 years to build.

④ **Nightingale Memorial**
The North Transept chapels contain some of the Abbey's finest monuments – this one, by Roubiliac, is for Lady Elizabeth Nightingale (1761).

⑤ **Tomb of Elizabeth I**
Inside the Lady Chapel you will find the huge tomb of Elizabeth I (reigned 1558–1603). It also houses the body of her sister, "Bloody" Mary I.

⑥ **The Lady Chapel**
The undersides of the choir stalls, dating from 1512, are beautifully carved with exotic and fantastic creatures.

⑦ **The Chapel of St. Edward the Confessor**
The shrine of the Saxon king Edward the Confessor and the tombs of many medieval monarchs are here.

⑧ **Poets' Corner**
Take time to explore the memorials to countless literary giants, such as Shakespeare and Dickens, which are gathered here.

⓫ Banqueting House

Whitehall SW1. **Map** 13 B4. **Tel** 0844 482 7777 (UK) or 020 3166 6000 (outside UK; possible closures – call ahead). ⊖ Charing Cross, Embankment, Westminster. **Open** 10am–5pm Mon–Sat (last adm 4:15pm). **Closed** Sun, public hols, Dec 24–Jan 1; for functions (phone first). 🎦 📖 📷 🆆 **hrp.org.uk**

This delightful building is of great architectural importance. It was the first in central London to embody the Classical Palladian style that designer Inigo Jones brought back from his travels in Italy. Completed in 1622, its disciplined stone facade marked a startling change from the Elizabethans' busy turrets and unrestrained external decoration. It was the sole survivor of the fire that destroyed most of the old Whitehall Palace in 1698.

The ceiling paintings by Rubens, a complex allegory on the exaltation of James I, were commissioned by his son, Charles I, in 1630. This blatant glorification of royalty was despised by Oliver Cromwell and the Parliamentarians, who executed King Charles I on a scaffold outside Banqueting House in 1649. Ironically, Charles II celebrated his restoration to the throne here 11 years later. The building is used for official functions.

Mounted sentries stationed outside Horse Guards Parade

⓬ Horse Guards Parade

Whitehall SW1. **Map** 13 B4. **Tel** 020 7766 7300. ⊖ Westminster, Charing Cross, Embankment. **Open** 8am–6pm daily. Changing the Guard 11am Mon–Sat, 10am Sun. Dismounting Ceremony 4pm daily. Times for both are subject to change (phone for details). Trooping the Colour *see Ceremonial London pp54–7.*

Once Henry VIII's tiltyard (tournament ground), nowadays the Changing of the Guard takes place here every morning. The elegant buildings, completed in 1755, were designed by William Kent. On the left is the Old Treasury, also by Kent, and

Dover House, completed in 1758 and now used as the Scottish Office. Nearby is a trace of the "real tennis" court where Henry VIII is said to have played the ancient precursor of modern lawn tennis. On the opposite side, the view is dominated by the ivy-covered Citadel. This is a bomb-proof structure that was erected in 1940 beside the Admiralty. During World War II, it was used as a communications headquarters by the Navy.

⓭ Trafalgar Studios

14 Whitehall SW1. **Map** 13 B3. **Tel** 0844 871 7627. ⊖ Charing Cross. **Open** for performances only. *See Entertainment pp336–7.*

Formerly the Whitehall Theatre and built in 1930, the plain white front seems to emulate the Cenotaph *(see p76)* at the other end of the street, but inside, the theater boasts fine Art Deco detailing. The studios comprise two intimate spaces.

⓮ Queen Anne's Gate

SW1. **Map** 13 A5. ⊖ St. James's Park.

The spacious terraced houses at the west end of this well-preserved enclave date from 1704 and are notable for the ornate canopies over their front doors. At the other end are houses built some 70 years later, sporting blue plaques that record former residents, such as Lord Palmerston, the Victorian Prime Minister. It is rumored that the British Secret Service, MI5, was formerly based in this unlikely spot. A small statue of Queen Anne stands in front of the wall separating Nos. 13 and 15. To the west, situated at the corner of Petty France, Sir Basil Spence's Home Office building (1976) is an architectural incongruity. Cockpit Steps, leading down to Birdcage Walk, mark the site of a 17th-century venue for the popular, yet bloodthirsty, sport of cockfighting.

Panels from the Rubens ceiling, Banqueting House

⑮ Guards Museum

Birdcage Walk SW1. **Map** 13 A5.
Tel 020 7414 3428. St. James's Park.
Open 10am–4pm daily (last adm:
3:30pm). **Closed** Christmas, ceremonies. (free for under-16s).
theguardsmuseum.com

Entered from Birdcage Walk, the
museum is under the parade
ground of Wellington Barracks,
headquarters of the five Guards
regiments. A must for military
buffs, the museum uses
tableaux and dioramas to
illustrate various battles in
which the Guards have taken
part, from the English Civil War
(1642–8) to the present.
Weapons and row after row
of colorful uniforms are on
display, as well as a fascinating
collection of models.

⑯ St. James's Park Station

55 Broadway SW1. **Map** 13 A5.
St. James's Park.

The station is built into
Broadway House, Charles
Holden's 1929 headquarters for
London Transport. It is notable
for its sculptures by Jacob
Epstein and reliefs by Henry
Moore and Eric Gill.

⑰ Blewcoat School

23 Caxton St SW1. **Map** 13 A5.
Tel 020 7222 2877. St. James's Park.
Closed to public.

A red-brick gem hemmed in
by the office towers of Victoria
Street, it was built in 1709 as a
charity school to teach pupils

Statue of a Blewcoat pupil above the
Caxton Street entrance

Baroque interior of St. John's, Smith Square

how to "read, write, cast accounts,
and the catechism." All pupils
were boys until 1713, when girls
were admitted. The attendance
of girls was discontinued in
1876. In 1899 it passed to
Christchurch National Schools.
It remained as a school until 1939,
became an army store during
World War II, and was bought
by the National Trust in 1954.

⑱ Westminster Cathedral

Ashley Place SW1. **Map** 20 F1.
Tel 020 7798 9055. Victoria.
Open 7am–7pm Mon–Fri,
8am–7pm Sat & Sun. for bell
tower elevator (9:30am–5pm Mon–Fri,
9:30am–6pm Sat & Sun). check
website for details of Mass and
services.
westminstercathedral.org.uk

One of London's rare Byzantine
buildings, it was designed by
John Francis Bentley for the
Catholic diocese and completed
in 1903 on the site of a former
prison. Its 285-ft- (87-m-) high
red-brick tower, with horizontal
stripes of white stone, stands
out on the skyline in sharp
contrast to the Abbey nearby.
A restful piazza on the north side
provides a good view of the
cathedral from Victoria Street.
The rich interior decoration,
with marble of varying colors
and intricate mosaics, makes
the domes above the nave

seem incongruous. They were
left bare because the project
ran out of money.
    Eric Gill's dramatic reliefs of
the 14 Stations of the Cross,
created during World War I,
adorn the pier of the nave,
which is the widest in Britain.
The organ is one of the finest
in Europe, and there are often
free recitals on Sunday
afternoons at 4:45pm.

⑲ St. John's, Smith Square

Smith Sq SW1. **Map** 21 B1. **Tel** 020
7222 1061. Westminster. Box office
Open 10am–5pm Mon–Fri. **Closed** to
public except for concerts.
phone first. **sjss.org.uk**

Described by artist and art
historian Sir Hugh Casson as one
of the masterpieces of English
Baroque architecture, Thomas
Archer's plump church, with its
turrets at each corner, looks as if
it is trying to burst from the
confines of the square, and
somewhat overpowers the
pleasing 18th-century houses
on its north side. Today it is
principally a concert hall. It has
an accident-prone history:
completed in 1728, it was burned
down in 1742, struck by lightning in 1773, and destroyed by a
World War II bomb in 1941. There
is a reasonably priced basement
restaurant that is open daily for
lunch and on concert evenings.

⑳ Tate Britain

Tate Britain displays the world's largest collection of British art from the 16th to the 21st centuries. In the Clore Galleries are works from the magnificent Turner Bequest, left to the nation by the great landscape artist J. M. W. Turner in 1851. The Clore Galleries have their own entrance, giving direct access to the Turner Collection and allowing a full appreciation of Sir James Stirling's Postmodernist design for the building. The Tate often loans out works or removes them for restoration, so exhibits described here may not always be on display.

Gallery Cafe

Main floor

★ **Three Studies for Figures at the Base of a Crucifixion** (c.1944, detail) Francis Bacon's famous triptych encapsulates an anguished vision of human existence. When it was first displayed, its savagery deeply shocked audiences.

Lower floor

Manton entrance

Gallery Guide

Tate Britain has undergone restoration and expansion, creating new spaces for displays and educational activities. Highlights from the collection are displayed chronologically around the outer perimeter of the galleries. More focused displays, "BP Spotlights," offer a more detailed look at specific artists or themes. The Duveen Galleries showcase the work of contemporary sculptors. Tate Britain also exhibits the annual Turner Prize nominees.

★ **Ophelia** (1851–2)
Taken from Shakespeare's play *Hamlet*, the scene of the drowning of Ophelia by Pre-Raphaelite John Everett Millais is one of the most famous – and popular – paintings at Tate Britain.

The Saltonstall Family (c.1637)
David Des Granges's life-size family portrait includes the dead first Lady Saltonstall as the second shows off her new baby.

Henry Moore Galleries
This permanent display holds valuable works by the famous sculptor.

Entrance to Clore Galleries

Rotunda

Stairs to lower floor
🖊 🔂 🖊 🖥 📷 🖊

★ **Peace – Burial at Sea** (1842)
This is J. M. W. Turner's tribute to his friend and rival David Wilkie. It was painted in 1842, the year after Wilkie died at sea.

Millbank entrance

Key to Floor Plan
- ▨ BP Walk Through British Art
- ▢ Duveen Galleries
- ▢ Clore Galleries
- ▨ Loan Exhibitions
- ▨ Non-exhibition space
- ▨ BP Spotlights
- ▢ Permanent displays

The Art of Good Food

The lower floor of Tate Britain boasts a café and an espresso bar, as well as a restaurant. Celebrated murals by Rex Whistler adorn the walls of the restaurant, telling the tale of the mythical inhabitants of Epicuriana and their expedition in search of rare foods. The extensive wine list has won awards. Open for lunch, weekend brunch, and afternoon tea.

Exploring Tate Britain

Tate Britain draws its displays from the massive Tate Collection. The variety of works on show, combined with a rigorous program of loan exhibitions and career retrospectives of British artists, results in a selection to suit all tastes – from Elizabethan portraiture to cutting-edge installation. The displays are changed frequently to explore many different aspects of the history and art of Britain from 1500 to the present day.

The Cholmondeley Ladies (c.1600–10), British School

BP Walk Through British Art

The national collection of British art has been rehung in a continuous chronological display from the 1500s to the present day. This presentation allows viewers to observe a range of art from any one historical moment and see how British art has changed over the last five hundred years. The walk comprises around 500 artworks in some 20 galleries, and covers a period of dramatic change in British history, from the Tudors and Stuarts through to the age of Thomas Gainsborough.

Included are important works by one of Britain's greatest painters, William Hogarth, known for his biting satire on the lifestyle and beliefs of his contemporaries. His *Marriage à la Mode* series satirized the marriage contracts of the upper classes. In contrast are the dramatic large-scale paintings in an idealized style by artists such as Benjamin West and Joshua Reynolds, the head of the newly established Royal Academy. Landscape painting lies at the heart of the revolution in British painting during the 19th century, when

images of the countryside changed ideas not only about art, but about what it means to be British. Works by the poet and artist William Blake reveal him as a seminal figure of the Romantic Age, though largely unrecognized in his lifetime.

The first half of the 19th century saw dramatic expansion and change in the arts in Britain. New themes began to emerge, and artists started working on a much larger scale as they competed for attention on the walls of public exhibitions. Monumental canvases by John Martin, Thomas Lawrence, and William Etty, as well as celebrated works by David Wilkie, are evidence of this. Storytelling was at the heart of Victorian art; the Victorians' belief in the power of art to convey moral messages produced such important works as Augustus Egg's series *Past and Present*. Pre-Raphaelite and Idealist works are perhaps the most popular works at Tate Britain; key examples are John Everett Millais's *Ophelia* and William Holman Hunt's *Awakening Conscience*. Painting and sculpture from the late Victorian period includes John Singer Sargent's haunting *Carnation, Lily, Lily, Rose*.

Modern British Art

The modern section of the gallery begins with the early 20th century. "Modern Figures" looks at artists' fascination with modern cities: cosmopolitan, noisy places with crowded streets, continually changing architecture, and fast, mechanized transportation, as well as new places of entertainment. It includes Jacob Epstein's *Torso in Metal from "The Rock Drill,"* a machine-like robot, visored and menacing, that became a symbol of the new age, as well as the work of Wyndham Lewis and his Vorticist group, who saw the artist at the still center of the vortex of modern life.

Work by celebrated British sculptors, such as Barbara Hepworth and Henry Moore, can also be seen in this section. Paintings by two of the most famous, and disturbing, modern British artists are also on display here: Francis Bacon, whose *Three Studies for Figures at the Base of a Crucifixion* (c.1944) depicts three mutant organisms in agony, confined in an apparently hostile and godless world; and Lucian Freud, whose expressive nudes are on display.

From the 1960s, Tate's funding for the purchase of works began to increase substantially, while artistic activity continued to pick up speed, encouraged by public funding. As a result, the Tate Collection is particularly rich on this time period, which means that the frequent rotation of displays is necessary.

There is, however, one room devoted to "Pop," one of the liveliest developments of British art in the 1960s, which focuses in particular on the beginnings of the movement through iconic works by artists such as Sir Peter Blake, Richard Hamilton, the early work of David Hockney, and Gerald Laing, deriving his inspiration for *Skydiver VI* (1964) from mass-produced images of the 1960s. A revolt against this movement took place at the end of the 1960s, with the emergence of Conceptual artists such as Gilbert & George, known as the

Self-Portrait with Knickers (2000) by Sarah Lucas

Living Sculptures, and Richard Long, who created a whole new approach to landscape painting by importing the land itself into the gallery.

Conceptual art in turn was rejected at the start of the 1980s by the School of London painters, including Howard Hodgkin, Frank Auerbach, and R. B. Kitaj, while Tony Cragg, Richard Deacon, and Antony Gormley pioneered a new kind of sculpture.

The 1990s saw a new surge in British art. Most recent British movements are well represented at Tate Britain. These include the work of the so-called Young British Artists (YBAs), who include Damien Hirst, perhaps the most notorious, as well as the controversial installations and photographic work of Tracey Emin and Sarah Lucas, exhibiting both individually and as a collective. Many contemporary British artists, including Tacita Dean, Douglas Gordon, Sam Taylor-Wood, Steve McQueen, and Jane and Louise Wilson, use film and video as their medium – the subject of a number of special displays at Tate Britain.

The frequently changing displays at Tate Britain include wider surveys as well as rooms devoted to single artists, and feature important newly acquired works. The Contemporary British Art

galleries reflect current developments in British art and are devoted to work by the latest up-and-coming artists.

The gallery also organizes the prestigious annual Turner Prize, which is presented to a British visual artist. Representing all sections of the art world, artists are selected on the basis of their work over the course of the preceding year. Works by all the artists shortlisted are showcased at Tate Britain, before a judging panel decides the winner.

Previous winners include Yoko Ono and British painter Howard Hodgkin. In the past, winners have often been surrounded by controversy, including Damien Hirst's *The Physical Impossibility*

of Death in the Mind of Someone Living (1991), which consists of a shark preserved in formaldehyde, and British artist Tracey Emin's *My Bed* (1998), which comprises a disheveled bed.

Clore Galleries

The Turner Bequest comprises some 300 oil paintings, 300 sketchbooks, and about 20,000 watercolors and drawings received by the nation from the great landscape painter J. M. W. Turner after his death in 1851. Turner's will had specified that a gallery be built to house his pictures, and this was finally done in 1987 with the opening of the Clore Galleries. Most of the oil paintings are on view in the main galleries, while the watercolors are the subject of changing displays.

Kids at the Tate

To encourage art appreciation from a young age, under-12s can visit any special exhibition at Tate Britain for free (when accompanied by an adult). Family-friendly events are held most weekends and during school breaks, including Open Studio, where families can get hands-on and creative; and the Families Welcome Area, with activities encouraging exploration of concepts such as scale, space, and architecture.

Shipping at the Mouth of the Thames (c.1806–7) by J. M. W. Turner

PICCADILLY AND ST. JAMES'S

Piccadilly is the main artery of the West End. Once called Portugal Street, it acquired its present name from the pickadills, or ruffs, worn by 17th-century dandies. St. James's still bears traces of the 18th century, when it surrounded the royal residences, and denizens of the court and society shopped and amused themselves here. Two shops in St. James's Street – James Lock the hatter and Berry Bros. & Rudd vintners – recall that era. Fortnum and Mason, on Piccadilly, has served high-quality food for nearly 300 years. Mayfair, to the north, is still the most fashionable address in London, while Piccadilly Circus marks the start of Soho.

Sights at a Glance

Historic Streets and Buildings
1 Piccadilly Circus
3 Albany
5 Burlington Arcade
6 Ritz Hotel
7 Spencer House
8 St. James's Palace
9 St. James's Square
10 Royal Opera Arcade
11 Pall Mall
14 The Mall
15 Marlborough House
17 Clarence House
18 Lancaster House
19 Buckingham Palace pp96–7
22 Wellington Arch
24 Shepherd Market

Museums and Galleries
4 Royal Academy of Arts
12 Institute of Contemporary Arts
20 The Queen's Gallery
21 Royal Mews
23 Apsley House
26 Faraday Museum

Churches
2 St. James's Church
16 Queen's Chapel

Parks and Gardens
13 St. James's Park
25 Green Park

Restaurants see pp292–295
1 Al Duca
2 Apsleys
3 Bentley's Oyster Bar and Grill
4 Le Caprice
5 Cecconi's
6 The Cut at 45 Park Lane
7 El Pirata
8 Hard Rock Café
9 Murano
10 Nobu
11 Noura
12 The Ritz Restaurant
13 Veeraswamy
14 The Wolseley

Street Finder, maps 12, 13

◄ Soldier at the Changing of the Royal Guard

For keys to symbols see back flap

Street by Street: Piccadilly and St. James's

As soon as Henry VIII built St. James's Palace in the 1530s, the area around it became the center of fashionable London, and it has remained so ever since. The most influential people in the land strut importantly along its historic streets as they press on with the vital business of lunching in their clubs, discussing matters of pith and moment, and brandishing their gold cards in the capital's most exclusive stores, or paying a visit to one of the many art galleries.

3 Albany
This has been one of London's most stylish addresses since it opened in 1803.

4 ★ Royal Academy of Arts
Sir Joshua Reynolds founded the Academy in 1768. Now it mounts large popular exhibitions.

Fortnum and Mason
was founded in 1707 by one of Queen Anne's footmen *(see p313)*.

5 ★ Burlington Arcade
Uniformed beadles discourage unruly behavior in this 19th-century mall.

6 The Ritz Hotel
Named after César Ritz, and opened in 1906, it still lives up to his name.

7 Spencer House
An ancestor of Princess Diana built this house in 1766.

8 St. James's Palace
This Tudor palace is still the Court's official headquarters.

To the Mall

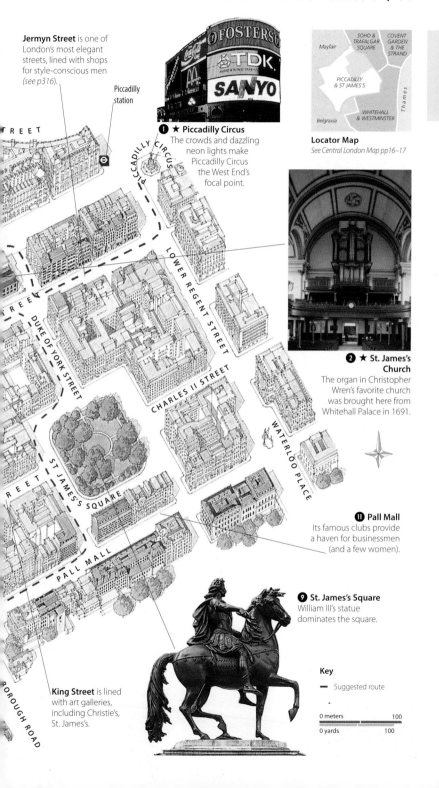

Jermyn Street is one of London's most elegant streets, lined with shops for style-conscious men (see p316).

Piccadilly station

FOSTER'S
Coca-Cola
TDK
AUDIO & VIDEO TAPE
McDonald's
SANYO

❶ ★ Piccadilly Circus
The crowds and dazzling neon lights make Piccadilly Circus the West End's focal point.

PICCADILLY CIRCUS

LOWER REGENT STREET

DUKE OF YORK STREET

CHARLES II STREET

ST JAMES'S SQUARE

WATERLOO PLACE

PALL MALL

BOROUGH ROAD

Locator Map
See Central London Map pp16–17

Mayfair
SOHO & TRAFALGAR SQUARE
COVENT GARDEN & THE STRAND
PICCADILLY & ST JAMES'S
Thames
Belgravia
WHITEHALL & WESTMINSTER

❷ ★ St. James's Church
The organ in Christopher Wren's favorite church was brought here from Whitehall Palace in 1691.

⓫ Pall Mall
Its famous clubs provide a haven for businessmen (and a few women).

❾ St. James's Square
William III's statue dominates the square.

King Street is lined with art galleries, including Christie's, St. James's.

Key
— Suggested route

| 0 meters | | 100 |
| 0 yards | | 100 |

Alfred Gilbert's statue of *Eros*

❶ Piccadilly Circus

W1. **Map** 13 A3. ⊖ Piccadilly Circus.

For years people have congregated beneath the symbolic figure of Eros, originally intended as an angel of mercy but renamed after the Greek god of love. Poised delicately with his bow, Eros has become almost a trademark for the capital. It was erected in 1892 as a memorial to the Earl of Shaftesbury, the Victorian philanthropist. Part of Nash's master plan for Regent Street, Piccadilly Circus has been considerably altered over the years and consists mostly of shops. One shopping mall can be found behind the facade of the London Pavilion (1885), once a popular music hall. The circus has London's gaudiest array of neon advertising signs marking the entrance to the city's lively entertainment district, with theaters, movie theaters, nightclubs, pubs, and restaurants.

❷ St. James's Church

197 Piccadilly W1. **Map** 13 A3. **Tel** 020 7734 4511. ⊖ Piccadilly Circus. **Open** 8am–6:30pm daily. Craft market 10am–6pm Wed–Sat, antiques market 10am–6pm Tue. ♿ 🖥 Concerts, talks, events. 🅦 **sjp.org.uk**

Among the many churches Wren designed *(see p49)*, this is said to be one of his favorites.

It has been altered over the years and was half-wrecked by a bomb in 1940, but it maintains its essential features from 1684: tall, arched windows, a thin spire (a 1966 replica of the original), and a light, dignified interior. The ornate screen behind the altar is one of the finest works of the 17th- century master carver Grinling Gibbons, who also made the exquisite marble font, with a scene depicting Adam and Eve standing by the Tree of Life. Artist and poet William Blake and Prime Minister Pitt the Elder were both baptized here. More of Gibbons's carvings can be seen above the grandiose organ, made for Whitehall Palace chapel but installed here in 1691. The church now has a full calendar of events, and houses a popular café.

❸ Albany

Albany Court Yard, Piccadilly W1. **Map** 12 F3. ⊖ Green Park, Piccadilly Circus. **Closed** to the public.

These desirable and discreet bachelor apartments, half hidden through an entrance off Piccadilly, were built in 1803 by Henry Holland. Notable residents have included the poet Lord Byron, novelist Graham Greene, two Prime Ministers (William Gladstone and Edward Heath), and the actor Terence Stamp. Married men were admitted in 1878 but could not bring their wives to live with them until 1919. Women are now allowed to live here in their own right.

Byron lived in Albany

Michelangelo's *Madonnna and Child*

❹ Royal Academy of Arts

Burlington House, Piccadilly W1. **Map** 12 F3. **Tel** 020 7300 8000. ⊖ Piccadilly Circus, Green Park. **Open** 10am–6pm Sat–Thu, 10am–10pm Fri. **Closed** Good Fri, Dec 24–26. **Adm charge some exhibitions.** 🖼 ♿ 🖥 🚭 🖥 📷 🅦 **royalacademy.org.uk**

The courtyard in front of Burlington House, one of the West End's few surviving mansions from the early 18th century, is often crammed with people waiting to get into one of the prestigious visiting art exhibitions on display at the Royal Academy (founded 1768). The famous annual summer exhibition, which has now been held for over 200 years, comprises around 1,200 new works by both established and unknown artists. Any artist, established or unknown, may submit work.

The airy Sackler Galleries (1991), designed by Norman Foster, show visiting exhibitions. There are permanent items in the sculpture promenade outside the galleries, notably a Michelangelo relief of the Madonna and Child (1505). The exceptional permanent collection (not all on display) includes one work by each current and former Academician; the highlights are displayed in the Madejski Rooms. Two shops adjacent to the gallery exits sell merchandise inspired by the current exhibitions, as well as a great range of art books.

❺ Burlington Arcade

Piccadilly W1. **Map** 12 F3. 🚇 Green Park, Piccadilly Circus. *See Shops and Markets p320.*

This is one of four 19th-century arcades of small shops that sell traditional British luxuries. (The Princes and Piccadilly Arcades are on the south side of Piccadilly, while the Royal Opera Arcade is off Pall Mall.) It was built for Lord Cavendish in 1819 to prevent garbage from being thrown into his garden. The arcade is still patrolled by beadles who make sure an atmosphere of refinement is maintained. They have authority to eject anyone who sings, whistles, runs, or opens an umbrella; those powers are infrequently invoked now, perhaps because the dictates of commerce take precedence over those of decorum.

❻ Ritz Hotel

Piccadilly W1. **Map** 12 F3. **Tel** 020 7493 8181. 🚇 Green Park. **Open** to non-residents for tea or restaurant (book ahead). ♿ *(See p284.)*
🌐 **theritzlondon.com**

Cesar Ritz, the famed Swiss hotelier who inspired the adjective "ritzy," had virtually retired by the time this hotel was built and named after him in 1906. The colonnaded frontal aspect of the imposing chateau-style building was meant to suggest Paris, where the very grandest and most fashionable hotels

The exquisite Palm Room of Spencer House

were to be found around the turn of the century. It maintains its Edwardian air of opulence and is a popular stop among those who are suitably dressed (no jeans or athletic shoes; jacket and tie for men), for afternoon tea, with daily servings in the Palm Court at 11:30am, 1:30, 3:30, and 5:30pm. Champagne tea is served at 7:30pm.

❼ Spencer House

27 St. James's Pl SW1. **Map** 12 F4. **Tel** 020 7514 1958. 🚇 Green Park. **Open** 10:30am–5:45pm Sun (last adm: 4:45pm). Garden: **Open** in spring and summer; call 020 7499 8620 to check dates. **Closed** Jan & Aug. No children under 10. 📷 📧 ♿ 🕐 required.
🌐 **spencerhouse.co.uk**

This Palladian palace, built in 1766 for the first Earl Spencer, an ancestor of the late Princess of Wales, has been completely restored to its 18th-century

splendor, thanks to a major renovation project. It contains some wonderful paintings and contemporary furniture; one of the highlights is the beautifully decorated Painted Room. The house is open to the public for guided tours, receptions, and meetings.

St. James's Tudor gatehouse

❽ St. James's Palace

Pall Mall SW1. **Map** 12 F4. 🚇 Green Park. **Closed** to the public.
🌐 **royal.gov.uk**

Built by Henry VIII in the late 1530s on the site of a former leper hospital, it was a primary royal residence only briefly, mainly during the reign of Elizabeth I and during the late 17th and early 18th centuries. In 1952, Queen Elizabeth II made her first speech as queen here, and foreign ambassadors are still officially accredited to the Court of St. James's. The northern gatehouse, seen from St. James's Street, is one of London's great Tudor landmarks. The palace buildings are now occupied by privileged Crown servants.

Afternoon tea served in the opulent Palm Court of the Ritz

Royal Opera Arcade

❾ St. James's Square

SW1. **Map** 13 A3. 🚇 Green Park, Piccadilly Circus.

One of London's earliest squares, it was laid out in the 1670s and lined by exclusive houses for those whose business made it vital for them to live near St. James's Palace. Many of the buildings date from the 18th and 19th centuries and have had many illustrious residents. During World War II, generals Eisenhower and de Gaulle both had headquarters here.

Today, No. 10 on the north side is Chatham House (1736), home of the Royal Institute for International Affairs, and in the northwest corner can be found the London Library (1896), a private lending library founded in 1841 by historian Thomas Carlyle *(see p198)* and others. The lovely gardens in the middle contain an equestrian statue of William III, here since 1808.

❿ Royal Opera Arcade

SW1. **Map** 13 A3. 🚇 Piccadilly Circus.

London's first shopping arcade was designed by John Nash and completed in 1818, behind the Haymarket Opera House (now called Her Majesty's Theatre). It beat the Burlington Arcade *(see p93)* by a year or so. The traditional shops that once used to be based here have since moved on: Farlows, selling

shooting and fishing equipment, and the famous Hunter's green Wellington boots, are now nearby, at No. 9 Pall Mall.

The Duke of Wellington (1842): a frequent visitor to Pall Mall

⓫ Pall Mall

SW1. **Map** 13 A4. 🚇 Charing Cross, Green Park, Piccadilly Circus.

This dignified street is named from the game of palle-maille – a cross between croquet and golf – which was played here in the 17th century. For more than 150 years Pall Mall has been at the heart of London's clubland. Here, exclusive gentlemen's clubs were formed to provide members with a refuge from their womenfolk.

The clubhouses now amount to a textbook of the most fashionable architects of the era. From the east end, on the left is the colonnaded entrance to No. 116, Nash's United Services Club (1827). This was the favorite club of the Duke of

Wellington and now houses the Institute of Directors. Facing it, on the other side of Waterloo Place, is the Athenaeum (No. 107), designed three years later by Decimus Burton, and long the power house of the British establishment. Next door are two clubs by Sir Charles Barry, architect of the Houses of Parliament *(see pp74–5)*; the Travellers' is at No. 106 and the Reform at No. 104. The clubs' stately interiors are well preserved but only members and their guests are admitted.

⓬ Institute of Contemporary Arts

The Mall SW1. **Map** 13 B3. **Tel** 020 7930 3647. 🚇 Charing Cross, Piccadilly Circus. **Open** 11am–11pm Tue–Sun. (Exhibition space closes 6pm, 9pm Thu, bookshop 9pm.) **Closed** Jan 1, Dec 24–26 & 31, public hols. 🎫 ♿ (movie theater and lower gallery) phone first. 🖥 📷 🏛 Concerts, theater, dance, lectures, films, exhibitions. *See Entertainment pp342–3.* 🌐 **ica.org.uk**

The Institute (ICA) was established in 1947 in an effort to offer British artists some of the same facilities that were available to artists at the Museum of Modern Art in New York. Originally on Dover Street, it has been situated in John Nash's Classical Carlton House Terrace (1833) since 1968. With its entrance on the Mall, this extensive warren contains a movie theater, an auditorium, a bookshop, an art gallery, a bar, and a restaurant. It also offers plays, concerts, and lectures. Non-members pay a charge.

Institute of Contemporary Arts, Carlton House Terrace

⑬ St. James's Park

SW1. **Map** 13 A4. **Tel** 0300 061 2350. ⊖ St. James's Park. **Open** 5am–midnight daily. 🚲 **Open** daily. ♿ Concerts twice daily on summer weekends in good weather.
🌐 **royalparks.org.uk**

In summer, office workers sunbathe between the dazzling flower beds of the capital's most ornamental park. In winter, overcoated civil servants discuss affairs of state as they stroll by the lake and eye its ducks, geese, and pelicans (who are fed at 1:30pm daily). Originally a marsh, the park was drained by Henry VIII and incorporated into his hunting grounds. Charles II redesigned it for pedestrian pleasures, with an aviary along its southern edge (hence Birdcage Walk, the street where the aviary was). It is still a popular place to go for a stroll, with an appealing view of Whitehall rooftops. In the summer there are concerts on the bandstand.

⑭ The Mall

SW1. **Map** 13 A4. ⊖ Charing Cross, Green Park, Piccadilly Circus.

This broad triumphal approach to Buckingham Palace was created by Aston Webb when he redesigned the front of the palace and the Victoria Monument in 1911 *(see picture p98)*. It follows the course of the old path at the edge of St. James's Park, laid out in the reign of Charles II, when it became London's most fashionable promenade. On the flagpoles down both sides of the Mall fly national flags of foreign heads of state during official visits.

⑮ Marlborough House

Pall Mall SW1. **Map** 13 A4. **Tel** 020 7747 6500. ⊖ St. James's Park, Green Park. **Open** Tue am tours subject to availability. 🎟 group tours by appt.

Marlborough House was designed by Christopher Wren *(see p49)* for the Duchess of Marlborough, and finished in 1711. It was substantially enlarged in the 19th century and used by members of the Royal Family. From 1863 until he became Edward VII in 1901, it was the home of the Prince (and Princess) of Wales and the social center of London. An Art Nouveau memorial in the Marlborough Road wall of the house commemorates Edward's queen, Alexandra. The building now houses the Commonwealth Secretariat.

Queen's Chapel

⑯ Queen's Chapel

Marlborough Rd SW1. **Map** 13 A4. **Tel** 020 7930 4832. ⊖ Green Park. **Open** during services only. ✝ Oct–Jul: 8:30am & 11:15am Sun.

This exquisite work of the architect Inigo Jones was built for Charles I's French wife, Henrietta Maria, in 1627, and was the first Classical church in England. It was initially intended to be part of St. James's Palace but is now separated from it by Marlborough Gate. George III married his queen, Charlotte of Mecklenburg-Strelitz (who was to bear him 15 children), here in 1761. The interior of the chapel, with its wonderful Annibale Carracci altarpiece and glorious 17th-century fixtures, is open to both regular worshippers and visitors during the spring and early summer.

The lake in St. James's Park with the London Eye in the background

⑲ Buckingham Palace

Buckingham Palace is both office and official London residence of the British monarchy. It is also used for ceremonial state occasions such as banquets for visiting heads of state. About 500 people work at the palace, including officers of the Royal Household and domestic staff.

John Nash converted the original Buckingham House into a palace for George IV (reigned 1820–30). Both he and his brother, William IV (reigned 1830–37), died before work was completed, and Queen Victoria was the first monarch to live at the palace. The present east front, facing the Mall, was added to Nash's conversion in 1913. The State Rooms are open to the public in summer.

Music Room
State guests are presented and royal christenings take place in this room, which boasts a beautiful, original parquet floor by Nash.

The Ballroom
The Victorian ballroom is used for state banquets and investitures.

The Queen's Gallery
Artworks from the Royal Collection (see p98), such as Canaletto's *Rome: The Pantheon*, are often on display.

KEY

① **The State Dining Room** is the setting for meals that are less formal than state banquets.

② **Blue Drawing Room** is decorated by imitation onyx columns created by architect John Nash.

③ **The White Drawing Room** is where the Royal Family assembles before passing into the State Dining Room or Ballroom.

④ **The Green Drawing Room** is the first of the large and magnificent state rooms entered by guests of the Queen at royal functions.

⑤ **The Royal Standard** flies when the Queen is in residence.

Changing of the Guard
Visitors can witness the Buckingham Palace grounds guard handing over duty regularly throughout the year in a colorful and musical royal military ceremony (see pp54–7).

Who Lives in Buckingham Palace?

The palace is the London residence of the Queen and her husband, the Duke of Edinburgh. The Princess Royal, the Duke of York, and the Earl of Wessex also have apartments here. About 50 domestic staff have rooms in the palace. There are more staff homes situated in the Royal Mews (see p98).

VISITORS' CHECKLIST

Practical Information
SW1.
Map 12 F5.
Tel 020 7766 7300.
W royalcollection.org.uk
State rooms **Open** end Jul–end Sep: 9:45am–6:30pm daily.
Changing of the Guard: May–Jul: 11:30am daily; Aug–Apr: alternate days. Tickets not required. ♿ 📷

Transportation
🚇 St. James's Park, Victoria.
🚌 2B, 11, 16, 24, 25, 36, 38, 52, 73, 135, C1. 🚆 Victoria.

The Throne Room
In a room lit by seven magnificent chandeliers sit the thrones used by the Queen and the Duke of Edinburgh during her coronation.

View over the Mall
Traditionally, the Royal Family waves to crowds from the balcony.

The garden is a haven for wildlife and is overlooked by most of the lavishly decorated state rooms at the back of the palace. It is also the venue for Royal Garden Parties, where guests enjoy tea and cakes.

⑰ Clarence House

Stable Yard SW1. **Map** 12 F4. **Tel** 020 7766 7303. 🚇 Green Park, St. James's Park. **Open** call or check website for opening times and dates. 📷 ♿ 🎧 mandatory. 🌐 **royalcollection.org.uk**

Designed by John Nash for William IV in 1827, this is Prince Charles's London home. Once a year, the public can visit the opulent ground floor.

Lancaster House

⑱ Lancaster House

Stable Yard SW1. **Map** 12 F4. 🚇 Green Park, St. James's Park. **Closed** to the public.

This royal residence was built for the Duke of York by Benjamin Wyatt, architect of Apsley House, in 1825. In 1848 Chopin played here for Queen Victoria, Prince Albert, and the Duke of Wellington. It is now a conference center.

⑲ Buckingham Palace

See pp96–7.

⑳ The Queen's Gallery

Buckingham Palace Rd SW1. **Map** 12 F5. **Tel** 020 7766 7301. 🚇 St. James's Park, Victoria. **Open** 10am–5:30pm daily (Aug & Sep: 9:30am–5:30pm). **Closed** dates vary; call or check website. 📷 ♿ 📼 🌐 **royalcollection.org.uk**

The Royal Family possesses one of the finest and most valuable art collections in the world, rich in the work of Old Masters, including Vermeer and Leonardo. In 2002 the galleries were expanded in the most extensive addition to Buckingham Palace in 150 years, resulting in three-and-a-half times more display space and an impressive entrance gallery with a striking columned portico.

Among the gallery's seven rooms, one is dedicated to a permanent display of some of the royal collection's masterpieces. Changing exhibitions include fine art, jewels, porcelain, furniture, and manuscripts.

㉑ Royal Mews

Buckingham Palace Rd SW1. **Map** 12 E5. **Tel** 020 7766 7302. 🚇 St. James's Park, Victoria. **Open** Apr–Oct: 10am–5pm daily; Nov, Feb–Mar: 10am–4pm Mon–Sat. Subject to closure at short notice (call first). **Closed** Dec–Jan. 📷 ♿ 🎧 🌐 **royalcollection.org.uk**

Although open for only a few hours each day, the Mews is worth catching for all lovers of horses and of royal pomp. The stables and coach houses, designed by Nash in 1825, accommodate the horses and coaches used by the Royal Family on state occasions. The star exhibit is the gold state coach, built for George III in 1761, with fine

Fabergé egg, Queen's Gallery

panels by Giovanni Cipriani. Among the other vehicles are the Irish state coach, bought by Queen Victoria for the State Opening of Parliament; the open-topped royal landau; and the glass coach, which was used for royal weddings and for transporting foreign ambassadors. The elaborate horses' harnesses are also on display, and so are some of the fine animals that wear them. The Mews has an exhibition that explains its history and current workings. Visitors may see carriages being prepared for use or limousines in action. A guided route around the mews includes a chance to view the 18th-century riding school where the horses are put through their paces. There is also a shop here selling royal souvenirs, open daily from 9:30am until 5pm.

The Victoria Monument outside Buckingham Palace

㉒ Wellington Arch

Hyde Park Corner SW1. **Map** 12 D4.
Tel 020 7930 2726. ⊖ Hyde Park
Corner. **Open** call or check website
for times and dates. **Closed** Jan 1,
Good Friday, Dec 24–26 & 31.
🎟 joint ticket with Apsley House
available. ♿ limited. 📷
W **english-heritage.org.uk**

After nearly a century of debate
about what to do with the
patch of land in front of Apsley
House, Wellington Arch,
designed by Decimus Burton,
was erected in 1828. The
sculpture, by Adrian Jones, was
added in 1912. Before it was
installed, Jones seated three
people for dinner in the body
of one of the horses.

The public now has access to
exhibitions in the inner rooms
of the arch. A viewing platform
beneath the sculpture has great
views over London.

Wellington Arch

㉓ Apsley House

Hyde Park Corner W1. **Map** 12 D4.
Tel 020 7499 5676. ⊖ Hyde Park
Corner. **Open** call or check website
for opening times and dates.
Closed Jan 1, Dec 24–26. 🎟 joint
ticket with Wellington Arch available.
📷 📷 pre-booked only. 📷
W **english-heritage.org.uk**

Apsley House, or Number One
London, as it is also known, on
the southeast corner of Hyde
Park, was completed by Robert
Adam for Baron Apsley in 1778.
Fifty years later it was enlarged
and altered by the architect
Benjamin Dean Wyatt, to
provide a grand home for the
Duke of Wellington, whose dual
career as soldier and politician
brought him victory against

Interior of Apsley House

Napoleon at Waterloo (1815),
and two terms as prime minister
(1828–30, 1834). Against a
sumptuous background of silk
hangings and gilt decoration
hangs the duke's art collection.
Paintings by Goya, Velázquez,
Brueghel, and Rubens stand
alongside displays of porcelain,
silver, and furniture. The duke's
memorabilia include swords
and medals, but are dominated
by Canova's colossal statue
of Napoleon, who was
Wellington's archenemy.

㉔ Shepherd Market

W1. **Map** 12 E4. ⊖ Green Park.

This attractive and petite
pedestrianized enclave of small
shops, restaurants, and outdoor
cafés, between Piccadilly and
Curzon Street, was named after
Edward Shepherd, who built it
in the middle of the 18th
century. During the 17th
century, the annual 15-day May
Fair (from which the name of
the area is derived) took place
on this site, and today Shepherd
Market is still very much the
center of Mayfair.

㉕ Green Park

SW1. **Map** 12 E4. **Tel** 0300 061 2350.
⊖ Green Park, Hyde Park Corner.
Open all day, year-round.
W **royalparks.org.uk**

Once part of Henry VIII's hunting
ground, it was, like St. James's
Park, adapted for public use by
Charles II in the 1660s, and is a
natural, undulating landscape
of grass and trees (with a good
spring show of daffodils). It was
a favorite site for duels during
the 18th century; in 1771 the
poet Alfieri was wounded here
by his mistress's husband,
Viscount Ligonier, but then
rushed back to the Haymarket
Theatre in time to catch the
last act of a play. Today the
park is popular with guests
staying at the Mayfair hotels
as a place to jog.

㉖ Faraday Museum

The Royal Institution, 21 Albemarle St
W1. **Map** 12 F3. **Tel** 020 7409 2992.
⊖ Green Park. **Open** 9am–6pm
Mon–Fri. **Closed** Dec 24–Jan 3. 📷 📷
📷 📷 call first. Lectures. **W** **rigb.org**

Michael Faraday was a
19th-century pioneer of
the uses of electricity. The
collections in the Michael
Faraday Museum include some
of his scientific apparatus and
personal effects, as well as the
work of other great scientists
across the lower three floors.

Michael Faraday

SOHO AND TRAFALGAR SQUARE

Soho has been renowned for pleasures of the table, the flesh, and the intellect ever since it was first developed in the late 17th century. For its first century, the area was one of London's most fashionable, and Soho residents of the time have gone down in history for their extravagant parties.

During the later part of the 20th century, Soho consolidated its reputation as a center for entertainment. With a cosmopolitan mix

of people, visitors here enjoy the many pleasant bars, restaurants, and cafés – popular with everyone from tourists to locals, office workers, and London's gay community.

Soho is one of London's most multi-cultural districts. The first immigrants were 18th-century Huguenots from France (*see Christ Church, Spitalfields p172*). Soho is also famous as a Chinatown; Gerrard Street is lined with Chinese restaurants.

Sights at a Glance

Historic Streets and Buildings
1 Trafalgar Square
2 Admiralty Arch
6 Leicester Square
8 Shaftesbury Avenue
9 Chinatown
10 Charing Cross Road
12 Soho Square
14 Carnaby Street

Shops and Markets
13 Berwick Street Market
15 Liberty

Churches
4 St. Martin-in-the-Fields

Museums and Galleries
3 *National Gallery pp106–9*
5 *National Portrait Gallery*
16 *Photographers' Gallery*

Theatres
7 Theatre Royal Haymarket
11 Palace Theatre

Restaurants *see pp292–295*
1 Andrew Edmunds
2 Asia de Cuba
3 Barrafina
4 Bocca di Lupo
5 Dehesa
6 Gopals of Soho
7 Haozhan
8 Inamo
9 Kulu Kulu Sushi
10 Mildred's
11 Nopi
12 Patara
13 Princi
14 Portrait
15 Refuel
16 Soho Joe
17 Tokyo Diner
18 Vasco and Piero's Pavilion
19 Yalla Yalla
20 Yauatcha

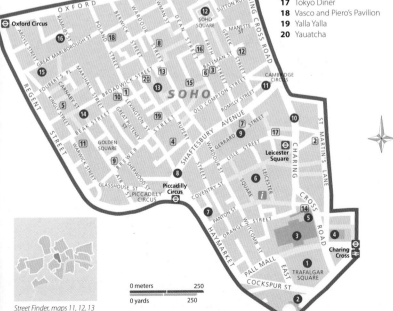

Street Finder, maps 11, 12, 13

◄ Chinatown, Soho

For keys to symbols *see back flap*

Street by Street: Trafalgar Square

This area buzzes both day and night with crowds enjoying the numerous restaurants, movies, and nightclubs. Broad avenues lined with regal office buildings converge at Trafalgar Square. Some of the roads that ring the square have now been pedestrianized, making this already popular meeting place far more accessible.

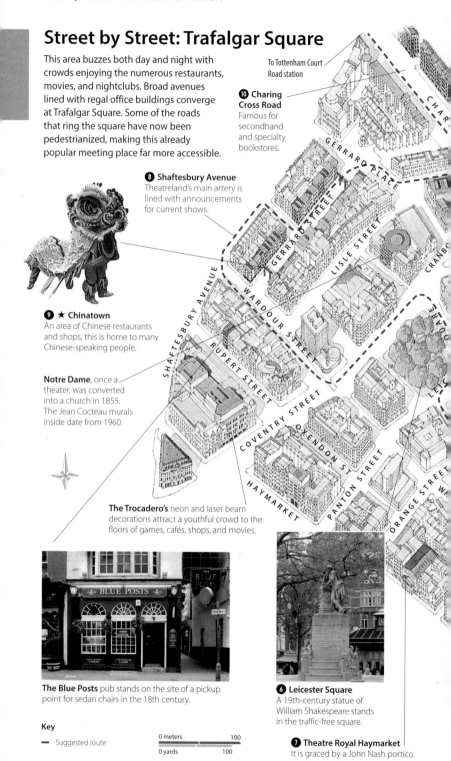

To Tottenham Court Road station

⑩ Charing Cross Road
Famous for secondhand and specialty bookstores.

⑧ Shaftesbury Avenue
Theatreland's main artery is lined with announcements for current shows.

⑨ ★ Chinatown
An area of Chinese restaurants and shops, this is home to many Chinese-speaking people.

Notre Dame, once a theater, was converted into a church in 1855. The Jean Cocteau murals inside date from 1960.

The Trocadero's neon and laser beam decorations attract a youthful crowd to the floors of games, cafés, shops, and movies.

The Blue Posts pub stands on the site of a pickup point for sedan chairs in the 18th century.

⑥ Leicester Square
A 19th-century statue of William Shakespeare stands in the traffic-free square.

⑦ Theatre Royal Haymarket
It is graced by a John Nash portico.

Key

— Suggested route

0 meters 100
0 yards 100

The Hippodrome, a former nightclub, was once a variety theater and is now a cabaret venue.

Leicester Square station

Cecil Court is lined with shops selling old books and prints.

Locator Map
See Central London Map pp14–15

4 ★ St Martin-in-the-Fields
James Gibbs's masterpiece set the US "colonial" style.

5 ★ National Portrait Gallery
Portraits of prominent Britons from Tudor times to the present-day adorn the walls here.

Charing Cross station

DUNCANNON ST

STRAND

NORTHUMBERLAND AVE

3 ★ National Gallery
The national collection of art is housed in these buildings.

TRAFALGAR SQUARE

CHARING CROSS

MALL EAST

COCKSPUR STREET

Nelson's Column

2 Admiralty Arch
The entrance to the Mall was designed in 1911.

1 ★ Trafalgar Square
Millions of tourists come here to admire the statues and the fountains.

❶ Trafalgar Square

WC2. **Map** 13 B3. ⊖ Charing Cross.

London's main venue for rallies and outdoor public meetings was conceived by John Nash and was mostly constructed during the 1830s. The 165-ft (50-m) column commemorates Admiral Lord Nelson, Britain's most famous sea lord, who died heroically at the Battle of Trafalgar against Napoleon in 1805. It dates from 1842; 14 stonemasons held a dinner on its flat top before the statue of Nelson was finally installed. Edwin Landseer's four lions were added to guard its base 25 years later. The north side of the square is now taken up by the National Gallery and its annex (see pp106–9), with Canada House on the west side, and South Africa House on the east. The restored Grand Buildings on the south side, with their fine arcade, were built in 1880 as the Grand Hotel. The square was partially pedestrianized in 2003, with other refurbishments including an enlarged central staircase descending from the National Gallery.

Nelson's statue overlooking the square

❷ Admiralty Arch

The Mall SW1. **Map** 13 B3. ⊖ Charing Cross.

Designed in 1911, this triple archway was part of Aston Webb's plan to rebuild the Mall as a grand processional route honoring Queen Victoria. The arch effectively seals the eastern end of the Mall, although traffic passes through the smaller side gates, and separates courtly London from the bustle of Trafalgar Square. The central gate is opened only for royal processions. There are plans to turn the preserved historic building into a five-star hotel.

Filming *Howard's End* at Admiralty Arch

❸ National Gallery

See pp106–9.

❹ St. Martin-in-the-Fields

Trafalgar Sq WC2. **Map** 13 B3. **Tel** 020 7766 1100. ⊖ Charing Cross. **Open** daily. 🛈 throughout the day; check website for details as times vary. ♿ 🎧 ▢ 📷 London Brass Rubbing Centre **Tel** 020 7766 1122 (leave a message with contact details). **Open** 10am–6pm Mon–Wed, 10am–8pm Thu–Sat, 11:30am–5pm Sun (last brass rubbing entry 1 hr before close). **Concerts** See Entertainment pp340–41. 🌐 **smitf.org**

There has been a church on this site since the 13th century. Many famous people were buried here, including Charles II's mistress, Nell Gwynne, and the painters William Hogarth and Joshua Reynolds. The present church was designed by James Gibbs and completed in 1726. In architectural terms, it was one of the most influential ever built; it was much copied in the United States, where it became a model for the Colonial style of church-building. An unusual feature of St. Martin's spacious interior is the royal box at gallery level on the left of the altar.

From 1914 until 1927 the crypt was used as a shelter for homeless soldiers and vagrants; during World War II it was an air-raid shelter. Today it helps the homeless by providing a lunchtime soup kitchen for them. It also has a café in the crypt, and a religious bookshop, as well as the London Brass Rubbing Centre. Lunchtime and evening concerts are held in the church and in the café.

❺ National Portrait Gallery

2 St Martin's Place WC2. **Map** 13 B3. **Tel** 020 7306 0055. ⊖ Leicester Sq, Charing Cross. **Open** 10am–6pm Sat–Wed, 10am–9pm Thu–Fri. **Closed** Dec 24–26. ♿ ♿ Orange St entrance. 🎧 ✏ ▢ 📷 Lectures. 🌐 **npg.org.uk**

Too often ignored in favor of the National Gallery next door, this fascinating museum recounts Britain's development through portraits of its main characters, giving faces to names that are familiar from history books. There are pictures of kings, queens, poets, musicians, artists, thinkers, heroes, and villains from all periods since the late 14th century. The oldest works,

William Shakespeare portrait on display in the Ondaatje Wing

on the fourth floor, include a Hans Holbein cartoon of Henry VIII and paintings of some of his wives.

The National Portrait Gallery's millennium development project, the Ondaatje Wing, opened in May 2000, allowing it 50 percent more exhibition and public space. It includes a Tudor Gallery, displaying some of the earliest and most important paintings, including one of Shakespeare (by John Taylor in 1651), and the Ditchley portrait of Elizabeth I. A balcony provides an extra display area for portraits from the 1960s to the 1990s.

The gallery has a rooftop restaurant, and a spacious lecture hall in the basement, which is also used for drama and film events.

The gallery also houses temporary exhibitions and has an excellent shop selling books on art and literature, as well as an extensive range of cards, prints, and posters featuring pictures from the main collection.

❻ Leicester Square

WC2. **Map** 13 B2. Leicester Sq, Piccadilly Circus.

It is hard to imagine that this, the perpetually animated heart of the West End entertainment district, was once a fashionable place to live. Laid out in 1670 south of Leicester House, a long-gone royal residence, the square's occupants included the scientist Isaac Newton and the artists Joshua Reynolds and William Hogarth. Reynolds made his fortune painting high society in his elegant salon at No. 46. Hogarth's house, in the southeast corner, became the Hôtel de la Sablionère in 1801, probably the area's first public restaurant.

In Victorian times, several popular music halls were established here, including the Empire (today the theater on the same site perpetuates the name) and the Alhambra, replaced in 1937 by the Art Deco Odeon. A booth selling discounted theater tickets

(see p336) sits in the square. There is also a statue of Charlie Chaplin, which was unveiled in 1981. The Shakespeare fountain dates from 1874.

Regeneration of the southwest corner of the square was completed in 2012, increasing public space and adding cafés, restaurants, and a state-of-the-art movie theater.

❼ Theatre Royal Haymarket

Haymarket SW1. **Map** 13 A3. **Tel** 020 7930 8800. Piccadilly Circus. **Open** performances and guided tours (call to check). trh.co.uk

The fine frontage of this theatre, with its portico of six Corinthian columns, dates from 1821, when John Nash designed it as part of his plan for a stately route from Carlton House to Regent's Park. The interior is equally grand.

❽ Shaftesbury Avenue

W1. **Map** 13 A2. Piccadilly Circus, Leicester Sq.

The main artery of London's theaterland, Shaftesbury Avenue has six theaters and two movie theaters, all on its north side. This street was cut through an area of terrible slums between 1877 and 1886 in order to improve communications across the city's busy West End; it follows the route of a much earlier highway. It is named after the Earl of Shaftesbury (1801–85), whose attempts to improve housing conditions had helped some of the local poor. (The Earl is also commemorated by the Eros statue in Piccadilly Circus – see p92.) The Lyric Theatre, which was designed by C. J. Phipps, has been open for almost the same length of time as the avenue.

London's West End: the facade of the Gielgud Theatre

❸ National Gallery

Trafalgar Square facade

The National Gallery has flourished since its inception in the early 19th century. In 1824 the House of Commons was persuaded to buy 38 major paintings, including works by Raphael and Rubens, and these became the start of a national collection. Contributions by rich benefactors have today resulted in a collection of some 2,300 Western European paintings. The main gallery building was designed in Greek Revival style by William Wilkins and built in 1833–8. To its left lies the Sainsbury Wing, financed by the grocery family and completed in 1991.

Stairs and elevator to lower galleries

★ The Burlington House Cartoon (c.1500)
The genius of Leonardo da Vinci glows through this chalk drawing of the Virgin and Child with St. Anne and St. John the Baptist.

Pigott Education Centre entrance

Stairs to lower floor

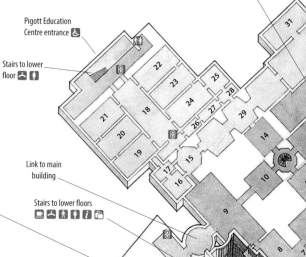

Link to main building

Stairs to lower floors

Doge Leonardo Loredan (1501–2)
Giovanni Bellini portrays this Venetian head of state as a serene father figure.

★ The Baptism of Christ
Piero della Francesca painted this tranquil masterpiece (1450s) of early Renaissance perspective for a church in his native Umbria.

Entrance to Sainsbury Wing

★ **The Rokeby Venus** (*1647–51*)
Diego Velázquez painted it to
match a lost Venetian nude.

★ **The Hay Wain** (*1821*)
John Constable brilliantly caught
the effect of distance and the
changing light and shadow of a
typically English cloudy summer
day in this famous classic.

VISITORS' CHECKLIST

Practical Information
Trafalgar Sq WC2.
Map 13 B3.
Tel 020 7747 2885.
ⓦ nationalgallery.org.uk
Open 10am–6pm daily (9pm Fri).
Closed Jan 1, Dec 24–26. ♿
Sainsbury Wing and Getty
entrances. 🎫 📷 📱 ✏ 🎒 🔲
🍴 Sainsbury Wing & temporary
exhibitions. Lectures, film
presentations, exhibitions,
special events.

Transportation
🚇 Charing Cross, Leicester Sq,
Piccadilly Circus. 🚌 3, 6, 9, 11, 12,
13, 15, 23, 24, 29, 88, 91, 139, 159,
176, 453. 🚆 Charing Cross.

Central
Hall

33

34

32

37   35

36

41

38   42

39   43

45   44

46

Getty entrance
♿

Trafalgar Square
entrance

At the Theater (*1876–7*)
Renoir was one of the greatest painters
of the Impressionist movement. The
theater was a popular subject among
artists of the time.

★ **The Ambassadors**
The strange shape in the
foreground of this Hans
Holbein portrait (1533) is
an anamorphic or distorted
skull, a symbol of mortality.

Key to Floorplan
- ▢ 13th- to 15th-century
- ▣ 16th-century
- ▢ 17th-century
- ▢ 18th- to early 20th-century
- ▣ Special exhibitions
- ▣ Non-exhibition space

Gallery Guide
*Most of the collection is housed on one floor divided into
four wings. The paintings hang chronologically, with the
earliest works (1250–1500) in the Sainsbury Wing. The
North, West, and East wings cover 1500–1600, 1600–
1700, and 1700–1900. Lesser paintings of all periods
are on the lower floor.*

Exploring the National Gallery

The National Gallery has over 2,300 paintings, most kept on permanent display. The collection ranges from early works by Cimabue, in the 13th century, to 19th-century Impressionists, but its particular strengths are in Dutch, early Renaissance Italian, and 17th-century Spanish painting. The bulk of the British collections are housed in Tate Britain (see pp84–7), while Tate Modern specializes in international modern art (pp180–83).

The Adoration of the Kings (1564) by Pieter Bruegel the Elder

Early Renaissance (1250–1500): Italian and Northern Painting

Three lustrous panels from the *Maestà*, Duccio's great altarpiece in Siena cathedral, are among the earliest paintings here. Other Italian works of the period include his outstanding *Madonna*.

The fine *Wilton Diptych* portraying England's Richard II is probably by a French artist. It displays the lyrical elegance of the International Gothic style that swept Europe.

Italian masters of this style include Pisanello and Gentile da Fabriano, whose *Madonna* often hangs beside another, by Masaccio – both date from 1425. Also shown are works by Masaccio's pupil, Fra Filippo Lippi, as well as Botticelli and Uccello. Umbrian paintings include Piero della Francesca's *Nativity* and *Baptism*, and there is an excellent collection of Mantegna, Bellini, and other works from the Venetian and Ferrarese schools. Antonello da Messina's *St. Jerome in His Study* has been mistaken for a van Eyck; it is not hard to see why, when you compare it with van Eyck's *Arnolfini Portrait*.

Important Netherlandish pictures, including some by Rogier van der Weyden and his followers, are also here, in the Sainsbury Wing.

St. Jerome in His Study by Antonello da Messina (c.1475)

High Renaissance (1500–1600): Italian, Netherlandish, and German Painting

Sebastiano del Piombo's *The Raising of Lazarus* was painted, with Michelangelo's assistance, to rival Raphael's great *Transfiguration*, which hangs in the Vatican in Rome. These and other well-known names of the High (or Late) Renaissance are extremely well represented, often with massive works. Look for Parmigianino's *Madonna and Child with Saints*, Leonardo da Vinci's charcoal cartoon of the *Virgin and Child* (a full-sized drawing used for copying as a painting), and his second version of the *Virgin of the Rocks*. There are also tender and amusing works by Piero di Cosimo, and several Titians, including *Bacchus and Ariadne* – which the public found too bright and garish when it was first cleaned by the gallery in the 1840s.

The Netherlandish and German collections are weaker. Even so, they include *The Ambassadors*, a fine double portrait by Holbein; and Altdorfer's superb *Christ Taking Leave of His Mother*, bought by the gallery in 1980. There is also a Hieronymus Bosch of *Christ Mocked* (sometimes known as *The Crowning with Thorns*), and an excellent Brueghel, *The Adoration of the Kings*.

The Annunciation (early 1450s) by Fra Filippo Lippi

The Sainsbury Wing

Plans for the Sainsbury Wing, opened in 1991, provoked a storm of dissent. An incensed Prince Charles dubbed an early design "a monstrous carbuncle on the face of a much-loved friend." The final building, by Venturi, has drawn criticism from other quarters for being a derivative compromise.

Major temporary exhibitions are held here – check the gallery's website for details. The wing also houses ArtStart, an interactive touch-screen guide to the Collection.

Dutch, Italian, French, and Spanish Painting (1600–1700)

The superb Dutch collection gives two entire rooms to Rembrandt. There are also works by Vermeer, Van Dyck (among them his equestrian portrait of King Charles I), and Rubens (including the popular *Chapeau de Paille*).

From Italy, the works of Carracci and Caravaggio are strongly represented, and Salvatore Rosa has a glowering self-portrait.

French works on display include a magnificent portrait of Cardinal Richelieu by Philippe de Champaigne. Claude's seascape, *Seaport with the Embarkation of the Queen of Sheba,* hangs beside Turner's rival painting *Dido Building Carthage,* as Turner himself had instructed.

The Spanish school has works by Murillo, Velázquez, Zurbarán, and others.

Young Woman Standing at a Virginal (1670–72) by Jan Vermeer

The Scale of Love (1715–18) by Jean-Antoine Watteau

Venetian, French, and English Painting (1700–1800)

One of the gallery's most famous 18th-century works is Canaletto's *The Stonemason's Yard.* Other Venetians here are Longhi and Tiepolo.

The French collection includes Rococo masters such as Chardin, Watteau, and Boucher, as well as landscapists and portraitists.

Gainsborough's early work *Mr. and Mrs. Andrews* and *The Morning Walk* are favorites with visitors; his rival, Sir Joshua Reynolds, is represented by some of his most Classical work and by more informal portraits.

English, French, and German Painting (1800–1900)

The great age of 19th-century landscape painting is amply represented here, with fine works by Constable and Turner, including Constable's *The Hay Wain* and Turner's *The Fighting Temeraire,* as well as works by the French artists Corot and Daubigny.

Of Romantic art, there is Géricault's vivid work, *Horse Frightened by Lightning,* and several interesting paintings by Delacroix. In contrast, the society portrait of *Madame Moitessier* by Ingres, though still Romantic, is more restrained and Classical.

Impressionists and other French avant-garde artists are well represented. Among the highlights are *The Water-Lily Pond* by Monet, and Renoir's *At the Theater,* Van Gogh's *Sunflowers,* not to mention one of Rousseau's famous jungle scenes, *Surprised!,* in which a tiger hunts explorers. In Seurat's *Bathers at Asnières* he did not originally use the pointillist technique he was later to invent, but subsequently reworked areas of the picture using dots of color.

Sunflowers (1888) by Vincent Van Gogh

❾ Chinatown

Streets around Gerrard St W1. **Map** 13 A2. ⊖ Leicester Sq, Piccadilly Circus.

There has been a Chinese community in London since the 19th century. Originally it was concentrated around the East End docks at Limehouse, where the opium dens of Victorian melodrama were sited. As the number of immigrants increased in the 1950s, many moved into Soho, where they created an ever-expanding Chinatown. It contains scores of restaurants, and mysterious aroma-filled shops selling Asian produce. Three Chinese arches straddle Gerrard Street, where a vibrant, colorful street festival, held in late January, celebrates Chinese New Year (see p61).

Rows of jars containing Chinese sweets in Chinatown

❿ Charing Cross Road

WC2. **Map** 13 B2. ⊖ Leicester Sq. See Shops and Markets pp312–13.

The road is a mecca for book-lovers, with a row of second-hand bookshops south of Cambridge Circus and, north of these, a clutch of shops that, between them, should be able to supply just about any recent volume. Visit the huge Foyle's and the smaller specialty shops: try Francis Edwards (see p322) for travel and art and Sportspages for sports. Sadly, rising rents have put this unique mix under threat.

At the junction with New Oxford Street rises the 1960s tower called Centrepoint. It lay empty for ten years after it was built, its owners finding this more profitable than renting it out.

At the Palace Theatre in 1898

⓫ Palace Theatre

Shaftesbury Ave W1. **Map** 13 B2. **Tel** Box office 0844 412 4656. ⊖ Leicester Sq. **Open** for performances only. See Entertainment pp336–7.
🅦 palace-theatre.co.uk

Most West End theaters are disappointingly unassertive. This one, which dominates the west side of Cambridge Circus, is a splendid exception, with its sparkling terra-cotta exterior and opulent furnishings. Completed as an opera house in 1891, it became a music hall the following year. The ballerina Anna Pavlova made her London debut here in 1910. Now the theater, owned by Andrew Lloyd Webber, whose own musicals are all over London, stages hit shows such as Spamalot.

⓬ Soho Square

W1. **Map** 13 A1. ⊖ Tottenham Court Rd.

Soon after it was laid out in 1681, this Square enjoyed a brief reign as the most fashionable address in London. Originally it was called King Square, after Charles II, whose statue was erected in the middle. The square went out of fashion by the late 18th century and is now surrounded by bland office buildings. The mock-Tudor garden shed in the center was added much later in Victorian times.

⓭ Berwick Street Market

W1. **Map** 13 A1. ⊖ Piccadilly Circus. **Open** 9am–6pm Mon–Sat. See Shops and Markets p331.

There has been a market here since the 1840s. Berwick Street trader Jack Smith introduced grapefruit to London in 1890. Today this is the West End's best street market, at its cheeriest and most crowded during the lunch hour. The freshest and least expensive produce for miles around is to be found here. There are also some interesting shops, including Borovick's, which sells extraordinary fabrics, and a growing number of cafés and restaurants. At its southern end the street narrows into an alley on which Raymond's Revue Bar (the comparatively respectable face of Soho sleaze) has presented its festival of erotica since 1958.

Some of London's cheapest produce at Berwick Street Market

⑭ Carnaby Street

W1. **Map** 12 F2. ⊖ Oxford Circus.

During the 1960s this street was so much the hub of swinging London that the Oxford English Dictionary recognized the term "Carnaby Street" as meaning "fashionable clothing for young people." Today fashion shops can be found on nearby streets such as Kingly Court and Fouberts Place.

⑮ Liberty

Regent St W1. **Map** 12 F2. ⊖ Oxford Circus. *See Shops and Markets p313.* **W** liberty.co.uk

Arthur Lasenby Liberty opened his first shop, selling Oriental silks, on Regent Street in 1875.

Liberty's mock-Tudor façade

Among his first customers were the artists Ruskin and Rossetti. Soon, Liberty prints and designs, by artists such as William Morris, epitomized the Arts and Crafts movement of the late 19th and early 20th centuries. They are still fashionable today.

The present mock-Tudor building with its country-house feel dates from 1925, and was built specifically to house the store.

Today the shop maintains its strong links with top quality craftsmanship of all kinds.

⑯ Photographers' Gallery

16-18 Ramillies St W1. **Map** 12 F1. ⊖ Oxford Circus. **Tel** 020 7087 9300. **Open** 10am–6pm Mon–Sat, till 8pm Thu, 11:30am–6pm Sun. 🚻 ▣ 🅿 **W** photonet.org.uk

Dedicated to photography, this gallery exhibits work from both new and more renowned artists, as well as putting on regular talks and events. The bookshop also sells cameras and prints.

The Heart of Soho

Old Compton Street is Soho's High Street. Its shops and restaurants reflect the variety of people who have lived in the area over the centuries. These include many great artists, writers, and musicians.

Maison Bertaux is known for producing delicious croissants and coffee and wonderful cakes as good as those found in Paris.

Ronnie Scott's opened in 1959, and nearly all the big names of jazz have played here *(see pp343–5).*

Bar Italia is a coffee shop situated under the room where John Logie Baird first demonstrated television in 1926. As a child, Mozart stayed next door with his family in 1764 and 1765.

The Coach and Horses pub has been a center of bohemian Soho since the 1950s and is still popular.

Algerian Coffee Stores is one of Soho's oldest shops. Delicious aromas of the world's coffees fill the shop.

Patisserie Valerie is a Hungarian-owned café serving delicious pastries *(see pp304–7).*

St. Anne's Church Tower is all that remains after a bomb destroyed the church in 1940.

The French House was frequented by Maurice Chevalier and General de Gaulle.

The Palace Theatre has hosted many successful musicals.

COVENT GARDEN AND THE STRAND

The open-air cafés, street entertainers, stylish shops, and markets make this area a magnet for visitors. At its center is the Piazza, site of a wholesale market until 1974. Since then, the Georgian and Victorian buildings here and in the surrounding streets have been converted into one of the city's liveliest districts. In medieval times the area was occupied by a convent garden that supplied Westminster Abbey with produce. Then in the 1630s, Inigo Jones laid out the Piazza as London's first square, with its west side dominated by his St. Paul's Church.

The Piazza was commissioned as a residential development by the Earl of Bedford, owner of one of the mansions that lined the Strand. Before the Embankment was built, the Strand ran along the river.

Sights at a Glance

Historic Streets and Buildings
1. The Piazza and Central Market
7. Neal Street and Neal's Yard
12. Savoy Hotel
14. Somerset House
16. Roman Bath
17. Bush House
20. Adelphi
21. Charing Cross

Museums and Galleries
3. London's Transport Museum

Churches
2. St. Paul's Church
13. Savoy Chapel
15. St. Mary-le-Strand

Monuments and Statues
9. Seven Dials
18. Cleopatra's Needle

Famous Theaters
5. Theatre Royal Drury Lane
6. Royal Opera House
11. Adelphi Theatre
22. The London Coliseum
10. Wyndham's Theatre
22. Parks and Garden
19. Victoria Embankment Gardens

Historic Pubs and Shopping Arcades
4. Lamb and Flag
8. Thomas Neal's

▢ Restaurants see pp292–295
1. Atelier de Joël Robuchon
2. Belgo Centraal
3. Clos Maggiore
4. Le Deuxieme
5. Food for Thought
6. J Sheekey
7. Porter's English
8. Rules
9. Sagar
10. The Ten Cases
11. Terroirs
12. Thai Pot
13. Wahaca

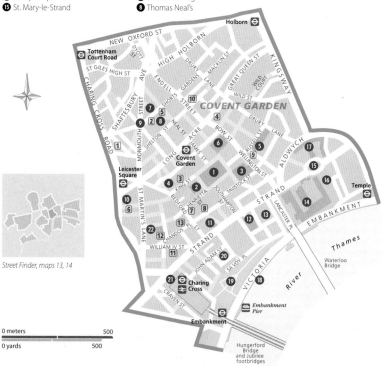

Street Finder, maps 13, 14

0 meters 500
0 yards 500

◀ Enzo Piazotta's statue *The Young Dancer* (1988), Covent Garden

For keys to symbols *see back flap*

Street-by-Street: Covent Garden

Once an area of decaying streets and
warehouses, Covent Garden came alive only
after dark when the fruit and vegetable market
traders went about their business. Now it is
completely revitalized. Day and night, visitors,
residents, and street entertainers of every
vocation throng the Piazza, much as they
would have done several centuries ago.

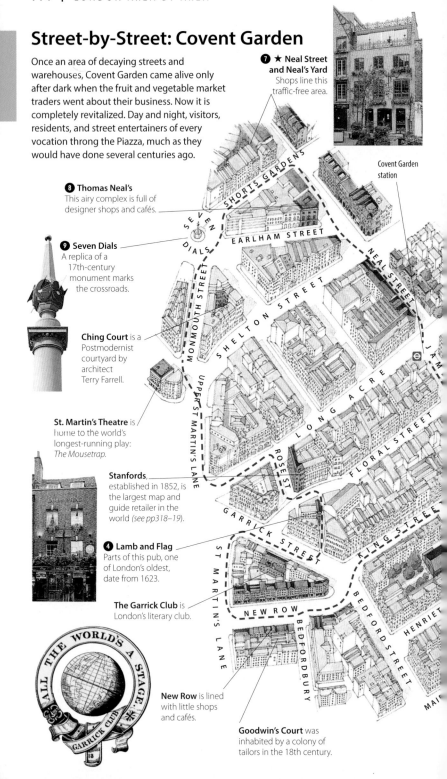

**❼ ★ Neal Street
and Neal's Yard**
Shops line this
traffic-free area.

Covent Garden
station

❽ Thomas Neal's
This airy complex is full of
designer shops and cafés.

❾ Seven Dials
A replica of a
17th-century
monument marks
the crossroads.

Ching Court is a
Postmodernist
courtyard by
architect
Terry Farrell.

St. Martin's Theatre is
home to the world's
longest-running play:
The Mousetrap.

Stanfords,
established in 1852, is
the largest map and
guide retailer in the
world *(see pp318–19)*.

❹ Lamb and Flag
Parts of this pub, one
of London's oldest,
date from 1623.

The Garrick Club is
London's literary club.

New Row is lined
with little shops
and cafés.

Goodwin's Court was
inhabited by a colony of
tailors in the 18th century.

THE WORLD'S A STAGE
GARRICK CLUB

❶ ★ The Piazza and Central Market
Performers of all kinds – jugglers, clowns, acrobats, and musicians – entertain the crowds in the square.

Locator Map
See Central London Map pp16–17

❻ Royal Opera House
Most of the world's greatest singers and dancers have appeared on its stage.

Bow Street Police Station housed London's first police force, the Bow Street Runners, in the 18th century. It closed in 1992.

❺ ★ Theatre Royal Drury Lane
A theater has stood on this site since 1663, making it London's oldest theater. The present theater was built in 1812. It is owned by composer Andrew Lloyd Webber and stages popular musicals.

Boswells, now a coffee house, is where Dr. Johnson first met his biographer, Boswell.

❸ ★ London's Transport Museum
The history of the city's Tube and buses is brought to life in this museum.

Jubilee Market sells clothes and bric-a-brac.

Key

— Suggested route

0 meters   100
0 yards   100

Rules is frequented by the rich and famous for its typically English food.

❷ ★ St. Paul's Church
Despite appearances, Inigo Jones's church faces away from the Piazza – the entrance is through the churchyard.

❶ The Piazza and Central Market

Covent Garden WC2. **Map** 13 C2.
⊖ Covent Garden. ♿ but cobbled streets. Street performers 10am–dusk daily. *See Shops and Markets p315.*
Ⓦ coventgardenlondonuk.com

The 17th-century architect Inigo Jones originally planned this area to be an elegant residential square, modeled on the piazza in Livorno, northern Italy. Today the buildings on and around the Piazza are almost entirely Victorian. The covered central market was designed by Charles Fowler in 1833 for fruit and vegetable wholesalers, the glass and iron roof anticipating the giant rail termini built later in the century – for instance, St. Pancras *(see p132)* and Waterloo *(see p193)*. It now makes a magnificent shell for an array of small shops selling designer clothes, books, arts, crafts, decorative items, and antiques, surrounded by bustling market stands that continue south in the neighboring Jubilee Hall, which was built in 1903.

The colonnaded Bedford Chambers, on the north side, give a hint of Inigo Jones's plan, although even they are not original: they were rebuilt and partially modified in 1879.

Street entertainment is a well-loved and now expected tradition of the area; in 1662, diarist Samuel Pepys wrote of watching a Punch and Judy show under the portico of St. Paul's Church.

West entrance to St. Paul's

❷ St. Paul's Church

Bedford St WC2. **Map** 13 C2.
Tel 020 7836 5221. ⊖ Covent Garden. **Open** 8:30am–5pm Mon–Fri, 9am–1pm Sun. ✝ 11am Sun, 2nd Sun of the month 4pm evensong.
♿ Ⓦ actorschurch.org

Inigo Jones built this church (completed in 1633) with the altar at the west end, so as to allow his grand portico, with its two square and two round columns, to face east into the Piazza. Clerics objected to this unorthodox arrangement, and the altar was moved to its conventional position at the east end. Jones went ahead with his original exterior design. Thus the church is entered from the west, and the east portico is a fake door, used now as an impromptu stage for street entertainers. In 1795 the interior was destroyed by fire but was rebuilt in Jones's airy, uncomplicated style. Today the church is all that is left of Jones's original plan for the Piazza. St. Paul's is known as "The Actors' Church" and plaques commemorate

Punch and Judy performer

distinguished men and women of the theater. A 17th-century carving by Grinling Gibbons, on the west screen, is a memorial to the architect.

❸ London's Transport Museum

The Piazza WC2. **Map** 13 C2. **Tel** 020 7379 6344 or 020-7565 7299 (24 hour infoline). ⊖ Covent Garden. **Open** 10am–6pm Sat–Thu, 11am–6pm Fri (last adm: 5:15pm). 📷 🖥 🏛 ♿ 🛍 book ahead.
Ⓦ ltmuseum.co.uk

You do not have to be a train spotter or a collector of bus numbers to enjoy this museum. The intriguing collection is housed in the picturesque Victorian Flower Market, which was built in 1872, and features public transportation from the past and present.

The history of London's mass transit is in essence a social history of the capital. Bus, streetcar, and underground route patterns first reflected the city's growth and then promoted it: the northern and western suburbs began to develop only after their tube connections were built. The museum houses a fine collection of 20th-century commercial art. London's bus and train companies have been, and still are, prolific patrons of contemporary artists, and copies of some of the finest posters on display can be bought at the well-stocked museum shop. They include the innovative Art Deco designs of E. McKnight Kauffer, as well as work by renowned artists of the 1930s, such as Graham Sutherland and Paul Nash.

A mid-18th-century view of the Piazza

This museum is excellent for children. There are plenty of hands-on exhibits, and these include the opportunity for children to put themselves in the driver's seat of a London bus, or a train from the underground system.

❹ Lamb and Flag

33 Rose St WC2. **Map** 13 B2. **Tel** 020 7497 9504. 🚇 Covent Garden, Leicester Sq. **Open** 11am–11pm Mon–Sat, noon–10:30pm Sun. *See Restaurants and Pubs p309.*

There has been an inn here since the 16th century, making the Lamb and Flag the oldest tavern in Covent Garden. Tucked away next to a narrow alleyway linking Garrick Street with Floral Street, the cramped bars are still largely unmodernized. A plaque concerns satirist John Dryden, attacked in the alley outside in 1679. He was set upon by hooligans sent by Charles II to uphold the honor of the Duchess of Portsmouth, one of his mistresses. Dryden had lampooned her in some of his verse. The upstairs bar is also named after Dryden.

The pub is popular with both downtown workers and savvy tourists, who spill out into the courtyard.

❺ Theatre Royal Drury Lane

Catherine St WC2. **Map** 13 C2. **Tel** 0844 871 8810. 🚇 Covent Garden, Holborn. **Open** for tours and performances. 🎭 *See Entertainment p336.* 🌐 **theatreroyaldrurylane.co.uk**

The first theater on this site was built in 1663 as one of only two venues in London where drama could legally be staged. Nell Gwynne acted here. Three of the theaters built here since then burned down, including one designed by Sir Christopher Wren *(see p49)*. The present one, by Benjamin Wyatt, was completed in 1812 and has one of the city's largest auditoriums. In the 1800s it was famous for pantomimes – now it stages blockbuster musicals. It is called

The glass Floral Hall, part of the Royal Opera House

the Theatre Royal Drury Lane even though its entrance is on Catherine Street.

❻ Royal Opera House

Covent Garden WC2. **Map** 13 C2. **Tel** 020 7304 4000. 🚇 Covent Garden. **Open** for tours and performances (call to check). *See Entertainment p340.* 🅿️ 📷 💻 ♿ 🌐 **roh.org.uk**

Built in 1732, the first theater on this site staged more spoken drama than music drama, although many of Handel's operas and oratorios were premiered here. Like its neighbor the Theatre Royal Drury Lane, the building proved prone to fire and was destroyed in 1808 and again in 1856. The present opera house was designed in 1858 by E. M. Barry. John Flaxman's portico frieze, depicting tragedy and comedy, survived from the previous building of 1809.

The Opera House has had both high and low points during its history. In 1892, the first British performance of Wagner's Ring was conducted here by Gustav Mahler. Later, during World War I, the building was used as a storehouse by the government. Today, it is home to the Royal Opera and Royal Ballet Companies – the best tickets can cost over £100. An extensive renovation project, completed in 1999, added a

second auditorium, along with rehearsal rooms for the Royal Opera and Royal Ballet companies. Backstage tours are available, and once a month visitors can watch the Royal Ballet attending its daily class.

❼ Neal Street and Neal's Yard

Covent Garden WC2. **Map** 13 B1. 🚇 Covent Garden. *See Shops and Markets pp314–15.*

In this attractive street, former warehouses from the 19th century can be identified by the hoisting mechanisms high on their exterior walls. The buildings have been converted into shops, art galleries, and restaurants. Off Neal Street in Short's Gardens is Neal's Yard Dairy, one of London's best cheese shops, which also sells delicious breads. Brainchild of the late Nicholas Saunders, it, and Neal's Yard itself, remain an oasis of alternative values amid the growing commercialism of the area.

A specialty shop on Neal Street

Entrance to Thomas Neal's

❽ Thomas Neal's

Earlham St WC2. **Map** 13 B2.
Covent Garden, Leicester Sq.
Open 10am–7pm Mon–Sat, noon–6pm Sun. ground floor only.

Opened in the early 1990s in an old converted banana warehouse, this upscale shopping complex offers an interesting range of shops, selling designer clothes and cosmetics, jewelry and accessories, antique clothing, and lace. When it is time for a break from shopping, there is a café and restaurant on the lower floor. The Donmar Warehouse theater *(see p338)* is also part of the complex, staging must-see productions such as *The Blue Room*.

❾ Seven Dials

Monmouth St WC2. **Map** 13 B2.
Covent Garden, Leicester Sq.

The pillar at this junction of seven streets incorporates six sundials (the central spike acted as a seventh). It was installed in 1989 and is a copy of a 17th-century monument. The original was removed in the 19th century because it had become a notorious meeting place for criminals who operated in an area that had become one of London's most infamous slums.
Today, Seven Dials is a vibrant shopping and dining area. Its streets and alleyways are known for their unique shops, funky boutiques, holistic medicine shops, restaurants, and bars.

❿ Wyndham's Theatre

32 Charing Cross Rd, WC2. **Map** 13 B2.
Tel 0871 976 0072. Leicester Square. **Open** for performances only.
 wyndhams-theatre.com
See Entertainment pp336–7.

The Wyndham's Theatre opened its doors in 1899 and takes its name from Charles Wyndham (1837–1919) – lauded as one of the greatest actors of his day. Designed by the architect William Sprague, the Wyndham was the first of seven theaters he completed that year. It boasts a Portland stone exterior and a turquoise, cream, and gold interior decorated in Louis XVI style, with a ceiling painted in the style of Boucher.
Many greats in British theater have graced the stage since Wyndham himself, Vanessa Redgrave, Sir Alec Guinness, and Sir John Gielgud among them. It has also seen such talents as Dame Judi Dench in *Madame de Sade* and Jude Law as Hamlet.

⓫ Adelphi Theatre

Strand WC2. **Map** 13 C3. **Tel** 0844 412 4651. Charing Cross, Embankment.
Open performances only.
 adelphitheatre.co.uk
See Entertainment pp336–7.

There has been a theater on this site since 1806, when the Sans Pareil Theatre opened here. It was set up by John Scott, a wealthy tradesman, who was helping to launch his daughter on the stage. After several refurbishments and name changes, the current Adelphi Theatre was remodeled in 1930 in Art Deco style by Ernest Schaufelburg. His modernist "straight-line" design resulted in a building without curves. Note the highly distinctive lettering on the frontage, and the well-kept lobby and auditorium with their stylized motifs.
The Adelphi now stages a variety of plays, from *The Body-guard*, featuring music of the late Whitney Houston, to *One Man, Two Guvnors*, which transferred to the Theatre Royal Haymarket *(see p103)* in 2011.

⓬ Savoy Hotel

Strand WC2. **Map** 13 C2. **Tel** 020 7836 4343. Charing Cross, Embankment.
 fairmont.com/savoy

Pioneer of private bathrooms and electric lighting, the grand Savoy was built in 1889 on the site of the medieval Savoy Palace. A lavish refurbishment project took place in 2008–2010, incorporating both the original Edwardian and the later Art Deco style. The forecourt is the only street in Britain where traffic drives on the right. Attached to the hotel are the Savoy Theatre built for D'Oyly Carte opera, famed for performing the operas of Gilbert and Sullivan; and Simpson's-in-the-Strand English restaurant.

Front entrance to the Savoy Hotel

⓭ Savoy Chapel

Strand WC2. **Map** 13 C2. **Tel** 020 7836 7221. Charing Cross, Embankment.
Open 9am–4pm Mon–Thu, 9am–1pm Sun. **Closed** Aug–Sep. 11am Sun.
 call to reserve.

The first Savoy Chapel was founded in the 16th century as the chapel for the hospital set up by Henry VII on the site of the old Savoy Palace. Parts of the outside walls date from 1512, but most of the present building dates from the mid-19th century. In 1890 it was London's first church to be electrically lit. It became the chapel of the Royal Victorian Order in 1937, and is now a private chapel of the Queen. Nearby on Savoy Hill were the first studios of the BBC.

⑭ Somerset House

Strand WC2. **Map** 14 D2. **Tel** 020 7845 4600. 🚇 Temple. Gallery & House **Open** 10am–6pm daily (last adm to galleries: 5:30pm). **Closed** Jan 1, Dec 24–26. 🎫 free guided tours. Ice rink **Open** 2 months in winter. 📞 call 0844-847 1520 for tickets. 💻 Courtauld Institute of Art Gallery: ♿ 💻 📷 ♿ Embankment Galleries: ♿ ♿ Tom's Kitchen **Tel** 020 7845 4646. **w somersethouse.org.uk**

This elegant Georgian building was the creation of Sir William Chambers. It was erected in the 1770s after the first Somerset House, a Renaissance palace built for the Duke of Somerset in the mid-16th century, was pulled down following years of neglect. The replacement was the first major building to be designed for use as government offices and has served to house the Navy Board (note that the classical grandeur of the Seamen's Waiting Hall and Nelson's Staircase are not to be missed), a succession of Royal Societies, and, for a substantial amount of time, the Inland Revenue. Today it is home to the Courtauld Institute of Art

Gallery. The courtyard of Somerset House was closed to the public for nearly a century, but on the Inland Revenue's departure in 1997 it was cleared, as part of a major restoration project. This created an attractive piazza with a 55-jet fountain. Films and concerts are often staged

Fountains at Somerset House

here in the summer, and for a few weeks in winter, there is an enchanting ice rink. From the courtyard visitors can stroll through the South Building, where the highly regarded Tom's Kitchen restaurant overlooks the Thames, onto a riverside terrace that includes an open-air summer café and a restaurant, with pedestrian access to Waterloo Bridge and the South Bank's theaters and other attractions.

Located in Somerset House, but famous in its own right, is the small but spectacular **Courtauld Institute of Art Gallery**. Its exquisite collection of paintings has been displayed here since 1990 and owes its existence to the bequest of textile magnate and philanthropist Samuel Courtauld. On display are works by Botticelli, Brueghel, Bellini, and Rubens (including one of his early masterpieces, *The Descent from the Cross*), but it is the Courtauld's collection of Impressionist and Post-Impressionist paintings that draws the most attention. As well as works by Monet, Gauguin, Pissarro, Renoir, and Modigliani, visitors can gaze captivated on Manet's *A Bar at the Folies-Bergères*, Van Gogh's *Self-Portrait with Bandaged Ear*, Cézanne's *The Card Players*, and some evocative studies of dancers by Degas. In addition to its permanent collection, the Courtauld Institute now hosts a series of world-class temporary exhibitions that take place throughout the year.

A modern riverside gallery was launched within Somerset House in 2008. The **Embankment Galleries** occupy 8,000 sq ft (750 sq m) of exhibition space on the two lower floors of the south wing. The changing exhibition program covers a broad range of contemporary arts, including photography, design, fashion, and architecture.

Van Gogh's *Self-Portrait with Bandaged Ear* (1889) at the Courtauld

⓯ St. Mary-le-Strand

Strand WC2. **Map** 14 D2. **Tel** 020 7836 3126. 🔵 Temple. **Open** 11am–4pm Tue–Thu, 10am–1pm Sun. 🕐 11am Sun, 1:05pm Thu. 📷
🌐 stmarylestrand.org

Now beached on a traffic island at the east end of the Strand, this pleasing church was consecrated in 1724. It was the first public building by James Gibbs, who designed St. Martin-in-the-Fields (*see p104*). Gibbs was influenced by Christopher Wren, but the exuberant external decorative detail here was inspired by the Baroque churches of Rome, where Gibbs studied. The multi-arched tower is layered like a wedding cake, and culminates in a cupola and lantern. St. Mary-le-Strand is now the official church of the Women's Royal Naval Service.

St. Mary-le-Strand

⓰ Roman Bath

5 Strand Lane WC2. **Map** 14 D2. **Tel** 020 7641 5264. 🔵 Temple, Embankment, Charing Cross. **Open** by appt only. ♿ via Temple Pl.

This little bath and its surround may be seen from a full-length window on Surrey Street, by pressing a light switch on the outside wall. It is almost certainly not Roman, for there is no other evidence of Roman habitation in the immediate

Bush House from Kingsway

area. It is more likely to have been part of Arundel House, one of several palaces that stood on the Strand from Tudor times until the 17th century, when they were demolished for new building. In the 19th century the bath was open to the public for cold plunges, believed to be healthy.

⓱ Bush House

Aldwych WC2. **Map** 14 D2. 🔵 Temple, Holborn. **Closed** to the public.

Situated at the center of the Aldwych crescent, this Neo-Classical building was first designed as manufacturers' showrooms by an American, Irving T. Bush, and completed in 1935. It appears especially imposing when viewed from Kingsway, its dramatic north entrance graced with various statues symbolizing Anglo-American relations. Since 1940 it has been used as radio studios, and was the headquarters of the BBC World Service until 2012. To most Londoners it still symbolizes the home of the BBC.

⓲ Cleopatra's Needle

Embankment WC2. **Map** 13 C3. 🔵 Embankment, Charing Cross.

Erected in Heliopolis in about 1500 BC, this incongruous pink granite monument is much older than London itself. Its inscriptions celebrate the deeds of the pharaohs of ancient Egypt. It was presented

to Britain by the then Viceroy of Egypt, Mohammed Ali, in 1819 and erected in 1878, shortly after the Embankment was built. It has a twin in New York's Central Park, behind the Metropolitan Museum of Art. The bronze sphinxes, added in 1882, are not Egyptian.

In the base is a Victorian time capsule of artifacts of the day, such as the day's newspapers, a train schedule, and photographs of 12 contemporary beauties.

⓳ Victoria Embankment Gardens

WC2. **Map** 13 C3. 🔵 Embankment, Charing Cross. **Open** 7:30am–dusk Mon–Sat, 9am–dusk Sun and public hols. ♿ 📷

This narrow sliver of a public park, created when the Embankment was built, boasts well-maintained flower beds, a clutch of statues of British worthies (including the Scottish poet Robert Burns), and, in summer, a season of concerts. Its main historical feature is the water gate at its northwest corner, which was built as a triumphal entry to the Thames for the Duke of Buckingham in 1626. It is a relic of York House, which used to stand on this site and was the home first of the Archbishops of York and then of the Duke. It is still in its original position, and although the water used to lap against it, because of the Thames Embankment the gate is now a good 330 ft (100 m) from the river's edge.

Victoria Embankment Gardens

The office building above Charing Cross station

The facade of No. 7 Adam Street

⑳ Adelphi

Strand WC2. **Map** 13 C3.
Embankment, Charing Cross.
Closed to the public.

Adelphi is a pun on *adelphoi*, the Greek word for "brothers" – this area was once an elegant riverside residential development designed in 1772 by brothers Robert and John Adam. The name now refers to the Art Deco office block, its entrance adorned with N. A. Trent's heroic reliefs of workers at toil, which in 1938 replaced the Adams' much admired Palladian-style apartment complex. That destruction is now viewed as one of the worst acts of 20th-century official vandalism. A number of the Adams' surrounding buildings survive, notably No. 8, the ornate Royal Society for the encouragement of Arts, Manufactures & Commerce just opposite (open first Sunday of the month, 10am–12:30pm, not January; 0207 930 5115). In the same exuberant idiom are Nos. 1–4 Robert Street, where Robert Adam lived for a time, and No. 7 Adam Street.

㉑ Charing Cross

Strand WC2. **Map** 13 C3. Charing Cross, Embankment.

The name derives from the last of the 12 crosses erected by Edward I to mark the funeral route in 1290 of his wife, Eleanor of Castile, from Nottinghamshire to Westminster Abbey. Today a 19th-century replica stands in the forecourt of Charing Cross station. Both the cross and the Charing Cross Hotel, built into the station frontage, were designed in 1863 by E. M. Barry, architect of the Royal Opera House *(see p117)*.

Above the station platforms has risen an assertive shopping center and office block, completed in 1991. Designed by Terry Farrell, it resembles a giant ocean liner, with portholes looking onto Villiers Street. The building is best seen from the river, where it dominates its neighbors. The railroad arches at the rear of the station have been modernized as a suite of small shops and cafés, as well as a venue for the Players Theatre, the last repository of Victorian music hall entertainment.

㉒ The London Coliseum

St. Martin's Lane WC2. **Map** 13 B3. **Tel** 020 7845 9300. Leicester Sq, Charing Cross. **Open** performances. Lectures. *See Entertainment pp340–41.* **W** eno.org

London's largest theater and one of its most elaborate, this flamboyant building, topped with a large globe, was designed in 1904 by Frank Matcham and equipped with London's first revolving stage. It was also the first theater in Europe to have elevators. A former variety house, today it is the home of the English National Opera, and well worth visiting, if only for the Edwardian interior with its gilded cherubs and heavy purple curtains. In 2003, the original glass roof was restored, providing dramatic views over Trafalgar Square.

London Coliseum

BLOOMSBURY AND FITZROVIA

Since the beginning of the 20th century, Bloomsbury and Fitzrovia have been synonymous with literature, art, and learning. The Bloomsbury Group of writers and artists were active from the early 1900s until the 1930s; the name Fitzrovia was invented by writers such as Dylan Thomas, who drank in the Fitzroy Tavern. Bloomsbury still boasts the University of London, the British Museum, and many fine Georgian squares. But it is now also noted for its Charlotte Street restaurants and the furniture and competitively priced electrical shops lining Tottenham Court Road.

Sights at a Glance

Historic Streets and Buildings

- ❷ Bloomsbury Square
- ❹ Russell Square
- ❺ Queen Square
- ❽ British Library
- ❾ St. Pancras International
- ⑪ Woburn Walk
- ⑬ Fitzroy Square
- ⑮ Charlotte Street

Museums

- ❶ British Museum pp126–9
- ❻ Charles Dickens Museum
- ❼ Foundling Museum
- ⑫ Wellcome Collection
- ⑯ Pollock's Toy Museum

Churches

- ❸ St. George's, Bloomsbury
- ⑩ St. Pancras Parish Church

Pubs

- ⑭ Fitzroy Tavern

Restaurants see pp297–298

1 Bam-Bou
2 Malabar Junction
3 Pied à Terre
4 Ragam
5 Roka
6 Salt Yard
7 Thai Metro

Street Finder, maps 4, 5, 6, 13

0 meters 500
0 yards 500

◀ The Great Court at the British Museum

For keys to symbols see back flap

Street-by-Street: Bloomsbury

The British Museum dominates Bloomsbury. Its earnestly intellectual atmosphere spills over into the surrounding streets, and to its north lies the main campus of London University. The area has been home to writers and artists, and is a traditional center of the book trade. Most of the publishers have left, but there are still many bookshops around.

The Senate House (1932) is the administrative headquarters of the University of London. It holds a priceless library.

Bedford Square is one of London's most complete Georgian squares. Its uniform doorways are fringed in artificial stone.

❶ ★ British Museum
Designed in the mid-19th century, it is extremely popular and attracts some five million visitors each year.

Key

— Suggested route

0 meters	100
0 yards	100

Museum Street is lined with small cafés and shops selling old books, prints, and antiques.

Pizza Express occupies a charming and little-altered Victorian dairy.

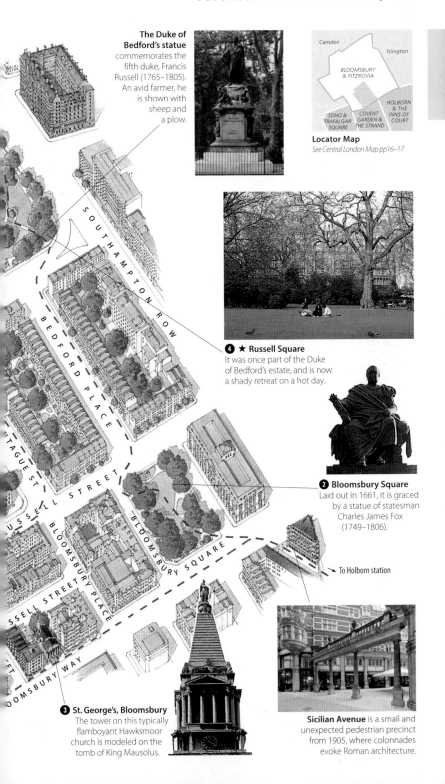

The Duke of Bedford's statue commemorates the fifth duke, Francis Russell (1765–1805). An avid farmer, he is shown with sheep and a plow.

Locator Map
See Central London Map pp16–17

❹ ★ **Russell Square**
It was once part of the Duke of Bedford's estate, and is now a shady retreat on a hot day.

❷ **Bloomsbury Square**
Laid out in 1661, it is graced by a statue of statesman Charles James Fox (1749–1806).

To Holborn station

❸ **St. George's, Bloomsbury**
The tower on this typically flamboyant Hawksmoor church is modeled on the tomb of King Mausolus.

Sicilian Avenue is a small and unexpected pedestrian precinct from 1905, where colonnades evoke Roman architecture.

❶ British Museum

The oldest public museum in the world, the British Museum was established in 1753 to house the collections of the physician Sir Hans Sloane (1660–1753), who also helped create the Chelsea Physic Garden *(see p199)*. Sloane's

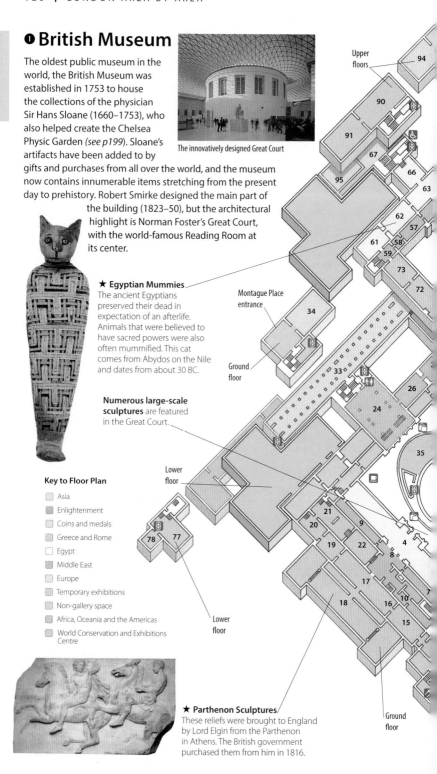

The innovatively designed Great Court

artifacts have been added to by gifts and purchases from all over the world, and the museum now contains innumerable items stretching from the present day to prehistory. Robert Smirke designed the main part of the building (1823–50), but the architectural highlight is Norman Foster's Great Court, with the world-famous Reading Room at its center.

★ **Egyptian Mummies**
The ancient Egyptians preserved their dead in expectation of an afterlife. Animals that were believed to have sacred powers were also often mummified. This cat comes from Abydos on the Nile and dates from about 30 BC.

Numerous large-scale sculptures are featured in the Great Court.

Upper floors

Montague Place entrance

Ground floor

Lower floor

Lower floor

Ground floor

Key to Floor Plan

▨ Asia
▨ Enlightenment
▨ Coins and medals
▨ Greece and Rome
▢ Egypt
▨ Middle East
▨ Europe
▨ Temporary exhibitions
▢ Non-gallery space
▨ Africa, Oceania and the Americas
▨ World Conservation and Exhibitions Centre

★ **Parthenon Sculptures**
These reliefs were brought to England by Lord Elgin from the Parthenon in Athens. The British government purchased them from him in 1816.

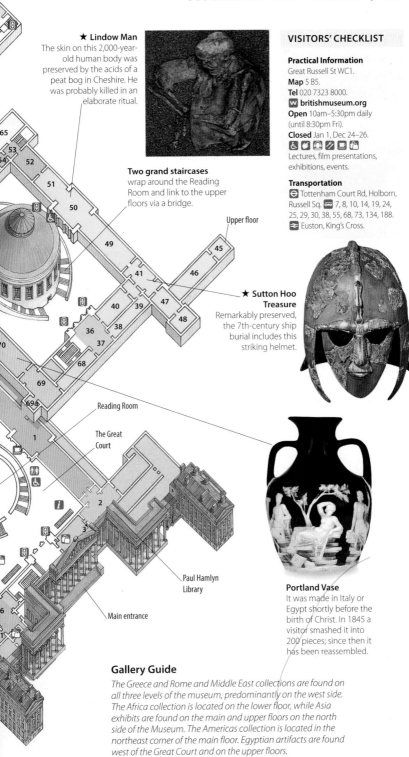

★ Lindow Man
The skin on this 2,000-year-old human body was preserved by the acids of a peat bog in Cheshire. He was probably killed in an elaborate ritual.

Two grand staircases
wrap around the Reading Room and link to the upper floors via a bridge.

Upper floor

★ Sutton Hoo Treasure
Remarkably preserved, the 7th-century ship burial includes this striking helmet.

Reading Room

The Great Court

Paul Hamlyn Library

Main entrance

Portland Vase
It was made in Italy or Egypt shortly before the birth of Christ. In 1845 a visitor smashed it into 200 pieces; since then it has been reassembled.

VISITORS' CHECKLIST

Practical Information
Great Russell St WC1.
Map 5 B5.
Tel 020 7323 8000.
🆆 britishmuseum.org
Open 10am–5:30pm daily
(until 8:30pm Fri).
Closed Jan 1, Dec 24–26.
Lectures, film presentations, exhibitions, events.

Transportation
Tottenham Court Rd, Holborn, Russell Sq. 7, 8, 10, 14, 19, 24, 25, 29, 30, 38, 55, 68, 73, 134, 188. Euston, King's Cross.

Gallery Guide

The Greece and Rome and Middle East collections are found on all three levels of the museum, predominantly on the west side. The Africa collection is located on the lower floor, while Asia exhibits are found on the main and upper floors on the north side of the Museum. The Americas collection is located in the northeast corner of the main floor. Egyptian artifacts are found west of the Great Court and on the upper floors.

Exploring the British Museum's Collections

The Museum's immense hoard of treasure spans 2 million years of history and culture. The 94 galleries, which stretch 2.5 miles (4 km), cover civilizations from ancient Egypt and Assyria to modern Japan.

1st-century BC bronze helmet dredged up from the Thames

Prehistoric and Roman Britain

Relics of prehistoric Britain are on display in six separate galleries. The most impressive items include the gold "Mold Cape," a Bronze Age ceremonial cape found in Wales; an antlered headdress worn by hunter-gatherers some 9000 years ago; and "Lindow Man," a 1st-century AD sacrificial victim who lay preserved in a bog until 1984. Some superb Celtic metalwork is also on display, alongside the silver Mildenhall Treasure and other Roman pieces. The Hinton St. Mary mosaic (4th century AD) features a roundel containing the earliest known British depiction of Christ.

Europe

The spectacular Sutton Hoo ship treasure, the burial hoard of a 7th-century Anglo-Saxon king, is on display in Room 41. This superb find, made in 1939, revolutionized our understanding of Anglo-Saxon life and ritual. The artifacts include a helmet and shield, Celtic hanging bowls, the remains of a lyre, and gold and garnet jewelry.

Adjacent galleries contain a collection of clocks, watches, and scientific instruments. Some exquisite timepieces are on view, including a 400-year-old clock from Prague, designed as a model galleon; in its day it pitched, played music, and even fired a cannon.

Also nearby are the famous 12th-century Lewis chessmen, and a gallery housing Baron Ferdinand Rothschild's (1839–98) remarkably varied treasures.

The museum's modern collection includes some Wedgwood pottery, glassware, and a series of Russian revolutionary plates.

Gilded brass late-16th-century ship clock from Prague

Ancient Near East

There are numerous galleries devoted to the Western Asian collections, covering 7,000 years of history. The most famous items are the 7th-century BC Assyrian reliefs from King Ashurbanipal's palace at Nineveh, but of equal interest are two large human-headed bulls from 7th-century BC Khorsabad, and an inscribed Black Obelisk of Assyrian King Shalmaneser III. The upper floors contain pieces from ancient Sumeria, part of the Oxus Treasure (which lay buried for over 2,000 years), and the museum's collection of clay cuneiform tablets. The earliest of these are inscribed with the oldest known pictographs (c.3300 BC). Also of interest is a skull discovered in Jericho in the 1950s; augmented with shells and lime plaster, the skull belonged to a hunter who lived in the area some 7,000 years ago.

Ornamental detail from a Sumerian Queen's lyre

Egypt

In Room 4 are Egyptian sculptures. These include a fine red granite head of a king, thought to depict Amenophis III, and a colossal statue of King Rameses II. Also on display is the Rosetta Stone, used by Jean-François Champollion (1790–1832) as a primer for deciphering Egyptian hieroglyphs. An extraordinary array of mummies, jewelry, and Coptic art can also be found upstairs. The various instruments that were used by embalmers to preserve bodies before entombment are all displayed. Room 61 houses paintings from the lost tomb-chapel of Nebamun.

Part of a colossal granite statue of Rameses II, the 13th-century BC Egyptian monarch

Greece and Rome

The Greek and Roman collections include the museum's most famous treasure, the Parthenon sculptures. These 5th-century BC reliefs were once part of a marble frieze that decorated the Parthenon, Athena's temple on the Acropolis in Athens. Much of it was ruined in battle in 1687, and most of what survived was removed between 1801 and 1804 by the British diplomat Lord Elgin, and sold to the British nation. Other highlights include the Nereid Monument and sculptures and friezes from the Mausoleum at

Ancient Greek vase illustrating the mythical hero Hercules's fight with a bull

Halicarnassus. The beautiful 1st-century BC cameo-glass Portland Vase is located in the Roman Empire section.

Asia

The Chinese collection boasts fine porcelain and ancient Shang bronzes (c.1500–1050 BC). Particularly impressive are the ceremonial ancient Chinese bronze vessels, with their enigmatic animal-head shapes.

The fine Chinese ceramics range from delicate tea bowls to a model pond, which is almost a thousand years old. In the Sir Percival David gallery, the Chinese ceramics date from the 10th to early 20th centuries.

Adjacent to these is one of the finest collections of South Asian religious sculpture outside India. A major highlight is an assortment of sculpted reliefs, which once covered the walls of the Buddhist temple at Amaravati, and recount stories from the life of the Buddha. A Korean section contains some gigantic works of Buddhist art.

The museum's collection of Islamic art, including a jade

Statue of the Hindu god Shiva as Nataraja, or Lord of the Dance (11th century AD)

terrapin found in a water tank, can be found in Room 34. Rooms 92 to 94 house the Japanese galleries, with a Classical teahouse in Room 92.

Africa

An interesting collection of African sculptures, textiles, and graphic art can also be found in Room 25 on the lower floor of the museum. Famous bronzes from the Kingdom of Benin stand alongside modern African prints, paintings, drawings, and colorful fabrics.

The Great Court and the Reading Room

Surrounding the Reading Room of the former British Library, the $150 million Great Court opened to coincide with the new millennium. Designed by Sir Norman Foster, the Court is covered by a wide-span, lightweight roof, creating London's first indoor public square. The Reading Room has been restored to its original design, so visitors can sample the atmosphere that Karl Marx, Mahatma Gandhi, and George Bernard Shaw found

so agreeable. From the outside, however, it is scarcely recognizable; it is housed in a multilevel construction that partly supports the roof, and also contains a Centre for Education, temporary exhibition galleries, bookshops, cafés, and restaurants. Part of the Reading Room also serves as a study suite where those wishing to learn more about the Museum's collections have access to information.

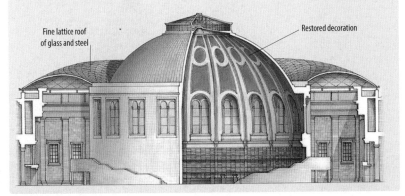
Fine lattice roof of glass and steel

Restored decoration

❷ Bloomsbury Square

WC1. **Map** 5 C5. ❸ Holborn.

This is the oldest of the Bloomsbury squares. It was laid out in 1661 by the fourth Earl of Southampton, who owned the land. None of the original buildings survive, and the shaded garden is encircled by a busy one-way traffic system. (Unusually for central London, you can nearly always find a space in the parking lot under the square.)

The literary and artistic avant-garde Bloomsbury Group lived in the area during the early years of the last century. It included many prominent figures, such as novelists Virginia Woolf and E.M. Forster, biographer Lytton Strachey, and artists Vanessa Bell, Duncan Grant, and Dora Carrington. Look for their individual plaques throughout the area (see p41).

St. George's Church

❸ St. George's, Bloomsbury

Bloomsbury Way WC1. **Map** 13 B1. **Tel** 020 7242 1979. ❸ Holborn, Tottenham Court Rd, Russell Sq. **Open** 1–4pm daily (times may vary – call to check). 🕐 1:10pm Wed & Fri, 10:30am Sun. Recitals. ♿ 🎫 🖥 **stgeorgesbloomsbury.org.uk**

A slightly eccentric church, St. George's was designed by Nicholas Hawksmoor, Wren's pupil, and completed in 1730. It was built as a place of worship for the prosperous residents of newly developed, fashionable Bloomsbury. The layered tower, modeled on the tomb of King

The flamboyant Russell Hotel on Russell Square

Mausolus (the original mausoleum in Turkey) and topped by a statue of George I, was for a long time an object of derision – the king was thought to be presented too heroically. In 1913, the funeral of Emily Davison, the suffragette who threw herself under King George V's horse, was held here.

Restored in 2006, it is now a thriving parish church, concert venue, and center for community art.

❹ Russell Square

WC1. **Map** 5 B5. ❸ Russell Sq. 🖥 **Open** 7:30am–10pm daily.

One of London's largest squares, Russell Square is a lively place, with a fountain, a café, and traffic roaring around its perimeter. The east side boasts perhaps the best of the Victorian grand hotels to survive in the capital. Charles Doll's Russell Hotel, which was opened in 1900, is a wondrous confection of red terra cotta, with colonnaded balconies and

prancing cherubs beneath the main columns. The exuberance is continued in the lobby, faced with marble of many colors.

Poet T. S. Eliot worked at the west corner of the square, from 1925 until 1965, in what were the offices of publishers Faber and Faber.

❺ Queen Square

WC1. **Map** 5 C5. ❸ Russell Sq.

In spite of being named after Queen Anne, this square contains a statue of Queen Charlotte. Her husband, George III, stayed at the house of a doctor here when he became ill with the hereditary disease that drove him mad before his death in 1820. Originally, the north side of the square was left open so that inhabitants had a clear view of Hampstead and Highgate. Today the square is almost completely surrounded by hospital buildings, with early Georgian houses on the west side.

Queen Charlotte's statue in Queen Square

❻ Charles Dickens Museum

48 Doughty St WC1. **Map** 6 D4.
Tel 020 7405 2127. ⊖ Chancery
Lane, Russell Sq. **Open** 10am–5pm
daily (last adm 4:30pm). 🎧 🖼
♿ ground floor. 🖼 📷 📹
🖥 **dickensmuseum.com**

The novelist Charles Dickens
lived in this early 19th-century
terraced house for three of his
most productive years (from
1837 to 1839). The popular
works *Oliver Twist* and *Nicholas
Nickleby* were entirely written
here, and *Pickwick Papers* was
finished. Although Dickens had
many London homes
throughout his lifetime, this is
the only one to have survived.
In 1923 it was acquired by
the Dickens Fellow-
ship, and it is now a
well-conceived
museum with
some of the
principal rooms
laid out exactly as
they were in
Dickens's time. Others
have been adapted to
display a varied collection of
articles associated with him.
The exhibits include papers,
portraits, and pieces of
furniture taken from his other
homes, as well as first
editions of many of his
best-known works.

A major
restoration project
was completed in
2011 in readiness
for the bicentennial
of Dickens' birth in 2012.

Portrait of Captain Coram (1740) by
William Hogarth

Horrified by the poverty on
London streets, he was
determined to alter the fate of
the city's foundlings by housing,
educating, and placing them
in private homes. Assisted
by his friend, the artist
William Hogarth, and the
composer George Frederick
Handel, Coram worked
tirelessly to raise funds for
the refuge. Finally, in 1739,
after much petitioning of
George II, he was granted
a Royal Charter to
establish a Foundling
Hospital. Hogarth donated
paintings to the hospital and
other artists followed suit,
creating Britain's first art
gallery. The wealthy
were encouraged to
view the works of
art and the children
at the hospital, in
the hope that they
would donate funds.

**Nautical publisher's trade sign,
Dickens Museum**

The original hospital located
at the end of Lambs Conduit
Street was demolished in the
1920s, but the interiors of two
of the 18th-century rooms were
saved and relocated to 40 Brunswick Square, the current location
of the museum. On the ground
floor, the story of the many
children who were cared for in
the Foundling Hospital is told.
The nationally important collection of 18th-century paintings,
sculpture, furniture, and interiors
is displayed on the first floor.

Adjacent to the museum,
with its entrance on Guilford
Street, is **Coram's Fields**, a

❼ Foundling Museum

40 Brunswick Square WC1. **Map** 5 C4.
Tel 020 7841 3600. ⊖ Russell
Square. **Open** 10am–5pm Tue–Sat,
11am–5pm Sun. **Closed** Jan 1, Dec
24–26 & 31. 🎧 🖼 ♿ 🖼 book
ahead. 🖥 📷 Coram's Fields: Guilford
St WC1. **Open** 9am–dusk.
🖥 **foundlingmuseum.org.uk**

In 1722, Captain Thomas Coram,
a retired sailor and shipbuilder
recently returned from the
Americas, vowed to establish a
refuge for abandoned children.

favorite central London
playground with lots of
space. It's highly popular with
children and a convenient pace-
changer for families visiting
the museums. Dogs are not
allowed, and all adults must
be accompanied by children.

❽ British Library

96 Euston Rd NW1. **Map** 5 B3.
Tel 0193 754 6060. ⊖ King's Cross
St. Pancras. **Open** 9:30am–6pm Mon–
Fri (8pm Tue), 9:30am–5pm Sat,
11am–5pm Sun. Regular events.
♿ 🖼 🖥 📷 📹 🖥 **bl.uk**

London's most important
building from the late 20th
century houses the national
collection of books, manuscripts,
and maps, as well as the British
Library Sound Archive.
Designed in red brick by Sir
Colin St John Wilson, it opened
in 1997 after nearly 20 years
under construction, involving
controversial cost overruns,
but is now widely admired.

A copy of nearly every printed
book in the United Kingdom is
held here – more than 14
million – and can be consulted
by those with a library card.
There are also exhibition
galleries open to everyone.
Visitors may view some of the
Library's most precious items,
including the Lindisfarne
Gospels, with the Turning the
Pages system, which shows
each page on a monitor. Other
volumes include a Gutenberg
Bible and Shakespeare's First
Folio. Running through six floors
is a spectacular glass tower
holding George III's library.

Page from the Lindisfarne Gospels

The massive St. Pancras Renaissance Hotel above St. Pancras Station

❾ St. Pancras International

Euston Rd NW1. **Map** 5 B2.
Tel 020 7843 7688. 🚇 King's Cross,
St. Pancras. **Open** 24 hours.
Closed Dec 25. *See Getting to London*
pp364–5. 🔲 stpancras.com

St. Pancras is the London
terminal for Eurostar services to
continental Europe. It is easily
the most spectacular of the
three rail termini along Euston
Road, thanks to the extravagant
frontage, in red-brick
gingerbread Gothic, of the
former Midland Grand Hotel,
opened in 1874 as one of the
most sumptuous hotels of its
time. By 1935 it was too
expensive to run and became
office space. It was threatened
with demolition in the 1960s,
but poet John Betjeman

Figures on St. Pancras Church

campaigned to save it (there is
a statue of him on the upper
level). It has since been lavishly
restored as a five-star hotel, plus
apartments, penthouses, and
Europe's longest champagne bar.

❿ St. Pancras Parish Church

Euston Rd NW1. **Map** 5 B3. **Tel** 020
7388 1461. 🚇 Euston. **Open** 8am–
6pm Mon–Thu, 8am–noon Fri.
🕇 8am, 10am, 6pm Sun. 🔲 Recitals
1:15pm Thu. 🔲 stpancraschurch.org

This is a stately Greek revival
church of 1822 designed by
William Inwood and his son
Henry, both great enthusiasts
for Athenian architecture.
The design is based on the
Erectheum on the Acropolis in
Athens, and even the wooden
pulpit stands on miniature
Ionic columns of its own.
The long, galleried interior has
a dramatic severity appropriate
to the church's style. The female
figures on the northern outer
wall were originally taller than
they are now; a chunk had to
be taken out of the middle of
each to make them fit under
the roof they were meant to
be supporting.
   The church hosts a festival of
contemporary church music in
May, and art exhibitions are
sometimes held in the
atmospheric crypt.

⓫ Woburn Walk

WC1. **Map** 5 B4. 🚇 Euston, Euston Sq.

A well-restored street of bow-
fronted shops, it was designed
by Thomas Cubitt in 1822.
The high sidewalk on the east
side was to protect shop fronts
from the mud thrown up by
carriages. The poet W. B. Yeats
lived at No. 5 from 1895
until 1919.

⓬ Wellcome Collection

183 Euston Rd NW1. **Map** 5 A4.
Tel 020 7611 2222. 🚇 Euston, King's
Cross, Warren St. **Open** 10am–6pm
Tue–Sat (to 10pm Thu), 11am–6pm
Sun, noon–6pm public hols.
Closed Dec 23–Jan 1. 🔲 🖵 🎦
🔲 wellcomecollection.org

Sir Henry Wellcome was a
pharmacist, entrepreneur, and
collector. His passionate interest
in medicine and its history,
as well as ethnography and
archaeology, led him to gather
more than a million objects
from around the world. The
Wellcome Collection is a
public venue used to house his
vast collection as well as to
explore the connections
between medicine, art, and the
human condition through
events and exhibitions.
   Exhibits range from the
bizarre to the beautiful, the
ancient to the futuristic.
More than 900 objects are on
permanent display, including
a used guillotine blade and
Napoleon's toothbrush.
Contemporary works include
a DNA sequencing robot and
a sculpture exploring HIV by
Mark Quinn. The Wellcome
library, on the upper floor, is
the world's largest devoted to
the history of medicine.

⓭ Fitzroy Square

W1. **Map** 4 F4. 🚇 Warren St, Great
Portland St.

Designed by Robert Adam in
1794, the square's south and
east sides survive in their
original form, in dignified
Portland stone. Blue plaques

record the homes of many artists, writers, and statesmen: George Bernard Shaw and Virginia Woolf both lived at No. 29 – although not at the same time. Shaw gave money to the artist Roger Fry to establish the Omega workshop at No. 33 in 1913. Here young artists were paid a fixed wage to produce Post-Impressionist furniture, pottery, carpets, and paintings for sale to the public.

No. 29 Fitzroy Square

⓮ Fitzroy Tavern

16 Charlotte St W1. **Map** 4 F5. **Tel** 020 7580 3714. ⓔ Tottenham Court Rd, Goodge St. **Open** 11am– 11pm Mon–Sat, noon–10:30pm Sun. ⓖ *See Pubs pp308–9.*

This traditional pub was a meeting place between the two word wars for a group of writers and artists who dubbed the area around Fitzroy Square and Charlotte Street "Fitzrovia." A basement "Writers and Artists Bar" contains pictures of former customers, including the writers Dylan Thomas and George Orwell, and the artist Augustus John.

⓯ Charlotte Street

W1. **Map** 5 A5. ⓔ Goodge St.

As the upper classes moved west from Bloomsbury in the early 19th century, a flood of artists and European immigrants moved in, turning the area into a northern appendage to Soho *(see pp100– 11).* The artist John Constable lived and worked for many years at No. 76. Some of the new residents established small workshops to service the clothing shops on Oxford

Street and the furniture stores on Tottenham Court Road. Others set up reasonably-priced restaurants. The street still boasts a great variety of eating places. It is overshadowed from the north by the 620-ft (189-m) Telecom Tower, built in 1964 as a vast TV, radio, and telecommunications aerial *(see p34).*

⓰ Pollock's Toy Museum

1 Scala St W1. **Map** 5 A5. **Tel** 020 7636 3452. ⓔ Goodge St, Warren St, Tottenham Court Rd. **Open** 10am–5pm Mon–Sat. ⓐ ⓑ Ⓦ pollockstoymuseum.com

Benjamin Pollock was a renowned maker of toy theaters in the late 19th and early 20th centuries – the

Telecom Tower

novelist Robert Louis Stevenson was an enthusiastic customer. The museum opened in Monmouth Street in Covent Garden in 1956 and relocated to these premises in 1969. The final room is devoted to stages and puppets from Pollock's theaters, together with a reconstruction of his workshop. This is a child-sized museum created in two largely unaltered 18th-century houses. The small rooms have been filled with a fascinating assortment of historic toys from all over the world. There are dolls, puppets, trains, cars, construction sets, a fine rocking horse, and a splendid collection of mainly Victorian dollhouses. Parents should be aware that the exit leads you through a very tempting toy shop.

Pearly king and queen dolls from Pollock's Toy Museum

HOLBORN & THE INNS OF COURT

This area is traditionally home to the legal and journalistic professions. The law is still here, in the Royal Courts of Justice and the Inns of Court, but the national newspapers left Fleet Street in the 1980s. Several buildings here predate the Great Fire of 1666 *(see pp26–7)*. These include the superb facade of Staple Inn, Prince Henry's Room, and the interior of Middle Temple Hall. Holborn used to be one of the capital's main shopping districts. Times have changed the face of the area, but the jewelry and diamond dealers of Hatton Garden are still here, as are the London Silver Vaults.

Sights at a Glance

Historic Buildings, Sights, and Streets
2 Lincoln's Inn
4 Old Curiosity Shop
5 Law Society
7 Royal Courts of Justice
9 Fleet Street
10 Prince Henry's Room
11 Temple
14 Dr. Johnson's House
16 Holborn Viaduct
18 Hatton Garden
19 Staple Inn
21 Gray's Inn

Museums and Galleries
1 Sir John Soane's Museum

Churches
6 St. Clement Danes
12 St. Bride's
15 St. Andrew, Holborn
17 St. Etheldreda's Chapel

Monuments
8 Temple Bar Memorial

Parks and Gardens
3 Lincoln's Inn Fields

Pubs
13 Ye Olde Cheshire Cheese

Shops
20 London Silver Vaults

Restaurants *see pp297–298*
1 De Palo's
2 The Chancery
3 Vanilla Black
4 The White Swan

Street Finder, maps 6, 13, 14

0 meters 500
0 yards 500

◀ Gothic facade of the Royal Courts of Justice

For keys to symbols *see back flap*

Street by Street: Lincoln's Inn

This is calm, dignified, legal London, packed with history and interest. Lincoln's Inn, adjoining one of the city's first residential squares, has buildings dating from the late 15th century. Dark-suited lawyers carry bundles of briefs between their offices here and the Neo-Gothic Law Courts. Nearby is the Temple, another historic legal district with a famous 13th-century round church.

❶ ★ Sir John Soane's Museum
The Georgian architect made this his London home and left it, with his collection, to the nation.

❸ ★ Lincoln's Inn Fields
The mock-Tudor archway, leading to Lincoln's Inn and built in 1845, overlooks the Fields.

❹ Old Curiosity Shop
This is a rare 16th-century, pre-Great Fire building which is now a shop.

To Kingsway

Lincoln's Inn

The Royal College of Surgeons was designed in 1836 by Sir Charles Barry. Inside there are laboratories for research and teaching as well as a museum of anatomical specimens.

Key

— Suggested route

| 0 meters | 100 |
| 0 yards | 100 |

Twinings has been selling tea here since 1706. The doorway dates from 1787, when the shop (216 Strand) was called the Golden Lion.

The Gladstone Statue was erected in 1905 to commemorate William Gladstone, the Victorian statesman who was prime minister four times.

2 ★ Lincoln's Inn
The Court of Chancery sat here, in Old Hall, from 1835 until 1858. Sir John Taylor Coleridge, nephew of the poet, was a well-known judge of the time.

Locator Map
See Central London Map pp16–17

7 Royal Courts of Justice
The country's main court for civil cases and appeals was built in 1882. It is made out of 35 million bricks faced with Portland stone.

5 Law Society
Look for the gold lions on the railings of this superb building.

9 Fleet Street
For two centuries this was the center of the national press. Today the newspaper offices are gone.

El Vino is a venerable wine bar, where journalists still mingle with lawyers.

10 Prince Henry's Room
There is an authentic 17th-century room in this former gatehouse.

6 St. Clement Danes
Designed by Wren (1679), it is the Royal Air Force church.

8 Temple Bar Memorial
A dragon marks where the City of London meets Westminster.

11 ★ Temple
It was built for the Knights Templar in the 13th century, but today lawyers stroll here.

The interior of the chapel in the grounds of Lincoln's Inn

❷ Lincoln's Inn

WC2. **Map** 14 D1. **Tel** 020 7405 1393.
🚇 Holborn, Chancery Lane.
Open Chapel: 9am–6pm Mon–Fri.
Other buildings: check website.
♿ 📷 1st Fri of month, 2pm.
🌐 **lincolnsinn.org.uk**

Some of the buildings in
Lincoln's Inn, the best-preserved
of London's Inns of Court, go
back to the late 15th century.
The coat of arms above the arch
of the Chancery Lane gatehouse
is Henry VIII's, and the heavy oak
door is of the same vintage.
Shakespeare's contemporary,
Ben Jonson, is believed to have
laid some of the bricks of
Lincoln's Inn during the reign of
Elizabeth I. The chapel is early
17th-century Gothic. Women
were not allowed to be buried
here until 1839, when the
grieving Lord Brougham
petitioned to have the rule
changed so that his beloved
daughter could be interred in
the chapel, to wait for him
to join her.
Lincoln's Inn has its share
of famous alumni. Oliver
Cromwell and John Donne,

❶ Sir John Soane's Museum

13 Lincoln's Inn Fields WC2. **Map** 14 D1.
Tel 0207 405 2107. 🚇 Holborn.
Open 10am–5pm Tue–Sat, 6–9pm
first Tue of month. **Closed** Sun, Mon,
bank hols & Christmas Eve. ♿ limited,
call first. 📷 Sat 11am; groups book
ahead. 📷 🌐 **soane.org**

One of the most surprising
museums in London, this house
was left to the nation by Sir
John Soane in 1837, with a far-
sighted stipulation that nothing
at all should be changed. One
of Britain's leading 19th-century
architects, Soane was responsible
for designing Dulwich Picture
Gallery, still the most influential
top-lit gallery. The son of a
bricklayer, he prudently married
the niece of a wealthy builder,
whose fortune he inherited. He
bought and reconstructed No. 12
Lincoln's Inn Fields, then No. 13,
which he and his wife moved
into in 1813. Later, in 1823–24,
he rebuilt No. 14, extending his

museum into the rear of this
building. Today, the collections
are much as Soane left them –
an eclectic gathering of beautiful,
peculiar, and instructional objects.

The building itself abounds
with architectural surprises and
illusions. In the main ground
floor room, with its deep red
and green coloring, cunningly
placed mirrors play tricks with
light and space. The picture
gallery is lined with layers of
folding panels to increase its
capacity. The panels open out
to reveal galleried extensions to
the room itself. Among other
works here are many of Soane's
own exotic designs, including
those for Pitzhanger Manor *(see
p260)* and the Bank of England
(see p149). Here also is William
Hogarth's *Rake's Progress* series.

In the center of the low-
ceilinged basement, an atrium
stretches up to the roof. A glass
dome lights galleries, on every
floor, that are filled with
Classical statuary.

A glass dome allows light
into the basement.

A vast sarcophagus
(1300 BC) stands on the
floor of the basement.

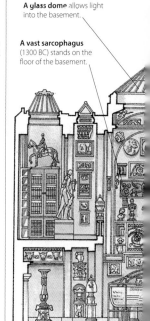

the 17th-century poet, were both students here, as was William Penn, founder of the state of Pennsylvania.

❸ Lincoln's Inn Fields

WC2. **Map** 14 D1. ⊖ Holborn. **Open** dawn–dusk daily. Public tennis courts.

This used to be a public execution site. Under the Tudors and the Stuarts, many religious martyrs, and those suspected of treachery to the Crown, perished here.

When the developer William Newton wanted to build here in the 1640s, students at Lincoln's Inn and other residents made him agree that the land in the center would remain a public area forever. Thanks to this early protest, lawyers today play tennis here throughout the summer, or read their briefs in the fresh air. For some years it has also been the site of an evening soup kitchen for some of London's homeless.

Old Curiosity Shop sign

❹ Old Curiosity Shop

13–14 Portsmouth St WC2. **Map** 14 D1. ⊖ Holborn.

Whether it is or is not the original for Charles Dickens's novel of the same name, this is a genuine 16th-century building and almost certainly the oldest shop in central London. With its overhanging first floor, it gives a rare impression of a London streetscape from before the Great Fire of 1666. The Old Curiosity Shop maintains its retailing tradition, and currently operates as a handmade shoe shop. A preservation order guarantees the building's long-term future.

❺ Law Society

113 Chancery Lane WC2. **Map** 14 E1. **Tel** 020 7242 1222. ⊖ Chancery Lane. **Closed** to the public.

The headquarters of the solicitors' professional body is, architecturally, one of the most interesting buildings in the legal quarter. The main part, dominated by four Ionic columns, was completed in 1832. More significant is the northern extension, an early work of Charles Holden, an Arts and Crafts enthusiast who later made his name as a designer of London Underground stations. In his window arches the four seated figures depict truth, justice, liberty, and mercy.

The building is on the corner of Carey Street, the site of the bankruptcy court whose name, corrupted to "Queer Street," entered the language to describe a state of destitution.

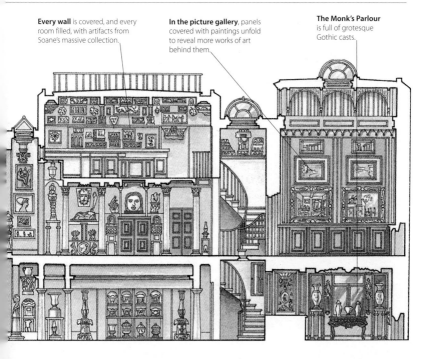

Every wall is covered, and every room filled, with artifacts from Soane's massive collection.

In the picture gallery, panels covered with paintings unfold to reveal more works of art behind them.

The Monk's Parlour is full of grotesque Gothic casts.

❻ St. Clement Danes

Strand WC2. **Map** 14 D2. **Tel** 020 7242
8282. 🚇 Temple. **Open** 9am–4pm
daily. **Closed** Dec 25 (noon), 26, 27,
public hols. 🕇 12:30am Wed & Fri,
11am Sun. 🚻 *See Ceremonial London
p57.* 🔲 raf.mod.uk/stclementdanes

Christopher Wren designed
this wonderful church in
1680. Its name derives from an
earlier church built here by the
descendants of Danish invaders
whom Alfred the Great had
allowed to remain in London in
the 9th century. From the 17th
to 19th centuries, many people
were buried here, and their
restplates are now in the crypt.
The chain now hanging on the
crypt wall was probably used to
secure coffin lids against body
snatchers who stole fresh
corpses and sold them to the
teaching hospitals.

St. Clement Danes sits
proudly isolated on a traffic
island. It is now the Royal Air
Force (RAF) church, and the
interior is dominated by

Clock at the Victorian law courts

RAF symbols, memorials, and
monuments. Outside, to the
east, is a statue (1910) of
Dr. Johnson *(see p142)*, who
often came to services here.
The church bells ring to the
tune of the English nursery
rhyme "Oranges and Lemons"
at 9am, noon, 3pm, and 6pm
Mon–Sat, and there is an
oranges and lemons
service each March.

❼ Royal Courts of Justice (the Law Courts)

Strand WC2. **Map** 14 D2. **Tel** 020 7947
6000. 🚇 Holborn, Temple, Chancery
Lane. **Open** 9am–4:30pm Mon–Fri.
Closed public hols. 🚻 🖥 📷
🔲 justice.gov.uk/courts

Knots of demonstrators and
television cameras can often
be seen outside this sprawling
and fanciful Victorian Gothic
building, waiting for the result
of a contentious case. These
are the nation's main civil
courts, dealing with such
matters as divorce, libel, civil
liability, and appeals. Criminals
are dealt with at the Old Bailey
(see p149), ten minutes' walk
to the east. The public is
admitted to all the courtrooms,
and a list tells you which case is
being heard in which court.

The massive Gothic building
was completed in 1882.
It is said to contain 1,000
rooms and 3.5 miles (5.6 km)
of corridors.

❽ Temple Bar Memorial

Fleet St EC4. **Map** 14 D2. 🚇 Holborn,
Temple, Chancery Lane.

The monument in the middle
of Fleet Street, outside the Law
Courts, dates from 1880 and
marks the entrance to the City
of London. On state occasions it
is a long-standing tradition for
the monarch to pause here and
ask permission of the Lord Mayor
to enter. Temple Bar, a huge archway designed by Wren, used to
stand here. You can see what it
used to look like from one of the
four reliefs that surround the
base of the present monument.

❾ Fleet Street

EC4. **Map** 14 E1. 🚇 Temple,
Blackfriars, St. Paul's.

England's first printing press
was set up here in the late
15th century by William Caxton's
assistant, and Fleet Street has
been a center of London's

The dragon, symbol of the City, at the entrance to the City at Temple Bar

William Capon's engraving of Fleet Street in 1799

publishing industry ever since. Playwrights Shakespeare and Ben Jonson were patrons of the old Mitre tavern, now No. 37 Fleet Street. In 1702 the first newspaper, *The Daily Courant*, was issued from Fleet Street – conveniently placed for the City and Westminster, which were the main sources of news. Later the street became synonymous with the Press.

The printing presses underneath the newspaper offices were abandoned in 1987, when new technology made it easy to produce papers away from the center of town in areas such as Wapping and the Docklands. Today the newspapers have left Fleet Street and the only remaining agency is the Commonwealth Broadcasting Association.

El Vino wine bar, at the western end opposite Fetter Lane, is a traditional haunt of journalists and lawyers.

Effigies in Temple Church

⑩ Prince Henry's Room

17 Fleet St EC4. **Map** 14 E1.
🚇 Temple, Chancery Lane.
Closed currently but check website for news. 🆆 **cityoflondon.gov.uk**

The site itself can be traced back to the 12th century, when it belonged to the Knights Templar, but this Fleet Street tavern is from 1610 and gets its name from the Prince of Wales' coat of arms and the initials PH in the ceiling, probably put there to mark the investiture as Prince of Wales of Henry, James I's eldest son, who died before he became king.

The fine half-timbered front, alongside the gateway to Inner Temple, is original, and so is some of the room's oak paneling.

⑪ Temple

Inner Temple, King's Bench Walk EC4.
Map 14 E2. **Tel** 020 7797 8250.
🚇 Temple. **Open** 12:30–3pm Mon–Fri (grounds only). ♿ Middle Temple Hall, Middle Temple Lane EC4. **Tel** 020 7427 4800. **Open** 10–11:30am, 3–4pm Mon–Fri. **Closed** at short notice for functions. ♿ 📷 book ahead. Temple Church **Tel** 020 7353 3470. **Open** Wed–Fri; call for times & services. 🆆 **templechurch.com**

This embraces two of the four Inns of Court, the Middle Temple and the Inner Temple. (The other two are Lincoln's and Gray's inns, *pp138, 143*.) The name derives from the Knights Templar, a chivalrous order that used to protect pilgrims to the Holy Land. The order was based here until it was suppressed by the Crown because its power was viewed as a threat. Initiations probably took place in the crypt of Temple Church, and there are 13th-century effigies of Knights Templar in the nave.

Among some other ancient buildings is the Middle Temple Hall. Its fine Elizabethan interior survives – Shakespeare's *Twelfth Night* was performed here in 1601. Behind Temple, peaceful lawns stretch lazily down toward the Embankment.

⑫ St. Bride's

Fleet St EC4. **Map** 14 F2. **Tel** 020 7427 0133. 🚇 Blackfriars. **Open** 9am–6pm Mon–Fri, 10am–6:30pm Sun (hours vary Sat). **Closed** public hols. ♿ 📷 🎵 11am & 6:30pm Sun. 🎵 Concerts check website for details. 🆆 **stbrides.com**

St. Bride's is one of Wren's best-loved churches. Its position just off Fleet Street has made it the traditional venue for memorial services to departed journalists. Wall plaques commemorate Fleet Street journalists and printers.

The marvelous octagonal layered spire has been the model for tiered wedding cakes since shortly after it was added in 1703. Bombed in 1940, the interior was faithfully restored after World War II. The fascinating crypt contains remnants of earlier churches on the site, and a section of Roman pavement.

St. Bride's, church of the Press

⑬ Ye Olde Cheshire Cheese

145 Fleet St EC4. **Map** 14 E1.
Tel 020 7353 6170. 🚇 Blackfriars.
Open 11am–11pm Mon–Fri,
noon–11pm Sat, noon–7pm Sun.
See Pubs pp308–11.

There has been an inn here for
centuries; parts of this building
date back to 1667, when the
Cheshire Cheese was rebuilt
after the Great Fire. The diarist
Samuel Pepys often drank here
in the 17th century, but it was
Dr. Samuel Johnson's association
with "the Cheese" that made
it a place of pilgrimage for
19th-century literati. These
included novelists Mark Twain
and Charles Dickens.

This is one of the few pubs
to have kept the 18th-century
arrangement of small rooms
with fireplaces, tables, and
benches, instead of combining
them into larger bars.

⑭ Dr. Johnson's House

17 Gough Sq EC4. **Map** 14 E1.
Tel 020 7353 3745. 🚇 Blackfriars,
Chancery Lane, Temple. **Open** May–
Sep: 11am–5:30pm Mon–Sat; Oct–
Apr: 11am–5pm Mon–Sat.
Closed Dec 24–Jan 3 & public hols.
📷 🎦 book ahead. 🅿️
🌐 drjohnsonshouse.org

Dr. Samuel Johnson was an
18th-century scholar famous
for the many witty (and often
contentious) remarks that his
biographer, James Boswell,
recorded and published.

Schoolgirl figure mounted on the facade of
St. Andrew church

Johnson lived here from 1748
to 1759. He compiled the first
definitive English dictionary
(1755) in the attic, where six
scribes and assistants stood all
day at high desks.

The house, built before
1700, is furnished with
18th-century pieces and a small
collection of exhibits relating to
Johnson and the times in which
he lived. These include a tea set
belonging to his friend Mrs.
Thrale and pictures of Johnson
and his contemporaries. It
also houses replica Georgian
costumes for children to try on.

⑮ St. Andrew, Holborn

5 St. Andrew St EC4. **Map** 14 E1.
Tel 020 7583 7394. 🚇 Chancery Lane.
Open 8:30am–5pm Mon–Fri. 📷 ♿
🌐 standrewholborn.org.uk

The medieval church here
survived the Great Fire of 1666.
In 1686 Christopher Wren was,
however, asked to redesign it,
and the lower part of the tower
is virtually all that remains of the
earlier church. One of Wren's
most spacious churches, it was
gutted during World War II but
faithfully restored as the church
of the London trade guilds.
Benjamin Disraeli, the Jewish-
born prime minister, was
baptized here in 1817, at the
age of 12. In the 19th century
a charity school was attached
to the church.

Civic symbol on Holborn Viaduct

⑯ Holborn Viaduct

EC1. **Map** 14 F1. 🚇 Farringdon,
St. Paul's, Chancery Lane.

This piece of Victorian ironwork
was erected in the 1860s as part
of a much-needed traffic plan.
It is best seen from Farringdon
Street, which is linked to the
bridge by a staircase. Climb up
and see the statues of City
heroes and bronze images of
Commerce, Agriculture, Science,
and Fine Arts.

⑰ St. Etheldreda's Chapel

14 Ely Place EC1. **Map** 6 E5.
Tel 020 7405 1061. 🚇 Farringdon.
Open 8am–5pm Mon–Sat, 8am–
12:30pm Sun. 📷 🎦 noon–2pm.
🌐 stetheldreda.com

This is a rare 13th-century
survivor, the chapel and crypt
of Ely House, where the
Bishops of Ely lived until the

Reconstructed interior of Dr. Johnson's house

Reformation. Then it was acquired by an Elizabethan courtier, Sir Christopher Hatton, whose descendants demolished the house but kept the chapel and turned it into a Protestant church. It passed through various hands and, in 1874, reverted to the Catholic faith.

⓲ Hatton Garden

EC1. **Map** 6 E5. 🚇 Chancery Lane, Farringdon.

Built on land that used to be the garden of Hatton House, this is London's diamond and jewelry district. Gems ranging from the priceless to the mundane are traded from scores of small shops with sparkling window displays, and even from the sidewalks. The city's only pawnbroker is here – look for its traditional sign of three brass balls above the door.

⓳ Staple Inn

Holborn WC1. **Map** 14 E1. 🚇 Chancery Lane. Courtyard **Open** 9am–5pm Mon–Fri.

This building was once the wool staple, where wool was weighed and taxed. The frontage overlooks Holborn and is the only real example of Elizabethan half-timbering left in central London. Although now much restored, it would still be recognizable by someone who had known it in 1586, when it was built. The shops at street level have the feel of the 19th century, and there are some 18th-century buildings in the courtyard.

⓴ London Silver Vaults

53–64 Chancery Lane WC2. **Map** 14 D1. **Tel** 020 7242 3844. 🚇 Chancery Lane, Holborn. **Open** 9am–5:30pm Mon–Fri, 9am– 1pm Sat. 🌐 thesilvervaults.com

These silver vaults originate from the Chancery Lane Safe Deposit Company, established in 1885. After descending a staircase you pass through

Staple Inn, a survivor from 1586

steel security doors and reach a nest of underground shops sparkling with antique and modern silverware. London silver makers have been renowned for centuries, reaching their peak in the Georgian era. The best examples sell for many thousands of pounds, but most shops also offer modest pieces at realistic prices.

Coffee pot (1716), Silver Vaults

㉑ Gray's Inn

Gray's Inn Rd WC1. **Map** 6 D5. **Tel** 020 7458 7800. 🚇 Chancery Lane, Holborn. Grounds **Open** noon– 2:30pm Mon–Fri. ♿ 🖥

This ancient legal center and law school goes back to the 14th century. Like many of the buildings in this area, it was badly damaged by World War II bombs, but much of it has been rebuilt. At least one of Shakespeare's plays (*A Comedy of Errors*) was first performed in Gray's Inn hall in 1594. The hall's 16th-century interior screen still survives.

More recently, the young Charles Dickens was employed as a clerk here in 1827–8. Today the garden, once a convenient site for staging duels, is open to lunchtime strollers for part of the year, and typifies the cloistered calm of the four Inns of Court. The buildings may be visited only by prior arrangement.

THE CITY

London's financial district is built on the site of the original Roman settlement. Its full title is the City of London, but it is usually referred to as the City. Most traces of the early City were obliterated by the Great Fire of 1666 and World War II *(see pp26–7 and 35)*. Today, glossy modern offices stand among a plethora of banks with marbled halls and stately pillars. It is the contrast between dour, warren-like Victorian buildings and shiny new ones that gives the City its distinctive character. Though it hums with activity in business hours, few people have lived here since the 19th century, when it was one of London's main residential centers. Today only the churches, many of them by Christopher Wren *(see p49)*, are a reminder of those past times.

Sights at a Glance

Historic Streets and Buildings
1 Mansion House
3 Royal Exchange
7 Old Bailey
8 Apothecaries' Hall
9 Fishmongers' Hall
16 *Tower of London pp156–7*
17 Tower Bridge
19 Stock Exchange
23 Lloyd's of London

Museums and Galleries
4 Bank of England Museum
24 Guildhall Art Gallery

Historic Markets
12 Old Billingsgate
22 Leadenhall Market

Monuments
11 Monument

Churches and Cathedrals
2 St. Stephen Walbrook
5 St. Mary-le-Bow
6 *St. Paul's Cathedral pp150–53*
10 St. Magnus the Martyr
13 St. Mary-at-Hill
14 St. Margaret Pattens
15 All Hallows by the Tower
20 St. Helen's Bishopsgate
21 St. Katharine Cree

Docks
18 St. Katharine's Dock

☐ Restaurants *see pp298–300*
1 Goodman
2 Haz
3 The Restaurant at St. Paul's Cathedral
4 Sauterelle

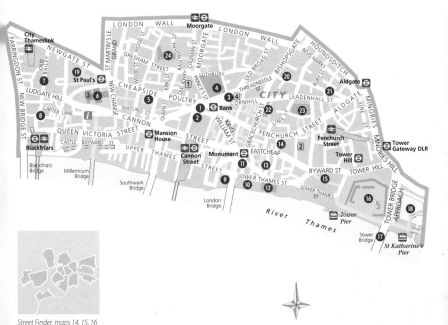

0 meters 500
0 yards 500

Street Finder, maps 14, 15, 16

◀ South side view of St. Paul's Cathedral with its impressive dome

For keys to symbols *see back flap*

Street by Street: The City

This is the business center of London, home to vast financial institutions such as the Stock Exchange and the Bank of England. But in contrast to these 19th- and 20th-century buildings are the older survivors. A walk through the City is in part a pilgrimage through the architectural visions of Christopher Wren, England's most sublime and probably most prolific architect. After the Great Fire of 1666 he supervised the rebuilding of 52 churches within the area, and enough survive to testify to his genius.

❺ St. Mary-le-Bow
Anyone born within earshot of the bells of this Wren church (the historic Bow Bells) is said to be a true Londoner or Cockney.

St. Paul's station

Mansion House station

ST PAUL'S CHURCHYARD

NEW CHANGE

WATLING STREET

BREAD STREET

CANNON STREET

FRIDAY ST

QUEEN VICTORIA

St. Nicholas Cole Abbey was the first church Wren built in the City (in 1677). Like many others, it had to be restored after World War II bomb damage.

St. James Garlickhythe contains unusual sword rests and hat stands, beneath Wren's elegant spire of 1717.

Key

— Suggested route

❻ ★ St. Paul's
Wren's masterpiece still dominates the City skyline.

COLLEGE · OF · ARMS

The College of Arms received its royal charter in 1484 from Richard III. Still active today, it assesses who has a legitimate claim to a British family coat of arms.

0 meters   100
0 yards   100

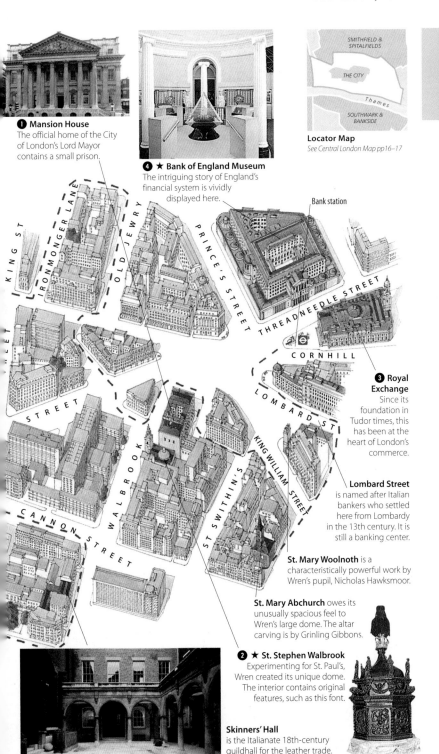

❶ Mansion House
The official home of the City of London's Lord Mayor contains a small prison.

❹ ★ Bank of England Museum
The intriguing story of England's financial system is vividly displayed here.

Bank station

Locator Map
See Central London Map pp16–17

SMITHFIELD & SPITALFIELDS

THE CITY

Thames

SOUTHWARK & BANKSIDE

KING ST

IRONMONGER LANE

OLD JEWRY

PRINCE'S STREET

THREADNEEDLE STREET

CORNHILL

LOMBARD ST

STREET

WALBROOK

ST SWITHIN'S

KING WILLIAM STREET

CANNON STREET

❸ Royal Exchange
Since its foundation in Tudor times, this has been at the heart of London's commerce.

Lombard Street
is named after Italian bankers who settled here from Lombardy in the 13th century. It is still a banking center.

St. Mary Woolnoth is a characteristically powerful work by Wren's pupil, Nicholas Hawksmoor.

St. Mary Abchurch owes its unusually spacious feel to Wren's large dome. The altar carving is by Grinling Gibbons.

❷ ★ St. Stephen Walbrook
Experimenting for St. Paul's, Wren created its unique dome. The interior contains original features, such as this font.

Skinners' Hall
is the Italianate 18th-century guildhall for the leather trade.

❶ Mansion House

Walbrook EC4. **Map** 15 B2. **Tel** 020 7626 2500. 🚇 Bank, Mansion House. **Open** to group tours only by appt or 2pm Tue on first-come-first-served basis. 🚫 📷 1:45pm Tue (near the entrance). 🌐 **cityoflondon.gov.uk**

The official residence of the Lord Mayor, it was completed in 1753 to the design of George Dance the Elder, whose work is now in John Soane's Museum *(see pp138–9)*. The Palladian front with its six Corinthian columns is one of the most familiar City landmarks. The state rooms have a dignity appropriate to the office of mayor, one of the most spectacular being the 90-ft (27-m) Egyptian Hall.

Formerly located here, and now in the Museum of London *(see pp168–9)*, were 11 holding cells, a reminder of the building's other function as a magistrate's court; the Mayor is chief magistrate of the City during his year of office. Emmeline Pankhurst, who campaigned for women's suffrage in the early 20th century, was once held here.

Egyptian Hall in Mansion House

❷ St. Stephen Walbrook

39 Walbrook EC4. **Map** 15 B2. **Tel** 020 7626 9000. 🚇 Bank, Cannon St. **Open** 10am–4pm Mon–Fri. ✝ 12:45pm Thu, sung Mass. Organ recitals 12:30pm Fri. 🌐 **ststephenwalbrook.net**

The Lord Mayor's parish church was built by Christopher Wren in 1672–9. Architectural writers consider it to be the finest of his City churches *(see p49)*. The deep, coffered dome, with its ornate plasterwork, was a forerunner of St. Paul's. St. Stephen's airy columned interior comes as a surprise after its plain exterior. The font cover and pulpit canopy are decorated with exquisite carved figures that contrast strongly with the stark simplicity of Henry Moore's massive white stone altar (1987).

However, perhaps the most moving monument of all is a telephone in a glass box. This is a tribute to Rector Chad Varah who, in 1953, founded the Samaritans, a voluntarily staffed telephone helpline for people in emotional need.

The church is also the home of the London Internet Church, which brings together people from all over the world to worship and relate.

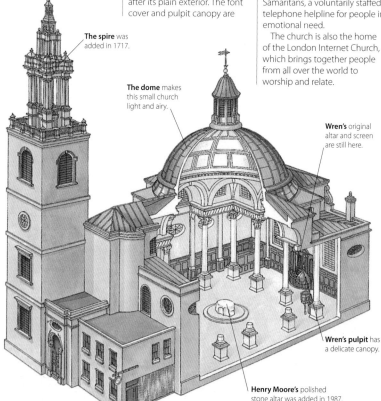

The spire was added in 1717.

The dome makes this small church light and airy.

Wren's original altar and screen are still here.

Wren's pulpit has a delicate canopy.

Henry Moore's polished stone altar was added in 1987.

❸ Royal Exchange

EC3. **Map** 15 C2. **Tel** 020 7623 0444. ⊖ Bank. Shopping center **Open** 10am–6pm daily.

Sir Thomas Gresham, the Elizabethan merchant and courtier, founded the Royal Exchange in 1565 as a center for commerce of all kinds. The original building was centered on a vast courtyard where merchants and tradesmen did business. Queen Elizabeth I gave it its Royal title, and it is still one of the sites from which new kings and queens are announced. Dating from 1844, this is the third splendid building on the site since Gresham's.

The building now contains a luxurious shopping center with such designer stores as Cartier, Hermès, and Paul Smith.

The facade of William Tite's Royal Exchange of 1844

The Duke of Wellington (1884) opposite the Bank of England

❹ Bank of England Museum

Bartholomew Lane EC2. **Map** 15 B1. **Tel** 020 7601 5545. ⊖ Bank. **Open** 10am–5pm Mon–Fri, Lord Mayor's Show (p57). **Closed** public hols. ♿ call first. ▣ 🎦 Films, lectures. 🅆 **bankofengland.co.uk/education/museum**

The Bank of England was set up in 1694 to raise money for foreign wars. It grew to become Britain's central bank, and also issues currency notes. Sir John Soane (see pp138–9) was the architect of the 1788 bank building on this site, but only the exterior wall of his design has survived. The rest was destroyed in the 1920s and 1930s when the Bank was enlarged. There is now a reconstruction of Soane's stock office of 1793.

Glittering gold bars, silver-plated decoration, and a Roman mosaic floor, discovered during the rebuilding, are among the items on display. The museum illustrates the work of the Bank and the financial system. The gift shop sells paperweights made out of used banknotes.

❺ St. Mary-le-Bow

(Bow Church) Cheapside EC2. **Map** 15 A2. **Tel** 020 7248 5139. ⊖ St. Paul's, Mansion Hse. **Open** 7:30am–6pm Mon–Wed, 7:30am–6:30pm Thu, 7:30am–4pm Fri. ✝ 7:30am Tue, 1pm Wed & Fri, 6pm Thu. 🎦 by arrangement. ♿ ✍ 🅆 **stmarylebow.co.uk**

The church takes its name from the bow arches in the Norman crypt. When Wren rebuilt the church (in 1670–80) after the Great Fire, he continued this pattern through the arches on the steeple. The weathervane, dating from 1674, is an enormous dragon.

The church was bombed in 1941, leaving only the steeple and two outer walls standing. It was restored in 1956–62 when the bells were recast and rehung. Bow bells are important to Londoners: traditionally only those born within their sound can claim to be true Cockneys.

❻ St. Paul's

See pp150–53.

❼ Old Bailey

EC4. **Map** 14 F1. **Tel** 020 7248 3277. ⊖ St Paul's. **Open** 10am–1pm, 2–5pm Mon–Fri (but opening hours vary from court to court). **Closed** Easter, Christmas, New Year, public hols. 🖂 🅆 **cityoflondon.gov.uk**

This short street has a long association with crime and punishment. The new Central Criminal Courts opened here in 1907 on the site of the notorious and malodorous Newgate prison (on special days in the legal calendar, judges still carry small posies to court as a reminder of those times). Across the road, the Magpie and Stump served "execution breakfasts" until 1868, when mass public hangings outside the prison gates were stopped.

Today, when the courts are in session, they are open to members of the public.

Old Bailey's rooftop Justice

❻ St. Paul's Cathedral

Following the Great Fire of London in 1666, the medieval cathedral of St. Paul's was left in ruins. The authorities turned to Christopher Wren to rebuild it, but his ideas met with considerable resistance from the conservative Dean and Chapter. Wren's 1672 Great Model plan was not at all popular with them, and so a watered-down plan was finally agreed upon in 1675. Wren's determination paid off, though, as can be witnessed from the grandeur of the present cathedral.

Stone urn outside the South Transept

Queen Anne's Statue
An 1886 copy of Francis Bird's 1712 original now stands on the forecourt.

KEY

① **The West Porch**, approached from Ludgate Hill, is the main entrance to St. Paul's.

② **The West Portico** comprises two tiers of columns rather than the single colonnade that Wren intended.

③ **The pediment** carvings, dating from 1706, show the Conversion of St. Paul.

④ **The balustrade** along the top was added in 1718 against Wren's wishes.

⑤ **The lantern** weighs a massive 850 tons.

⑥ **The golden gallery** lies at the highest point of the dome.

⑦ **The brick cone** located inside the outer dome supports the heavy lantern.

⑧ **The oculus** is an opening through which the lantern can be seen.

⑨ **The stone gallery** offers a splendid view over London.

⑩ **Upper screen wall** masks the flying buttresses.

⑪ **Flying buttresses** support the nave walls and the dome.

⑫ **The North and South Transepts** cross the nave in a medieval style that contrasts with Wren's original plan *(see p152)*.

★ **The West Front and Towers**
The towers were not on Wren's original plan – he added them in 1707, when he was 75 years old. Both were designed to have clocks.

Main Entrance

★ **The Dome**
At 360 ft (110 m) high, the dome at St. Paul's is the second-biggest in the world after St. Peter's in Rome, as spectacular from inside as outside.

VISITORS' CHECKLIST

Practical Information
Ludgate Hill EC4.
Map 15 A2.
Tel 020 7246 8357.
w stpauls.co.uk
Cathedral: **Open** 8:30am–4pm Mon–Sat.
Galleries: **Open** 9:30am–4:15pm Mon–Sat. Crypt & ambulatory **Open** 9:15am–4:15pm Mon–Sat.
Closed for sightseeing on Sun
times vary.
Concerts.

Transportation
St. Paul's, Mansion House.
6, 8, 11, 15, 22, 23, 25, 76.
City Thameslink.

★ **Whispering Gallery**
The unusual acoustics here cause whispers to echo around the dome.

South Porch
Wren took the idea of a semi-circular porch from a Baroque church in Rome.

604 Bishop Mellitus built the first St. Paul's. It burned down in 1087

Detail on Tijou gate (see p153)

1666 St. Paul's reduced to a burned ruin after the Great Fire

1708 Wren's son Christopher lays the last stone on the lantern

2011 Extensive restorations finished

| 600 | 800 | 1000 | 1200 | 1400 | 1600 | 1800 | 2000 |

1087 Bishop Maurice began Old St. Paul's: a Norman cathedral of stone

1675 Foundation stone of Wren's design laid

1940–1 Slight bomb damage to the cathedral

1981 Prince Charles marries Lady Diana Spencer

A Guided Tour of St. Paul's

Visitors to St. Paul's will be immediately impressed by its cool, beautifully ordered, and extremely spacious interior. The nave, transepts, and choir are arranged in the shape of a cross, as in a medieval cathedral, but Wren's Classical vision shines through this conservative floor plan, forced on him by the cathedral authorities. Aided by some of the finest craftsmen of his day, he created an interior of grand majesty and Baroque splendor, a worthy setting for the many great ceremonial events that have taken place here. These include the funeral of Winston Churchill in 1965 and the wedding of Prince Charles and Lady Diana Spencer in 1981.

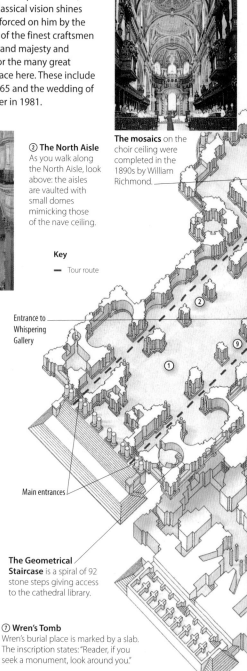

The mosaics on the choir ceiling were completed in the 1890s by William Richmond.

② The North Aisle
As you walk along the North Aisle, look above: the aisles are vaulted with small domes mimicking those of the nave ceiling.

Key

— Tour route

① The Nave
Take in the full glory of the massive arches and the succession of saucer domes that open out into a huge space below the main dome.

⑨ South Aisle
From here the brave can ascend the 259 steps to the Whispering Gallery and test the acoustics.

Entrance to Whispering Gallery

Main entrances

⑧ Florence Nightingale's Tomb
Famous for her pioneering work in nursing standards, Florence Nightingale was the first woman to receive the Order of Merit.

The Geometrical Staircase is a spiral of 92 stone steps giving access to the cathedral library.

⑦ Wren's Tomb
Wren's burial place is marked by a slab. The inscription states: "Reader, if you seek a monument, look around you."

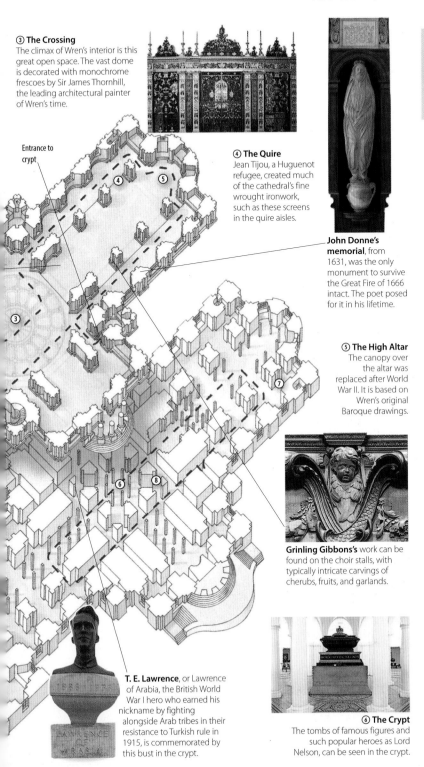

③ The Crossing
The climax of Wren's interior is this great open space. The vast dome is decorated with monochrome frescoes by Sir James Thornhill, the leading architectural painter of Wren's time.

④ The Quire
Jean Tijou, a Huguenot refugee, created much of the cathedral's fine wrought ironwork, such as these screens in the quire aisles.

Entrance to crypt

John Donne's memorial, from 1631, was the only monument to survive the Great Fire of 1666 intact. The poet posed for it in his lifetime.

⑤ The High Altar
The canopy over the altar was replaced after World War II. It is based on Wren's original Baroque drawings.

Grinling Gibbons's work can be found on the choir stalls, with typically intricate carvings of cherubs, fruits, and garlands.

T. E. Lawrence, or Lawrence of Arabia, the British World War I hero who earned his nickname by fighting alongside Arab tribes in their resistance to Turkish rule in 1915, is commemorated by this bust in the crypt.

⑥ The Crypt
The tombs of famous figures and such popular heroes as Lord Nelson, can be seen in the crypt.

Apothecaries' Hall, rebuilt in 1670

❽ Apothecaries' Hall

Blackfriars Lane EC4. **Map** 14 F2. **Tel** 020 7236 1189. ⊖ Blackfriars. Courtyard **Open** 9am–5pm Mon–Fri. **Closed** public hols, end Aug. Phone Hall for appt to visit (groups only). ♿

London has had livery companies, or guilds, to protect and regulate specific trades since early medieval times. The Apothecaries' Society was founded in 1617 for those who prepared, prescribed, or sold drugs. It has some surprising alumni, including Oliver Cromwell and the poet John Keats. Now nearly all the members are physicians or surgeons.

❾ Fishmongers' Hall

London Bridge EC4. **Map** 15 B3. **Tel** 020 7626 3531. ⊖ Monument. **Closed** to the public. Limited tours by appt only. 🌐 fishhall.org.uk

This is one of the oldest livery companies, established in 1272. Lord Mayor Walworth, a member of the Fishmongers' Company, killed Wat Tyler, leader of the Peasants' Revolt, in 1381 *(see p164)*.
Today it still fulfills its original role; all the fish sold in the City must be inspected by Company officials.

❿ St. Magnus the Martyr

Lower Thames St EC3. **Map** 15 C3. **Tel** 020 7626 4481. ⊖ Monument. **Open** 10am–4pm Tue–Fri. 🕆 11am Sun. ♿ 🌐 stmagnusmartyr. org.uk

There has been a church here for over 1,000 years. Its patron saint, St. Magnus, Earl of the Orkney Islands and a renowned Norwegian Christian leader, was brutally murdered in 1116. When Christopher Wren built this church in 1671–6, it was at the foot of old London Bridge, until 1738 the only bridge across the Thames River in London. Anyone going south from the city would have passed under Wren's magnificent arched porch spanning the flagstones leading to the old bridge.
Highlights of St. Magnus the Martyr include the carved musical instruments that decorate the organ case. Wren's pulpit, with its slender supporting stem, was restored in 1924.

⓫ Monument

Monument St EC3. **Map** 15 C2. **Tel** 020 7626 2717. ⊖ Monument. **Open** 9:30am–5:30pm daily (6pm in summer). **Closed** Jan 1, Dec 24–26. 🚷 🌐 themonument.info

The column designed by Christopher Wren to commemorate the Great Fire of London, which devastated the original walled city in September 1666, is the tallest isolated stone column in the world. It is 205 ft (62 m) high and is said to be 205 ft west of where the fire started in Pudding Lane. It was sited on the direct approach to old London Bridge, which was a few steps downstream from the present one. Reliefs around the column's base show Charles II

The altar of St. Magnus the Martyr

restoring the city. The 311 steps to the top lead to a viewing platform. In 1842 this was enclosed with railings after a suicide. The views are spectacular.

Fish weathervane at Billingsgate

⓬ Old Billingsgate

Lower Thames St EC3. **Map** 15 C3. ⊖ Monument. **Closed** to the public.

London's main fish market was based here for 900 years, on one of the city's earliest quays. During the 19th and early 20th centuries, 400 tons of fish were sold here every day, much of it delivered by boat. It was London's noisiest market, renowned, even in Shakespeare's day, for foul language. In 1982 the market moved from this building (1877) to the Isle of Dogs.

⓭ St. Mary-at-Hill

Lovat Lane EC3. **Map** 15 C2. **Tel** 020 7626 4184. ⊖ Monument. **Open** 11am–4pm Tue, Wed, Thu. 🕆 1pm Wed, 1:05pm Thu. Concerts. 🌐 stmary-at-hill.org

The interior and east end of St. Mary-at-Hill were Wren's first church designs (1670–76). The Greek cross design was a prototype for his St. Paul's proposals. Ironically, the delicate plasterwork and rich 17th-century fixtures, which had survived both the Victorian mania for refurbishment and the bombs of World War II, were lost in a fire in 1988. The building was then restored to its original appearance, only to be damaged again by an IRA bomb in 1992.

⑭ St. Margaret Pattens

Rood Lane and Eastcheap EC3. **Map** 15 C2. **Tel** 020 7623 6630.
🚇 Monument. **Open** 7:30am–6pm Mon–Fri. **Closed** Christmas week.
✝ 1:05pm Thu. Concerts and recitals.
♿ 🖳 stmargaretpattens.org

Wren's church of 1684–7 was named after a type of overshoe made near here. Its rendered brickwork and Portland stone contrast with the Georgian stucco shopfront in the forecourt. It retains 17th-century canopied pews and an ornate font.

⑮ All Hallows by the Tower

Byward St EC3. **Map** 16 D3. **Tel** 020 7481 2928. 🚇 Tower Hill. **Open** 8am–6pm Mon–Fri, 10am–5pm Sat, 10am–1pm Sun. **Closed** Dec 26–Jan 2.
✝ 11am Sun. ♿ 🖳 📷 🏛 📷 undercroft museum.
🖳 allhallowsbythetower.org.uk

The first church on this site was Saxon. The arch in the southwest corner, which contains Roman tiles, dates from that period, as do some crosses in the crypt. There is a Roman pavement in the crypt. William Penn, founder of Pennsylvania, was baptized here in 1644. Most of the interior has been altered, but a lindenwood font cover, carved by Grinling Gibbons in 1682, survives. John Quincy Adams married here in

Roman tile from All Hallows

1797 before he was US president. Samuel Pepys watched the Great Fire from the church tower. There is a small museum, a brass rubbing center, concerts, and a bookstand.

⑯ Tower of London

See pp156–9.

⑰ Tower Bridge

SE1. **Map** 16 D3. **Tel** 020 7403 3761.
🚇 Tower Hill. The Tower Bridge Exhibition: **Open** Apr–Sep: 10am–6pm daily; Oct–Mar: 9:30am–5:30pm daily (open from noon on Jan 1).
Closed Dec 24–26. 📷 🎞 ♿ 🏛
🖳 towerbridge.org.uk

Completed in 1894, this flamboyant piece of Victorian engineering quickly became a symbol of London. Its pinnacled towers and linking catwalk support the mechanism for raising the roadway when big ships have to pass through, or for special and historic occasions.

The bridge now houses The Tower Bridge Exhibition, with interactive displays bringing the bridge's history to life, river views from the catwalk, and a close-up look at the steam engine that powered the lifting machinery until 1976, when the system was electrified.

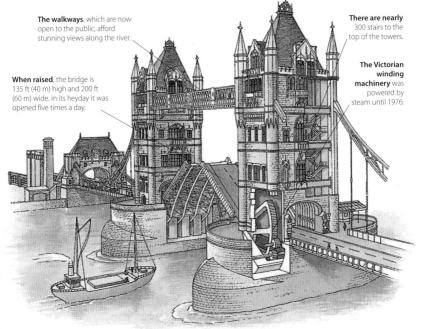

The walkways, which are now open to the public, afford stunning views along the river.

When raised, the bridge is 135 ft (40 m) high and 200 ft (60 m) wide. In its heyday it was opened five times a day.

There are nearly 300 stairs to the top of the towers.

The Victorian winding machinery was powered by steam until 1976.

⑯ Tower of London

For much of its 900-year history the Tower was an object of fear. Those who had committed treason or threatened the throne were held within its dank walls. A lucky few lived in comparative comfort, but the majority had to endure appalling conditions. Many did not get out alive, and some were tortured before meeting violent deaths on nearby Tower Hill.

"Beefeaters"
Thirty-seven Yeoman Warders guard the Tower and live here.

★ The Jewel House
The magnificent Crown Jewels are housed here (see p158).

Queen's House
This is the official residence of the constables.

KEY

① **Beauchamp Tower** was used for high-ranking prisoners, who were often allowed to keep their own retinues of servants.

② **Tower Green** was where the aristocratic prisoners were executed, away from the ghoulish crowds on Tower Hill. But while only seven people died here – including two of Henry VIII's six wives – there were hundreds of public executions on Tower Hill.

③ **Wakefield Tower**, part of the Medieval Palace, has been carefully refurbished to match its original appearance in the 13th century.

④ **The Bloody Tower** is associated with the legend of the two princes and other deaths (see p159).

Main entrance

The Ravens

The Tower's most celebrated residents are a small colony of ravens. It is not known when they first settled here, but there is a legend that should they desert the Tower, the kingdom will fall. In fact, the birds have part of their wings trimmed on the right side, making full flight impossible. The Ravenmaster, one of the Yeoman Warders, looks after the birds.

A memorial in the moat commemorates some of the ravens who have died at the Tower since the 1950s.

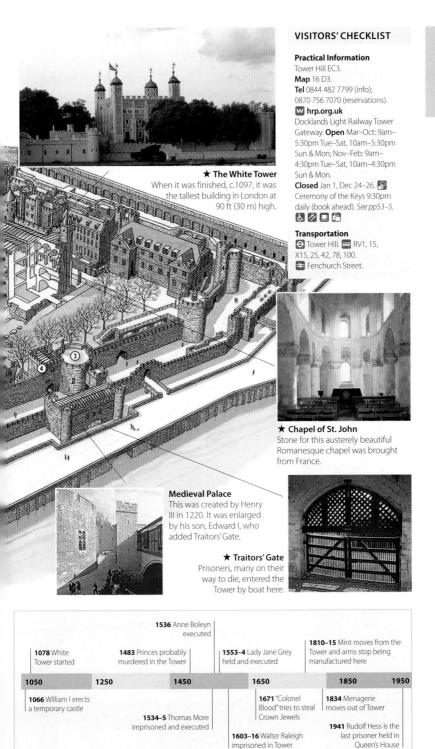

★ **The White Tower**
When it was finished, c.1097, it was
the tallest building in London at
90 ft (30 m) high.

★ **Chapel of St. John**
Stone for this austerely beautiful
Romanesque chapel was brought
from France.

Medieval Palace
This was created by Henry
III in 1220. It was enlarged
by his son, Edward I, who
added Traitors' Gate.

★ **Traitors' Gate**
Prisoners, many on their
way to die, entered the
Tower by boat here.

		1536 Anne Boleyn executed			**1810–15** Mint moves from the Tower and arms stop being manufactured here
1078 White Tower started	**1483** Princes probably murdered in the Tower		**1553–4** Lady Jane Grey held and executed		
1050	**1250**	**1450**	**1650**	**1850**	**1950**
1066 William I erects a temporary castle			**1671** "Colonel Blood" tries to steal Crown Jewels	**1834** Menagerie moves out of Tower	
	1534–5 Thomas More imprisoned and executed		**1603–16** Walter Raleigh imprisoned in Tower	**1941** Rudolf Hess is the last prisoner held in Queen's House	

Inside the Tower

The Tower has been a tourist attraction since the reign of Charles II (1660–85), when both the Crown Jewels and the collection of armor were first shown to the public. They remain powerful reminders of royal might and wealth.

The Orb, symbolizing the power and Empire of Christ the Redeemer

The Crown Jewels

The Crown Jewels comprise the regalia of crowns, scepters, orbs, and swords used at coronations and other state occasions. They are impossible to price, but their worth is irrelevant beside their enormous significance in the historical and religious life of the kingdom. Most of the Crown Jewels date from 1661, when a new set was made for the coronation of Charles II; Parliament had destroyed the previous crowns and scepters after the execution of Charles I in 1649. Only a few pieces survived, hidden by the clergy of Westminster Abbey until the Restoration.

The Coronation Ceremony

Many elements in this solemn and mystical ceremony date from the days of Edward the Confessor. The king or queen proceeds to Westminster Abbey, accompanied by objects of the regalia, including the State Sword, which represents the monarch's own sword. He or she is then anointed with holy oil, to signify divine approval, and invested with ornaments and royal robes. Each of the jewels represents an aspect of the monarch's role as head of the state and church. The climax comes when St. Edward's Crown is placed on the sovereign's head; there is a cry of "God Save the King" (or Queen), the trumpets sound, and guns at the Tower are fired. The last coronation was Elizabeth II's in 1953.

The Imperial State Crown, containing more than 2,800 diamonds, 273 pearls, and other gems

The crowns

There are 10 crowns on display at the Tower. Many of these have not been worn for years, but the Imperial State Crown is in frequent use. The Queen wears it at the Opening of Parliament *(see p75)*. The crown was made in 1937 for George VI, and is similar to the one made for Queen Victoria. The sapphire set in the cross is said to have been worn in a ring by Edward the Confessor (ruled 1042–66).

The most recent crown is not at the Tower, however. It was made for Prince Charles's investiture as Prince of Wales at Caernarvon Castle in north Wales in 1969, and is kept at the Museum of Wales in Cardiff.

The Queen Mother's crown was made for the coronation of her husband, George VI, in 1937. It is the only one to be made out of platinum – all the other crowns on display at the Tower are made of gold.

Other regalia

Apart from the crowns, there are other pieces of the Crown Jewels that are essential to coronations. Among these are three Swords of Justice, symbolizing mercy and spiritual and temporal justice. The orb is a hollow gold sphere encrusted with jewels and weighing about 3 lb (1.3 kg). The Sceptre with the Cross contains the biggest cut diamond in the world, the 530-carat First Star of Africa. The rough stone it comes from weighed 3,106 carats.

The Sovereign's Ring, sometimes referred to as "the wedding ring of England"

Plate Collection

The Jewel House also holds a collection of elaborate gold and silver plate. The Maundy Dish is still used on Maundy Thursday when the monarch distributes money to selected old people. The Exeter Salt (a very grand saltcellar from the days when salt was a valuable commodity) was given by the citizens of Exeter, in west England, to Charles II; during the 1640s Civil War, Exeter was a Royalist stronghold.

The hilt and solid-gold scabbard of the jeweled State Sword, one of the most valuable swords in the world

The Sceptre with the Cross (1660), rebuilt in 1910 after Edward VII was presented with the First Star of Africa diamond

The White Tower

This is the oldest surviving building in the Tower of London, begun by William I in 1075 and completed before 1079. For centuries it served as an armory, and much of the national collection of arms and armor is held here. Fit for a King showcases 500 years of royal arms and armor, while Hands on History allows visitors literally to get to grips with items of weaponry.

The Power House exhibition tells the stories of what went on behind the Tower's walls from 1100 to the present day, and the personalities that lived here are brought to life.

The Royal Castle and Armour Gallery

These two chambers on the first floor were the main ceremonial rooms of the original Norman castle. The first one, to the east, is the smaller, probably an antechamber to the Banqueting Hall beyond, and contains exhibits setting out the history of the White Tower. It adjoins St. John's Chapel, a rare surviving early Norman chapel, virtually intact, with a powerfully solid interior with little ornamentation. Originally, the two main rooms were twice their present height; a pitched roof was removed in 1490 to allow extra floors to be built on top. Suits of armor from Tudor and Stuart times are here, including three made for Henry VIII, one covering his horse as well. A suit made in Holland for Charles I is decorated in gold leaf.

Japanese armor presented to James I in 1613

The Ordnance Gallery

This and the temporary exhibition gallery next door were chambers created in 1490 when the roof was raised. They were used chiefly for storage, and in 1603 a new floor was installed to allow gunpowder to be kept here: by 1667, some 10,000 barrels of it were stored in the Tower. Among the displays are gilt panels and ornament from the barge of the Master of the Ordnance built in 1700.

The Small Armoury and Crypt

The westerly room on the ground floor may originally have been a living area, and has traces of the oldest fireplaces known in England. Pistols, muskets, swords, pikes, and bayonets are mounted on the walls and panels in elaborate symmetrical patterns based on displays in the Tower armories in the 18th and 19th centuries. They were shown in the Grand Storehouse until it burned down in 1841. A collection of weapons taken from the men who planned to assassinate William III in 1696 is on display, and a wooden block made in 1747 for the execution of Lord Lovat – the last public beheading in England – is on the third floor. The crypt now houses a shop.

The Line of Kings

The Line of Kings, ten life-size carvings of prominent English Monarchs, wearing armor and seated on horseback, originated in Tudor times, when eight such figures adorned the royal palace at Greenwich. Two more had been added by the time they first appeared in the Tower in 1660, celebrating the Restoration of Charles II. In 1688, 17 new horses and heads were commissioned, some from the great carver Grinling Gibbons (the third from the left is reputed to be his work).

Henry VIII's armor (1540)

The Princes in the Tower

Now explored in a display in the Bloody Tower, one of the Tower's darkest mysteries concerns two boy princes, sons and heirs of Edward IV. They were put into the Tower by their uncle, Richard of Gloucester, when their father died in 1483. Neither was seen again and Richard was crowned later that year. In 1674 the skeletons of two children were found nearby.

The yacht haven of the restored St. Katharine's Dock

⑱ St. Katharine's Dock

E1. **Map** 16 E3. **Tel** 020 7488 0055.
🚇 Tower Hill. ♿ ✏️ 🖥️ 📷
🌐 **skdocks.co.uk**

This most central of all London's docks was designed by Thomas Telford and opened in 1828 on the site of St. Katharine's hospital. Commodities as diverse as tea, marble, and live turtles (turtle soup was a Victorian delicacy) were unloaded here.

During the 19th and early 20th centuries, the docks flourished, but by the mid-20th century, cargo ships were delivering their wares in massive containers. The old docks became too small, and new ones had to be built downstream. St. Katharine's closed in 1968.

St. Katharine's is now one of London's most successful developments, with its commercial, residential, and entertainment facilities, including a hotel and a yacht marina. Old warehouse

St. Helen's Bishopsgate

buildings have shops and restaurants on their ground floors, and offices above.

On the north side of the dock is LIFFE Commodity Products, trading in commodities such as coffee, sugar, and oil. There is no public gallery, but if you ask at the door, you may be able to look down from the glass-walled reception area onto the frenzied trading floors. The dock is worth wandering through after visiting the Tower or Tower Bridge (see pp155–9).

⑲ Stock Exchange

Paternoster Sq EC4. **Map** 15 A1.
🚇 Bank, Farringdon.
Closed to the public.

The first Stock Exchange was established in Threadneedle Street in 1773 by a group of stockbrokers who previously met and did business in nearby City coffee houses. By the 19th century the rules of exchange were laid down, and for a hundred years London's was the biggest stock exchange in the world. Nevertheless, the rise of the American and Japanese economies during the 20th century gradually challenged London's dominance.

In 1986 the deregulation of the UK market, known as the "Big Bang," resulted in the computerization of trades, making the trade floor obsolete and setting London's financial markets on a course of rapid growth. Today, London has reclaimed its position as the market of choice for companies around the world wishing to raise capital.

⑳ St. Helen's Bishopsgate

Great St. Helen's EC3. **Map** 15 C1.
Tel 020 7283 2231. 🚇 Liverpool St, Bank. **Open** 9:30am–12:30pm Mon–Fri; some afternoons (call to check).
🕐 1pm Tue & Thu, 10:30am, 6pm Sun. ♿ 🌐 **st-helens.org.uk**

The curious appearance of this 13th-century church is due to its origins as two places of worship: one a parish church, the other the chapel of a long-gone nunnery next door. (The medieval nuns of St. Helen's were notorious for their "secular kissing.")

Among its monuments is the tomb of Sir Thomas Gresham, who founded the Royal Exchange (see p149).

The organ at St. Katharine Cree

㉑ St. Katharine Cree

86 Leadenhall St EC3. **Map** 16 D1.
Tel 020 7283 5733. 🚇 Aldgate, Tower Hill. **Open** 10:30am–4pm Mon–Fri. 🕐 1:05pm Thu.
🌐 **london.anglican.org**

A rare pre-Wren 17th-century church with a medieval tower, this was one of only eight churches in the City to survive the fire of 1666. Some of the elaborate plasterwork on and beneath the high ceiling of the nave portrays the coats of arms of the guilds, with which the church has special links. The 17th-century organ, supported on magnificent carved wooden columns, was played by both Purcell and Handel.

❷ Leadenhall Market

Whittington Ave EC3. **Map** 15 C2. **Tel** 020 7332 1523. 🚇 Bank, Monument. **Open** 7am–4pm Mon–Fri (stands: 10am–4pm). *See Shops and Markets pp324–33* 🅦 cityoflondon.gov.uk

There has been a food market here, on the site of the Roman forum *(see pp20–21)*, since the Middle Ages. Its name comes from a lead-roofed mansion that stood nearby in the 14th century. The ornate, Victorian covered shopping precinct of today was designed in 1881 by Sir Horace Jones, the architect of Billingsgate fish market *(see p154)*. Essentially a food market, offering traditional game, poultry, fish, and meat, Leadenhall also has a number of independent shops, which offer all kinds of fare from chocolates to wine. The area is busiest during breakfast and lunch hours, and is best seen at Christmas when all the stores are decorated. Next door is the Lloyd's of London building.

❷ Lloyd's of London

1 Lime St EC3. **Map** 15 C2. **Tel** 020 7327 1000. 🚇 Bank, Monument, Liverpool St, Aldgate. **Closed** to the public. 🅦 lloyds.com

Lloyd's was founded in the late 17th century and takes its name from the coffee house where underwriters and shipowners used to meet to arrange marine insurance contracts. Lloyd's soon became the world's main insurers, issuing policies on everything from oil tankers to Betty Grable's legs.

The present building, by Richard Rogers, dates from 1986 and is one of the most interesting modern buildings in London *(see p34)*. Its exaggerated stainless steel external piping and high-tech ducts echo Rogers' forceful Pompidou Center in Paris. Lloyd's is a far more elegant building and particularly worth seeing floodlit at night. Nearby is 30 St. Mary Axe, otherwise known as "the Gherkin," one of the most recognizable land-marks on the London skyline.

Leadenhall Market in 1881

❷ Guildhall Art Gallery

Guildhall Yard EC2. **Map** 15 B1. **Tel** 020 7332 3700. 🚇 St. Paul's. **Open** 10am–5pm Mon–Sat, noon–4pm Sun (last adm: 30 min prior). **Closed** Jan 1, Dec 25–26. 📷 for temporary exhibitions. 📷 ♿ 📷 Guildhall Gresham St EC2. **Tel** 020 7606 3030. **Open** phone to check. 🅦 cityoflondon.gov.uk

The Guildhall Art Gallery was built in 1885 to house the art collection of the Corporation of London, but was destroyed in World War II. The present gallery houses the studio collection of 20th-century artist Sir Matthew Smith, portraits from the 16th century to the present day, a gallery of 18th-century works, including John Singleton Copley's *Defeat of the Floating Batteries at Gibraltar*, and numerous Victorian works.

In 1988, the foundations of a Roman amphitheater were discovered beneath the gallery. Built in 70 AD and capable of holding about 6,000 spectators, the arena would have featured animal hunts, executions, and gladiatorial combat. Access to the atmospheric ruins is free.

The adjacent Guildhall itself has been the administrative center of the City for at least 800 years. For centuries the hall was used for trials, and many people were condemned to death here, including Henry Garnet, one of the Gunpowder Plot conspirators *(see p26)*. Today, a few days after the Lord Mayor's parade *(see pp56–7)*, the Prime Minister addresses a banquet here.

Richard Rogers' Lloyd's building illuminated at night

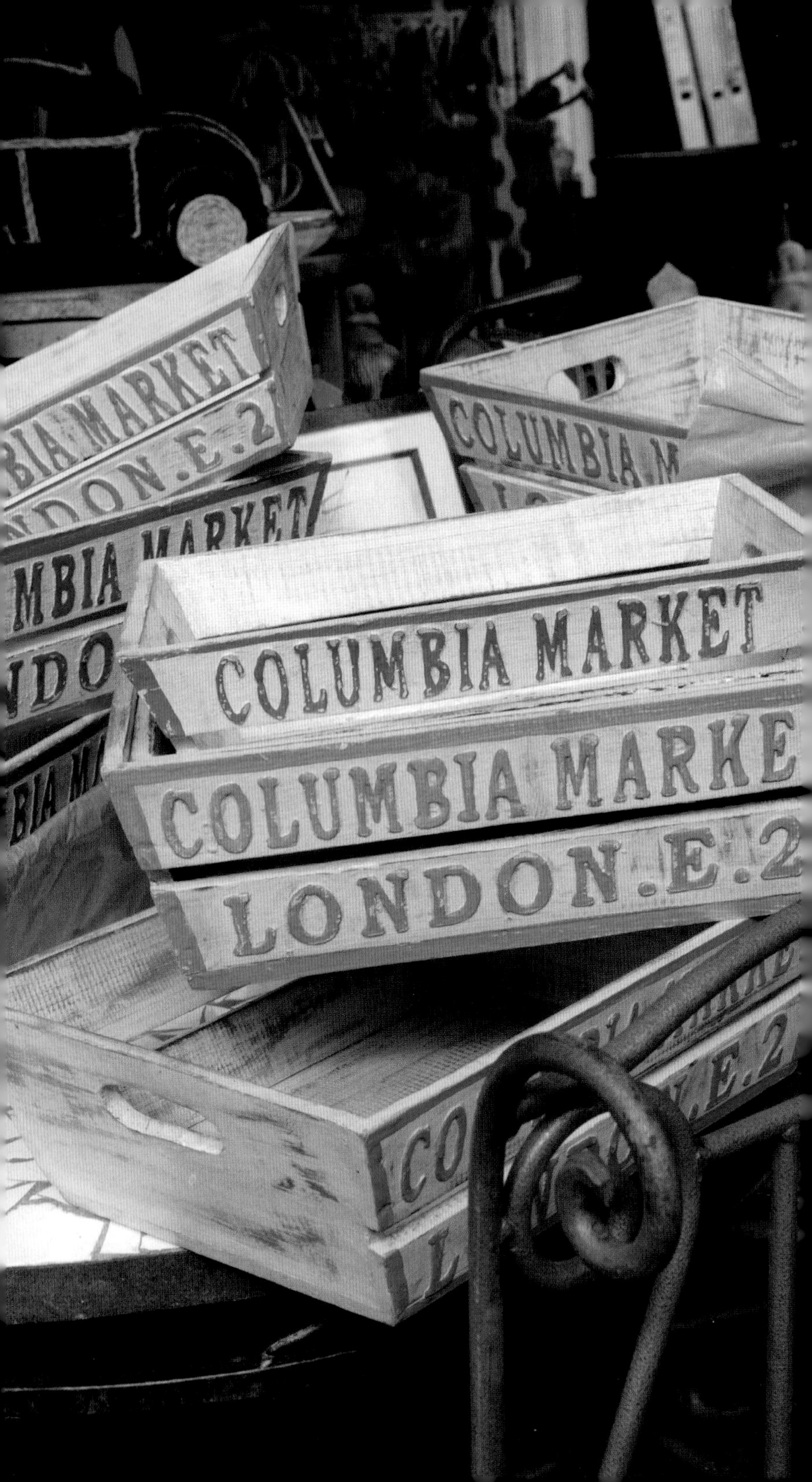
COLUMBIA MARKET
COLUMBIA MARKE
LONDON.E.2

SMITHFIELD AND SPITALFIELDS

The areas just north of the City walls have always been a refuge for those who did not want to come under its jurisdiction, or were not welcome there. These included Huguenots in the 17th century and, in later times, other immigrants from Europe and then Bengal. They founded small industries and brought with them their restaurants and places of worship. The name Spitalfields comes from the medieval priory of St. Mary Spital. Middlesex Street became known as Petticoat Lane in the 16th century, for its clothing stands; it is still the hub of a popular Sunday morning street market that spreads as far east as Brick Lane, today lined with aromatic Bengali food shops. London's meat market is at Smithfield, and nearby is the Barbican, a late-20th-century residential and arts complex.

Sights at a Glance

Historic Streets and Buildings

4 Charterhouse
5 Cloth Fair
7 Barbican
9 Whitbread's Brewery
11 Wesley's Chapel–Leysian Mission
13 Petticoat Lane
17 Fournier Street
19 Spitalfields Centre Museum of Immigration & Diversity
20 Brick Lane
21 Dennis Severs House

Museums and Galleries

3 *Museum of London pp168–9*
14 Whitechapel Gallery

Churches and Mosques

2 St. Botolph, Aldersgate
6 St. Bartholomew-the-Great
8 St. Giles, Cripplegate
12 St. Leonard's Church
16 Christ Church, Spitalfields
18 London Jamme Masjid

Cemeteries

10 Bunhill Fields

Markets

1 Smithfield Market
15 Old Spitalfields Market
22 Columbia Road Market

Restaurants *see pp298–300*

1 L'Anima
2 The Boundary
3 Café du Marché
4 Carnevale
5 Casa Negra
6 Cây Tre
7 Club Gascon
8 Galvin la chapelle
9 Hawksmoor
10 Leon Spitalfields
11 Pham Sushi
12 St John
13 Vinoteca

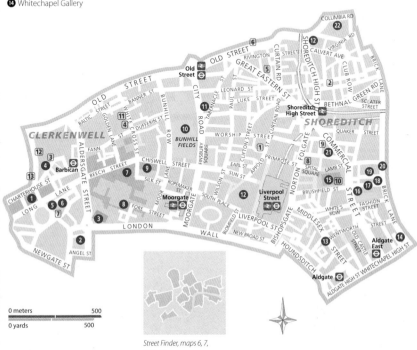

Street Finder, maps 6, 7, 8, 15, 16

0 meters 500
0 yards 500

◄ Columbia Road flower and plant market

For keys to symbols *see back flap*

Street-by-Street: Smithfield

This area is among the most historic in London. It contains one of the capital's oldest churches, some rare Jacobean houses, vestiges of the Roman wall (near the Museum of London), and central London's only surviving wholesale food market.

Smithfield's long history is also bloody. In 1381 the rebel peasant leader Wat Tyler was killed here by an ally of Richard II as he presented the king with demands for lower taxes. Later, in the reign of Mary I (1553–8), scores of Protestant religious martyrs were burned at the stake here.

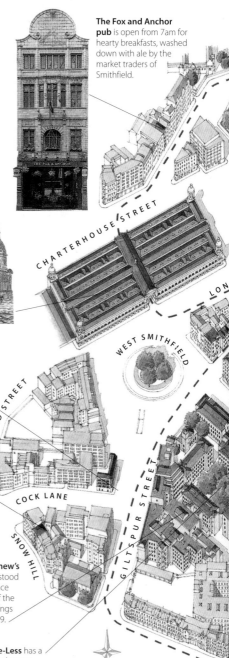

The Fox and Anchor pub is open from 7am for hearty breakfasts, washed down with ale by the market traders of Smithfield.

❶ ★ Smithfield Market
A contemporary print shows Horace Jones's stately building for the meat market when it was completed in 1867.

Key

— Suggested route

The Saracen's Head, a historic inn, stood on this site until the 1860s, when it was demolished to make way for Holborn Viaduct *(see p142)*.

Golden Boy of Pye Corner

St. Bartholomew's Hospital has stood on this site since 1123. Some of the existing buildings date from 1759.

St. Bartholomew-the-Less has a 15th-century tower and vestry. Its links to the hospital are shown by this early-20th-century stained glass of a nurse, a gift of the Worshipful Company of Glaziers.

0 meters		100
0 yards		100

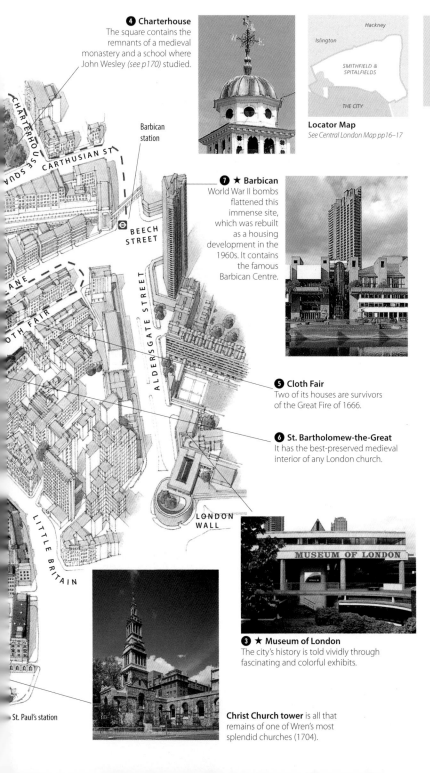

❹ Charterhouse
The square contains the remnants of a medieval monastery and a school where John Wesley *(see p170)* studied.

Barbican station

Locator Map
See Central London Map pp16–17

❼ ★ Barbican
World War II bombs flattened this immense site, which was rebuilt as a housing development in the 1960s. It contains the famous Barbican Centre.

❺ Cloth Fair
Two of its houses are survivors of the Great Fire of 1666.

❻ St. Bartholomew-the-Great
It has the best-preserved medieval interior of any London church.

❸ ★ Museum of London
The city's history is told vividly through fascinating and colorful exhibits.

Christ Church tower is all that remains of one of Wren's most splendid churches (1704).

St. Paul's station

Smithfield Market, now officially known as London Central Markets

❶ Smithfield Market

Charterhouse St EC1. **Map** 6 F5.
🚇 Farringdon, Barbican. **Open** 3–9am Mon–Fri. **Closed** public hols.
w smithfieldmarket.com

Animals have been traded here since the 12th century, but the site was granted its first official charter in 1400. In 1648 it was officially established as a cattle market, and live cattle continued to be sold here until the mid-19th century. It now confines itself to wholesale trading in dead meat and poultry. It was originally sited in Smithfield outside the city walls. Although moved to its present location in Charterhouse Street in the 1850s and called the London Central Meat Market, the original name stuck. The old buildings are by Horace Jones, the Victorian architect, but there are 20th-century additions. Some pubs in the area keep market hours and, from dawn, serve hearty breakfasts. After much-needed modernization, the market is now one of the best-equipped meat markets in the world. Aim to arrive by 7am.

❷ St. Botolph, Aldersgate

Aldersgate St EC1. **Map** 15 A1. **Tel** 020 7283 1670. 🚇 St. Paul's, Barbican, Moorgate. **Open** 10am–3pm Mon–Fri (to 2pm Mon & Wed). ✝ 1pm Tue. ♿

A modest late Georgian exterior (completed in the late 18th century) conceals a flamboyant, well-preserved interior that has a finely decorated plaster ceiling, a rich brown wooden organ case and galleries, and an oak pulpit resting on a carved palm tree. The original box pews have been kept in the galleries rather than in the body of the church. Some of the memorials come from a 14th-century church that originally existed on the site.

The former churchyard alongside was converted in 1880 into a relaxing green space known as Postman's Park, because it was used by workers from the nearby Post Office headquarters. In the late 19th century, the Victorian artist G. F. Watts dedicated one of the walls to a quirky collection of plaques that commemorate acts of bravery and self-sacrifice by ordinary people. Some of these plaques are still here and can be viewed. There are three St. Botolph churches in the City; the other two can be found at Aldgate and in Bishopsgate.

❸ Museum of London

See pp168–9.

❹ Charterhouse

Charterhouse Sq EC1. **Map** 6 F5.
🚇 Barbican. **Open** for 📷 Apr–Aug: reserve well in advance (see website for details). **w** thecharterhouse.org

The Tudor gateway on the north side of the square leads to the site of a former Carthusian monastery, which was dissolved under Henry VIII. In 1611 the buildings were converted into a hospital for poor pensioners, and a charity school – called Charterhouse – whose pupils included John Wesley (*see p170*), writer William Thackeray, and Robert Baden-Powell, founder of the Boy Scouts. In 1872 the school, now a top boarding school, relocated to Godalming, Surrey. Part of the original site was subsequently taken over by St. Bartholomew's Hospital medical school. Some of the old buildings survived. These include the chapel and part of the cloisters. Today Charterhouse is still home to more than 40 pensioners, who are supported by the charitable foundation.

Charterhouse: stone carving

❺ Cloth Fair

EC1. **Map** 6 F5. 🚇 Barbican.

This pretty street is named after the notoriously rowdy Bartholomew Fair, which was the main cloth fair in medieval and Elizabethan England, held annually at Smithfield until 1855. Nos. 41 and 42 are fine 17th-century houses and have distinctive two-story wooden bay windows, although their ground floors have since been modernized. The former poet laureate John Betjeman, who died in 1984, lived in No. 43 for most of his life. It has now been turned into a wine bar named after him.

17th-century houses: Cloth Fair

❻ St. Bartholomew-the-Great

West Smithfield EC1. **Map** 6 F5. **Tel** 020 7600 0440. 🚇 Barbican. **Open** 8:30am–5pm Mon, Tue, 8:30am–9:30pm Wed–Fri, 10:30am–4pm Sat, 8:30am–8pm Sun. **Closed** Christmas week. ✝ 9am, 11am, 6:30pm Sun. 📷 ♿ 🎧 by appt. 📷 🎵 Concerts. 🆆 greatstbarts.com

One of London's oldest churches was founded in 1123 by the monk Rahere, whose tomb is inside. A courtier of Henry I, he dreamed that St. Bartholomew saved him from a winged monster.

The 13th-century arch used to be the door to the church until the nave of that earlier building was pulled down when Henry VIII dissolved the priory. Today the arch leads from West Smithfield to the burial ground –

the gatehouse above it is from a later period. The present building retains the crossing and chancel of the original, with its round arches and other fine Norman detailing. There are also some fine Tudor monuments. The painter William Hogarth was baptized here in 1697.

Parts of the church have been used for secular purposes. In 1725, US statesman Benjamin Franklin worked for a printer in the Lady Chapel. The church also featured in the movies *Four Weddings and a Funeral*, *Shakespeare in Love*, and *The Other Boleyn Girl*.

❼ Barbican

Silk St EC2. **Map** 7 A5. **Tel** 020 7638 4141. **Tel** 020 7638 4141. 🚇 Barbican, Moorgate. Barbican Centre **Open** 9am–11pm Mon–Sat, noon–11pm Sun, public hols. 📷 🖥 🎧 🅿 📷 ♿ induction loop. *See Entertainment pp334–45.* 🆆 barbican.org.uk

An ambitious piece of 1960s city planning, this residential, commercial, and arts complex was begun in 1962 on a site devastated by World War II bombs, and not completed for nearly 20 years. Residential high-rises surround the Barbican Centre, the arts complex, which also includes an ornamental lake and fountains.

The old city wall turned a corner here, and substantial remains are still clearly visible (particularly so from the Museum of London – *see pp168–9*). The word "barbican" means a defensive tower over a gate –

St. Bartholomew's gatehouse

perhaps the architects were trying to live up to the name when they designed this self-sufficient community with formidable defenses against the outside world. Obscure entrances and raised walkways remove pedestrians from the cramped bustle of the City, but, in spite of the signposts and yellow lines on the sidewalks, the complex can be difficult to navigate.

As well as two theaters and a concert hall, the Barbican Centre has two movie theaters, two galleries, an excellent library, and a surprising conservatory. It is home to the London Symphony Orchestra and the Guildhall School of Music and Drama.

Pretty lake with fountains in the Barbican Centre

❸ Museum of London

Opened in 1976 on the edge of the Barbican, this museum provides a lively account of London life from prehistoric times to the present day. Reconstructed interiors and street scenes are alternated with displays of original domestic artifacts and items found on the museum's archaeological digs. The museum underwent a huge redevelopment of its lower galleries in 2010, which opened up 25 percent more gallery space.

★ **Marble Head of Serapis**
This statue of the Egyptian god of the underworld (2nd–3rd century) was discovered in the temple of Mithras (see p146).

Stairs to Galleries of Modern London

Oliver Cromwell's Death Mask
This plaster copy made from a wax impression acts as a permanent record of how he looked.

Boy's Leather Jerkin
This practical sleeveless jacket (c.1560), decorated with punched hearts and stars, would have been worn over a doublet for extra warmth.

Main entran

Flint Hand Ax
Thousands of these cutting tools (c.350,000–120,000 BC) have been found in the gravels beneath modern London.

Key

- ☐ 450,000BC–AD50: London before London
- ☐ AD50–410: Roman London
- ☐ AD410–1558: Medieval London
- ☐ 1550s–1660s: War, Plague and Fire
- ☐ 1670s–1850s: Expanding City
- ☐ Victorian Walk
- ☐ Sackler Hall
- ☐ 1850s–1940s: People's City
- ☐ 1950s–Today: World City
- ☐ Inspiring London
- ☐ Linbury Gallery
- ☐ City Gallery
- ☐ Temporary Exhibitions

Gallery Guide

The galleries are laid out chronologically, starting on the entrance level with prehistory. Visitors can walk through Roman and medieval London galleries to the War, Plague, and Fire gallery, which includes a special display on the Great Fire. On the lower level, they can learn about London from 1666 to the present day, and see the Lord Mayor of London's spectacular State Coach.

Tobacconist
The Victorian Walk uses several original shop fronts and objects to recreate the atmosphere of late 19th-century London.

The Expanding City Gallery explores London after the Great Fire.

Ignazio Pluchino Shoes
The Sicilian opened his shoemaking business in London in 1900. He made high-quality shoes for the wealthy.

Selfridges Elevators
These bronze and cast iron Brandt Edgar elevators were installed in 1928.

Beatles Dress
Made in 1964, this cotton dress is printed with the Beatles' heads alongside a guitar that features their signatures.

★ Lord Mayor's Coach
Finely carved and painted, this gilded coach (c.1757) is paraded once a year during the Lord Mayor's Show (see p57.)

St. Giles, Cripplegate

❽ St. Giles, Cripplegate

Fore St EC2. **Map** 7 A5. **Tel** 020 7638 1997. ⊖ Barbican, Moorgate. **Open** 11am–4pm Mon, Fri. 🕇 8:30am Mon–Thu, 10am, 4pm Sun. 🎦 2–5pm Tue. 🚹 🇼 stgilescripplegate.co.uk

Completed in 1550, this church survived the ravages of the Great Fire in 1666, but was so badly damaged by a World War II bomb that only the tower survived. St. Giles was refurbished during the 1950s to serve as the parish church of the Barbican, and now stands awkwardly amid the stark modernity of the Barbican. It is one of the few UK churches with two complete organs.

Oliver Cromwell married Elizabeth Bourchier here in 1620, and the poet John Milton was buried here in 1674. Well-preserved remains of London's Roman and medieval walls can be seen to the south.

❾ Whitbread's Brewery

Chiswell St EC1. **Map** 7 B5. ⊖ Barbican, Moorgate. **Closed** to the public.

In 1736, when he was just 16, Samuel Whitbread became an apprentice brewer in Bedford. By the time of his death in 1796, his Chiswell Street brewery (which he bought in 1750) was brewing 240,000 gallons (909,000 liters) per year. The building has not been used as a brewery since 1976, when it was converted into rooms rented out for private functions – they are

no longer open to the public. The Porter Tun room, which is now used as a banqueting suite, boasts the largest timber post roof in Europe, and has a huge span of 60 ft (18 m).

The street's 18th-century buildings are well-preserved examples of their period, and are worth a look from the outside. A plaque on one commemorates a visit to the brewery in 1787 by George III and Queen Charlotte.

❿ Bunhill Fields

City Rd EC1. **Map** 7 B4. **Tel** 020 7374 4127 (City Gardens). ⊖ Old St. **Open** Apr–Sep: 7:30am–7pm Mon–Fri, 9:30am–7pm Sat, Sun & public hols; Oct–Mar: 7:30am–4pm Mon–Fri; 9:30am–4pm Sat, Sun & public hols. **Closed** Jan 1, Dec 25–26. 🎦 see website for details. 🚹 call first. 🇼 **cityoflondon.gov.uk/ openspaces**

This spot was first designated a cemetery after the Great Plague of 1665 *(see p27)*, when it was

William Blake's gravestone at Bunhill Fields

enclosed by a brick wall and gates. Twenty years later it was allocated to Nonconformists, who were banned from being buried in churchyards because of their refusal to use the Church of England prayer book. The cemetery is situated on the edge of the City and shaded by large plane trees. There are monuments to the well-known writers Daniel Defoe, John Bunyan and William Blake, as well as to members of the Cromwell family. John Milton wrote his epic poem *Paradise Lost* while he lived in Bunhill Row, located on the west side of the cemetery. The website has further information on the burial records of Bunhill Fields.

Wesley's Chapel

⓫ Wesley's Chapel– Leysian Mission

49 City Rd EC1. **Map** 7 B4. **Tel** 020 7253 2262. ⊖ Old St, Moorgate. **Open** 10am–4pm Mon–Sat, 12:30–1:45pm Sun. **Closed** between Christmas & New Year, public & bank hols (except Good Friday). 🚹 ground floor of John Wesley's house. 🕇 9:45am (not 1st Sun of month), 11am Sun, 12:45pm Wed. 🎦 groups book ahead. 🎵 Free lunchtime recitals: Tue. 🇼 **wesleyschapel.org.uk**

John Wesley, the founder of the Methodist church, laid the chapel's foundation stone in 1777. He preached here until his death in 1791, and is buried behind the chapel. Next door is the house where he lived, and today some of his furniture, books, and other assorted possessions are on display there.

The chapel, adorned in a spartan style, in accordance with Wesley's austere religious principles, has columns made from ships' masts. Baroness Thatcher, the first British woman prime minister (1979–90), was married here. Beneath it is a small museum about the history of the Methodist church.

Facade of St. Leonard's Church

⓬ St. Leonard's Church

Shoreditch High St E1. **Map** 8 D3. 🚇 Old Street, Liverpool Street. **Open** noon–2pm Mon–Fri. 🕆 10:30am Sun. 🎵 Concerts and theatrical performances. 🌐 **shoreditchchurch.wordpress.com**

Standing as it does on the spot where several major Roman roads converged, this has been a site of worship for millennia. The Norman St. Leonard's was the original "actors' church" and many famous names of Tudor theater are buried in the crypt, including Richard Burbage, who played the first Hamlet, Macbeth, and Romeo, and his brother Cuthbert, founder of the Globe Theatre.

The current Palladian-style church was erected in 1736–40, making it the oldest building in Shoreditch. Its fine acoustics make it popular as a performance space with musicians.

⓭ Petticoat Lane

Middlesex St E1. **Map** 16 D1. 🚇 Aldgate East, Aldgate, Liverpool St. **Open** 10am–2:30pm Mon–Fri, 9am–2pm Sun. *See Shops and Markets pp324–33.*

In Queen Victoria's prudish reign, the name of this street, long famous for its market, was changed to the respectable but colorless Middlesex Street. That is still its official designation, but the old name, derived from the petticoats and lace sold here by the Huguenots who came from France, has stuck, and is now applied to the market held every Sunday morning in this and the surrounding streets. Numerous attempts were made to stop the market, but it was allowed by Act of Parliament in 1936. A great variety of goods is sold, but there is still a bias toward clothing, especially leather coats. The atmosphere is noisy and cheerful, with Cockney vendors making use of their wit to attract customers. There are scores of snack bars, and many of these sell traditional Jewish food such as salt beef sandwiches and bagels with smoked salmon.

Entrance to Whitechapel Gallery

⓮ Whitechapel Art Gallery

77–82 Whitechapel High St E1. **Map** 16 E1. **Tel** 020 7522 7888. 🚇 Aldgate East, Aldgate. **Open** 11am–6pm Tue–Sun, (to 9pm Thu). **Closed** Jan 1, Dec 25–26. 🅿 occasionally for exhibitions. ♿🄲🄳🄼 Wide range of talks & events. 🌐 **whitechapelgallery.org**

A striking Art Nouveau facade by C. Harrison Townsend fronts this light, airy gallery, founded in 1901 and expanded in the 1980s and again in 2007–9. Situated close to Brick Lane and the area's burgeoning art scene, this independent gallery was founded with the aim of bringing great art to the people of East London. Today it enjoys an excellent international reputation for high-quality shows of major contemporary artists. In the 1950s and 1960s the likes of Jackson Pollock, Robert Rauschenberg, Anthony Caro, and John Hoyland all displayed their work here. In 1970 David Hockney's first exhibition was held here.

The gallery has a well-stocked arts bookshop, a relaxed whole food café, and an award-winning restaurant.

Bustling Petticoat Lane Market

18th-century Fournier Street

industry). Completed in 1729, the building was mauled by alterations in the 1850s. By 1960 it was derelict, narrowly escaping demolition. In 1976 the Friends of Christ Church Spitalfields was formed to restore the building to its former glory – a goal achieved in 2004. It is now used as a music venue.

Christ Church still dominates the surrounding streets. The impression of size and strength created by its portico and spire is continued inside by such features as the high ceiling and the gallery.

Bengali sweet factory: Brick Lane

⓯ Old Spitalfields Market

Commercial St E1. **Map** 8 E5. 🔵 Liverpool St, Aldgate. **Open** General Market Stands: 10am–5pm Sun–Wed (from 9am Sun); Antiques & Vintage: 9am–5pm Thu; Fashion & Art: 10am–4pm Fri; Themed Market Day: 11am–5pm Sat. *See Shops and Markets pp324–33.*
W oldspitalfieldsmarket.com

One of the oldest markets in London, Spitalfields started life as a produce market in 1682, and foods such as organic greens, breads, and preserves can still be purchased here. It is open during the week, but on Sundays crowds come in search of vintage clothing, bric-a-brac, crafts, and innovative fashion.

⓰ Christ Church, Spitalfields

Commercial St E1. **Map** 8 E5. **Tel** 020 7377 2440. 🔵 Liverpool St. **Open** 10am–4pm Mon–Fri (unless in use as venue), 1–4pm Sun. 🕆 1:10pm Tue; 8:30am & 10:30amSun. Concerts ♿ 📷 book ahead. **W** ccspitalfields.org

The finest of Nicholas Hawksmoor's six churches, Christ Church was commissioned by parliament in the Fifty New Churches Act of 1711, aimed at combating the threat of Nonconformism. It was intended to make a powerful statement in an area fast becoming a Huguenot stronghold. (The Protestant Huguenots had fled from persecution in Catholic France and came to Spitalfields to work in the local silk-weaving

⓱ Fournier Street

E1. **Map** 8 E5. 🔵 Aldgate East, Liverpool Street.

The 18th-century houses on the north side of this street have attics with broad windows that were designed to give maximum light to the silk-weaving French Huguenot community who lived here. Even now, the textile trade lives on, in this and nearby streets, still dependent on immigrant labor. Today it is Bengalis who toil at sewing machines in workrooms that are as cramped as they were when the Huguenots used them. Working conditions have improved, however, and many of the sweatshops have been converted into showrooms for companies that now have modern factories away from the central city.

Christ Church, Spitalfields

⓲ London Jamme Masjid

59 Brick Lane E1. **Map** 8 E5. 🔵 Liverpool St, Aldgate East.

Muslims now worship here, in a building whose life story as a religious site reflects the history of immigration in the area. Built in 1743 as a Huguenot chapel, it was a synagogue in the 19th century, a Methodist chapel in the early 20th century, and has been a mosque since 1976.

⓳ Spitalfields Centre Museum of Immigration & Diversity

19 Princelet St E1. **Map** 8 E5. **Tel** 020 7247 5352. 🔵 Liverpool St. **Open** some days & by appt (call to check).
W 19princeletstreet.org.uk

A little Victorian synagogue hidden behind a 1719 Huguenot silk merchant's house with exhibitions celebrating the Jewish and other peoples who arrived as immigrants and settled in London's East End. This historic gem is under constant threat of closure due to lack of funding.

⓴ Brick Lane

E1. **Map** 8 E5. 🔵 Liverpool St, Aldgate East, Shoreditch. Market **Open** dawn–noon Sun. *See Shops and Markets pp324–33.*

Once a lane running through brickfields, this is now the busy center of London's Bengali district. Its shops and houses,

The grand bedroom of Dennis Severs House

some dating from the 18th century, have seen waves of immigrants of many nationalities, and most now sell food, spices, silks, and saris. The first Bengalis to live here were sailors who came in the 19th century. In those days it was a predominantly Jewish quarter, and a few Jewish shops remain, including a 24-hour bagel shop at No. 159.

On Sundays a large market is held here and in the surrounding streets, complementing Petticoat Lane (see p169). At the northern end of Brick Lane is the former Black Eagle Brewery, a medley of 18th- and 19th-century industrial architecture, now reflected in, and set off by, a sympathetic mirror-glassed extension.

㉑ Dennis Severs House

18 Folgate St E1. **Map** 8 D5. **Tel** 020 7247 4013. ⊖ Liverpool St. **Open** noon–4pm Sun (book ahead); noon–2pm 1st & 3rd Mon of month; for further dates see website. Private and group bookings welcome. ♿ W **dennissevershouse.co.uk**

At No. 18 Folgate Street, built in 1724, the late designer and performer Dennis Severs recreated a historical interior that takes you on a journey from the 17th to the 19th centuries. It offers what he called "an adventure of the imagination … a visit to a time-mode rather than … merely a look at a house." The rooms are like a series of *tableaux vivants*, as if the occupants had simply left for a

18th-century portrait: Dennis Severs House

moment. There is broken bread on the plates, wine in the glasses, fruit in the bowl; the candles flicker and horses' hooves clatter on the cobbles outside. This highly theatrical experience is far removed from more usual museum recreations and is not suitable for children under 12. Praised by many, including artist David Hockney, it is truly unique. The house's motto is "you either see it or you don't." Around the corner on Elder Street are two of London's earliest surviving terraces, where many of the Georgian red-brick houses have been carefully restored.

㉒ Columbia Road Market

Columbia Rd E2. **Map** 8 D3. ⊖ Liverpool St, Old St, Bethnal Green. **Open** 8am–3pm Sun. *See Shops and Markets pp324–33.*

A visit to this flower and plant market is one of the most delightful things to do on a Sunday morning in London, whether you want to take advantage of the exotic species offered there or not. Set in a well-preserved street of small Victorian shops, it is a lively, sweet-smelling, and colorful event. Apart from the stands, there are several shops selling, among other things, home-made bread and farmhouse cheese, antiques, and interesting objects, many of them flower-related. There is also a Spanish delicatessen and an excellent snack bar that sells bagels and welcome mugs of hot chocolate on chilly winter mornings.

Columbia Road flower market

SOUTHWARK AND BANKSIDE

Southwark once offered an escape route from the City, where many forms of entertainment were banned. Borough High Street was lined with taverns: the medieval courtyards that still run off it mark where they stood. The George survives as the only galleried London inn. Among the illicit pleasures that thrived here were brothels in houses by the river, as well as theaters and bear and cock pits, which were established in the late 16th century. Shakespeare's company was based at the Globe Theatre, which has now been rebuilt close to its original site. Today the south bank of the river has undergone extensive renovation. Riverside attractions range from the Design Museum and Tate Modern, next to the Millennium Bridge, to historic pubs, Borough Market, Southwark Cathedral, and London's tallest building, The Shard.

Sights at a Glance

Historic Streets and Areas
2 Hop Exchange
5 The Old Operating Theatre
7 Cardinal's Wharf
13 Bermondsey

Museums and Galleries
6 Shakespeare's Globe
8 Bankside Gallery
9 Tate Modern
11 Vinopolis
12 Clink Prison Museum
14 The Shard
15 Design Museum

Cathedrals
1 Southwark Cathedral

Pubs
4 George Inn
10 The Anchor

Markets
3 Borough Market

Historic Ships
16 HMS *Belfast*

Restaurants *see pp300–301*
1 Blueprint Café
2 Champor-Champor
3 Dim T - London Bridge
4 José
5 Roast
6 Tapas Brindisa
7 Tito's Peruvian Restaurant
8 Wright Brothers
9 Zucca

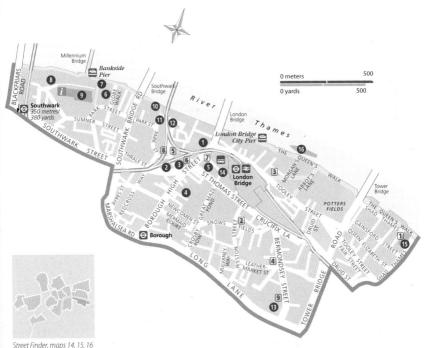

Street Finder, maps 14, 15, 16

◄ Seasonal fruit and vegetables for sale at Borough Market

For keys to symbols *see back flap*

Street-by-Street: Southwark

From medieval times until the 18th century, Southwark
was a venue for the pursuit of illicit pleasures; south of the
Thames, it was out of the jurisdiction of the City authorities.
The 18th and 19th centuries brought docks, warehouses, and
factories. Now it is once again one of London's most exciting
boroughs, with the arrival of Tate Modern, a regenerated
Borough Market, the stunning recreation of Shakespeare's
Globe Theatre, and The Shard, soaring through the clouds.

Southwark Bridge was opened in
1912 to replace a bridge of 1819.

Millennium Bridge

BLACKFRIARS BRIDGE

HOLLAND STREET

SUMNER STREET

PARK STREET

EMERSON STREET

SOUTHWARK BRIDGE ROAD

Key

— Suggested route

| 0 meters | 100 |
| 0 yards | 100 |

❾ ★ Tate Modern
The former Bankside Power Station is
now a powerhouse of contemporary
art, its spectacular open spaces
showing off exhibits to perfection.

❻ ★ Shakespeare's Globe
This brilliant recreation of an
Elizabethan theater has open-air
performances in the summer months
and a year-round exhibition.

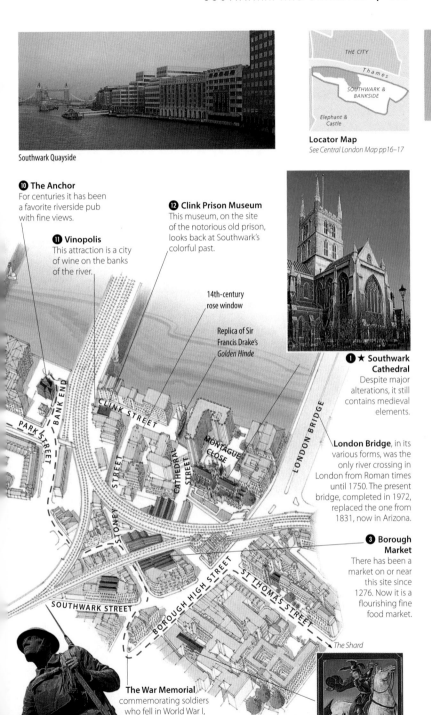

Southwark Quayside

Locator Map
See Central London Map pp16–17

⑩ The Anchor
For centuries it has been a favorite riverside pub with fine views.

⑪ Vinopolis
This attraction is a city of wine on the banks of the river.

⑫ Clink Prison Museum
This museum, on the site of the notorious old prison, looks back at Southwark's colorful past.

14th-century rose window

Replica of Sir Francis Drake's *Golden Hinde*

① ★ Southwark Cathedral
Despite major alterations, it still contains medieval elements.

London Bridge, in its various forms, was the only river crossing in London from Roman times until 1750. The present bridge, completed in 1972, replaced the one from 1831, now in Arizona.

③ Borough Market
There has been a market on or near this site since 1276. Now it is a flourishing fine food market.

The Shard

The War Memorial, commemorating soldiers who fell in World War I, was erected in 1924 on Borough High Street, where it has become a powerful landmark.

④ George Inn
This is London's only surviving traditional, galleried inn.

THE GEORGE

❶ Southwark Cathedral

Montague Close SE1. **Map** 15 B3.
Tel 020 7367 6700. London
Bridge. **Open** 8am–6pm Mon–Fri,
8:30am–6pm Sat & Sun. daily
(check website).
Concerts. **cathedral.southwark.
anglican.org**

This church did not become a
cathedral until 1905. However,
some parts of it date back to the
12th century, when the building
was attached to a priory, and
many of its medieval features
remain. The memorials are
fascinating, including a late-
13th-century wooden effigy
of a knight. John Harvard, the
first benefactor of Harvard
University, was baptized here
in 1607, and there is a chapel
named after him.

In 2000 the cathedral was
restored in a multi-million-
dollar restoration program,
including the addition of new
buildings, which house a shop
and a refectory. The exterior has
been landscaped to create an
herb garden and an attractive
Millennium Courtyard that leads
to the riverside.

Southwark Cathedral's Shakespeare Window

❷ Hop Exchange

Southwark St SE1. **Map** 15 B4.
London Bridge. **Closed** to the public.

Southwark, with its easy access
to Kent where hops are grown,
was a natural venue for brewing
beer and trading hops. In 1866
this building was constructed as
the center of that trade. Now a
hospitality venue, it retains its
original pediment complete

The George Inn, now owned by the National Trust

with carved scenes showing
the hop harvest, and iron gates
with a hop motif.

❸ Borough Market

8 Southwark St SE1. **Map** 15 B4.
London Bridge. Retail market:
Open 10am–5pm Wed–Thu,
10am–6pm Fri, 8am–5pm Sat.
boroughmarket.org.uk

Borough Market was once an
exclusively wholesale fruit and
vegetable market, which had
its origins in medieval times,
and moved to its current
atmospheric position beneath
the railroad tracks in 1756. A
popular fine food market, it sells
gourmet foods from Britain and
Europe, as well as quality fruit
and vegetables, and organic
meat, fish, and dairy products.

❹ George Inn

77 Borough High St SE1. **Map** 15 B4.
Tel 020 7407 2056. London Bridge,
Borough. **Open** 11am–11pm Mon–Sun.
See Restaurants and Pubs pp308–11.

Dating from the 17th century,
this building is the only example
of a traditional galleried
coaching inn left in London and
is mentioned by Dickens in *Little
Dorrit*. It was rebuilt after the
Southwark fire of 1676 in a style
that dates back to the Middle
Ages. Originally there would
have been three wings around
a courtyard where plays were

staged in the 17th century. In
1889 the north and east wings
were demolished, so there is
only one wing remaining.

The inn, now owned by
the National Trust, is still a
restaurant. Perfect on a cold,
wet day, the pub has a well-
worn, comfortable atmosphere.
In the summer, the yard fills
with picnic tables, and patrons
are occasionally entertained by
actors and morris dancers.

Ancient remedies, the Old Operating Theatre

❺ The Old Operating Theatre

9a St Thomas St SE1. **Map** 15 B4.
Tel 020 7188 2679. London Bridge.
Open 10:30am–5pm daily.
Closed Dec 15–Jan 5.
limited. **thegarret.org.uk**

Guy's & St. Thomas' Hospital,
one of the oldest in Britain,
stood here from its foundation
in the 12th century until it was
moved west in 1862. At this
time nearly all of its buildings
were demolished in order to
make way for the railroad.
The women's operating room
(The Old Operating Theatre

Museum and Herb Garret) survived only because it was located away from the main buildings, in a garret over the hospital church. The UK's oldest operating room, dating back to 1822, it lay bricked up and forgotten until the 1950s. It has now been equipped just as it would have been in the early 19th century, before the discovery of either anesthetics or antiseptics. The display shows how patients were blindfolded, gagged, and bound to the wooden operating table, while a box of sawdust underneath was used to catch the blood.

Shakespeare's Henry IV (performed at the Globe Theatre around 1600)

❻ Shakespeare's Globe

New Globe Walk SE1. **Map** 15 A3. **Tel** 020 7902 1400. Box Office: **Tel** 020 7401 9919. 🚇 Southwark, London Bridge. Exhibition open May–Sep: 9am–5pm; Oct–Apr: 10am–5pm daily. 🎫 📷 every 30 min. (Rose Theatre tours for groups of 15 or more by appt only.) Performances Apr–early Oct. 🅿️ 🚻 🍴 📷
Ⓦ **shakespearesglobe.com**

Built on the banks of the Thames, Shakespeare's Globe is an impressive reconstruction of the Elizabethan theater where many of his plays were first performed. The circular wooden structure is open in the middle, leaving some of the audience exposed to the elements. Those holding seat tickets have a roof over their heads. The performances happen only in summer, and seeing a play here is a thrilling experience, with top-quality acting. There is an informative tour for visitors, and groups may make arrangements to see the foundations of the nearby Rose Theatre. Beneath the theater, and open year-round, is Shakespeare's Globe Exhibition, which brings his work and times to life.

❼ Cardinal's Wharf

SE1. **Map** 15 A3. 🚇 London Bridge.

A small group of 17th-century houses still survives here in the shadow of Tate Modern art gallery (see pp180–83). A plaque commemorates Christopher Wren's stay here while St. Paul's Cathedral (see pp150–53) was being built. He would have had a particularly fine view of the works. It is thought that the wharf got its name from Cardinal Wolsey, who was Bishop of Winchester in 1529.

❽ Bankside Gallery

48 Hopton St SE1. **Map** 14 F3. **Tel** 020 7928 7521. 🚇 Blackfriars, Southwark. **Open** 11am–6pm daily. **Closed** Jan 1, Dec 24–26. ♿ 📷 Lectures.
Ⓦ **banksidegallery.com**

This modern riverside gallery is the headquarters of two historic British societies, namely the Royal Watercolour Society and the Royal Society of Painter-Printmakers. The members of

View from the Founders' Arms

these societies are elected by their peers in a tradition that dates back over 200 years. Their work embraces both established and experimental practices. The gallery's permanent collection is not on display here, but there are constantly changing temporary displays of contemporary water-colors and original artists' prints. The exhibitions feature the work of both societies, and many of the pieces on display are for sale. There is also a superb specialty art shop that sells both books and materials.

There is an unparalleled view of St. Paul's Cathedral from the nearby pub, the Founders' Arms, built on the site of the foundry where the cathedral's bells were cast. South of here, on Hopton Street, is a series of almshouses that date from 1752.

Row of 17th-century houses on Cardinal's Wharf

❾ Tate Modern

Looming over the south bank of the Thames River, Tate Modern occupies the converted Bankside power station, a dynamic space for one of the world's premier collections of contemporary art. Up until 2000, the Tate collection was shown at three galleries: Tate St. Ives, Tate Liverpool, and the former Tate Gallery, now Tate Britain *(see pp82–85)*. With the addition of Tate Modern, space was made for a growing acquisition of contemporary art. Tate Modern continually rehangs its collection, so works and exhibitions may vary. A new extension is currently under construction.

The lightbeam, a two-story glass box, allows light to filter into the upper galleries.

Restaurant at Tate Modern
The restaurant on level 6 of the Tate Modern boasts a view that's a veritable work of art in its own right, with floor-to-ceiling windows overlooking the Thames and St. Paul's Cathedral.

The Turbine Hall
The massive scale of this space – it covers 35,520 sq ft (3,300 sq m) – presents an unusual challenge for the artists who install pieces here.

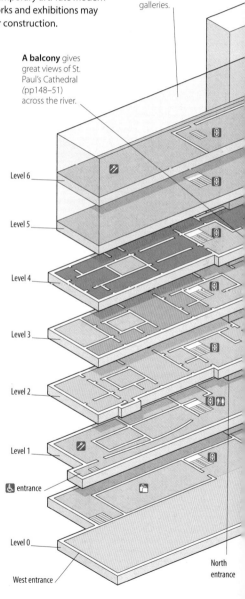

A balcony gives great views of St. Paul's Cathedral (pp148–51) across the river.

Level 6

Level 5

Level 4

Level 3

Level 2

Level 1

♿ entrance

Level 0

West entrance

North entrance

Key to Floor Plan

- Turbine Hall
- Transformed Visions
- Poetry and Dream
- Energy and Process
- Structure and Clarity
- Temporary exhibition space
- Non-exhibition space

Facade of Tate Modern
The imposing former power station is a recognizable building along the river. It is the perfect space to house a vast collection of contemporary art.

Interacting with Art
Tate Modern has won awards for its handheld multimedia guides, which present audio commentary alongside images, film clips, and games. The gallery's latest digital project, Bloomberg Connects, enables members of the public to actively connect with art, artists, and other visitors. A digital drawing bar allows people to respond visually and see large-scale

versions of their art projected on the wall. Visitors can compose captions to artworks, bringing their own experiences to bear. Screens on the walls throughout the building display visitors' ideas and comments. Through this interactive digital space, visitors become participants and co-creators of modern art.

Quattro Stagioni
(1993–4)
Cy Twombly's four paintings depict the changes of light and color over the seasons.

★ Fish (1926)
Constantin Brancusi attempted to portray the "spirit" of a fish in this abstract work constructed from bronze, metal and wood.

Gallery Guide
The main west entrance opens into the expansive, sloped Turbine Hall. From here, a flight of stairs leads to the café and foyer of level 1, and an escalator whisks visitors straight up to gallery level 2. Temporary exhibitions are on levels 2 and 3, while level 4 is again devoted to galleries. Level 5 is members' access only, but a superb restaurant and spectacular city views can be found on level 6.

Exploring Tate Modern

Tate Modern's displays are arranged into four thematic wings, each of which revolves around a large central room that focuses on a key period of modern art: Cubism, Surrealism, postwar painting and sculpture, and Minimalism. Around these focal points, smaller, changing displays explore how each movement reflects earlier artistic practice or influenced subsequent developments. Works shown here are examples of what might be on display.

Transformed Visions

The Transformed Visions wing is largely devoted to works from 1945–60, which demonstrates how new forms of abstraction and expressive figuration arrived in the US and Europe in the aftermath of World War II. Artists showcased in these rooms – such as Francis Bacon, Willem de Kooning, and Germaine Richier – were all associated with the existentialist movement, and their works deal with a new image of the human form in primitive and thought-provoking ways. Germaine Richier's *Chessboard* (1959) is one such key work on display here. This group of five sculpted and painted plaster figures is semi-abstracted, combining human and animal characteristics.

Mark Rothko's Seagram murals (1958–9) are also featured in this wing. This series of canvases had originally been commissioned by the opulent Four Seasons restaurant, located in the Seagram building in New York. The group of paintings, entitled *Red on Maroon* and *Black on Maroon*, are of open, rectangular, windowlike forms and are somber in mood. Rothko eventually decided to withhold the murals from the restaurant as he did not want them to be enjoyed only by the privileged. Rothko ultimately donated the murals to the late in 1970.

This wing also displays new works that focus on conflict and redemption.

Poetry and Dream

The central concept of Poetry and Dream is the process by which modern and contemporary art develops out of what has gone before, while also fueling our understanding of these past movements. Poetry and Dream illustrates this primary concept using the key artists of the Surrealist movement, including Salvador Dalí, René Magritte, and Pablo Picasso. After identifying key Surrealist themes, techniques, and principles, the wing invites visitors to examine works by more modern figures such as Cindy Sherman, Louise Bourgeois, and Francis Bacon and illustrates how these artists invoke the legacy of their Surrealist predecessors. Further rooms focus on the use of film as a Surrealist medium; Cy Twombly and Joseph Beuys; Susan Hiller and her installation piece *From the Freud Museum* (1991–6); and the survival of Realism alongside the burgeoning Surrealist movement using works by André Derain, Max Beckman, and Diego Rivera.

Section of *From the Freud Museum* (1991–6) by Susan Hiller

Energy and Process

"Artists' interest in transformation and natural forces" is the concept behind this fascinating sequence of 11 rooms. Room 1 contrasts the work of painter Kasimir Malevich, a pioneer of the early-20th-century avant-garde, and contemporary

The facade, chimney, and lightbeam of Tate Modern

Bankside Power Station

This forbidding fortress was designed in 1947 by Sir Giles Gilbert Scott, the architect of Battersea Power Station, Waterloo Bridge, and London's famous red telephone boxes. The power station is of steel-framed brick skin construction, comprising over 4.2 million bricks. The Turbine Hall was designed to accommodate huge oil-burning generators, and three vast oil tanks are still in situ, buried under the ground just south of the building. The tanks are to be employed in a future stage of Tate Modern development. The power station itself was converted by Swiss architects Herzog and de Meuron, who designed the two-story glass box, or lightbeam, which runs the length of the building. This serves to flood the upper galleries with light and also provides wonderful views of London.

sculptor Richard Serra, known for his sheet-metal assemblages. Nontraditional approaches to canvas are explored in room 2. Sculptures made from everyday materials – sometimes organic, sometimes industrial – are featured in room 3. Photography is the focus in room 4, with work from Ana Mendieta. More sculpture follows in room 5 with work by the Italian sculptor Marisa Merz, who applies craft techniques to industrial materials. Room 6 brings together three representatives of the Arte Povera school – Boetti, Fabro, and Pistoletto. Magdalena Abakanowicz's striking, sculptural textiles are found in room 7. Room 8 documents artistic "interventions" in the natural landscape, and room 9 highlights a video installation by Brazilian artist Lucia Nogueira. In Room 10 you can view an early video art piece – Juan Downey's *Video Trans Americas*. Finally, room 11 has an installation by artists Peter Fischli and David Weiss, whose work re-creates cheap, mass-produced objects.

Dynamic Suprematism (1915 or 1916) by Kazimer Malevich

Structure and Clarity

The Structure and Clarity wing begins with two large-scale masterpieces in room 1: Henri Matisse's *Snail* (1953) and Bridget Riley's *Deny II* (1967). Both works are experiments in color, shape, and tonality. Room 2 focuses on the abstract art of the interwar years. Following World War I, artists sought a utopian ideal

Untitled (1964) by Larry Bell

for art and society, and aimed to remove art from human conflict. This resulted in producing nonfigurative works of cool geometric compositions. The movement is represented with major works by figures such as Wassily Kandinsky and Constantin Brancusi, whose bronze, metal, and wood sculpture *Fish*, created in 1926, is on display here.

The surrounding rooms explore the impact of abstraction on various media including film and photography with works by Werner Mantz and Sameer Makerius in room 4. Room 5 presents artists from the mid-20th century whose works dealt with form, space, and movement. The minimalist art of the 1960s, which not only echoed the works of the 1920s and 1930s but also had its own distinct style, is featured in this wing

too. Works by Larry Bell, Jo Baer, and Carl Andre can be found in rooms 7 and 8, including the latter's *Equivalent III* (1966) – the last in a series of *Equivalent* sculptures, each consisting of a rectangular arrangement of 120 firebricks.

Special Exhibitions

To complement its permanent collection, Tate Modern presents a program of exhibitions including three large shows a year (retrospectives of modern masters or surveys of important movements). Smaller-scale projects are dotted around, and occasionally outside, the gallery. Once a year Tate Modern challenges an artist to create a work capable of occupying the vast Turbine Hall. This has resulted in a spectacular display of innovative sculptures and interactive works of art.

Louise Bourgeois was the first artist to exhibit here, with works that included her sculpture *Maman* (1999), a monumental steel spider. Others have included Olafur Eliasson's *The Weather Project* (2003), which lit the Turbine Hall with a giant glowing sun. In 2010, Ai Weiwei's *Sunflower Seeds* filled the hall with 100 million handcrafted porcelain seeds, and in 2012, Tate Modern staged its first live commission using actors – *These associations* created by Tino Sehgal.

Ai Weiwei holds painted ceramic "seeds" from his *Sunflower Seeds* installation (2010)

Pub sign at the Anchor Inn

❿ The Anchor

34 Park St SE1. **Map** 15 A3. **Tel** 020 7407 1577. ⊖ London Bridge. **Open** 11am–11pm Mon–Wed, 11am–midnight Thu–Sat, noon–10:30pm Sun. ♿ ⏸

This is one of London's most famous riverside pubs. It dates from after the Southwark fire of 1676, which devastated the area (see pp26–7). The present building is 18th-century, but traces of much earlier hostelries have been found beneath it. The inn was once connected with a brewery across the road that belonged to Henry Thrale, a close friend of Dr. Johnson (see p142). When Thrale died in 1781, Johnson went to the brewery sale and encouraged the bidders with a phrase that has passed into the English language: "The potential of growing rich beyond the dreams of avarice."

⓫ Vinopolis

1 Bank End SE1. **Map** 15 B3. **Tel** 020 7940 8300. ⊖ London Bridge. **Open** phone or check website for details. **Closed** Jan 1, Dec 25–26. 🅿 ♿ ⏸ ⏸ 🎧 📷 **W** vinopolis.co.uk

Vinopolis is a unique attraction devoted to the enjoyment of wine. Its blend of interactive fun and educational exhibits has made it a popular destination for anyone who wishes to know more about making and drinking wine. Set within cavernous Victorian railroad arches, Vinopolis explores the history of the grape from earliest times and illuminates the process of winemaking from planting the vines through to labeling the bottles. "Tasting stations" provide an opportunity to savor the subject matter along the way.

A selection of choice vintages can be purchased from the wine warehouse after the tour, while the shop has a vast assortment of wine-related merchandise. Cantina Vinopolis offers good food, great service, and, unsurprisingly, high-quality wines.

Replica of Civil War trooper's helmet made in the Clink

⓬ Clink Prison Museum

1 Clink St SE1. **Map** 15 B3. **Tel** 020 7403 0900. ⊖ London Bridge. **Open** Jul–Sep: 10am–9pm daily; Oct–Jun: 10am–6pm Mon–Fri, 10am–7:30pm Sat & Sun. **Closed** Dec 25. 🎧 📷 ⏸ for groups (call first). **W** clink.co.uk

Now a macabre museum, the prison that was once located here first opened in the 12th century. It was owned by successive Bishops of Winchester, who lived in the adjoining palace just east of the museum, of which all that now remains is a lovely rose window. During the 15th century, the prison became known as the "Clink." It finally closed in 1780.

The museum illustrates the history of the prison. Tales of the inmates are told, including those of the numerous prostitutes, debtors, and priests who were incarcerated here. Hands-on displays of instruments of torture leave little to the imagination and are not for the faint-hearted.

⓭ Bermondsey

SE1. **Map** 15 C5. ⊖ London Bridge, Borough. Market **Open** 4am–1pm Fri, starts closing noon. Fashion and Textile Museum: 83 Bermondsey St SE1. **Tel** 020 7407 8664. **Open** 11am–6pm Tue–Sat. 🎧 ♿ ⏸ on request. 🏠 🖥 **W** ftmlondon.org

Bermondsey's winding streets still hold traces of its historic past in the form of medieval, 18th-century, and Victorian buildings. Today it is famous for its antique market. Each Friday at dawn, seriously committed antique dealers trade their latest acquisitions at Bermondsey. There are occasional press reports about long-lost masterpieces changing hands here for a song, and optimists are welcome to try their luck and test their judgment. However, trading starts at the crack of dawn, and the best bargains tend to go before most people are even awake. The **Fashion and Textile Museum** in Bermondsey Street combines an education, exhibition, and visitor center and is a cutting-edge creative hub for contemporary fashion, textiles, and jewelry. A shop sells products by up-and-coming designers.

Antique stand at Bermondsey Market

The Shard, London's tallest building, soaring above Tower Bridge

⑭ The Shard

London Bridge Street. **Map** 15 B4.
🚇 London Bridge. The View: Entrance via Joiner Street. **Tel** 0844 499 7111.
Open 10am–10pm Thu–Sat, 10am–7pm Sun–Wed. **Closed** Dec 25.
🅿 reservations recommended. 🅖
🅓 🆆 theviewfromtheshard.com

Designed by Renzo Piano, the Shard is the tallest building in Western Europe and dominates the London skyline. At 1,016 ft (310-m) high with a crystalline facade, the 95-story building houses offices, restaurants, the five-star Shangri-La hotel, exclusive apartments, and the country's highest observation gallery, the View. Take a high-speed elevator to the top of the building for unobstructed views of the capital. The public galleries on the top four floors have multimedia exhibits.

⑮ Design Museum

Butlers Wharf, Shad Thames SE1.
Map 16 E4. **Tel** 020 7403 6933.
🚇 Tower Hill, London Bridge.
Open 10am–5:45pm daily (last adm: 5:15pm). **Closed** Dec 25–26. 🅿
🅿 Blueprint Café: **Tel** 020 7940 8785
(reservations recommended). 🅓 🅖
🅑 🅖 🆆 designmuseum.org

This museum was the first in the world to be devoted solely to modern and contemporary design when it was founded in 1989. A frequently changing program of exhibitions explores landmarks in modern design history and the most exciting innovations in contemporary design, set against the context of social, cultural, economic, and technological changes.

The Design Museum embraces every area of design, from furniture and fashion, to household products, cars, graphics, websites, and architecture in exhibitions and new design commissions. Each spring the museum hosts Designer of the Year, a national design prize, with an exhibition at which the public can vote for the winner.

The museum is arranged on three floors, with major exhibitions on the first floor. There are smaller displays on the second, which also has an Interaction Space, where visitors can play vintage video games and learn about the designers featured in the museum in the Design at the Design Museum online research archive. The shop and café are on the ground floor. On the first floor is the **Blueprint Café** restaurant, which has stunning views of the Thames.

⑯ HMS Belfast

Morgan's Lane, Tooley St SE1. **Map** 16 D3. **Tel** 020 7940 6300. 🚇 London Bridge, Tower Hill. **Open** Mar–Oct: 10am–6pm daily (last adm 5:45pm); Nov–Feb: 10am–5pm. **Closed** Dec 24–26. 🅿 🅖 limited. 🅓 🅖
🆆 hmsbelfast.iwm.org.uk

Originally launched in 1938 to serve in World War II, HMS *Belfast* was instrumental in the destruction of the German battle cruiser *Scharnhorst* in the battle of North Cape, and also played an important role in the Normandy Landings.

After the war, the battle cruiser, designed for offensive action and for supporting amphibious operations, was sent to work for the United Nations in Korea. The ship remained in service with the British navy until 1965.

Since 1971, the cruiser has been used as a floating naval museum. Part of it has been recreated to show what the ship was like in 1943, when it participated in sinking the German battle cruiser. Other displays portray life on board during World War II, and there are also exhibits relating to the history of the Royal Navy, as well as an interactive Operations Room.

It is also possible for children to take part in educational activity weekends on board the ship.

The now familiar sight of the naval gunship HMS *Belfast* on the Thames

SOUTH BANK

Following the Festival of Britain in 1951, the Southbank Centre grew up around the newly erected Royal Festival Hall. The architecture has been criticized over the years, especially the chunky concrete building that houses the Hayward Gallery, but is now accepted as an important part of London's river frontage. The area is popular with locals and tourists, and is crowded with culture-seekers most evenings and afternoons. As well as the National Theatre and the Old Vic theater, concert halls, and galleries, the South Bank has the BFI Southbank and London's most striking movie theater, the BFI IMAX *(see p339)*. In keeping with Festival of Britain tradition, the South Bank was a focal point for the new millennium, with the raising of the world's highest observation wheel, the London Eye.

Sights at a Glance

Historic Streets and Buildings
9 Lambeth Palace
12 Gabriel's Wharf
13 Waterloo Station

Museums and Galleries
2 Hayward Gallery
7 Florence Nightingale Museum
8 Museum of Garden History
10 Imperial War Museum

Attractions
4 County Hall
5 London Dungeon
6 The London Eye

Theaters and Concert Halls
1 Royal National Theatre
3 Royal Festival Hall
11 The Old Vic

Restaurants *see pp300–301*
1 Anchor and Hope
2 The Laughing Gravy
3 Oxo Tower Restaurant

Street Finder, maps 13, 14, 22

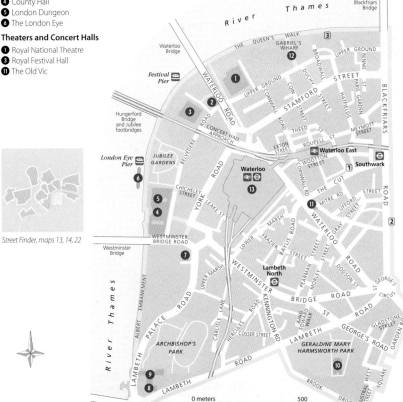

◄ The London Eye on the South Bank

For keys to symbols *see back flap*

Street by Street: Southbank Centre

Originally this was an area of wharves and factories that was badly damaged by bombing during World War II. It was chosen as the site of the 1951 Festival of Britain *(see p34)*, celebrating the centennial of the Great Exhibition *(see pp30–31)*. The Royal Festival Hall is the only building from 1951 to remain, but since then, London's main arts center has been created around it, including the national showplaces for theater, music, and film, and a major art gallery.

To the Strand

❶ ★ National Theatre
Its three auditoriums offer a choice of plays ranging from the classics to the sharpest modern writing.

BFI Southbank, previously the National Film Theatre, was established in 1953 to show historic films *(see p339)*.

Festival Pier

The Queen Elizabeth Hall stages more intimate concerts than the Festival Hall. The adjoining Purcell Room is for chamber music *(see pp340–41)*.

❷ Hayward Gallery
The concrete interior of this venue for important exhibitions is well suited to many modern works.

❸ ★ Royal Festival Hall
The London Philharmonic is one of many world-class orchestras to perform here in the focal point of the Southbank Centre.

0 meters		100
0 yards		100

Hungerford Bridge was built in 1864 to carry both trains and pedestrians to Charing Cross. It now includes two footbridges, the Golden Jubilee Bridges.

❺ ★ The London Eye
The world's tallest cantilevered observation wheel offers passengers a unique view of London.

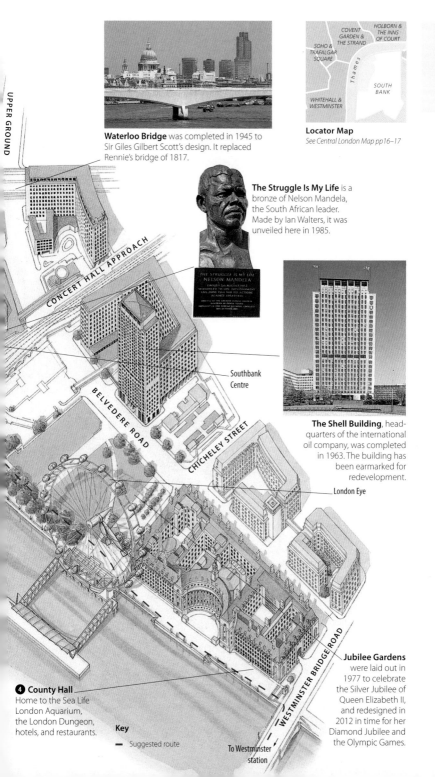

Waterloo Bridge was completed in 1945 to Sir Giles Gilbert Scott's design. It replaced Rennie's bridge of 1817.

Locator Map
See Central London Map pp16–17

HOLBORN & THE INNS OF COURT

COVENT GARDEN & THE STRAND

SOHO & TRAFALGAR SQUARE

Thames

SOUTH BANK

WHITEHALL & WESTMINSTER

UPPER GROUND

The Struggle Is My Life is a bronze of Nelson Mandela, the South African leader. Made by Ian Walters, it was unveiled here in 1985.

THE STRUGGLE IS MY LIFE
NELSON MANDELA

CONCERT HALL APPROACH

Southbank Centre

The Shell Building, headquarters of the international oil company, was completed in 1963. The building has been earmarked for redevelopment.

BELVEDERE ROAD

CHICHELEY STREET

London Eye

4 County Hall
Home to the Sea Life London Aquarium, the London Dungeon, hotels, and restaurants.

WESTMINSTER BRIDGE ROAD

Jubilee Gardens were laid out in 1977 to celebrate the Silver Jubilee of Queen Elizabeth II, and redesigned in 2012 in time for her Diamond Jubilee and the Olympic Games.

Key

— Suggested route

To Westminster station

The facade of the Hayward Gallery

❶ National Theatre

South Bank SE1. **Map** 14 D3. **Tel** 020 7452 3400. 🚇 Waterloo. **Open** 9:30am–8pm Mon–Sat, noon–6pm Sun (performance days). **Closed** Good Fri, Dec 24–25, bank hols. 🈲 during performances. 🅿 🖭 📷 ♿ 🎞 Foyer concerts (free) 5:45pm Mon–Sat, 1pm Sat & Sun, exhibitions. *See Entertainment p336.* 🆆 **nationaltheatre.org.uk**

Even if you don't want to see a play, this well-appointed complex is worth a visit. Sir Denys Lasdun's building was opened in 1976 after 200 years of debate about whether there should be a national theater and where it should be. The company was formed in 1963, under Laurence (later Lord) Olivier, Britain's leading 20th-century actor. The largest of the three theaters is named after him; the others are the Cottesloe and the Lyttleton.

❷ Hayward Gallery

South Bank SE1. **Map** 14 D3. **Tel** 020 7960 4200. 🚇 Waterloo. **Open** noon–6pm Mon, 10am–6pm Tue, Wed, Sat & Sun (to 8pm Thu & Fri). **Closed** Jan, Dec 24–26, between exhibitions. 🈲 ♿ 🖭 📷 🆆 **southbankcentre.co.uk**

The Hayward Gallery is one of London's main venues for large art exhibitions. Its slabby gray concrete exterior is too starkly modern for some tastes, but it is also considered by many as an icon of 1960s "Brutalist" architecture. The Waterloo Sunset Pavilion by Dan Graham

shows a selection of cartoons and artists' videos.

Hayward exhibitions cover classical and contemporary art, but the work of British contemporary artists is particularly well represented.

❸ Royal Festival Hall

South Bank SE1. **Map** 14 D4. **Tel** 0844 875 0073. 🚇 Waterloo. **Open** 10am–11pm daily. **Closed** Dec 25. 🈲 during performances. 🅿 🖭 📷 ♿ Pre-concert talks, exhibitions, free concerts. *See Entertainment p338.* 🆆 **southbankcentre.co.uk**

The Royal Festival Hall was the only structure in the 1951 Festival of Britain (*see p34*) that was designed for permanence. Sir Robert Matthew and Sir Leslie Martin's concert hall was the first major public building project undertaken in London following World War II. It has stood the test of time so well that many of the capital's major arts institutions have gathered around it, and the preserved historic building is today one of the world's leading performance venues. As well as the main auditorium, there is the Clore Ballroom, the poetry-library Spirit Level of three rooms – Blue, White, and Yellow – and also a gift shop, the Riverside Terrace Cafe, Central Bar, and Skylon restaurant. Skylon offers a modern European menu, with an extensive wine and cocktail list.

❹ County Hall

Westminster Bridge Rd SE1. **Map** 13 C4. Aquarium **Tel** 0871 663 1678. 🚇 Waterloo. **Open** 10am–7pm daily (aquarium). **Closed** Dec 25. 🈲 ♿ 🖭 📷 🆆 **visitsealife.com/london**

Once the home of London's elected government, this imposing building now houses a leisure complex. The Sea Life London Aquarium, London Dungeon (*see below*) and *Namco Station*, a computer games hall, occupy the space alongside two hotels, several restaurants, and a health club.

The Aquarium is home to hundreds of aquatic species from all over the world, including stingrays, turtles, and sea scorpions. Special features include an 80-ft (25-m) glass tunnel walkway through a tropical ocean environment, and, for the brave, a Shark Walk across a suspended glass platform.

Shark in a tank at the Sea Life London Aquarium

❺ London Dungeon

Westminster Bridge Rd SE1. **Map** 13 C4. **Tel** 0871 423 2240. 🚇 Waterloo. **Open** 10am–5pm Mon–Fri (from 11am Thu), 10am–6pm Sat–Sun. Extended hours during school breaks. **Closed** Dec 25. 🈲 ♿ 🖭 📷 🆆 **thedungeons.com**

This museum is a great hit with children. It illustrates the most bloodthirsty events in British history, with live actors and special effects. It is played strictly for terror, and screams abound with experiences such as Gruesome Goings-On, which includes live actors and shows; the Great Plague; and Jack the Ripper. Don't miss Henry's Wrath: cruise along a black River Thames to find out what happened to Anne Boleyn and her co-conspirators – but be careful not to get wet.

❻ The London Eye

The EDF Energy London Eye is a 443-ft- (135-m-) high observation wheel. Opened in 2000 as part of London's millennium celebrations, it immediately became one of the city's most recognizable landmarks, notable not only for its size, but for its circularity amid the block-shaped buildings flanking it. Thirty-two capsules, each holding up to 25 people, take a gentle 30-minute round trip. On a clear day, the Eye affords a unique 25-mile (40-km) view, which sweeps over the capital in all directions and on to the countryside and hills beyond.

Houses of Parliament
Seventeen minutes into the flight, the spectacular aerial view of Westminster should not be missed.

The glass capsules are mounted on the outside of the rim, allowing unobstructed 360-degree views.

80 spokes made from 3.7 miles (6 km) of cable hold the structure in tension, strengthening the wheel.

Battersea Power Station
After 15 minutes, the distinctive white smokestacks of this old power station are visible.

Two cables, 197 ft (60 m) long, support the entire structure from concrete bases in Jubilee Gardens.

The wheel rim was floated down the Thames in sections and then assembled on site.

Buckingham Palace
Ten minutes into the journey, the Queen's official residence glides into view.

The Eye turns continuously and moves slowly enough that the capsules are boarded here while moving. The wheel is stopped for those requiring assistance.

❼ Florence Nightingale Museum

2 Lambeth Palace Rd SE1. **Map** 14 D5. **Tel** 020 7620 0374. 🚇 Waterloo, Westminster. **Open** 10am–5pm daily (last adm 4:30pm). **Closed** Dec 25 (and some other dates; call to check). 🎦 📷 🎦 ♿ Videos, lectures.
W florence-nightingale.co.uk

This determined woman captured the nation's imagination as the "Lady of the Lamp," who nursed the wounded soldiers of the Crimean War (1853–6). She also founded Britain's first school of nursing at old St. Thomas' Hospital in 1860.

Obscurely sited near the entrance to St. Thomas' Hospital, this museum gives an account of Nightingale's career through displays of original documents and personal memorabilia. They illustrate her life and the developments she pioneered in health care, until her death in 1910 at the age of 90.

Florence Nightingale

❽ Museum of Garden History

Lambeth Palace Rd SE1. **Map** 21 C1. **Tel** 020 7401 8865. 🚇 Waterloo, Lambeth North, Westminster. **Open** 10:30am–5pm Sun–Fri, 10:30am–4pm Sat. **Closed** 1st Mon of month; Dec 22–Jan 1. 🎦 ♿ 🎦 last Tue of month (free). 🎦 🎦 Library by appt, lectures, films.
W gardenmuseum.org.uk

The world's first museum of garden history is housed in the restored church of St. Mary of Lambeth Palace, and set around a central knot garden. In the grounds are the tombs of John Tradescant, father and son, who, as well as being gardeners to Charles I and Charles II, were adventurous plant hunters and collectors of curiosities. The tomb of William Bligh of *The Bounty* can also be seen here. The museum presents a history of gardening in Britain, illustrated by a selection of

historic garden tools, artifacts, and curiosities. It also runs a program of exhibitions, events, lectures, and educational activities. There is a shop offering garden-related items for freshly inspired gardeners.

❾ Lambeth Palace

SE1. **Map** 21 C1. 🚇 Lambeth North, Westminster, Waterloo, Vauxhall. **Open** for guided tours only. 🎦 Tue & Fri (reservations essential).
W archbishopofcanterbury.org

This palace has housed Archbishops of Canterbury since the 13th century and today remains the Archbishop's official London residence.

The chapel and its undercroft contain elements from the 13th century, but a large part of the rest of the building is far more recent. It has been frequently restored, most recently by Edward Blore in 1828. The Tudor gatehouse, however, dates from 1485 and is one of London's most familiar riverside landmarks.

Until the first Westminster Bridge was built, the horse ferry that operated between here and Millbank was a principal river crossing. The revenues from it went to the archbishop, who received compensation when the bridge opened in 1750.

The Tudor gatehouse

❿ Imperial War Museum

Lambeth Rd SE1. **Map** 22 E1. **Tel** 020 7416 5000. 🚇 Lambeth North, Elephant & Castle. **Open** 10am–6pm daily. **Closed** Dec 24–26. ♿ 🎦 🎦 🎦 Films, lectures.
W iwm.org.uk

This museum is not just concerned with the engines of modern warfare, though massive tanks, artillery, bombs, and aircraft are on show. Some of the most fascinating exhibits in the museum relate more to the impact on the lives of people at home than to the business of fighting. There are displays about food rationing, air raid precautions, censorship, and morale-boosting.

Extracts from wartime films, radio programs, and literature are shown alongside hundreds of photographs, paintings by John Singer Sargent, Graham Sutherland, and Paul Nash, and sculpture by Jacob Epstein. Henry Moore did some evocative

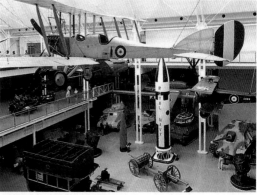

The machinery of war through the ages

drawings of life during the Blitz of 1940, when many Londoners slept in Underground stations to protect themselves from falling bombs. There is also a library with a fascinating archive. The Holocaust exhibition is a major permanent display, using historical material and original artifacts to tell its story.

The museum is housed in part of what used to be the Bethlehem Royal Hospital for the Insane ("Bedlam"), built in 1811. Visitors would come for the afternoon to enjoy the antics of the patients. The hospital moved out to new premises in Surrey in 1930, leaving this vast building empty. Its two large flanking wings were pulled down and this central block converted into the museum, which moved here from its former South Kensington site in 1936.

To mark the centennial of World War I in 2014, the museum has rebuilt its First World War Galleries and Atrium, improving visitor facilities.

The memorial to the dead of World War I at Waterloo Station

and other acts. In 1912 Lillian Baylis became manager, and from 1914 to 1923 she staged all of Shakespeare's plays here. In the 1960s the National Theatre (see p190) was founded and based at this site.

In 1997, Sally Greene, with director Stephen Daldry and others, set up a charitable trust to secure the theatre's future. The Trust set up The Old Vic Theatre Company as a resident company in 2003, with Kevin Spacey as artistic director. There are cheap seats for younger people and pantomimes at Christmas.

⓬ Gabriel's Wharf

56 Upper Ground SE1. **Map** 14 E3. ⊖ Waterloo. *See Shops and Markets pp312–33.*

This pleasant enclave of boutiques, craft shops, and cafés was the product of a long and stormy debate over the future of what was once an industrial riverside area. Residents of Waterloo strongly opposed various proposals for office developments before a community association was able to acquire the site in 1984 and build cooperative housing around the wharf.

Adjoining the market is a small garden and a riverside walkway with marvelous views to the north of the City. The OXO Tower to the east, built in 1928 to surreptitiously advertise a meat extract by means of its window shapes, is now the setting for a fine restaurant (see p301).

⓭ Waterloo Station

York Rd SE1. **Map** 14 D4. **Tel** 08457 484950. ⊖ Waterloo. *See Getting to London p364.*

The terminus for trains to southwest England, Waterloo station was originally built in 1848 but completely remodeled in the early 20th century, with the addition of a grand formal entrance on the northeast corner. Today the spacious concourse, lined with shops, cafés, and bars, makes it one of the most practical of the London rail terminals.

Toward the end of the 20th century, the station was enlarged again to serve as London's first Channel Tunnel rail link to Europe. In the fall of 2007, the Eurostar terminal moved from Waterloo station to its present home at St. Pancras International (see p132).

The area around Waterloo has a great community feel, and it is worth passing down Lower Marsh with its shops, eateries, and street market.

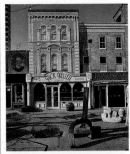

Illusionistic painting on the buildings around Gabriel's Wharf

The Old Vic's facade from 1816

⓫ The Old Vic

Waterloo Rd SE1. **Map** 14 E5. **Tel** 0844 871 7628. ⊖ Waterloo. **Open** for performances only. ♿ ⃠ *See Entertainment pp344–5.*
🆆 oldvictheatre.com

This splendid building dates back to 1818, when it was opened as the Royal Coburg Theatre. In 1833 the name was changed to the Royal Victoria, in honor of the future queen. Shortly after this, the theater became a center for "music hall," the immensely popular Victorian entertainment, which included singers, comedians,

CHELSEA

The showy young shoppers who paraded along the King's Road from the 1960s until the 1980s are more or less gone, along with Chelsea's reputation for extreme behavior established by the bohemian Chelsea Set of writers and artists in the 19th century. Formerly a riverside village, Chelsea became fashionable in Tudor times. Henry VIII liked it so much that he built a small palace (long vanished) here. Artists, including Turner, Whistler, and Rossetti, were attracted by the river views from Cheyne Walk. The historian Thomas Carlyle and the essayist Leigh Hunt arrived in the 1830s and began a literary tradition continued by writers such as the poet Swinburne. Yet Chelsea has always had a raffish element, too: in the 18th century, the pleasure gardens were noted for beautiful courtesans, and the Chelsea Arts Club has held riotous balls for nearly a century. The Chelsea of today is home to expensive boutique shops, upscale restaurants, and exclusive residential areas.

Sights at a Glance

Historic Streets and Buildings
- ❶ King's Road
- ❷ Carlyle's House
- ❺ Cheyne Walk
- ❽ Royal Hospital
- ❿ Sloane Square

Museums
- ❼ National Army Museum
- ❾ Saatchi Gallery

Churches
- ❸ Chelsea Old Church

Gardens
- ❹ Roper's Garden
- ❻ Chelsea Physic Garden

Restaurants *see pp295–297*
- 1 Buona Sera Jam
- 2 Caraffini
- 3 Gallery Mess
- 4 Gordon Ramsay

Street Finder, maps 19, 20

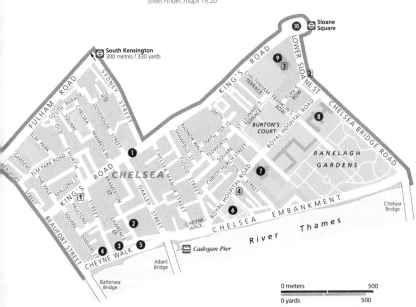

For keys to symbols *see back flap*

Street by Street: Chelsea

Once a peaceful riverside village, Chelsea has been fashionable since Tudor times, when Sir Thomas More, Henry VIII's Lord Chancellor, lived here. Artists, including Turner, Whistler, and Rossetti, were attracted by the views from Cheyne Walk, before a busy main road disturbed its peace. Chelsea's artistic connection is maintained by upscale galleries and antique shops, while enclaves of 18th-century houses preserve a genteel atmosphere.

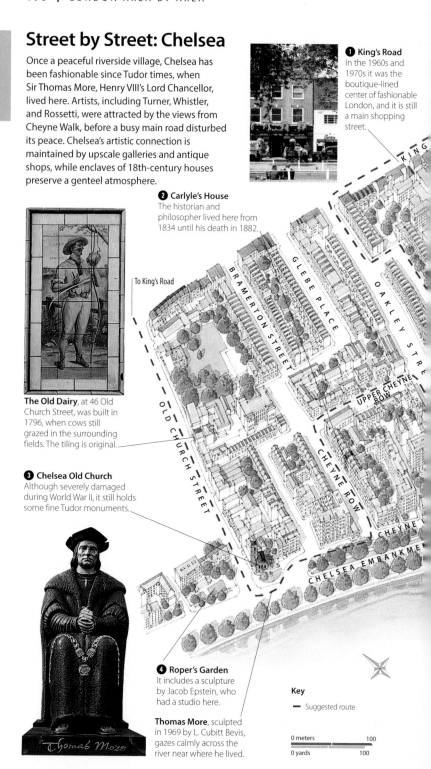

① King's Road
In the 1960s and 1970s it was the boutique-lined center of fashionable London, and it is still a main shopping street.

② Carlyle's House
The historian and philosopher lived here from 1834 until his death in 1882.

To King's Road

The Old Dairy, at 46 Old Church Street, was built in 1796, when cows still grazed in the surrounding fields. The tiling is original.

③ Chelsea Old Church
Although severely damaged during World War II, it still holds some fine Tudor monuments.

④ Roper's Garden
It includes a sculpture by Jacob Epstein, who had a studio here.

Thomas More, sculpted in 1969 by L. Cubitt Bevis, gazes calmly across the river near where he lived.

Key

— Suggested route

0 meters   100
0 yards   100

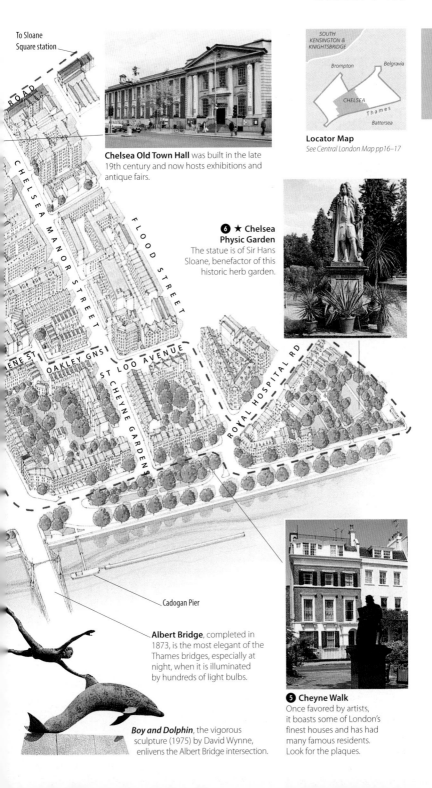

To Sloane
Square station

Chelsea Old Town Hall was built in the late 19th century and now hosts exhibitions and antique fairs.

Locator Map
See Central London Map pp16–17

SOUTH
KENSINGTON &
KNIGHTSBRIDGE

Brompton

Belgravia

CHELSEA

Thames

Battersea

❻ ★ **Chelsea Physic Garden**
The statue is of Sir Hans Sloane, benefactor of this historic herb garden.

Cadogan Pier

Albert Bridge, completed in 1873, is the most elegant of the Thames bridges, especially at night, when it is illuminated by hundreds of light bulbs.

Boy and Dolphin, the vigorous sculpture (1975) by David Wynne, enlivens the Albert Bridge intersection.

❺ **Cheyne Walk**
Once favored by artists, it boasts some of London's finest houses and has had many famous residents. Look for the plaques.

The Pheasantry, King's Road

❶ King's Road

SW3 and SW10. **Map** 19 B3.
🚇 Sloane Square. *See Shops and Markets pp312–33.*

This is Chelsea's central artery, with its wealth of small fashion shops packed with young people looking for designer fashions. The miniskirt revolution of the 1960s began here, and so have many subsequent style trends, perhaps the most famous of them being punk.

Look for the Pheasantry at No. 152, with its columns and statuary. It was built in 1881 as the shop front of a furniture maker's premises, but now conceals a modern restaurant.

This was once also a vibrant area for antiques, but most of the Kings Road's merchants have left. Nearby Kensington Church Street is where to go to find high-quality art and antiques today.

❷ Carlyle's House

24 Cheyne Row SW3. **Map** 19 B4.
Tel 020 7352 7087. 🚇 Sloane Sq, South Kensington. **Open** Mar–Oct: 11am–5pm Wed–Sun (last adm: 4:30pm). 🐾 ♿ 📷 tours 11am–12:30pm Wed–Fri (by appt).
W nationaltrust.org.uk/
carlyleshouse

The historian and founder of the London Library *(see St. James's Square p94),* Thomas Carlyle moved into this modest 18th-century house in 1834, and wrote many of his best-

known books here, notably *The French Revolution* and *Frederick the Great.* His presence made Chelsea more fashionable, and the house became a mecca for some great literary figures. The novelists Charles Dickens and William Thackeray, poet Alfred Lord Tennyson, and naturalist Charles Darwin were all regular visitors here. The house has been restored and looks as it did during Carlyle's lifetime.

Chelsea Old Church in 1860

❸ Chelsea Old Church

64 Cheyne Walk SW3. **Map** 19 A4.
Tel 020 7795 1019. 🚇 Sloane Sq, South Kensington. **Open** 2–4pm, Tue–Thu. ♿ 📷 by appt. ✝ 8am Thu, noon Fri, 8am, 10am, 11am, 12:15pm, 6pm Sun.
W chelseaoldchurch.org.uk

Rebuilt after World War II, this square-towered building does not look old from the outside. However, early prints confirm that it is a careful replica of the medieval church that was largely destroyed by World War II bombs.

The glory of this church is its Tudor monuments. One, to Sir Thomas More, who built a chapel here in 1528, contains an inscription he wrote (in Latin), asking to be buried next to his wife. Among other monuments is a chapel to Sir Thomas Lawrence, who was an Elizabethan merchant, and a 17th-century memorial to Lady Jane Cheyne, after whose husband Cheyne Walk was named. Outside the church is a statue in memory of Sir Thomas More, "statesman, scholar, saint," gazing piously across the river.

❹ Roper's Garden

Cheyne Walk SW3. **Map** 19 A4.
🚇 Sloane Square, South Kensington.

This is a small park outside Chelsea Old Church. It is named after Margaret Roper, Thomas More's daughter, and her husband William, who wrote More's biography. The sculptor Jacob Epstein worked at a studio on the site between 1909 and 1914, and there is a stone carving by him commemorating the fact. The park also contains a figure of a nude woman by Gilbert Carter.

❺ Cheyne Walk

SW3. **Map** 19 B4. 🚇 Sloane Square, South Kensington.

Until Chelsea Embankment was constructed in 1874, Cheyne Walk was a pleasant riverside promenade. Now it overlooks a busy road that has destroyed much of its charm. Many of the 18th-century houses remain, though, bristling with blue plaques celebrating some of the famous people who have lived in them. Most were writers and artists, including J. M. W. Turner, who lived incognito at No. 119; George Eliot, who died at No. 4; and a clutch of writers (Henry James, T. S. Eliot, and Ian Fleming) in Carlyle Mansions.

Thomas More on Cheyne Walk

❻ Chelsea Physic Garden

66 Royal Hospital Road SW3. **Map** 19 C4. **Tel** 020 7352 5646. 🚇 Sloane Square. **Open** 1st week Feb; Apr–Oct: 11am–6pm Sun–Fri, occasional late openings. 🅿️ ♿ call in advance. 🎫 🖥️ 🌿 Gardening school. 🌐 **chelseaphysicgarden.co.uk**

Established by the Society of Apothecaries in 1673 to study plants for medicinal use, this garden was saved from closure in 1722 by a gift from Sir Hans Sloane, whose statue adorns it. Many new varieties have been nurtured in its greenhouses, including cotton sent to the plantations of the southern United States. Visitors to London's oldest botanic garden can see ancient trees and one of Britain's first rock gardens, installed in 1772.

Chelsea Physic Garden in fall

❼ National Army Museum

Royal Hospital Rd SW3. **Map** 19 C4. **Tel** 020 7730 0717. 🚇 Sloane Square. **Open** 10am–5:30pm daily; see website for celebrity speaker programme. **Closed** Jan 1, Dec 24–26. ♿ 🖥️ 🌿 🌐 **nam.ac.uk**

A lively account of the history of British land forces from 1485 to the present can be found here. Tableaux, dioramas, archive film, and interactive displays illustrate major engagements and give a taste of life behind the lines. There are fine paintings of battle scenes and portraits of soldiers. The shop sells a range of books and model soldiers.

❽ Royal Hospital

Royal Hospital Rd SW3. **Map** 20 D3. **Tel** 020 7881 5298. 🚇 Sloane Sq. **Open** Museum: 10am–noon, 2–4pm Mon–Fri. **Closed** Sun Oct–Mar, public hols, functions (check first). 📷 10am & 1:30pm Mon–Fri, reserve in advance. 🌿 🌐 **chelsea-pensioners.co.uk**

This graceful complex was commissioned by Charles II

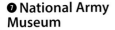
A Chelsea Pensioner in uniform

from Christopher Wren in 1682 as a retirement home for old or wounded soldiers, who have been known as Chelsea Pensioners ever since. The hospital opened ten years later and is still home to about 330 retired soldiers, whose distinctive uniforms of scarlet coats and tricorne hats date from the 17th century. Flanking the northern entrance are Wren's two main public rooms: the chapel, notable for its wonderful simplicity, and the paneled Great Hall, still used as the dining room. A small museum explains the history of the Pensioners.

A statue of Charles II by Grinling Gibbons is to be found on the terrace outside, and there is a fine view of the decommissioned Battersea Power Station across the river.

❾ Saatchi Gallery

Duke of York's HQ, King's Road, Chelsea. **Map** 19 C3. 🚇 Sloane Square. **Open** 10am–6pm daily. **Closed** for private events. ♿ call in advance 020 7811 3085. 📷 🖥️ 🌐 **saatchi-gallery.co.uk**

The Saatchi Gallery is famous for presenting the best in contemporary art and showcasing talent from the UK and international art world. The gallery now receives over 600,000 visitors each year.

Many of the featured artists are unknown when first exhibited at the gallery but then rise to fame as a result. Relocated from its original site on the South Bank, the Saatchi Gallery's present home at the Duke of York's HQ offers an ideal environment in which to view contemporary art. Admire pieces by established names such as Tracy Emin and Jenny Saville while also keeping an eye open for up-and-coming talent.

Sloane Square fountain

❿ Sloane Square

SW1. **Map** 20 D2. 🚇 Sloane Square.

This pleasant small square (or rectangle, to be precise) has a paved center with a flower stand and a fountain depicting Venus. Laid out in the late 18th century, it was named after Sir Hans Sloane, the wealthy physician and collector who bought the manor of Chelsea in 1712. Opposite Peter Jones, the 1936 department store on the square's west side, is the Royal Court Theatre, which for over a century has fostered new drama.

SOUTH KENSINGTON AND KNIGHTSBRIDGE

Bristling with embassies and consulates, South Kensington and Knightsbridge are among London's most desirable, and expensive, areas. With Kensington Palace being a royal residence, the surrounding area has remained fairly unchanged.

The prestigious shops of Knightsbridge serve their wealthy residents. With Hyde Park to the north, and museums that celebrate Victorian learning at its heart, visitors to this part of London can expect to find a unique combination of the serene and the grandiose.

Sights at a Glance

Historic Streets and Buildings
5 Royal College of Music
7 Royal College of Art
10 Kensington Palace
13 Speakers' Corner

Churches
4 Brompton Oratory

Museums and Galleries
1 Natural History Museum pp204–5
2 Science Museum pp208–9
3 Victoria and Albert Museum pp212–15
9 Serpentine Gallery

Parks and Gardens
11 Kensington Gardens
12 Hyde Park

Monuments
8 Albert Memorial
14 Marble Arch

Concert Halls
6 Royal Albert Hall

Shops
15 Harrods

Restaurants see pp295–297
1 Bar Boulud
2 Dinner
3 Zuma

Street Finder, maps 10, 11, 19

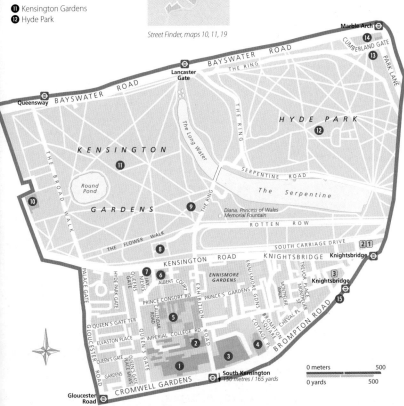

◀ The Royal Albert Hall and the Albert Memorial

For keys to symbols see back flap

Street by Street: South Kensington

A clutch of museums and colleges provide
this area with its dignified character.
The Great Exhibition of 1851 in Hyde Park
was so successful that in the following years,
smaller exhibitions were held here, just to its
south. By the end of the 19th century, some
of these had become permanent museums,
housed in grandiose buildings celebrating
Victorian self-confidence.

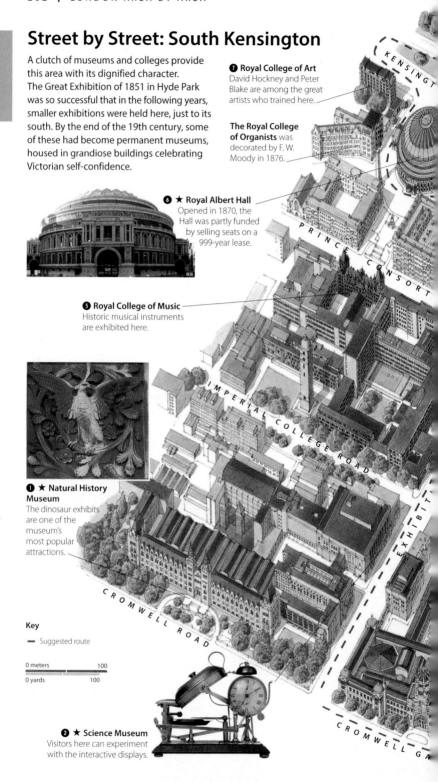

❼ Royal College of Art
David Hockney and Peter
Blake are among the great
artists who trained here.

**The Royal College
of Organists** was
decorated by F. W.
Moody in 1876.

❻ ★ Royal Albert Hall
Opened in 1870, the
Hall was partly funded
by selling seats on a
999-year lease.

❺ Royal College of Music
Historic musical instruments
are exhibited here.

**❶ ★ Natural History
Museum**
The dinosaur exhibits
are one of the
museum's
most popular
attractions.

Key

— Suggested route

| 0 meters | 100 |
| 0 yards | 100 |

❷ ★ Science Museum
Visitors here can experiment
with the interactive displays.

The Albert Hall Mansions, built by Norman Shaw in 1879, started a fashion for red brick.

Locator Map
See Central London Map pp16–17

❽ **Albert Memorial**
This memorial was built to commemorate Queen Victoria's consort.

The Royal Geographical Society was founded in 1830. Scottish missionary and explorer David Livingstone (1813–73) was a member.

Imperial College, part of London University, is one of the country's leading scientific institutions.

❸ ★ **Victoria and Albert Museum**
A range of objects and a stunning photo gallery illustrate the nation's history of design and decoration.

Holy Trinity church dates from the 19th century and is located in a calm oasis among cottages.

❹ **Brompton Oratory**
The Oratory was built during the 19th-century Catholic revival.

Brompton Square, begun in 1821, established this as a fashionable residential area.

To Knightsbridge station

● Natural History Museum

Life on Earth and the Earth itself are vividly explained at the Natural History Museum. Using the latest interactive techniques and traditional displays, exhibits tackle such issues as how human beings evolved and how we can safeguard our planet. The Images of Nature exhibit showcases 350 years of wildlife artwork and photography. The vast museum building is a masterpiece in itself. It opened in 1881 and was designed by Alfred Waterhouse using revolutionary Victorian building techniques. It is built on an iron and steel framework concealed behind arches and columns, richly decorated with sculptures of plants and animals.

★ Mammals
The life-size model of a blue whale dwarfs everything else in this vast gallery.

The Darwin Centre features an eight-story cocoon in a glass atrium. It is home to 20 million insect and plant specimens and a research center.

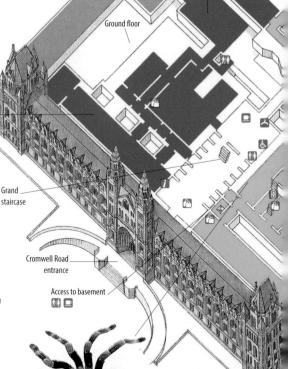

Ground floor

★ Dinosaurs
T Rex, one of the museum's impressively lifelike animatronic models, lurches and roars in this hugely popular gallery. More traditional exhibits of fossilized skeletons and eggs are also on display.

Grand staircase

Cromwell Road entrance

Access to basement

Gallery Guide

The museum is divided into four sections: the Blue Zone, the Green Zone, the Red Zone, and the Orange Zone.

An 85-ft (26-m) skeleton of the dinosaur Diplodocus dominates Central Hall. Beyond, in the Blue Zone, Human Biology, Mammals, Dinosaurs, and Images of Nature are to the left, while Creepy Crawlies and Ecology are to the right. On the first floor are found Our Place in Evolution and The Vault.

The giant escalator in Visions of Earth leads through a stunning globe to Red Zone highlights The Power Within and Earth's Treasury.

Creepy Crawlies
Eight out of ten animal species are arthropods – insects, crustaceans, centipedes, and spiders, like this tarantula.

Key to Floor Plan

- ■ Blue Zone
- ■ Green Zone
- ■ Red Zone
- ■ Orange Zone

The Vault
The Vault contains a dazzling collection of the finest gems, crystals, meteorites, and metals from around the world, such as this Latrobe gold nugget.

Treasures is a showcase for the best of the museum's collections.

Second floor

Second floor Red Zone

The Power Within has a convincing earthquake simulator that is hugely popular.

Earth's Treasury gallery glitters with thousands of gems, rocks, and minerals, including some of the rarest on Earth.

First floor Red Zone

First floor

Access to Red Zone

Exhibition Road entrance – Earth Galleries ♿

Birds
This traditional display, with many species in Victorian glass cases, includes a model of the legendary dodo. A flightless bird from Mauritius, it was extinct by the mid-1600s.

★ **Visions of Earth**
Specimens are recessed into the etched slate walls of this beautiful gallery. Access to the rest of the Red Zone is via an escalator that runs through a massive model of the Earth.

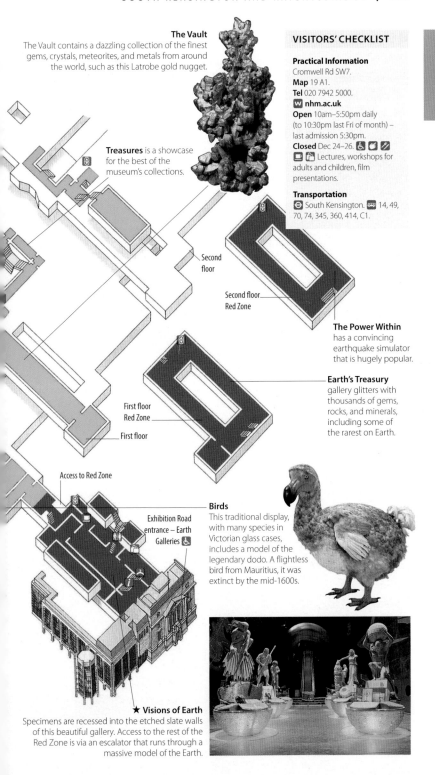

❷ Science Museum

See pp208–209.

Children captivated by the exhibits on display in the Science Museum

❸ Victoria and Albert Museum

See pp212–15.

❹ Brompton Oratory

Brompton Rd SW7. **Map** 19 A1. **Tel** 020 7808 0900. ⊖ South Kensington. **Open** 6am–8pm daily. 🕇 11am Sun sung Latin Mass (see website for other times). ♿ 🎦 Ⓦ bromptonoratory.com

The Italianate Oratory is a rich (some think a little too rich) monument to the English Catholic revival of the late 19th century. The Oratory was established by John Henry Newman (who later became Cardinal Newman). Father Frederick William Faber (1814–63) had already founded a London community of priests at Charing Cross. The group had moved to Brompton, then an outlying London district, and this was to be its oratory. Newman and Faber (both Anglican converts to Catholicism) were following the example of St. Philip Neri, who set up a community of city-based secular priests living without vows.

The present church was opened in 1884. Its facade and dome were added in the 1890s, and the interior has been progressively enriched ever since. Herbert Gribble, the architect, who was also a Catholic convert, was only 29 when he triumphed in the highly prestigious competition to design it. Inside, all the most eye-catching treasures predate the church – many of them were transported here from Italian churches. Giuseppe Mazzuoli carved the huge marble figures of the 12 apostles for Siena Cathedral in the late 17th century. The beautiful Lady Altar was originally created in 1693 for the Dominican church in Brescia, and the 18th-century altar in St. Wilfrid's Chapel was actually imported from a church in Rochefort, Belgium.

The Oratory has always been famous for its splendid musical tradition.

❺ Royal College of Music

Prince Consort Rd SW7. **Map** 10 F5. **Tel** 020 7591 4300. ⊖ Knightsbridge, South Kensington. Museum of Instruments: **Tel** 020 7591 4842. **Open** 11:30am–4:30pm Tue–Fri in term-time or by appointment. ♿ call 020 7591 4322 before visit. 🎦🖵Ⓦ rcm.ac.uk

Sir Arthur Blomfield designed the turreted Gothic palace, with Bavarian overtones, that has housed this distinguished institution since 1894.

The college was founded in 1882 by George Grove, who also compiled the famous *Dictionary of Music*; pupils have included English composers Benjamin Britten and Ralph Vaughan Williams. The **Museum of Musical Instruments** has limited opening hours; if you do manage to get inside, you will see instruments from the earliest times and from many parts of the world. Some of the exhibits were played by such greats as Handel and Haydn.

17th-century viol at the Royal College of Music

The sumptuous interior of Brompton Oratory

Joseph Durham's statue of Prince Albert (1858) by the Royal Albert Hall

❻ Royal Albert Hall

Kensington Gore SW7. **Map** 10 F5.
Tel 020 7589 8212. ⊜ High St
Kensington, South Kensington.
Open for performances. ✉ ✐ to
book, call 0845 401 5045; charge for
tour. ♿ ✐ ▢ *See Entertainment
pp340–41.* **W** royalalberthall.com

Designed by an engineer,
Francis Fowke, and completed
in 1871, this huge concert hall
was modeled on Roman
amphitheaters and is easier on
the eye than most Victorian
structures. On the red-brick
exterior the only ostentation is
a pretty frieze symbolizing the
triumph of arts and science.
In plans the building was called
the Hall of Arts and Science, but
Queen Victoria changed it to
the Royal Albert Hall, in memory
of her husband, when she laid
the foundation stone in 1868.
    The hall is often used for
Classical concerts, most
famously the "Proms," but it also
accommodates other large
gatherings, such as tennis
matches, comedy shows, rock
concerts, circus shows, and
major business conferences.

❼ Royal College of Art

Kensington Gore SW7. **Map** 10 F5.
Tel 020 7590 4444. ⊜ High St
Kensington, South Kensington.
Open 10am–5:30pm daily (call
first). ♿ ▢ ▣ Lectures, events,
film presentations, exhibitions.
W rca.ac.uk

Sir Hugh Casson's mainly glass-
fronted building (1962) is in
stark contrast to the Victoriana
around it. The college was
founded in 1837 as a school of
design and practical art for the
manufacturing industries. It
became noted for modern art
in the 1950s and 1960s when
David Hockney, Peter Blake, and
Eduardo Paolozzi were there.

❽ Albert Memorial

South Carriage Drive, Kensington
Gdns SW7. **Map** 10 F5. ⊜ High St
Kensington, South Kensington.

This grandiose but dignified
memorial to Queen Victoria's
beloved consort was completed
in 1876, 15 years after his death.
Albert was a German prince and
a cousin of Queen Victoria's.
When he died of typhoid in
1861, he was only 41, but they
had been happily married for
21 years, producing nine
children. It is fitting that the
monument is near the site of
the 1851 Exhibition *(see pp30–
31)*, for Prince Albert was closely
identified with the Exhibition
itself and with the scientific
advances it celebrated. The
larger-than-life statue, by John
Foley, shows him with an
exhibition catalog on his knee.
    The desolate Queen chose
Sir George Gilbert Scott to
design the monument that
stands 175 ft (55 m) high. It is
loosely based on a medieval
market cross – although many
times more elaborate, with a
black and gilded spire, multicolored marble canopy, stones,
mosaics, enamels, wrought iron,
and nearly 200 sculpted figures.
In October 1998 the re-gilded
statue was unveiled by Elizabeth
II; it had not been gilded since
1915, when it was painted black
to avoid attracting attention
during World War I.

Victoria and Albert at the Great
Exhibition opening (1851)

❷ Science Museum

Centuries of continuing scientific and technological development lie at the heart of the Science Museum's massive collections. The variety of objects displayed is magnificent: from steam engines to aeroengines, spacecraft to the first mechanical computers. Equally important is the social context of science – what discoveries and inventions mean for day-to-day life – and the process of discovery itself. The high-tech Wellcome Wing has interactive displays, an IMAX Cinema, a 4D theater, and galleries devoted to new advances in science.

★ Science and Art of Medicine
A 17th-century Italian vase for storing snake bite treatment is part of this interesting collection.

Science in the 18th Century
The original orrery, a mechanical model of the solar system, is one of many beautiful scientific instruments in this gallery.

Computing
Babbage's Difference Engine No. 1 (1832), the first automatic calculator and a magnificent example of precision engineering, is a highlight of this gallery.

Energy: Fuelling the Future
explores how energy powers every aspect of our lives.

Media Space
looks at relationships between photography, science, art, and technology.

★ The Energy Hall
Dedicated to steam power, this gallery includes the still-operational Harle Syke Mill Engine (1903).

Key to Floor Plan

- Basement
- Ground floor
- First floor
- Second floor
- Third floor
- Fourth floor
- Fifth floor
- Wellcome Wing

Stairs to lower level

Exploring Space
Rockets, satellites, space probes, landers, and more.

Main entrance

★ Flight

This gallery is packed with early flying contraptions, fighter planes, and aeroengines, many of them suspended as if in mid-flight.

VISITORS' CHECKLIST

Practical Information
Exhibition Rd SW7.
Map 19 A1.
Tel 0870 870 4868.
W sciencemuseum.org.uk
Open 10am–6pm daily.
Closed Dec 24–26. 🎫 some exhibitions & IMAX Cinema. 🚻 Lectures, films, workshops. 🖥 📷

Transportation
🚇 South Kensington. 🚌 9, 10, 14, 49, 52, 70, 74, 345, 360, 414, 430, 452, C1.

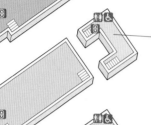

Atmosphere

This interactive gallery allows visitors to explore the science behind our changing climate – how it works, why it changes, and what might happen in the future.

Escalator to
Imax Cinema

★ Who Am I?

Find out what makes you unique and explore the science of being human. The exhibition utilizes intriguing objects, displays, and hands-on exhibits.

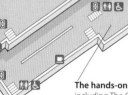

★ Making the Modern World

Apollo 10 took US astronauts around the moon in May 1969, and now forms part of this stunning gallery of museum highlights.

The hands-on galleries, including The Garden, are very popular with children.

Gallery Guide

The Science Museum is spread over seven floors, balconies, and mezzanine levels. The Wellcome Wing, offering four floors of interactive technology, is at the west end of the museum and is accessible from the ground floor and third floor of the main building. Power dominates the ground floor; here too are Exploring Space and Making the Modern World. The first floor has the Challenge of Materials gallery as well as Telecommunications and Agriculture. On the second floor a range of diverse galleries look at energy, mathematics, and computing. The third floor includes Flight, Health Matters, and Launchpad. The fourth and fifth floors (accessible by only one of the elevators) house the medical history galleries.

Statue of young Queen Victoria by her daughter Princess Louise outside Kensington Palace

❾ Serpentine Gallery

Kensington Gdns W2. **Map** 11 A4. **Tel** 020 7402 6075. 🚇 Lancaster Gate, South Kensington. **Open** 10am–6pm Tue–Sun. **Closed** Jan 1, Dec 24–26 & 31 & between exhibitions. Lectures. ♿ 🔲 summer only. 📷 art bookshop. 🆆 **serpentinegallery.org**

The Serpentine Gallery houses temporary exhibitions of major contemporary artists' work. Past exhibitors include Gilbert & George, Rachel Whiteread, and Felix Gonzalez-Torres. This exciting gallery transforms its space to suit the exhibits, sometimes spilling out into the park. Every summer, a temporary pavilion (open daily) is commissioned from a major architect; this is where you will find the café.

❿ Kensington Palace

Kensington Palace Gdns W8. **Map** 10 D4. **Tel** 0844 482 7777. 🚇 High St Kensington, Queensway, Notting Hill Gate. **Open** Mar–Oct: 10am–6pm daily; Nov–Feb: 10am–5pm daily (last adm: 1 hr earlier). **Closed** Dec 24–26. 📷 🔲 ✏ 📷 ♿ Exhibitions. 🆆 **hrp.org.uk**

Half of this spacious palace is used as royal apartments; the other half, which includes the 18th-century state rooms, is open to the public. When William III and his wife Mary came to the throne in 1689

they bought a mansion, dating from 1605, and commissioned Christopher Wren to convert it into a royal palace. He created separate suites of rooms for the king and queen.

The palace has seen some important royal events. In 1714 Queen Anne died here from a fit of apoplexy brought on by overeating and, on June 20, 1837, Princess Victoria of Kent was woken at 5am to be told that her uncle William IV had died and she was now queen – the start of her 64-year reign. After the death in 1997 of Diana, Princess of Wales, the gold gates south of the palace became a focal point for mourners by the thousands, who turned the surrounding area into a field of bouquets.

A major renovation project has seen the palace gardens connected to Kensington Gardens for the first time since the 19th century. The palace interior has been rearranged into four "story zones" focusing on the lives of William and Mary; George II; Victoria's Story, told in her own words; and Margaret and Diana, some of whose dresses are on display. Visitors can try to master the games of the royal court in the King's State Apartments.

Detail of the Coalbrookdale gate, Kensington Gardens

⓫ Kensington Gardens

W8. **Map** 10 E4. **Tel** 0300 061 2000. 🚇 Bayswater, High St Kensington, Queensway, Lancaster Gate. **Open** 6am–dusk daily. 🔲 🆆 **royalparks.org.uk**

The former grounds of Kensington Palace became a public park in 1841. A small part of it has been dedicated as a memorial playground to Diana, Princess of Wales (see p219). The gardens are full of charm, starting with Sir George Frampton's statue (1912) of J. M. Barrie's fictional Peter Pan, the boy who never grew up, playing his pipes to the bronze fairies and animals that cling to the column below. Often surrounded by parents, nannies, and their charges, the statue stands near the west bank of the Serpentine, not far from where Harriet, wife of the poet Percy Bysshe Shelley, drowned herself in 1816.

Just north of here (in Hyde Park) are the ornamental fountains and statues, including Jacob Epstein's *Rima*, at the lake's head. George Frederick Watts's statue of a muscular horse and rider, *Physical Energy*, stands to the south. Not far away is a summer house designed by William Kent in 1735, and the Serpentine Gallery. The Round

Pond, created in 1728 just east of the palace, is often packed with model boats navigated by children and older enthusiasts. In winter it is occasionally fit for skating. In the north, near Lancaster Gate, is a dog cemetery, started in 1880 by the Duke of Cambridge while mourning one of his pets.

Riding on Rotten Row, Hyde Park

⑫ Hyde Park

W2. Map 11 B3. Tel 0300 061 2000. 🚇 Hyde Park Corner, Knightsbridge, Lancaster Gate, Marble Arch. Open 5am–midnight daily. 🖥 Sports facilities. 🌐 royalparks.gov.uk

The ancient manor of Hyde was part of the lands of Westminster Abbey seized by Henry VIII in the Dissolution of the Monasteries in 1536. It has remained a royal park ever since. Henry used it for hunting, but James I opened it to the public in the early 17th century. The Serpentine, an artificial lake used for boating and bathing, was created when Caroline, George II's queen, dammed the flow of the Westbourne River in 1730.

In its time the park has been a venue for dueling, horse racing, highwaymen, demon-strations, and music. The 1851 Exhibition was held here in a vast glass palace (see pp28–9). The Princess Diana Memorial fountain is to the south of the Serpentine. Hyde Park is the setting for one of the UK's largest Christmas markets, complete with an ice rink and amusement park.

⑬ Speakers' Corner

Hyde Park W2. Map 11 C2. 🚇 Marble Arch.

An 1872 law made it legal to assemble an audience and address them on whatever topic you chose; since then, this corner of Hyde Park has become the established venue for budding orators and a fair number of eccentrics. It is well worth spending time here on a Sunday: speakers from fringe groups and one-member political parties reveal their plans for the betterment of mankind while the assembled onlookers heckle them without mercy.

⑭ Marble Arch

Park Lane W1. Map 11 C2. 🚇 Marble Arch.

John Nash designed the arch in 1827 as the main entrance to Buckingham Palace. It was, however, too narrow for the grandest coaches and was moved here in 1851. Historically, only senior members of the Royal Family and one of the royal artillery regiments are allowed to pass under it.

The arch stands near the site of the old Tyburn gallows (marked by a plaque), where until 1783 the city's most notorious criminals were hanged in front of crowds of bloodthirsty spectators.

An orator at Speakers' Corner

⑮ Harrods

Knightsbridge SW1. Map 11 C5. Tel 020 7730 1234. 🚇 Knightsbridge. Open 10am–8pm Mon–Sat, 11:30am–6pm Sun. 📧 🚻 🖥 ♿ See Shops and Markets p313. 🌐 harrods.com

London's most famous department store began in 1849 when Henry Charles Harrod opened a small grocery shop nearby on Brompton Road. By concentrating on good quality and impeccable service, the store was soon popular enough to expand.

It used to be claimed that Harrods could supply anything from a packet of pins to an elephant – not quite true today, but the range of stock is still vast. A dress code applies, so shorts, bare midriffs, and flip-flops are not permitted.

Harrods at night, lit by 11,500 lights

❸ Victoria and Albert Museum

The Victoria and Albert Museum (the V&A) contains one of the world's widest collections of art and design, ranging from early Christian devotional objects to cutting-edge furniture design. Originally founded in 1852 as the Museum of Manufactures to inspire design students, it was renamed by Queen Victoria in 1899 in memory of Prince Albert. The museum is undergoing a dramatic redisplay of some of its collection, including work on a number of galleries and the Sackler Education Centre. To find out if a particular gallery is open, call the bookings office at 020 7942 2211.

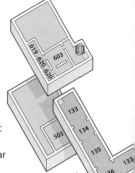

British Galleries (1760–1900)
This charming candy jar (1770) is one of many pieces on display that were crafted in the workshops of Britain.

Silver Galleries
Radiant pieces such as the Burgess Cup (Britain, 1863) fill these stunning galleries.

★ British Galleries (1500–1760)
Displays of evocative objects, such as this writing desk from King Henry VIII's court, illustrate Britain's fascinating history.

★ Fashion Gallery
European fashion, fabrics, and accessories from 1750 to the present day are on display, including these floral 1920s Lilley & Skinner shoes.

Exhibition Road entrance

Key to Floor Plan

- ▨ Level 0
- ▨ Level 1
- ▨ Level 2
- ▨ Level 3
- ▨ Level 4
- ▨ Level 6
- ▨ Henry Cole Wing
- ▨ Non-exhibition space

Gallery Guide

The V&A has a 7-mile (11-km) layout spread over six levels, and the museum incorporates approximately 150 different galleries. The main floor, level 1, houses the China, Japan, and South Asia Galleries, as well as the Fashion Gallery and the Cast Courts. The British Galleries are on levels 2 and 4. Level 3 contains the 20th Century Galleries and displays of silver, ironwork, paintings, photography, and design works. The glass display is also on level 4. The Ceramics Galleries and Furniture are on level 6. The Henry Cole Wing houses the Sackler Education Centre, RIBA Architecture Study Rooms, and the Prints and Drawings Study Rooms.

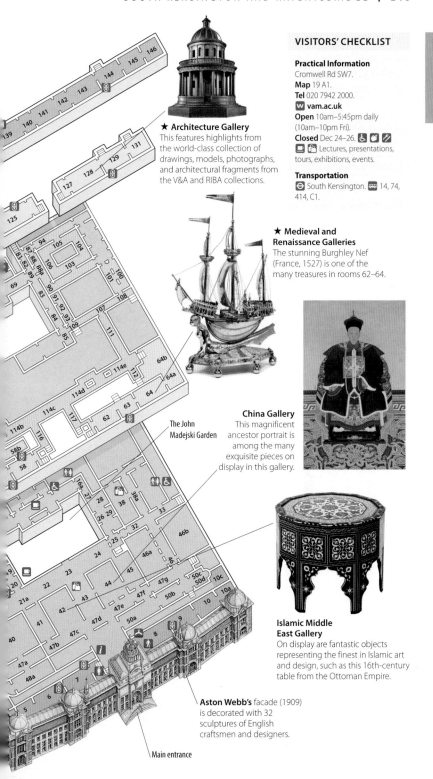

★ Architecture Gallery
This features highlights from the world-class collection of drawings, models, photographs, and architectural fragments from the V&A and RIBA collections.

VISITORS' CHECKLIST

Practical Information
Cromwell Rd SW7.
Map 19 A1.
Tel 020 7942 2000.
w vam.ac.uk
Open 10am–5:45pm daily
(10am–10pm Fri).
Closed Dec 24–26. ♿ 🚫 🚫
🔲 📷 Lectures, presentations, tours, exhibitions, events.

Transportation
🔵 South Kensington. 🚌 14, 74, 414, C1.

★ Medieval and Renaissance Galleries
The stunning Burghley Nef (France, 1527) is one of the many treasures in rooms 62–64.

China Gallery
This magnificent ancestor portrait is among the many exquisite pieces on display in this gallery.

The John Madejski Garden

Islamic Middle East Gallery
On display are fantastic objects representing the finest in Islamic art and design, such as this 16th-century table from the Ottoman Empire.

Aston Webb's facade (1909) is decorated with 32 sculptures of English craftsmen and designers.

Main entrance

Exploring the V&A's Collections

The sheer size of the V&A means you should plan your visit carefully to avoid missing an area of particular interest. The following sections offer highlights but are by no means exhaustive. Be sure to visit the museum's original refreshment rooms off room 16a (one of which was designed by William Morris), now being used again as a café. If the weather is good, don't miss the John Madejski Garden. The Photographs galleries (rooms 38a and 100) display a changing selection of 300,000 photographs from 1856 to the present.

Covering the millennia from 3000 BC to the present, the impressive collection includes a giant Buddha's head from 700–900 AD, a huge yet elegant Ming canopied bed, and rare jade and ceramics.

Japanese art is concentrated in the Japan gallery in room 45, and is particularly notable for lacquer, Samurai armor, and woodblock prints.

British Galleries

A sequence of grand rooms starting on level 2 and continuing on level 4 are devoted to the luxurious British Galleries. By presenting design and decorative arts from 1500 to 1900, the galleries chart Britain's rise from obscure island to "workshop of the world." The galleries present the evolution of British high design and the numerous influences, whether technological or aesthetic, absorbed from all over the world.

Beautiful textiles, furniture, costumes, and household objects illustrate the tastes and lifestyles of Britain's ruling classes. Among the highlights are James II's wedding suit, the opulent State Bed from Melville House, and a number of carefully preserved period rooms, including the stunning Rococo Norfolk House Music Room. Discovery Areas give visitors a chance to delve even deeper into the past

by sporting a Tudor ruff or viewing 3-D images through a Victorian stereoscope.

China, Japan, and South Asia

The Jameel Gallery of Islamic Art was opened in July 2006 and houses a significant collection of more than 400 objects including ceramics, textiles, carpets, metalwork, glass, and woodwork. The exhibits date from the great days of the Islamic caliphate of the 8th and 9th centuries through to the years preceding the First World War.

Middle Eastern art from Syria, Iraq, Iran, Turkey, and Egypt is found in room 42. Beautifully crafted textiles and ceramics illustrate the Islamic influence on fine and decorative arts. A dramatic arc of burnished steel fins, representing the spine of a Chinese dragon, spans the China gallery (room 44).

Gilt copper ice chest (Qing Dynasty, 1700s), room 44

Architecture Gallery

The Architecture Gallery features highlights from the world-class collections of drawings, models, photographs, and architectural fragments of the V&A and the Royal Institute of British Architects (RIBA).

The gallery explores the architecture that shapes our world through five themes. "The Art of Architecture" explores the history and ideas behind architectural styles. A superb collection of artifacts and illustrations is on display, grouped by period and spanning world cultures, including Asian, Spanish Islamic, Classical, Gothic, and Modernist. "The Function of Buildings" looks at the way in

Waistcoat (1734) in room 52b

The Great Bed of Ware

Made in about 1590 of oak with inlaid and painted decoration, the Great Bed of Ware measures some 12 by 12 ft (3.6 by 3.6 m) and is 8 ft 9 inches (2.6 m) high. It is the V&A's most celebrated piece of furniture. Elaborately carved and decorated, the bed is a superb example of the art of the English woodworker. Its name derives from the town of Ware in Hertfordshire, about a day's ride north of London, where it resided in a number of inns. The Great Bed's enormous size made it an early tourist attraction, and no doubt interest was boosted by Shakespeare's reference to it in *Twelfth Night*, which he wrote in 1601.

Redecorated and refurbished, the bed is located in room 57.

Detail of the Ardabil Carpet (c.1539–40) from the Jameel Gallery of Islamic Art

which the design of a building is informed not only by its function but also by the demands of climate.

"Architects and Architecture" examines the team effort involved in designing a building, and how this has evolved over the centuries. A huge range of sketches, models, and drawings used by architects supports the theme.

"Structures" examines the different structures needed to create different buildings, from chunky low-rise to tall buildings.

"Buildings in Context" takes a look at the construction of London's Trafalgar Square, from the original maps in 1730 to the present day, in order to explore the relationship that exists between a building and its surroundings.

Medieval and Renaissance

Ten galleries, occupying an entire wing of the museum, house some of the world's greatest treasures of this era. Among the many remarkable exhibits are the notebooks of Leonardo da Vinci; sculptures by Italian masters such as Donatello and Giambologna, some in a Renaissance courtyard garden setting; the fine enamel Becket Casket (c.1180); and the reconstructed Santa Chiara Chapel, the only one of its kind outside Italy.

Textiles and Fashion

The popular Fashion Gallery displays items from the largest and most comprehensive collection of dress in the world. Around 100 exhibits, spanning over three centuries, are arranged chronologically. They include a magnificent mantua from the 1760s; an 1850s wedding dress with veil and shoes; a Schiaparelli evening coat embroidered with a design by Jean Cocteau; and a punk outfit designed by Vivienne Westwood. The equally fine Textiles collection is currently featured in galleries across the museum, but there are plans to create a custom-built, dedicated gallery.

Ruby glass flagon (c.1858–9)

Metalwork

This group of galleries is located on level 3. In the Silver Galleries, 3,500 pieces from 1400 to the present day are displayed in the beautifully refurbished Victorian rooms 65 to 69. Arms and armor, European metalwork from the 1500s to the present, and Islamic brass and bronze can be found in rooms 81, 82 and 87 to 89.

The Sacred Silver and Stained Glass galleries in rooms 83 and 84 display devotional treasures. The highlight of the ironwork galleries, which are located in rooms 113 to 114e, is the dazzling Hereford Screen designed by Sir George Gilbert Scott in 1862, and displayed at the International Exhibition of that year. The screen became the V&A's largest conservation project.

The Gilbert Collection of gold, silver, micromosaics, and gold boxes, formerly housed at Somerset House, reopened here in 2009.

Glass and Ceramics

Examples of 2,000 years of glass are exhibited across galleries on level 4. These contain superb porcelain from European china factories and a stunning balustrade by glass artist Danny Lane in room 131. Displays of international contemporary glass are on display in this room as well as in room 129.

The museum holds the world's largest and most comprehensive collection of ceramics. The introductory gallery presents the history and development of ceramics across the world.

Stained glass roundel entitled *Susanna Accused by the Elders* (c.1520)

KENSINGTON AND HOLLAND PARK

The western and northern perimeters of Kensington Gardens are a rich residential area and include many foreign embassies. The shops on Kensington High Street are almost as stylish as those in Knightsbridge, and Kensington Church Street is a good source of quality antiques. Around Holland Park are some magnificent late Victorian houses, two of them open to the public. But as you cross into Bayswater and Notting Hill, you enter a more vibrant, cosmopolitan part of London. Its stucco terraces are lined with medium-priced hotels and inexpensive restaurants.

Westbourne Grove has become increasingly popular with the young, designer-clad crowd. Whiteleys, in Queensway, is one of the many historic buildings in the area. Built in 1912 by Belcher and Joass as a fashionable department store, it was converted in the 1980s into a vibrant shopping center. To the west, Portobello Road is a popular street market selling anything from food to antiques. Notting Hill is known for its flamboyant Caribbean carnival, which took to the streets in 1966 and has been staged every year since, on the last weekend in August *(see p59)*.

Sights at a Glance

Historic Streets and Buildings
2 Holland House
3 Leighton House
4 Linley Sambourne House
6 Kensington Square
7 Kensington Palace Gardens
9 Queensway

Parks and Gardens
1 Holland Park
5 Kensington Roof Gardens
8 The Diana, Princess of Wales Memorial Playground

Markets
10 Portobello Road

Historic Areas
11 Notting Hill

Street Finder, maps 9, 17

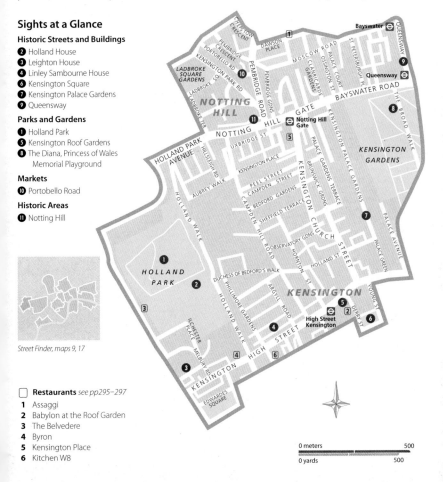

0 meters 500
0 yards 500

◀ Antiques for sale at Portobello Road market

For keys to symbols *see back flap*

Street by Street: Kensington and Holland Park

Although now part of central London, as recently as the 1830s this was a country village of market gardens and mansions. Outstanding among these was Holland House; part of its grounds are now Holland Park. The area grew up rapidly in the mid-19th century, and most of its buildings date from then – mainly expensive apartments, mansion flats, and fashionable shops.

❷ Holland House
The rambling Jacobean mansion, started in 1605 and pictured here in 1795, was largely demolished in the 1950s.

❶ ★ Holland Park
Parts of the old formal gardens of Holland House have been retained to grace this delightful public park.

The Orangery, now a restaurant, has parts that date from the 1630s, when it was within the grounds of Holland House.

Melbury Road is lined with large Victorian houses. Many were built for fashionable artists of the time.

The Victorian mailbox on High Street is one of the oldest in London.

❸ ★ Leighton House
It is preserved as it was when the Victorian painter Lord Leighton lived here. He had a passion for Middle Eastern tiles.

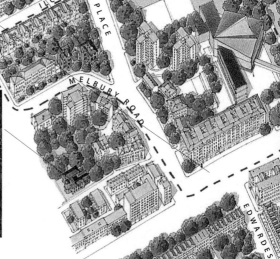

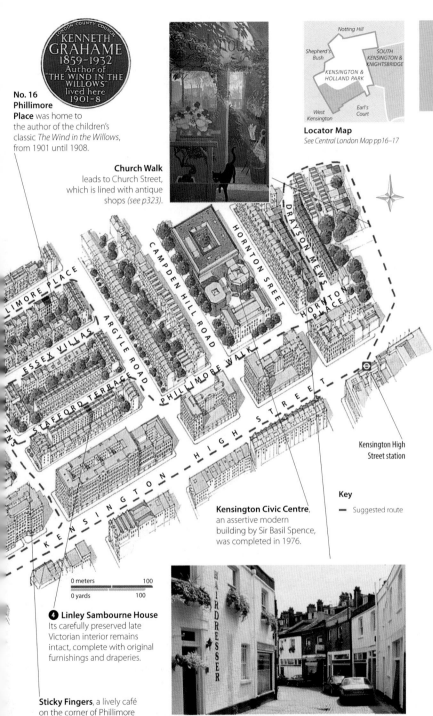

No. 16 Phillimore Place was home to the author of the children's classic *The Wind in the Willows*, from 1901 until 1908.

Church Walk leads to Church Street, which is lined with antique shops *(see p323)*.

Locator Map
See Central London Map pp16–17

Kensington High Street station

Key

— Suggested route

Kensington Civic Centre, an assertive modern building by Sir Basil Spence, was completed in 1976.

0 meters 100
0 yards 100

④ Linley Sambourne House
Its carefully preserved late Victorian interior remains intact, complete with original furnishings and draperies.

Sticky Fingers, a lively café on the corner of Phillimore Gardens, is owned by Bill Wyman, former bass guitarist of the Rolling Stones.

Drayson Mews is one of the quaint alleys that were built behind large town houses for the stabling of horses and coaches. Today most have been converted into small houses.

The café in Holland Park

❶ Holland Park

Abbotsbury Rd W14. **Map** 9 B4.
Tel 020 7602 2226 to reserve facilities.
🚇 Holland Park, High St Kensington,
Notting Hill Gate. **Open** 7:30am–dusk
daily (hours are flexible depending on
light). **Closed** Dec 25. 🏛 💻 Open-
air opera, theater, dance. Box Office:
Tel 0300 999 1000. Art exhibitions
Apr–Oct. *See Entertainment pp336–7.*

This small but delightful park,
more wooded and intimate
than the large royal parks
to its east (Hyde Park and
Kensington Gardens,
see pp210–11), was opened in
1952 on what remained of the
grounds of Holland House –
the rest had been sold off in
the late 19th century for the
construction of large houses
and terraces to the north and
west. The park still contains
some of the formal gardens,
laid out in the early 19th
century for Holland House.
There is also a Japanese
garden, created for the 1991
London Festival of Japan.
The park has an abundance of
wildlife, including peacocks.

❷ Holland House

Holland Park W8. **Map** 9 B5. Youth
Hostel **Tel** 020 7937 0748. 🚇 Holland
Park, High Street Kensington.

During its heyday in the 19th
century, this was a noted center
of social and political intrigue.
Statesmen such as Lord
Palmerston mixed here with
the likes of the poet Byron.

The remains of the house are
now used as a youth hostel.
The outbuildings are put to
various uses: exhibitions are
held in the orangery and the
ice house (a forerunner of the
refrigerator), and the old Garden
Ballroom is now a restaurant.

❸ Leighton House

12 Holland Park Rd W14. **Map** 17 B1.
Tel 020 7602 3316. 🚇 High St Kensington. **Open** 10am–5:30pm Wed–
Mon. **Closed** Jan 1, Dec 25.
🏛 📷 3pm Wed & Sun or by
appt for groups. 🎭 Concerts,
exhibitions. 🌐 **rbkc.gov.uk/
leightonhousemuseum**

Built for respected Victorian
painter Lord Leighton in 1864–79,
the house has been preserved
with its opulent decoration as an
extraordinary monument to
Victorian aesthetics. The highlight
is the Arab hall, added in 1879 to
house Leighton's collection of
Islamic tiles, some of which are
inscribed with quotes from the
Koran. The best paintings include
some by Edward Burne-Jones,
John Millais, G. F. Watts, and many
works by Leighton himself.

Original tiling in Holland House

❹ Linley
Sambourne House

18 Stafford Terrace W8. **Map** 9 C5.
Tel 020 7602 3316 Mon–Fri; 020 7938
1295 Sat & Sun. 🚇 High St
Kensington. **Open** for guided tours
only: 11:15am & 2:15pm Wed; 11:15am
Sat & Sun; costumed tours 1pm,
2:15pm, 3:30pm Sat & Sun; call to
reserve. 🏛 📷 🌐 **rbkc.gov.uk/
linleysambournehouse**

The house, built in about
1870, has undergone a major
renovation, but remains much
as Linley Sambourne furnished
it, in the Victorian manner, with
china ornaments and heavy
velvet drapes. Sambourne was
a cartoonist for the satirical
magazine *Punch*; drawings cram
the walls of the house. Some
rooms are decorated with William
Morris wallpaper *(see p251)*.

❺ Kensington Roof
Gardens

99 Kensington High Street W8
(entrance in Derry Street). **Map** 10 D5.
Tel 020 7937 7994. **Open** 9am–5pm
daily (but call ahead, as sometimes
closed for private functions). 🏛
🌐 **roofgardens.virgin.com**

High above the bustle of
Kensington High Street is one
of London's best-kept secrets –
a 1.5-acre (6,000-sq-m) roof
garden. First planted in the
1930s by the owners of Derry &
Toms department store below
(now housing many different
stores), the themed gardens are
a lavish flight of fancy and

feature a woodland garden, a Spanish garden (with palm trees), and a formal English garden (with a pond, live ducks, and a pair of pink flamingos). Best of all, it's free to wander around, though there is no access when the gardens have been reserved for events.

❻ Kensington Square

W8. **Map** 10 D5. 🚇 High St Kensington.

This is one of London's oldest squares. It was laid out in the 1680s, and a few early 18th-century houses still remain. (Nos. 11 and 12 are the oldest.) The philosopher John Stuart Mill lived at No. 18, and the Pre-Raphaelite painter and illustrator Edward Burne-Jones at No.41.

❼ Kensington Palace Gardens

W8. **Map** 10 D3. 🚇 High St Kensington, Notting Hill Gate, Queensway.

This private road of luxury mansions occupies the site of the former kitchen gardens of Kensington Palace *(see p210)*. It changes its name halfway down; the southern part is known as Palace Green. It is open to pedestrians but closed to cars, unless they have specific business here. Most of the houses are occupied by embassies and their staff. At cocktail hour, you can watch black limousines with diplomatic license plates sweep beneath the raised barriers at each end of the road.

Queensway shop front

❽ The Diana, Princess of Wales Memorial Playground

Kensington Gardens. **Map** 10 E3. **Tel** 0300 061 2001. 🚇 Bayswater, Queensway. **Open** daily, Feb & Oct: 10am–4:45pm; Mar: 10am–5:45pm; Apr & Sep: 10am–6:45pm; May–Aug: 10am–7:45pm; Nov–Jan: 10am–3:45pm. **Closed** Dec 25. 📷 ♿ 🌐 **royalparks.org.uk**

The newest of Kensington Gardens' three playgrounds was opened in 2000. Dedicated to the memory of the late Princess Diana, it is located close to the Bayswater Road, on the site of an earlier playground funded by Peter Pan's creator, J. M. Barrie. Diana's innovative adventure playground takes the boy who didn't want to grow up as its theme and is packed with novel ideas and activities, including a beach cove with a 50-ft pirates' galleon, a tree house with walkways and ramps, and a mermaid's fountain with a half-submerged slumbering crocodile (careful not to rouse him!). Though all children up to the age of 12 must be accompanied by an adult, staff are on duty to make sure the children are safe. Many features of the playground are accessible to children with special needs.

❾ Queensway

W2. **Map** 10 D2. 🚇 Queensway, Bayswater.

One of London's most cosmopolitan streets, Queensway has the heaviest concentration of eating places outside Soho. Newsstands are abundantly stocked with foreign news-papers. At the northern end is Whiteley's shopping center. Founded by William Whiteley, who was born in Yorkshire in 1863, it was probably the world's first

Antique shop on Portobello Road

department store. The present building dates from 1911.

The street is named after Queen Victoria, who rode here as a princess.

❿ Portobello Road

W11. **Map** 9 C3. 🚇 Notting Hill Gate, Ladbroke Grove. Antique market **Open** 9:30am–4pm Fri, 8am–5pm Sat. *See also Shops and Markets p333.*

There has been a market here since 1837. These days the southern end consists almost exclusively of stands that sell antiques, jewelry, souvenirs, and many other collectibles. The market is extremely popular with tourists and tends to be very crowded on summer weekends. However, it is well worth visiting just to experience its bustling and cheerful atmosphere, even if you don't intend to buy anything. If you do decide to buy, be warned: you are unlikely to get a real bargain, since the vendors are well aware of the value of what they are selling.

⓫ Notting Hill

W11. **Map** 9 C3. 🚇 Notting Hill Gate.

Now the home of Europe's biggest street carnival, most of this area was farmland until the 19th century.

In the 1950s and 1960s Notting Hill became a center for the Caribbean community, many of whom lived here when they first arrived in Britain. The carnival started in 1966 and takes over the area every August over the bank holiday weekend *(see p59)*, when costumed parades flood through the streets.

REGENT'S PARK AND MARYLEBONE

The area south of Regent's Park, incorporating the medieval village of Marylebone, has London's highest concentration of quality Georgian housing. It was developed by Robert Harley, Earl of Oxford, as London shifted west in the 18th century. Terraces by John Nash adorn the southern edge of Regent's Park, the busiest of the Royal Parks, while to the northwest lies St. John's Wood, a stylish inner suburb.

Sights at a Glance

Historic Streets and Buildings
4 Harley Street
5 Portland Place
6 Broadcasting House
15 Cumberland Terrace

Museums and Galleries
10 Wallace Collection
11 Sherlock Holmes Museum

Churches and Mosques
3 St. Marylebone Parish Church
7 All Souls, Langham Place
12 London Central Mosque

Parks and Gardens
2 Regent's Park

Entertainment
1 Madame Tussauds
9 Wigmore Hall
14 London Zoo

Historic Hotels
8 Langham Hotel

Historic Waterways
13 Regent's Canal

Street Finder, maps 3, 4, 12

Restaurants *see pp297–298*
1 Galvin Bistrot de Luxe
2 Golden Hind
3 Orrey
4 The Povidores and Tapa Room
5 Texture

0 meters   500
0 yards   500

◀ Georgian-style architecture, Regent's Park

For keys to symbols *see back flap*

Street by Street: Marylebone

South of Regent's Park lies the medieval village of Marylebone (originally Maryburne, the stream by St. Mary's church). Until the 18th century it was surrounded by fields, but these were built over as fashionable London drifted west. In the mid-19th century, professional people, especially doctors, used the spacious houses to receive wealthy clients. The area has maintained both its medical connections and its elegance. Marylebone High Street is full of interesting, high-quality food and clothes shops, bookshops, and cafés.

2 ★ Regent's Park
John Nash laid out the royal park in 1812 as a setting for classically designed villas and terraces.

The Royal Academy of Music, England's first music academy, was founded in 1774. The present brick building, with its own concert hall, is from 1911.

1 ★ Madame Tussauds
The wax museum of famous people, historical and contemporary, has been in business since 1835 and remains one of London's most popular attractions. It moved to its present location in 1884.

To Regent's Park

YORK BRIDGE

OUTER CIRCLE

YORK TERRACE EAST

YORK TERRACE WEST

YORK GATE

MARYLEBONE

MARYLEBONE HIGH STREET

ALLSOP PLACE

NOTTINGHAM PLACE

NOTTINGHAM STREET

LUXBOROUGH STREET

3 St. Marylebone Parish Church
Poets Robert Browning and Elizabeth Barrett married in this church.

Key

— Suggested route

0 meters	100
0 yards	100

Baker Street station

Park Crescent's breathtaking facades by Nash have been preserved, although the interiors were rebuilt as offices in the 1960s. The crescent seals the north end of Nash's ceremonial route from St. James's to Regent's Park, via Regent Street and Portland Place.

Locator Map
See Central London Map pp16–17

The London Clinic is one of the best-known private hospitals in this medical district.

Regent's Park station

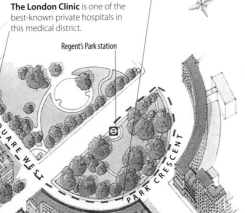

5 Portland Place
In the center of this broad street stands a statue of Field Marshal Sir George Stuart White, who won the Victoria Cross for gallantry in the Afghan War of 1879.

The Royal Institute of British Architects is housed in a striking Art Deco building designed by Grey Wornum in 1934.

4 Harley Street
Consulting rooms of eminent medical specialists have been located here for more than a century.

❶ Madame Tussauds

Marylebone Rd NW1. **Map** 4 D5.
Tel 0871 894 3000. 🚇 Baker St.
Open 9:30am–5:30pm Mon–Fri, 9am–
6pm Sat & Sun (Aug: 9am–6pm daily).
Closed Dec 25. 🎭 💻 🏛 ♿ phone
first. 🆆 **madametussauds.com**

Madame Tussaud began her
wax-modeling career rather
morbidly, taking death masks of
many of the best-known victims
of the French Revolution. In 1835
she set up an exhibition of her
work in Baker Street, not far from
the collection's present site.

The attraction still uses traditional wax-modeling techniques
to recreate politicians, royals,
movie and television actors,
rock stars, and sports heroes.

The main sections of the
exhibition are "A-List Party,"
where visitors get to feel what it
is like to be at a celebrity party;
"Film," devoted to giants of the
entertainment world such as
Marilyn Monroe and ET; and
"World Leaders," including

Traditional wax-modelling at Madame Tussauds

Barack Obama, David Cameron,
and Martin Luther King Jr.

The "Culture" area has the
likes of Shakespeare and
Picasso, and the "Music Zone"
includes Madonna, Rihanna,
and The Beatles.

"Scream" is the most
renowned part of Madame
Tussauds, featuring gruesome
episodes in the grim catalog of
crime and punishment: the
murderer Dr. Crippen; Vlad the
Impaler; and the chill gloom of

an east London Victorian street
during Jack the Ripper's time in
the late 19th century.

The "Spirit of London" is the
finale. Visitors travel in stylized
London taxicabs and participate
in momentous events of the
city, from the Great Fire of 1666
to 1960s Swinging London.

Ticket prices also include
entry to the thrilling
Marvel Superheroes
4D Movie
Experience.

There are also
educational tours
designed for
groups and
schools – check
the website
for further
information.

Wax figure of Elizabeth II

Tulip time at Queen Mary's Gardens in Regent's Park

❷ Regent's Park

NW1. **Map** 3 C2. **Tel** 0300 061 2300.
🚇 Regent's Park, Baker St, Great
Portland St. **Open** 5am–dusk daily.
♿ 💻 Open-air theater *See
Entertainment pp336–7*. Zoo *See p229*.
Sports facilities.
🆆 **royalparks.gov.uk**

This area of land became
enclosed as a park in 1812. John
Nash designed the plan and
originally envisaged a kind of
garden suburb, dotted with

56 villas in a variety of Classical
styles, with a pleasure palace for
the Prince Regent. In the end,
only eight villas – and no
palace – were built inside the
park (three survive around the
edge of the Inner Circle).

The boating lake, which has
many varieties of water birds,
is marvelously romantic,
especially when music drifts
across from the bandstand in
the distance. Queen Mary's
Gardens are a mass of

wonderful sights and smells in
summer, when visitors can
enjoy Shakespeare productions
at the **Open Air Theatre** nearby.

Nash's master plan for the
park continues just beyond its
northeastern edge in Park
Village East and West. These
elegant stucco buildings
date from 1828.

The park is also renowned for
its excellent sports facilities.

❸ St. Marylebone Parish Church

Marylebone Rd NW1. **Map** 4 D5.
Tel 020 7935 7315. 🚇 Regent's Park.
Open call to check. ♿ ✝ 11am Sun.
💻 🆆 **stmarylebone.org**

This is where the poets Robert
Browning and Elizabeth Barrett
were married in 1846 after
eloping from her strict family
home on nearby Wimpole
Street. The large, stately church
by Thomas Hardwick was
consecrated in 1817 after the
former church, where Lord
Byron was christened in 1778,
became too small. Hardwick

was determined that the same thing should not happen to his new church – so everything is on a grand scale.

Commemorative window in St. Marylebone Parish Church

❹ Harley Street

W1. **Map** 4 E5. ☻ Regent's Park, Oxford Circus, Bond St, Great Portland St.

The large houses on this late 18th-century street were popular with successful doctors and specialists in the middle of the 19th century when it was a rich residential area. The doctors' practices stayed, and lend the street an air of hushed order, unusual in central London. There are very few private houses or apartments here now, but William Gladstone lived at No. 73 from 1876 to 1882.

❺ Portland Place

W1. **Map** 4 E5. ☻ Regent's Park, Oxford Circus.

The Adam Brothers, Robert and James, laid out this street in 1773. Only a few of the original houses remain, the best being 27 to 47 on the west side, south of Devonshire Street. John Nash added the street to his processional route from Carlton House to Regent's Park and sealed its northern end with Park Crescent.

The building of the Royal Institute of British Architects (1934) at No. 66 is adorned with symbolic statues and reliefs. Its bronze front doors depict London's buildings and the Thames River.

❻ Broadcasting House

Portland Place W1. **Map** 12 E1. ☻ Oxford Circus. **Open** daily for guided tours only. Reservations essential; call 0370 901 1227. 🅿 ♿ 🚫 No children under 9. 🆆 bbc.co.uk

Broadcasting House was built in 1931 as a suitably modern Art Deco headquarters for the brand-new medium of broadcasting. Its front, curving with the street, is dominated by Eric Gill's stylized relief of Prospero and Ariel. As the invisible spirit of the air, Shakespeare's Ariel was considered an appropriate personification of broadcasting. The character appears in two other sculptures on the western frontage, and again over the eastern entrance in "Ariel Piping to Children."

Broadcasting House is now partly occupied by management, as some radio studios moved to west London in the 1990s. Fascinating tours of Broadcasting House (and also of BBC TV Centre in White City) are available. Each tour is unique, as the itinerary depends on programming and events of the day.

In partnership with English Heritage, a major refurbishment in 2011 opened a public piazza, a BBC shop, a café, and an exhibition/interactive area.

Relief on the Royal Institute of British Architects on Portland Place

❼ All Souls, Langham Place

Langham Place W1. **Map** 12 F1. **Tel** 020 7580 3522. ☻ Oxford Circus. **Open** 9:30am–6pm Mon–Fri; 9am–3pm, 5:30–8:30pm Sun. ✝ 9:30, 11:30am, 6:30pm Sun. ♿ 📷 Sun. 🆆 allsouls.org

John Nash designed this church in 1824. Its quirky round frontage is best seen from Regent Street. When it was first built, the spire was ridiculed because it appeared too slender and flimsy.

The only Nash church in London, it had close links with the BBC, based opposite at Broadcasting House, and ten years ago used to double as a recording studio for the daily broadcast church service.

❽ Langham Hotel

1 Portland Place W1. **Map** 12 E1. **Tel** 020 7636 1000. ☻ Oxford Circus. . 🆆 langhamhotels.com

This was London's grandest hotel after opening in 1865. The writers Oscar Wilde and Mark Twain and composer Antonín Dvořák were among its many distinguished guests. It was, for a time, used by the BBC as a record library and as a venue for recording shows. It has since been restored, bringing it boldly into the 21st century with its luxurious rooms, chic Artesian bar, and the exquisite fine-dining restaurant, Roux at the Landau.

All Souls, Langham Place (1824)

❾ Wigmore Hall

36 Wigmore St W1. **Map** 12 E1. **Tel** 020 7258 8200. Box Office: **Tel** 020 7935 2141. ⊖ Bond St, Oxford Cir. ♿ ⧗ *See Entertainment p341.* 🔳 **wigmore-hall.org.uk**

This appealing little concert hall for chamber music was designed by T. E. Collcutt, architect of the Savoy Hotel, in 1900. At first it was called Bechstein Hall because it was attached to the Bechstein piano showroom; the area used to be the heart of London's piano trade. Opposite is the Art Nouveau emporium built in 1907 as Debenham and Freebody's department store – now Debenham's on Oxford Street.

The Mosque on the edge of Regent's Park

Late 18th-century Sèvres porcelain vase at the Wallace Collection

❿ Wallace Collection

Hertford House, Manchester Sq W1. **Map** 12 D1. **Tel** 020 7563 9500. ⊖ Bond St, Baker St. **Open** 10am–5pm daily. **Closed** Dec 24–26. Lectures. ♿ ⧉ ⧗ ⌂ 🔳 **wallacecollection.org**

This is one of the world's finest private collections of art. It has remained intact since it was bequeathed to the government in 1897 with the stipulation that it should go on permanent public display with nothing added or taken away. The product of passionate collecting for four generations of the

Hertford family, it is a must for anyone with even a passing interest in the progress of European art up to the late 19th century. In 2000 four more galleries were opened so that even more of the collection could be shown.

Among the 70 master works are Frans Hals's *The Laughing Cavalier*, Titian's *Perseus and Andromeda*, and Rembrandt's *Titus*. There are superb portraits by Reynolds, Gainsborough, and Romney. Other highlights include Sèvres porcelain and sculpture by Houdon and Roubiliac. The fine European and Asian armor collection is the second largest in the UK.

⓫ Sherlock Holmes Museum

221b Baker St NW1. **Map** 3 C5. **Tel** 020 7224 3688. ⊖ Baker St. **Open** 9:30am–6pm daily. **Closed** Dec 25. ⧉ ⌂ 🔳 **sherlock-holmes.co.uk**

Sir Arthur Conan Doyle's fictional detective lived at 221b Baker Street. This building, dating from 1815, has been converted to resemble Holmes's flat, and is furnished exactly as described in the books. Visitors are greeted by Holmes's "housekeeper" and shown to his recreated rooms on the first floor. The shop sells the novels and deerstalker hats.

⓬ London Central Mosque

146 Park Rd NW8. **Map** 3 B3. **Tel** 020 7724 3363. ⊖ Marylebone, St. John's Wood, Baker St. **Open** dawn–dusk daily. ♿ ⌂ Lectures. 🔳 **iccuk.org**

Surrounded by trees on the edge of Regent's Park, this large, golden-domed mosque was designed by Sir Frederick Gibberd and completed in 1978. Built to cater to the increasing number of Muslim residents and visitors in London, the mosque is capable of holding 1,800 worshippers. The main hall of worship is a plain square chamber with a domed roof and a magnificent carpet. Visitors must remove their shoes before entering the mosque, and women should remember to cover their heads.

Conan Doyle's Sherlock Holmes

A boat trip on Regent's Canal

⓭ Regent's Canal

NW1 & NW8. **Map** 3 C1. **Tel** 020 7482
2660 (waterbus). ⊖ Camden Town,
St. John's Wood, Warwick Ave. Canal
towpaths: **Open** dawn–dusk daily.
See Six Guided Walks pp266–7.
ⓦ londonwaterbus.com

John Nash was extremely
enthusiastic about this
waterway, opened in 1820 to
link the Grand Junction Canal,
which ended at Little Venice in
Paddington in the west, with
the London docks at Limehouse
in the east. He saw it as an
added attraction for his new
Regent's Park, and originally
wanted the canal to run
through the middle of that park.
He was persuaded out of that
by those who thought that the
bargees' bad language would
offend the genteel residents of
the area. Perhaps this was just
as well – the steam tugs that
hauled the barges were dirty
and sometimes dangerous.
In 1874, a barge carrying
gunpowder blew up in the
cutting by London Zoo, killing
the crew, destroying a bridge,
and terrifying the populace
and the animals. After an initial
period of prosperity for the
canal, increasing competition
from new railroads saw it
gradually slip into decline.

Today it has been revived as a
leisure amenity; the towpath is
paved as a pleasant walkway,
and short boat trips are offered
between Little Venice and
Camden Lock, where there is a
thriving crafts market. Visitors to
the zoo can use the landing stage
that is situated alongside it.

⓮ London Zoo

Regent's Park NW1. **Map** 4 D2.
Tel 0844 225 1826. ⊖ Camden Town.
Open 10am–5:30pm (4:30pm Nov–
Mar) daily. **Closed** Dec 25. ♿ 🚻 🏠
📷 ⓦ zsl.org

Opened in 1828, the zoo has
been one of London's biggest
tourist attractions ever since,
and is also a major research and
conservation center. London
Zoo has over 600 species of
animals, from Sumatran tigers to
Mexican red-kneed bird-eating
spiders. Exhibits include
Penguin Beach, with over

London Zoo's aviary, designed by
Lord Snowdon (1964)

60 birds, and B.U.G.S!, which
covers the vast range of life
forms found in Earth's major
habitats. There are also plenty
of interactive activities.

⓯ Cumberland Terrace

NW1. **Map** 4 E2. ⊖ Great Portland St,
Regent's Park, Camden Town.

James Thomson is credited with
the detailed design of this, the
longest and most elaborate
of the Nash terraces around
Regent's Park. Its imposing central
block of raised Ionic columns
is topped with a decorated
triangular pediment. Completed
in 1828, it was designed to be
visible from the palace Nash
planned for the Prince Regent
(later George IV). The palace
was never built because the
Prince was too busy with his
plans for Buckingham Palace
(*see pp96–7*).

Nash's Cumberland Terrace, dating from 1828

HAMPSTEAD

Hampstead has always stayed aloof from London, looking down from its site on the high ridge north of the metropolis. Today it is essentially a Georgian village. The heath separating Hampstead from Highgate

reinforces its appeal, isolating it further from the hurly-burly of the modern city. A stroll around the charming village streets, followed by a hike across the Heath, makes for one of the finest walks in London.

Sights at a Glance

Historic Streets and Buildings
1 Flask Walk and Well Walk
5 Church Row
6 Downshire Hill
13 Vale of Health

Museums and Galleries
2 Burgh House
4 Fenton House
7 Keats House
10 Kenwood House

Parks and Gardens
8 Hampstead Heath
9 Parliament Hill
12 The Hill Garden

Pubs and Restaurants
3 Old Bull and Bush
12 Spaniards Inn

☐ Restaurants *see pp301–303*
1 Jin-Kichi
2 Gaucho Hampstead
3 The Wells

0 meters 500
0 yards 500

Street Finder, maps 1, 2

For keys to symbols *see back flap*

Street-by-Street: Hampstead

Perched awkwardly on a hilltop, with its broad heath to the north, Hampstead has kept its villagey atmosphere and sense of being out of the city. This has attracted artists and writers since Georgian times and made it one of London's most desirable residential areas. Its mansions and town houses are perfectly maintained and a stroll through Hampstead's narrow streets is one of London's quieter pleasures.

❸ Old Bull and Bush
This pub on the edge of the Heath was a former haunt for writers and artists.

To Old Bull and Bush

❽ ★ Hampstead Heath
A welcome retreat from the city, its broad open spaces include bathing ponds, meadows and lakes .

Whitestone Pond takes its name from the old white milestone nearby. It is 4.5 miles (7 km) from Holborn *(see pp134–43)*.

Grove Lodge was home to novelist John Galsworthy (1867–1933), author of the *Forsyte Saga*, for the last 15 years of his life.

Admiral's House dates from about 1700. Built for a sea captain, its name derives from its external maritime motifs. No admiral ever actually lived in it.

Key

— Suggested route

0 meters		100
0 yards		100

❹ ★ Fenton House
Summer visitors should seek out this late 17th-century house and its exquisite walled garden, which are well hidden in the jumble of streets near the Heath.

2 ★ Burgh House
Built in 1702 but much altered
since, the house contains an
intriguing local history museum
and a café overlooking the
small garden.

Locator Map
See Central London Map pp16–17

The New End Theatre
produces rare but significant
work. The building used to
be a morgue.

LCC
JOHN
CONSTABLE
(1770-1837)
Painter
Lived
here

No. 40 Well Walk
is where artist John Constable
lived while working on his
many Hampstead pictures.

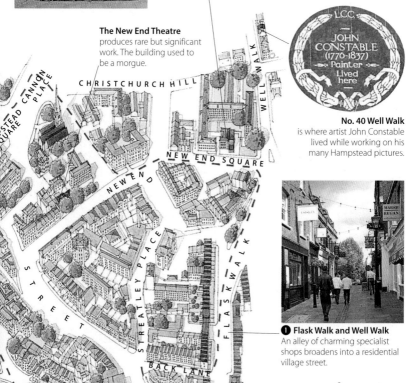

1 Flask Walk and Well Walk
An alley of charming specialist
shops broadens into a residential
village street.

Hampstead station

The Everyman Cinema has been
an art cinema
since 1933.

5 ★ Church Row
The tall houses are rich in
original detail. Notice the
superb ironwork on what is
probably London's finest
Georgian street.

Old Bull and Bush in 1900

❶ Flask Walk and Well Walk

NW3. **Map** 1 B5. ⊖ Hampstead.

Flask Walk is named after the Flask pub. Here, in the 18th century, therapeutic spa water from what was then the separate village of Hampstead was put into flasks and sold to visitors or sent to London. The water, rich in iron salts, came from nearby Well Walk, where a disused fountain now marks the site of the well. The Wells Tavern, almost opposite the spring, used to be a hostelry that specialized in accommodating those who engaged in the illicit liaisons for which the spa became notorious.

In later times, there have been many notable residents of Well Walk, including artist John Constable (at No. 40), novelists D. H. Lawrence and J. B. Priestley, and the poet John Keats, before he moved to his better-known house in what is now Keats Grove. At the High Street end,

Site of the well on Well Walk

Flask Walk is narrow and lined with old shops. Beyond the pub (note the Victorian tiled panels outside), it broadens into a row of Regency houses, one of which used to belong to the novelist Kingsley Amis.

❷ Burgh House

New End Sq NW3. **Map** 1 B4. **Tel** 020 7431 0144. ⊖ Hampstead. **Open** noon–5pm Wed–Sun (Sat ground floor art gallery & café only), 2–5pm public hols. **Closed** Christmas week. 🖵 📷 Music recitals. 🔲 **burghhouse.org.uk**

The last private tenant of Burgh House was the son-in-law of the writer Rudyard Kipling, who visited here occasionally in the last years of his life until 1936. After a period under the ownership of Hampstead Borough Council, the house was rented to the independent Burgh House Trust. Since 1979, the Trust has run it as the Hampstead Museum, which illustrates the history of the area and concentrates on some of its most celebrated residents.

One room is devoted to the life of John Constable, who painted an extraordinary series of studies of clouds from Hampstead Heath. The house also has sections on Lawrence, Keats, the artist Stanley Spencer, and others who lived and worked in the area. There is a display about Hampstead as a spa in the 18th and 19th centuries, which is also worth a visit. Burgh House often has exhibitions by contemporary local artists. The house itself was

built in 1703 but is named after a 19th-century resident, the Reverend Allatson Burgh. It has been much altered inside, and today the marvelously carved staircase is a highlight of the interior. Also worth seeing is the music room, which was reconstructed in 1920 but contains good 18th-century pine paneling from another house. In the 1720s, Dr. William Gibbons, chief physician to the then thriving Hampstead spa, lived here.

A licensed café serves delicious food and has a terrace overlooking the pretty garden.

Burgh House staircase

❸ Old Bull and Bush

North End Rd NW3. **Map** 1 A2. **Tel** 020 8905 5456. ⊖ Golders Green. **Open** 11am–11pm Mon–Sat, 11am–10:30pm Sun. ♿ 🚫

This pub, one of London's oldest and most famous, dates back to 1645, when it was a farmhouse. It received its license to sell ale in 1721 and quickly became a haunt for artists and literary figures, including the famous artist William Hogarth *(see p261)* and the writer Austin Dobson. It is reputed that Hogarth planted a tree in the pub's garden. Located next to Hampstead Heath, the pub serves food at lunchtime and in the evening, and has barbecues in the summer in the garden. The interior is comfortably furnished.

❹ Fenton House

20 Hampstead Grove NW3. **Map** 1 A4.
Tel 020 7435 3471. 🚇 Hampstead.
Open Mar–Oct: 11am–5pm Wed–Sun
& public hols (2–5pm some Thu due
to lunchtime concerts). 🎫 🚻
ground floor only. 📷 book ahead.
📅 💻 **nationaltrust.org.uk/
fentonhouse**

Built in 1686, this splendid William
and Mary house is the oldest
mansion in Hampstead. It
contains two specialized exhibitions that are open to the
public during the summer:
the Benton-Fletcher
collection of early
keyboard instruments,
which includes a
harpsichord dating from
1612, said to have been
played by Handel; and a
fine collection of porcelain.
The instruments are kept in full
working order and are actually
used for concerts held in the
house. The porcelain collection
was largely accumulated by
Lady Binning, who, in 1952,
bequeathed the house and its
contents to the National Trust.

❺ Church Row

NW3. **Map** 1 A5. 🚇 Hampstead.

The row is one of the most
complete Georgian streets in
London. Much of its original
detail has survived, notably
the ironwork.
    At the west end is St. John's,
Hampstead's parish church,
built in 1745. The iron gates are
earlier and come from Canons
Park in Edgware. Inside the
church is a bust of John Keats.
John Constable's grave is
in the churchyard, and many
Hampstead luminaries are
buried in the adjoining cemetery.

❻ Downshire Hill

NW3. **Map** 1 C5. 🚇 Hampstead.

A beautiful street of mainly
Regency houses, it lent its name
to a group of artists, including
Stanley Spencer and Mark
Gertler, who would gather at
No. 47 between the two world
wars. That same house had

been the meeting place of
Pre-Raphaelite artists, among
them Dante Gabriel Rossetti
and Edward Burne-Jones. A
more recent resident, at No. 5,
was the late Jim Henson, the
puppeteer and producer who
created the Muppets.
    The church on the corner (the
second Hampstead church to be
called St. John's) was built in 1823
to serve the Hill's residents. Inside,
it still has its original box pews.

Lock of Fanny Brawne's hair

❼ Keats House

Keats Grove NW3. **Map** 1 C5. **Tel** 020
7332 3868. 🚇 Hampstead, Belsize
Park. **Open** Apr–Oct: 1–5pm
Tue–Sun, Nov–Apr: 1–5pm Fri–Sun.
Closed Good Fri, Christmas week.
🎫 📷 3pm daily. 🚻 ground floor
only. 📅 Poetry readings, lectures.
💻 **keatshouse.cityoflondon.gov.uk**

Originally two semidetached
houses built in 1816, the smaller
one became Keats's home in
1818 when a friend persuaded
him to move in. Keats spent two

St. John's, Downshire Hill

productive years here: *Ode to a
Nightingale*, perhaps his most
celebrated poem, was written
under a plum tree in the garden.
The Brawne family moved into
the larger house a year later,
and Keats became engaged to
their daughter, Fanny. However,
the marriage never took
place because Keats died of
consumption in Rome before
two years had passed. He was
only 25 years old.
    A copy of one of Keats's
love letters to Fanny, the
engagement ring he offered
her, and a lock of her hair are
among the mementos that are
exhibited at the house – it was
first opened to the public in
1925. Visitors are also able to
see facsimiles of some of Keats's
manuscripts, part of a collection
that serves as an evocative and
memorable tribute to his
life and work.

Fenton House's 17th-century facade

People relaxing in the open space of Hampstead Heath

❽ Hampstead Heath

NW3. **Map** 1 C2. **Tel** 020 7332 3322.
🚇 Belsize Park, Hampstead.
Open 24 hrs daily. Special walks
on Sundays. ♿ call for disability
buggies. 🎭 Concerts, some children's
activities in summer. Sports facilities,
swimming ponds. Sports bookings
Tel 020 7332 3773.
🌐 **cityoflondon.gov.uk**

The best time to stride across
these broad 3 sq miles (8 sq km)
is Sunday afternoon, when the
local residents walk off their roast
beef lunches, discussing the
contents of the Sunday papers.
Separating the hilltop villages
of Hampstead and Highgate

(see p248), the Heath was made
from the grounds of several,
formerly separate, properties
and embraces a variety of
landscapes – woods, meadows,
hills, ponds, and lakes. It remains
uncluttered by the haphazard
buildings and statues that
embellish the central London
parks, and its open spaces have
become increasingly precious
to Londoners as the areas
around it get more crowded.
There are ponds for swimming
and fishing and, on three holiday
weekends – Easter, late spring,
and late summer – the southern
part of the Heath is taken over
by a fair (see pp58–61).

❾ Parliament Hill

NW5. **Map** 2 E4. **Tel** 020 7332 3773.
🚇 Belsize Park, Hampstead. ♿
Concerts, children's activities in
summer. Sports facilities. 🎭

An unlikely but romantic
explanation for the area's name
is that it is where Guy Fawkes's
fellow plotters gathered on
November 5, 1605 in the vain
hope of watching the Houses
of Parliament blow up after they
had planted gunpowder there
(see p26). More probably it was
a gun emplacement for the
Parliamentary side during the
Civil War 40 years later. The
gunners would have enjoyed

❿ Kenwood House

Hampstead Lane NW3. **Map** 1 C1.
Tel 020 8348 1286. 🚇 Golders Green,
Archway, then 210 bus. Estate:
Open 7am–dusk daily. **Closed** Jan 1,
Dec 24–26. 🎭 Lakeside concerts in
summer. Regular events. ♿ ground
floor. 🎭 🎦 See Entertainment pp340–
41. 🌐 **english-heritage.org.uk**

This is a magnificent Adam
mansion, filled with Old Master
paintings, including works by
Vermeer, Turner, and Romney
(who lived in Hampstead). It is
situated in landscaped grounds
high on the edge of Hampstead
Heath. There has been a house
here since 1616 – the present
one was remodeled by Robert

Adam in 1764 for the Earl of
Mansfield. Adam refurbished
existing rooms and added to
the original building. Most of his
work has survived, the highlight
being the library. A Rembrandt
self-portrait is the star attraction
of the collection, and there are
also works by Van Dyck, Hals,
and Reynolds.

The orangery is now
used for occasional
concerts and recitals.

a broad view across London: even today, when tall buildings intervene, it provides one of the most spectacular views over the capital. From here the dome of St. Paul's is prominent. Parliament Hill is also a popular place for flying kites and sailing model boats on the boating pond.

The historic Spaniards Inn

⓫ Spaniards Inn

Spaniards Rd NW3. **Map** 1 B1.
Tel 020 8731 8406. 🚇 Hampstead, Golders Green. **Open** 11am–11pm Mon–Fri, 10am–11pm Sat, 10am–10:30pm Sun. ♿
🌐 thespaniardshampstead.co.uk

Dick Turpin, the notorious 18th-century highwayman, is said to have frequented this pub. When he wasn't holding up stagecoaches on their way to and from London, he stabled his horse, Black Bess, at the Kenwood stables. The building certainly dates from Turpin's

time and, although the bar downstairs has been altered frequently, the small upstairs Turpin Bar is original. A pair of guns over the bar were reputedly taken from anti-Catholic rioters, who came to Hampstead to burn the Lord Chancellor's house at Kenwood during the Gordon Riots of 1780. The landlord detained them by offering pint after pint of free beer and, when they were drunk, disarmed them.

Among the pub's noted patrons have been the poets Shelley, Keats, and Byron, the actor David Garrick, and the artist Sir Joshua Reynolds.

The tollhouse has been restored; it juts into the road so that, in the days when tolls were levied, traffic could not race past without paying.

⓬ The Hill Garden

North End Way NW3. **Map** 1 A2.
🚇 Hampstead, Golders Green.
Open dawn to dusk daily.

This charming garden was created by Edwardian soap manufacturer and patron of the arts Lord Leverhulme. It was originally the grounds to his house, and is now part of Hampstead Heath. It boasts a raised pergola walkway, best seen in summer when the plants are in flower; the garden also has a beautiful formal pond.

Pergola walk at The Hill Garden

⓭ Vale of Health

NW3. **Map** 1 B4. 🚇 Hampstead.

This area was famous as a distinctly unhealthy swamp before it was drained in 1770; until then it was known as Hatches Bottom. Its newer name may derive from people fleeing here from cholera in London at the end of the 18th century. Alternatively, the name could have been the hype of a property developer when it was first recorded in 1801.

The poet James Henry Leigh Hunt put it on the literary map when he moved here in 1815, and played host to Coleridge, Byron, Shelley, and Keats.

D. H. Lawrence lived here briefly and Stanley Spencer painted in a room above the Vale of Health Hotel, demolished in 1964.

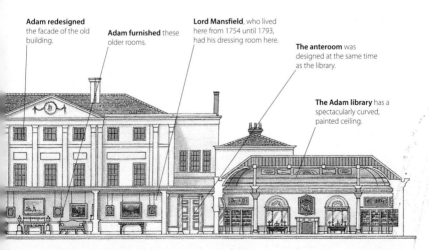

Adam redesigned the facade of the old building.

Adam furnished these older rooms.

Lord Mansfield, who lived here from 1754 until 1793, had his dressing room here.

The anteroom was designed at the same time as the library.

The Adam library has a spectacularly curved, painted ceiling.

GREENWICH
AND BLACKHEATH

Best known as the place from which the world's time is measured, Greenwich marks the historic eastern approach to London by land and water. Home to the National Maritime Museum and the Queen's House, the Royal Observatory and the Cutty Sark, Greenwich has a village feel, with charming shops, markets, and museums to explore.

Sights at a Glance

Historic Streets and Buildings
❷ The Queen's House
❼ Old Royal Naval College
❾ Royal Observatory Greenwich
⓬ Croom's Hill

Museums
❶ National Maritime Museum
❹ Ranger's House – The Wernher Collection
⓭ The Fan Museum

Churches
❸ St. Alfege Church

Parks and Gardens
❿ Greenwich Park
⓫ Blackheath

Walkway
❻ Greenwich Foot Tunnel

Pubs and Restaurants
❽ Trafalgar Tavern

Ships
❺ Cutty Sark

0 meters		500
0 yards		500

Street Finder, maps 23, 24

◀ View of Canary Wharf from Greenwich Park

For keys to symbols *see back flap*

Street-by-Street: Greenwich

This historic town, granted UNESCO World Heritage Site status, marks the eastern approach to London and is best visited by river *(see pp62–7)*. In Tudor times it was the site of a palace much enjoyed by Henry VIII, near a fine hunting ground and his naval base. The old palace is gone, leaving Inigo Jones's exquisite Queen's House, built for James I's wife. Museums, shops, cafés, and markets, Wren's architecture, and the magnificent Royal Park all make Greenwich an enjoyable day's excursion.

❻ Greenwich Foot Tunnel, leading to the Isle of Dogs, is one of two tunnels built solely for pedestrians.

Greenwich Pier is a boarding point for boats to Westminster, the O2, and the Thames Barrier.

❺ Cutty Sark

Clipper ships such as this once traded across the oceans. The impressively restored Cutty Sark has been raised to allow visitors to explore above and below decks.

To Cutty Sark DLR →

COLLEGE APPROACH

KING WILLIAM WALK

GREENWICH CHURCH STREET

NELSON ROAD

STOCKWELL STREET

NEVA STRE

Greenwich Market

Selling crafts, antiques, and books, this market is open Tuesday to Sunday.

❸ St. Alfege Church

There has been a church here since 1012.

Spread Eagle Yard

Once a stopping point for horse-drawn carriages. The Spread Eagle restaurant is next to the site of the ticket office.

Locator Map
See Greater London Map pp14–15

❼ ★ Old Royal Naval College
Wren's stately structure was built in two halves so that the Queen's House would keep its river view.

George II Statue
Sculpted by John Rysbrack in 1735, this statue depicts the king as a Roman emperor.

The Painted Hall
contains 18th-century murals by Sir James Thornhill, who painted the interior of the dome at St. Paul's Cathedral.

❷ ★ The Queen's House
On his return from Italy, this was the first building Inigo Jones designed in the Palladian style.

Key

— Suggested route

0 meters	100
0 yards	100

❶ National Maritime Museum
Real and model boats, paintings, and instruments like this 18th-century compass illustrate naval history.

❶ National Maritime Museum

Romney Rd SE10. **Map** 23 C2.
Tel 020 8858 4422. 🚇 Cutty Sark DLR.
🚆 Greenwich. **Open** 10am–5pm
daily. **Closed** Dec 24–26. 🖼 special
exhibitions. 🎫 ♿ 🖥 📷 Lectures.
w rmg.co.uk

The sea has always played an important role in British history, and this museum – built in the 19th century as a school for sailors' children – celebrates this seafaring heritage, from early British trade and empire to the exploratory expeditions of Captain Cook, and from the Napoleonic Wars through to the modern day.

The Sammy Ofer wing, the biggest development in the museum's history, boasts "the Wave," a 65-ft (20-m) audiovisual installation in which images and films from the museum's vast archives unfurl in dramatic, thematic journeys.

The Nelson gallery looks at the course of British maritime history over the tumultuous 18th century, a period when seafaring heroes were national celebrities. A star exhibit is the uniform that Lord Horatio Nelson was wearing when he was shot at the Battle of Trafalgar in October 1805.

More spectacular is the royal barge built for Prince Frederick in 1732, decorated with gilded mermaids and his Prince of Wales's feathers on the stern. Throughout the museum are scores of finely crafted models of ships and historic paintings.

St. Alfege's altar with rails attributed to Jean Tijou

❷ The Queen's House

Romney Rd SE10. **Map** 23 C2. **Tel** 020
8858 4422. 🚇 Cutty Sark DLR.
🚆 Greenwich. **Open** 10am–5pm
daily. Closes early for special events –
call to check. **Closed** Dec 24–26. 🎫
♿ 🚭 🖥 📷 **w** rmg.co.uk

The house was designed by Inigo Jones and was completed in 1637. It was originally meant to be the home of Anne of Denmark, wife of James I, but she died while it was still being built, and it was finished for Charles I's queen, Henrietta Maria. She fell in love with it and called it her house of delights. After the Civil War, it was briefly occupied by Henrietta as dowager queen, but was not much used by the royal family after that.

The building has been refurbished, and now displays the art collection of the National Maritime Museum. On the ground floor is a permanent exhibition, Historic Greenwich, which includes two models showing how the house looked in 17th-century Greenwich. The paintings on display include early views of Greenwich and portraits of historical figures associated with the house, including Inigo Jones. Visitors can also see the spiral "tulip staircase," which curves sinuously upwards without a central support. The staircase is reputed to be haunted.

❸ St. Alfege Church

Greenwich Church St SE10. **Map** 23
B2. **Tel** 020 8853 0687. 🚇 Cutty Sark
DLR. **Open** 11am–4pm Mon–Wed,
11am–2pm Thu & Fri, 10am–4pm Sat,
noon–4pm Sun. 🕈 8am, 10am Sun.
♿ if accompanied. Concerts.
w st-alfege.org

This is one of Nicholas Hawksmoor's most distinctive and powerful designs, with its gigantic columns and pediments topped by urns. It was

Prince Frederick's barge at the National Maritime Museuum

completed in 1714 on the site of an older church, which marked the martyrdom of St. Alfege, the then Archbishop of Canterbury, killed on this spot by Danish invaders in 1012. A second church here was the site of Henry VIII's baptism in 1491 and of 16th-century composer and organist Thomas Tallis's burial in 1585. Today a stained-glass window commemorates Tallis.

Some of the carved wood inside is by Grinling Gibbons, but much of it was badly damaged by a World War II bomb and has been restored. The wrought iron of the altar and gallery rails is original, attributed to Jean Tijou.

❹ Ranger's House – the Wernher Collection

Chesterfield Walk, Greenwich Park SE10. **Map** 23 C4. **Tel** 020 8294 2548. ⊖ Cutty Sark DLR. 🚊 Blackheath. **Open** See website. 🅿 🖼 guided tours by appointment; call for details. 🚻 🖼 🌐 english-heritage.org.uk

The Wernher Collection is located in Ranger's House (1688), an elegant building southeast of Greenwich Park (see p245). It is an enchanting array of over 650 pieces accumulated by South African mine owner Sir Julius Wernher in the late 19th century. The collection is displayed in 12 rooms and includes paintings, jewelry, furniture and porcelain. Highlights include Renaissance masterworks by Hans Memling and Filippo Lippi, over 100 Renaissance jewels, and an opal-set lizard pendant jewel. Other curiosities include enameled skulls.

Opal-set lizard pendant at the Wernher Collection

The domed entrance of the Greenwich Foot Tunnel

❺ Cutty Sark

King William Walk SE10. **Map** 23 B2. **Tel** 020 8858 2698. ⊖ Cutty Sark DLR. 🚢 Greenwich Pier. **Open** 10am–5pm daily (last adm 4:30pm). **Closed** Dec 25–26. 🎦 **Tel** 020 8312 6608 🖥 📷 🚻 book ahead 🌐 cuttysark.org.uk

This majestic vessel is a survivor of the clippers that crossed the Atlantic and Pacific Oceans in the 19th century. Launched in 1869 as a tea carrier, it was something of a speed machine in its day, winning the annual clippers' race from China to London in 1871 in a time of 107 days. It made its final voyage in 1938 and was put on display here in 1957. In 2006 the Cutty Sark was closed to visitors for renovation work, which suffered a major setback in May 2007 when the ship was severely damaged by fire. It was reopened by the Queen in spring 2012, fully restored.

❻ Greenwich Foot Tunnel

Between Greenwich Pier SE10 and Isle of Dogs E14. **Map** 23 B1. ⊖ Island Gardens, Cutty Sark DLR. 🚢 Greenwich Pier. **Open** 24 hours daily; elevators 7am–7pm Mon–Sat, 10am–5:30pm Sun. 🚻 when elevators are open.

This 1,200-ft- (370-m-) long tunnel was opened in 1902 to allow south London laborers to walk to work in Millwall Docks. Today it is worth crossing for the wonderful views, across the river, of Christopher Wren's Royal Naval College and of Inigo Jones's Queen's House.

Matching round red-brick terminals, with glass domes, mark the top of the elevator shafts on either side of the river. The tunnel is about 9 ft (2.5 m) high and is lined with 200,000 tiles. Both ends of the tunnel are close to stations on the Docklands Light Railway (DLR), with trains to Canary Wharf (see p251), Limehouse, East London, Tower Hill, and Lewisham. Although there are security cameras, the tunnel can be eerie at night.

A late-19th-century figurehead from the Cutty Sark

ⓧ Old Royal Naval College

King William Walk SE10. **Map** 23 C2.
Tel 020 8269 4747. 🚉 Cutty Sark DLR,
Greenwich DLR. 🚆 Greenwich, Maze
Hill. **Open** 10am–5pm daily. **Closed**
Dec 24–26 & some Sat. Grounds:
Open 8am–6pm daily. Chapel: **Open**
10am–5pm Mon–Sat, 12:30am–5pm
Sun. 📷 call 020 8269 1799 to book.
♿ 🚻 🖥 📷 🌐 **ornc.org**

These ambitious buildings by
Christopher Wren were built on
the site of the old 15th-century
royal palace, where Henry VIII,
Mary I, and Elizabeth I were
born. The Painted Hall, Chapel,
Discover Greenwich Visitor
Centre, and grounds are open
to the public. The west front
was completed by Vanbrugh.

Wren's Chapel was destroyed
by fire in 1779. The present
Greek Revival interior, by James
Stuart, is light and airy. The
Painted Hall was opulently
decorated by Sir James Thornhill
in the early 18th century.
The ceiling paintings are
supported by his illusionistic
pillars and friezes.

Next to the visitor center is a
bar-restaurant and Greenwich
Tourist Information Centre.

ⓧ Trafalgar Tavern

Park Row SE10. **Map** 23 C1. **Tel** 020
8858 2909. 🚉 Cutty Sark DLR, Greenwich DLR. **Open** noon–11pm Mon–Thu,
noon–midnight Fri–Sat, noon–10:30pm
Sun. ♿ *See Restaurants and Pubs
pp307–11.* 🌐 **trafalgartavern.co.uk**

This charming paneled pub
was built in 1837 and quickly
became established, along
with other waterside inns in

Thornhill's painting of King William III in the Painted Hall of the Old Royal Naval College

Greenwich, as a venue for
"whitebait dinners." Government
ministers, legal luminaries, and
the like would arrive from
Westminster and Charing
Cross by water on celebratory
occasions and feast on the tiny
fish. The last such meeting of
government ministers was held
here in 1885. Whitebait still
feature, when they are in
season, on the menu at the
pub's restaurant, although
they are no longer fished from
the Thames.

This was another of Charles
Dickens's haunts. He drank
here with one of his novels'
most famous illustrators,
George Cruickshank.

In 1915 the pub became an
institution for old merchant
seamen. It was restored in 1965
after a spell as a social club for
working men.

ⓧ Royal Observatory Greenwich

Greenwich Park SE10. **Map** 23 C3.
Tel 020 8858 4422. 🚉 Cutty Sark DLR.
🚆 Blackheath, Greenwich. **Open**
10am–5pm daily (last adm: 4:30pm).
Closed Dec 24–26. 📷 for Planetarium shows (last show 4pm). 🎟 ♿
📷 🌐 **rmg.co.uk**

The meridian (0° longitude) that
divides the Earth's eastern and
western hemispheres passes
through here, and millions of
visitors have taken the opportunity to be photographed
standing with a foot on either
side of it. In 1884, Greenwich
Mean Time became the basis of
time measurement for most of
the world, following the
International Meridian
Conference in Washington, DC.

The original building,
Flamsteed House, was designed
by Christopher Wren. Above one
of the building's two turrets is a
ball on a rod, which has dropped
at 1pm every day since 1833 so
that sailors on the Thames, and
makers of chronometers
(navigators' clocks), could set
their clocks by it. The house now
contains a display of John
Harrison's marine timekeepers
and an intriguing exhibition
about Greenwich Mean Time.
Flamsteed was the first
Astronomer Royal, appointed
by Charles II, and this was the

Trafalgar Tavern viewed from the Thames

official government observatory from 1675 until 1948, when the lights of London became too bright and the astronomers moved to darker Sussex.

A state-of-the-art planetarium, the only one in London, opened here in 2007.

A rare 24-hour clock at the Royal Observatory Greenwich

⑩ Greenwich Park

SE10. **Map** 23 C3. **Tel** 0300 061 2380. 🔵 Cutty Sark DLR, Greenwich DLR. 🚉 Greenwich, Maze Hill, Blackheath. **Open** 6am–7pm daily. 📷 ♿ Children's shows, playground, boating lake, and sports facilities. 🌐 **royalparks.gov.uk** Ranger's House, Chesterfield Walk, Greenwich Park SE10. **Map** 23 C4. 🌐 **english-heritage.co.uk** See also Wernher Collection, p243.

Originally the grounds of a royal palace and still a Royal Park, Greenwich Park was enclosed in 1433 and its brick wall built in the reign of James I. Later, in the 17th century, the French royal landscape gardener André Le Nôtre, of Versailles and Fontainebleau fame, was invited to design one at Greenwich. The broad avenue, rising south up the hill, was part of his plan.

There are great river views from the hilltop and on a clear day, most of London can be seen. In 2012, the park played host to the London Olympic equestrian events.

To the south-east of the park, and on the edge of the park's rose garden, is the Ranger's House (1688), which now houses the art collection of Julius Wernher (see p243).

From here the walk to the charming village of Blackheath is flat, compared with the steep walk down to the village of Greenwich at the bottom of the hill.

⑪ Blackheath

SE3. **Map** 24 D5. 🚉 Blackheath.

This open heath used to be a rallying point for large groups who were entering London from the east, including Wat Tyler's band of rebels at the time of the Peasants' Revolt in 1381.

Blackheath is also the place where King James I of England (who was also King James VI of Scotland) introduced the game of golf from his native Scotland, to the then largely skeptical English.

Today the heath is well worth exploring for the stately Georgian houses and terraces that surround it. The prettily-named Tranquil Vale to the south of the heath is the main shopping strip.

Ranger's House in Greenwich Park

⑫ Croom's Hill

SE10. **Map** 23 C3. 🔵 Cutty Sark DLR, Greenwich DLR. 🚉 Greenwich.

One of the best-kept 17th- to early 19th-century streets in London. Famous residents include Irish actor Daniel Day Lewis. The oldest buildings are at the Blackheath end: the original Manor House of 1695; No. 68, from about the same date; and No. 66, the oldest of all.

⑬ The Fan Museum

12 Croom's Hill SE10. **Map** 23 B3. **Tel** 020 8305 1441. 🚉 Greenwich. **Open** 11am–5pm Tue–Sat, noon–5pm Sun. **Closed** Jan 1, Dec 24–26. 📷 no flash. 🌂 by appt. 🏠 📷 🎁 ♿ Lectures, fan-making workshops first Sat of the month. 🌐 **thefanmuseum.org.uk**

One of London's most unlikely museums – the only one of its kind in the UK – opened in 1991. It owes its existence and appeal to the enthusiasm of Helene Alexander MBE, whose personal collection of about 4,000 fans from the 17th century onward has been augmented by donations, including several fans that were made for the stage. If there, Alexander will act as a guide.

Stage fan used in a D'Oyly Carte operetta

FARTHER AFIELD

Many of the great houses originally built as country retreats for London's elite were overrun by sprawling suburbs in the Victorian era. Fortunately, several have survived as museums in these now less-rustic surroundings. Most are less than an hour's journey from central London. Richmond Park and Wimbledon Common give a taste of the country, or go on an adventure to explore the Docklands and Thames Barrier.

Sights at a Glance

Historic Streets and Buildings
11 Sutton House
21 Charlton House
22 Eltham Palace
30 *Hampton Court pp256–7*
31 Ham House
32 Orleans House Gallery
33 Marble Hill House
35 Syon House
37 Osterley Park House
38 PM Gallery and House
41 Strand on the Green
42 Chiswick House
44 Fulham Palace

Churches
13 St. Mary, Rotherhithe
14 St. Anne's, Limehouse
26 St. Mary's, Battersea

Markets
2 Camden Market

0 kilometers 5
0 miles 3

Museums and Galleries
1 Lord's Cricket Ground
3 Freud Museum
6 The Jewish Museum
7 St. John's Gate
8 Crafts Council Gallery
10 Geffrye Museum
12 V&A Museum of Childhood
15 Museum of London Docklands
17 William Morris Gallery
23 Horniman Museum
24 Dulwich Picture Gallery
27 Wimbledon Lawn Tennis Museum
28 Wimbledon Windmill Museum
36 Musical Museum
39 Kew Bridge Steam Museum
43 Hogarth's House

Parks and Gardens
25 Battersea Park
29 Richmond Park
40 *Kew Gardens pp262–3*

Cemeteries
5 Highgate Cemetery

Modern Architecture
16 Canary Wharf
20 The O2 Arena
45 Chelsea Harbour

Historic Districts
4 Highgate
9 Islington
34 Richmond

Modern Technology
18 Emirates Air Line Cable Car
19 Thames Barrier

Key
■ Main sightseeing areas
▬ Motorway
▬ Main road
═ Minor road

All the sights in this section lie inside the M25 motorway *(see pp14–15).*

◀ Red deer frequently spotted at Richmond Park

For keys to symbols *see back flap*

North of the Center

❶ Lord's Cricket Ground

NW8. **Map** 3 A3. **Tel** 020 7616 8595 or 020 7616 8500. ⊖ St. John's Wood. Museum: **Open** 10am–4:30pm on non-match days. On match days, museum is open to ticket holders only. **Closed** Jan 1, Dec 25–26 & 29. ♿ 🅿 📷 see website; groups call to reserve. 🎫 See Entertainment pp346–7. 🌐 **lords.org**

The headquarters of Britain's chief summer sport contains a museum, including a stuffed sparrow killed by a cricket ball, as well as the Ashes (burned wood in an urn), the object of ferocious competition between the English and Australian national teams. The museum explains the history of the game, and mementos of notable cricketers make it a place of pilgrimage for devotees of the sport. Entrance to the museum is included in the tour.

Cricket pioneer Thomas Lord moved his ground here in 1814. The Pavilion (1890), from which women were excluded until 1999, is late Victorian.

The Ashes at Lord's

❷ Camden Market

NW1. ⊖ Camden Town, Chalk Farm. **Open** 10am–6pm daily.

Camden Market is really six markets located close to each other along Chalk Farm Road and Camden High Street. Packed with shoppers on weekends, most of the shops and some of the stands are open on weekdays. Many units are housed in restored Victorian buildings alongside Camden Lock and the canal. The first market here was a craft market at Camden Lock in 1975. Today all the markets sell a wide range of exciting goods, from arts and crafts and street fashion, to new age remedies and body piercing.

Sigmund Freud's famous couch

❸ Freud Museum

20 Maresfield Gdns NW3. **Tel** 020 7435 2002. ⊖ Finchley Rd. **Open** noon–5pm Wed–Sun. **Closed** Dec 24–26. 📷 no flash. ♿ limited. 🎫 Events. 🌐 **freud.org.uk**

In 1938 Sigmund Freud, the founder of psychoanalysis, fled from Nazi persecution in Vienna to this Hampstead house. Making use of the possessions he brought with him, his family recreated the atmosphere of his Vienna consulting rooms. After Freud died in 1939, his daughter Anna (who was a pioneer of child psychoanalysis) kept the house as it was. In 1986 it was opened as a museum dedicated to Freud. The most famous item is the couch on which patients lay for analysis. A series of 1930s home movies shows cheerful moments with his dog as well as scenes of Nazi attacks on his apartment. The bookshop has a large collection of his works.

❹ Highgate

N6. ⊖ Highgate.

There has been a settlement here since at least the early Middle Ages, when an important staging post on the Great North Road from London was established with a gate to control access. Like Hampstead across the Heath (see pp236–7), it soon became fashionable for its unpolluted air, and noblemen built country houses here.

It still has an exclusive feel, with a Georgian High Street and expensive houses. It was on Highgate Hill in medieval times, that Dick Whittington (a poor young lad) and his pet cat were persuaded to turn back and try their fortune in the city by the sound of Bow Bells. Whittington went on to become Lord Mayor of London. A statue of a black cat marks the spot of his epiphany (see p41).

❺ Highgate Cemetery

Swain's Lane N6. **Tel** 020 8340 1834. ⊖ Archway. Eastern Cemetery: **Open** 10am–5pm Mon–Fri, 11am–5pm Sat & Sun. 📷 2pm Sat. Western Cemetery: **Open** 📷 only Mar–Nov: 1:45pm Mon–Fri, hourly 11am–4pm Sat & Sun; Nov–Feb: half-hourly 11am– 3pm Sat & Sun. No children under 8 years admitted; first come first served. **Closed** Dec 25–26 & during funerals (phone to check). ♿ ♿ Eastern only. 🌐 **highgate-cemetery.org**

The western section of this High Victorian gem opened in 1839. For many years it lay neglected, until a voluntary group, the Friends of Highgate Cemetery, stepped in to save it from further decline. They have restored the Egyptian Avenue, a street of family vaults styled on ancient Egyptian tombs, and the Circle of Lebanon, more vaults in a ring, topped by a cedar tree. In the eastern section lie Karl Marx, Herbert Spencer, and novelist George Eliot (real name Mary Anne Evans).

George Wombwell's memorial at Highgate Cemetery

Jewish Bakers' Union banner, c.1926, Jewish Museum, Camden

❻ The Jewish Museum

129–31 Albert Street, NW1. **Map** 4 E1.
Tel 020 7284 7384. ⊖ Camden Town.
Open 10am–5pm Sat–Thu, 10am–2pm Fri. **Closed** Jewish hols, Dec 25–26. 🚹 🚻 🖵 📷
W jewishmuseum.org.uk

When London's Jewish Museum was founded in 1932, it was split between two sites, in Finchley and Camden. In 2007 the museum celebrated its 75th anniversary with the commencement of works to bring the two collections together in a single building. The project has created enlarged galleries, education facilities, and hands-on displays for children.

Celebrating Jewish life in England from the Middle Ages, the museum is packed with memorabilia. It also has important collections of Jewish ceremonial art, which includes Hanukkah lamps, a collection of Jewish marriage rings, and some illuminated marriage contracts. The highlight of this collection is a 16th-century Venetian synagogue ark.

❼ St. John's Gate

St. John's Lane EC1. **Map** 6 F4.
Tel 020 7324 4005. ⊖ Farringdon.
Open 10am–5pm Mon–Sat.
Closed Christmas week & bank holiday weekends. 🎥 11am, 2:30pm Tue, Fri, Sat (donation). 📷 🚻 limited.
W museumstjohn.org.uk

The Tudor gatehouse and parts of the 12th-century church are all that remain of the priory of the Knights of St. John, which flourished here for 400 years and was the precursor of the St. John Ambulance. Over the years, the priory buildings have had many uses, such as offices for Elizabeth I's Master of the Revels, a pub, and a coffee shop run by the artist William Hogarth's father. A museum of the order's history has been renovated, with support from the Heritage Lottery Fund, to create an exhibition space showing hidden parts of the gatehouse and a learning space in the priory church. To see the rest of the building, join a guided tour.

The Crafts Council

❽ Crafts Council

44a Pentonville Rd N1. **Map** 6 D2.
Tel 020 7806 2500. ⊖ Angel. 📖
library, 10am–5pm Wed & Thu.
Closed Dec 25–Jan 1. 🚻 📷
Lectures. **W** craftscouncil.org.uk

The Crafts Council is the national agency for promoting the creation and appreciation of contemporary crafts in the UK. It has a collection of contemporary British crafts, some of which are loaned to touring exhibitions, and there is a library. They also organize two large craft fairs – one at the Saatchi Gallery (see p199) in May and the other at Somerset House (see p119) in September/October.

❾ Islington

N1. **Map** 6 E1. ⊖ Angel, Highbury & Islington.

Islington was once a highly fashionable spa, but the rich began to move out in the late 18th century, and the area deteriorated rapidly. During the 20th century, writers such as Evelyn Waugh, George Orwell, and Joe Orton lived here. Now Islington has again returned to fashion as one of London's first areas to become gentrified, with many young professionals buying and refurbishing old houses.

An older relic is Canonbury Tower, the remains of a medieval manor house that was converted into apartments in the 18th century. Writers such as Washington Irving and Oliver Goldsmith lived here, and today it houses the Tower Theatre. On Islington Green there is a statue of Sir Hugh Myddleton, who built a canal through Islington in 1613 to bring water to London from Hertfordshire; today a landscaped walk along its banks runs between Essex Road and Canonbury stations. There is a market, Chapel Market, close to the Angel station (see p333), antique shops at Camden Passage, and a shopping and movie complex, the N1 Centre.

St. John's Priory: today, only the gatehouse remains intact

East of the Center

⑩ Geffrye Museum

Kingsland Rd E2. **Tel** 020 7739 9893.
🚇 Liverpool St, Old St. **Open** 10am–5pm Tue–Sun, noon–5pm bank hols. **Closed** Jan 1, Good Fri, Dec 24–26. Garden **Open** Apr–Oct. ♿ ▯ ▨ 🏠 Exhibitions & events.
w geffrye-museum.org.uk

This delightful museum is housed in a set of 18th-century almshouses. They were built in 1715 on land bequeathed by Sir Robert Geffrye, a 17th-century Lord Mayor of London who made his fortune through trade. Inside, you take a trip through a series of 11 rooms, chronologically arranged, which have been decorated in different period styles, each one providing an insight into the domestic interiors of the urban middle classes. The historic room settings begin with Elizabethan (which contains magnificent paneling) and run through various major styles, including High Victorian, while an attractive extension houses more modern settings, such as an example of 1990s loft living. Each room contains superb

examples of British furniture of the period. Outside, there is a series of garden "rooms" that show the designs and planting plans popular in urban gardens between the 16th and 20th centuries. There is a good café, which has a children's menu.

⑪ Sutton House

2–4 Homerton High St E9. **Tel** 020 8986 2264. 🚇 Bethnal Green then bus 253. **Open** see website for opening times. 🏠 ♿ limited. 📷 call first. ▯ 🏠 Regular events.
w nationaltrust.org.uk

One of the few London Tudor merchants' houses to survive in something like its original form. Built in 1535 for Ralph Sadleir, a courtier to Henry VIII, it was owned by several wealthy families before becoming a girls' school in the 17th century. In the 18th century the front was altered, but the Tudor fabric remains surprisingly intact, with much original brickwork, large fireplaces, and linenfold paneling.

⑫ V&A Museum of Childhood

Cambridge Heath Rd E2. **Tel** 020 8983 5200. 🚇 Bethnal Green. **Open** 10am–5:45pm daily (to 9pm 1st Thu of month). **Closed** Jan, Dec 25–26. ♿ ▯ 🏠 Workshop, children's activities.
w vam.ac.uk/moc

This East London branch of the Victoria and Albert Museum (see pp212–15) has the largest collection of childhood-related objects in the UK. Its array of toys, games, lavish dollhouses, model trains, theaters, and costumes dates from the 16th century to the present day, and is well explained and enticingly displayed. The upper floor has lots of fun activities, such as dressing up, a playable jukebox, and a funhouse mirror.

The specially built museum building was originally erected on the V&A site. In 1872, it was dismantled and reassembled here to bring the light of learning to the East End. The toy collection began in the early 20th century and became a dedicated museum of childhood at Bethnal Green in 1974.

⑬ St. Mary, Rotherhithe

St. Marychurch St SE16. **Tel** 0207 394 3394. 🚇 Rotherhithe. **Open** 9am–6pm daily. ✝ 10am, 6pm Sun. ♿
w stmaryrotherhithe.org

This church was built in 1715 on the site of a medieval church. It has nautical connotations, most notably a memorial to Christopher Jones, captain of the Mayflower, on which the Pilgrim Fathers sailed to North America. The communion table is made from the timbers of the Temeraire, a warship whose final journey to the breaker's yard at Rotherhithe was evocatively recorded in Turner's painting at the National Gallery (see pp106–109).

The church also contains a fine example of 18th-century organ-building by John Byfield.

A typical Victorian-era room at the Geffrye Museum

⓮ St. Anne's, Limehouse

3 Colt St E14. **Tel** 020 7987 1502. 🚇 Westferry (DLR). **Open** 9:30am–1pm Sun. 🚌 10:30am Sun. ⬤ Concerts, lectures see website for details. 🌐 stanneslimehouse.org

This is one of a group of East End churches designed by Nicholas Hawksmoor, completed in 1724. Its 130-ft (40-m) tower became a landmark for ships using the East End docks – St. Anne's still has the highest church clock in London. Damaged by fire in 1850, the church interior was subsequently Victorianized. It was bombed in World War II and is today in need of further restoration.

⓯ Museum of London Docklands

No. 1 Warehouse, West India Quay E14. **Tel** 020 7001 9844. 🚇 Barbican, St. Paul's **Open** 10am–6pm daily. **Closed** Dec 24–26. ⬤ ⬤ ⬤ ⬤ 🌐 museumoflondon.org.uk/docklands

Occupying a late Georgian warehouse, this museum tells the story of London's docks and their links from Roman times to the present. Recreations let visitors step back in time: notably the dark and dangerous "Sailor-town" of Wapping in the 1850s.

⓰ Canary Wharf

E14. 🚇 Canary Wharf or West India Quay (DLR). ⬤ ⬤ ⬤ 🏛 Information centre, concerts.

London's most ambitious commercial development opened in 1991, when the first tenants moved into the 50-story Canada Tower, designed by Argentine architect César Pelli. At 800 ft (250 m), it dominates the city's eastern skyline. The tower stands on what was the West India Dock, closed, like all the London docks, between the 1960s and the 1980s, when trade moved to the modern port down river at Tilbury. Today, Canary Wharf is thriving. A major shopping complex, with offices and restaurants, is located in and around Canada Tower.

⓱ William Morris Gallery

Lloyd Park, Forest Rd E17. **Tel** 020 8496 4390. 🚇 Walthamstow Central. **Open** 10am–5pm Wed–Sun. **Closed** Dec 24–26 and public hols. ⬤ ⬤ 🏛 Lectures. 🌐 wmgallery.org.uk

The most influential designer of the Victorian era, born in 1834, lived in this 18th-century house as a youth in 1848–56. It is now a beguiling and well-presented museum giving a full account of William Morris the artist, designer, writer, craftsman, and socialist.

It has examples of his work and that of other members of the Arts and Crafts movement – tiles by William de Morgan, and paintings by members of the Pre-Raphaelite Brotherhood.

Interactive exhibits introduce visitors to techniques such as hand-printing and dyeing.

⓲ Emirates Air Line Cable Car

Western Gateway E16/Edmund Halley Way SE10. 🚇 Royal Victoria (DLR), North Greenwich/The O2 Arena. **Open** 7am–9pm Mon–Fri, 8am–9pm Sat, 9am–9pm Sun. 🏛 🌐 emiratesairline.co.uk

Connecting the Royal Victoria Dock and The O2, this cable car provides spectacular views over the river during the 5-minute trip.

Intricate detail visible on a William Morris tapestry (1885)

⓳ Thames Barrier

Unity Way SE18. **Tel** 020 8305 4188. 🚂 Charlton, Silvertown. **Open** 10:30am–5pm Thu–Sun (last adm 4:30pm). **Closed** Dec 25–Jan 1. ⬤ ⬤ ⬤ 🏛 exhibition.

In 1236 the Thames rose so high that people rowed across Westminster Hall; London flooded again in 1663, 1928, and 1953. Something had to be done, and in 1965 the Greater London Council invited proposals. The Thames Barrier opened in 1984. It is 1,700 ft (520 m) across. Its 10 gates, which pivot from being flat on the river bed, swing up to 6 ft (1.6 m) above the level reached by the tide in 1953. The barrier has been raised over 100 times since 1984, and can be visited by boat in summer.

Unique structure of the O2 Arena

⓴ The O2 Arena

North Greenwich SE10. **Tel** 020 8463 2000 or 0844 856 0202 (to buy tickets). 🚇 North Greenwich/The O2 Arena (Jubilee Line). **Open** 9am–late. 🌐 theo2.co.uk

The former Millennium Dome was the focal point of Britain's celebration of the year 2000. Controversial from its earliest days, it is nonetheless a spectacular feat of engineering. Its base is ten times that of St. Paul's Cathedral, and Nelson's Column could stand beneath its roof. Its canopy is made from 109,000 sq yards (100,000 sq m) of Teflon-coated spun fiberglass, and is held by over 43 miles (70 km) of steel cable rigged to twelve 328-ft (100-m) masts.

Now one of London's most popular concert venues, the O2 boasts an entertainment complex with bars, restaurants, movie theater, sports arena, and IndigO2, a smaller venue.

South of the Center

A Jacobean fireplace at Charlton House

❶ Charlton House

Charlton Rd SE7. **Tel** 020 8856 3951.
🚈 Charlton. Main house not open to public. Exhibition area: **Open** 8:30am–6pm Mon–Fri. Peace Garden: **Open** 10am–5pm daily. **Closed** public hols.
🎫 book ahead. ♿ limited.
🖥 9am–4pm Mon–Fri. Concerts; 1–2pm free. 🅦 charlton-house.org

The house was completed in 1612 for Adam Newton, tutor to Prince Henry. It has good river views and is the best-preserved Jacobean mansion in London – well worth the tricky journey for enthusiasts of that period. It is now used as a community center and library, but many of the original ceilings and fireplaces survive, as does the carved main staircase. Parts of the wood paneling, too, are original, and the ceilings have been restored using the original molds. The summer house in the grounds was reputedly designed by Inigo Jones, and a mulberry tree (probably the oldest in England) is said to have been planted by James I in 1608 as part of his failed attempt to start an English silk industry.

❷ Eltham Palace

Court Yard SE9. **Tel** 020 8294 2548.
🚈 Eltham, then a 15-minute walk.
Open Sun–Wed. Apr–Oct: 10am–5pm; Nov–Dec & Feb–Mar: 11am–4pm. **Closed** Dec 31–Jan 31. 🅿
♿ ♿ 🎫 🖥 📷
🅦 english-heritage.org.uk

This unique property lets visitors relive the grand life of two very different eras. In the 14th century, English kings spent Christmas in a splendid palace here. The Tudors used it as a base for deer hunting, but it fell to ruin after the Civil War (1642–8). In 1935, Stephen Courtauld, of the wealthy textile family, restored the Great Hall, which, apart from the bridge over the moat, was the only part of the medieval palace to survive. Next to it he built a house described as "a wonderful combination of Hollywood glamour and Art Deco design." It has been superbly restored and is open, along with the Great Hall, the carp-filled moat, and the 1930s garden.

❸ Horniman Museum

100 London Rd SE23. **Tel** 020 8699 1872. 🚈 Forest Hill. Gardens: **Open** 7:15am–sunset Mon–Sat, 8am–sunset Sun. Museum & Library: **Open** 10:30am–5:30pm daily. **Closed** Dec 24–26. 🖥 📷 ♿ Events & activities. 🅦 horniman.ac.uk

Frederick Horniman, the tea merchant, had this museum built in 1901 to house the curios he had collected on his travels around the world in the 1860s. The museum features a music gallery, aquarium, world culture displays, and a history gallery. There is a good shop with toys that represent the popular range of the museum's collections.

❹ Dulwich Picture Gallery

College Rd SE21. **Tel** 020 8693 5254.
🚈 West Dulwich, North Dulwich.
Open 10am–5pm Tue–Fri, 11am–5pm Sat, Sun & bank hol Mon. (last adm 4:30pm). **Closed** Mon, Jan 1, Dec 25–26. 📷 🎫 3pm Sat & Sun. ♿ 🖥 📷
🅦 dulwichpicturegallery.org.uk

England's oldest public art gallery, which was opened in 1817 and designed by Sir John Soane (see pp138–9). Its imaginative use of skylights made it the prototype of most art galleries built since. The gallery was originally commissioned to house the royal collection of the King of Poland. The superb collection has works

Rembrandt's *Jacob II de Gheyn* at Dulwich Picture Gallery

by Rembrandt (his *Jacob ll de Gheyn* has been stolen from here four times), Canaletto, Poussin, Watteau, Claude, Murillo, and Raphael. The building houses Soane's mausoleum to Desenfans and Bourgeois, who were the original founders of the collection.

㉕ Battersea Park

Albert Bridge Rd SW11. **Map** 19 C5. **Tel** 020 8871 7530. 🚇 Sloane Sq then bus 137. 🚆 Battersea Pk. **Open** 8am–dusk daily. 🚻 📷 Sports facilities. *See Six Guided Walks pp268–9.* 🅦 batterseapark.org

This was the second public park created to relieve the growing urban stresses on Victorian Londoners (the first was Victoria Park in the East End). It opened in 1858 on the former Battersea Fields – a swampy area notorious for every kind of vice, centered around the Old Red House, a disreputable pub.

The new park immediately became popular, especially for its artificial boating lake, with its romantic rocks, gardens, and waterfalls.

In 1985 a peace pagoda was opened, a 100-ft (35-m) high monument built by Buddhist nuns and monks. There is also an excellent children's zoo (entry fee payable), a children's playground, sports activities, and an art gallery, the Pumphouse.

Tennis racket and net from 1888, Wimbledon Lawn Tennis Museum

㉖ St. Mary's, Battersea

Battersea Church Rd SW11. **Tel** 020 7228 9648. 🚇 Sloane Sq then bus 19 or 219. **Open** daily by arrangement. ✝ 8:30am Mon–Wed; 8:30am, 11am, & 6:30pm Sun. 🚻 Concerts. 🅦 stmarysbattersea.org.uk

There has been a church here since at least the 10th century. The present brick building dates from 1775, but the 17th-century stained glass, commemorating Tudor monarchs, comes from the former church.

In 1782 the poet and artist William Blake was married in the church. Later, J. M. W. Turner painted views of the Thames from the tower. Benedict Arnold, who served George Washington in the American Revolutionary War before defecting to the British side, was buried in the crypt.

㉗ Wimbledon Lawn Tennis Museum

Church Rd SW19. **Tel** 020 8247 3142. 🚇 Southfields. **Open** Apr–Sep: 10am–5:30pm, Oct–Mar: 10am–5pm daily (during championships, ticket holders only). **Closed** Jan 1, Jun 23 & 30, Jul 8–9, Dec 24–26. 🚫 🚻 📷 📱 📷 🅦 wimbledon.com/museum

Even those with only a passing interest in the sport will find plenty to enjoy at this museum. It traces tennis's development from its invention in the 1860s as a diversion for country house parties, to the sport it is today. Alongside strange 19th-century equipment are film clips showing the great

players of the past. More recent matches may be viewed in the video theater.

㉘ Wimbledon Windmill Museum

Windmill Rd SW19. **Tel** 020 8947 2825. 🚇 🚆 Wimbledon then 30-min walk. **Open** Apr–Oct: 2–5pm Sat, 11am–5pm Sun & pub hols (Nov–Mar: groups only, by arrangement). 🚫 📷 📱 📷 🅦 wimbledonwindmill.org.uk

The mill on Wimbledon Common was built in 1817. The building at its base was turned into cottages in 1864. Boy Scouts founder Lord Baden-Powell lived in the mill house. Today the site is a museum housing model windmills.

St. Mary's, Battersea

Peace Pagoda, Battersea Park

West of the Center

Ham House

㉙ Richmond Park

Kingston Vale SW15. **Tel** 0300 061 2200. 🚆 🚊 Richmond then bus 65 or 71. **Open** 7am–6:45pm daily. 🚻 🚾 📵 **royalparks.gov.uk**

In 1637, Charles I built a wall 8 miles (13 km) around to enclose the royal park as a hunting ground. Today the park is a national nature preserve, and deer still graze warily among the chestnuts, birches, and oaks, no longer hunted but still discreetly culled. They have learned to coexist with the thousands of human visitors who stroll here on sunny weekends.

In late spring the highlight is the Isabella Plantation with its spectacular display of azaleas, while the nearby Pen Ponds are very popular with optimistic anglers. (Adam's Pond is for model boats.) The rest of the park is heath, bracken, and trees (some of them hundreds of years old). Richmond Gate, in the northwest corner, was designed by the landscape gardener Capability Brown in 1798. Nearby is Henry VIII Mound, where in 1536 the king,

Deer in Richmond Park

staying in Richmond Palace, awaited the signal that his former wife, Anne Boleyn, had been executed. The Palladian White Lodge, built in 1729, is home to the Royal Ballet School.

㉚ Hampton Court

See pp256–9.

㉛ Ham House

Ham St, Richmond. **Tel** 020 8940 1950. 🚆 🚊 Richmond then bus 65 or 371. **Open** Apr–Oct: 🚻 📵 **Closed** Jan 1, Dec 25–26. 🏛 🚾 by appt. 🚻 partial. 📵 & 📷 11am–4pm daily (mid-Feb–Oct: to 5pm). Gardens: **Open** Jan–mid-Feb: 11am–4pm daily; mid-Feb–Oct: 11am–5pm daily; Nov–Dec: 11am–4pm daily. 🚾 **nationaltrust.org.uk**

This magnificent house by the Thames was built in 1610, but its heyday came when it was home to the Duke of Lauderdale, confidant to Charles II and Secretary of State for Scotland. His wife, the Countess of Dysart, inherited it from her father, who had been Charles I's whipping boy (punished for the future king's misdemeanors). From 1672 the Duke and Countess modernized the house, and it was regarded as one of Britain's finest. The garden has been restored to its 17th-century form.

On some days in summer, a foot passenger ferry runs from

here to Marble Hill House and Orleans House at Twickenham.

㉜ Orleans House Gallery

Orleans Rd, Twickenham. **Tel** 020 8831 6000. 🚆 🚊 Richmond then bus 33, 90, 290, R68 or R70. **Open** Apr–Sep: 1–5:30pm Tue–Sat, 2–5:30pm Sun & bank hols; Oct–Mar: 1–4:30pm Tue–Sat, 2–4:30pm Sun & bank hols. **Closed** Jan 1, Good Fri, Dec 24–26. Gardens: **Open** 9am–dusk daily. 🚻 ground floor. 📵 📷 🚾 **richmond.gov.uk/ orleans_house_gallery**

This gallery is on the site of the original Orleans House, named after Louis Philippe, Duke of Orleans, who lived there from 1815 to 1817. Adjacent is the Octagon Room, designed by James Gibbs for James Johnson in 1720. The gallery shows exhibitions of local history.

Marble Hill House

㉝ Marble Hill House

Richmond Rd, Twickenham. **Tel** 020 8892 5115. 🚆 🚊 Richmond then bus 33, 90, 290, R68 or R70. **Open** by guided tour only (call or visit website to check). **Closed** Nov–Mar. 🚻 restricted. 📵 📵 📷 Fireworks on weekends. *See Entertainment p341.* 🚾 **english-heritage.org.uk**

Built in 1729 for George II's mistress, Henrietta Howard, the house and its grounds have been open to the public since 1903. It has now been fully restored to its Georgian appearance. There are paintings by William Hogarth and a view of the river and house in 1762 by Richard Wilson, who is regarded as the father of English landscape painting. The café is especially good.

Richmond side street

34 Richmond

SW15. ⊖ ⇄ Richmond.

This attractive London suburb took its name from the palace that Henry VII built here in 1500. Many early 18th-century houses survive near the river and off Richmond Hill, notably Maids of Honour Row, which was built in 1724. The beautiful view of the river from the top of the hill has been captured by many artists, and is largely unspoiled.

35 Syon House

London Rd, Brentford. **Tel** 020 8560 0882. ⊖ Gunnersbury then bus 237 or 267. House: **Open** mid-Mar–Oct: 11am–5pm Wed–Thu, Sun. House: **Closed** Nov–mid-Mar. Gardens: **Open** mid-Mar–Oct: 10:30am–5pm daily; Nov–mid-Mar: 10:30am–4pm Sat & Sun. ♿ ✉ ⬚ ⬚ ⬚ ⬚ ⬚ gardens only. **W** syonpark.co.uk

The Earls and Dukes of Northumberland have lived here for 400 years – it is the only large mansion in the London area still under hereditary ownership. The interior was remodeled in

1761 by Robert Adam and is considered one of his masterpieces. The five Adam rooms house original furnishings and a collection of Old Master paintings.

The 200-acre (80-ha) park was landscaped by Capability Brown, and it includes a lovely 40-acre (16-ha) garden with more than 200 species of rare trees. The park's Great Conservatory inspired Joseph Paxton's designs for the Crystal Palace.

36 Musical Museum

399 High St, Brentford. **Tel** 020 8560 8108. ⊖ Gunnersbury, South Ealing then bus 65, 237 or 267. **Open** 11am–5:30pm Tue–Sun & bank hol Mondays. ♿ ⬚ ⬚ ⬚ ⬚ **W** musicalmuseum.co.uk

The collection is arranged over three floors and comprises chiefly large instruments, including player (or automatic) pianos and organs, miniature and cinema pianos, and what is thought to be the only surviving self-playing Wurlitzer organ in Europe.

Drawing room: Osterley Park House

37 Osterley Park House

Jersey Rd, Isleworth. **Tel** 020 8232 5050. ⊖ Osterley. **Open** Mar–Nov: noon–4:30pm Wed–Sun; 1st 2 weeks Dec: noon–3:30pm Sat & Sun. ♿ ⬚ ⬚ Park **Open** 8am–dusk daily. **W** nationaltrust.org.uk/osterley

Osterley is ranked among Robert Adam's finest works, and its colonnaded portico and elegant library ceiling are the proof. Much of the furniture is by Adam; the garden and temple are by William Chambers, the architect of Somerset House. The garden house is by Adam.

Robert Adam's red drawing room at Syon House

⓾ Hampton Court

Hampton Court was not orginally built as a royal palace but begun in 1514 by Cardinal Wolsey, Henry VIII's Archbishop of York, as his riverside country house. Later, in 1528, in the hope of retaining royal favor, Wolsey offered it to the king. After the royal takeover, Hampton Court was twice rebuilt and extended, first by Henry himself and then, in the 1690s, by William and Mary, who employed Christopher Wren as architect.

There is a striking contrast between Wren's Classical royal apartments and the Tudor turrets, gables, and chimneys elsewhere. The inspiration for the gardens as they are today comes largely from the time of William and Mary, who created a vast, formal Baroque landscape, with radiating avenues of majestic lindens and many collections of exotic plants.

★ The Maze
Lose yourself in one of the garden's most popular features.

Main entrance

★ The Great Vine
The vine was planted in the 1760s, and, in the 19th century, produced up to 2,000 lb (910 kg) of black grapes.

The Pond Garden
This sunken garden was once a pond to store fresh fish for Henry VIII's Court.

KEY

① River boat pier
② Royal tennis court
③ Privy Garden
④ Thames River

★ The Mantegna Gallery
Andrea Mantegna's nine canvases depicting *The Triumphs of Caesar* (c.1484–1505) are housed here.

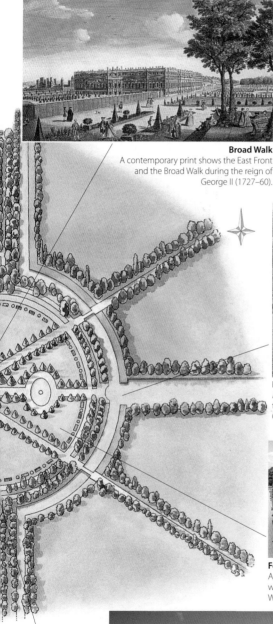

Broad Walk
A contemporary print shows the East Front and the Broad Walk during the reign of George II (1727–60).

VISITORS' CHECKLIST

Practical Information
Surrey KT8 9AU.
Tel 0844 482 7777.
🆆 hrp.org.uk
Open Apr–Oct: 10am–6pm daily;
Nov–Mar: 10am–4:30pm daily
(last adm: 1 hour before closing).
Closed Dec 24–26.
🖼🔊🛈🍽🚻🎁

Transportation
🚌 R68 from Kew, Richmond or Twickenham. 🚆 Hampton Court. 🚢 Hampton Court pier.

Long Water
An artificial lake runs parallel to the Thames, from the Fountain Garden across the Home Park.

Fountain Garden
A few of the clipped yews here were planted in the reign of William and Mary.

The East Front
The windows of the Queen's Drawing Room, designed by Wren, overlook the central avenue of the Fountain Garden.

Exploring the Palace

As a historic royal palace, Hampton Court bears traces of many of the kings and queens of England from Henry VIII to the present day. The building itself is a harmonious blend of Tudor and English Baroque architecture. Inside, visitors can see the Great Hall, built by Henry VIII, as well as state apartments of the Tudor court. Many of the Baroque state apartments, including those above Fountain Court by Christopher Wren, are decorated with furniture, tapestries, and old masters from the Royal Collection.

Tudor Chimneys
Ornate chimneys, some original, some careful restorations, adorn the roof of the Tudor palace.

★ Chapel Royal
The Tudor chapel was refurbished by Wren, except for the carved and gilded vaulted ceiling.

★ Great Hall
The stained-glass window in the Tudor Great Hall shows Henry VIII flanked by the coats of arms of his six wives.

KEY

① Haunted Gallery

② Queen's Presence Chamber

③ Queen's Guard Chamber

④ Wren's east facade

★ Clock Court
Anne Boleyn's Archway is at the entrance to Clock Court. The Astronomical Clock, created for Henry VIII in 1540, is also located here.

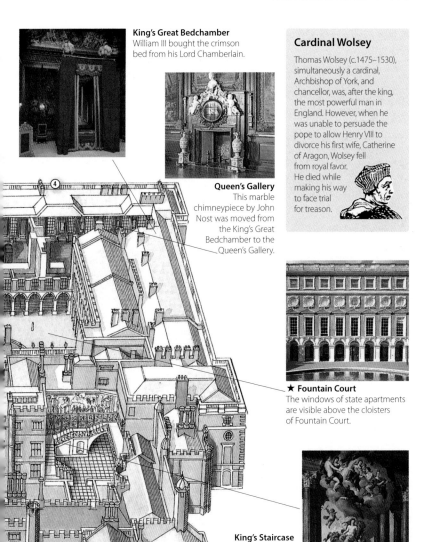

King's Great Bedchamber
William III bought the crimson bed from his Lord Chamberlain.

Queen's Gallery
This marble chimneypiece by John Nost was moved from the King's Great Bedchamber to the Queen's Gallery.

Cardinal Wolsey
Thomas Wolsey (c.1475–1530), simultaneously a cardinal, Archbishop of York, and chancellor, was, after the king, the most powerful man in England. However, when he was unable to persuade the pope to allow Henry VIII to divorce his first wife, Catherine of Aragon, Wolsey fell from royal favor. He died while making his way to face trial for treason.

★ Fountain Court
The windows of state apartments are visible above the cloisters of Fountain Court.

King's Staircase
Leading to the state apartments, the King's Staircase has wall paintings by Antonio Verrio.

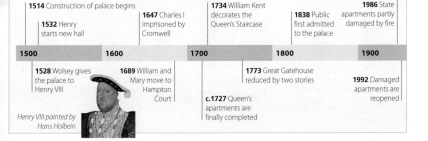

1514 Construction of palace begins
1532 Henry starts new hall
1647 Charles I imprisoned by Cromwell
1734 William Kent decorates the Queen's Staircase
1838 Public first admitted to the palace
1986 State apartments partly damaged by fire

1500 **1600** **1700** **1800** **1900**

1528 Wolsey gives the palace to Henry VIII
1689 William and Mary move to Hampton Court
1773 Great Gatehouse reduced by two stories
1992 Damaged apartments are reopened
c.1727 Queen's apartments are finally completed

Henry VIII painted by Hans Holbein

❸ PM Gallery and House

Mattock Lane W5. **Tel** 020 8567 1227. ⊖ Ealing Broadway. **Open** 1–5pm Tue–Fri, 11am–5pm Sat; Summer: 1–5pm Sun. **Closed** public hols. ♿ Exhibitions. 🆆 **ealing.gov.uk/pmgalleryandhouse**

Sir John Soane, architect of the Bank of England (see p147), designed this house, Pitzhanger Manor, on the site of an earlier one. Completed in 1803, it was to become his own country residence. There are clear echoes of his elaborately constructed townhouse in Lincoln's Inn Fields (see pp138–9), especially in the library, with its imaginative use of mirrors; in the darkly-painted breakfast room opposite; and in the "monk's dining room," which is located on the basement level.

Soane retained two of the principal formal rooms: the drawing room and the dining room. These were designed in 1768 by George Dance the Younger, with whom Soane had worked before establishing his own reputation.

A sympathetic 20th-century extension has been refurbished as a gallery offering a wide range of contemporary art exhibitions and associated events. The house also contains a large exhibition of Martinware, highly decorated glazed pottery made in nearby Southall

between 1877 and 1915 and fashionable in late Victorian times. The gardens of Pitzhanger Manor are now a pleasant public park and offer a welcome contrast to the bustle of nearby Ealing.

❸ Kew Bridge Steam Museum

Green Dragon Lane, Brentford. **Tel** 020 8568 4757. ⊖ Kew Bridge, Gunnersbury then bus 65, 237, or 267. **Open** 11am–4pm Tue–Sun (engines operate at set times – check website for details). **Closed** Mon (except bank hols). 🎦 📷 book ahead. 🖥 Sat & Sun. 🏠 ♿ 🆆 **kbsm.org**

The 19th-century water pumping station, near the north end of Kew Bridge, is now a museum of steam power and water in London. Its main exhibits are five giant Cornish beam engines that pumped water here from the river, to be distributed in London. The earliest engines, dating from 1820, are similar to those built to pump water out of Cornish mines. See them working on weekends and public holidays.

Martinware bird at PM Gallery

❹ Kew Gardens

See pp262–3.

City Barge: Strand on the Green

❹ Strand on the Green

W4. ⊖ Gunnersbury then bus 237 or 267. 🚃 Kew Bridge.

This charming Thames-side walk passes some fine 18th-century houses as well as rows of more modest cottages once inhabited by fishermen. The oldest of its three pubs is the City Barge (see pp308–11), parts of which date from the 15th century: the name is older and derives from the time when the Lord Mayor's barge was moored on the river outside.

❹ Chiswick House

Burlington Lane W4. **Tel** 020 8995 0508. ⊖ Chiswick. **Open** Apr–Oct: 10am–5pm Sun–Wed & bank hols; Nov: pre-booked visits only. **Closed** end Dec–Mar. 🎦 📷 ♿ phone ahead. 🖥 9am–5:30pm (to 4pm winter). 🏠 Gardens **Open** 7am–dusk daily (free admission). 🆆 **chgt.org.uk**

Completed in 1729 to the design of its owner, the third Earl of Burlington, this is a fine

Chiswick House

example of a Palladian villa. Burlington revered both Palladio and his disciple Inigo Jones, and their statues stand outside. Built around a central octagonal room, the house is packed with references to ancient Rome and Renaissance Italy, as is the garden.

Chiswick was Burlington's country residence and this house was built as an annex to a larger, older house (since demolished). It was designed for recreation and entertaining – Lord Hervey, Burlington's enemy, dismissed it as "too little to live in and too big to hang on a watch chain." Some of the ceiling paintings are by William Kent, who also contributed to the garden design.

The house was a private mental home from 1892 until 1928, when a long process of restoration began. The layout of the garden, now a public park, is much as Burlington designed it.

The Belvedere takes center stage at Chelsea Harbour

WILLIAM
HOGARTH
Painter & Engraver
1697 – 1764
LIVED AND WORKED
HERE FOR 15 YEARS
COUNTY OF MIDDLESEX

Plaque on Hogarth's House

🄳 Hogarth's House

Hogarth Lane, W4. **Tel** 020 8994 6757. 🚇 Turnham Green. **Open** noon–5pm Tue–Sun & bank hol Mon **Closed** Jan, Good Fri, Dec 25 & 26. 🖼 🚻 ground floor only. 🖼 🆆 **hounslow.info/arts/hogarthshouse**

When the painter William Hogarth lived here from 1749 until his death in 1764, he called it "a little country box by the Thames" and painted bucolic views from its windows – he had moved from Leicester Square (*see p105*). Today, traffic roars by along the Great West Road, on its way to and from Heathrow Airport – rush hour traffic is also notoriously bad here. In an environment as hostile as this, and following

years of neglect and then bombing during World War II, it is surprising that the house has survived. It has now been turned into a small museum and gallery, which is filled mostly with a collection of engraved copies of the moralistic cartoon-style pictures with which Hogarth made his name. Salutary tales such as *The Rake's Progress* (in Sir John Soane's Museum – *see pp138–9*), *Marriage à la Mode, An Election Entertainment*, and many others can all be seen here.

🄴 Fulham Palace

Bishops Ave SW6. **Tel** 020 7736 3233. 🚇 Putney Bridge. **Open** 1–4pm Sat–Wed. **Closed** Good Fri, Dec 25 & 26. Park **Open** daylight hours daily. 🚻 🖼 2–3 times each month; check website for days and times. 🖼 🆆 Events, concerts, lectures. 🆆 **fulhampalace.org**

The home of the bishops of London from the 8th century until 1973, the oldest surviving parts of Fulham Palace date from the 15th century. The palace stands in its own landscaped gardens northwest of Putney Bridge. A restoration project completed in 2007 revealed a grand, long-hidden Rococo ceiling.

🄵 Chelsea Harbour

SW10. 🚇 Fulham Broadway. 🖼 Exhibitions. 🖼 🖼

This is an impressive development of modern apartments, shops, offices, restaurants, a hotel, and a marina. It is near the site of Cremorne Pleasure Gardens, which closed in 1877 after more than 40 years as a venue for dances and circuses. The centerpiece is the Belvedere, a 20-story apartment tower with an external glass elevator and pyramid roof, topped with a golden ball on a rod that rises and falls with the tide.

Eye-catching entrance to Fulham Palace dating from Tudor times

⑳ Kew Gardens

The Royal Botanic Gardens, Kew, are a World Heritage Site and the most complete public gardens in the world. Their reputation was first established by Sir Joseph Banks, the British naturalist and plant hunter, who worked here in the late 18th century. The former royal gardens were given to the nation in 1841 and now display about 30,000 plants. Garden enthusiasts will want a full day to visit. Kew is also a center for scholarly research.

Princess Augusta
King George III's mother established the first garden on a 9-acre (3.6 ha) site here in 1759.

★ **Pagoda**
William Chambers's pagoda, built in 1762, reflects the fashion of the time.

KEY

① Cherry Walk
② Waterlily Pond
③ Queen Charlotte's Cottage
④ Thames River
⑤ Sackler Crossing
⑥ Fall foliage
⑦ Witch hazels
⑧ Azalea Garden
⑨ Climbers and Creepers soft play area
⑩ Kew Palace
⑪ Nash Conservatory
⑫ The Orangery restaurant
⑬ Duke's Garden
⑭ Princess of Wales Conservatory
Encompassing ten climatic zones, this greenhouse contains cacti, giant waterlilies, and orchids.
⑮ Davies Alpine House
⑯ Rock Garden
⑰ Winter Garden
⑱ Campanile
⑲ Rose Garden
⑳ Crocus carpet
㉑ Temple of Bellona

Lion Gate entrance

★ **Rhizotron and Xstrata Treetop Walkway**
This 220-yd (200-m) walkway meanders through the tree canopy and offers fine views.

Minka House
This minka (traditional wooden Japanese house), built around 1900, was shipped from Japan and reconstructed in the Bamboo Garden in 2001.

Brentford Gate entrance

Elizabeth Gate entrance

Victoria Gate entrance

★ Palm House
Designed by Decimus Burton in the 1840s, this famous jewel of Victorian engineering houses exotic plants in tropical conditions.

SIX GUIDED WALKS

London is an excellent city for walkers. Although it is much more spread out than most European capitals, many of the main tourist attractions are fairly close to each other *(see pp16–17)*. Central London is full of parks and gardens *(see pp50–53)*, and there are also several walk routes planned by the tourism board and local history societies. These include footpaths along canals and the Thames River, and the Silver Jubilee Walk. Planned in 1977 to commemorate the Queen's Silver Jubilee, the walk runs for 12 miles (19 km) between Lambeth Bridge in the west and Tower Bridge in the east; Visit London *(see p354)* has maps of the route, which is marked by silver plaques placed at intervals in the sidewalks.

Each of the 16 areas described in the *Area-by-Area* section of this book has a short walk marked on its *Street-by-Street* map. These walks will take you past many of the most interesting sights in that area. On the following twelve pages are routes for six walks that take you through areas of London not covered in detail elsewhere. These range from the bustling, fashionable King's Road *(see pp268–69)* to the wide open spaces of riverside Richmond and Kew *(see pp270–71)*.

Several companies offer guided walking tours of London *(www.walks.com)*. Most of these have themes, such as ghosts, Jack the Ripper, or Shakespeare's London. Look in listings magazines *(see p334)* for details.

The Six Walks

This map shows the location of the six guided walks in relation to the main sightseeing areas of London.

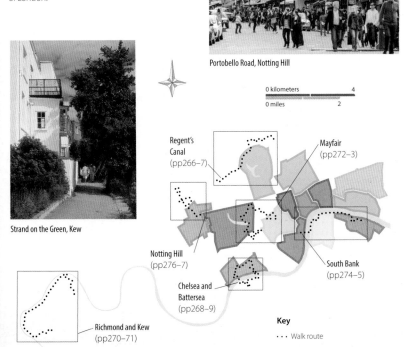

Portobello Road, Notting Hill

Strand on the Green, Kew

0 kilometers 4
0 miles 2

Regent's Canal (pp266–7)

Mayfair (pp272–3)

Notting Hill (pp276–7)

South Bank (pp274–5)

Chelsea and Battersea (pp268–9)

Richmond and Kew (pp270–71)

Key

••• Walk route

◀ Traditional narrow boats on Regent's Canal, Little Venice

A Two-Hour Walk Along the Regent's Canal

Master builder John Nash wanted the Regent's Canal to pass through Regent's Park, but instead it circles north of the park. Opened in 1820, it is long defunct as a commercial waterway but is today a valuable leisure amenity. This walk starts at Little Venice and ends at Camden Lock market, diverting briefly to take in the view from Primrose Hill. For more details on the sights near the Regent's Canal, see pages 222–29.

Houseboat on the canal ③

Houseboats moored at Little Venice ③

From Little Venice to Lisson Grove

At Warwick Avenue station ① take the left-hand exit and walk straight to the traffic lights by the canal bridge at Blomfield Road. Turn right and descend to the canal through an iron gate ② opposite No. 42, marked "Lady Rose of Regent." The pretty basin with moored narrow boats is Little Venice ③. At the foot of the steps, turn left to walk back beneath the blue iron bridge ④. You soon have to climb up to street level again because this stretch of the towpath is reserved for access to the barges. Cross Edgware Road and walk down Aberdeen

Place. When the road turns to the left by a pub, Crockers ⑤, follow the signposted Canal Way down to the right of some modern apartments. Continue along the canal towpath, crossing Park Road at street level. The scenery along this stretch is unremarkable, but it is not long before a splash of green to your right announces that you are now walking alongside Regent's Park ⑥.

Regent's Park

Soon you see four mansions ⑦. A bridge on huge pillars marked "Coalbrookdale" ⑧ carries

Key

••• Walk route

0 meters   500

0 yards   500

(Map showing walk route through Warwick Avenue, Maida Vale, Clifton Gdns, Blomfield Road, Edgware Rd, St John's Wood Road, Lisson Grove, Wellington Rd, Grove End Rd, Lord's Cricket Ground)

Tips for Walkers

Starting point: Warwick Avenue Underground station.
Length: 3 miles (5 km).
Getting there: Warwick Avenue and Camden Town Underground stations are at either end of the walk. Buses 16, 16A, and 98 go to Warwick Avenue; 24, 29, and 31 go to Camden Town.
Stopping points: Crockers, Queens, and The Princess of Wales (corner of Fitzroy and Chalcot Roads) are good pubs. At the intersection of Edgware Road and Aberdeen Place is Café La Ville. Camden Town has many cafés, restaurants, and sandwich shops.

Avenue Road into the park. Cross the next bridge, with London Zoo ⑨ on your right, then turn left up a slope. A few steps later, take the right fork, and turn left to cross Prince Albert Road. Turn right before entering Primrose Hill through a gate ⑩ on your left.

Primrose Hill

From here there is a view of the zoo aviary ⑪, designed by Lord

Mansion with riverside gardens ⑦

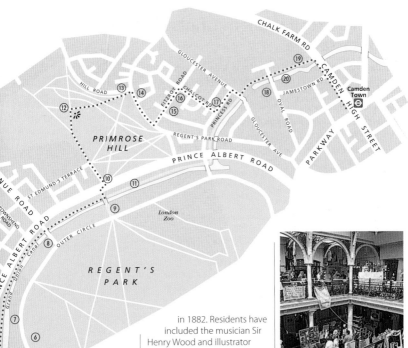

Indoor market, Camden Lock ⑲

Snowdon and opened in 1965.
Inside the park, keep to the left-hand path that climbs to the top of the hill. Soon you fork right to the summit, which offers a fine view of the city skyline. A viewing panel ⑫ helps identify the landmarks, but it does not include the 1990 skyscraper at Canary Wharf, with its pyramid crown, on the left. Descend on the left, heading for the park gate at the intersection of Regent's Park Road and Primrose Hill Road.

Toward Camden
Almost opposite the gate is the Queens ⑬, a Victorian pub, and just to the left is No. 122 Regent's Park Road ⑭. This was for 24 years the home of the communist philosopher Friedrich Engels; he was often visited here by his friend Karl Marx.
Turn right and walk down Regent's Park Road for 150 yd (135 m), then turn left up Fitzroy Road. On the right, between Nos. 41 and 39, is the entrance to Primrose Hill Studios ⑮, built

in 1882. Residents have included the musician Sir Henry Wood and illustrator Arthur Rackham, famous for his fairy pictures.
Continue down Fitzroy Road past No. 23 ⑯, once home to the poet W. B. Yeats, then go right onto Chalcot Road and left down Princess Road, past a Victorian board school ⑰. Turn right and rejoin the canal down steps across Gloucester Avenue. Turn left under the railroad bridge and past the Pirate Castle ⑱, a water sports center. Cross a hump bridge and enter Camden Lock

Market ⑲ (see p324) through an arch on your left. After browsing there, you can take the water bus ⑳ back to Little Venice or turn right into Chalk Farm Road and walk up to Camden Town Underground station.

Pedestrian bridge over the canal at Camden Lock ⑲

A Three-Hour Walk in Chelsea and Battersea

This delightful circular walk ambles through the grounds of the Royal Hospital and across the river to Battersea Park, with its romantic Victorian landscaping. It then returns to the narrow village streets of Chelsea and the stylish shops on the King's Road. For more details on the sights in Chelsea see pages 194–9.

Royal Hospital ③

Sloane Square to Battersea Park

From the station ①, turn left and walk down Holbein Place. The Renaissance painter's connection with Chelsea stems from his friendship with Sir Thomas More, who lived nearby. Pass the cluster of good antique shops ② as you turn on to Royal Hospital Road. Enter the grounds of the Royal Hospital ③, designed by Christopher Wren, and turn left into the informal Ranelagh Gardens ④. The small pavilion by John Soane ⑤ displays a history of the gardens as a Georgian pleasure resort – it was the most fashionable meeting place for London society. Leave the gardens for fine views of

Charles II statue in Royal Hospital ⑥

the hospital and Grinling Gibbons's bronze of Charles II ⑥. The granite obelisk ⑦ commemorates the 1849 battle at Chilianwalla, in what is now Pakistan, and forms the centerpiece of the main marquee at the Chelsea Flower Show (see p58).

Battersea Park

When crossing the Chelsea Bridge ⑧ (1937), look up at the four gilded galleons on top of the pillars at each end. Turn into Battersea Park ⑨ (see p253), one of London's liveliest, and follow the main path along the river to enjoy the excellent views of Chelsea. Turn left at the exotic Buddhist Peace Pagoda ⑩ to the main part of the park.

Past the bowling greens lies Henry Moore's carving of *Three Standing Figures* ⑪ (1948) and the lake, a favored spot for wildfowl. (There are boats for rent.) Just beyond the sculpture, head northwest and, after crossing the central avenue, fork right and head for the wooden gate into the rustic Old English Garden ⑫. Leave the garden by the metal gate and return to Chelsea via the Victorian Albert Bridge ⑬.

Tips for Walkers

Starting point: Sloane Square. **Length:** 4 miles (6.5 km). **Getting there:** Sloane Square is the nearest tube. There are frequent buses 11, 19, 22, and 349 to Sloane Square and along the King's Road. **Royal Hospital Grounds** are open only 10am–6pm Mon–Sat, 2–6pm Sun. **Stopping points:** There is a café in Battersea Park, by the lake. The Eight Bells, on Cheyne Walk, is a well-known local pub. There are several other pubs, restaurants, and sandwich shops to be found along the King's Road. The Chelsea Farmers' Market on Sydney Street has several cafés.

Key

••• Walk route

Old English Garden in Battersea Park ⑫

Albert Bridge ⑬

Place ㉒ has retained much of its original character. Where Glebe Place meets the King's Road are three pretty, early-18th-century houses ㉓. Cross Dovehouse Green opposite (it used to be a burial ground), to Chelsea Farmers' Market ㉔, an enclave of cafés and craft shops.

The King's Road

Leave the market on Sydney Street and cross into the garden of St. Luke's Church ㉕, where the writer Charles Dickens was married. The walk then winds through pretty back streets until it rejoins the King's Road ㉖ *(see p198)*, which was very fashionable in the 1960s. On the left is The Pheasantry ㉗. Look down the side streets on both left and right to see the squares and terraces: Wellington Square ㉘, then Royal Avenue ㉙, intended as a triumphal way to the Royal Hospital, and Blacklands Terrace ㉚, where book-lovers will want to visit John Sandoe's shop. The Duke of York's Territorial Headquarters ㉛ (1803) on the right – now home to the Saatchi Gallery – marks the approach to Sloane Square ㉜ and the Royal Court Theatre *(see Sloane Square p199)*.

Thomas Carlyle statue ⑮

The Back Streets of Chelsea

Over the bridge is David Wynne's sculpture of a boy and dolphin ⑭ (1975). Pass the sought-after residences on Cheyne Walk and the statues of historian Thomas Carlyle ⑮ and Sir Thomas More ⑯. The area was renowned for gatherings of intellectuals. Past Chelsea Old Church ⑰ is Roper's Gardens ⑱ with its carving by Jacob Epstein. Just beyond these is the medieval Crosby Hall ⑲. Justice Walk ⑳ has a nice view of two early Georgian houses – Duke's House and Monmouth House. Turn left to pass the site of the Chelsea porcelain factory ㉑, which used to make highly fashionable (and today very highly collectible) wares in the late 18th century. Glebe

Royal Court Theatre ㉜

For keys to symbols *see back flap*

A 90-Minute Walk Around Richmond and Kew

This delightful riverside walk begins in historic Richmond by the remains of Henry VII's once-splendid palace and ends at Kew, Britain's premier botanic garden. For more details on the sights in Richmond and Kew, turn to pages 254–60.

The river at low tide

Richmond Green

From Richmond station ①, proceed to Oriel House ②, which is practically opposite. Take the alleyway beneath it, and turn left toward the red-brick and terra-cotta Richmond Theatre ③, built in 1899. The remarkable Edmund Kean, whose brief, meteoric career in the early 19th century had a lasting impact on English acting, was closely associated with the previous theater on the site. Opposite is Richmond Green ④. Cross it diagonally and go through the entrance arch ⑤ of the old Tudor palace, which is adorned with the arms of Henry VII.

Richmond

Richmond owes much of its importance – as well as its name – to Henry, victor of the Wars of the Roses and the first Tudor monarch. On becoming king in 1485, he spent a lot of time at an earlier residence on this site, Sheen Palace, dating from the 12th century. The palace burned down in 1499 and Henry had it rebuilt, naming it Richmond after the town in Yorkshire where he held an earldom. In 1603 Henry's granddaughter, Elizabeth I, died here. The houses inside the archway on the left contain remnants, much modified,

of the 16th-century buildings. Leave Old Palace Yard at the right-hand corner ⑥, following a sign "To the River," and turn left to pass the White Swan pub ⑦. At the river, go right along the towpath under the iron railroad bridge and then the concrete Twickenham Bridge ⑧, completed in 1933, to reach Richmond Lock ⑨, with its cast-iron footbridge built in 1894. The Thames is tidal as far as Teddington, some 3 miles (5 km) upstream, and the lock is used to make the river continuously navigable.

The Riverside

Do not cross the bridge but continue along the wooded path by the river to Isleworth Ait ⑩, a large island where herons may be standing warily on the river bank. Just beyond it, on the far shore, is All Saints' Church ⑪, where the 15th-century tower has survived several rebuildings, most recently in the 1960s. Farther around the inlet, Isleworth ⑫, once a small riverside village with a busy harbor, is now a bedroom suburb of central London. Here there is river traffic to watch: barges, yachts, and, in summer, the passenger boats that head upriver to Hampton Court (see pp256–9). Rowers are out at most times of year,

training for races. The most prestigious occasions are the Henley Regatta in July and the Oxford vs. Cambridge boat race, every spring from Putney to Mortlake (see p58).

Richmond Theatre ③

Kew

After a while the appearance of iron railings on your right marks where Old Deer Park ⑬ turns into Kew Gardens ⑭ (officially known as the Royal Botanic Gardens – *see pp262–3*). There used to be a riverside entrance for visitors arriving on foot or by water, but the gate ⑮ is now

Kew Palace in Kew Gardens ⑲

18th century. Just beyond are modern waterside apartments at Brentford ⑰. This was originally an industrial suburb, sited where the Grand Union Canal runs into the Thames, and its residential potential has only recently been exploited. You can pick out the tall chimney of the waterworks ⑱, now a museum dedicated to steam power. On the right, behind the Kew Gardens parking lot, there is soon a view of Kew Palace ⑲, now fully restored and open to the public.

Beyond the parking lot, leave the river by Ferry Lane on to Kew Green ⑳. Now you could spend the rest of the day in Kew Gardens, or cross Kew Bridge and turn right onto Strand on the Green ㉑, a fine riverside walkway with atmospheric pubs, the oldest of them the City Barge ㉒. Head south down Kew Road if you need to get back, then turn left at Kew Gardens Road to depart from Kew Gardens Underground station (District line).

Tips for Walkers

Starting point: Richmond station, District Line.
Length: 3 miles (5 km).
Getting there: Richmond Underground or train station. Buses 391 and R68 come here from Kew.
Stopping points: There are many cafés, pubs, and tearooms in Richmond. The famous Maids of Honour tearoom is at Kew, and Kew Grill is one of several good eateries on Kew Green.

closed and the nearest entrance is to the north, near the parking lot. Across the river, there are magnificent views of Syon House ⑯, seat of the Dukes of Northumberland since 1594. Part of the present house dates from the 16th century, but it was largely redesigned by Robert Adam in the 1760s. You are looking at it across the garden Capability Brown laid out in the

The river bank between Richmond and Kew

A Two-Hour Walk Through Mayfair to Belgravia

This walk takes you from Green Park to Hyde Park, through the hearts of Mayfair and Belgravia, two of London's most elegant Georgian residential districts. It includes a bracing stroll through Hyde Park and, if you're feeling energetic, a row on the Serpentine.

⑦ L'Artiste Musclé restaurant, Shepherd Market, Mayfair

Green Park to Berkeley Square

Exit Green Park station ① following the signs for Piccadilly North. With Green Park opposite you, turn left. Pass Devonshire House ②, a 1920s office block that replaced the 18th-century mansion designed by William Kent. Only Kent's gates survive, now at the park entrance across Piccadilly. Turn left and walk up Berkeley Street to Berkeley Square ③. To the south, Lansdowne House by Robert Adam has been replaced by an advertising agency ④. There are still a few splendid 18th-century houses to the west, including No. 45 ⑤, home of the soldier and governor, Lord Clive of India.

Mayfair

Keep to the south of the square and turn into Charles Street, noting the evocative lampholders at Nos. 40 and 41 ⑥. Turn left into Queen Street and cross Curzon Street to enter Shepherd Market ⑦ (*see p99*) through Curzonfiel;d House alleyway. Turn right up a pedestrian-only street then right onto Hertford Street, passing the Curzon Cinema ⑧ on the corner of Curzon Street. Here you are almost facing Crewe House ⑨, built in 1730 by Edward Shepherd who also laid out the market.

Turn left and walk up Curzon Street, then turn right onto Chesterfield Street. A left turn at Charles Street brings you to Red Lion Yard ⑩, where a pub stands opposite one of the few clapboard buildings in the West End. Turn right into Hay's Mews and left up Chesterfield Hill. Cross Hill Street and South Street and head left until you reach an alley leading to the peaceful haven of Mount Street Gardens ⑪. The gardens back on to the Church of the Immaculate Conception ⑫. Cross the garden and turn left onto Mount Street; then right onto South Audley Street and left at Grosvenor Square ⑬ into Upper Grosvenor Street, passing to the left of the US Embassy. Look out for the statue of Franklin D Roosevelt. Turn right up Park Lane and walk past houses that are the remnants of what used to be the city's most

③ Grand Georgian doorway in Berkeley Square

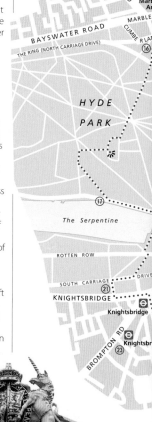

Royal coat of arms above the door of Auckley House

desirable residential street before the traffic got so heavy ⑭. At the end you can see Marble Arch *(see p211)*.

Hyde Park

Enter the pedestrian subway ⑮ at exit No. 6 and follow signs for Park Lane West Side, exit No. 5. You will emerge at Speakers' Corner ⑯ *(see p211)*, where on Sundays anyone can make a speech on any topic. Cross Hyde Park *(see p211)* south–southwest, enjoying the views on all sides,

⑰ The Serpentine, on a fine day

and head for the boat house ⑰ on the Serpentine (an artificial lake created by Queen Caroline in 1730), where you rent a rowboat. Turn left and follow the path to Serpentine Bar and Kitchen ⑱ for refreshments. From there, take the stone bridge ⑲ and cross Rotten Row ⑳, where the very fashionable exercise their horses. Leave the park at Edinburgh Gate ㉑.

Knightsbridge

Cross Knightsbridge and, resisting the temptations of two of London's great department stores – Harvey Nichols ㉒ and Harrods ㉓ *(see p211)* on Brompton Road – head down Sloane Street to turn left at Harriet Street. At Lowndes Square turn right and leave the square on the far side, turning left into Motcomb Street. On your left is the Pantechnicon, an eccentric structure fronted by colossal Doric columns, built in 1830. A path beside it leads to Halkin Arcade ㉔, built in the 1830s and adorned by Geoffrey Wickham's fountain built in 1971.

Belgravia

Turn left out of the arcade onto Kinnerton Street, which boasts one of London's smallest pubs, the Nag's Head ㉕. A street of pretty mews houses runs off to the left of this street at its northern end: look for Ann's Close and Kinnerton Place North. Almost opposite the latter, the street makes a sharp right turn to emerge into Wilton Place opposite St Paul's Church (1843). Turn right here and follow Wilton Crescent round to the left before turning left into Wilton Row, where there is another small pub, the Grenadier ㉖, once the officers' mess of the Guards' barracks and reputedly frequented by the Duke of Wellington. Up Old Barracks Yard to its right there are some old officers' billets and a worn stone said to have been used by the Iron Duke when mounting his horses. The alley leads to a T-junction. To finish the walk, turn right onto Grosvenor Crescent Mews, then left onto Grosvenor Crescent, which leads you to Hyde Park Corner Underground station.

Key

••• Walk route

0 meters 400
0 yards 400

㉖ Once the officers' mess, now the Grenadier pub, Belgravia

For keys to symbols *see back flap*

A 90-Minute Walk Along the South Bank

The Riverside Walk along the South Bank from Westminster Bridge *(see page 187)* via Bankside to Southwark Cathedral is one of the most entertaining excursions in town. From County Hall to Shakespeare's Globe, the South Bank's well-known music, theater, and film venues, the shops and galleries of Gabriel's Wharf, and the Oxo Tower, there's something for everyone. For more details on the sights in Southwark and Bankside, see pages 175–85.

on the level above. Moving on along the Riverside Walk, past Waterloo Bridge, you reach BFI Southbank ⑪ *(see p339)* where films are shown throughout the day. Outside its lively café, rows of tables stacked with second-hand books shelter beneath the bridge. The National Theatre ⑫ *(see p190)* also has exhibitions and musical events as well as a good bookshop, while in summer there are free outdoor performances. Several of the theater's

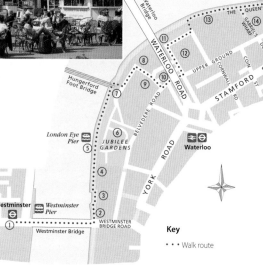

Cafés and shops at Gabriel's Wharf ⑭

Key

• • • Walk route

Westminster

Begin at Westminster station ① by the statue of Queen Boudica (or Boadicea), and walk over Westminster Bridge. Once on the south side ②, there is a fine view back over the river to the Houses of Parliament *(see pp74–5)*. The main building on this side is the former County Hall ③, now offering two hotels, several restaurants, and a range of entertainment *(see p190)*, the highlights being the Sea Life London Aquarium ④ to see the vibrant underwater world, and Namco Station, a games

Tips for Walkers

Starting point: Westminster Bridge.
Length: 1.75 miles (2.75 km)
Getting there: Westminster Underground station on the District, Circle, and Jubilee lines.
Stopping points: All the South Bank's art centers have cafés, bars, and restaurants. Also: Gourmet Pizza, Gabriel's Wharf; EAT, Riverside House (snacks and sandwiches); Anchor pub with river terrace (bars and restaurant).

hall with computer games, cars, and pool tables. For the best city view, the London Eye ⑤ *(see p191)* is beside Jubilee Gardens ⑥, where buskers and mime artists perform. Walk past Hungerford Bridge ⑦ with its modern walkways and trains to Charing Cross Station, on the site of the former Hungerford market. Ahead is the Southbank Centre ⑧ *(see pp188–9)*, the capital's main arts showcase. Music and exhibitions fill the Royal Festival Hall ⑨ *(see p190)*, created for the Festival of Britain in 1951. Check to see what's showing at the Hayward Gallery ⑩ *(see p190)* too, just beyond,

View from the Oxo Tower ⑮

Art at the Hayward Gallery,
South Bank ⑩

where he had a good view of
it. Next door to his house is
the exhibition and tour center
for Shakespeare's Globe ㉔
(see p179). A tour around the
theater is the next best thing
to attending a performance.

Bankside

Bankside becomes more
cramped here, as the historic
streets pass the Anchor ㉕
riverside pub and Vinopolis ㉖
to reach the Clink Prison
Museum ㉗ *(see p184)*, on the
site of one of London's first
lock-ups. At St. Mary Ovarie
Dock, climb aboard a replica
(1973) of *Golden Hinde* ㉘, in

restaurants, cafés, and bars offer
outside seating overlooking the
South Bank. Past the London
Studios (ITV) ⑬ is Gabriel's
Wharf ⑭ *(see p193)*, a pleasant
diversion of art and craft shops
and lively cafés.

The Oxo Tower

The next landmark you come
to is the Oxo Tower ⑮, a red-
brick industrial building, with
contemporary designer shops
and galleries, such as gallery@.
Take the elevator to the top of
the tower for an excellent, free
view of the city: the Inner Temple
and Fleet Street lie opposite.
Once down again, the Riverside
Walk passes by Sea Containers
House ⑯, with gold trimmings
(built as a hotel, but now offices)
and Doggett's Coat and Badge
pub ⑰ *(see p65)*, then continue
under Blackfriars Bridge ⑱,
emerging by the remaining
piers and railroad emblem of a
former bridge. On the right,
opposite the Founders Arms ⑲,
is the esteemed Bankside

Gallery ⑳ *(see p179)*, which
has regular exhibitions of its
members' work. Behind it,
opposite Falcon Point Piazza is
Marcus Campbell, an excellent
art bookshop, a stone's throw
from Tate Modern ㉑ *(see
pp180–83)*, the best free show
on the river. Drop in for a coffee
if nothing else. The Millennium
Bridge ㉒ leads over to St. Paul's
(see pp150–51) and the City.
Architect Sir Christopher Wren
had a house by Cardinal Cap
Alley in Cardinal's Wharf ㉓,

which the Elizabethan
buccaneer Sir Francis Drake
became the second man to
circumnavigate the world.
Southwark Cathedral ㉙ *(see
p178)*, is a quiet place to end
the walk – there is a good tea
shop here. Or, if you still feel
energetic, browse around
Borough Market *(see p178)*
and take a look up at London's
new landmark, the Shard
(www.the-shard.com), before
heading to the tube or train
at London Bridge station ㉛.

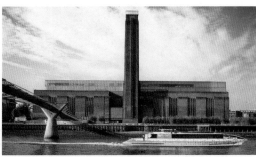

Tate Modern: a vast space for contemporary British art ㉑

A Two-Hour Walk Around Notting Hill

This walk centers around Portobello Road, the city's most famous antique and bric-a-brac shopping area in one of the ultra-fashionable parts of London. Great for original souvenirs, the neighborhood is fascinating at any time, though the streets are busiest on Fridays and Saturdays, when all the shops are open and the market stands laid out (see page 325). This is the heart of Notting Hill, renowned for its carnival and also favored as a movie setting and a prestigious address.

Terrace ⑩ the daily fruit and vegetable market begins. On the left is the Electric Cinema ⑪, said to be the oldest working movie theater in Britain (1910), and certainly one of the most delightful. If there is not a film showing, you can go in and try the comfortable armchair seats and sofas.

The Notting Hill Bookshop

Turn left down Blenheim Crescent to find The Notting Hill Bookshop ⑫, formerly The Travel

Sun in Splendour pub frontage ⑤

Portobello Road

Leaving Notting Hill Gate tube station ①, follow the signs to Portobello Road (see p221), taking Pembridge Road ②. Intriguing shops here include Retro Woman ③ (Nos. 20 and 32) and Retro Man ④ (No. 34) for period clothes and accessories. At the Sun in Splendour pub ⑤, turn left into Portobello Road. No. 22, among the attractively painted row houses on the right, was where George Orwell lived in 1927 before his writing career began ⑥. Cross Chepstow Villas ⑦

and the serious antique shops begin. Near the Portobello Arcade ⑧, signposted with a large teapot, is Portobello Gold (Nos. 95–7), a guest house where Bill, Hillary, and Chelsea Clinton dropped in for a beer and a snack in 2000. At No. 115 ⑨ is a plaque to June Aylward, who opened the first antique shop in the street. At Colville

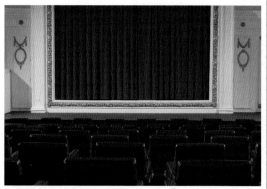

The Electric Cinema, the UK's oldest working movie theater ⑪

Tips for Walkers

Starting point: Notting Hill Gate underground station.
Length: 1.85 miles (3 km)
Getting there: Notting Hill Underground station on Central, District, and Circle lines.
Stopping points: The area is known for its pubs and restaurants. Try Grove Café at 253a Portobello Road; Eve's Market Café at 222 Portobello Road; Toms at 127 Westbourne Grove (great sandwiches and snacks); Ottolenghi's Patisserie at 63 Ledbury Road (superb pastries).

Bookshop, a location of the 1999 movie *Notting Hill*, in which Hugh Grant was the assistant. Books for Cooks ⑬ (No. 4) is where recipes from the latest books are prepared and sold. Head back to Portobello Road and pass the local Salvation Army center ⑭. Amble for several blocks to Grove Café ⑮ (No. 253a) on the corner (opposite the Market Bar ⑯). If you can find a table on the upstairs terrace, you'll have a good view of the street. All-day breakfasts are a specialty. Excitement dwindles once you pass under the Westway overpass, except on Fridays and Saturdays,

Ottolenghi Patisserie display ㉓

Lady of Walsingham – an unusual feature in a Protestant church. Just beyond the red-brick Tabernacle Centre for Arts and Education ⑳, where Pink Floyd made their debut in 1966, is My Beautiful Laundrette ㉑, named after the successful 1986 movie. Turn right into Ledbury Road to

find high-fashion shops, and also, at its end, the still-functioning Westbourne Grove Church ㉒. As you are passing No. 63, try the pastries in Ottolenghi Patisserie ㉓ for a snack to hit the spot. Turn right into Westbourne Grove for more stylish shopping. Dinny Hall ㉔ at No. 200 stocks award-winning jewelry. Detour to Toms deli and café ㉕ at 127, which claims the best toasted sandwiches in town, and is run by Tom Conran, son of the style guru Terence Conran. The Wild at Heart flower stand on Turquoise Island ㉖ opposite, has won awards for its designer, Piers Gough. On the far side is the Oxfam thrift shop ㉗, where its bargains reflect the good taste of the locals. Head back to Portobello Road ㉘ and Notting Hill Gate tube.

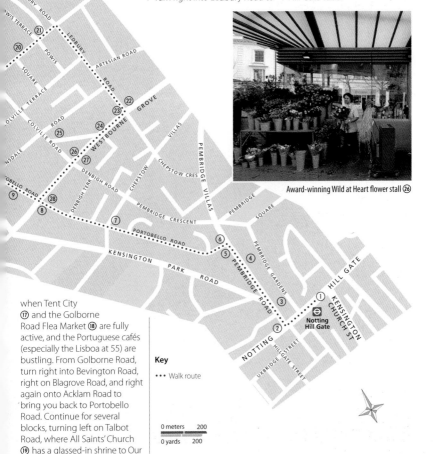

Award-winning Wild at Heart flower stall ㉖

when Tent City ⑰ and the Golborne Road Flea Market ⑱ are fully active, and the Portuguese cafés (especially the Lisboa at 55) are bustling. From Golborne Road, turn right into Bevington Road, right on Blagrove Road, and right again onto Acklam Road to bring you back to Portobello Road. Continue for several blocks, turning left on Talbot Road, where All Saints' Church ⑲ has a glassed-in shrine to Our

Key

••• Walk route

0 meters 200
0 yards 200

For keys to symbols *see back flap*

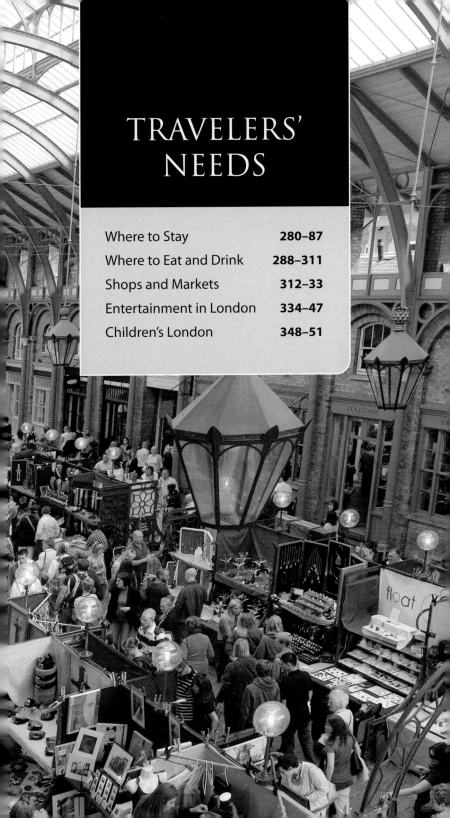

TRAVELERS' NEEDS

WHERE TO STAY

The high cost of accommodations in London is one of the biggest drawbacks for visitors. At the top end of the market, there is no shortage of expensive pedigree hotels, such as Claridge's and the Ritz. Midrange hotels, while there are many, tend to be slightly farther out of the center of town. Budget hotels are few and far between thanks to rising property prices. However, there are ways to stay in the capital without breaking the bank. Low-cost chains such as Premier Inn, Novotel, and Tune have hotels in convenient locations throughout the city, many concentrated in the center of town,

offering good-quality accommodations at affordable prices. We have inspected more than 250 hotels and apartment complexes across a range of price brackets and localities and chosen 70 of the best of their kind. For further details on these, turn to the listings on pages 284–87. If you don't need a hotel's facilities, consider self-service apartments and private homes *(see pp282–3)*, available at a wide range of prices. Student halls and hostels, and even a few campsites on London's outskirts, are additional possibilities for those traveling on a budget *(see p283)*.

Where to Look

The most expensive hotels tend to be in smart West End areas such as Mayfair and Belgravia. Often large and opulent, with uniformed staff, they are not always the most relaxing places to stay. For smaller, more personal, but still luxurious hotels, try South Kensington or Holland Park.

The streets off Earl's Court Road are full of hotels at the lower end of the price range. Several of the major train stations are well served by budget hotels too. Try Ebury Street near Victoria, or Sussex Gardens near Paddington. Close to Euston or Waterloo and in the City and Docklands,

well-known hotel chains cater to travelers at a range of prices.

There are also inexpensive hotels in the suburbs, such as Ealing, Hendon, Richmond, or Harrow. From here you can get into town on public transportation and by suburban train services. Be sure to check the train times for the last train service leaving central London.

If you get stranded at an airport or have to catch an early morning flight, consult the list on page 369. For further information, advice, and reservation services, contact visitlondon. com, which publishes several annually updated booklets on the different types of accommodations in Greater London.

Discount Rates

Prices in the capital tend to stay high year-round, but there are bargains. Many hotels, especially the chains, offer reduced rates for weekends and special breaks *(see p282)*. Others work on a more ad hoc basis, depending on how busy they are. If a hotel isn't full, it is always worth trying to negotiate a discount, especially if it is off-season. Older budget hotels may have rooms without showers or private bathrooms. These usually cost less than those with private facilities.

Hidden Extras

Read the small print carefully. Most hotels quote room rates rather than rates per person, but not all. Service charges and VAT are usually included in the quoted price but in some cases they are added on later, which means that the final bill can come as a shock to visitors. Also be aware of high mark-ups on telephone calls made in your hotel room. Breakfast may not be included in room rates, though it generally is in cheaper hotels. Single travelers are usually charged a "supplement" and end up paying about 80 percent of the double room rate, even if they are occupying a "single" room – so don't accept anything substandard.

Tipping is expected in the more expensive hotels, but

Comfortable foyer area in Charlotte Street Hotel *(see p284)*

◀ Apple Market, Covent Garden Piazza

Attractive facade of the London Bridge Hotel *(see p285)*

there is no need to tip staff other than porters, except perhaps a helpful concierge for arranging theater tickets or calling for taxis.

Facilities

Room sizes in London hotels tend to be on the small side whatever the price range, but the majority of hotels provide telephones, televisions, and private baths or showers in all their rooms. At the top end of the scale, hotels compete to offer the very latest sound-and-video systems, computer equipment, and high-tech gadgetry. Most hotel rooms come equipped with Wi-Fi. Whatever the hotel, you will be expected to vacate your room by noon on the day you leave, sometimes even earlier.

The elegant hallway of The Gore, Kensington *(see p286)*

How to Book

It is always advisable to reserve your accommodations well in advance, as room availability and prices are likely to fluctuate, with the better quality hotels being more popular. Direct bookings can be made by phone, via the hotel website booking form, or by email. This generally entails giving a guarantee: either a credit card number from which a cancellation fee can be deducted, or a one-night deposit (some hotels will expect more for longer stays). Don't forget that if you subsequently cancel, part or all of the room price may be charged unless the hotel can fill the room. Insurance coverage is advised.

The visitlondon.com website offers an excellent guide to finding accommodations in London, from self-service apartments and budget hostels to luxury hotels. To make a reservation by phone, call Expedia at 0203 564 5657. Visitors can also book in person at the London Visitor Centre at No. 1 Regent Street. There is no fee for this service but you will be asked for a credit card number. During high season there may be a one-night deposit to pay. Alternatively, travelers can use a similar booking service at www.superbreak.com, or call or email the service directly at 0871 221 3344 or bookings@superbreak.com. There is no fee if booking online.

Accommodations booking services are also available at the British Hotel Reservation Centre in Victoria train station. A number of non-LTB booking agencies operate from booths in the major train stations, charging a small fee to personal callers. You may come across unidentified scalpers who often hang around at train and coach stations offering cheap accommodations; these offers should be avoided.

Online booking is the easiest way to book hotels, with the best prices often only available via the Internet. Many hotels have their own online advance

Impeccably stylish interior of the Hotel 41 *(see p286)*

purchase rate, while Internet travel sites, vacation retailers, and hotel wholesalers such as Expedia (www.expedia.co.uk) and Travelocity (www.travelocity.co.uk) also quote good rates, particularly if you book a hotel and flight together. Increasingly, the Internet demonstrates the fluidity of many hotel "rack rates" (i.e., the rates printed on the price sheet), which, far from being fixed in stone, fluctuate widely according to the laws of supply and demand.

Special Breaks

Many travel agencies carry brochures from the major hotel chains listing special offers, which are usually priced on a minimum two-night stay. Some are extraordinary bargains compared to the normal rate. For most leisure travelers or families with children, this is the best way to get the best value out of London hotels so that you can spend time in the city without breaking the bank.

City-break packages are organized by specialty operators, ferry companies, and airlines, and some privately owned hotels too. Sometimes the same hotel may be featured in several brochures at widely differing prices and with different perks. It's worth asking the hotel directly what special rates they offer, and checking their websites too.

Opulent bathroom interiors at the Goring Hotel *(see p286)*

Disabled Travelers

Information about wheelchair access is based largely on hotels' own assessments, so travelers with special needs should always confirm when booking whether an establishment is suitable. If forewarned, many hotels will go out of their way to help disabled visitors. The nationwide Tourism for All program provides details on accommodation standards and facilities for elderly visitors or those with mobility problems. For information on hotels that meet the three-tier "National Accessible Standard," contact **DisabledGo** or **Tourism For All**. A guide book for people with access needs, Open Britain, can be obtained from **RADAR**.

Traveling with Children

London hotels are very welcoming to children and make a concerted effort to cater to the needs of people traveling with children, providing cribs, high chairs, babysitting services (always make sure sitters have had a Criminal Records Bureau check), and special meal arrangements. Ask whether the hotel offers special deals for children – some have special rates, or allow children to stay free of charge in their parents' room.

Self-Service Flats

Many agencies offer self-service accommodation in flats, usually for stays of a week or more. Prices, depending on size and location, start at about £300 per

week. Some luxury complexes are fully serviced, so you don't need to cook, shop, or clean. **Bridge Street Worldwide** has over 550 London apartments in good locations. It caters mainly to corporate and professional travelers, but its properties can be rented for short-term stays whenever they are available.

The **Landmark Trust** rents apartments in historic or unusual buildings. These include apartments in Hampton Court *(see pp256–9)* and in a pretty 18th-century terrace in the City: one of them was the home of the late poet laureate Sir John Betjeman. A handbook of Landmark Trust properties is available for a charge via their website.

Staying in Private Homes

A number of agencies organize stays in private homes; several are registered with Visit London. Reservations can be made directly with Visit London, with credit card reservations made by

telephone. Several agencies have minimum stays of up to a week. Prices depend on location, starting at around £25 per person per night. Sometimes you will enjoy family hospitality, but this isn't guaranteed, so inquire when you book. **Airbnb** offers accommodation for one night's stay or longer in private homes in London and the UK. Deposits may be requested and cancellation fees imposed. The **Bed & Breakfast and Homestay Association** (BBHA) is an umbrella organization for several reputable agencies whose properties are inspected regularly. For details of members, visit the BBHA website *(see box)*.

Uptown Reservations arranges B&B stays in interesting London homes that have been inspected for their welcome, security, and comfort. Prices start at £125 per night for a double room. It works in tandem with **Wolsey Lodges**, a nationwide consortium of distinctive private homes, often of historic or architectural interest, offering individual hospitality. Wolsey Lodges lists charming properties.

Chain Hotels

Chain hotels are an important feature of the London hotel market. Though they can lack character, they offer some of the best value accommodations in town. Some also offer particular facilities; Novotel, for example, caters to both business guests and families. Other good-value chains include Express by Holiday Inn and easyHotel.

Imaginative dining suite, W hotel *(see p284)*

Budget Accommodations

Despite the high cost of many London hotels, budget accommodations do exist, and not only for young travelers.

Dormitory accomodation and youth hostels can be booked through the LTB's information center at Victoria Station for a small fee plus a refundable deposit. Some private hostels near Earl's Court charge little more than £10 a night for a dormitory bed with breakfast. The **London Hostels Association** has a selection of reasonably priced accommodations throughout central London. **The Youth Hostels Association** (YHA) runs seven hostels in London. There is no age limit, though non-members pay a joining fee. Of the seven, two are located in the heart of London. The Oxford Street hostel is actually in Noel Street, Soho, while the London St. Paul's hostel is located near St. Paul's Cathedral *(see pp150–53)*. One of the most popular hostels is

City of London Youth Hostel

Holland House, a Jacobean mansion in Holland Park. The easiest way to book a bed online is through the **Hostelling International** (HL) website, which offers a range of global hostels to stay at.

Many student rooms are available at Easter and from July to September. Some of these are in central locations such as South Kensington. **London University Rooms** arranges stays in halls, or, if you need a room in a hurry,

King's College or **Imperial College** may be able to find you one.

Recommended Hotels

The hotels on pages 284–7 of this guide are a selection of the best luxury, boutique, character, bed & breakfast, and budget hotels in London. They are first listed according to theme, and then alphabetically by area. Most of the hotels are spread across the main tourist areas, although a number that are farther afield are included if they offer particularly good value, facilities, service, or charm.

There are also B&Bs, guesthouses and apartments, as well as pubs and restaurants with rooms. What they all have in common is that, regardless of category and price, they have something special to offer.

Where a hotel has an exceptional feature, such as bargain rates or spectacular views it has been highlighted as a DK Choice.

DIRECTORY

Reservations and Information

British Hotel Reservation Centre
Victoria Railway Station, East Concourse, SW1V 1JU.
Tel 020 7828 1027.
W bhrconline.com
W visitlondon.com
Tel 020 3564 5657.
W visitlondon.com

Disabled Travelers

DisabledGo
Tel 0845 270 4627.
W disabledgo.com

Radar
Unit 12, City Forum, 250 City Road EC1V 8AF.
Tel 020 7250 3222.
W radar.org.uk

Tourism For All
7A Pixel Mill, 4 Appleby Road, Kendal, Cumbria LA9 6ES.
Tel 0845 124 9971; 0044 1539 726 111 (overseas).
W tourismforall.org.uk

Self-Service Agencies

Bridge Street Worldwide
Compass House, 22 Redan Place W2 4SA.
Tel 020 7792 2222.
W bridgestreet.com

Landmark Trust
Shottesbrooke, Maidenhead, Berks SL6 3SW.
Tel 01628 825925.
W landmarktrust.org.uk

Agencies for Stays in Private Homes

Airbnb
W airbnb.com

At Home in London
70 Black Lion Lane W6 9BE. Tel 020 8748 1943.
W athomeinlondon.co.uk

Bed & Breakfast & Homestay Assoc.
8 Kelso Place W8 5OP.
Tel 020 7937 2001.
W bbha.org.uk

Uptown Reservations
8 Kelso Place W8 5QD.
Tel 020 7937 2001.
W uptownres.co.uk

Wolsey Lodges
9 Market Place, Hadleigh, Ipswich, Suffolk, IP7 5DL.
Tel 01473 822058.
W wolseylodges.com

Hostel Booking

Hostelling International
Tel 01707 324170.
W hihostels.com

London Hostels Association
54 Eccleston Sq SW1V 1PG. Tel 020 7727 5665.
W london-hostels.co.uk

Youth Hostels Association
Trevelyan House, Dimple Rd, Matlock, Derbyshire DE4 3YH.
Tel 01629 592700.
W yha.org.uk

Booking Addresses for Residence Halls

Imperial College Summer Accommodation Centre
Sherfield Building, Level 3 SW7 2AZ.
Tel 020 7594 9507.
W imperial.ac.uk/conferenceandevents/accommodation

King's Conference & Vacation Bureau
26–29 Drury Lane, 1st floor WC2B 5RL.
Tel 020 7848 1700.
W kingsvenues.com

London University Rooms
Tel 020 7040 8037.
W londonuniversityrooms.co.uk

Where to Stay

Luxury

Westminster and the West End

Flemings Hotel and Apartments ££
7–12 Half Moon Street, W1J 7BH
Tel *020 7499 0000* **Map** 12 E4
🆆 flemings-mayfair.co.uk
This tranquil oasis is stylish without being pretentious. Choose between charming rooms and apartments.

The Athenaeum £££
116 Piccadilly, W1J 7BJ
Tel *020 7499 3464* **Map** 12 E4
🆆 athenaeumhotel.com
An established hotel, but with up-to-date, airy bedrooms and family-friendly apartments. A great on-site spa.

Claridge's £££
49 Brook Street, W1K 4HR
Tel *020 7629 8860* **Map** 12 E2
🆆 claridges.co.uk
One of London's greats: seamless service and understated luxury in a dazzling Art Deco building. Perfect for a special occasion.

Covent Garden £££
10 Monmouth Street, WC2H 9HB
Tel *020 7806 1000* **Map** 13 B2
🆆 firmdalehotels.com/london/covent-garden-hotel
A vibrant, sexy, and designer-dressed hotel from the Firmdale stable. Combines old-world style with metropolitan chic.

Four Seasons Hotel London at Park Lane £££
Hamilton Place, W1J 7DR
Tel *020 7499 0888* **Map** 12 E4
🆆 fourseasons.com/london
Sumptuously glossy and in a fantastic location, this hotel boasts immaculate service. It also has a stunning glass-walled rooftop spa.

St John £££
1 Leicester Street, WC2H 7BL
Tel *020 3301 8069* **Map** 13 A2
🆆 stjohnhotellondon.com
Dine at the sumptuous restaurant and stay in one of the calm, white, minimalist rooms.

The Ritz £££
150 Piccadilly, W1J 9BR
Tel *020 7493 8181* **Map** 12 F3
🆆 theritzlondon.com
Perfectly preserved in its original Louis XVI style: glamor and glitz rolled into one. Don't miss the famous afternoon tea.

W £££
10 Wardour Street, W1D 6QF
Tel *020 7758 1000* **Map** 12 A2
🆆 wlondon.co.uk
All glass outside, sleek and bright inside, this luxury global brand hotel is the ultimate in cool.

Bloomsbury and Regent's Park

Charlotte Street £££
15–17 Charlotte Street, W1T 1RJ
Tel *020 7806 2000* **Map** 13 A1
🆆 firmdalehotels.com/london/charlotte-street-hotel
The groovy favorite of media people, with lively public areas and a stylish, private movie theater.

The Langham £££
1c Portland Place, W1B 1JA
Tel *020 7636 1000* **Map** 12 E1
🆆 london.langhamhotels.co.uk
A *grande dame* hotel with an Eastern look. Rooms have a relaxing private-home feel.

The City and the East End

DK Choice

Boundary Rooms £££
2–4 Boundary Street, E2 7DD (entrance in Redchurch Street)
Tel *020 7729 1051* **Map** 8 D4
🆆 theboundary.co.uk
A converted Victorian warehouse in trendy Shoreditch is the setting for Terence Conran's hotel. It exudes style, from the retro cellar bar to each perfectly designed bedroom. All rooms are customized and decorated with designer objects. Don't miss the spectacular views from the rooftop brasserie, which hums on summer weekends.

Individually designed room at Charlotte Street hotel

Shoreditch Rooms £££
Ebor Street, E1 6AW
Tel *020 7739 5040* **Map** 8 D4
🆆 www.shoreditchhouse.com
An imaginatively renovated warehouse, home to 26 bright, fresh-looking rooms decorated in a New England vintage style.

Kensington and Chelsea

The Capital ££
22–24 Basil Street, SW3 1AT
Tel *020 7589 5171* **Map** 11 C5
🆆 capitalhotel.co.uk
All the luxury and service of a grand hotel, but much more intimate and personal. The bedrooms are a good size and traditionally elegant.

Belgraves £££
20 Chesham Place, SW1X 8HQ
Tel *020 7858 0100* **Map** 20 D1
🆆 thompsonhotels.com/hotels/london/belgraves
New York "boho" in Belgravia, with bold, eclectic design. There's a terrace with a retractable roof, a buzzy lobby, and Mark Hix's restaurant.

DK Choice

Mandarin Oriental Hyde Park £££
66 Knightsbridge, SW1X 7LA
Tel *020 7235 2000* **Map** 11 C5
🆆 mandarinoriental.com/london
Mandarin Oriental is a byword for luxury and impeccable Eastern-style service, and this vast Edwardian red-brick pile is no exception. A happy blend of the old and new, it has traditional, swagged bedrooms with mahogany furniture and marble fireplaces, a sleek, contemporary ground floor, and a fabulous high-spec granite spa.

Royal Garden £££
2–24 Kensington High Street, W8 4PT
Tel *020 7937 8000* **Map** 10 D5
🆆 royalgardenhotel.co.uk
A 1960s hotel favored by celebrities and well-suited to families. Go for a room with an unrivaled park view. Service throughout is courteous and very efficient.

The studio suite at the W hotel, Leicester Square

The Halkin by COMO £££
5 Halkin Street, SW1X 7DJ
Tel *020 7333 1059* **Map** 12 D5
W comohotels.com/thehalkin
Welcoming service, fresh flowers, soft lighting, and exquisite beds – the perfect place to chill out.

The Levin £££
28 Basil Street, SW3 1AS
Tel *020 7589 6286* **Map** 11 C5
W thelevinhotel.co.uk
A little gem, from the pistachio-colored reception area to the gorgeous, cozy bedrooms.

Boutique

Westminster and the West End

The Arch £££
50 Great Cumberland Place, W1H 7FD
Tel *020 7724 4700* **Map** 11 C2
W thearchlondon.com
Cleverly converted from a row of townhouses. Popular bar and laid-back dining.

Bloomsbury and Regent's Park

Megaro, King's Cross ££
Belgrove Street, WC1H 8AB
Tel *020 7843 2222* **Map** 5 C3
W hotelmegaro.co.uk
A buzzing urban hangout with striking contemporary rooms.

Montagu Place ££
2–3 Montagu Place, W1H 2ER
Tel *020 7467 2777* **Map** 11 C1
W montagu-place.co.uk
Go for a "Comfy," "Swanky," or "Fancy" room. An intimate hotel that stands out from the crowd. Decorated in neutral shades and with plentiful facilities.

No. Ten Manchester Street ££
10 Manchester Street, W1U 4DG
Tel *020 7317 5900* **Map** 12 D1
W tenmanchesterstreethotel.com
A handsome Edwardian townhouse with a gentleman's club feel. All-weather cigar terrace and comfy bar.

The City and the East End

The Hoxton ££
81 Great Eastern Street, EC2A 3HU
Tel *020 7550 1000* **Map** 7 C4
W hoxtonhotels.com
The earlier you book this hip hotel, the less you pay. The vast open-plan lobby has a real buzz.

King's Wardrobe by Bridge Street ££
6 Wardrobe Place, EC4V 5AF
Tel *020 7792 2222* **Map** 14 F2
W bridgestreet.com/The_Kings_Wardrobe_by_BridgeStreet_Worldwide.htm
Flagship building with apartments, ranging from studios to three bedrooms, all well equipped.

The Zetter Townhouse ££
49–50 St John's Square, EC1V 4JJ
Tel *020 7324 4567* **Map** 6 E2
W thezettertownhouse.com
Get your toothpaste and Champagne from the same vending machine at this hip hotel with playful touches. Ultra-cool and very welcoming.

Threadneedles £££
5 Threadneedle Street, EC2R 8AY
Tel *020 7657 8080* **Map** 15 B2
W theetoncollection.co.uk/content.aspx
Immaculate service and luxurious rooms in a stylish former bank. A spectacular glass dome dominates the reception area.

Southwark and the South Bank

Bermondsey Square ££
Bermondsey Square, Tower Bridge Road, SE1 3UN
Tel *020 7378 2450* **Map** 16 D4
W bermondseysquarehotel.co.uk
Treat yourself to a loft suite and hot tub with a view at this wittily furnished hotel.

DK Choice

London Bridge ££
8–18 London Bridge Street, SE1 9SG
Tel *020 7855 2200* **Map** 15 B4
W londonbridgehotel.com
Through the handsome 19th-century entrance, a modern lobby sets the scene for this hip yet intimate, independently owned four-star hotel. Bedrooms are über cool, each with a black-and-white bathroom. There's also a well-equipped gym, three restaurant/bars, and great weekend rates.

Kensington and Chelsea

The Ampersand ££
10 Harrington Road, SW7 3ER
Tel *020 7589 5895* **Map** 19 A2
W ampersandhotel.com
A whimsical interior inspired by music, science, and nature.

Baby ABode Sydney House ££
9–11 Sydney Street, SW3 6PU
Tel *020 7376 7711* **Map** 19 A3
W abodehotels.co.uk/chelsea
A chic bolthole: pale pistachio walls, blonde wood floors, and Frette linen sheets.

myhotel Chelsea ££
35 Ixworth Place, SW3 3QX
Tel *020 7225 7500* **Map** 19 B2
W myhotels.com/my-hotel-chelsea
Designed along Feng Shui principles: you feel a sense of well-being as soon as you arrive.

Grand Plaza Serviced Apartments £££
42 Princes Square, W2 4AD
Tel *020 7985 8000* **Map** 10 D2
W www.grand-plaza.co.uk
Snug studios for couples; airy apartments for groups. Access to the square's gardens is a big plus.

Space Apart Hotel £££
36–37 Kensington Gardens Square, W2 4BQ
Tel *020 7908 1340* **Map** 10 D2
W aparthotel-london.co.uk
Practical, comfortable apartments with funky details.

For more information on types of hotels *see page 283*

Farther Afield

Avo £
82 Dalston Lane, E8 3AH
Tel *020 3490 5061*
W avohotel.com
DVDs for rent, memory-foam beds, and a host of thoughtful extras are available at this trendy crash pad.

High Road House ££
162–70 Chiswick High Road, W4 1PR
Tel *020 8742 1717*
W highroadhouse.co.uk
Enjoy breakfast in the brasserie, after a night in a chic, Scandinavian-inspired room.

Rafayel on the Left Bank ££
34 Lombard Road, SW11 3RF
Tel *020 7801 3600*
W www.hotelrafayel.com
Large relaxing rooms, a spa, and conscientious staff single out this eco-friendly Battersea hotel.

Town Hall Hotel and Apartments ££
8 Patriot Square, E2 9NF
Tel *020 7871 0460*
W townhallhotel.com
Edwardian architecture, Art Deco interiors, and hip furnishings – a winning combination.

Character

Westminster and the West End

Dean Street Townhouse ££
69–71 Dean Street, W1D 3SE
Tel *020 7434 1775* **Map** 13 A1
W deanstreettownhouse.com
A dynamic hotel with its Georgian heritage intact. A lively restaurant and charming bedrooms.

The Fox Club ££
46 Clarges Street, W1J 7ER
Tel *020 7495 3656* **Map** 12 E3
W foxclublondon.com
Decorated with eye-catching fabrics, this charming hotel is open to non-club members.

Hazlitt's ££
6 Frith Street, W1D 3JA
Tel *020 7434 1771* **Map** 13 A2
W hazlittshotel.com
Furnished with antiques, busts, and prints, this is a distinctive hotel with loads of charm.

The Orange ££
37 Pimlico Road, SW1W 8NE
Tel *020 7881 9844* **Map** 20 D2
W theorange.co.uk
Calls itself a "Public House and Hotel," but really it's a rustic restaurant with four cozy rooms.

The elegant exterior of the Goring Hotel

Hotel 41 £££
41 Buckingham Palace Road, SW1W 0PS
Tel *020 7300 0041* **Map** 20 E2
W 41hotel.com
A stunning hotel with a clubby atmosphere, black-and-white bedrooms, and dark wood.

The Goring £££
Beeston Place, SW1W 0JW
Tel *020 7396 9000* **Map** 20 E1
W thegoring.com
There are liveried doormen and a lovely private garden at this great English institution. It's where the Duchess of Cambridge stayed before her wedding.

The Stafford London by Kempinski £££
16–18 St. James's Place, SW1A 1NJ
Tel *020 7493 0111* **Map** 12 F4
W kempinski.com/en/london/the-stafford-london
A class act. Traditional English country house furnishings and an American bar.

Bloomsbury and Regent's Park

Durrants ££
26–32 George Street, W1H 5BJ
Tel *020 7935 8131* **Map** 12 D1
W durrantshotel.co.uk
An English classic, from the venerable paneled entrance to the tiny snug bar. The uniformed staff and Edwardian lobby set the scene for the rest of the hotel.

Rough Luxe ££
1 Birkenhead Street, WC1H 8BA
Tel *020 7837 5338* **Map** 5 C3
W roughluxe.co.uk
Quirky, creative, and full of surprises: friendly service, original art, and a touch of luxury.

Montague on the Gardens £££
15 Montague Street, WC1B 5BJ
Tel *020 7637 1001* **Map** 5 B5
W montaguehotel.com
Full of charm, from the tartan-walled bar to the chintzy rooms.

The City and the East End

DK Choice

The Rookery ££
12 Peter's Lane, Cowcross Street, EC1M 6DS
Tel *020 7336 0931* **Map** 6 F5
W rookeryhotel.com
A romantic venue, The Rookery consists of three restored 18th-century houses, crammed with curiosities. Its seductive bedrooms have antique beds and bathrooms with roll-top baths. Downstairs, in the foyer, you'll find an open fire.

Kensington and Chelsea

The Gore ££
190 Queen's Gate, SW7 5EX
Tel *020 7584 6601* **Map** 10 F5
W gorehotel.com
A hotel that explodes with character: pictures jostle for wall space; bedrooms are all unique.

Twenty Nevern Square ££
20 Nevern Square, SW5 9PD
Tel *020 7565 9555* **Map** 17 C2
W 20nevernsquare.com
Some deliciously over-the-top rooms at this calm refuge with colonial and Asian decor.

Vancouver Studios ££
30 Prince's Square, W2 4NJ
Tel *020 7243 1270* **Map** 10 D2
W vancouverstudios.co.uk
Elegant modern studios in a stylish townhouse; each has a mini kitchen with all accessories.

Farther Afield

The Alma ££
499 Old York Road, SW18 1TF
Tel *020 8870 2537*
W almawandsworth.com
A Victorian tavern, now one of Wandsworth's new-breed pub-restaurants, with 23 rooms.

Bingham ££
61–63 Petersham Road, Richmond upon Thames, Surrey, TW10 6UT
Tel *020 8940 0902*
W thebingham.co.uk
A Georgian townhouse overlooking the Thames, with a great restaurant. Located close to Richmond's shops.

Fox and Grapes ££
9 Camp Road, SW19 4UN
Tel *020 8619 1300*
ⓦ foxandgrapeswimbledon.co.uk
This chic getaway offers small
bedrooms above a gastropub.

The Rose and Crown ££
*199 Stoke Newington Church Street,
N16 9ES*
Tel *020 7923 3337*
ⓦ roseandcrownn16.co.uk
Stay in a king-sized room above
this classic oak-paneled pub.

Bed & Breakfast

Westminster and the West End

Luna Simone £
47–49 Belgrave Road, SW1V 2BB
Tel *020 7834 5897*   **Map** 20 F2
ⓦ lunasimonehotel.com
 A family-run business since the
1980s. Prices include breakfast.

Lime Tree ££
135–7 Ebury Street, SW1W 9QU
Tel *020 7730 7865*   **Map** 20 E2
ⓦ limetreehotel.co.uk
Real value for money at this
established, family-run venture.

The Sumner ££
54 Upper Berkeley Street, W1H 7QR
Tel *020 7723 2244*   **Map** 11 C1
ⓦ thesumner.com
A Georgian townhouse full of
warmth and charm. The
decoration is elegant.

Bloomsbury and Regent's Park

Arosfa £
83 Gower Street, WC1E 6HJ
Tel *020 7636 2115*   **Map** 5 A5
ⓦ arosfalondon.com
Guests are made to feel like part
of the family at this simple B&B.

Hart House ££
51 Gloucester Place, W1U 8JF
Tel *020 7935 2288*   **Map** 11 C1
ⓦ harthouse.co.uk
Spotless rooms and an excellent
breakfast at this award-winning
townhouse. Rooms are cozy and
appealingly decorated.

Kensington and Chelsea

Hyde Park Rooms £
137 Sussex Gardens, W2 2RX
Tel *020 7723 0225*   **Map** 11 A1
ⓦ hydeparkrooms.com
No-frills rooms (some with
shared bath), all kept spick-and-
span. Generous breakfasts.

Amsterdam ££
7 Trebovir Road, SW5 9LS
Tel *020 7370 5084*   **Map** 17 C3
ⓦ amsterdam-hotel.com
A prize-winning B&B with pastel
rooms and apartments. The
garden is perfect for summer.

Aster House ££
3 Sumner Place, SW7 3EE
Tel *020 7581 5888*   **Map** 19 A2
ⓦ asterhouse.com
A peaceful, eco-friendly
sanctuary. Victorian architecture
and traditional furnishings.

Rhodes ££
195 Sussex Gardens, W2 2RJ
Tel *020 7262 0537*   **Map** 11 A1
ⓦ rhodeshotel.com
You are assured of a warm
welcome at this eclectic hotel.

Budget

Bloomsbury and Regent's Park

No. 5 Doughty Street £
5 Doughty Street, WC1N 2PL
Tel *020 7373 9120*   **Map** 6 D4
ⓦ www.blueprintlivingapartments.
com/no-5-doughty-street
Apartments with pizzazz:
Blueprint Living's complex offers
comfort at reasonable rates.

The City and the East End

DK Choice

Fleet River Bakery Rooms £
71 Lincolns Inn Fields, WC2A 3JF
Tel *020 7691 1457*   **Map** 14 D1
ⓦ fleetriverbakery.com
Above the bustle and graceful
arched windows of this busy
bakery, these well-appointed,

good-sized studios with their
own kitchen areas are stylish in
a low-key way. Excellent, fresh
breakfast is served every day by
friendly bakery staff – except for
Sundays, when delicious
hampers are provided. Terrific
value for money.

**Premier Inn London City
(Tower Hill)** £
24 Prescot Street, E1 8BB
Tel *0871 527 8646*   **Map** 16 E2
ⓦ premierinn.com/en/hotel/
LONCIT/london-city-tower-hill
Plain but pleasant rooms with
comfortable king-size beds.
Bathrooms have power showers.

Southwark and the South Bank

Tune – Westminster £
*118–20 Westminster Bridge Road,
SE1 7RW*
Tel *020 7633 9317*   **Map** 14 D5
ⓦ tunehotels.com
London outpost of a modest
Asian chain. Smart, simple,
spotless accommodation.

**Premier Inn London
County Hall** ££
County Hall, Belvedere Road, SE1 7PB
Tel *0871 527 8648*   **Map** 13 C5
ⓦ premierinn.com/en/hotel/
LONCOU/london-county-hall
Larger-than-average bedrooms,
some with river views.

Farther Afield

The Westport Inn £
166 Malden Road, NW5 4BS
Tel *020 7916 4959*
ⓦ thewestportinn.co.uk
Unwind in the traditional
pub, before snuggling down
in one of the simple rooms.
No children.

Self-contained apartment above the Fleet River Bakery

For more information on types of hotels *see page 283*

WHERE TO EAT AND DRINK

Hailed as the world's dining capital, London thrives on an extraordinary culinary diversity. With a long tradition of Indian, Chinese, French, and Italian restaurants, eating out in London can nowadays take you on a gastronomic journey around the world, from the Americas to Africa, taking in a pan-European tour, as well as the Middle East, Asia, and the Pacific Rim.

London has a dynamic café scene, with good coffee and snacks readily available throughout the day. Good-quality chains have also sprung up all over the capital, offering a variety of food options and often seating for large groups. London's pubs have evolved into some of the most popular places to eat. "Gastropubs" are a key part of the London food scene, often serving modern British classics, including traditional Sunday lunch. For a selection of mainly informal places to eat and drink, including pubs, see pages 304–11.

Diners at a Leon Restaurant *(see p299)*

London Restaurants

The broadest choice of restaurants can be found in Covent Garden, Piccadilly, Mayfair, Soho, and Leicester Square. Knightsbridge, Kensington, and Chelsea also offer a good range of restaurants. In Central London, the South Bank, including the area around Butler's Wharf, has a variety of riverside restaurants. Farther up the river, there is a cluster along Chelsea Harbour. Chefs such as Fergus Henderson at St John are revitalizing British cooking, combining top notch traditional ingredients with a variety of culinary influences and techniques from around the world. Homegrown British chefs such as Heston Blumenthal, Bruce Poole, and Angela Hartnett have been instrumental in helping to elevate London's restaurants to world-class status.

Londoners have long had a tremendously cosmopolitan appetite for Indian, Chinese, French, and Italian food, with many restaurants specializing in regional cuisine. Asian food is also increasingly popular, particularly Thai, Korean, Malaysian, Indonesian, Japanese, and combinations known as "Asian fusion." Popular Spanish tapas bars have opened up around the capital, offering smaller sharing plates.

Most restaurants provide at least one vegetarian option, and some have a separate vegetarian menu. A number of specialty vegetarian restaurants offer more adventurous dishes. Some restaurants exclusively serve fish and seafood.

The range of cuisines offered by London restaurants is matched by the diversity of their location and decor. You'll find all styles from classical ornate and traditional wood-paneled to luxurious contemporary and hard-edged minimalist.

Other Places to Eat

Many hotels have excellent restaurants open to non-residents, which in some cases include a menu devised by, or even actually prepared by, a star chef. These restaurants range from the very formal to the fun and flamboyant, and prices tend to be at the top end of the scale.

In the 1990s an increasing number of pizza, pasta, and brasserie chains sprang up across the city, and they continue to serve reliable, good-value food. Gastropubs and wine bars are also still strong London favorites. Both serve anything from standard British dishes to Thai curries and more imaginative International food, complemented by global wine lists. If you're in a hurry, you can grab a quick snack from one of the many popular chain sandwich bars or cafés spread all over the capital.

Attendant at the Hard Rock Café *(see p293)*

Entrance to the Gallery Mess *(see p296)*

Tips on Eating Out

Most London restaurants serve lunch between noon and 2:30pm, with dinner from 6:30pm until 11pm, which usually means that last orders are taken at 11pm. Even after midnight you can usually find somewhere open to grab a snack. Some restaurants may close for either lunch or dinner during the weekend, so it is always best to check opening times first. Many restaurants and some cafés and brasseries serve alcohol without restriction during licensing hours (11am–11pm).

The traditional British Sunday lunch appears in many pubs and restaurants, although more informal brunches are also very popular. It is worth checking the menu beforehand, however, unless traditional Sunday lunch is what you particularly want, since even high-class restaurants may suspend their normal menu on Sundays.

Most formal restaurants require neat casual dress (no jeans, shorts, or athletic shoes). Some insist on a jacket, or a jacket and tie. Reservations are recommended, especially at gourmet restaurants and between Friday and Sunday.

Smoking is banned in all London pubs and restaurants.

Price and Service

Since London is one of the world's most expensive cities, restaurant prices can often seem exorbitant to visitors, with an average three-course meal and a few glasses of house wine at a medium-priced central London restaurant costing £35–50 per person. Many restaurants have set-price menus that are generally significantly less expensive than ordering à la carte. Similarly, various West End restaurants serve pre-theater set menus (typically from around 5:30–6pm). Prices may be lower (around £15–25 a head) at smaller, more modest ethnic and vegetarian restaurants, wine bars, and pubs.

Before ordering, check the fine print on the menu. Prices may include an optional service charge (10–15 percent).

Be aware that some restaurant staff may leave the "total" box on your credit slip blank, even when service is included in the final bill.

Eating with Children

Many London restaurants, particularly chain restaurants and fast-food establishments, welcome children. A few venues, such as the Rainforest Café on Shaftesbury Avenue, create a unique dining experience especially for kids.

With the growing trend for a more informal style of dining, more restaurants, including those at the top end of the market, have become child-friendly, offering children's menus, smaller portions, and high chairs. Some provide coloring books and even put on live entertainment to keep the little diners happy. See page 357 for suggested places that cater particularly to children with a wide range of ages.

Recommended Restaurants

The restaurants on pages 292–303 of this guide cover a comprehensive range of cuisine styles and prices, and are the best of their kind. They are listed by area, mostly in the main tourist districts, although there are a number that merit a special trip farther afield. Within these areas, they are listed alphabetically in each of the three price categories.

Some London restaurants have moved away from classic three-course dining toward a tapas or mezze style, offering a selection of numerous small dishes for sharing. Fusion food is ever popular, with chefs borrowing from different cuisines, particularly Southeast Asian, to produce eclectic menus. Restaurants specializing in British or French cuisine feature either classic or modern dishes. You can choose between places that serve traditional dishes, such as steak and kidney pudding or *coq au vin*, and those where you might find scallop ravioli or seared duck *foie gras*.

Where a restaurant is in some way exceptional – perhaps for its cooking, bargain menus, or family-friendly facilities – it has been highlighted as a DK Choice.

Bibendum, a popular choice for sophisticated French cuisine *(see p297)*

The Flavors of London

"Modern European cooking" describes much of what's offered in London, a reflection of the capital's cosmopolitan nature. However, as competitive restaurateurs vie for customers, they often look to traditional foods, from once-unfashionable beets to pig's trotters and organ meats. Increasing concern about what goes into the growing and rearing of food is also reflected on London menus. Even pub food, once limited to Sunday roasts, the ubiquitous "ploughman's lunch" (cheese or ham with bread and pickles), or sandwiches, has been given a fresh twist by "gastropubs" and a new breed of sandwich bars offering fresh, top-quality snacks.

Chef and customer at Clerkenwell's St John restaurant

Scottish beef, Welsh lamb, Devon cider, Suffolk oysters – as well as from the rest of the world. Visitors can snack as they browse, on anything from Cornish scallops to grilled Spanish chorizo.

Modern British Food

London menus will often detail the provenance of ingredients with obvious pride. Ancient or "rare" breeds of meat animals are name-checked, such as Gloucester Old Spot pork. Once-overlooked, old-fashioned ingredients like rhubarb and black (blood) pudding are being used in creative new ways. Seasonal and organic produce is also taking more of a center stage. The new breed of "gastropubs" were among

London's Pantry

Nowhere better exemplifies the city's love affair with good food than Borough Market *(see p331)*. Its busy stands of both regional and continental food are a microcosm of what Londoners today like to eat. There is produce from all over Britain – English and Irish cheeses,

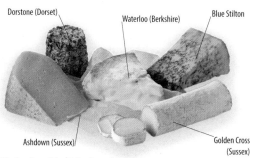

Dorstone (Dorset)
Waterloo (Berkshire)
Blue Stilton
Ashdown (Sussex)
Golden Cross (Sussex)

Selection of superb English farmhouse cheeses

Traditional English Food

You can still find traditional dishes, such as jugged hare, roast beef, or brown Windsor soup, but even fish and chips can be harder to hunt down than tapas, pizza, or chicken tikka masala. A "full English breakfast" is a fry-up of sausages, eggs, bacon, tomatoes, mushrooms, and toast, perhaps with black (blood) pudding. Baked beans and fried potatoes may be included, as can bubble and squeak (refried cabbage and potatoes). There is an English heritage of heavy "nursery" puddings. These are a favorite of gentlemen's clubs and include such treats as treacle tart, jam roly-poly (suet and jam), spotted dick (suet and currants), and fruit crumbles with custard. Teatime may be a thing of the past, but some top hotels still offer "cream teas" with scones, cakes, and perhaps cucumber sandwiches.

Celery and Stilton soup The king of English cheeses makes an excellent winter soup when combined with celery.

Bountiful vegetable stand at south London's Borough Market

the first to adopt these trends, offering good, imaginative, well-prepared, sensibly-priced food, as well as fine wines and beers, in the relaxed surroundings of the traditional London pub.

Chef Fergus Henderson of St John *(see p299)* is a pioneer of "head-to-toe" eating, espousing anything from ox cheek and tail to entire roast suckling pig.

London's historic seafood favorites, such as cockles and whelks, are increasingly hard to find at present, but as capital of an island nation, the city offers many fine fish restaurants. Concern about overfishing and farmed fish means that you are likely to see more of such local catches as bream, bass, sole, and gurnard alongside cod and haddock, as well as salmon being billed as wild, and scallops as diver-caught.

Eastern Flavors

Britain has long had a love affair with both Asian and Indian food, and some of the best examples of each can be found in London. While chicken tikka masala has been voted the nation's favorite dish (invented here, the legend

A mouthwatering pint of traditional London bitter beer

goes, to satisfy the national passion for gravy by pairing tandoori dry-roasted meat with a mild, creamy sauce), regional Indian food is now more prominent, notably southern cuisine strong on coconut, fish, and fruits. The balti is another British take on the food of the subcontinent – named for the bowl-shaped dish in which they are cooked and served, fresh-tasting stews are served alongside vast naan breads for dunking.

In Chinatown, you can enjoy everything from a simple bowl of noodles to gourmet dishes featuring rare ingredients such as razor clams and sea urchins.

WHAT TO DRINK

Beers There are two large brewers in London – Young's and Fuller's – and some microbrewers, too. The main varieties found in Britain are:
Bitter Brewed from malted barley, hops, yeast, and water; drunk at room temperature.
Mild ale Sweeter than bitter.
Lager Hundreds of varieties of this pale carbonated beer are available. Served chilled.
Stout Thick, dark, creamy Guinness is the most famous.
Cider English cider has undergone a revival, with producers often featuring single old English apple varieties and using traditional methods.

Dover sole This is the tastiest flatfish, best served simply grilled with lemon, spinach, and new potatoes.

Roast beef Horseradish sauce is a traditional accompaniment, as are crisp Yorkshire puddings made of batter.

Summer pudding Lightly cooked fruits fill a basin lined with bread, which absorbs the sweet juices.

Where to Eat and Drink

Westminster and the West End

Belgo Centraal £
Belgian **Map** 13 B2
50 Earlham Street, WC2H 9LJ
Tel *020 7813 2233*
A bustling branch of a quirky chain, where staff dress as monks. Team the excellent lobster or *moules frites* with a Trappist beer.

Food for Thought £
Vegetarian **Map** 13 B1
31 Neal Street, WC2H 9PR
Tel *020 7836 0239*
Be prepared to line up for tasty vegetarian dishes, including perfectly cooked wild mushroom gnocchi and hearty vegan soups, at this snug basement café.

Kulu Kulu Sushi £
Japanese **Map** 13 A2
76 Brewer Street, W1F 9TU
Tel *020 7734 7316*
Sit on a stool in the bar area and help yourself to tasty sushi and sashimi from a conveyor belt. Perfect for a quick bite.

Princi £
Italian **Map** 13 A2
135 Wardour Street, W1F 0UT
Tel *020 7478 8888*
A stylish Milan import. Help yourself to handmade bread, wood-oven pizzas, and mouthwatering pastries; eat at communal tables or at the gleaming counters.

Regency Café £
British **Map** 21 A2
17–19 Regency Street, SW1P 4BY
Tel *020 7821 6596*
A 1950s-style "caff," featured in the movie *Layer Cake*. Heavenly hash browns and eggs Benedict for breakfast or brunch.

DK Choice

Sagar £
Indian vegetarian **Map** 13 C2
31 Catherine Street, WC2B 5JS
Tel *020 7836 6377*
Subtle flavors distinguish a broad range of dishes from southern India at this simple, cafeteria-style restaurant. Curries are freshly made and the lunch *thali* (selection of small dishes) not only tastes good, it's also a great deal. Don't overlook the delicious crispy *dosas* (potato-filled pancakes). Efficient, friendly service.

Soho Joe £
Mediterranean **Map** 13 A1
22–25 Dean Street, W1D 3RY
Tel *07534 134398*
Thin-crust pizzas are the stars of the show at this great-value Italian. Pasta, burgers and toasted sandwiches also feature.

Tokyo Diner £
Japanese **Map** 13 B2
2 Newport Place, WC2H 7JJ
Tel *020 7287 8777*
Authentic food, including *katsu* curry, sushi, and bento boxes, at this functional three-story diner. Strictly no tipping.

Wahaca £
Mexican **Map** 13 B3
66 Chandos Place, WC2N 4HG
Tel *020 7240 1883*
Colorful and cool, this is the original branch of a mini chain serving a seasonal menu of tasty Mexican street food. No bookings.

Al Duca ££
Italian **Map** 13 A3
4–5 Duke of York Street, SW1Y 6LA
Tel *020 7839 3090* **Closed** *Sun*
A reasonably priced and popular

local. Using the freshest of ingredients, classic Italian dishes are given a modern twist.

Andrew Edmunds ££
European **Map** 13 A2
46 Lexington Street, W1F 0LW
Tel *020 7437 5708*
A tiny, candlelit, romantic retreat. Imaginative dishes, including well-balanced seafood and game, feature on a daily-changing menu.

Barrafina ££
Spanish tapas **Map** 13 A2
54 Frith Street, W1D 4SL
Tel *020 7813 8016*
Take pot luck at this hip joint – there are just 23 bar stools and no reservations. Fabulous, intensely flavored tapas.

Bocca di Lupo ££
Italian **Map** 13 A2
12 Archer Street, W1D 7BB
Tel *020 7734 2223*
A small place (only 14 tables) with a big Italian heart. Chef Jacob Kennedy specializes in robust, little-known traditional regional recipes.

Chisou ££
Japanese **Map** 12 F2
4 Princes Street, W1B 2LE
Tel *020 7629 3931*
Simple decor teamed with delectable sushi at this bona fide Japanese bistro. There's also a mind-blowing selection of saké available.

DK Choice

Clos Maggiore ££
European **Map** 13 B2
33 King Street, WC2E 8JD
Tel *020 7379 9696*
Try for a table in the courtyard conservatory at Clos Maggiore, with its blossom-laden branches, for a magical experience. On balmy evenings, the roof is opened to the stars, while a fire is lit when it's chilly – sheer romance. French regional food inspires the modern European cooking. Fixed-price pre- and post-theater menus are quite a bargain.

The traditional dining rooms of Clos Maggiore

Dehesa ££
Tapas Map 12 F2
25 Ganton Street, W1F 9BP
Tel *020 7494 4170*
A buzzy vibe paired with stand-out tapas. Make sure you taste the famous charcuterie and signature dish – stuffed zucchini flower.

El Pirata ££
Tapas Map 12 E4
5–6 Down Street, W1J 7AQ
Tel *020 7491 3810* **Closed** *Sun*
There's a deft hand in the kitchen at this lively, laid-back restaurant. All the classic Spanish and Portuguese favorites are here.

Gopals of Soho ££
Indian Map 13 A2
12 Bateman Street, W1 5TD
Tel *020 7434 1621*
You don't come to this traditional family-run curry house for the surroundings, but for the intense flavors of the expertly spiced food. Excellent vegetarian *thalis*.

Haozhan ££
Chinese Map 13 A2
8 Gerrard Street, W1D 5PJ
Tel *020 7434 3838*
A pioneer of superb, inventive cuisine. Try delicate black cod dumplings or wasabi shrimp – a world away from the standard sweet-and-sour staples.

Hard Rock Café ££
American Map 12 E4
150 Old Park Lane, W1K 1QZ
Tel *020 7514 1700*
Try American staples at this legend with a fascinating collection of rock memorabilia. Still rocking after more than 40 years.

Inamo ££
Asian fusion Map 13 A2
134–136 Wardour Street, W1F 8ZP
Tel *020 7851 7051*
An Asian eatery with a difference. Order your meal on a touch-screen pad and play games while you wait. Fun for groups and large parties.

Le Deuxième ££
French Map 13 B2
65a Long Acre, WC2E 9JD
Tel *020 7379 0033*
A solid choice, particularly for pre-opera or theater dining. The bistro-style menu concentrates on interesting combinations and strong flavors.

Mildred's ££
Vegetarian Map 13 A2
45 Lexington Street, W1F 9AN
Tel *020 7494 1634* **Closed** *Sun*
Inspired vegetable dishes, fit to

The tables double as touch-screen menus at Asian-inspired Inamo

convert the most confirmed carnivore. Try the ale and porcini mushroom pie. No bookings.

Nopi ££
Middle Eastern Map 12 F2
21–22 Warwick Street, W1B 5NE
Tel *020 7494 9584*
Cooking writer Yotam Ottolenghi's grown-up restaurant. A blend of aromatic flavors, bold colors, and exciting textures in dishes designed for sharing.

Noura ££
Lebanese Map 20 E1
16 Hobart Place, SW1W 0HH
Tel *020 7235 9696*
Exceptional mezzes and kebabs at the flagship of an award-winning small chain. Classy decor and a tempting brasserie-style menu.

Patara ££
Thai Map 13 A2
15 Greek Street, W1D 4DP
Tel *020 7437 1071*
An enticing all-arounder, spread over two dimly lit, soothingly romantic floors. Specialties include several shrimp dishes, each an explosion of flavor.

Porter's English Restaurant ££
British Map 13 C2
17 Henrietta Street, WC2E 8QH
Tel *020 7836 6466*
Fill up on hearty English classics, such as steak and kidney pudding, fish pie, and spotted dick. Casual dining and a great choice for families.

Rasa ££
Indian Map 12 E2
6 Dering Street, W1S 1AD
Tel *020 7629 1346* **Closed** *Sun*
Unusual and exquisitely fragrant specialties from Kerala, each served on a huge fresh banana leaf. The vegetarian and fish dishes are exceptional.

Refuel ££
British Map 13 A2
The Soho Hotel, 4 Richmond Mews, W1D 3DH
Tel *020 7559 3000*
Rub shoulders with the glitterati at this stylish media-land hangout. A diverse menu of modern European cuisine. Great service.

Terroirs ££
Mediterranean Map 13 B3
5 William IV Street, WC2N 4DW
Tel *020 7036 0660* **Closed** *Sun*
An impressive selection of biodynamic wines, teamed with wholesome organic food (pork, snails, lentils, and charcuterie). Reminiscent of a Parisian wine bar.

Thai Pot ££
Thai Map 13 B2
1 Bedfordbury, WC2N 4BP
Tel *020 7379 4580* **Closed** *Sun*
Thai staples full of fragrant flavor. Dashes of warm color jazz up the sleek, contemporary decoration.

DK Choice

The Portrait ££
British Map 13 B3
National Portrait Gallery, 2 St Martin's Place, WC2H 0HE
Tel *020 7312 2490*
Spot London's famous monuments from a window seat at Searcys' airy top-floor restaurant: they're almost all on view. The excellent food served here is contemporary British: the sea bass with marsh samphire stands out. The main dining area is chic and modern, in complete contrast to the historical surroundings. Before or after your meal, be sure to take a stroll around the splendid National Portrait Gallery.

The elegant afternoon tea at the Wolseley

The Ten Cases ££
British   Map 13 B1
16 Endell Street, WC2H 9BD
Tel *020 7836 6801*
Outstanding wines – ten reds, ten whites – plus three choices per course at this exciting restaurant. British cooking with European overtones.

The Wolseley ££
European   Map 12 F3
160 Piccadilly, W1J 9EB
Tel *020 7499 6996*
The glorious 1920s Wolseley Motors car showroom makes a stunning home for this glamorous café/restaurant. The afternoon tea is legendary.

Vasco and Piero's Pavilion ££
Italian   Map 13 A2
15 Poland Street, W1F 8QE
Tel *020 7437 8774*   **Closed** *Sun*
Homemade pasta is used in their own excellent recipes, often with truffles when in season. Umbrian specialties, such as pork and lentils, are favorites.

Yalla Yalla ££
Lebanese   Map 13 A2
1 Green's Court, W1F 0HA
Tel *020 7287 7663*
Be transported to Beirut at this little gem, where the spicy street food packs a punch. Heartier meals are also offered.

Apsleys, a Heinz Beck Restaurant £££
Italian   Map 12 D5
The Lanesborough Hotel, Hyde Park Corner, SW1X 7TA
Tel *020 7333 7254*
If you're celebrating, go all out and order the impressive seven-course tasting menu. The Venetian-style dining room is sumptuous.

Asia de Cuba £££
Fusion (Asian/Cuban)   Map 13 B2
45 St Martin's Lane, WC2N 4HX
Tel *020 7300 5588*
Combines Asian and Cuban cuisine, served sharing-style in a high-energy, sophisticated and yet relaxed environment.

Atelier de Joël Robuchon £££
French   Map 13 B2
13–15 West Street, WC2H 9NE
Tel *020 7010 8600*
Try for a front-row seat at the Japanese-inspired counter in this contemporary two-Michelin-starred temple. Flawless modern French cuisine.

Bellamy's £££
French   Map 12 E3
18 Bruton Place, W1J 6LY
Tel *020 7491 2727*   **Closed** *Sun*
A mews house makes a quietly traditional dining room and clubby Oyster Bar. Exclusively French wines accompany a well-executed menu.

Bentley's Oyster Bar and Grill £££
Seafood   Map 12 F3
11 Swallow Street, W1B 4DG
Tel *020 7734 4756*   **Closed** *Sun*
A civilized island of calm, in business since 1916. Chef Richard Corrigan's inventive creations keep it firmly on the map. There are plenty of meat dishes if you're not in the mood for seafood.

Cecconi's £££
Italian   Map 12 F3
5A Burlington Gardens, W1S 3EP
Tel *020 7434 1500*
The beautiful people even come to this captivating Italian for breakfast. Virtuoso versions of standard dishes. Gets busy at peak times, so make reservations if you can.

Cinnamon Club £££
Indian   Map 21 B1
The Old Westminster Library, 30–32 Great Smith Street, SW1P 3BU
Tel *020 7222 2555*   **Closed** *Sun*
Delicately spiced North Indian cuisine, using the freshest ingredients. Housed in a former library with an atmosphere of hushed sophistication.

DK Choice

CUT at 45 Park Lane £££
Steakhouse   Map 12 D4
45 Park Lane, W1K 1PN
Tel *020 7493 4554*
US celebrity chef Wolfgang Puck's first European venture is a paradise for carnivores. Choose a raw cut from a platter brought to your table before it is whisked away and expertly cooked. The surroundings are as grand, and the waiters as courteous and well-informed, as you'd expect from the price tag.

Hakkasan Mayfair £££
Chinese   Map 12 E3
17 Bruton Street, W1J 6QB
Tel *020 7907 1888*
Glitzy, adeptly lit showcase for exquisite Cantonese cuisine, including some of the finest dim sum you're likely to taste.

DK Choice

J Sheekey £££
Fish and seafood   Map 13 B2
28–32 St Martin's Court, WC2N 4AL
Tel *020 7240 2565*
London's finest fish restaurant dates back to the 1890s. It still occupies a warren of Dickensian rooms, but now offers a wonderfully varied menu of sustainably sourced fish, oysters, and shellfish. Most fun is to sit on a high stool at the horseshoe-shaped bar for the signature oysters and Champagne. Or dine in the elegant banquette seating area and admire the open kitchen. Perfect for pre- and post-theater dining. Friendly and attentive service.

La Petite Maison £££
French   Map 12 E2
53–54 Brook's Mews, W1K 4EG
Tel *020 7495 4774*
Come to this exhilarating spot in a group: the small Mediterranean dishes and Southern French flavors combine seasonal ingredients and are ideal for sharing. Cutting-edge cuisine.

Le Caprice £££
International Map 12 F3
Arlington House, Arlington Street,
SW1A 1RJ
Tel *020 7629 2239*
Classy yet vibrant rendezvous for
media types, where everyone is
made to feel like a star by the
delightful staff. Bistro food.

Le Gavroche £££
French Map 12 D2
43 Upper Brook Street, W1K 7QR
Tel *020 7408 0881* **Closed** *Sun*
Come to Michel Roux Jr's flagship
restaurant for exceptional *haute*
cuisine and supremely professional
service. The set lunch is well priced.

Murano £££
European Map 12 E3
20 Queen Street, W1J 5PP
Tel *020 7495 1127* **Closed** *Sun*
The clue's in the name. Angela
Hartnett's sublime cooking is
Venetian-influenced. Nothing
disappoints, from *amuse-bouches*
to *petits fours*.

Nobu £££
Japanese Map 12 E4
Metropolitan Hotel W1,
19 Old Park Lane, W1K 1LB
Tel *020 7447 4747*
Sample beautifully prepared
sashimi, tempura, and many
more contemporary, ground-
breaking dishes at this Japanese
restaurant. The seafood and fish
are of the highest quality.

Pollen Street Social £££
British Map 12 F2
10 Pollen Street, W1S 1NQ
Tel *020 7290 7600* **Closed** *Sun*
Opened by Gordon Ramsay
protégé Jason Atherton in 2011.
It's all hard surfaces and cutting-
edge art. The food is ravishing
too. A well-priced set menu and
efficient service.

Rules £££
British Map 13 C2
35 Maiden Lane, WC2E 7LB
Tel *020 7836 5314*
Robust British food in an opulent
setting– rib of beef, oysters, and
game from its own country
estate – at the capital's oldest
restaurant, established in 1798.

Scott's £££
Fish and seafood Map 12 D3
20 Mount Street, W1 2HE
Tel *020 7495 7309*
Join the league of celebrities
who have dined here, from
Winston Churchill to Marilyn
Monroe. Its sensational seafood
makes it as popular as ever.
The roasted shellfish platters
are outstanding.

The Ritz Restaurant £££
British Map 12 F3
150 Piccadilly, W1J 9BR
Tel *020 7493 8181*
This gilded and frescoed room,
with its profusion of chandeliers,
is a glamorous setting for
impressive cuisine.

The Square £££
French Map 12 E3
6–10 Bruton Street, W1J 6PU
Tel *020 7495 7100*
A luxurious haunt of wine-lovers
and foodies alike. All down to its
encyclopedic wine list and
complex, wonderful food.

Veeraswamy £££
Indian Map 12 F3
Victory House, 99 Regent Street,
W1B 4RS
Tel *020 7734 1401*
A mix of contemporary and
classic cooking at this London
institution, opened in 1926.

Yauatcha £££
Chinese Map 13 A2
15 Broadwick Street, W1F 0DL
Tel *020 7494 8888*
A reinterpretation of a traditional
Chinese teahouse, serving sublime
dim sum.

Kensington and Chelsea

DK Choice

Alounak £
Persian Map 10 D2
44 Westbourne Grove, W2 5SH
Tel *020 7229 4158*
Lines often snake down the
street, so popular is this bazaar-
style café. It specializes in
deliciously light Middle Eastern
food at low prices. Inside, it's all
bare wood tables and exposed
brick walls. There's no wine
available, so bring your own. The
presence of so many
Iranians speaks for itself.

Buona Sera Jam £
Italian Map 19 A4
289 King's Road, SW3 5EW
Tel *020 7352 8827*
A lively trattoria that's fun for the
whole family. Climb miniature
ladders to reach the top-tier
tables and try the terrific pizzas.

Café Mona Lisa £
French Map 18 E5
417 King's Road, SW10 0LR
Tel *020 7376 5447*
A much-loved neighborhood
café with friendly service and a
warm feel. Specials chalked up
on the blackboards are always
a good option.

El Pirata Detapas £
Spanish tapas Map 10 D2
115 Westbourne Grove, W2 4UP
Tel *020 7727 5000*
There's a real buzz to this spot,
with its on-trend zinc bar and
wood floor. The modern tapas
offer big flavors for small prices.

Jak's £
Mediterranean Map 19 B2
77 Walton Street, SW3 2HT
Tel *020 7584 3441*
Choose from a splendid array of
healthy, organic dishes and
tempting desserts and eat in
the diminutive country-style
back room.

Raison d'Etre £
European Map 18 F2
18 Bute Street, SW7 3EX
Tel *020 7584 5008* **Closed** *Sun*
They bake their own bread at this
very French, very popular café.
Sandwiches, made with super-
fresh ingredients, are delicious.
Good selection of fillings.

DK Choice

Assaggi ££
Italian Map 9 C2
39 Chepstow Place, W2 4TS
Tel *020 7792 5501* **Closed** *Sun*
Hidden away above a pub, this
alluring restaurant feels like a
discovery. In fact, it's all the rage
and often difficult to get a table.
The bright, simply furnished
room reflects the vivid colors
of chef Nino Sassu's native
Sardinia. Enthusiastic wait staff.

The sleek interior of Hakkasan Mayfair

For more information on types of restaurants *see page 289*

Bar Boulud ££
French **Map** 11 C5
Mandarin Oriental Hyde Park, 66 Knightsbridge, SW1X 7LA
Tel 020 7201 3899
The look is chic but the mood is relaxed at US star chef Daniel Boulud's London venture. A French-inspired bistro with unforgettable terrines.

Byron ££
American **Map** 9 C5
222 Kensington High Street, W8 7RG
Tel 020 7361 1717
The secret is that Byron's burgers are the best in town; simple and tasty and made from quality, freshly minced beef. A stylish branch with eager staff.

Caraffini ££
Italian **Map** 20 D3
61–63 Lower Sloane Street, SW1 8DH
Tel 020 7259 0235 **Closed** *Sun*
Service Italian-style at this old favorite, still hopping at lunchtimes. Plump for the lobster tagliarini or one of the specials.

Chez Patrick ££
French **Map** 18 D1
7 Stratford Road, W8 6RF
Tel 020 7937 6388
Front-of-house owner Patrick gives excellent advice on ordering at this intimate restaurant. Classic French recipes, mostly fish, flawlessly executed.

E&O ££
Asian fusion **Map** 9 A2
14 Blenheim Crescent, W11 1NN
Tel 020 7229 5454
Dine on dim sum, tempura, sushi, or sashimi in glossy black surroundings. Specials might include pad thai or crispy sea bass. Dim sum is available all day at the bar.

Gallery Mess ££
European **Map** 19 C2
Saatchi Gallery, Duke Of York's HQ, King's Road, SW3 4RY
Tel 020 7730 8135
A desirable lunch spot after an exhibition. Try for the most attractive tables, in the airy cloister, overlooking a leafy square. Appetizing lunches.

Hunan ££
Chinese **Map** 20 D2
51 Pimlico Road, SW1W 8NE
Tel 020 7730 5712 **Closed** *Sun*
Taiwanese tapas-size portions keep arriving at your table, as fiery or mild as you like, until you're full. Try the signature dish of hearty broth with minced pork, mushrooms, and ginger.

The stylish Asian fusion restaurant E&O

Kensington Place ££
Fish **Map** 9 C4
201 Kensington Church Street, W8 7LX
Tel 020 7727 3184
Fresh decoration and a classic menu, including superb beer-battered fish and chips, game, and steaks at this famous goldfish-bowl brasserie.

Kitchen W8 ££
British **Map** 17 C1
11–13 Abingdon Road, W8 6AH
Tel 020 7937 0120
A benchmark of quality: Philip Howard's creative Michelin-starred cooking in a sleek, comfortable environment. And it won't break the bank.

La Poule au Pot ££
French **Map** 20 E2
231 Ebury Street, SW1W 8UT
Tel 020 7730 7763
Full of romance and rustic French charm, which complements the honest cooking. Serves all the classics, such as *boeuf bourguignon* and *tarte tatin*.

Le Cercle ££
French **Map** 19 C2
1 Wilbraham Place, SW1X 9AE
Tel 020 7901 9999 **Closed** *Mon & Sun*
A tall, mellow basement, evocative of a swanky cocktail bar. Even the set menus provide exquisitely complex flavors. Grown-up dining.

Le Metro at the Levin Hotel ££
British **Map** 11 C5
28 Basil Street, SW3 1AS
Tel 020 7589 6286
A basement brasserie with delectable food and the ambience of a contemporary European tearoom. It has comfy banquettes, and an open kitchen. Feels like a well-kept secret.

Lucky Seven ££
American **Map** 10 D1
127 Westbourne Park Road, W2 5QL
Tel 020 7727 6771
Typical US fare, from burgers to shakes, at this archetypal East Coast diner. So tiny, you might have to share a booth.

Maroush II ££
Lebanese **Map** 19 B1
38 Beauchamp Place, SW3 1NU
Tel 020 7581 5434
The perfect spot for a late-night bite; tender, tasty grilled dishes available until 3am. Fine dining on the first floor.

The Abingdon ££
International **Map** 17 C1
54 Abingdon Road, W8 6AP
Tel 020 7937 3339
A converted pub with a refined feel. Try to get one of the comfortable booths for high-end, brasserie-style food.

The Belvedere ££
French **Map** 9 B5
Holland Park (off Abbotsbury Road), W8 6LU
Tel 020 7602 1238
Enjoy modern European fare in a sumptuous former ballroom overlooking lawns and flower gardens. A treat, whether you eat inside or out.

The Enterprise ££
European **Map** 19 B2
35 Walton Street, SW3 2HU
Tel 020 7584 3148
A humble local pub converted into a well-groomed restaurant/bar. Don't miss out on the impeccably cooked squid and zucchini tempura starter.

The Markham Inn ££
British **Map** 19 B2
2 Elystan Street, SW3 3NS
Tel 020 7581 9139
In Victorian times, travelers would congregate in this popular pub. Now tastefully clubby, with red Chesterfields and a superior seasonal menu.

DK Choice

The Painted Heron ££
Indian **Map** 19 A5
112 Cheyne Walk, SW10 0DJ
Tel 020 7351 5232
Not a run-of-the-mill Indian restaurant. A stylish modern room, hung with contemporary artworks, is the setting for succulent dishes using unconventional ingredients, such as game, wild sea trout, black cod, and soft-shell crab.

Key to prices *see page 292*

Spicing is complex but not overstated. For the health conscious, there's a vegetarian menu based on Ayurvedic principles.

DK Choice

**Babylon at the
Roof Garden** £££
British **Map** 10 D5
*99 Kensington High Street,
W8 5SA*
Tel *020 7368 3993*
The "hanging gardens,"
overlooked by this fashionable restaurant, sprawl high above the street. Eat here and explore three themed areas filled with trees, flamingos, and a fish-stocked stream (call first to make sure they're not fully booked). Enjoy the modern British cuisine and the panorama. Best in summer, when you can dine al fresco on the terrace.

Bibendum £££
French **Map** 19 A2
*Michelin House, 81 Fulham Road,
SW3 6RD*
Tel *020 7581 5817*
Seasonal food, assiduous service, and Michelin House's Art Nouveau stained glass, a stunning backdrop to this airy first-floor dining room. Head chef Matthew Harris produces classic French food with a strong British influence and 21st-century style.

Blakes £££
Asian **Map** 18 F3
33 Roland Gardens, SW7 3PF
Tel *020 7370 6701*
Fans, orchids, and Asian touches decorate this seductive downstairs sanctuary. The imaginative menu mingles Mediterranean and Eastern flavors. Specials include the angel-hair pasta with black cod.

**Dinner
by Heston Blumenthal** £££
British **Map** 11 C5
*Mandarin Oriental Hyde Park, 66
Knightsbridge, SW1X 7LA*
Tel *020 7201 3833*
London's most hyped restaurant showcases this celebrity chef's inspired take on classic cuisine. Blumenthal is well-known for juxtaposing different flavors. Only for those with deep pockets, but unforgettable.

Launceston Place £££
British **Map** 18 E1
1a Launceston Place, W8 5RL
Tel *020 7937 6912*
Imaginative modern cooking in a series of traditional, carpeted rooms. An oasis of calm, where staff pay attention to detail. The menu is designed to complement the setting and features British classics given a flamboyant twist.

**Marcus Wareing at
the Berkeley** £££
European **Map** 12 D5
*The Berkeley Hotel, Wilton Place,
SW1X 7RL*
Tel *020 7235 1200* **Closed** *Sun*
Sample delectable cooking from a superstar chef in the claret red dining room. Sheer genius. Sophisticated fine dining. Has two Michelin stars.

One-0-One £££
Fish and seafood **Map** 11 C5
*Sheraton Park Tower Hotel,
101 Knightsbridge, SW1X 7RN*
Tel *020 7290 7101*
Seafood's the thing at this exquisite restaurant. Try Norwegian halibut or crab in stunning recipes from head chef Pascal Proyart, or the signature crab risotto. *Petits plats* make an ideal light lunch. The key to the standout menu is the chef's use of the freshest ingredients.

Restaurant Gordon Ramsay £££
French **Map** 19 C4
68 Royal Hospital Road, SW3 4HP
Tel *020 7352 4441* **Closed** *Sat & Sun*
Standards remain high at this triple-Michelin-starred shrine to *haute cuisine*. Eye-wateringly expensive, but the menu is truly exciting.

The Ledbury £££
European **Map** 9 C2
127 Ledbury Road, W11 2AQ
Tel *020 7792 9090*
Possibly London's most happening restaurant, the realm of thrilling Australian chef Brett Graham. Expect two-Michelin-starred culinary fireworks.

Zuma £££
Japanese **Map** 11 B5
5 Raphael Street, SW7 1DL
Tel *020 7584 1010*
Spot the celebrities at this cool joint. They're drawn – like everyone – by divine robata-grilled dishes, tempura, nigiri sushi, and sashimi.

Bloomsbury and Regent's Park

Golden Hind £
British **Map** 12 E1
73 Marylebone Lane, W1U 2PN
Tel *020 7486 3644* **Closed** *Sun*
Devotees claim its fish and chips are unequaled. A welcoming, no-frills family-run place with no license; bring your own wine. The homemade fishcakes make an enticing alternative.

DK Choice

Thai Metro £
Thai **Map** 5 A5
38 Charlotte St, W1T 2NN
Tel *020 7436 4201*
The exemplary Thai cooking at this down-to-earth corner café has made it a smash hit. Choose carefully if you can't take your curries too hot: some of the specialties are guaranteed to make you sweat. Service is speedy and efficient, and the bill shouldn't be a nasty shock.

Bam-Bou ££
Vietnamese **Map** 13 A1
1 Percy Street, W1T 1DB
Tel *020 7323 9130* **Closed** *Sun*
Stop off for a drink in the romantic red bar before descending to the candlelit restaurant. Well-crafted French-Vietnamese dishes with Thai and Chinese influences.

Rustic charm and traditional French cuisine at La Poule au Pot

For more information on types of restaurants *see page 289*

Galvin Bistrot de Luxe £££

French
66 Baker Street, W1U 7DJ
Tel *020 7935 4007*
You could be in Paris in the Galvin brothers' high-class bistro. Beautifully cooked classics in a room bristling with happy customers. Top quality French cuisine at affordable prices.

Malabar Junction £££

Indian **Map** 13 B1
107 Great Russell Street, WC1B 3NA
Tel *020 7580 5230*
An atrium with wood floors and wicker chairs. The wide-ranging menu features specialties from Kerala, all tender, fragrant, and skilfully prepared.

Ragam £££

Indian **Map** 4 F5
57 Cleveland Street, W1T 4JN
Tel *020 7636 9098*
Not much to look at, but this veteran offers Keralan specialties zinging with aromatic flavor. The filled pancakes are guaranteed to wow. Choose from side dishes such as beet *baji* or spinach with lentils.

DK Choice

Salt Yard £££

Tapas **Map** 5 A5
54 Goodge Street, W1T 4NA
Tel *020 7637 0657* **Closed** *Sun*
Fans claim this go-to place offers the best tapas in London. What's unique is the combination of Spanish and Italian cuisines. Fresh, top-quality ingredients are center stage in such small delights as duck and spinach *gnocchetti* and the signature zucchini flowers stuffed with goat cheese and drizzled with honey. Always packed.

The Chancery £££

European **Map** 14 E1
9 Cursitor Street, EC4A 1LL
Tel *020 7831 4000* **Closed** *Sun*
A small legal-land treasure, tempting for lazy lunches. Fabulous hake, muntjac, and slow-cooked pork belly. Well-priced too.

The White Swan £££

British **Map** 14 E1
108 Fetter Lane, EC4A 1ES
Tel *020 7242 9696* **Closed** *Sat & Sun*
You'll find this place above a no-nonsense pub. The room is light and sunny, the cooking sophisticated, with an innovative menu with dishes such as braised octopus *carpaccio*.

Diners enjoying lunch on the outdoor deck at Clerkenwell Kitchen

Vanilla Black £££

Vegetarian **Map** 14 E1
17–18 Tooks Court, EC4A 1LB
Tel *020 7242 2622* **Closed** *Sun*
Exciting vegetarian dishes in an elegant setting. Warm walnut pannacotta and blue stilton dumplings – proof positive that you don't need meat.

Orrery £££

French **Map** 4 D5
55–57 Marylebone High Street, W1U 5RB
Tel *020 7616 8000*
Outstanding modern cuisine on the first floor of a converted stable block. Great attention to detail in both cooking and service. Ask for a table beside the arched windows.

Pied à Terre £££

French **Map** 5 A5
34 Charlotte Street, W1T 2NH
Tel *020 7636 1178* **Closed** *Sun*
Adventurous and impeccable food tops the bill at this discreet haven. A comfortable dining room and friendly staff.

Roka £££

Japanese **Map** 5 A5
37 Charlotte Street, W1T 1RR
Tel *020 7580 6464*
Sit at the wood counter in this goldfish bowl restaurant, graze on luscious sushi and watch the chefs at the robata grill. Riveting and theatrical.

Texture £££

European **Map** 11 C2
34 Portman Street, W1H 7BY
Tel *020 7224 0028* **Closed** *Mon & Sun*
Bold, experimental cookery from Icelandic chef Agnar Sverrisson. Expect to find cod, lamb, and herbs from his homeland.

The Providores and Tapa Room £££

International fusion **Map** 4 D5
109 Marylebone High Street, W1U 4RX
Tel *020 7935 6175*
The global fusion food has won plaudits at this showcase establishment. For lighter fare, try the downstairs tapas bar.

The City and the East End

Cây Tre £

Vietnamese **Map** 7 A4
301 Old Street, EC1V 9LA
Tel *020 7729 8662*
The menu's short, but dishes are authentic and high quality. Surprises include Cornish scallops and anchovied chicken wings plus unusual combinations like the beef *carpaccio* and tamarind soup special.

Clerkenwell Kitchen £

British **Map** 6 E4
27–31 Clerkenwell Close, EC1R 0AT
Tel *020 7101 9959* **Closed** *Sat & Sun*
A good choice for lunch. Organic produce, gutsy home cooking, and appealingly modern brick-and-wood surroundings.

De Palo's £

Italian **Map** 14 F2
8 Bride Court, EC4Y 8DU
Tel *020 7583 8440* **Closed** *Sat & Sun*
Fresh ingredients and authentic Sicilian flavors are the stars at this intimate, family-owned restaurant. Try the amazing *tortiglioni* special.

Kolossi Grill £

Greek **Map** 6 E4
56–60 Rosebery Avenue, EC1R 4RR
Tel *020 7278 5758* **Closed** *Sun*
Homemade Cypriot classics have been served in this cozy, unpretentious restaurant for more than 50 years. Service is warm and friendly.

The stylish interior of Salt Yard, serving Spanish and Italian tapas

Lahore Kebab House £
Pakistani **Map** 16 E1
2–10 Umberston Street, E1 1PY
Tel *020 7481 9737*
A traditional but spartan Pakistani spot, open late and with the kitchen on view. Spiced curries and kebabs set taste buds tingling in this warehouse-style space. Bring your own alcohol.

Leon–Spitalfields £
European **Map** 8 D5
3 Crispin Place, E1 6DW
Tel *020 7247 4369*
Healthy "superfood" salads and Mediterranean-inspired fast food in a large, bright, colorful space. Open from breakfast to dinner.

Tayyabs £
Punjabi **Map** 16 F1
83 Fieldgate Street, E1 1JU
Tel *020 7247 6400*
A local favorite serving delicious spiced curries and sizzling mixed grills. Don't miss the Kahari lamb chops. Make a reservation to avoid the very long lines.

DK Choice

Brawn ££
French **Map** 8 E3
49 Columbia Road, E2 7RG
Tel *020 7729 5692*
Big, bold, full-bodied flavors can be found in abundance in Brawn's seasonal cuisine. Dishes you might find on the daily written menu are venison pie, pig's trotters, and ceps with Bordelaise sauce. Accompany your choice with one of the many organic wines. The industrial-rustic dining room has an eclectic charm.

Carnevale ££
Vegetarian **Map** 7 A4
135 Whitecross Street, EC1Y 8JL
Tel *020 7250 3452* **Closed** *Sun*
Stellar culinary creations in a modest little café. Delicious Middle Eastern-inspired risottos, casseroles, and curries.

Casa Negra ££
Mexican **Map** 7 C4
54–6 Great Eastern Street, EC2A 3QR
Tel *020 7613 4545* **Closed** *Sun*
An understated pop-up style Mexican restaurant and bar in Shoreditch. Friendly staff.

Haz Plantation Place ££
Turkish **Map** 15 C2
6 Mincing Lane, EC3M 3BD
Tel *020 7929 3173* **Closed** *Sun*
Order the marvelous *mezze* for a range of authentic dishes, or try the perfectly-cooked tuna steak

Contemporary dining area, L'Anima

with homemade chili sauce. The set menus are a bargain for the City.

L'Anima ££
Italian **Map** 7 C5
1 Snowden Street, EC2A 2DQ
Tel *020 7422 7000* **Closed** *Sun*
Francesco Mazzei's food is as elegant as the minimalist glass and white setting. Stunning regional recipes from Sicily and Sardinia.

Le Café du Marché ££
French **Map** 6 F5
22 Charterhouse Square, EC1M 6DX
Tel *020 7608 1609* **Closed** *Sun*
Very French: a hideaway with accomplished classic cooking and a simple, stylish look.

Pham Sushi ££
Japanese **Map** 7 A4
159 Whitecross Street, EC1Y 8JL
Tel *020 7251 6336* **Closed** *Sun*
Exquisite sushi, sashimi, tempura, and California rolls, all so fresh and full of flavor, you hardly notice the uninspiring interior.

The Peasant ££
British **Map** 6 E2
240 St John Street, EC1V 4PH
Tel *020 7336 7726*
Finely executed brasserie cooking in an agreeable Victorian pub dining room. Enjoy the Chilean chef's first-rate pub food in the cavernous bar below. Splendid Sunday roasts.

The Restaurant at St. Paul's Cathedral ££
British **Map** 15 A1
St. Paul's Cathedral, St Paul's Churchyard, EC4M 8AD
Tel *020 7248 2469*
Have a substantial or light lunch or afternoon tea in the beautifully-lit crypt. Imaginative seasonal menus of fine British produce are served daily.

DK Choice

Vinoteca ££
European **Map** 6 E2
7 St John Street, EC1M 4AA
Tel *020 7253 8786* **Closed** *Sun*
Admirers come from far and wide to this Farringdon wine bar. The list of 300 outstanding wines might be the draw, but the excellence of the modern European food keeps bringing them back. Pairing suggestions are made for every dish. Arrive early for dinner; reservations are only accepted for lunch.

Club Gascon £££
French **Map** 14 F1
57 West Smithfield, EC1A 9DS
Tel *020 7600 6144* **Closed** *Sun*
Dinner here is an experience to savor. Try the creamy signature *foie gras*, paired with a recommended wine.

Galvin La Chapelle £££
French **Map** 8 D5
35 Spital Square, E1 6DY
Tel *020 7299 0400*
A sensitive conversion of a school hall, which certainly has the wow factor, with an elegant menu.

Goodman £££
Steakhouse **Map** 15 B1
11 Old Jewry, EC2R 8DU
Tel *020 7600 8220* **Closed** *Sat & Sun*
Melt-in-the-mouth steaks are the staple at this all-American steak house. You can see the meat dry-aging in the kitchen.

Hawksmoor £££
Steakhouse **Map** 16 E1
157 Commercial Street, E1 6BJ
Tel *020 7426 4850*
Astonishing, dictionary-thick steaks. They're from traditionally reared Longhorn cattle, dry-aged and cooked simply on a charcoal grill – scrumptious.

For more information on types of restaurants *see page 289*

Sauterelle
French   £££
The Royal Exchange, EC3V 3LR   **Map** 15 C2
Tel *020 7618 2480*   **Closed** *Sat & Sun*
Stylish cuisine in a captivating setting: on a mezzanine overlooking the glorious courtyard of the Grade I–listed Neo-Classical Royal Exchange.

St John
British   £££
26 St. John Street, EC1M 4AY   **Map** 6 E2
Tel *020 7251 0848*
Not for the squeamish. Fergus Henderson's celebrated kitchen makes the most of organ meats including heart, lung, kidney, and more obscure animal parts.

The Boundary
French   £££
2 Boundary Street, E2 7DD   **Map** 8 D4
Tel *020 7729 1051*
Faultless modern versions of traditional recipes at style-guru Terence Conran's sexy, subterranean hideout. Staff are very attentive.

Impressive view of St. Pauls Cathedral from the Oxo Tower Restaurant

Southwark and the South Bank

Anchor and Hope
British   £
36 The Cut, SE1 8LP   **Map** 14 E4
Tel *020 7928 9898*   **Closed** *Sun*
Turn up with a good appetite. Large portions of such gutsy fare as calf brains, pumpkin risotto, and braised venison.

Dim T – London Bridge
Asian fusion   £
2 More London Place,   **Map** 16 D4
Tooley Street, SE1 2DB
Tel *020 7403 7000*
Be creative by choosing noodles, toppings, and sauces to make your own dish. Fun for the family, plus spectacular river views.

The Laughing Gravy
British   £
154–156 Blackfriars Road, SE1 8EN   **Map** 14 F3
Tel *020 7998 1707*
A laid-back restaurant, with a more lively bar, in an old foundry building. A well-chosen wine list complements the changing seasonal menu.

DK Choice

Blueprint Café
European   ££
1st Floor, Design Museum, 28   **Map** 16 E4
Shad Thames, SE1 2YD
Tel *020 7378 7031*
Grab a window seat and enjoy the view of Tower Bridge to the full, using the signature blue binoculars to zoom in on the river traffic. With bentwood chairs and a sleek wood floor, the café is right at home on top of the Design Museum. Chef Mark Jarvis puts an individual stamp on classic dishes made with seasonal produce.

Champor-Champor
Malaysian   ££
62–64 Weston Street, SE1 3QJ   **Map** 15 C4
Tel *020 7403 4600*
The name means "mix and match" – a perfect depiction of its exotic, yet wacky decoration, and wonderfully eclectic cuisine.

José
Spanish   ££
104 Bermondsey Street, SE1 3UB   **Map** 15 C4
Tel *020 7403 4902*
Team extraordinarily good Barcelona-style tapas with a choice from the varied list of sherries and wines. The real thing.

Kennington Tandoori
Indian   ££
313 Kennington Road, SE11 4QE   **Map** 22 E1
Tel *020 7735 9247*
A calm refuge serving some of the best curries in London, according to aficionados. Novel dishes mixed in with classics.

Lobster Pot
French   ££
3 Kennington Lane, SE11 4RG   **Map** 22 D3
Tel *020 7582 5556*   **Closed** *Mon & Sun*
Walk through the door and you're in Brittany, complete with piped seagulls. Try the eight-course "surprise" menu.

Tapas Brindisa
Spanish   ££
18–20 Southwark Street, SE1 1TJ   **Map** 15 B4
Tel *020 7357 8880*
Hearty flavors steal the show at this animated tapas bar. Fantastic Serrano hams, Cantabrian anchovies, and piquillo peppers.

Tito's Peruvian Restaurant
Peruvian   ££
4–6 London Bridge Street, SE1 9SG   **Map** 15 B4
Tel *020 7407 7787*
Drink a pisco sour while you wait for robust and spicy regional dishes, many meat-based, at this brightly lit local favorite.

Wright Brothers Oyster and Porter House
Seafood   ££
11 Stoney Street, SE1 9AD   **Map** 15 B3
Tel *020 7403 9554*
Fast food with a difference: market-fresh fish and shellfish from Cornwall. The oysters are sublime. Very informal.

Zucca
Italian   ££
184 Bermondsey Street, SE1 3TQ   **Map** 15 C4
Tel *020 7378 6809*   **Closed** *Mon*
All white, hard-edged and ultra-cool, with an open kitchen and mind-blowing menu. Excellent pasta – including fennel and lemon tagliatelle – and polenta.

The relaxed dining area of the Laughing Gravy, in Southwark

DK Choice

Oxo Tower Restaurant, Bar and Brasserie   £££
European   **Map** 14 E3
Oxo Tower Wharf, Barge House Street, SE1 9GY
Tel 020 7803 3888
Whether you're lunching or dining, the eighth-floor view will take your breath away: colorful by day, glittering by night. Eat on the terrace in summer, but when it's cold the picture windows bring the outside in. Choose between the relaxed brasserie and the sophisticated restaurant, both serving modern British classics.

Roast   £££
British   **Map** 15 B3
The Floral Hall, Stoney Street, SE1 1TL
Tel 0845 034 7300
A chic, light-filled, modern dining room in the eaves of Floral Hall. Come for a whopping breakfast or succulent roasts.

Farther Afield

Anarkali   £
Indian
303–5 King Street, W6 9NH
Tel 020 8748 1760
A Hammersmith restaurant in a class of its own. Unique, subtle spicing and a great choice for vegetarians. Delightful service.

DK Choice

Brady's   £
British
Dolphin House, Smugglers Way, SW18 1DG
Tel 020 8877 9599   **Closed** Sun
"The best fish and chips in London," assert enthusiasts of this cheerful Wandsworth bistro with a suitably seaside atmosphere. Choose from line-caught, fresh fish, battered or grilled with perfect chips – crunchy outside and fluffy inside – a pint of shrimp, or smoked salmon. Finish with a traditional English dessert of treacle tart or apple crumble.

Gem   £
Turkish   **Map** 6 F1
265 Upper Street, N1 2UQ
Tel 020 7359 0405
Gem by name and by nature. Fragrant *mezze* at bargain prices in a charming white-painted room decorated with Kurdish farm implements. The specialty

is the wonderful *qatme* (stuffed Kurdish bread). No reservations.

Mandalay   £
Burmese   **Map** 3 A5
444 Edgware Road, W2 1EG
Tel 020 7258 3696
This basic eatery is an ideal introduction to Burmese food. Stir-fries and curries fuse Chinese, Indian, and Thai cuisines.

Taiwan Village   £
Taiwanese   **Map** 17 A5
85 Lillie Road, SW6 1UD
Tel 020 7381 2900
If you're hungry, opt for the 13-course "set feast." Dishes draw on regional cuisines, providing a concentration of flavors.

The Greenwich Union   £
British   **Map** 23 B3
56 Royal Hill, SE10 8RT
Tel 020 8692 6258
A local landmark, this pub showcases a unique range of beers. Menus recommend ale pairings for each delicious traditional dish.

Buen Ayre   ££
Steakhouse   **Map** 8 F1
50 Broadway Market, E8 4QJ
Tel 020 7275 9900
A back-to-basics Hackney hot spot where Argentine steak and grilled meats are the order of the day. The wine list is huge. Friendly staff.

DK Choice

Canton Arms   ££
British   **Map** 21 C4
177 South Lambeth Road, SW8 1XP
Tel 020 7582 8710

In a culinary desert, this stand-out gastropub is worth crossing the river for. Its style is plain and countrified – bar at the front, restaurant at the back – and the food is knockout: gutsy, meaty flavors, interesting textures and combinations. Don't miss the signature "toasties," unusual but extraordinarily good; try the one filled with haggis.

El Parador   ££
Tapas   **Map** 4 F2
245 Eversholt Street, NW1 1BA
Tel 020 7387 2789
Simplicity is key, in both the sunny decoration – yellow walls, terra-cotta floor, wooden chairs – and the market-fresh ingredients.

Emile's   ££
European
98 Felsham Road, SW15 1DQ
Tel 020 8789 3323   **Closed** Sun
A Putney treasure: good, simple food in an uncluttered room. A blackboard, brought to your table, displays the seasonal, monthly changing menu.

Enoteca Turi   ££
Italian
28 Putney High Street, SW15 1SQ
Tel 020 8785 4449   **Closed** Sun
A convivial restaurant owned and run by a dedicated couple. Main attractions are the relaxed mood and rustic, wholesome cooking.

Indian Zing   ££
Indian
236 King Street, W6 0RF
Tel 020 8748 5959
A noteworthy wine list and contemporary Indian cuisine, prepared with panache at this upmarket gem.

Argentine grill and steakhouse, Buen Ayre

For more information on types of restaurants *see page 289*

A selection of tempting salads on display at Ottolenghi

Inside
European   **££**   **Map** 23 A4
19 Greenwich South Street,
SE10 8NW
Tel *020 8265 5060*   **Closed** *Mon*
A minimalist space where a
constantly changing menu offers
modern European dishes for
fairly reasonable prices.

Jin-Kichi
Japanese   **££**   **Map** 1 A4
73 Heath Street, NW3 6UG
Tel *020 7794 6158*   **Closed** *Sun*
A tiny piece of Tokyo in
Hampstead. With a grill as a focus,
well-spaced tables, efficient
service, and sublime sushi. The
food is authentic and delicious.

Lamberts
British   **££**
2 Station Parade, Balham
High Road, SW12 9AZ
Tel *020 8675 2233*   **Closed** *Mon*
Harmonious cuisine, top-notch
organic ingredients, and
comfortable, easy surroundings.
Classic favorites sit side by side
with modern variations. The wine
list excels and prices are sensible.

Fine dining establishment Chez Bruce,
Wandsworth Common

L'Aventure
French   **££**
3 Blenheim Terrace, NW8 0EH
Tel *020 7624 6232*   **Closed** *Sun*
A diminutive hideaway with a
French heart in well-heeled
St. John's Wood. Classic cuisine,
with traditional favorites, and a
romantic interior and terrace.

Le Sacré Coeur
French   **££**   **Map** 6 E1
18 Theberton Street, N1 0QX
Tel *020 7354 2618*
Montmartre comes to Islington
in this cozy Parisian spot. Classic
French style, with poster-lined
walls, wooden beams, blue-and-
white checked tablecloths, and
superior traditional dishes.
Unfailingly friendly service.

Le Vacherin
French   **££**
76–77 South Parade, W4 5LF
Tel *020 8742 2121*
A neighborhood bistro with a
refined, intimate air. It boasts a
sure hand in the kitchen and old-
fashioned service. The set menu
affords good value.

North China
Chinese   **££**
305 Uxbridge Road, W3 9QU
Tel *020 8992 9183*
A family affair set up in 1976 by
the current owner's father, this
tasteful little restaurant offers
mouthwatering dishes with
specialties from both northern
and southern China.

Ottolenghi
Mediterranean   **££**   **Map** 6 F1
287 Upper Street, N1 2TZ
Tel *020 7288 1454*
The Islington flagship restaurant
of a popular chain. A designer
space where divine, healthy
dishes are the *raison d'être*. A chic
yet relaxed place serving daring
Mediterranean food.

Ransome's Dock
European   **££**   **Map** 19 B5
35–37 Parkgate Road, SW11 4NP
Tel *020 7223 1611*
A long-established local serving
fresh, seasonal food, simply
cooked. Ingredients are sourced
from small specialty producers
throughout the UK. Wine buffs
from all over the world enthuse
about the wide selection. Order
wine by the glass or bottle.

DK Choice

Sam's Brasserie   **££**
European
11 Barley Mow Passage, W4 4PH
Tel *020 8987 0555*
Rick Stein protégé Sam Harrison
chose a former paper factory in
Chiswick for his brasserie and
bar. It has a hectic vibe, but is
welcoming to all ages. Menus
offer a welcome range, from
light salads to serious roasts.
There is a special menu for kids
and coloring sheets to keep
them busy.

Singapore Garden
Singaporean   **££**
83 Fairfax Road, NW6 4DY
Tel *020 7328 5314*
A jovial Swiss Cottage veteran
serving the best soft-shelled
crabs, with chili peppers and
garlic, you're likely to taste – pure
magic. Also recommended is the
beef *rendang* (slow cooked beef
in thick coconut sauce).

Tatra
Polish   **££**
24 Goldhawk Road, W12 8DH
Tel *020 8749 8193*
This Shepherd's Bush local blends
the most appetizing tastes from
Eastern Europe. At dinner, be
prepared: flavored vodka is
almost compulsory.

The Depot
British   **££**
*Tideway Yard, 125 Mortlake High
Street, SW14 8SN*
Tel *020 8878 9462*
A tranquil riverside setting,
informal air and superior cooking
have made this brasserie a sure-
fire hit. Try for a window table or
enjoy the outdoor dining terrace
in the summer.

The Glasshouse
European   **££**
14 Station Parade, Kew, TW9 3PZ
Tel *020 8940 6777*
Asian overtones jazz up the
contemporary European food at
this light, urban, award-winning
restaurant. An alluring wine list

complements the menu. Comfortable, relaxed, and excellent value.

DK Choice

The Wells ££
British **Map** 1 B4
30 Well Walk, NW3 1BX
Tel *020 7794 3785*
Take a ramble on Hampstead Heath before heading to this splendid gastropub. Either grab a snack or light bite in the easygoing bar, or, for a more stylish affair, dine in the upstairs room. Modern European specialties are on the menu in the warmly decorated dining room, and traditional bar snacks in the downstairs area. Enjoy the pretty summer terrace when the weather is good. Busy at weekends. Friendly staff.

Trinity ££
British
4 The Polygon, SW4 0JG
Tel *020 7622 1199*
The wonderfully complex flavors of Adam Byatt's cooking draw people to this Clapham staple with handsome looks and exemplary service. Smoked rabbit leg, roast cod, and pan-fried sea bream are satisfying specialties.

Upstairs Bar and Restaurant ££
French
89B Acre Lane, SW2 5TN
Tel *020 7733 8855* **Closed** *Mon & Sun*
Ring a buzzer to get into this Brixton house that serves as a restaurant and bar. The menu is simple and robust (cod with black cabbage and smoked garlic, for example). All food is cooked from market produce and served on the top floors.

Bustling atmosphere of Sam's Brasserie

DK Choice

Chez Bruce £££
British
2 Bellevue Road, SW17 7EG
Tel *020 8672 0114*
Bruce Poole's modern British food has strong classical French notes with an emphasis on organ meats, fish, and remarkable flavor combinations. Specialties include homemade *charcuterie* and bread, and slow-cooked braises. Overlooking Wandsworth Common, this light, refined restaurant has a reputation for its food, wine, and service.

Gaucho – Hampstead £££
Steakhouse **Map** 1 A4
64 Heath Street, NW3 1DN
Tel *020 7431 8222*
Hearty steaks are cooked on a genuine Argentine *asado* barbecue at this stylish chain restaurant. Non-meat-eaters might plump for the *ceviche*, a citrus marinated seafood salad.

The sunny outdoor terrace at the River Café

La Trompette £££
French
5–7 Devonshire Road, W4 2EU
Tel *020 8747 1836*
Sister of the Chez Bruce outlet, La Trompette is perfectly placed close to Kew Gardens. The menu at Bruce Poole's Chiswick outpost has roots in regional France. Defined by *charcuterie* and *confits*; rounded off with comforting desserts. Relaxed, and a great deal. Staff are knowledgeable.

DK Choice

River Café £££
Italian
Thames Wharf, Rainville Road, W6 9HA
Tel *020 7386 4200*
First-rate seasonal ingredients, cooked simply, is Ruth Rogers' ethos at her famous Hammersmith eatery – one of the first in London to make the sourcing of sustainable ingredients a priority. It is sophisticated, in a cafeteria style, with a wood-burner and open kitchen. The rustic Italian meals rarely disappoint and sit alongside the more refined dishes on the menu. A pricey option, but worth every penny.

Zumbura £
Indian
36 Old Town, SW4 0LB
Tel *020 7720 7902*
Off the beaten tourist track, this place serves up authentic Punjabi food in a wonderfully stylish setting; the owners were previously interior designers. Sip top-notch cocktails and sample a range of delicious tasting dishes. Don't miss the *Karela* (bitter gourd cooked with lentils).

For more information on types of restaurants *see page 289*

Light Meals and Snacks

When you want to make the most of the available sightseeing time, it doesn't always make sense to stop for a lengthy restaurant meal. Or perhaps you don't have the budget or the appetite for a full sit-down meal. London has several eateries for every taste and occasion – many of them unmissable institutions – from traditional fish-and-chips and pie-and-mash shops to elegant tearooms and cool cafés.

Breakfast

A good breakfast prepares you for a solid day's sightseeing, with the traditional British breakfast including staples such as bacon and eggs, smoked salmon, and grilled kippers. Many hotels (see pp284–87) serve traditional breakfasts to nonresidents, but to start the day like a 19th-century lord, head for **Simpson's-in-the-Strand**, which on weekdays offers an old-fashioned breakfast menu (as well as classic lunchtime and dinner roasts) in a historic paneled dining room. Porridge, lamb's kidneys, Cumberland sausage, and black pudding are just part of the multicourse "10 deadly sins" set breakfast.

Several pubs around Smithfield serve the all-night meat market workers. The most famous of these is the **Cock Tavern**, dishing up bargain fare from 6am onward. Traditional cafés also fry up artery-clogging working-men's morning meals including eggs, sausage, mushrooms, and baked beans.

For Continental breakfasts such as pastries and a cappuccino, there are many cafés to choose from. **The Wolseley** serves croissants, brioches, and cooked breakfasts in opulent surround-ings. Brunch has become increasingly popular in London. The spacious, modern restaurant in the back of popular French grocer/delicatessen **Villandry** serves one of the best on Saturday and Sunday. American restaurants such as **Joe Allen** and **Christopher's** also offer brunch, or head for well-heeled Westbourne Grove, where it's a weekend ritual at relaxed eateries such as **202** and **Tom's** delicatessen.

Coffee and Tea

For a cappuccino or espresso at any time of day, step into round-the-clock Soho stalwart **Bar Italia**, which also serves a range of pastries and paninis. It's a legendary late-night pit stop, full of colorful characters (but do keep a hand on your bag/wallet). There is no shortage of coffee-bar chains, but one of the best is **Caffè Nero**, which dispenses authentic Italian coffee at reasonable prices across town.

If you're out shopping, many of London's department stores have their own cafés; Harvey Nichols has one of the most stylish, while Selfridges has a branch of the cool Moroccan tearoom **Momo** among its many eating options. Designer stores such as Emporio Armani, Nicole Farhi, and Joseph have trendy cafés – from the outside **202** looks like a chic French-style café, but it showcases Nicole Farhi's fashion and home designs downstairs. **Joe's**, surrounded by Joseph's three boutiques at Brompton Cross, is a small but slick refreshment option; there are a few branches around town. In Portobello Market, quaint tearoom **Still Too Few**, below the antique kitchenalia shop of the same name, serves tea, sandwiches, and cakes to bric-a-brac hunters on Saturdays.

Patisseries such as **Maison Bertaux** and **Patisserie Valerie** are a delight, with mouth-watering window displays of French pastries. **Richoux** in Piccadilly is another popular refreshment spot. Chic French bakery/patisserie **Paul** offers delicious tarts and other treats in a Parisian café atmosphere. The elegantly old-world **The**

Wolseley (see p294) in Piccadilly has an all-day café menu of sandwiches and salads. If you're strolling in picturesque Little Venice, **Café Laville** commands a spectacular view over Regent's Canal. **Bluebird**, Terence Conran's multifaceted food center in the converted 1920s Bluebird motor garage on the King's Road, has a café with tables on its cobbled forecourt, as well as a more formal restaurant, bar, and market.

No visit to London would be complete without afternoon tea. Top hotels such as the **Ritz** and **Brown's** offer pots of your choice of tea, scones with jam and cream, delicious thin cucumber sandwiches, and cakes galore. For a relaxed place in beautiful Kensington Gardens, there's nothing to beat **The Orangery**. Its selection of English teas and cakes tastes even better in the elegant surroundings of Sir John Vanbrugh's 18th-century building. Good coffee (and cakes) can also be found at the **Monmouth Coffee House** in Covent Garden. **Fortnum and Mason** (see p313) serves both afternoon and high teas. In Kew, the **Maids of Honour** tearoom offers pastries reputedly enjoyed by Henry VIII. For a more modern experience, **Sketch** offers exquisite contemporary confections in a restyled Georgian room.

Traditional Cafés

These basic greasy spoons all over the city are a London institution, serving up fried breakfasts and such British staples as sausages, pies, and grills. They are usually only open until about 5pm; some close earlier. Granddaddy of them all is East End legend **E Pellicci**, with its wonderful Art Deco interior. A vogue for simple British fare has spawned numerous versions of the "caff," including **River Café** at Putney Bridge station – a quintessential British café with Formica tables and great service.

Museum and Theater Cafés

Most museums and galleries have cafés, including the Royal Academy, Tate Modern (with wonderful views over the Thames), the National Portrait Gallery, and the British Museum. The National Film Theatre on the South Bank has a buzzing bar/café frequented by film fanatics, while St. Martin-in-the-Fields church in Trafalgar Square, famous for its concerts, has a capacious self-service café in its vaulted crypt.

Sandwich Bars

A leading sandwich chain in London is **Prêt à Manger**, with branches throughout the center decked out with metalwork features and serving a range of delicious prepacked sandwiches, salads, cakes, and soft drinks. Another popular sandwich chain is **Eat**, which offers a daily changing menu of innovative soups and salads using seasonal ingredients as well as sandwiches made with homemade breads and tortilla wraps. Quality Italian sandwich fillings in focaccia and ciabatta breads can be had at Soho's **Carlton Coffee House**. For a quick bite try **Kappacasein**, a popular stand in Borough Market – come here for delicious raclette and toasted cheese sandwiches.

Delis

With Londoners becoming more and more interested in high-quality foods from small producers in Britain and abroad, there has been a boom in stylish delis, many of which provide seating so that you can sample their wares on site. **Tom's** is a one-stop deli and café. The chic deli **Luigi's** sells delicious Italian fare, from fresh pasta to farmhouse cheeses to freshly roasted vegetables and salads, while deli/cheese shop **La Fromagerie** has a large communal table in the back for light bites. Nearby is the family-run delicatessen/lunchroom **Paul Rothe & Son**, which

opened in the early 1900s and serves sandwiches and soups among shelves of "British and foreign provisions."

Diners

London is full of American-style fast-food joints, serving burgers, fries, fried chicken, apple pie, milk shakes, and cola, particularly around Soho, Leicester Square, Shaftesbury Avenue, and Covent Garden. Some time-honored establishments include family favorite **Maxwell's**, in Covent Garden, the **Hard Rock Café**, and the fun, 1950s-kitsch **Ed's Easy Diner**, but thanks to the continuing vogue for retro burger restaurants, new ones keep popping up. GBK (Gourmet Burger Kitchen) and Byron are some of the best, while **Lucky 7** and The Diner serve up burgers and breakfasts in a dice-and-cards-themed diner, complete with vinyl-seated booths and blaring rock'n'roll.

Pizza and Pasta

Italian food has now become a staple of the British diet. Street-side stands offer variable quality, while there are well-established chains with several branches, including **Ask**. **Pizza Express** offers thin-crust pizzas that are a step up from the norm. Try the elegant Georgian townhouse outlet on Chelsea's King's Road, or the branch in a converted dairy in Soho where there's also live jazz. **Kettners**, also part of the group, offers casual, inexpensive eating in a legendary old dining room (there's also a champagne bar). The **Carluccio's Caffè** chain, which has a branch with al fresco tables in pedestrianized St. Christopher's Place, serves good-quality, freshly made pastas and salads. **Marine Ices** near Camden Market serves great pizza and pasta in addition to its famous ice cream (see Street Food pp306–7). Other reliable pasta chains are **Spaghetti House** and **Café Pasta**. Inexpensive pasta is also served at bustling trattorias such as **Pollo** in Soho.

Food in Pubs

Perhaps the biggest – and most popular – change in the London dining scene in the last 15 years has been the transformation in the food found in pubs. Before the early 1990s, most pubs that provided food at all offered a pretty simple range of salads and sandwiches, put together with no great imagination. The last two decades, though, have seen the rapid rise of the "gastropub," in which the food range is treated with as much care as the beer selection. Grilled steaks, fresh fish, or English classics like sausage and mash have been reinvigorated by the use of first-rate, organic ingredients, and the menus have become increasingly sophisticated, mixing Mediterranean, Asian, and other global influences.

The neighborhood gastropub has become an essential London institution. Some have separate dining rooms, while others have stayed more pub-style, where you order at the bar from a chalkboard. All tend to be more relaxed than formal restaurants, but they can get busy, so make reservations. Among the best are **The Eagle**, **The Engineer**, **The Lansdowne**, **The Queen's Head & Artichoke**, and **The Wells** in Hampstead. (See also pp308–11).

Fish and Chips

Fish and chips is typically considered the national dish of Britain, with a "chippy" serving a choice of fish (typically cod or plaice) deep-fried in batter, accompanied by chips (thicker cut than French fries). A range of accompaniments includes bread baps (rolls) for a "chip buttie" (a chip sandwich), mushy peas, pickled eggs, or onions. Four of the best places for such fare are the **North Sea Fish Restaurant**, **Rock & Sole Plaice**, **Faulkner's**, and **Fish Central**. Fish and chips is now considered very "trendy" and is increasingly available on the menu in various chic restaurants and chains such as **Fish!**

Bars and Wine Bars

The range and quality of London's bars has grown over the past five years. There are numerous wine bars in the center, such as **Café des Amis du Vin** in Covent Garden (downstairs from its ground-floor brasserie), and the legendary **El Vino**, as well as chains such as **Corney & Barrow** and **Balls Bros**, which also serve good food. The cozy **Tapa Room** on the ground floor of acclaimed **The Providores** restaurant serves globally influenced tapas. Good-value food is also part of the success of such chain bars as **All Bar One**. Capitalizing on young Londoners' habit of spending an entire evening out drinking, many style-conscious, modern bars serve food, such as the chic wine bar **28°–50°** in Marylebone, which has French bistro-style food. **Gordon's Wine Bar** is London's oldest (c.1890), located in an underground cellar. *(See also pp309–11.)*

Brasseries

Now that informal dining is an integral aspect of life in London, brasseries have become part of the landscape. These are based on the classic French blueprint, with its Parisian ambience and decor, serving such favorites as steak frites and seafood platters – a classic example is long-established **La Brasserie** in South Kensington. Among the chains is **Café Rouge**. **Randall & Aubin** is a buzzy oyster and lobster (plus champagne) bar in a former delicatessen that has retained its period charm and overlooks Soho's lively Brewer Street. Relative newcomer **The Electric Brasserie**, next to Portobello's luxurious art-house movie theater of the same name, is a popular update on the traditional model.

Juice Bars and Organic Cafés

The healthy-diet trend has made juice bars and organic food shops very popular. Longstanding Lebanese favorite **Ranoush Juice** has added outlets to its original Edgware Road location, and chains such as **Crussh** have branches all over London. Organic food chains

---

DIRECTORY

Breakfast

202
202 Westbourne Grove W11. **Map** 9 C2.

Christopher's
18 Wellington St WC2.
Map 13 C2.

Cock Tavern
East Poultry Avenue, Smithfield Market EC1.
Map 6 F5.

Joe Allen
13 Exeter St WC2.
Map 13 C2.

Simpson's-in-the-Strand
100 Strand WC2.
Map 13 C2.

Tom's
226 Westbourne Grove W11. **Map** 9 B2.

Villandry
170 Great Portland Street W1.
Map 4 F5.

The Wolseley
160 Piccadilly W1.
Map 12 F3.

Coffee and Tea

Bar Italia
22 Frith St W1.
Map 13 A2.

Bluebird Café
350 King's Rd SW3.
Map 19 A4.

Café Laville
Little Venice Parade, 453 Edgware Rd W2.

Emporio Armani Caffè
191 Brompton Rd SW3.
Map 19 B1.

Joe's
126 Draycott Ave SW3.
Map 19 B2.

Maids of Honour
288 Kew Rd
Richmond, Surrey.

Maison Bertaux
28 Greek St W1.
Map 13 A1.

Monmouth Coffee House
27 Monmouth St WC2.
Map 13 B2.

The Orangery
Kensington Palace, Kensington Gardens W8.
Map 10 D3.

Patisserie Valerie
17 Motcombe St, Belgravia SW1.
Map 12 D5.

Paul
29 Bedford St WC2.
Map 13 B2.

Richoux
172 Piccadilly W1.
Map 12 F3.

Sketch
9 Conduit St W1. **Map** 12 F2.

Still Too Few
300 Westbourne Grove W11. **Map** 9 B2.

Traditional Cafés

E Pellicci
332 Bethnal Green Rd E2.

River Café
Station Approach South SW6.

Museum and Theater Cafés

Café in the Crypt
St Martin-in-the-Fields, Duncannon St WC2.
Map 13 B3.

Riverfront Bar & Kitchen
BFI Southbank, South Bank SE1. **Map** 14 D3.

Sandwich Bars

Carlton Coffee House
41 Broadwick St W1.
Map 13 A2.

Eat
12 Oxo Tower Wharf, Barge House St SE1.
Map 14 E3.

Kappacasein
Borough Market SE1.
Map 5 A5.

Prêt à Manger
421 Strand WC2.
Map 13 C3.

Delis

La Fromagerie
2–6 Moxon St W1.
Map 4 D5.

Luigi's
349 Fulham Rd SW6.
Map 18 F4.

Paul Rothe & Son
35 Marylebone Lane W1.
Map 12 D1.

Diners

Ed's Easy Diner
12 Moor St W1.
Map 13 B2.

Hard Rock Café
150 Old Park Lane W1.
Map 12 E4.

Lucky 7
127 Westbourne Park Rd W2. **Map** 9 C1.

Maxwell's
8 James St WC2.
Map 13 C2.

such as **Planet Organic** and **Whole Foods Market** do a roaring trade in hot and cold fare and freshly squeezed juices alongside their groceries, baked goods, and vitamins. With tables on the premises, you can enjoy the freshly prepared food and drinks immediately.

Noodle Bars

Popular chain **Wagamama** still draws crowds for its well-priced noodles and other Asian dishes in airy yet basic environs; customers sit at long communal tables. **Dim T Café** serves dim sum and mix-and-match noodles, meat, and toppings in a modern café setting. **Taro** is a busy Japanese diner offering cheap sushi, ramen, and teriyaki.

Street Food

During summer, many parks have ice-cream vans parked by the entrances, with **Marine Ices** serving some of the town's best ice cream. Hot roasted chestnuts, made on mini-barbecues, are a winter delight found along Oxford Street. Shellfish stands, selling ready-to-eat potted shrimp, crab, whelks, and jellied eels, are a feature of many street markets. At Camden Lock and Old Spitalfields Market, you can wander among the stands choosing from falafel, satay chicken, veggie burgers, and honey balls. In the East End, Jewish bakeries such as **Brick Lane Beigel Bake** are open 24 hours a day. Fresh plain bagels as well as ones with

a wide range of fillings are available here. The East End also has the largest number of pie-and-mash shops, which provide an inexpensive and satisfying "nosh-up" of jellied eels and potatoes, or meat pie with mash and liquor (green parsley sauce). Two classic venues, both on Bethnal Green Road, are **G Kelly** and **S&R Kelly**. Or try **Manze's** on Tower Bridge Road. For the real East End experience, you should drench your food in vinegar and wash it all down with a couple of mugs of strong, hot tea.

Modern pie-maker **The Square Pie Company** sells superior pies with gourmet fillings in Old Spitalfields Market and Selfridges.

DIRECTORY

Pizza and Pasta

Ask
56–60 Wigmore St W1.
Map 12 D1.

Café Pasta
184 Shaftesbury Ave WC2.
Map 13 2B.

Carluccio's Caffè
St Christopher's Place W1.
Map 12 E2.
One of many branches.

Kettner's
29 Romilly St W1.
Map 13 A2.

Pizza Express
30 Coptic St WC1.
Map 13 B1.
One of many branches.

Pollo
20 Old Compton St W1.
Map 13 A2.

Fish and Chips

Faulkner's
424–426 Kingsland
Rd E8.

Fish!
Borough Mkt SE1.
Map 15 B4.

Fish Central
149–155 Central
St EC1.
Map 7 A3.

North Sea Fish Restaurant
7–8 Leigh St WC1. **Map** 5 B4.

Rock & Sole Plaice
47 Endell St WC2.
Map 13 B1.

Wine Bars

28°–50°
15–17 Marylebone Lane
W1. **Map** 12 D1.

All Bar One
103 Cannon St EC4.
Map 15 A2.

Balls Bros
Hays Galleria, Tooley St
SE1. **Map** 15 B3.

Café des Amis du Vin
11–14 Hanover Place
WC2. **Map** 13 C2.

Corney & Barrow
19 Broadgate Circle EC2.
Map 7 C5.

Dickens Inn
St Katharine's Dock E1.
Map 16 E3.

Gordon's Wine Bar
47 Villiers St WC2.
Map 13 C3.

Providores Tapa Room
109 Marylebone High St
W1. **Map** 4 D5.

El Vino
1–2 Hare Place, Fleet St
EC4. **Map** 14 E1.

Brasseries

La Brasserie
272 Brompton Rd SW3.
Map 19 B2.

Café Rouge
27 Basil St SW3.
Map 11 C5.
One of many branches.

The Electric Brasserie
191 Portobello Rd W11.
Map 9 B2.

Randall & Aubin
16 Brewer St W1.
Map 13 A2.

Juice Bars and Organic Cafés

Crussh
Unit 1, 1 Curzon
Street W1.
Map 12 E3.

Fluid Juice Bar
208 Fulham Rd SW3.
Map 19 A2.

Planet Organic
22 Torrington Place WC1.
Map 5 A5.

Ranoush Juice
43 Edgware Rd W2.
Map 11 C2.

Whole Foods Market
20 Glasshouse St W1.
Map 13 A3.

Noodle Bars

Dim T Café
32 Charlotte St W1.
Map 13 A1.

Taro
59–61 Brewer St W1.
Map 13 A2.

Wagamama
101 Wigmore St W1.
Map 12 D1.

Street Food

Brick Lane Beigel Bake
159 Brick Lane E1.
Map 8 E5.

G Kelly S&R Kelly
526 Roman Road E3.
Map 8 D4.

Manze's
87 Tower Bridge Rd SE1.
Map 16 D5.

Marine Ices
8 Haverstock Hill NW3.

London Pubs and Bars

Affectionately known as a "pub" as well as "boozer" and "the local," a public house was originally just that – a house in which the public could eat, drink, and even stay the night. Large inns with courtyards, such as the George Inn, were originally stopping points for horse-drawn coach services. Some pubs stand on historic public house sites – for instance, the Ship, the Lamb and Flag, and the City Barge. However, many of the finest ones date from the emergence of "gin palaces" in the late 1800s, where Londoners took refuge from the misery of their poverty amid lavish interiors, often with stunning mirrors (the Salisbury) and elaborate decorations. Since the 1990s cocktail-bar boom, the traditional pub has been given an image makeover, restoring the British institution's popularity with a fashionable crowd.

Rules and Conventions

Visitors to London have long been bemused by early pub closing times, which made a night out a bit tricky – an after-theater nightcap, for example, was usually out of the question outside of your hotel. In theory, reforms to the licensing laws, which came into effect in 2005, mean pubs can now stay open up to 24 hours, as long as they obtain permission from their local authority, and many extend their hours beyond the 11am–11pm standard. Some may close in the afternoon or early evening and also on weekends. You must be at least 18 to buy or drink alcohol, and at least 14 to enter a pub without an adult. Children can be taken into pubs that serve food, or can use outside areas. Order at the bar and pay when you are served; tips are not customary unless you are served food and drink at a table. "Last orders" are usually called 10 minutes before closing, then "time" is called, and a further 20 minutes is then allowed for finishing up drinks. Since July 2007, smoking has been banned from all pubs and clubs.

British Beer

The most traditional beers are available in various different strengths and styles, and are flat (not fizzy), and served only lightly cooled. The spectrum of bottled beers goes from "light"

ale, through "pale," "brown," "bitter," and the strong "old." A sweeter, lower-alcohol alternative is shandy, a classic mixture of draft beer or lager and lemon soda. Many traditional methods of brewing and serving beer have been preserved over the years, and there is a great variety of "real ale" in London pubs. Serious beer drinkers should look for free houses, pubs that are not tied to any particular brewery. The main London brewers are Young's (try their strong Winter Warmer beer) and Fuller's. The **Orange Brewery** serves a good pint and excellent food, and offers tours of the brewery.

Other Pub Drinks

Cider is another traditional English drink found in every pub. Made from apples, it comes in a range of strengths and degrees of dryness. Blended Scotch whiskey and malt whiskeys are also staples, together with gin, usually drunk with tonic water. During the winter, mulled wine (warm and spicy) or hot toddies (brandy or whiskey with hot water and sugar) may be served. Non-alcoholic drinks are also always available.

Historic Pubs

Many pubs have a fascinating history and decor, whether it is a beamed medieval snug,

Victorian fantasy, or an extraordinary Arts and Crafts interior, as at the **Black Friar**, a must-see temple to imbibing, featuring bronze bas-reliefs, and an intimate, marble-and-mosaic chamber at the back. While many of the "gin palaces" of the 19th century have been revamped or abandoned, there are some notable survivors. At the **Prince Alfred** in Maida Vale, the bar is divided by "snobscreens," a feature that allowed the upper crust to enjoy a drink without mixing with their servants. The semicircular **Viaduct Tavern**, opposite the Old Bailey, is a suitably stately setting for distinguished barristers and judges, ablaze with mirrors, chandeliers, and etched glass, while the **Princess Louise** retains its magnificent central mahogany bar, complete with original clock, molded ceiling, and vivid wall tiles. Less grand but just as lovingly decorated is the tiny, tiled **Dog & Duck** in Soho – but you may have to battle for a seat or (in warm weather) stand outside with its many devotees.

Many pubs have strong literary associations, such as the **Fitzroy Tavern**, a meeting place for writers and artists in the 1930s and 40s, including Dylan Thomas, George Orwell, and Augustus John. **Ye Olde Cheshire Cheese** is associated with Dr. Johnson; Charles Dickens frequented the **Trafalgar Tavern**; and Oscar Wilde often went to **The Salisbury**. Samuel Pepys witnessed the Great Fire of London from the **Anchor**, on the river at Bankside. The less literary **Old Bull and Bush** in north London was the subject of a well known old music-hall song, while the 17th- century **Lamb and Flag** – one of central London's few surviving timber-framed buildings down an alleyway – was known as the Bucket of Blood because it was the venue for bare-knuckle prize fights. Some pubs have sinister associations – for example, some of Jack the Ripper's victims were found near the **Ten Bells**. Dick Turpin, the 18th-century highwayman, took refreshment at the **Spaniards Inn** in north London, and the **French House** in Soho was a meeting point for the French Resistance during World War II.

Pub Names

Signs have hung outside public houses since 1393, when King Richard II decreed they should replace the usual bush outside the door. As most people were illiterate, names that could easily be illustrated were chosen, such as the Rose & Crown, coats of arms (Freemasons' Arms), historical figures (Princess Louise), or heraldic animals (White Lion).

Pub Entertainment

Fringe theater productions (see p338) are staged at the **King's Head**, the **Latchmere,** and the **Gate Theatre** above the Prince Albert. Some pubs have live music: there is excellent modern jazz at the **Bull's Head** in Barnes and a wide variety of music styles at the popular **Mean Fiddler** (see pp343–5). The diminutive **Golden Eagle**, on a winding back street in Marylebone, is a rare central London piano pub with nostalgic singalongs a few nights a week.

Outdoor Drinking

Most pubs with outdoor seating tend to be located slightly outside central London. The **Freemason's Arms,** for example, near Hampstead Heath, has a very pleasant garden, as does the **Hampshire Hog** in Hammersmith. Some pubs enjoy riverside locations with fine views, from the **Prospect of Whitby** in Wapping and the **Grapes** in Limehouse to the **White Cross** in Richmond.

Microbreweries

Delicious beer is brewed on the premises at microbreweries such as **Mash,** where a space-age interior makes you forget that real ale tends to be the domain of older drinkers.

This bar is frequented by a young and trendy crowd. Huge orange vats indicate where the actual brewing takes place. The **Bünker Bier Hall Bar and Kitchen** in Covent Garden has three signature beers, and a good atmosphere.

Themed Pubs and Bars

Big, brash Irish pubs such as **Filthy McNasty's** and **Waxy O'Connor's** (mocked up like a Catholic church, complete with confessional) attract a young, fun-loving crowd, as does Australian bar chain **Walk-about**. Sports bars are popular as well. The **Sports Café**, near Piccadilly, has three bars, a dance floor, and 120 screens showing global sporting events on satellite TV. More low-key is **Kick** in Shoreditch (there's a smaller sister establishment, **Café Kick**, in Exmouth Market), which features table-soccer games and organic food in a relaxed setting. Pool players can take their cue at a branch of slick pool-bar chain the **Elbow Room**.

Gastropubs

Since the early 1990s, many old pubs have been given gleaming makeovers and kitchens turning out superior fare. Among the first gastropubs was the **Eagle**, which offers gourmet dishes from the open kitchen that occupies half of the bar. Many, like **The Lansdowne,** have dedicated dining rooms as well as laid-back pub rooms where you can eat, drink, or do both. TV foodie Roxy Beaujolais serves simple bistro dishes in tiny, quirky old pub the **Seven Stars** near the Royal Courts of Justice. **The Cow** is known for its oysters and Guinness, while the **Chapel**, the **Fire Station,** and the **Dusk** are popular with both drinkers and diners. (See also pp305–7.)

Bars

London's bar scene has been gradually transformed since the mid-1990s; up until then, the choice was limited to either

hotel bars, wine bars, or pubs (see pp306–7). Propelled by a cocktail revival, as well as the fact that eating and drinking out is now deeply ingrained in daily London life, new bars are opening all the time.

Eagerly sought out by style-conscious connoisseurs, the latest watering holes are now as much a talking point as new restaurants. Soho and Covent Garden are brimming with bars, but to sample the hottest night spots, head either east or west. In the past decade, Shoreditch has been transformed from a no-go area to an evening destination, which is spilling into neighboring Bethnal Green.

One of the earliest pioneers – basement lounge, no-frills **The Shoreditch Electricity Showrooms** – is still hopping. Though slightly farther afield, it's since been joined by the gloriously camp **Loungelover**, decorated with crystal chandeliers, vintage handbags, and stuffed animals. The hip **Book Club** is an eclectic space in which to eat, drink, and enjoy events from arts and science to crafts and DIY.

Across town in Notting Hill, sip good-value Scorpion Bowls and Zombies in the kitsch tiki-lounge ambience of **Trailer Happiness** or go for classic or more inventive cocktails at the **Lonsdale** with its bronze bubble-studded walls and hazy violet lighting. The area's style bars are in contrast with down-to-earth pubs frequented by the market traders, such as the bustling **Portobello Star**.

If you want to stick to the center of town, fashionable options include the **Lab Bar**, which serves excellent cocktails, especially Central American drinks such as caipirinhas and mojitos, or **Match Bar**, an East End lounge bar behind the West End's Oxford Circus. Heading south, the **Fridge Bar** in Brixton has DJs playing decent hip-hop and deep house, with lots of dancing and drinking.

Many restaurants feature excellent bars. The bar at **Green's Restaurant and Oyster Bar** is a very special place to go, to drink champagne and eat oysters and lobster in elegant surroundings. **Smiths of Smithfield**, opposite the famous meat market, has a large, industrial-style café/bar at ground level, a sleek cocktail and champagne bar on the next floor, topped by two restaurants upstairs; nearby, **St John** *(see p299)* has a stylish bar serving excellent wine and bar food. A drink in the bar is the less-expensive way to experience the **Criterion** brasserie's sumptuous, gilded neo-Byzantine decor. Contemporary Chinese restaurant **Hakkasan** *(see p294)* serves exotic cocktails flavored

with the likes of ginger and lemongrass in its glamorous Asian-style bar.

Specialty Bars

Aficionados of particular spirits are well served in London. Scottish restaurant Boisdale's **Macdonald Bar** boasts 170 Scotch malt whiskeys (and an impressive selection of Cuban cigars), while the **Rockwell**, an upscale bar in the Trafalgar Hotel, offers London's largest bourbon selection. **Salt** is a slick, modern whiskey bar, and **Dollar Grills & Martinis**, in the basement of a glitzed-up former pub, serves a lengthy martini "library." Mexican bar/restaurant

La Perla in Covent Garden has an extensive range of tequilas for your shooting pleasure.

Chain Bars

They may not be the most exciting places to drink, but London's chain bars are a reliable option. Halfway between a bar and a pub, with large windows and white walls, they are also far more female-friendly than traditional pubs. **All Bar One** is very popular, with chunky wood furniture. **Pitcher & Piano** has sofas and blonde wood surrounds, while the **Slug & Lettuce** chain features paintings on the walls and quiet rooms for talking.

DIRECTORY

Hotel Bars

London's hotel bars continue to offer an elegant setting for classic and innovative cocktails, with **The Blue Bar** at the Berkeley Hotel and the **Long Bar** at the Sanderson Hotel prime examples. The **American Bar** at the Savoy, decorated in an Art Deco style, has a pianist, a terrific atmosphere, and classic cocktails (try the signature White Lady or the Dry Martini, which the bar introduced to Britain), while another Jazz Age gem, the **Rivoli Bar** at the Ritz, has been resplendently restored. **Claridge's Bar** offers excellent champagne cocktails (among other concoctions) in a glamorous, contemporary-classic setting. **Trader Vic's** in the Park Lane Hilton offers an exotically tropical setting in which to enjoy an amazing range of rum cocktails. **The Bar**, in the Rosewood London, is a lively bar with a traditional soul, evoking the atmosphere of a London gentlemen's club with a roaring fire at one end and a wooden bar running along the other. Warm, intimate, and sophisticated, with plush furniture and handwoven rugs on a parquet floor, **Brasserie Max** in the Covent Garden Hotel is always buzzing and is very popular with theater and film people.

Gay Bars

Old Compton Street in Soho has a well-established gay scene. Tables spill out on to the sidewalks and there is a lively atmosphere tolerant of all sexual preferences. **Compton's of Soho**, a busy pub, is across the road from the gay bar and eatery **Balans** and close to the well-known gay pub, **The Admiral Duncan**. The **Edge** is a sprawling bar and club over four floors, while **Rupert Street** is a stylishly low-key option for a relaxed drink. The **Candy Bar** is a popular lesbian bar, while, away from the West End, the **Royal Vauxhall Tavern** hosts Duckie's outrageous cabaret and DJs on Saturday nights.

DIRECTORY

Kick
127 Shoreditch High St E1.
Map 8 D3.

Loungelover
1 Whitby St E1.
Map 8 D4.

Ship Tavern
23 Lime St EC3.
Map 15 C2.

The Shoreditch Electricity Showrooms
39a Hoxton Sq N1.
Map 7 C3.

Smiths of Smithfield
67–77 Charterhouse St EC1.
Map 6 F5.

Ten Bells
84 Commercial St E1.
Map 8 D5.

Viaduct Tavern
126 Newgate St EC1.
Map 14 F1.

Ye Olde Cheshire Cheese
145 Fleet St EC4.
Map 14 E1.

Southwark and South Bank

Anchor
34 Park Street SE1.
Map 15 A3.

Fire Station
150 Waterloo Rd SE1.
Map 14 E4.

George Inn
77 Borough High St SE1.
Map 15 B4.

Hampstead

Freemasons Arms
32 Downshire Hill NW3.
Map 1 C5.

Old Bull and Bush
North End Way NW3.
Map 1 A3.

Spaniards Inn
Spaniards Rd NW3.
Map 1 A3.

Knightsbridge, Belgravia

Blue Bar
The Berkeley, Wilton Pl
SW1. **Map** 12 D5.

Boisdale
15 Eccleston St SW1.
Map 20 E1.

The Lansdowne
90 Gloucester Ave NW1.
Map 4 D1.

Primrose Hill, Marylebone

Chapel
48 Chapel St NW1.
Map 3 B5.

Coco Momo
79 Marylebone High
St W1. **Map** 4 D5.

Golden Eagle
59 Marylebone Lane W1.
Map 12 D1.

Bayswater, Notting Hill

The Cow
89 Westbourne
Park Rd W11.
Map 9 B1.

Lonsdale
44–48 Lonsdale Rd W11.
Map 9 B2.

Portobello Star
171 Portobello Rd W11.
Map 9 B2.

Prince Albert
11 Pembridge Rd W11.
Map 9 C3.

Trailer Happiness
177 Portobello Rd W11.
Map 9 B2.

Farther Afield

Bull's Head
373 Lonsdale Rd SW13.

City Barge
27 Strand-on-the-
Green W4.

Fridge Bar
1 Town Hill Parade SW2.

Grapes
76 Narrow St E14.

The Hampshire Hog
227 King St W6.

King's Head
115 Upper St N1.
Map 6 F1.

Latchmere
503 Battersea
Pk Rd SW11.

Prince Alfred
5a Formosa St W9.

Prospect of Whitby
57 Wapping Wall E1.

Royal Vauxhall Tavern
372 Kennington
Lane SE11.
Map 22 D3.

Trafalgar Tavern
Park Row SE10.

White Cross
Water Lane, Richmond,
Surrey.

SHOPS AND MARKETS

London is one of the most lively shopping cities in the world. Ultramodern stores sit comfortably alongside the old-fashioned emporia presided over by tailcoated staff. You can buy anything here, as long as you're prepared to pay. Luxury goods are expensive, although bargain-hunters will find a wealth of cheap goods in the thriving markets, which often exude a carnival atmosphere. Explore the famous department stores, which encompass a huge breadth of merchandise, or seek out specialty shops. In general, you'll find upscale designer stores around Knightsbridge, Chelsea, Regent Street, and Bond Street, while Oxford Street is the frenetic center for mid-priced labels as well as mainstream department stores. Notting Hill, Islington, Soho, and Covent Garden are all rich in small, independent shops and specialty shops. Merchandise found in these areas includes clothes, from raincoats and traditional tweeds to cutting-edge design and catwalk copies; books and records; perfumes; art and antiques; and craft goods such as jewelry, ceramics, and leather.

When to Shop

In central London, most shops open from 10am and close between 5:30–6pm from Monday to Saturday, and are also open 11am–4pm Sunday. Many department stores have longer hours. "Late night" shopping until 7 or 8pm is on Thursdays and Fridays in Oxford Street and the rest of the West End, and on Wednesdays in Knightsbridge and Chelsea. Some shops in tourist areas, such as Covent Garden (see pp112–21) and the Trocadero, are open until 7pm or later every day and on Sundays. Some street markets (see pp331–3) are usually open on Sundays as well.

Bags from two of the most famous West End shops

How to Pay

Most shops accept all major credit cards, including MasterCard, American Express, Diners Club, Japanese Credit Bureau, and Visa. However, smaller shops and street markets do not. A few of the stores also accept traveler's checks, especially if they're in sterling; for other currencies the rate of exchange is less favorable than in a bank. You need your passport.

Most shops no longer accept payment by personal check, and their use is likely to be phased out completely by 2018. Debit cards are accepted in many major stores, as are euros.

Rights and Services

On a defective purchase, you usually get a refund, if proof of purchase is produced and the goods are returned. This isn't always the case with sales goods, so inspect them carefully. Most large stores, and some small ones, will pack goods up for you and send them anywhere in the world.

VAT Exemption

VAT (Value Added Tax) is a sales tax of 20%, which is charged on virtually all goods sold in Britain. The exceptions are books, food, and children's clothes. VAT is mostly included in the advertised or marked price, although business suppliers, including some stationers and electrical goods shops, often charge separately.

Non-European Union visitors to Britain who stay no longer than three months may claim back VAT. If you plan to do so, carry your passport when shopping. You must complete a form in the store when you buy the goods and then give a copy to Customs while leaving the country. The tax refund may be returned by check or refunded to your credit card, but then a service charge will be deducted and most stores have a minimum purchase threshold (often £50 or £75). If you arrange to have your goods shipped directly home from the store, VAT should be deducted before you pay.

Harrods' elaborate Edwardian tiled food halls

Twice-Yearly Sales

The traditional sale season is after Christmas to February and again in June to July, when shops slash their prices and sell off unwanted stock. The department stores have some of the best reductions; for sales at the famous **Harrods** (see p211), lines start to form outside long before opening.

Best of the Department Stores

The traditional king of London's department stores is **Harrods**, with over 300 departments and a staff of 5,000. The spectacular food hall with Edwardian tiles displays fish, cheese, fruit, and vegetables. The specialties also include fashions for all ages, china and glass, kitchenware, and electronics. **Harvey Nichols** aims to stock the best of everything. Clothes are particularly strong on high fashion, with emphasis on talented British, European, and American names. There's also an impressive menswear section. The food hall, opened in 1992, is one of London's most stylish.

Some well-known names in British clothes design

    Selfridges, on Oxford Street, has a wide choice of labels, a great lingerie department, and a section devoted to emerging designers. A melange of chain-store concessions on the ground-floor caters to young women. It also has a food hall featuring global delicacies.

    The original **John Lewis** was a draper, and even today his shop has a good selection of fabrics and sewing notions. Its china, glass, and household items make John Lewis, and its popular Sloane Square partner, Peter Jones, equally popular with Londoners. **Liberty** (see p111) near Carnaby Street still sells the beautiful silks and other Asian goods for which it was famed after opening in

1875. Look for the famous scarf department. **Fortnum and Mason's** ground-floor food department is so engrossing that the upper floors of classic fashion and luxury items often remain free of crowds. The food section has everything from Fortnum's tins of cookies and tea to the lovely wicker hampers. The latest addition to the retail scene is **Westfield London**, an impressive, upscale shopping destination with over 250 retailers, as well as several restaurants.

Marks and Spencer

Marks and Spencer has come a long way since 1882, when Russian emigré Michael Marks had a single stand in Leeds' Kirkgate market with the sign, "Don't ask the price – it's a penny!" It now has more than 690 stores worldwide, and most stock is "own label" – Marks and Spencer's underwear, in particular, is a staple of the British wardrobe. The food department mostly stocks convenience foods. The main Oxford Street branches at the Pantheon (near Oxford Circus) and Marble Arch are best for clothes and household goods.

Shopping Areas

As well as offering a wealth of delights for the discerning bargain hunter, London's thriving markets also provide an atmospheric glimpse into the past, with many dating back to medieval times.

    Soak up the colors, aromas, and flavors at specialty food stands, browse quaint antique shops for curios, or pick up a retro bargain at one of the many vintage clothes outlets that spill onto the streets. Early risers have a better chance of finding a bargain (see also pp331–3).

Doorman at Fortnum and Mason

Penhaligon's for scents (see p325)

London's Best: Shopping Streets and Markets

London's best shopping areas range from the elegance of Knightsbridge, where porcelain, jewelry, and *couture* clothes come at the highest prices, to colorful markets such as Brick Lane, Spitalfields, and Portobello. Meccas for those who enjoy searching for a bargain, London's markets also reflect the vibrant street life engendered by its enterprising multicultural community. The city is fertile ground for specialty shoppers: there are streets crammed with antique shops, antiquarian booksellers, and art galleries. Turn to pages 316–30 for more details of shops, grouped according to category.

Kensington Church Street
Home to over 60 antique dealers with one of the largest selections of art and antiques in London. *(See p217)*

Portobello Road Market
Over 1,000 stands sell *objets d'art*, jewelry, medals, paintings, and silverware – plus fresh fruit and vegetables. *(See p333)*

Regent's Park and Marylebone

See inset map

South Kensington and Knightsbridge

Kensington and Holland Park

Piccadilly and St. James

0 kilometers 1
0 miles 0.5

Chelsea

Knightsbridge
Exclusive designer wear is on sale here, at Harrods as well as smaller stores. *(See p211)*

King's Road
Once a center for avant-garde fashion in the 1960s and 1970s, the street is now home to chain stores and designer shops. There is also a good antique market. *(See p198)*

LONDON'S WEST END SHOPS

Oxford Street could be considered London's "Main Street," and many of the shops that line it are branches of national or international chains. The big department stores, such as Selfridges and John Lewis, also loom along this street, as do smaller shops selling clothes and tourist souvenirs. On Regent Street, Piccadilly, and Bond Street, prices rise and shoppers search for specialty purchases among the designer clothes shops, jewelers, and art and antique dealers, while Carnaby Street has a more eclectic vibe.

Bloomsbury and Fitzrovia

Holborn and the Inns of Court

Covent Garden and the Strand

Smithfield and Spitalfields

The City

Southwark and Bankside

South Bank

Whitehall and Westminster

Brick Lane Market
In this East End street, everything from old books to new shoes is on sale. *(See p331)*

Petticoat Lane
London's most famous market has leather, clothes, watches, jewelry, and toys. *(See p333)*

Gabriel's Wharf
The wharf has been converted into small shops selling art, jewelry, and crafts. *(See p193)*

Charing Cross Road
Crammed shops selling old and new books line this long street. *(See p322)*

Covent Garden and Neal Street
Street entertainers perform in this lively and historic market. The specialty shops of Neal Street are nearby. *(See p117)*

Clothes

London has never been better for clothes shopping, offering a virtually inexhaustible range of styles, price levels, and quality, across a far-reaching and varied geographical area. Besides the traditional British style famous the world over, you'll also find international designers, global and home-grown chains, and an ever-increasing number of independent boutiques catering to every taste. While old-fashioned tailors, shirt-makers, and cobblers still thrive, often in their original premises, shops are increasingly design-led. The hugely popular national chains have perfected the art of producing good-quality catwalk knockoffs, while a new generation of British design talent has revitalized the fashion scene.

Traditional Clothing

British tailoring and fabrics are world-renowned for their high quality. In Savile Row, you can follow in the sartorial footsteps of Winston Churchill and the Duke of Windsor, among other dapper luminaries, and have a suit made to measure or buy one off the rack. Established in 1806, **Henry Poole** was the first tailor in the Row. At **H Huntsman & Sons**, you can choose from three options – bespoke, custom-made, and ready-to-wear. The bespoke suits are painstakingly hand-stitched on the premises, which partly explains the exorbitant £3,000-plus price tag. In addition to making suits to order, **Gieves & Hawkes** has two ready-to-wear lines.

A new generation of fashion-conscious tailors, known for modern cuts and vibrant fabrics, has joined the distinguished and traditional lineup, including **Ozwald Boateng** and **Richard James**. Jermyn Street is famous for sharp shirts. At venerable shops such as **Turnbull & Asser** or the family-run **Harvie & Hudson**, you can either have them custom-made or choose the less expensive standard-sized options. Many manufacturers, including the popular shirt chain **Pink**, now also sell a wide variety of classic women's blouses.

In the past few years, several bastions of classic British style have completely reinvented themselves as fashion labels. **Burberry** is the best example of this, although it still does a brisk trade in its famous trenchcoats,

checked clothing (for children too), and distinctive accessories. **Daks** is also a good choice for classic raincoats, suits, and accessories for both sexes, with its high-fashion takes on traditional British looks. **Dunhill** specializes in immaculate, if expensive, menswear and accessories, while at the **Crombie**

outlet, you can buy the famous fitted overcoat that came to be known by the company's name. The famous menswear emporium **Hackett** caters to a younger, yet still conservative, clientele. Designers **Margaret Howell** and **Nicole Farhi** create updated versions of relaxed British country garments for men and women, such as knitwear, tweeds, and sheepskin coats. You can still find a more traditional, stylish country look in the Regent Street, Piccadilly, or Knightsbridge areas. Waxed Barbour jackets are on sale at Harrods (see p313). **Cordings**, established 1839, is good for country-gent/lady gear, such as check shirts, moleskin trousers, and Covert coats.

While **Liberty** (see p111) now has a good selection of contemporary designers, it still uses its famous patterned prints to make blouses and stylish men's shirts as well as scarves and ties. Floral

Size Chart

For Australian sizes follow British and American convention

Children's clothing

British	2–3	4–5	6–7	8–9	10–11	12	14	14+ (years)	
American	2–3	4–5	6–6X	7–8	10–12	14	16 (size)		
Continental	2–3	4–5	6–7	8–9	10–11	12	14	14+ (years)	

Children's shoes

British	7½	8	9	10	11	12	13	1	2
American	7½	8½	9½	10½	11½	12½	13½	1½	2½
Continental	24	25½	27	28	29	30	32	33	34

Women's dresses, coats, and skirts

British	6	8	10	12	14	16	18	20
American	4	6	8	10	12	14	16	18
Continental	32	34	36	38	40	42	44	46

Women's blouses and sweaters

British	30	32	34	36	38	40	42
American	6	8	10	12	14	16	18
Continental	34	36	38	40	42	44	46

Women's shoes

British	3	4	5	6	7	8
American	5	6	7	8	9	10
Continental	36	37	38	39	40	41

Men's suits

British	34	36	38	40	42	44	46	48
American	34	36	38	40	42	44	46	48
Continental	44	46	48	50	52	54	56	58

Men's shirts

British	14	15	15½	16	16½	17	17½	18
American	14	15	15½	16	16½	17	17½	18
Continental	36	38	39	41	42	43	44	45

Men's shoes

British	7	7½	8	9	10	11	12
American	7½	8	8½	9½	10½	11	11½
Continental	40	41	42	43	44	45	46

print "English rose" dresses and feminine blouses can be found at **Laura Ashley**, although the store has introduced more contemporary looks as well.

Modern British Design and Street Fashion

London designers are known for their eclectic, irreverent style. Grand dames Vivienne Westwood and Zandra Rhodes have been on the scene since the 1970s – the latter opened the **Fashion and Textile Museum** in southeast London in 2003. It features 3,000 of her own garments as well as examples by other influential fashion figures. Many British designers of international stature have their flagship stores in the capital, including the popular **Paul Smith** and **Stella McCartney**, both of whom showcase their collections in fabulous townhouses. **Matthew Williamson** and the late **Alexander McQueen** also have standalone stores. Young homegrown talent such as Alice Temperley, whose feminine frocks are beloved of the London party set, Eley Kishimoto, characterized by bold prints, and avant-garde design duo Boudicca, can be found in most of the capital's boutiques.

Selfridges (see p313) also has an impressive selection of emerging designers. **Dover Street Market**, conceived by Comme des Garçons' Rei Kawakubo, revives the age-old London tradition of the covered clothes market, but in a much more upscale setting. Its four minimalist floors showcase a varied array of goods, from glitzy shoes by king of the platform Terry de Havilland to cool art books and vintage and contemporary designer clothes.

If you want to take home a bit of British design, but can't afford the high prices, it's worth visiting **Debenhams**, which has harnessed the talents of numerous leading designers, including Jasper Conran, Julien Macdonald, and Ben De Lisi, to create cheaper collections exclusive to the store. Young

designers often start out with a stand on Portobello Road or Old Spitalfields Market (see p333), both good sources of interesting clothing. There are also a few good designer sale shops: **Paul Smith Sale Shop** is located in central London. Those shoppers looking for **Burberry** bargains at its factory outlet will have to travel a bit farther afield, to the East End.

Boutiques

London is home to an extensive variety of boutiques – hot new shops crop up and, it must be said, close down with dizzying regularity. The mother of them all is **Browns**. Established in the 1970s, it occupies several storefronts in South Molton Street and stocks a wide selection of international labels. But the highest concentration of boutiques is in Notting Hill, near the intersection of Westbourne Grove and Ledbury Road. Because of the numerous cafés in the area, and the relaxed, affluent atmosphere away from the crowded West End shopping districts, it's an extremely pleasant place to browse.

JW Beeton embodies quirky British style, while **Matches**, which also has outposts in Richmond and Wimbledon, dominates Ledbury Road with three separate shops – one for both sexes, another just for women, plus one specializing in dresses by Diane von Furstenberg. Like Browns in the West End, Matches stocks international designer labels, including Balenciaga, Prada, and Chloé, interspersed with a variety of British talent such as Temperley, Bella Freud, Matthew Williamson, and Georgina Goodman. **Question Air** and **Feathers** also stock designer labels, while **Aimé** specializes in French clothes and homewares. A short walk away in a quiet residential street, celebrity favorite **The Cross** is a delightfully understated little shop, packed with women's fashion, cute children's clothes and toys, toiletries, and varied displays of unusual accessories. **Cross The Road**,

located opposite, caters to chic interiors while **The Dispensary** in Kensington Park Road is much loved by locals for its Notting Hill style. Primrose Hill, Islington, Soho, and the streets radiating off Seven Dials near Covent Garden are also dotted with independent fashion shops. Some, such as **Labour of Love** in Islington, combine clothes with a careful selection of interior items, art books, and CDs. **Diverse**, also in Islington, caters to both sexes with a great selection of labels.

Chain Stores and Street Fashion

In Britain, designer looks are no longer, as they once were, the exclusive preserve of the rich. National fashion chains – or "high street" stores – have never been better, in terms of both quality and design. Moreover, the cheaper versions of all the latest styles appear in the shops almost as soon as they have been sashayed down the catwalk. **Oasis** and **Topshop** have both won celebrity fans for their up-to-the-minute, young womenswear. The latter, which proudly claims to be "the world's largest fashion store," is a mine of inexpensive clothes and beautiful accessories; there is even an in-store "boutique" with latest collections by hip designers, and a vintage section as well.

Vintage fashion (see p318) has become so popular, many national chains either sell it or feature collections that recreate the style.

The upscale chains **Jigsaw** and **Whistles** are more expensive, with the emphasis on beautiful fabrics and shapes that, while stylish, don't slavishly copy the catwalk. **Jigsaw Junior**, available in larger branches, offers delectable mini versions of its designs for little girls. **Reiss** and **Ted Baker** are more popular with trend-conscious young men, though they also have good women's collections. More streetwise shops can be found in and around Newburgh Street, behind Carnaby Street. **Cecil Gee** in Covent Garden is among the trail-blazers for men.

Vintage Fashion

The city offers a vast hunting ground for aficionados of vintage style, from market stands to the exclusive shops showcasing immaculately preserved designer-wear. Head east for funky emporia such as **Rokit**, which also has other branches in Camden and Covent Garden, in addition to the huge warehouse **Beyond Retro**. Grays Antique Market (see p332) covers all the bases with the award-winning Vintage Modes, spanning the styles of the past century as well as fashion-conscious Advintage, run by a former department store personal shopper. Glamorous evening gowns and pinup lingerie for the girls, flashy Hawaiian shirts and novelty bar accessories for the guys, can be found at Sparkle Moore's gloriously kitsch string of stands, **The Girl Can't Help It** in Alfies Antique Market, which also houses excellent vintage shop **Persiflage**.

For mint-condition 1930s bias-cut silk slips and 1920s flapper dresses, head to **Annie's Vintage Clothes** in Camden Passage. Those looking for old designer gems should pay a visit to **Appleby** in West London, which is pretty much strong on the 1950s through 80s. Be warned, neither of these shops is cheap – they both charge quite handsomely.

Knitwear

From the sought-after Fair Isle sweaters to Aran knits, traditional British knitwear is famous. The best places for this are in Piccadilly, Regent Street, and Knightsbridge. Heritage label **Pringle** has been revitalized with more contemporary shapes and vivid colors. Luxurious, casual labels **Joseph** and **The White Company** feature modern chunky knits, while **John Smedley** concentrates on simpler designs in fine-gauge wool and sea island cotton. For cashmere, **N Peal**, which has both men's and women's shops at opposite ends

of the Burlington Arcade, has a great selection – including a fairly cheap, fashion-conscious line, npealworks. The popular chain **Brora** offers an affordable range of contemporary Scottish cashmere for the entire family. **Marilyn Moore** designs hip interpretations of classic knitwear.

Underwear and Lingerie

Marks & Spencer (see p313) is the most popular source of reasonably priced basics; it now has several fashionable lingerie lines as well. **Agent Provocateur**, owned by the famous designer Vivienne Westwood's son and his wife, oozes retro pinup glamour, from the slightly kinky pink uniforms worn by the staff to the nostalgically seductive bra sets. **Tallulah Lingerie** sells wispy negligées, handmade silk undergarments, and sumptuous bridal lingerie. For top-quality bra sets head to **Rigby and Peller**. This British institution holds a Royal Warrant of Appointment and has experts on hand to help you find the perfect lingerie for your shape.

Children's Clothes

You can get traditional hand-smocked dresses and romper suits from Liberty, **Young England**, and **Rachel Riley**, which stock smocks, gowns, and tweed coats. Burberry's New Bond Street store has a children's section showcasing adorable mini macs, kilts, and other items featuring the famous check. **Trotters** offers everything from shoes and clothes to haircuts, while **Their Nibs** sells eclectic designer children's clothing. The **Little White Company** makes soft, comfortable, and traditional clothes for boys and girls in pure cotton and wool. They also sell delightful bedding and sleepwear.

Shoes

Some of the most famous names in the footwear industry are based in Britain. If you have a few thousand pounds to spare, you can have a pair custom-made by the Royal Family's shoemaker, **John Lobb**. Ready-made

traditional brogues and Oxfords are the mainstay of **Church's Shoes**, while **Oliver Sweeney** gives classics a contemporary edge. For traditional, bench-made shoes at bargain prices, it's worth traveling farther afield to Battersea to splurge at the **Shipton & Heneage** outlet. It offers an exceptionally wide range of Oxfords, Derbys, loafers, and boots crafted in the same Northamptonshire factories as some of the most celebrated names, for considerably lower prices; the out-of-the-way location keeps costs down.

Fans of the Fab Four can step into their idols' shoes; **Anello & Davide** designed the original Beatle Boot and still sells custom-made shoes in a range of materials. **The British Boot Company** in funky Camden has the widest range of Dr. Martens, which were originally designed as hard-wearing work boots and appropriated by skinheads and punk rockers.

Jimmy Choo and **Manolo Blahnik** are two celebrated shoe designers, popular with some of most fashionable women worldwide. Their sophisticated high heels and cutting-edge designs are much sought after.

While **French Soles** produces stunning, quality ballet flats and pumps in numerous colors and materials, **Emma Hope** in Sloane Square is best known for simple, timeless shapes embellished with embroidery or beadwork. Less expensive yet good-quality designs can be found in **Hobbs** or **Pied à Terre**, while **Faith** and **Office** turn out young fashion-led styles; the latter also sells men's shoes.

If you are on the lookout for something that's a bit different, it's worth visiting London designer **Georgina Goodman's** shop in the picturesque Shepherd Market, where she showcases her unique ready-to-wear range.

The Natural Shoe Store, a Covent Garden institution of more than 30 years' standing, sells exactly what its name says – shoes crafted from natural products. Vegan shoes and Birkenstocks are among its top sellers.

DIRECTORY

Traditional Clothing

Burberry
21–23 New Bond St W1.
Map 12 F2.
Tel 020 7930 3343.

Cordings
19–20 Piccadilly W1.
Map 13 A3.
Tel 020 7734 0830.

Crombie
48 Conduit St W1.
Map 12 F2.
Tel 020 7434 2886.
One of two branches.

Daks
10 Old Bond St W1.
Map 12 F3.
Tel 020 7409 4000.

Dunhill
48 Jermyn St W1.
Map 12 F3.
Tel 0845 458 0779.

Gieves & Hawkes
1 Savile Row W1.
Map 12 E3.
Tel 020 7432 6403.

H Huntsman & Sons
11 Savile Row W1.
Map 12 F3.
Tel 020 7734 7441.

Hackett
87 Jermyn St SW1.
Map 13 A3.
Tel 020 7930 1300.
One of several branches.

Harvie & Hudson
77 Jermyn St SW1.
Map 12 F3.
Tel 020 7930 3949.
One of three branches.

Henry Poole & Co
15 Savile Row W1.
Map 12 F3.
Tel 020 7734 5985.

Jaeger
200–206 Regent St W1.
Map 12 F2.
Tel 020 7979 1100.

Laura Ashley
House of Fraser, 318
Oxford St W1.
Map 12 F1.
Tel 0844 800 3752.
One of several branches.

Liberty
Regent St W1.
Map 12 F2.
Tel 020 7734 1234.

Margaret Howell
34 Wigmore St W1.
Map 12 E1.
Tel 020 7009 9009.

Nicole Farhi
25 Conduit St W1.
Map 10 F2.
Tel 020 7499 8368.
One of several branches.

Ozwald Boateng
30 Savile Row &
9 Vigo St W1.
Map 12 F3.
Tel 020 7437 2030.

Pink
85 Jermyn St SW1.
Map 12 F3.
Tel 020 7930 6364.
One of several branches.

Richard James
29 Savile Row W1.
Map 12 F2.
Tel 020 7434 0605.

Turnbull & Asser
71–72 Jermyn St SW1.
Map 12 F3.
Tel 020 7808 3000.

Modern British Design and Street Fashion

Alexander McQueen
4–5 Old Bond St W1.
Map 12 F3.
Tel 020 7355 0088.

Browns Labels for Less
50 South Molton St W1.
Map 12 E2.
Tel 020 7514 0052.

Burberry Factory Shop
29–53 Chatham Place E9.
Tel 020 8985 3344.

Debenhams
334–348 Oxford St W1.
Map 12 E2.
Tel 08445 616 161.

Dover Street Market
17–18 Dover Street W1.
Map 12 F3.
Tel 020 7518 0680.

Fashion and Textile Museum
83 Bermondsey St SE1.
Map 15 C4.
Tel 020 7407 8664.

Matthew Williamson
28 Bruton St W1.
Map 12 E3.
Tel 020 7629 6200.

Paul Smith
Westbourne House 120 &
122 Kensington Park Rd
W11. **Map** 9 B2.
Tel 020 7727 3553.
One of several branches.

Paul Smith Sale Shop
23 Avery Row W1.
Map 12 E2.
Tel 020 7493 1287.

Stella McCartney
30 Bruton St W1.
Map 12 E3.
Tel 020 7518 3100.

Vivienne Westwood
44 Conduit St W1.
Map 12 F2.
Tel 020 7439 1109.

Boutiques

Aimé
32 Ledbury Rd W11.
Map 9 C2.
Tel 020 7221 7070.

Anna
126 Regent's Park Rd
NW1. **Tel** 020 7483 0411.

Browns
23–27 South Molton St
W1. **Map** 12 E2.
Tel 020 7514 0039.

The Cross
141 Portland Rd W11.
Map 9 A3.
Tel 020 7727 6760.

Diverse
286 & 294 Upper St,
Islington N1. **Map** 6 F1.
Tel 020 7359 8877.

Feather & Stitch
16 King St TW9.
Tel 020 8332 2717.

Feathers
176 Westbourne Grove
W11. **Map** 9 C2.
Tel 020 7243 8800.

JW Beeton
48–50 Ledbury Road W11.
Map 9 C2.
Tel 020 7229 8874.

Koh Samui
65–67 Monmouth St
WC2. **Map** 13 B2.
Tel 020 7240 4280.

Lamuète Boutique
37 Marshall St W1.
Map 12 F2.
Tel 020 7287 0221.

Matches
60–64, 83 & 85 Ledbury
Rd W11. **Map** 9 C2.
Tel 020 7221 0255.

Question Air
28 Rosslyn Hill NW3.
Map 1 C5.
Tel 020 7435 9921.

Chain Stores and Street Fashion

Cecil Gee
36 Long Acre WC2.
Map 13 B2.
Tel 020 7379 0061.

The Dispensary
200 Kensington Park Rd
W11. **Map** 9 B2.
Tel 020 7727 8797.

Hobbs
84–88 King's Rd SW3.
Map 19 C2.
Tel 020 7581 2914.
One of many branches.

Jigsaw
6 Duke of York Sq, Kings
Rd SW3. **Map** 19 C2.
Tel 020 7730 4404.
One of many branches.

Karen Millen
247 Regent St W1. **Map**
12 F1. **Tel** 020 7629 1901.
One of several branches.

Oasis
12–14 Argyll St W1.
Map 12 F2.
Tel 020 7434 1799.
One of several branches.

Reiss
Kent House, 14-17 Market
Place W1.
Map 12 F1.
Tel 020 7637 9112.
One of several branches.

DIRECTORY

Ted Baker
9–10 Floral St WC2.
Map 13 C2.
Tel 020 7836 7808.
One of several branches.

Topshop
Oxford Circus W1.
Map 12 F1.
Tel 0844 848 7487.
One of several branches.

Whistles
12–14 St. Christopher's Pl
W1. **Map** 12 D1.
Tel 020 7487 4484.
One of several branches.

Vintage Fashion

**Annie's Vintage
Clothes**
12 Camden Passage N1.
Map 6 F1.
Tel 020 7359 0796.

Appleby
95 Westbourne Park
Villas W2. **Map** 9 C1.
Tel 020 7229 7772.

Beyond Retro
110–112 Cheshire St E2.
Map 8 E4.
Tel 020 7613 3636.

The Girl Can't Help It
Alfies Antiques Market,
13–25 Church
Street NW8. **Map** 3 A5.
Tel 020 7724 8984.

Persiflage
Alfies Antiques Market,
13–25 Church
St NW8. **Map** 3 A5.
Tel 020 7724 7366.

Rokit
101 & 107 Brick
Lane E1. **Map** 8 E4.
Tel 020 7247 3777.
One of three branches.

Knitwear

Brora
81 Marylebone High St
W1. **Map** 4 D5.
Tel 020 7224 5040.
One of several branches.

John Smedley
24 Brook St W1.
Map 12 E2.
Tel 020 7495 2222.

Joseph
299 Fulham Rd SW10.
Map 18 F3.
Tel 020 7352 6776.
One of several branches.

Marilyn Moore
7 Elgin Crescent W11.
Map 9 B2.
Tel 020 7727 5577.

N Peal
Burlington Arcade,
Piccadilly, W1.
Map 12 F3.
Tel 020 7499 6485.

Pringle Scotland
112 New Bond St W1.
Map 12 E2.
Tel 020 7297 4580.

The White Company
Unit 5, Slingsby Pl,
St. Martin's Courtyard
WC2. **Map** 13 B2.
Tel 020 8166 0200.

Underwear and Lingerie

Agent Provocateur
6 Broadwick St W1.
Map 13 A2.
Tel 020 7439 0229.
One of several branches.

Myla
77 Lonsdale Rd W11.
Map 9 B2.
Tel 020 7221 9222.
One of several branches.

Rigby & Peller
22A Conduit St W1.
Map 12 F2.
Tel 020 7491 2200.

Tallulah Lingerie
65 Cross St, Islington N1.
Map 6 F1.
Tel 020 7704 0066.

Children's Clothes

Little White Company
90 Marylebone High St W1.
Map 4D5.
Tel 020 7486 7550.

Rachel Riley
82 Marylebone High St
W1. **Map** 4 D5.
Tel 020 7935 7007.

Their Nibs
46-47 Upper Berkeley
St W1. **Map** 11C1.
Tel 020 7101 0351.

Trotters
34 King's Rd SW3.
Map 19 C2.
Tel 020 7259 9620.

Young England
The Old Imperial Laundry,
71 Warrior Gardens SW11.
Tel 07960 698 269. By
appointment only.

Shoes

Anello & Davide
15 St. Alban's Grove,
Kensington W8.
Map 10 E5.
Tel 020 7938 2255.

**The British Boot
Company**
5 Kentish Town Rd NW1.
Map 4 F1.
Tel 020 7485 8505.

Church's Shoes
108–10 Jermyn St W1.
Map 12 F3.
Tel 020 7930 8210.

Emma Hope
53 Sloane Sq SW1.
Map 19 C2.
Tel 020 7259 9566.
One of three branches.

Faith
192–194 Oxford St W1.
Map 12 F1.
Tel 020 7580 9561.
One of several branches.

French Soles
6 Ellis St SW1.
Map 19 C2.
Tel 020 7730 3771.

Georgina Goodman
12–14 Shepherd St W1.
Map 12 E4.
Tel 020 7499 8599.

Gina
189 Sloane St SW1.
Map 19 C1.
Tel 020 7235 2932.

Hobbs
124 Long Acre WC2.
Map 13 B2.
Tel 020 7836 0625.
One of several branches.

Jimmy Choo
27 New Bond St W1.
Map 12 F2.
Tel 020 7493 5858.

John Lobb
88 Jermyn St SW1.
Map 12 F3.
Tel 020 7930 8089.

Kate Kuba
Unit 3, Cabot Pl,
Canary Wharf E14.
Tel 020 7715 5305.

Manolo Blahnik
49–51 Old Church St,
Kings Road SW3.
Map 19 A4.
Tel 020 7352 3863.

Office
57 Neal St WC2.
Map 13 B1.
Tel 020 7379 1896.
One of several branches.

Oliver Sweeney
5 Conduit St W1.
Map 12 F2.
Tel 020 7491 9126.

Pied à Terre
19 South Molton St W1.
Map 12 E2.
Tel 020 7629 1362.

Shelly's
12 The Broadway SW19.
Tel 020 8947 6162.
One of several branches.

Shipton & Heneage
117 Queenstown Rd SW8.
Map 20 E5.
Tel 020 7738 8484.

**The Natural Shoe
Store**
13 Neal St WC2
Map 13 B1.
Tel 020 7836 5254.

Specialty Shops

London may be famed for grand department stores such as Harrods, but there are many specialty shops that deserve a place on the visitor's itinerary. Some have expertise built up over a century or more, while others are new and fashionable or cater to the whims of eccentric collectors. Whether you are looking for traditional British products and food, high-tech gadgets, or the latest trends in music, London has a wide range of stores to suite everyone's tastes.

Food

Britain's reputation for terrible food is proving hard to shake off, but over the past decade, not only has the national cuisine improved immeasurably, but London has become one of the culinary capitals of the world. There is an unprecedented interest in local and organic produce, as well as delicacies imported from all over Europe. This is reflected in the growing number of food markets, the main one being Borough Market (see p331). Specialties that are well worth sampling include a variety of chocolates, cookies, preserves, cheeses, and teas (see pp290–91).

The food halls of Fortnum & Mason, Harrods, and Harvey Nichols (see p313) are good outlets for all of these, but it's also worth visiting the gastro-nomic gems dotted around town. Of these, **A Gold**, housed in an atmospheric old milliner's shop near Spitalfields Market, specializes in traditional foods from across Britain. Its wares, including cheeses, sausages, jams, baked goods, English wines, and mead, are advertised on chalkboards. **Paxton & Whitfield**, a delightful shop dating from 1797, stocks more than 300 cheeses, including baby Stiltons and Cheshire truckles, along with pork pies, cookies, oils, and preserves.

The shelves of tiny **Neal's Yard Dairy** groan with huge British farmhouse cheeses. **Paul Rothe & Son** is a family-run deli that has hardly changed since it opened more than a century ago. Besides selling "British and foreign provisions," such as preserves, old-fashioned candy, and cookies, the white-coated proprietors also serve morning toast and sandwiches on real china. For traditional English chocolates, such as violet or rose creams and after-dinner mints in beautiful gift boxes, head for **Charbonnel et Walker** in Royal Arcade off Old Bond Street. It has been in business for more than 100 years and holds Royal warrants. True chocoholics will be in their element at **The Chocolate Society's** shop/café, where only the finest pure chocolate is available. Also committed to "real" chocolate, **Rococo** is well-known for its unique blue-and-white Victorian-esque packaging.

Drinks

Tea, the most British of drinks, comes in all kinds of flavors. Fortnum & Mason's traditional teas come in appealingly refined gift selections. **The Tea House** is packed with myriad varieties from classic to creative (such as "summer pudding"), colorful tourist-oriented tins, and teapots. **Postcard Teas** is another specialty retailer of high-quality teas.

The quaint 19th-century **Algerian Coffee Stores** manages to pack more than 140 varieties of coffee and 200 teas into its small shop. Family business **HR Higgins** sells fine coffees and teas from around the world. There are many attractive gift boxes, and you can try before you buy in the coffee room downstairs.

For whiskey lovers, **The Vintage House** displays the widest array of single malts in England, including some very old bottles. **Berry Bros & Rudd** is one of the oldest wine merchants in the world, still trading in wines, fortified wines, and spirits from its ancient, paneled shop in St. James's. In contrast, **Vinopolis** (see p184), Bankside's "wine city," which charges admission, has a vast range of wines to choose from once you been on their interactive world wine tour and enjoyed five tastings. You can continue to imbibe in the restaurant or wine bar.

One-Offs

Sadly, many of London's quirky old specialty shops have closed, but there are still some fascinating anachronisms, as well as interesting newcomers, to be found across the city. A large number of specialty traders operate from stands in antique markets such as Alfies and Portobello Road (see p333), where you can find everything from old military medals to commemorative china and vintage luggage. A notable survivor is **James Smith & Sons**, the largest and oldest umbrella shop in Europe. It first opened for business in 1830. Behind its mahogany and glass-paneled facade lies an array of high-quality umbrellas and walking sticks, including the once-ubiquitous city gent brolly.

Halcyon Days specializes in little enameled copper boxes, the delightful products of a revived English 18th-century craft. Top-quality wooden chess sets and boards, including an ornamental design featuring Sherlock Holmes characters, are available at **Chess & Bridge Ltd**. **VV Rouleaux**, on the other hand, is festooned with every imaginable type of ribbon and flamboyant trimming.

For serious collectors of model-making kits and historic TV character dolls and toys, **Comet Miniatures** has the largest selection in London. **Honeyjam** sells traditional toys and games for all ages. Without a Gameboy in sight, **Benjamin Pollock's Toyshop** has a nifty line in miniature self-assembly paper theaters as well as other traditional toys and antique teddy bears. **Flower Space** specializes in 1960s and 1970s furniture and classic movie prints.

At **The Bead Shop** in Covent Garden you will find two floors stocked with everything from Swarovski crystals to semiprecious beads and sterling silver. The tasteful erotic boutique **Coco de Mer** banishes the seedy sex-shop cliché with its exquisite handmade lingerie and esthetically pleasing sex toys.

Fans of Doctor Who and all things science fiction will love **ScifiCollector** on the Strand. It stocks a huge range of Doctor Who, Red Dwarf, and other collectible toys and merchandise. There is also a section for first-day covers, stamp sheets, and signed items. Special events held at the store include appearances by science fiction authors, artists, and actors.

Books and Magazines

Bookshops are high among London's specialties. Charing Cross Road (see p110) is undoubtedly the focal point for those searching for new, antiquarian, and secondhand volumes. Although film buffs won't be able to browse in the shop that inspired the book and movie *84 Charing Cross Road*, they will be consoled by a commemorative plaque marking the site of the now-defunct Marks & Co., which bore the celebrated address.

On the strip there are plenty of other antiquarian booksellers, shelves groaning with dusty finds. **Francis Edwards** here has a good selection covering travel, natural history, naval and military history, and art and literature. Many shops offer a book-finding service if the title you want is no longer in print.

Charing Cross Road is famously the home of **Foyles**, once known for its massive but notoriously badly organized stock; it was given a facelift and is now much easier to navigate. Here, you'll find everything from the latest bestsellers to academic tomes.

London's largest women's interest bookshop, **Silver Moon**, is on the third floor; there's a jazz shop and a cool café (see below), plus an art gallery and real live piranhas in the children's department. As well as large branches of chains **Waterstone's** and **Blackwell**, many specialty bookshops are based here. A popular one is **Magma**, which is excellent for design subjects and avant-garde illustrated books.

Stanfords (see p114), which stocks maps and guides to cover the globe, is on Long Acre; more travel books can be found at the **Travel Bookshop** in Notting Hill. Nearby is **Books for Cooks**, complete with café and test kitchen.

The beautiful Edwardian **Daunt Books** in Marylebone has a soaring, galleried back room devoted entirely to travel titles and, unusually, related fiction organized by country. Graphic novels and American and European comics are the specialty at **Gosh!** and **Orbital Comics**, while fantasy and science fiction abound in **Forbidden Planet**. For gay writing, visit the pioneering **Gay's The Word**, near Russell Square. The best selection of books on movies is found at the **Cinema Store**.

London's oldest bookshop, **Hatchards** in Piccadilly, is also one of the best, offering a well-organized and extensive choice. **Grant & Cutler** is an unrivaled source of foreign books and videos, while **Watkins Books**, located alongside other antiquarian bookshops in Cecil Court, specializes in all manner of esoteric subjects.

Cecil Court (see p103) is a charming pedestrian alleyway lined with dealers specializing in everything from illustrated children's books to modern first editions. There are also shops selling old prints covering every theme – great for gifts – and especially theatrical memorabilia.

The French Bookshop in South Kensington is stocked full of best-selling French titles. If you are looking for newspapers and magazines from abroad, **Capital Newsagents** stocks, among others, American, Italian, French, Spanish, and Middle Eastern publications. **Gray's Inn News** is also worth a visit for European press. For those with an avid interest in vintage magazines, there are more than 200,000 in the basement of **Vintage Magazines** in Soho, dating from the early 1900s all the way through to the present day. There are also all manner of movie and popular-culture memorabilia and gifts on the ground floor of the shop.

CDs and Records

As one of the world's greatest centers of recorded music, London has a huge and excellent selection of record shops catering to fans of all musical styles. **Fopp** sells a wide range of music from pop to punk to peaceful easy listening, and their Covent Garden branch stocks a comprehensive range.

Small specialty shops tend to cater to the more esoteric tastes. **Rough Trade** was at the center of the emerging punk scene and still sniffs out interesting indie talent today, found in both East and West London. For jazz, check out **Ray's Jazz**, which is now housed in Foyle's bookshop along with a cool café where you can chill out to the vibe.

A shop that specializes in jazz, **Honest Jon's** (established in 1974) also offers various types of music in both vinyl and CD form. In particular, it carries an extensive selection of soul and reggae. **Haggie Vinyl** sells rare music and collectible records, from reggae to pop.

EGEA UK: Alternative Music Shop is based in North London, specializing in world, folk, and international jazz music. It carries mainly CDs, as well as books and DVDs.

There is a high concentration of indie vinyl and CD shops on and around Berwick Street. **Sister Ray** is the largest indie record store in the West End. For 12-inch singles, the medium of club and dance music, one of the top places to go is **BM Music**.

DIRECTORY

Foods

A Gold
42 Brushfield St E1.
Map 8 D5.
Tel 020 7247 2487.

Charbonnel et Walker
1 Royal Arcade, 28 Old
Bond St W1. Map 12 F3.
Tel 020 7318 2075.

The Chocolate Society
36 Elizabeth St SW1.
Map 20 E2.
Tel 020 7259 9222.

Neal's Yard Dairy
17 Short's Gardens WC2.
Map 13 B2.
Tel 020 7240 5700.

Paul Rothe & Son
35 Marylebone
Lane W1. Map 12 E1.
Tel 020 7935 6783.

Paxton & Whitfield
93 Jermyn St SW1.
Map 12 F3.
Tel 020 7930 0259.

Rococo
321 King's Rd SW3.
Map 19 A4.
Tel 020 7352 5857.

Drinks

Algerian Coffee Stores
52 Old Compton St W1.
Map 13 A2.
Tel 020 7437 2480.

Berry Bros & Rudd
3 St. James's St SW1.
Map 12 F4.
Tel 0207 396 9600.

HR Higgins
79 Duke St W1.
Map 12 D2.
Tel 020 7629 3913.

Postcard Teas
9 Dering St W1.
Map 12 E2.
Tel 020 7629 3654.

The Tea House
15A Neal St WC2.
Map 13 B2.
Tel 020 7240 7539.

Vinopolis
1 Bank End SE1.
Map 15 B3.
Tel 020 7940 8333.

The Vintage House
42 Old Compton St W1.
Map 13 A2.
Tel 020 7437 5112.

One-Offs

Benjamin Pollock's Toyshop
44 The Market, Covent
Garden Piazza WC2.
Map 13 C2.
Tel 020 7379 7866.

Chess & Bridge Ltd
44 Baker St W1.
Map 12 D1.
Tel 020 7486 7015.

Coco de Mer
23 Monmouth St WC2.
Map 13 B2.
Tel 020 7836 8882.

Comet Miniatures
44–48 Lavender Hill SW11.
Tel 020 7228 3702.

Flower Space
301 Portobello Rd W10.
Map 9 A1.
Tel 020 8968 9966.

Halcyon Days
14 Brook St W1.
Map 12 E2.
Tel 020 7629 8811.

Honeyjam
267 Portobello Rd W11.
Map 9 A1.
Tel 020 7243 0449.

James Smith & Son
53 New Oxford St W1.
Map 13 B1.
Tel 020 7836 4731.

SciFiCollector
79 Strand WC2.
Map 13 C3.
Tel 020 7836 2341.

The Bead Shop
21a Tower St WC2.
Map 13 B2.
Tel 020 7240 0931.

VV Rouleaux
102 Marylebone Lane W1.
Map 4 D5.
Tel 020 7224 5179.

Books and Magazines

Blackwell
100 Charing Cross Rd
WC2. Map 13 B2.
Tel 020 7292 5100.

Books for Cooks
4 Blenheim Crescent W11.
Map 9 B2.
Tel 020 7221 1992.

Capital Newsagents
48 Old Compton St W1.
Map 13 A2.
Tel 020 7437 2479.

Cinema Store
Unit 4B, Upper St. Martin's
Lane WC1. Map 13 B2.
Tel 020 7379 7838.

Daunt Books
83–84 Marylebone High
St W1. Map 4 D5.
Tel 020 7224 2295.

Forbidden Planet
179 Shaftesbury Ave W1.
Map 13 A2.
Tel 020 7420 3666.

Foyles
113–119 Charing Cross
Rd WC2. Map 13 B1.
Tel 020 7437 5660.

Francis Edwards
72 Charing Cross Rd WC2.
Map 13 B1.
Tel 020 7379 7669.

The French Bookshop
28 Bute St SW7.
Map 18 F2.
Tel 020 7584 2840.

Gay's The Word
66 Marchmont St WC1.
Map 5 B4.
Tel 020 7278 7654.

Gosh!
1 Berwick St W1.
Map 13 B1.
Tel 020 7636 1011.

Gray's Inn News
50 Theobalds Rd WC1
Map 6 D5.
Tel 020 7405 5241.

Hatchards
187 Piccadilly W1.
Map 12 F3.
Tel 020 7439 9921.

Magma
8 Earlham St WC2.
Map 13 B2.
Tel 020 7240 8498.

Orbital Comics
8 Great Newport St WC2.
Map 13 B2.
Tel 020 7240 0591.

Stanfords
12–14 Long Acre WC2.
Map 13 B2.
Tel 020 7836 1321.

Waterstone's
421 Oxford St W1.
Map 11 D2.
Tel 020 7495 8507.

Watkins Books
19–21 Cecil Court WC2.
Map 13 B2.
Tel 020 7229 5260.

Vintage Magazines
39–43 Brewer St W1.
Map 13 A2.
Tel 020 7836 2182.

CDs and Records

BM Music
25 D'Arblay St W1.
Map 13 A2.
Tel 020 7437 0478.

EGA UK: Alternative Music Shop
267 Archway Rd N6.
Tel 020 8347 5555.

Fopp
1 Earlham St WC2.
Map 13 B2.
Tel 020 7379 0883.

Haggie Vinyl
114 Essex Rd N1.
Map 6 F1.
Tel 020 7704 3101.

Honest Jon's
278 Portobello Rd W10.
Map 9 B2.
Tel 020 8969 9822.

Ray's Jazz
(See Foyles).
Tel 020 7437 5660.

Rough Trade West
130 Talbot Rd W11.
Map 9 C1.
Tel 020 7229 8541.

Rough Trade East
91 Brick Lane E1.
Map 8 E5.
Tel 020 7392 7788.

Sister Ray
34–5 Berwick St W1.
Map 13 A1.
Tel 020 7734 3297.

Gifts and Souvenirs

London is a wonderful place to shop for gifts. It presents an impressive array of original ceramics, jewelry, perfume, and glassware, and exotic merchandise from around the world, including jewelry from India and Africa, stationery from Europe, and kitchenware from France and Italy. The elegant, Regency-period Burlington Arcade (see p93), the largest of several covered shopping arcades in the area, is popular for its high-quality clothes, antique and new jewelry, leather goods, and other items, many of which are made in the UK. It is also a real boon when the famously unpredictable weather turns nasty.

The shops at big museums, such as the Victoria and Albert (see pp212–15), the Natural History Museum (see pp204–5), and the Science Museum (see pp208–9) often have unusual items to take home as mementoes, while Contemporary Applied Arts and the market in Covent Garden Piazza (see p116) sell a range of British pottery, knitwear, pictures, clothing, and other crafts. To buy all your gifts under one roof, go to Liberty (see p111), where beautiful stock from the world over fills every department, and the classic Liberty print features on many goods.

Gift Shops

If the phrase "gift shop" conjures up images of tacky tourist souvenirs, think again. A number of interesting shops bringing together a variety of present-friendly goods under one roof have sprung up in the capital. Just off Brick Lane, one-room **Shelf** showcases stationery, prints, ceramics, and other objects by local and European artists and designers. It's only open Thursday to Sunday; call for hours before making a special trip. There are several other quirky, small shops in this street good for gift-hunting, including **Labour & Wait**.

A short walk away, **Story**, in a beautifully preserved 18th-century residential street, looks more like a gallery space than a shop. The fascinating mix of wares unites vintage dresses, organic bath products, and modern and classic furnishings.

Across town in Notting Hill, **Coco Ribbon** is a girly emporium, decked out with antique armoires and chandeliers, selling everything from 1950s-influenced embroidered cushions and scented candles to prettily packaged toiletries, hand-made lingerie, and Australian designer fashion.

The **Design Museum Shop** is a museum gift shop with a difference. It displays postmodern toys, games, and innovative – and in some cases surprisingly affordable – accessories for home and office by big design names such as Arne Jacobsen, Tord Boontje and Eames. There are some wonderfully witty items, such as shoe-shaped shoe brushes and a doorstop in the form of a figure holding it open. Boutiques **Saloon** and **Labour of Love** (see p319) also sell an eclectic range of items.

Jewelry

There are styles to suit every taste, from the fine traditional jewelry found in the exclusive shops of Bond Street to unusual pieces by independent designers in areas like Covent Garden (see pp112–21), Gabriel's Wharf (see p193), and Camden Lock (see p331). Antique jewelry can be found in Hatton Garden and the Silver Vaults (see p143). The Crown Jeweler, **Garrard** in Albemarle Street, has been brought up-to-date under creative director Jade Jagger. Be warned, the spectacular creations have price tags to match. Its former business partner **Asprey** sells updated classics, while **Butler & Wilson** specializes in reproductions of vintage jewelry and accessories. **Nude Jewellery London**, tucked away in Mayfair's Shepherd Market, deals mainly in handmade pieces, and **Kabiri**, with stores in Covent Garden and Marylebone and a stand in Selfridges, aims to bring works of previously unseen jewelry designers to London. Popular London design house **Erickson Beamon**, which is also sold in Harrods (see p313), typically features dramatic chokers and earrings dripping with beads. The husband and wife duo **Wright & Teague** design covetable modern silver and gold charm bracelets and necklaces, among other things.

The **Victoria & Albert shop** sells modern replicas of ancient British designs, as does the shop at the British Museum (see pp128–9). The **Lesley Craze Gallery**, which also deals in other handmade accessories and crafts, sells jewelry by designers from around the globe. Liberty (see p111) stocks a wide range of attractive jewelry as well.

Hats

Traditional men's headgear, from flat caps to trilbies and toppers, can be found at **Edward Bates**. Venerable hatter **Lock & Co**, established in 1672, caters to both men and women, while Swaine Adeney Brigg sells hats for both sexes by well-known name **Herbert Johnson**.

Philip Treacy is Britain's most celebrated milliner, and his fabulous creations are on display at his shop on Elizabeth Street and in upmarket department stores. Established name **Stephen Jones** also has some very eye-catching looks, while **Rachel Skinner's** beautifully made, slightly nostalgic designs range from cute cloches to extravagant Ascot confections, which are less expensive than more famous names. **Fred Bare's** funky, affordable designs can be bought from the shop on Columbia Road on Sundays when the weekly flower market is in bloom, or from high-end department stores.

Bags and Leather Goods

Traditional British luggage, bags, and small leather goods can be found in the streets and arcades off Piccadilly. **Swaine Adeney Brigg** sells umbrellas, hats, classic bridle-leather bags, old-fashioned walking sticks, and other accoutrements for the country gent and lady. Well known for its classic, hard-wearing bags and luggage is upmarket **Mulberry**. Established in 1971, its modern interpretations of English country clothes and accessories are sought after by fashion folk as well as anyone who appreciates fine quality.

The ultimate luxury is **Connolly**, a name famous for crafting sleek leather interiors for Rolls-Royce. Its two swanky shops sell items that hark back to the golden age of motoring, such as leather driving jackets and shoes, magnificent tool cases and stylish luggage, bound diaries, and other extravagant home accessories and clothes.

J&M Davidson, owned by an Anglo-French couple, produces beautifully crafted, slightly retro bags, belts, and small leather goods, often in unusual colors or skins. The shop in Notting Hill also stocks a line of clothes and interior items. In Piccadilly, **Bill Amberg's** shop sells simple, contemporary bags in various types of leather, suede, and other skins, plus gloves, wallets, leather boxes, and unusual items such as a stylish leather and sheepskin baby "papoose."

Lulu Guinness and **Anya Hindmarch** both bring British wit and eccentricity to their handbags. Guinness's elaborate designs include a bag in the shape of a flowerpot topped with red roses and a circular purse resembling an old-fashioned rotary telephone dial, and there are also many London-themed items.

Hindmarch is famous for personalized, digitally printed photo bags, but also produces classic leather ones. For less expensive but still high-quality unique bags, try **Radley**.

Scarves

The luxury French designer store **Hermès** sells beautiful silk and cashmere scarves, often using vibrant colors. Of course, Liberty's famous print scarves are perennially popular. Small, stylish **Fenwick** is also known for its accessories department, which includes a wide array of interesting scarves by the likes of Pucci and Missoni, as well as bags, hats, and a huge range of hair decorations. The **V&A Museum** shop has a good selection of scarves, including William Morris print silk scarves and stunning replica scarves inspired by V&A collections. N Peal (see p320) has an extensive choice of cashmere scarves and shawls.

Perfumes and Toiletries

Many British perfumeries use recipes that are hundreds of years old. **Floris** and **Penhaligon's**, for example, still manufacture the same flower-based scents and toiletries for men and women that they sold in the 19th century. The same goes for men's specialists **Truefitt & Hill** and **George F Trumper**, where you can buy some wonderful reproductions of antique shaving equipment as well. Perfumer **DR Harris** has been making its own range of toiletries for over two centuries; it's worth stopping in just to look around the old-fashioned shop.

Neal's Yard Remedies employs traditional herbal and floral remedies as bases for its natural, therapeutic products. Former facialist **Jo Malone** uses such delicious aromas as herbs, fruit, even coffee, as well as traditional floral essences in her fragrances, skincare, and candles, which come in simple yet sophisticated packaging. If you're looking for an unusual

scent, head for **Miller Harris**; young Grasse-trained perfumer Lyn Harris creates fragrances with remarkable depth, which come in boxes decorated with botanical prints. **Scent Systems** is a contender for the smallest shop in the capital, but its fragrances are worn by some of London's biggest names. The tiny shop near Carnaby Street brings together an exclusive selection of marvelously packaged perfumes from Europe and the US, including Mandy Aftel's Pink Lotus, which was specially commissioned for Madonna.

Space NK stocks the best and the most up-to-date collection of beauty products from around the world, along with its popular own-brand range. **The Body Shop** uses recyclable plastic packaging for its affordable natural cosmetics and toiletries, and encourages staff and customers alike to take an interest in environmental issues. **Molton Brown** sells a range of natural cosmetics and body- and hair-care products in branches throughout London. **Kiehl's** American luxury toiletries and skincare brand has its own store in Covent Garden.

Stationery

For luxurious writing paper and desk accessories, try the Queen's stationer, **Smythson** of Bond Street. The little bound notebooks and address books, embossed with a wide selection of amusing and practical titles, such as "Travel Notes" and "Blondes, Brunettes, Redheads" make great gifts and souvenirs. Fortnum and Mason (see p313) has handsome leather-bound diaries, blotters, and pencil holders, while Liberty (see p111) embellishes desk accessories with its famous Art Nouveau prints. For personal organizers covered in anything from vinyl to iguana skin, try **The Filofax Centre**. **Asprey** also has a chic line of pocket diaries, organizers, key fobs, and jewelry boxes in a variety of eye-catching skins.

Aspinal of London, known for its fine leather goods, such as handcrafted wallets and purses, produces leather-bound high-end stationery. Beautiful photo albums, diaries, iPad and iPhone cases and sleeves, pencil cases, and even leather-encased tape measures are sold out of their Marylebone store alongside all manner of other leather and non-leather gift ideas, such as silk and cashmere scarves.

Shepherd's Bookbinders stocks a range of handmade and decorative papers. Its marbled paper can make a glorious giftwrap for a very special present. Finally, for greeting cards, pens, gift wrapping paper, and general stationery, pop into one of the branches of **Paperchase**.

Interiors

Wedgwood still makes the famous pale blue Jasper china that Josiah Wedgwood designed in the 18th century. You can buy this and the Irish Waterford crystal at **Waterford Wedgwood** on Piccadilly. For a fine variety of original pottery, visit **Contemporary Ceramics**, the gallery of the Craft Potters Association, or go to **Contemporary Applied Arts**. **Mint's** hand-picked selection of unique furniture, home accessories, china, and glassware by established names and up-and-coming design talent is a pleasure to browse. Large interiors stores **Heal's** and the

Conran Shop have a great display of stylish, modern accessories for the home. Those with more traditional tastes may prefer **Thomas Goode**, presided over by courteous tail-coated staff, which sells exquisite china, glassware, crystal, linen, and gifts, including some antique pieces. The **Nicole Farhi Home** line exudes the same laid-back luxury as her clothes. If you're on a tighter budget, check out **Graham & Green**, which stocks a huge array of attractive items from around the globe, ranging from Moroccan tea glasses to Mongolian cushions and pretty nightwear.

Labour & Wait is a wonderful source of solid, functional British

---

DIRECTORY

Gift Shops

Coco Ribbon
21 Kensington Park Rd W11. **Map** 9 B2.
Tel 020 7229 4904.

Design Museum Shop
Shad Thames SE1.
Map 16 E4.
Tel 020 7940 8787.

Labour & Wait
85 Rechurch St E2.
Map 8 E4.
Tel 020 7729 6253.

Shelf
40 Cheshire St E2.
Map 8 E4.
Tel 020 7739 9444.

Story
4 Wilkes St E1. **Map** 8 E5.
Tel 020 7377 0313.

Jewelry

Asprey
167 New Bond St W1.
Map 12 F3.
Tel 020 7493 6767.

Butler & Wilson
20 South Molton St W1.
Map 12 E2.
Tel 020 7409 2955.

Erickson Beamon
38 Elizabeth St SW1.
Map 20 E2.
Tel 020 7259 0202.

Garrard
24 Albemarle St W1.
Map 12 F3.
Tel 0870 871 8888.

Kabiri
37 Marylebone High St W1. **Map** 4 D5.
Tel 020 7317 2150.

Lesley Craze Gallery
33–35a Clerkenwell Green EC1. **Map** 6 E4.
Tel 020 7608 0393.

Nude Jewellery
36 Shepherd Market, Mayfair W1. **Map** 12 E4.
Tel 020 7629 8999.

Wright & Teague
35 Dover St W1.
Map 12 F3.
Tel 020 7629 2777.

Hats

Edward Bates
73 Jermyn St SW1.
Map 13 A3.
Tel 020 7734 2722.

Fred Bare
118 Columbia Rd E2.
Map 8 E3.
Tel 020 7229 6962.

Herbert Johnson
54 St. James's Street SW1.
Map 12 F3.
Tel 020 7409 7277.

Lock & Co
6 St. James's St SW1.
Map 12 F4.
Tel 020 7930 8874.

Philip Treacy
69 Elizabeth Street SW1.
Map 20 E2.
Tel 020 7730 3992.

Rachel Skinner
13 Princess Rd NW1.
Map 4 D1.
Tel 020 7209 0066.

Stephen Jones
36 Great Queen St WC2.
Map 13 C1.
Tel 020 7242 0770.

Bags and Leather Goods

Anya Hindmarch
15–17 Pont St SW1.
Map 20 D1.
Tel 020 7838 9177.

Bill Amberg
9 Shepherd Market W1.
Map 12 E4.
Tel 020 7499 0962.

Connolly
41 Conduit St W1.
Map 12 F2.
Tel 020 7439 2510.

J&M Davidson
97 Goldborne Rd W10.
Tel 020 8969 2244.

Lulu Guinness
3 Ellis St SW1.
Map 19 C2.
Tel 020 7823 4828.

Mulberry
50 New Bond St W1. **Map** 12 E2.
Tel 020 7491 3900.

Radley
37 Floral St WC2.
Map 13 B2.
Tel 020 7379 9709.

Swaine Adeney Brigg
7 Piccadilly Arcade (at St James) SW1. **Map** 12 F3.
Tel 020 7409 7277.

Scarves

Fenwick
63 New Bond St W1.
Map 12 E2.
Tel 020 7629 9161.

Hermès
179 Sloane St SW1.
Map 11 C3.
Tel 020 7823 1014.
One of several branches.

V&A Enterprises
V&A Museum, Cromwell Rd SW7. **Map** 19 A1.
Tel 020 7942 2696.

Perfumes and Toiletries

The Body Shop
64, 360 & 374, Oxford St W1. **Map** 12 D2–F1.
Tel 020 7631 0027.

DR Harris
52 Piccadilly W1.
Map 12 F3.
Tel 020 7930 3915.

Floris
89 Jermyn St SW1.
Map 13 A3.
Tel 020 7930 2885.

items for home and garden, such as old-fashioned stainless steel kettles, Welsh blankets, and Guernsey sweaters. **David Mellor** is famous for his streamlined modern cutlery designs, while **Divertimenti** sells all manner of kitchen equipment and has a pleasant cafe at the back.

Bridgewater Pottery has chunky mugs, crockery, and tea towels, which are decorated with traditional motifs and amusing mottoes. **The Cloth Shop** in Notting Hill stocks beautiful new and antique British wool and cashmere blankets and throws, as well as cottons, velvets, and soft

furnishings. **Cath Kidston** designs fresh, nostalgic, English-style prints that adorn everything from humble household items to fashion accessories. There's a huge range of pretty, giftable goods such as toiletries, ironing-board covers, laundry bags, eiderdowns, clothes for women and children, bags, china, and stationery.

Several interiors stores on Upper Street in the affluent Islington offer an impressive cache of gifts. **After Noah** is a big warehouse-like space bursting with vintage and retro-look items that also include Bakelite rotary telephones,

nostalgic toiletries, old metal tins and street signs, classic board games, and a huge assortment of children's toys. There is another branch in King's Road and a stand in Harvey Nichols *(see p313)*.

The modern interiors emporium **Aria** has two stores in the same vicinity. One of these concentrates entirely on furniture and housewares by designers such as Alessi and Philippe Starck, while its satellite across the street sells gifts, including stationery, frames, bags, and jewelry. Also on the same stretch is the contemporary-design heavyweight **twentytwentyone**.

DIRECTORY

George F Trumper
9 Curzon St W1.
Map 12 E3.
Tel 020 7499 1850.

Jo Malone
23 Brook St W1.
Map 12 E2.
Tel 0870 192 5181.

Kiehl's
29 Monmouth St WC2.
Map 13 B1.
Tel 020 7240 2411.

Molton Brown
58 South Molton St W1.
Map 12 E2.
Tel 020 7493 7319.

Miller Harris
21 Bruton St W1.
Map 12 E3.
Tel 020 7629 7750.

Neal's Yard Remedies
15 Neal's Yard WC2.
Map 13 B1.
Tel 020 7379 7222.

Penhaligon's
13 Market Building,
Covent Garden Piazza
WC2. **Map** 13 C2.
Tel 020 3040 3030.

Scent Systems Studio
13 Rugby St WC1.
Map 6 D5.
Tel 020 7404 7070.

Space NK
131 Westbourne Grove
W2. **Map** 9 C2.
Tel 020 7727 8063.

Truefitt & Hill
71 St. James's St SW1.
Map 12 F3.
Tel 020 7493 2961.

Stationery

Aspinal of London
46 Marylebone High St W1.
Map 4 D5.
Tel 020 7224 0413.

Asprey
167 New Bond St W1.
Map 12 F3.
Tel 020 7493 6767.

The Filofax Centre
21 Conduit St W1.
Map 12 F2.
Tel 020 7499 0457.

Paperchase
213 Tottenham Court Rd
W1. **Map** 5 A5.
Tel 020 7467 6200.

**Shepherd's
Bookbinders**
30 Gillingham Street SW1.
Map 20 F2.
Tel 020 7233 9999.

Smythson
40 New Bond St W1.
Map 12 E2.
Tel 020 7629 8558.

Interiors

After Noah
121 Upper Street N1.
Map 6 F1.
Tel 020 7359 4281.

Aria
Barnsbury Hall, Barnsbury
St N1. **Map** 6 F1.
Tel 020 7704 6222.

Cath Kidston
51 Marylebone High St W1.
Map 4 D5.
Tel 020 7935 6555.

The Cloth Shop
290 Portobello Rd W10.
Map 9 A1.
Tel 020 8968 6001.

Conran Shop
Michelin House, 81
Fulham Rd SW3.
Map 19 A2.
Tel 020 7589 7401.

**Contemporary
Applied Arts**
89 Southwark St SE1.
Map 14 E3.
Tel 020 7436 2344.

**Contemporary
Ceramics**
63 Great Russell St WC1.
Map 13 B1.
Tel 020 7845 4600.

David Mellor
4 Sloane Sq SW1.
Map 20 D2.
Tel 020 7730 4259.

Divertimenti
33–34 Marylebone High
St W1. **Map** 4 D5.
Tel 020 7935 0689.

Emma Bridgewater
81a Marylebone High St.
Map 4 D5. **Tel** 020 7486
6897. Also: 739 Fulham
Road. **Map** 17 C5.
Tel 020 7371 5264.

Graham & Green
4 Elgin Crescent W11.
Map 9 B2.
Tel 020 7243 8908.

Heal's
196 Tottenham Court Rd
W1. **Map** 5 A5.
Tel 020 7636 1666.

Mint
2 North Terrace SW3. **Map**
19 A1. **Tel** 020 7225 2228.

Nicole Farhi Home
115 Fulham Rd SW3.
Tel 020 7838 0937.

Thomas Goode
19 South Audley St W1.
Map 12 D3.
Tel 020 7499 2823.

twentytwentyone
274 Upper St N1. **Map** 6
F1. **Tel** 020 7288 1996.

**Waterford
Wedgwood**
Sold at John Lewis, 300
Oxford St. **Map** 12 E1.
Tel 0844 693 1765.

Art and Antiques

London's art and antique shops are spread across the length and breadth of the capital city. While the more fashionable and more expensive dealers are mainly concentrated in a relatively small area bounded by Mayfair and St. James's, other shops and galleries catering to a relatively modest budget are scattered over the rest of the city. Whether your taste is for Old Masters or young modern artists, Boule or Bauhaus, you are bound to find something of beauty in London that is within your financial means.

Mayfair

Cork Street is the center of the British contemporary art world. The huge lineup of galleries offers work in varying degrees of the avant-garde. The biggest name to look for is **Waddington Custot Galleries**; if you want to discover the flavor of the month, a stop here is a must. However, purchasing is only for the serious and rich collector. The **Mayor Gallery**, famous for Dada and Surrealism, was the first gallery to open in the street. **Redfern Gallery** shows mainstream modern art, while **Flowers Central**, part of a growing modern gallery chain, has some unusual British pieces. A couple of doors down, **Browse and Darby Gallery** sells 19th- and 20th-century British and French paintings as well as contemporary works.

Also look into Clifford Street, where **Maas Gallery** excels in Victorian masters, and Sackville Street for **Henry Sotheran's** rare books and prints. On Albemarle Street, the **Albemarle Gallery** specializes in contemporary prints and sculptures, showcasing the works of international and British artists. Established and up-and-coming talents are featured in the gallery's frequent, stunning installations.

Nearby, New Bond Street is the center of the fine antiques trade in London. If it's Turner watercolors or Louis XV furniture you're after, this is the place. A walk up from Piccadilly takes you past the lush portals of **Richard Green** (which also has a gallery in Dover Street) and the **Fine Art Society**, among other extremely smart galleries. For jewelry and objets d'art visit **David Aaron Ancient Art** and **Grays Antique Market**; for silver go to **S J Phillips**; and for 18th-century British furniture and art, try **Mallett Antiques**.

Even if you are not a buyer, these galleries are fascinating places to visit, so don't be afraid to walk in – you can learn more from an hour spent here than you can from weeks of studying textbooks. Also on New Bond Street are two of the big London auction houses, Bonhams and Sotheby's.

St. James's

South of Piccadilly lies a maze of 18th-century streets. This is gentlemen's club country (see Pall Mall p94) and the galleries mostly reflect the traditional nature of the area. The center is Duke Street, home of Old Master dealers **Johnny van Haeften** and **Derek Johns**. Nearby, on King Street, you will find the main sale rooms of **Christie's**, the well-known auction house where Van Goghs and Picassos change hands for millions. On the corner of Bury Street, celebrating past masculine pleasures, is the sophisticated **Pullman Gallery**, which specializes in automobile art and collectibles, vintage cocktail shakers, racy cigarette cases, and other bar accessories.

Walk back up Bury Street past several interesting galleries, including the **Tryon Gallery** for traditional British sporting pictures and fine sculptures. Also duck into Ryder Street to take in **Chris Beetle's** gallery of works by illustrators and caricaturists.

Knightsbridge

If you walk around to the back of **Harrods** (see p313), you'll find the beginning of pretty Walton Street, which is lined with art galleries, traditional interiors shops, and boutiques. As you would expect in this exclusive area, prices are high. On nearby Brompton Road the **Crane Kalman** gallery shows an enticing variety of contemporary art. Not far away is **Harvey Nichols** (see p313), Knightsbridge's other swanky department store. Motcomb Street houses some notable galleries, including the fascinating **Mathaf Gallery**, which features 19th-century British and European paintings of the Arab world.

Pimlico Road

The antique shops that line this road tend to cater predominantly to the pricy requirements of the interior decorator. This is where to come if you are searching for an Italian leather screen or a silver-encrusted ram's skull. Of particular fascination is **Westenholz**. While he doesn't deal in antiques, the Queen's nephew, furniture designer **Viscount Linley**, produces some beautiful pieces that could pass as such, as well as contemporary designs. The finely crafted accessories, such as inlaid wooden boxes and frames, make great gifts.

East and West

London's East End is a growth area for contemporary art. In addition to the famous **White Cube Gallery** in Hoxton Square and **Flowers East** in Kingsland Road, there is a cluster of art dealers and galleries in **The Tea Building** on nearby Shoreditch High Street. **The Approach** combines an upstairs gallery with a good pub, frequented by local artists.

On the other side of the river in southeast London, **Purdy Hicks**, based in a converted warehouse near Tate Modern, is great for contemporary British painting. Over in Mayfair, **Eyestorm** is a gallery that shows the work of both leading and emerging artists.

The **Oxo Tower Wharf**, in a landmark Thameside building topped by a good restaurant, is a hive of creativity, housing over 30 design and craft studios. You can find everything from hand-woven textiles and jewelry to homewares and fashion. Among the highlights are Black + Blum's innovative, affordable interior designs – for example, a lamp in the shape of a reading figure, made up of a lightbulb "holding" a book shade. Bodo Sperlain's delicate modern china and Studio Fusion's striking enamel pieces are also a draw for the visitors.

There are also some very interesting contemporary galleries in the vicinity of Portobello Road and Westbourne Grove. Some of the popular names include **East West Gallery** for contemporary art; **Themes & Variations**, which combines striking postwar and contemporary furniture and decorative art; and **Gallery 85**, stylishly refurbished and boasting a range of the finest antiques, including some exceptional Meissen porcelain.

A browse along Kensington Church Street in west London will reveal everything from Arts and Crafts furniture to Staffordshire dogs in a concen-tration of small antiques emporia.

North

High-profile American dealer Larry Gagosian has been at the forefront of the regen-eration of famously sleazy King's Cross by opening his second gallery here, in a capacious former garage. Expect world-class contemporary names as well as lesser-known artists at **Gagosian Gallery. Victoria Miro's** massive Victorian warehouse in Islington is a showcase for British as well as young international talent. At its two spaces in the same quiet Marylebone Street, the **Lisson Gallery** often features cutting-edge installations.

Thompson's Gallery has locations in Marylebone and the City, selling a diverse mix of appealing if somewhat mainstream current British art.

Affordable Art

For the chance to acquire a work by what could become one of the big names of the future, visit the **Contemporary Art Society**. Its annual ARTFutures market showcases the work of more than 100 artists; prices run from £100 into the thousands.

Open seven days a week year-round, **Will's Art Warehouse** in Putney sells pieces from £50 to £3,000. This friendly gallery offers a wide variety of art to choose from and holds a new exhibition every six weeks. The owner founded the aptly named Affordable Art Fair, which takes place twice a year in Battersea Park.

Photography

The largest collection of original photographs for sale in the country is to be found in the print sales room of the **Photographers' Gallery**. The gallery displays work from emerging global talent and established artists, as well as works from its historical archives over its three floors of exhibition space. There are also talks, events, workshops, and courses, as well as a bookshop and a café.

Atlas Gallery is one of the foremost galleries in London, dealing exclusively with fine art photography. It is also the official gallery for Magnum photographs. **Hamiltons Gallery** is worth visiting, especially during its major exhibitions.

Michael Hoppen's three-floor space in Chelsea shows both vintage and current works. If you want to take home a piece of London's rock 'n' roll heritage, the **Rock Archive**, near Camden Passage in Islington, is a great source of limited-edition prints of British music legends such as Paul Weller posing with Pete Townshend or Mick Jagger jamming with Ronnie Wood.

Bric-a-Brac and Collectibles

For smaller, more affordable pieces, it's worth going to one of the established London markets, such as Portobello Road, Camden Passage (see p332), or Bermondsey (see p331), which is the main antiques market, catering to the trade. Conveniently situated in the city's main shopping district, Grays Antique Markets (see p332) have some great specialty dealers, but the prices are a bit higher than elsewhere, given the location; farther afield, Greenwich Market (see p332) is well worth a rummage and may throw up some bargains. Many main streets outside of central London have covered markets of specialty stands.

Alfies Antique Market is London's largest indoor market for antiques and collectibles. The dealers are experienced specialists, and anyone interested in 20th-century design and vintage fashion especially will enjoy browsing among the eclectic mix on sale.

Auctions

If you are confident enough, auctions are a much cheaper way to buy art or antiques, but be sure to read the small print in the catalog, which usually costs around £15. Bidding is simple – you need to register, take a number, then raise your hand when the lot you want comes up. The auctioneer will see your bid. It's as easy as that, and can be great fun.

The main auction houses in London are **Christie's Fine Art Auctioneers**, **Sotheby's Auctioneers**, and **Bonhams**. Don't forget Christie's sale room in Kensington, and Sotheby's premises in Olympia, which both offer art and antiques for the modest budget. Bonhams' second London saleroom in Knightsbridge holds weekly auctions of affordable antiques and collectibles.

DIRECTORY

Mayfair

Albemarle Gallery
49 Albemarle St W1.
Map 12 F3.
Tel 020 7499 1616.

Browse and Darby Gallery
19 Cork St W1.
Map 12 F3.
Tel 020 7734 7984.

David Aaron Ancient Art
22 Berkeley Square W1.
Map 12 E3.
Tel 020 7491 9588.

Fine Art Society
148 New Bond St W1.
Map 12 E2.
Tel 020 7629 5116.

Flowers Central
21 Cork St W1. **Map** 12 F3.
Tel 020 7439 7766.

Grays Antique Markets
58 Davies St & 1-7 Davies Mews W1. **Map** 12 E2.
Tel 020 7629 7034.

Henry Sotheran
2 Sackville St W1.
Map 12 F3.
Tel 020 7439 6151.

Maas Gallery
15a Clifford St W1.
Map 12 F3.
Tel 020 7734 2302.

Mallett Antiques
141 New Bond St W1.
Map 12 E2.
Tel 020 7499 7411.

Mayor Gallery
22a Cork St W1.
Map 12 F3.
Tel 020 7734 3558.

Redfern Gallery
20 Cork St W1. **Map** 12 F3.
Tel 020 7734 1732.

Richard Green
33 & 147 New Bond St.
Also: 39 Dover St W1.
Map 12 E2.
Tel 020 7493 3939.

S J Phillips
139 New Bond St W1.
Map 12 E2.
Tel 020 7629 6261.

Waddington Custot Galleries
11, 12, 34 Cork St W1.
Map 12 F3.
Tel 020 7851 2200.

St. James's

Chris Beetle
8 & 10 Ryder St SW1.
Map 12 F3.
Tel 020 7839 7551.

Derek Johns
12 Duke St SW1.
Map 12 F3.
Tel 020 7839 7671.

Johnny van Haeften
13 Duke St SW1.
Map 12 F3.
Tel 020 7930 3062.

Pullman Gallery
14 King St SW1.
Map 12 F4.
Tel 020 7930 9595.

Tryon Gallery
7 Bury St SW1. **Map** 12 F3.
Tel 020 7839 8083.

Knightsbridge

Crane Kalman
178 Brompton Rd SW3.
Map 19 B1.
Tel 020 7584 7566.

Mathaf Gallery
24 Motcomb St SW1.
Map 12 D5.
Tel 020 7584 2396.

Pimlico Road

Linley
60 Pimlico Rd SW1. **Map** 20 D2. **Tel** 020 7730 7300.

Westenholz
80–82 Pimlico Rd SW1.
Map 20 D2.
Tel 020 7824 8090.

East and West

The Approach
1st Floor, 47 Approach Rd E2. **Tel** 020 8983 3878.

East West Gallery
8 Blenheim Cres W11.
Map 8 D4.
Tel 020 7229 7981.

Eyestorm
27 Hill St W1. **Map** 12 E3.
Tel 0845 643 2001.

Flowers East
82 Kingsland Rd E2.
Tel 020 7920 7777.

Gallery 85

85 Portobello Rd W11.
Map 9 A1.
Tel 020 7243 6365.

Oxo Tower Wharf
Bargehouse St SE1.
Map 14 E3.
Tel 020 7021 1600.

Purdy Hicks
65 Hopton St SE1. **Map** 14 F3. **Tel** 020 7401 9229.

The Tea Building
56 Shoreditch High St E1.
Map 8 D4.
Tel 020 7729 2973.

Themes & Variations
231 Westbourne Grove W11. **Map** 9 B2.
Tel 020 7727 5531.

White Cube Gallery
Hoxton Square N1.
Map 7 C3.
Tel 020 7930 5373.

North

Gagosian Gallery
6–24 Britannia St WC1.
Map 5 C3.
Tel 020 7841 9960.

Lisson Gallery
29 & 52-54 Bell St NW1.
Map 3 B5.
Tel 020 7724 2739.

Thompson's Gallery
15 New Cavendish St W1.
Map 4 E5.
Tel 020 7935 3595.

Victoria Miro
16 Wharf Rd N1.
Map 7 A2.
Tel 020 7336 8109.

Affordable Art

Contemporary Art Society
59 Central Street EC1.
Map 7 A3.
Tel 020 7017 8400

Will's Art Warehouse
180 Lower Richmond Rd SW15. **Tel** 020 8246 4840.

Photography

Atlas Gallery
49 Dorset St W1.
Map 3 C5.
Tel 020 7224 4192.

Hamiltons Gallery
13 Carlos Place London W1. **Map** 12 E3.
Tel 020 7499 9493.

Michael Hoppen
3 Jubilee Place SW3.
Map 19 B3.
Tel 020 7352 3649.

Photographers' Gallery
16–18 Ramilies St W1.
Map 12 F1.
Tel 020 7087 9300.

Rock Archive
110 Islington High St N1.
Map 6 F2.
Tel 020 7267 4716.

Bric-a-Brac and Collectibles

Alfies Antique Market
13–25 Church St NW8.
Map 3 A5.
Tel 020 7723 6066.

Auctions

Bonhams, W & FC, Auctioneers
Montpelier St SW7.
Map 11 B5.
Tel 020 7393 3900. Also: 101 New Bond St W1.
Map 12 E2.
Tel 020 7447 7447.

Christie's Fine Art Auctioneers
8 King St SW1.
Map 12 F4.
Tel 020 7839 9060. Also: 85 Old Brompton Road SW7.
Map 18 F2.
Tel 020 7930 6074.

Sotheby's Auctioneers
34–35 New Bond St W1.
Map 12 E2.
Tel 020 7293 5000. Also: Hammersmith Rd W14.
Map 17 A1.
Tel 020 7293 5555.

Markets

Even if you're not looking for cut-price cabbages or a silk sari, it's worth paying a visit to one of London's crowded, colorful markets. Many mix English traditions with those of more recent immigrants, creating an exotic atmosphere and a fascinating patchwork quilt of merchandise. At some, the seasoned cockney hawkers have honed their sales patter to an entertaining art, which reaches fever pitch just before closing time as they advertise ever-plummeting prices. Keep your wits about you and your hand on your purse and join in the fun. For details, go to www.visitlondon.com.

Archway Market

Holloway Rd N19. ◉ *Archway.* 🚌 *4, 17, 41, 43, 143, 271.* **Open** *11am–7pm Thu, 10am–5pm Sat.*

This young and growing market is one of North London's best-kept secrets. Its specialty traders are committed to offering shoppers things that can't be bought anywhere else, including organic cheeses, breads and cakes, gourmet pickles and chutneys, farm-pressed juices, and much more. Tasty lunch options include Breton crêpes, spicy curries, and organic hot dogs. Several craft stands sell unusual objects and gifts.

Bermondsey Market (New Caledonian Market)

Long Lane and Bermondsey St SE1. **Map** *15 C5.* ◉ *London Bridge, Borough.* **Open** *4am–1pm Fri. Starts closing midday. See p184.*

Bermondsey is the gathering point for London's antique traders every Friday. Serious collectors start early and scrutinize the paintings, the silver, and the vast array of old jewelry. Browsers might uncover some interesting curiosities but most bargains go before 9am.

Berwick Street Market

Berwick St W1. **Map** *13 A1.* ◉ *Piccadilly Circus, Leicester Sq.* **Open** *9am–6pm Mon–Sat. See p110.*

The spirited costermongers of Soho's Berwick Street sell some of the cheapest and most attractive fruit and vegetables in the West End. Spanish black radishes, star fruit, and Italian plum tomatoes are among the produce you might find here, in addition to the various nuts and sweets. The market is good for fabrics and cheap household goods, too, as well as for leather handbags and delicatessen. Separated from Berwick Street by a seedy passageway is the quieter Rupert Street market, where vendors sell cheap street fashions.

Borough Market

Southwark St SE1. **Map** *14 F3.* ◉ *London Bridge.* **Open** *10am–3pm Mon–Wed, 11am–5pm Thu, noon–6pm Fri, 8am–5pm Sat. See p178.*

On one of London's most ancient trading sites, Borough has for many years been a wholesale market catering to the restaurant and hotel trade. Now open to the public from Thursday to Saturday, the award-winning market has a reputation as London's premier center for fine foods, selling a vast array of British and international foodstuffs. Among the cornucopia is organic meat, fish and produce, top-quality handmade cheeses, breads, sweets, chocolates, coffees and teas, and also soaps. It's a favorite foraging ground for the city's celebrity chefs.

Brick Lane Market

Brick Lane E1. **Map** *8 E5.* ◉ *Shoreditch, Liverpool St, Aldgate East.* **Open** *11am– 6pm Sat, 9am–5pm Sun. See pp172–73.*

This massively popular East End jamboree is at its best around its gloriously frayed edges. Pick through the mishmash of junk sold on Bethnal Green Road or head east on Cheshire Street, past the new outcrop of fashionable home-design and gift shops, to explore the indoor stands, packed with shabby furniture and old books. Much of the action takes place in cobbled Sclater Street and the lots on either side. Here you'll find everything from fresh shellfish and shoes to old power tools and new bicycles. Farther south on Brick Lane itself, the trendy boutiques and cafés give way to spice shops and curry restaurants in this center for London's Bangladeshi community.

Brixton Market

Electric Ave SW9. ◉ *Brixton.* **Open** *8am– 6pm Mon, Tue, Thu–Sat; 8am–3pm Wed.*

This market offers a wonderful assortment of Afro-Caribbean food, from goat meat, pigs' feet, and salt fish to plantains, yams, and breadfruit. There is an abundance of produce in the large Brixton Village and Market Row arcades, where exotic fish are a highlight. You'll also find Afro-style wigs, strange herbs and potions, traditional African ensembles and fabrics, and children's toys. From record stands, the bass of raw reggae pounds through this cosmopolitan market like a heartbeat.

Broadway Market

Broadway Market, between Andrews Rd & Westgate St E8. 🚌 *386.* **Open** *8am–6pm Sat.*

Although this market is a bit tricky to get to because it's not served by the tube, it's worth getting a bus from Islington or walking from Bethnal Green tube. One of London's oldest, Broadway Market had gone into decline until its rebirth as a popular organic farmers' market. On Saturdays, the historic street running between London Fields and the Regent's Canal comes alive with around 40 stands selling fruit and vegetables, cheeses, baked goods, meats, and confectionery. Also lining Broadway Market are some interesting, arty shops, catering to the young creative types who have been colonizing this part of Hackney over the past couple of decades. Black Truffle (No. 74), owned by shoemaker Melissa Needham, stocks a range of accessories made by independent designers – both local and international – while textile designer Barley Massey sells her own unusual designs and those of others at Fabrications (No. 7). L'Eau à la Bouche (No. 49) is a superior deli offering everthing from charcuterie to fruit tarts. There are also a couple of contemporary galleries such as Flaca (No. 69) and Seven Seven (No. 75–77). When it's time to refuel, duck into the Dove pub (No. 24–28) for a choice of Belgian beers.

Camden Lock Market

Chalk Farm Road NW1. ◉ *Camden Town.* **Open** *9:30am–6pm daily.*

Camden Lock Market has grown swiftly since its opening in 1974, spreading along Chalk Farm Road and Camden High Street. Crafts, new and secondhand street fashions, whole foods, books, records, and antiques form the bulk of the goods that a shopper can choose from. Its setting alongside the Regent's Canal is a bonus, too. Often, thousands of young people come here simply to enjoy the vibrant atmosphere, especially on weekends, when Camden Lock is abuzz with activity (see p248).

Camden Passage Market

Camden Passage N1. **Map** *6 F1.* 🚇 *Angel.* **Open** *9am–6pm Wed, Sat.*

Camden Passage is a quiet walkway where cafés nestle among petite antique shops. Prints, silverware, 19th-century magazines, jewelry, and toys are among the many collectibles for sale. Don't miss the tiny shops tucked away in the atmospherically poky Pierrepont Arcade; one is precariously stacked with 18th- and 19th-century porcelain; another specializes in antique puzzles and games. Jubilee Photographica deals in photographs from the 19th century onward. The passage is also lined with shops – Annie's Vintage Clothes is known for pristine 1920s–40s frocks, while Origin sells classic 20th-century furniture. There's a specialty book market on Thursdays.

Chapel Market

Chapel Market N1. **Map** *6 E2.* 🚇 *Angel.* **Open** *9am–6pm Tue–Sat, 8:30am–4pm Sun.*

This is one of London's most traditional and exuberant street markets. Weekends are best; the fruit and vegetables are varied and cheap, the fish is the finest in the area, and there are also stands selling European delicacies and cheeses and a wealth of bargain household goods.

Church Street Market

Church St NW8 and Bell St NW1. **Map** *3 A5.* 🚇 *Edgware Rd.* **Open** *8am–6pm Mon–Sat.*

Like many of London's markets, Church Street reaches a crescendo on the weekend. On Friday and Saturday, stands selling cheap clothes, household goods, fish, cheese, and antiques join the everyday fruit and vegetable stands. Alfies Antique Market (No.13–25) houses around 100 dealers selling everything from jewelry to furniture. There is also a cluster of interesting standalone antique furniture shops, plus the fascinating Gallery of Antique Costume and Textiles (No. 2), showcasing 17th-century garments.

Columbia Road Market

Columbia Rd E2. **Map** *8 D3.* 🚇 *Shoreditch, Old St.* **Open** *8am–3pm Sun. See p173.*

This is the perfect place to come to buy greenery and blossoms, or just to enjoy the fragrances and colors. Cut flowers, plants, shrubs, seedlings, and pots are all sold at about half their normal prices on a Sunday morning in this charming Victorian street. (During December, as you might expect, there's a brisk trade in Christmas trees.) There are also some lovely shops that keep market hours, such as Angela Flanders' pretty perfumerie (No. 96), Salon for vintage jewelry and cufflinks (No. 142) and hip hatter Fred Bare (No. 118). When you're shopped out, take tea at Treacle (No. 160), which turns out cute retro cupcakes and classic jam sponge cakes, plus cups of proper tea to wash them down. There is also a selection of vintage and modern china for sale. Shoppers with the munchies can snack on deep-fried shrimp from hole in the wall Lee's Seafoods (No.134).

Earlham Street Market

Earlham St WC2. **Map** *13 B2.* 🚇 *Covent Garden.* **Open** *10am–4pm Mon–Sat.*

Situated on a short road just off Shaftesbury Avenue, this market is a small affair. Several stands sell a range of items from secondhand clothes to fashion jewelry and accessories.

East Street Market

East St SE17. 🚇 *Elephant and Castle.* **Open** *8am–5pm Tue–Fri, 8am–6:30pm Sat; 8am–2pm, Sun.*

East Street Market's high point is Sunday, when more than 250 stands fill the narrow street and a small plant and flower market is set up on Blackwood Street. The majority of traders sell clothes, accessories, and household goods, although there is plenty of British and Afro-Caribbean produce, fish, and other delicacies. Charlie Chaplin (see p39) was born on this street and sought inspiration for his characters in the area.

Gabriel's Wharf and Riverside Walk Markets

56 Upper Ground and Riverside Walk SE1. **Map** *14 E3.* 🚇 *Waterloo. Gabriel's Wharf* **Open** *11am–6pm Tue–Sun; Riverside Walk* **Open** *noon–7pm Sat, Sun. See p193.*

Little shops filled with ceramics, paintings, and jewelry surround a bandstand in Gabriel's Wharf where jazz groups sometimes play in the summer. A few stands are set up around the courtyard, selling ethnic clothing and handmade jewelry and pottery. The book market under Waterloo Bridge includes a good selection of new and old Penguin paperbacks.

Grays Antique Markets

58 Davies St & 1–7 Davies Mews W1. **Map** *12 E2.* 🚇 *Bond Street.* **Open** *10am–6pm Mon–Fri; 11am–5pm Sat.*

Conveniently placed in the West End, Grays probably isn't the place to bag a bargain – the liveried doorman is a tipoff that this place is posh – but it makes a pleasant place to browse. There are some lovely pieces here, from costume jewelry and fabulous vintage fashion to enamel boxes and modern first editions from Biblion bookseller.

Greenwich Market

College Approach SE10. **Map** *23 B2.* 🚄 *Greenwich.* 🚇 *Cutty Sark DLR.* **Open** *10am–5:30pm Wed–Sun.*

On weekends, the area west of Hotel Ibis accommodates dozens of trestle tables piled with coins, medals, banknotes, secondhand books, Art Deco furniture, assorted bric-a-brac, and vintage clothing. The covered crafts market specializes in wooden toys, clothes made by young designers, handmade jewelry, and accessories.

Jubilee and Apple Markets

Covent Gdn Piazza WC2. **Map** *13 C2.* 🚄 *Covent Gdn.* **Open** *9am–5pm daily.*

Covent Garden has become the center of London streetlife, with some of the capital's best busking. Both these markets sell crafts and designs. The Apple Market, inside the Piazza where the famous fruit and vegetable market was housed (see p116), has knitwear, jewelry, and novelty goods. Jubilee Hall sells antiques on Monday, crafts on weekends, and a large selection of clothes, handbags, cosmetics, and tacky mementoes in between. The East Colonnade Market also has a variety of stands, from handmade soaps to hand-knitted children's clothing. Every Thursday on the East Piazza, the Real Food Market, a.k.a. the "Larder of London," trades in sustainably and ethically produced gourmet delicacies, including prepared meals and street food.

Leadenhall Market

Whittington Ave EC3. **Map** *15 C2.* 🚇 *Bank, Monument.* **Open** *7am–4pm Mon–Fri. See p161.*

There has been a marketplace on this site since medieval times, but the present spectacular, glass-roofed structure was built in 1881. Leadenhall Market was traditionally famous for fish, meat, and poultry, but only fishmonger HS Linwood & Sons remains. The stylish red and green facades now bear the names of upscale clothing chains, restaurants, pubs, and gift shops. Leadenhall does, however, retain something of its reputation as a center for fine food. More than a dozen stands set up shop on the cobblestones beneath this dramatic structure Monday to Friday from 11am to 4pm. Wares include European cheeses, cured meats, baked goods, condiments, and other gourmet goods as well.

Leather Lane Market

Leather Lane EC1. **Map** *6 E5.* 🔵 *Farringdon, Chancery Lane.* **Open** *10am–2pm Mon–Fri.*

This ancient street, originally called Leveroun Lane, has played host to a market for over 300 years. The history of the Lane, however, has nothing to do with leather. Stands here sell cut-price chain-store clothes, plus shoes, bags, jewelry, and accessories. All are well worth a browse.

Marylebone Farmers' Market

Cramer St parking lot, behind Marylebone High St W1. **Map** *4 D5.* 🔵 *Baker Street, Bond Street.* **Open** *10am–2pm Sun.*

In response to Britain's interest in local organic produce, weekly markets have sprung up all over the city. This enables farmers and other producers to sell directly to the public. Locations include Islington Green and the parking lot behind Waterstone's, Notting Hill, but Marylebone is the largest and most central, offering seasonal fruit and vegetables, dairy products, fish, meat, breads, preserves, and sauces. There is also a lineup of excellent gourmet shops in adjacent Moxon Street, including a renowned rare-breed pork butcher, the Ginger Pig, and La Fromagerie delicatessen with its extensive cheese cave.

Old Spitalfields Market

Commercial St E1. **Map** *8 E5.* 🔵 *Aldgate East, Liverpool Street.* **Open** *10am–5pm Mon–Fri, 9am–5pm Sun. See p172.*

The main market is on a Sunday, and is a mecca for those interested in the latest street fashion trends. Many young designers have stands, and prices are also reasonable.

The stands are of mixed quality, so you have to search for the gems. The organic food stands and a selection of cafés make it a good brunch venue any day. A varying number of stands are open during the week.

Petticoat Lane Market

Middlesex St E1. **Map** *16 D1.* 🔵 *Liverpool St, Aldgate, Aldgate East.* **Open** *9am–2pm Sun (Wentworth St 10am–4:30pm Mon–Fri). See p171.*

Probably the most famous of all London's street markets, Petticoat Lane continues to attract many thousands of visitors and locals every Sunday. The prices may not be as cheap as some of those to be found elsewhere, but the sheer volume of leather goods, clothes (the Lane's traditional strong point), watches, cheap jewelry, and toys more than make up for that. A variety of fast-food sellers do a brisk trade catering to the bustling crowds that throng the market on a weekend.

Piccadilly Crafts Market

St. James's Church, Piccadilly W1. **Map** *13 A3.* 🔵 *Piccadilly Circus, Green Park.* **Open** *antiques: 10am–6pm Tue. Arts and crafts: 10am–6pm Wed–Sat.*

Many of the markets in the Middle Ages were held in churchyards, and Piccadilly Crafts Market is rekindling that ancient tradition. It is aimed mostly at visitors rather than locals, and the merchandise on display ranges from tacky T-shirts to wooden toys. All are spread out in the shadow of Sir Christopher Wren's beautiful church *(see p90).*

Portobello Road Market

Portobello Rd W10. **Map** *9 C3.* 🔵 *Notting Hill Gate, Ladbroke Grove.* **Open** *antiques and junk: 5:30am–5:30pm Sat. General market: 9am–6pm Mon–Wed, 9am–1pm Thu, 9am–7pm Fri & Sat. See p221.*

Portobello Road is really three or four markets rolled into one. The Notting Hill end has more than 1,000 stands in numerous arcades and on the street, displaying a compendium of objets d'art, jewelry, old medals, paintings, and silverware. Most stands are managed by experts, so bargains are very rare. Farther down the gentle hill, antiques give way to fruit and vegetables. The next transformation comes under the Westway overpass, where young fashion designers sell inexpensive creations alongside secondhand clothing, record, and food stands on Fridays and Saturdays. It's also worth venturing into the covered Portobello Green market,

which has an interesting mix of small shops selling everything from avant-garde fashion to kitsch cushions and lingerie. From this point on, the market becomes increasingly shabby.

Ridley Road Market

Ridley Rd E8. 🚃 *Dalston.* **Open** *6am–6pm Mon–Thu, 6am–7pm Fri & Sat.*

Early last century, Ridley Road was a center of the Jewish community. Since then, Asians, Greeks, Turks, and West Indians have also settled in the area, and the market is a lively celebration of this cultural mix. Highlights include the 24-hour bagel bakery, shanty-town shacks selling green bananas and reggae records, colorful drapery stands, and cheap fruit and vegetables.

Roman Road Market

Roman Rd, between Parnell Rd and St. Stephen's Rd E3. 🔵 *Bethnal Green.* 🚌 *8.* **Open** *10am–3pm Tue & Thu; 9am–4pm Sat. Farmers' market 1st Sat of month.*

This lively market established in the 19th century has a real East End flavor and traditionally sells everything from cheap bedding and fashion to discount cleaning products and fruit and vegetables. Chances are that you'll be treated to some colorful cockney patter from the vendors trying to drum up business. As well as the standard market traders, some more unusual vendors, street entertainers, and special events add variety to the mix. When you pay a visit to the Roman Road Market, you may just be tempted to buy some of the handmade jewelry, vintage clothes, or antiques being sold at the stands.

Shepherd's Bush Market

Goldhawk Rd W12. 🔵 *Goldhawk Road, Shepherd's Bush.* **Open** *9am–6pm Mon–Sat.*

A focal point for many of the local ethnic communities, this rambling market contains an impressive volume of eclectic wares. West Indian food, Afro wigs, Asian spices, exotic fish, rugs, and other household goods are just some of the major attractions. There are acres of cheap clothing for every occasion, from floral flannel nighties and men's suits to clubwear and elaborately beaded wedding gowns. Cheap fabric stands are a highlight of the Shepherd's Bush Market, and there is even an on-site tailor and barber.

ENTERTAINMENT IN LONDON

London has the enormous, multilayered variety of entertainment that only the great cities of the world can provide, and, as always, the city's historical backdrop adds depth to the experience. While few things could be more contemporary than dancing the night away in style at a famed nightclub such as Café de Paris or Heaven, you could also choose to spend the evening picturing the ghosts of long-dead Hamlets pacing ancient boards in the shadow of one of the living legends that grace the West End theaters today. There's a healthy, innovative fringe theater scene too, plus world-class ballet and opera in fabled venues such as Sadler's Wells, the Royal Opera House, and the Coliseum. In London you'll be able to hear the best music,

ranging from classical, jazz, and rock to rhythm and blues, while dedicated movie buffs can choose from hundreds of different films each night, in both large multiplexes and excellent small independent theaters. Sports fans can watch a game of cricket at Lords, cheer on oarsmen on the Thames, or eat strawberries and cream at Wimbledon. Should you be feeling adventurous and sporty yourself, you could try going for a horse ride along Rotten Row in Hyde Park. There are festivals, celebrations, and sports to attend, and there's plenty for children to do, too – in fact, there's plenty for everyone to do. Whatever you want, you'll be sure to find it in London; it's just a question of knowing where to look.

Top; Cultural classics: a concert at Kenwood House; Above left; open-air theater at Regent's Park; Above right; performers at the Coliseum

Information Sources

For details of events in London, check the comprehensive weekly listings and review magazine *Time Out* (published every Tuesday), sold at most newsstands and many bookshops. The commuter newspaper *Metro* (week days) and London's evening newspaper, the *Evening Standard*, are both free and give

brief daily listings. The *Independent* has daily listings and also reviews a different arts sector every day, plus a weekly round-up section, "The Information"; the *Guardian* has arts reviews in its G2 section every day and weekly listings in "The Guide" on

Saturday. The *Independent*, the *Guardian*, and *The Times* all have lists of ticket availability.

Specialty flyers, brochures, and advance listings are distributed free in the lobbies of theaters, concert halls, movie theaters, and arts complexes such as the Southbank and Barbican. Tourist information offices and hotel lobbies often have the same publications. Posters advertise forthcoming events on billboards everywhere.

The Society of London Theatre (SOLT) publishes an informative free broadsheet every two weeks, available in many theater lobbies. It tends to concentrate on mainstream theaters, but does provide invaluable information about what's on. The National Theatre and the Royal Shakespeare Company also publish free broadsheets detailing future performances, distributed at the theaters. SOLT's website (www.officiallondontheatre.co.uk) provides full details of current productions. It also has news, interviews, access information and online ticket booking. Many theaters operate a

Café sign advertising free live music

faxback service that lets you see a seating plan showing the unsold seats for any performance.

Getting Tickets

Some of the more popular shows and plays in London's West End – the latest Lloyd Webber musical, for instance – can be totally booked out for weeks and even months ahead and you will find it impossible to purchase any tickets. This is not the norm, though, and most tickets will be available on the day of the performance, especially if you are prepared to line up in front of the theater for returns. However, for a stress-free vacation it helps to book tickets in advance; this will ensure that you get the day, time, and seats that you want. You can book tickets from the box office in person, by telephone, online or by mail. Quite a few hotels have concierges or porters who will give advice on where to go and arrange tickets for you.

Box offices are usually open about 10am–8pm, and accept payment by cash, credit card, traveler's check, or personal UK check when supported by a check guarantee card. Many venues

Lineup from the Royal Ballet, on stage at Covent Garden

will now sell unclaimed or returned tickets just before the performance; ask at the box office when you should get in line. To reserve seats by telephone, call the box office and either pay on arrival or send payment – seats are usually held for three days. Some venues now have separate phone numbers for credit card bookings – check before you call. Reserve your seat, and always take your credit card with you when you pick up your ticket. Some smaller venues do not accept credit cards.

Palace Theatre plaque

Disabled Visitors

Many London venues are old buildings and were not originally designed with disabled visitors in mind, but a lot of facilities have been updated, particularly to give access to those using wheelchairs, or for those with hearing difficulties.

Call the box office prior to your visit to reserve the special seating places or equipment, which are often limited. Special discounts may be available: for details and information on facilities, call Artsline (020 7388 2227, www.artsline.org.uk).

Transportation

Night buses (see p375) are the preferred late-night mode of transportation, or call for a cab from the venue. If you find yourself outside central London late at night, do not rely on being able to hail a black cab quickly in the street. Never take an unlicensed minicab. The Underground usually runs until just after midnight, but check the timetables in the stations (see pp372–73).

Ticket Agencies

Tickets are also available from agencies. Try the theater box office first; if no seats are available there, find out the standard prices before going to an agency. Most, but not all, are reputable. Agencies advertising top show tickets for "tonight" may really have them, and they may be fairly priced. If you order by phone, tickets will be mailed to you or sent to the theater for you to pick up. Commission should be a standard 22%. Some shows waive the agency fee by paying the commission themselves; this is usually advertised, and agencies should then charge standard box office prices. Always compare prices, try to avoid agencies in bureaux de change, and do not be tempted to buy from ticket scalpers or unofficial Internet sources.

Ticket booth in Leicester Square

London's Theaters

London offers an extraordinary range of theatrical entertainment – this is one of the world's great stages, and, at its best, standards of quality are extremely high. Despite their legendary reputation for reserve, the British are passionate about theater, and London's theaters reflect every nuance of this passion. You can stroll along a street of West End theaters and find a somber Samuel Beckett, Brecht, or Chekhov play showing next door to some absurdly frothy farce like *No Sex Please, We're British!* Amid such diversity, there is always something to appeal to everyone.

West End Theater

There is a distinct glamour to the West End theaters. Perhaps it is the glittering lights of the lobbies and the impressively ornate interiors, or maybe it is their hallowed reputations – but whatever it is, the old theaters retain a magic all of their own.

The West End billboards always feature a generous sprinkling of world-famous performers such as Judi Dench, Kenneth Branagh, John Malkovich, and Kevin Spacey.

The major commercial theaters cluster along Shaftesbury Avenue and the Haymarket and around Covent Garden and Charing Cross Road. Unlike the national theaters, most West End theaters survive only on profits; they do not receive any state subsidy. They rely on an army of ever-hopeful "angels" (financial backers) and producers to keep the old traditions alive.

Many theaters are historical landmarks, such as the classic **Theatre Royal Drury Lane**, established in 1663 *(see p117)*, and the elegant **Theatre Royal Haymarket** – both superb examples of early 19th-century buildings. Another to note is the **Palace** *(see p110)*, with its terra-cotta exterior and imposing position right on Cambridge Circus.

National Theatre

The **National Theatre** is based in the Southbank Centre *(see p190)*. Here, the large, open-staged Olivier, the proscenium-staged Lyttelton, and the small, flexible Cottesloe offer a range of sizes and styles, making it possible to produce every kind of theater from large, extravagant works to miniature masterpieces. The complex is also a lively social center. Enjoy a drink with your friends before your play begins; watch the crowds and the river drift by; wander around the many free art exhibitions; relax during the free early evening concerts in the foyer; or browse through the theater bookshop.

The **Royal Shakespeare Company** is Britain's national theater company, one of the world's great theater ensembles, with an unparalleled reputation for its dramatic interpretation of Shakespeare and other leading dramatists. Although its official home since the 19th century has been in Stratford-upon-Avon, the company has maintained a regular London presence since the 1960s. Its London base used to be the Barbican Centre, but now the RSC enjoys regular London seasons in the West End, at the Novello Theatre and other smaller venues. If you want to find out where the RSC is performing in London, call their ticket hotline.

National Theatre Booking Addresses

National Theatre
(Lyttelton, Cottesloe, Olivier) South Bank SE1. **Map** 14 D3. **Tel** 020 7452 3000.
W nationaltheatre.org.uk

Royal Shakespeare Company
Tel 01789 403 4444 (information).
Tel 0844 800 1110 (tickets).

Pantomime

Should you happen to be visiting London between December and February, one unmissable experience for the whole family is pantomime. "Panto" is an absurd tradition in which major female characters are played by men and male characters by women, and the audience has to participate, shouting encouragement according to a set formula. Whatever adults may think of it, children love the experience.

Open-Air Theater

A performance of one of Shakespeare's airier creations, such as *A Midsummer Night's Dream*, takes on an atmosphere of pure enchantment among the green vistas of **Regent's Park** *(see p226)*. Lavish opera productions are staged during the summer months in **Holland Park** *(see p220)*. Wear warm clothing, and take a blanket and, to be safe, an umbrella. Refreshments are available, or pack a picnic.

Open-air performances of a different kind can be experienced at **Shakespeare's Globe** on Bankside *(see p179)*. This authentic reproduction of an Elizabethan playhouse, open to the skies – but with protected seating – is open to visitors all year but only puts on performances in the summer months.

Open-Air Theater Booking Addresses

Holland Park Theatre
Holland Park. **Map** 9 B4.
Tel 020 7361 3570. **Open** Jun–Aug.
W operahollandpark.com

Open Air Theatre
Inner Circle, Regent's Park NW1. v 4 D3.
Open Jun–Sep.
Tel 0844 826 4242.
W openairtheatre.org

Shakespeare's Globe
New Globe Walk SE1. **Map** 15 A3.
Tel 020 7401 9919. **Performances** Apr–Oct. W shakespearesglobe.com

DIRECTORY

West End Theaters

Adelphi ⑬
Strand WC2.
Tel 0844 811 0053.

Aldwych ⑱
Aldwych WC2.
Tel 0844 847 1712.

Ambassadors ㉖
West St WC2.
Tel 0844811 2334.

Apollo ㉜
Shaftesbury Ave W1.
Tel 0844 482 9671.

Cambridge ㉔
Earlham St WC2.
Tel 0844 412 4652.

Criterion ⑦
Piccadilly Circus W1.
Tel 020 7839 8811.

Dominion ㉓
Tottenham Court Rd.
Tel 0844 847 1775.

Duchess ⑯
Catherine St WC2.
Tel 0844 482 9672.

Duke of York's ③
St Martin's Lane WC2.
Tel 0844 871 7623.

Fortune ⑳
Russell St WC2.
Tel 0844 871 7626.

Garrick ④
Charing Cross Rd WC2.
Tel 0844 482 9673.

Gielgud ㉛
Shaftesbury Ave W1.
Tel 0844 482 5141.

Harold Pinter ⑧
Panton St SW1.
Tel 0844 871 7627.

Her Majesty's ⑩
Haymarket SW1.
Tel 0844 412 2707.

Lyceum ⑮
Wellington St WC2.
Tel 0844 844 0005.

Lyric ㉝
Shaftesbury Ave W1.
Tel 0844 482 9674.

New Leicester Square Theatre ⑤
Leicester Pl W1.
Tel 0844 873 3433.

New London ㉑
Drury Lane WC2.
Tel 0871 230 1547.

Noel Coward ①
St Martin's Lane WC2.
Tel 0844 482 5120.

Novello ⑰
Aldwych WC2.
Tel 0844 482 5170.

Palace ㉘
Shaftesbury Ave W1.
Tel 0844 482 9676.

Phoenix ㉗
Charing Cross Rd WC2.
Tel 0844 871 7629.

Piccadilly ㉞
Denman St W1.
Tel 0844 412 6666.

Playhouse ⑫
Northumberland Ave WC2.
Tel 0844 871 7631.

Prince Edward ㉙
Old Compton St W1.
Tel 0844 482 5151.

Prince of Wales ⑥
Coventry St W1.
Tel 0844 482 5115.

Queen's ㉚
Shaftesbury Ave W1.
Tel 0844 482 5160.

Shaftesbury ㉒
Shaftesbury Ave WC2.
Tel 020 7379 5399.

St Martin's ㉕
West St WC2.
Tel 0844 499 1515.

Theatre Royal Drury Lane ⑲
Catherine St WC2.
Tel 0844 871 8810.

Theatre Royal Haymarket ⑨
Haymarket SW1.
Tel 020 7930 8800.

Trafalgar Studios ⑪
Whitehall SW1.
Tel 0844 871 7632.

Vaudeville ⑭
Strand WC2.
Tel 0844 482 9675.

Wyndham's ②
Charing Cross Rd WC2.
Tel 0844 482 5138.

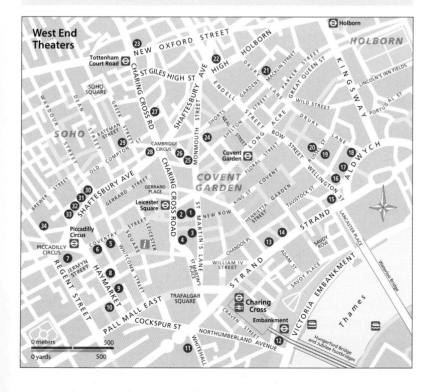

West End Theaters

Fringe Theater

London's fringe theater acts as an outlet for new, adventurous writing and for writers from other cultures and lifestyles – works by Irish writers appear regularly, as do plays by Caribbean and Latin American authors and feminist and gay writers.

The plays are usually staged in tiny theaters based in pubs, such as the **Gate Theatre** above the Prince Albert pub in Notting Hill, the **King's Head** in Islington, and the **Latchmere** pub in Battersea, or in warehouses and vacant spaces in larger theaters, such as the **Donmar Warehouse** and the **Lyric**.

Venues like the **Bush Theatre**, the **Almeida,** and the **Jerwood Theatre Upstairs** at the Royal Court have earned their reputations for discovering outstanding new works, some of which have subsequently transferred successfully to the West End.

Foreign-language plays are sometimes performed at national cultural institutes; for example, you might be able to catch Molière at the **Institut Français** or Brecht at the **Goethe Institute**; check the listings magazines.

For alternative stand-up comedy and cabaret, where you can encounter the sharp edge of satire with its brash, newsy style, try the **Comedy Store**, the birthplace of so-called "alternative" comedy, or the **Hackney Empire**, a former Victorian music hall that showcases local talent and hosts theater, music and comedy events.

Budget Tickets

There is a wide range of prices for seats in London theaters. The cheaper West End tickets, for example, can cost under £10, while the best seats for musicals hover around £35–50. However, it is usually quite possible to get cheaper tickets.

"tkts" (see p337) is the only official discount theater ticket shop in London, and sells tickets on the day of the performance for a wide range of mainstream shows. Located on the south side of Leicester Square, the booth is open Monday to Saturday (10am–7pm) for matinee and evening shows, and Sunday (noon–3:30pm) for matinees only. Payment is by cash or credit card, and there is a strict limit of up to four tickets per purchase, with a small service charge.

You can sometimes get reduced-price seats for matinee performances and press and preview nights – it is always worth checking with the box office to see what they currently have available.

Choosing Seats

If you go to the theater in person, you will be able to see its seating plan and note where you can get a good view at an affordable price. If you book by telephone, you should note the following: stalls are in front of the stage and expensive. The back stalls are slightly cheaper; dress, grand, or royal circles are above the stalls and cheaper again; the upper circle or balcony are the cheapest seats, but you will have to climb several flights of stairs; the slips are seats that run along the edges of the theater; boxes are the most expensive option.

It is also wise to bear in mind that some of the cheap seats have a restricted view.

Theater-Related Activities

If you are curious about how the mechanics of the theater work, you would probably enjoy a back-stage tour. The National Theatre organizes tours (see p336). The tour includes the Lyttleton, Olivier, and Cottesloe auditoria, as well as the workshops and dressing rooms. The London Palladium also offers a backstage guided tour of the theater's history.

Irate Ghosts

Many of London's oldest theaters are said to have ghosts; however, the two most famous specters haunt the environs of the Garrick and the Duke of York's (see p337). The Garrick is heavily atmospheric, and the ghost of Arthur Bourchier, a manager at the turn of the 20th century, is reputed to make fairly regular appearances. He hated critics and many believe he is still trying to frighten them away. The ghost occupying the Duke of York's theater was Violet Melnotte, an actress manager during the 1890s, who was famed for her extremely fiery temper.

Fringe Theater

Almeida
Almeida St N1.
Tel 020 7359 4404.

Bush Theatre
Shepherds Bush Green W12.
Tel 020 8743 5050.

Comedy Store
1a Oxendon St WC2.
Map 13 B3.
Tel 0844 871 7699.

Donmar Warehouse
41 Earlham St WC2.
Map 13 B2.
Tel 0844 871 7624.

Gate Theatre
The Prince Albert Pub,
11 Pembridge Rd W11.
Map 9 C3.
Tel 020 7229 0706.

Goethe Institute
50 Prince's Gate,
Exhibition Rd SW7.
Map 11 A5.
Tel 020 7596 4000.

Hackney Empire
291 Mare St E8.
Tel 020 8985 2424.

Institut Français
17 Queensberry Pl SW7.
Map 18 F2.
Tel 020 7871 3515.

King's Head
115 Upper St N1. **Map** 6
F1. **Tel** 020 7478 0160.

Lyric
King St, Hammersmith
W6. **Tel** 020 8741 6850.

Theatre 503
The Latchmere Pub, 503
Battersea Park Rd SW11.
Tel 020 7978 7040.

Royal Court
Sloane Sq SW1.
Map 19 C2.
Tel 020 7565 5000.

Movie Theaters

If you can't find a movie you like in London, then you don't like movies. The huge choice of British, American, foreign-language, new, classic, popular, and special-interest films makes London a major international film center, with about 250 different films showing at any one time. There are about 50 theaters in the central district of London alone, many of them ultramodern multiplexes. The big commercial theater chains show current blockbusters, and a healthy number of independent theaters offer inventive programs drawing on the whole history of film. London's listings magazines carry full details of what's playing where.

West End Theaters

"West End" is a loose term for the main theaters in the West End of London, which show new releases, such as the **Odeon Leicester Square** and the **Cineworld** Shaftesbury Avenue at the Trocadero, but it also includes the theaters found in Chelsea, Fulham, and Notting Hill. Programs begin around midday and are then repeated every two or three hours, with the last showing around 8:30pm; there are often late-night screenings on Fridays and Saturdays.

West End theaters are very expensive, but admission is often cheaper for afternoon performances or on Mondays. Reserve your seats well in advance for screenings of the more popular movies on Friday and Saturday evenings and Sunday afternoon.

BFI London Imax

The largest IMAX screen in Britain shows specially created movies accompanied by surround sound. Subjects like space flight or the undersea

world suit this breathtaking format well, as do animations.

Repertory Theaters

These theaters often show foreign-language and slightly more offbeat art films, and sometimes change programs daily or even several times each day. Some theaters show two or three films, often on the same theme, for one entrance charge.

These include the **Prince Charles**, which is situated centrally, close to Leicester Square; the **Everyman,** in locations across north London; the ICA in the Mall; the **Ritzy** in Brixton, South London; and the BFI Southbank.

BFI Southbank

Formerly known as the National Film Theatre, BFI Southbank is located in the Southbank Centre, near Waterloo Station. It has two screens of its own, which together offer a huge and diverse selection of films, both British and international. The BFI Southbank also holds regular screenings of rare and restored films and television

programs. It is absolutely essential for movie buffs to pay a visit.

Foreign-Language Films

These are screened at a number of repertory and independent theaters, including the **Renoir**, the **Prince Charles**, the **Curzon Soho** in Shaftesbury Avenue, the **Screen** theater chain, and the **Ciné Lumière**. Films are shown in the original language, with English subtitles.

Movie Ratings

Children are allowed to go unaccompanied by an adult to movies that have been awarded either a U (universal) or a PG (parental guidance advised) certificate for viewing. Children must be accompanied by an adult to see a movie that is rated 12A.

With other movies, the numbers 12, 15, or 18 denote the minimum ages allowed for admission to the theater.

London Film Festival

The most important cinema event in Britain is held every November, when over 100 films – some of which will have already won awards abroad – from a number of countries are screened. The BFI Southbank, several of the repertory theaters, and some of the big West End theaters have special showings of these films. Details are published in the listings magazines. Tickets are quite hard to come by, but some standby tickets will generally be available to the public 30 minutes before a showing.

Movie Theater Addresses

BFI London IMAX
Waterloo Rd SE1.
Map 14 D4.
Tel 0330 333 7878.

BFI Southbank
Southbank Centre, SE1.
Map 14 D3.
Tel 020 7928 3232.

Ciné Lumière
Institut Français, 17 Queensberry Pl SW7. **Map** 18 F2. **Tel** 020 7871 3515.

Cineworld (at the Trocadero)
Coventry St W1. **Map** 13 A3. **Tel** 0871 200 2000.

Curzon Soho
93–107 Shaftesbury Ave W1. **Map** 13 B2. **Tel** 0330 500 1331.

Everyman
Hollybush Vale NW3. **Map** 1 A5. **Tel** 0871 906 9060.

Odeon Leicester Sq
Leicester Sq, WC2. **Map** 13 B2. **Tel** 0871 224 4007.

Prince Charles
Leicester Pl, WC2. **Map** 13 B2. **Tel** 020 7494 3654.

Renoir
Brunswick Sq WC1. **Map** 5 C4. **Tel** 0330 500 1331.

Ritzy
Coldharbour Lane SW2. **Tel** 0871 902 5739.

Screen Cinemas
96 Baker St NW1. **Map** 3 C5. **Tel** 0871 906 9060.

Opera, Classical, and Contemporary Music

Opera has always been tarred with a somewhat elitist reputation in Britain. However, televised concerts and free outdoor concerts in Hyde Park and the Piazza, Covent Garden, have greatly increased its popularity. London is home to five world-class orchestras and a host of smaller music companies and contemporary music ensembles; it also houses three permanent opera companies and numerous smaller opera groups, and leads the world with its period orchestras. It is a major center for the classical recording industry, which helps to support a large community of musicians and singers. Mainstream, obscure, traditional, and innovative music are all to be found in profusion. *Time Out* magazine *(see p334)* has the most comprehensive listings of the classical music being presented around the capital.

London Music Festivals

The BBC-run Promenade concerts are mostly held at the Royal Albert Hall *(see p341)* between July and September. More than 70 concerts feature soloists, orchestras, and conductors from around the world, performing a wide repertoire from much-loved classics to newly commissioned pieces. Every concert is broadcast live both on the radio and online. Tickets are best bought in advance, but 500 standing or "promming" places are sold on the day, one-and-a-half hours before the performance. The City of London Festival is held annually in June and July, when churches and public buildings in the City host a range of varied musical events. Venues such as the Tower of London *(see p156)* and Goldsmiths' Hall lend a special atmosphere to the events. Many concerts are free. For more details, contact the information office (0845 401 5040) from May onward.

Royal Opera House

Floral Street WC2. **Map** 13 C2. **Tel** 020 7304 4000. *See p117.* **W** roh.org.uk
The building, with its elaborate red, white, and gold interior, is opulent; it looks, and is, expensive. It is the home of the Royal Opera and the Royal Ballet, but visiting opera and ballet companies also perform here. Many productions are shared with foreign opera houses, so check that you haven't already seen the same production at home. Works are always performed in the original language, but English translations are projected above the stage.

Seats are usually booked well in advance, particularly if major stars such as Placido Domingo or Anna Netrebko are performing. Tickets range from about £5 to £200 or more for a world-class star. The cheapest seats tend to go first, although a number of these tickets are reserved for sale on the day. Some of the cheaper seats have extremely restricted views. Standing passes can often be obtained right up to the time of a performance. Standby information is available on the day, and there are often concessions on tickets.

London Coliseum

St. Martin's Lane WC2. **Map** 13 B3. **Tel** 0871 911 0200 (24 hrs). *See p121.* **W** eno.org
The Coliseum, home of the English National Opera (ENO), was founded in 1961. The company's hallmarks are performances in English, high musical standards, and a permanent ensemble

complemented by guest appearances. Productions range from the classic to the adventurous. For weekday performances, there are 500 pre-bookable seats at £10 and under.

Southbank Centre

Southbank Centre SE1. **Map** 14 D4. **Tel** 0844 875 0073. *See pp188–89.* **W** southbankcentre.co.uk
The Southbank Centre includes the **Royal Festival Hall (RFH)**, the **Queen Elizabeth Hall**, the **Purcell Room**, and the **Hayward Gallery**. There are nightly performances, mostly of classical music, interspersed with opera, jazz, ballet, and modern dance seasons, as well as festivals of contemporary and ethnic music. The largest concert hall on the South Bank is the RFH. Built in the 1950s, it is now considered one of the best modernist structures in London. The RFH is ideal for major orchestras and large-scale choral works. The airy halls outside the auditorium are also used to house exhibitions, a number of cafés, a book and music shop, and the occasional free performance.

The Purcell Room is comparatively small and tends to host chamber and contemporary music, in addition to many debut recitals of young artists. The Queen Elizabeth Hall lies somewhere in between. It stages medium-sized ensembles whose audiences, while too large for the Purcell Room, would not fill the Festival Hall. Jazz and ethnic music are performed here, and

the innovative and often controversial Opera Factory makes several appearances throughout the year. It performs a range of modern interpretations of the classics, and often commissions new works. The London Philharmonic Orchestra and the Philharmonia are resident at the South Bank. The Royal Philharmonic and the BBC Symphony Orchestra are frequent visitors, along with leading ensembles and soloists such as Angela Gheorghiu, Mitsuko Uchida, Stephen Kovacevich, and Anne-Sofie von Mutter. World-class conductors who have played here include Daniel Barenboim, Kurt Masur, and Simon Rattle.

The Academy of St. Martin-in-the-Fields, the London Festival Orchestra, Opera Factory, the London Classical Players, and the London Mozart Players all have regular seasons. There are also frequent free foyer concerts, and throughout the summer the center is well worth visiting.

Barbican Concert Hall

Silk Street EC2. **Map** 7 A5. **Tel** 020 7638 8891. See p167. **W** barbican.org.uk

The Barbican is the home of the London Symphony Orchestra (LSO). Classical concerts are performed by the resident LSO and the BBC Symphony Orchestra, as well as many other visiting orchestras and ensembles, as part of the Barbican's own international concert seasons. The concert hall is also renowned for its performances of contemporary music, including jazz, blues, and world music.

Royal Albert Hall

Kensington Gore SW7. **Map** 10 F5. **Tel** 020 7589 8212. See p207. **W** royalalberthall.com

Each year the Royal Albert Hall hosts over 300 concerts, from ballet to rock, pop, opera, and national events. From mid-July to mid-September it is devoted to the Henry Wood Promenade Concerts, the "Proms." Organized by the BBC, the season features the BBC Symphony Orchestra performing modern symphonies and other works as well as classics. Tickets for the Proms can be bought on the day of performance or booked in advance, but long lines build up early in the day, so Promenaders take cushions to sit on. Tickets sell out weeks ahead for the "Last Night of the Proms," which has become a national institution.

The hall is also open for tours that take you on a journey of its extraordinary history.

Handel House Museum

25 Brook St W1. **Map** 12 E2. **Tel** 020 7495 1685. **Open** 10am–6pm Tue–Sat (until 8pm Thu), noon–6pm Sun. **W** handelhouse.org

Located in the finely restored Georgian house where George Frideric Handel lived from 1723 until his death in 1759, the Handel House Museum provides an intimate venue for performances. Thursday night recitals of baroque music on period instruments are held in the paneled rehearsal and performance room, where Handel himself would have entertained his guests. Concert tickets include access to the museum. Check the website for more details.

Outdoor Music

London has many outdoor musical events in summer. At Kenwood House on Hampstead Heath (see p236), a grassy hill leads down to a lake, beyond which is the concert platform. Arrive early – the concerts are popular, particularly if fireworks are to accompany the music. Deck chairs tend to be reserved early, so most people sit on the grass. Take a sweater and a picnic. Purists beware – people walk around, eat, and talk throughout, and the music is amplified, so it can be a little distorted. You don't get your money back if it rains, since they have never abandoned a performance yet.

Other venues include Marble Hill House in Twickenham (see p254), with offerings similar to Kenwood's; Crystal Palace Park; and Holland Park.

Wigmore Hall

36 Wigmore St W1. **Map** 12 E1. **Tel** 020 7935 2141. See p228. **W** wigmore-hall.org.uk

Because of its excellent acoustics, the Wigmore Hall is a favorite with visiting artists, and attracts international names such as Andreas Scholl and András Schiff for a wide-ranging program of events. It presents seven evening concerts a week, BBC Monday lunchtime concerts, and a Sunday morning concert from September to July.

St. Martin-in-the-Fields

Trafalgar Sq WC2. **Map** 13 B3. **Tel** 020 7766 1100. See p102. **W** smitf.org

This elegant Gibbs church is where the famous Academy of St. Martin-in-the-Fields and the famous choir of the same name began life. Orchestras as disparate as the Delmont Ensemble and the London Oriana Choir provide evening concerts. The choice of each program is partly dictated by the religious year; for example, Bach's *St. John Passion* is played at Ascensiontide. Free lunchtime concerts are given on Mondays, Tuesdays, and Fridays by young artists.

St. John's, Smith Square

Smith Sq SW1. **Map** 21 B1. **Tel** 020 7222 1061. See p81. **W** sjss.org.uk

This converted Baroque church has good acoustics and seating. It hosts concerts by groups such as the Academy of Ancient Music, the London Mozart Players, the Monteverdi Choir, and Polyphony. The concert season runs from September to mid-July.

Broadgate Arena

3 Broadgate EC2. **Map** 7 C5. **W** broadgateinfo.net

This open-air venue in the City offers a summer season of lunchtime concerts, with varied programs from up-and-coming musicians.

Music Venues

Orchestral

Barbican Concert Hall
Broadgate Arena
Queen Elizabeth Hall
Royal Albert Hall
Royal Festival Hall
St. Martin-in-the-Fields
St. John's, Smith Square

Chamber and Ensemble

Barbican Concert Hall
Broadgate Arena
Handel House Museum
LSO St. Luke's
Purcell Room
Royal Festival Hall foyer
St. Martin-in-the-Fields
St. John's, Smith Square
Wigmore Hall

Soloists and Recitals

Barbican Concert Hall
Handel House Museum
Purcell Room
Royal Albert Hall
St. Martin-in-the-Fields
St. John's, Smith Square
Wigmore Hall

Children's

Barbican Concert Hall
Royal Festival Hall

Free

Barbican Concert Hall
Royal Festival Hall foyer
Royal National Theatre foyer (see p344)
St. Martin-in-the-Fields (lunchtime)

Early Music

Purcell Room
Wigmore Hall

Contemporary Music

Barbican Concert Hall
Southbank Centre

Dance

London-based dance companies present a range of styles from classical ballet to mime, jazz, experimental, and ethnic dance. London is also host to visiting companies as diverse as the classic Bolshoi Ballet and the innovative Jaleo Flamenco. Most dance companies (with the exception of the resident ballets) have short seasons that seldom last longer than two weeks and often less than a week – check the listings magazines for details (see p334). Theaters that regularly feature dance are the Royal Opera House, the London Coliseum, Sadler's Wells, and The Place Theatre. There are also performances at the Southbank Centre and other arts centers throughout the city.

Ballet

The **Royal Opera House** (see p117) and the **London Coliseum** in St. Martin's Lane are by far the best venues for classical ballet, providing the stage for foreign companies when they visit London. The Opera House is home to the Royal Ballet, which usually invites major international guest artists to take up residence. Book well in advance for classics such as Swan Lake and Giselle. The company also has an unusual repertoire of modern ballet; triple bills provide a mixture of new and old, and seats are normally readily available.

The English National Ballet holds its summer season at the **London Coliseum**. It has a repertoire to that of the Royal Ballet and stages some very popular productions.

Visiting companies also perform at **Sadler's Wells**, which, although it is London's premier venue for contemporary dance, also hosts a few companies with a classical repertoire.

Contemporary

A plethora of new and young companies is flourishing in London, each one with a distinctive style. **Sadler's Wells** in Islington, near Angel, has a proud reputation as the host of contemporary dance companies from around the world. There are regular visits from such luminaries of dance as the Nederlands Dance Theatre and the Alvin Ailey Company from New York. The Rambert Dance Company, an innovative English ensemble, has a regular, twice-a-year slot at the theater – usually in May and November. A stunning modern theater was built on the historic site of the Sadler's Wells Ballet in 1998. The **Peacock Theatre** (the West End home of Sadler's Wells) also features contemporary dance as part of its program.

The Place is the home of contemporary and ethnic dance companies and has a year-round program of performances from these and a number of visiting dancers. A custom-built space in Deptford, south London, the **Bonnie Bird Theatre**, presents a rich and diverse mix of dance, music, and physical theater. Other venues include the **Institute of Contemporary Arts** (ICA) (see p94) and the **Chisenhale Dance Space**, a center for small companies currently regarded as being on the experimental fringes of dance.

Ethnic

There is a constant stream of visiting groups coming to perform traditional dance from all over the world. Both **Sadler's Wells** and the **Riverside Studios** are major venues, while classical ethnic dance companies, including Indian and East Asian, have seasons at the Southbank Centre, often in the **Queen Elizabeth Hall**. Check the listings magazines for details.

Dance Festivals

There are two major contemporary dance festivals each year in London, featuring many different companies. Spring Loaded runs from February to April, while Dance Umbrella runs from early October to early November. The listings magazines carry all details.

Other smaller festivals include Almeida Dance, from the end of April to the first week of May at the **Almeida Theatre**, and The Turning World, a festival running in April and May, offering dance from all over the world.

Dance Venues

Almeida Theatre
Almeida St N1.
Tel 020 7359 4404.

Bonnie Bird Theatre
Creekside SE8.
Map 23 A2.
Tel 020 8691 8600.

Chisenhale Dance Space
64 Chisenhale Rd E3.
Tel 020 8981 6617.

ICA
Nash House, Carlton House Terrace, The Mall SW1.
Map 13 A4.
Tel 020 7930 3647.

London Coliseum
St Martin's Lane WC2.
Map 13 B3.
Tel 020 7845 9300.

Peacock Theatre
Portugal St WC2.
Map 14 D1.
Tel 020 7863 8198.

The Place
17 Duke's Rd WC1.
Map 5 B3.
Tel 020 7121 1100.

Queen Elizabeth Hall
Southbank Centre SE1.
Map 14 D4.
Tel 0844 875 0073.

Riverside Studios
Crisp Rd W6.
Tel 020 8237 1111.

Royal Opera House
Floral St WC2. **Map** 13 C2.
Tel 020 7304 4000.

Sadler's Wells
Rosebery Ave EC1.
Map 6 E3.
Tel 020 7863 8198.

Rock, Pop, Jazz, Reggae, and World Music

You will find the whole range of popular music being strummed and hummed, howled, growled, or synthesized in London. There may be as many as 80 listed concerts on an ordinary weeknight, featuring rock, reggae, soul, folk, country, jazz, Latin, and world music. In addition to the gigs, there are music festivals in the summer at parks, pubs, halls, and stadiums throughout the capital *(see p345)*. Check the listings magazines and keep your eyes open for publicity posters *(see p334)*.

Major Venues

The largest venues in London are host to an extraordinary variety of music.

Places where pop idols hope to draw enormous crowds of adoring fans include the **O2 Arena** in Greenwich, the indoor **Wembley Arena**, the **Hammersmith Apollo**, or, if they take themselves seriously, the grand **Royal Albert Hall**.

The **O2 Academy Brixton** and the **Town and Country Club** are next in prominence and size. Each can hold well over 1,000 people, and for many Londoners these former movie theaters are the capital's best venues, with seating upstairs, large dance-floors downstairs, and accessible bars.

Rock and Pop

Indie music is one of the mainstays of London's live music output. Following the leads of Manchester and Bristol, the capital has a healthy, cross-fertilized rock scene: venues all over town offer Britpop, bratpop, hip-hop, trip-hop, and the many other variations on pop that have yet to be labeled for the mass market. The **Union Chapel** in Islington hosts a variety of bands. Kentish Town's **Bull and Gate** is good for goth, and rock is the order of the day at venues such as **The Bullet Bar** and **The Shepherd's Bush Empire** among others.

The **Underworld** in Camden is a famous live venue for up-and-coming bands as well as big-name artists such as Sheryl Crow, Radiohead, and The Darkness. The venue is also home to two nightclubs. London is the home of pub-rock, which is a vibrant blend of rhythm and blues, rock, and punk that has been evolving since the 1960s as a genre in which bands frequently develop before finding their real musical identity. Such diverse bands as the Clash, Dr. Feelgood and Dire Straits all started as pub rockers. While there's usually no entrance fee to pub gigs, drinks tend to be surcharged.

New bands have a popular showcase at the **Betsey Trotwood** in Clerkenwell most weeknights, while **Borderline**, near Leicester Square, is frequented by record company talent scouts.

The **Barfly** in Chalk Farm delivers a good range of indie acts. **Koko** in Camden is a great intimate venue in a restored theater dating from 1900. Here you can listen to the finest established artists, such as Madonna or Coldplay, and live performances from up-and-coming indie bands. Another good venue for stimulating rock bands in North London is **The Garage** at Highbury Corner.

Jazz

The number of jazz venues in London continues to grow – both the music and the lifestyle romantically imagined to go with it are officially hip once again. **Ronnie Scott's** in the West End is still the pick of the vintage crop, and since the 1950s, many of the finest performers in the world have come to play here. The **100 Club** in Oxford Street is another very popular venue for confirmed jazzniks. Jazz and food have formed a partnership at venues such as the **Palookaville** in Covent Garden, the **Dover Street Wine Bar and Club**, and the largely vegetarian **Jazz Café**. Others include the **Pizza Express** on Dean Street and the **Mau Mau Bar**, on Portobello Road.

The **Southbank Centre** *(see pp188–89)* and also the **Barbican** *(see p167)* feature formal jazz concerts and free jazz in the foyers.

Reggae

London's large West Indian community has made the city the European reggae capital. At the **Notting Hill Carnival** *(see p59)*, late in August, many top bands perform free.

Reggae has now become integrated with the main-stream rock music scene, and bands appear at most of London's rock venues.

World Music

Musicians from every corner of the globe live in London. "World music" includes African, Latin, South American, or anything exotic, and its popularity has sparked a revitalization of British and Irish folk music. **Cecil Sharp House** has regular shows for folk purists, while the **ICA** *(see p94)* hosts innovative acts. **Cargo** in Shoreditch has an eclectic program of live music that includes African beats and Latin funk. Hot Latin nights can be found at **Cuba Libre** in Islington, and laid-back vibes pervade the **Notting Hill Arts Club**. For all French Caribbean and African sounds, you could check **Le Café de Piaf** inside Waterloo Station; and for the widest selection of African sounds and food in town, try visiting the **Africa Centre** in Covent Garden. The **Barbican Centre**, the **Royal Festival Hall**, and the **Queen Elizabeth Hall** at the Southbank Centre all offer plenty of world music.

Clubs

The old cliché that London dies when the pubs shut no longer holds true. Europe has long scoffed at Londoners going to bed at 11pm when the night is only just beginning in Paris, Madrid, and Rome, but London has caught on at last, and you can revel all night if you want to. The best clubs are not all confined to the downtown – initial disappointment that your hotel is a half-hour tube-ride from Leicester Square can be offset by the discovery of a trendy club right on your doorstep.

Etiquette

Fashions and club nights change very rapidly, and night spots open and close down all the time. Some of the best club nights are one-nighters – check the listings magazines (see p334). Be aware that there are sometimes bouncers at the door, enforcing a variety of dress or other appearance codes for a particular club. If you are set on visiting one of these, do some research before you go.

A few clubs require that you arrange membership 48 hours in advance, and you may also find that you have to be introduced by a member. Again, check these details in the listings magazines. Groups of men may not be welcome, so split up and find a woman to go in with; expect to line up to get in. Entrance fees may seem reasonable, but drinks tend to be overpriced.

Opening times are usually 10pm–3am Monday to Saturday, although many clubs stay open until 6am at the weekend and some open on Sunday from about 8pm to midnight.

Mainstream

London offers a broad selection of nightclubs that cater to all musical tastes and budgets.

Most of the more upscale nightclubs in London – for example, **Annabel's** – have a strict members-only policy; they require nominations by current members and have long waiting lists, so unless you move in privileged circles, you are unlikely to get in.

Traditional disco-type clubs that are easier to enter include the **Café de Paris**, where you can dine and boogie the night away. For those with a lust for samba and Latin beats, **Guanabara** in Covent Garden is friendly, unpretentious, and fun.

Farther north, the **Forum** hosts popular club nights, which feature classic soul, funk, and rhythm and blues. Similar clubs are **East Village** in Shoreditch and the **Tattershall Castle**, a disco boat moored on the bank of the Thames.

Fashionable Venues and Club Nights

Over the last few years, London has become one of the most innovative and sought-after club capitals in the world. It is now a major stage where trends are set. **Heaven** hosts England's premier house night. With its huge dance floor, excellent lasers, sound systems, and light shows, it's very popular, so line up early. **Punk** in Soho is a trendy spot playing a mixture of sounds (you might even spot a celebrity). The **Ministry of Sound** is a New York–style club that set the pattern for others to follow, hosting some of the world's best-known DJs. If you are feeling energetic, club nights are also run at the **Queen of Hoxton** in Shoreditch. Try **Envy Nightclub** for funky house, electro, and old skool, and for die-hard clubbers there's always **Fabric. Electric Brixton**, formely the much-loved Fridge, hosts club events and live music.

As with many clubs, **Bar Rumba** has different themes on different evenings, but if you like your dancing with a dash of spice and a lot of sauce, sashay along to its salsa night, with dance classes also available.

Cargo, the pioneering live/mixed music venue, features some of London's funkiest sounds. **93 Feet East** showcases a variety of live music and club nights from indie and rock to techno beats. Dress in uniform for the School Disco Night with 70s, 80s, and 90s sounds. It takes place on Saturdays in the **HMV Forum**, but check listings – it moves sometimes.

In Kensington, **The Roof Gardens** is London's only roof-top private members' club. It opens on Friday and Saturday nights, admits over-21s only, and has a "no effort, no entry" dress code. Apply for entry via the website, at www.roofgardensclub.com.

Gay

London has a number of gay nightclubs. The best-known and most popular is **Heaven**, with its huge dance floor and bar and video lounge under the arches of Charing Cross station. The **Queen of Hoxton** hosts mixed gay nights.

Transvestite

Watch for the occasional "Kinky Gerlinky" night in the listings magazines, an outrageously kitsch collection of drag queens and assorted exotica. In Soho, **Madame Jojo's** revue is a fabulous whirl of glittering color and extreme high camp.

Casinos

To gamble in London, you must be a member, or at least the guest of a member, of a licensed gaming club. Most clubs are happy to let you join, but membership must be arranged 48 hours in advance. Many will let you in to use facilities other than the gambling tables until about 4am, when most close. Try the excellent restaurants and bars, which are often subject to the usual licensing laws (see p310). Many clubs also have "hostesses" – beware the cost of their company.

DIRECTORY

Major Music Venues

Hammersmith Apollo
Queen Caroline St W6.
Tel 0844 249 4300 (tickets),
020 8563 3800 (venue).

The Forum
9–17 Highgate Rd NW5.
Tel 020 7428 4080.

O2 Academy Brixton
211 Stockwell Rd SW9.
Tel 0844 477 2000.

Royal Albert Hall
See p203.

Wembley Arena
Empire Way, Wembley,
Middlesex HA9.
Tel 0844 800 2755
(tickets), 020 8782 5500
(inquiries).

Rock and Pop Venues

Barfly
49 Chalk Farm Rd NW1.
Map 4 F1.
Tel 020 7424 0800.

Betsey Trotwood
56 Farringdon Rd EC1.
Map 6 E4.
Tel 020 7253 4285.

Borderline
Orange Yard, Manette St
WC2. Map 13 B1.
Tel 020 7734 5547.

Hoxton Square Bar and Kitchen
2–4 Hoxton Sq N1.
Tel 020 7613 0709.

Koko
1a Camden High St NW1.
Map 4 F2.
Tel 0870 432 5527.

The Garage
20–22 Highbury Corner,
N5. Tel 0844 847 1678.

Shepherd's Bush Empire
Shepherd's Bush Green
W12. Tel 0905 020 3999.

The Underworld
174 Camden High St
NW1. Map 4 F1.
Tel 020 7482 1932.

Union Chapel
The Vestry, Compton Ave
N1. Tel 020 7226 1686.

Jazz Venues

100 Club
100 Oxford St W1.
Map 13 A1.
Tel 020 7636 0933.

Barbican Hall
See p165.

Dover Street Wine Bar and Club
8–10 Dover St W1.
Map 12 F3.
Tel 020 7629 9813.

Jazz Café
5 Parkway NW1.
Map 4 E1.
Tel 020 7485 6834.

Mau Mau Bar
265 Portobello Rd W11.
Map 9 A1.
Tel 020 7229 8528.

Pizza Express
10 Dean St W1.
Map 13 A1.
Tel 0845 602 7017.

Ronnie Scott's
47 Frith St W1.
Map 13 A2.
Tel 020 7439 0747.
W ronniescotts.co.uk

Royal Festival Hall
See p348.

Vortex Jazz Club
Dalston Culture House
Gillett St, N16.
Map 8 1D.
Tel 020 7245 4097.

World Music

Africa Centre
38 King St WC2.
Map 13 C2.
Tel 020 7836 1973.

Barbican Centre
See p349.

Cargo
83 Rivington St EC2.
Map 7 C3.
Tel 020 7739 3440.

Cecil Sharp House
2 Regent's Park Rd NW1.
Map 4 D1.
Tel 020 7485 2206.

Cuba Libre
72 Upper St N1.
Map 6 F1.
Tel 020 7354 9998.

ICA
See p350.

Notting Hill Arts Club
21 Notting Hill Gate W11.
Map 9 C3.
Tel 020 7460 4459.

Queen Elizabeth Hall
Southbank Centre SE1.
Map 14 D4.
Tel 020 7960 4200.

Royal Festival Hall
See p348.

Clubs

93 Feet East
150 Brick Lane,
Shoreditch E1.
Map 8 E4.
Tel 020 7770 6006.

Annabel's
44 Berkeley Sq W1.
Map 12 E3.
Tel 020 7629 1096.

Bar Rumba
36 Shaftesbury Ave WC2.
Map 6 E2.
Tel 020 7287 6933.

Café de Paris
3 Coventry St W1.
Map 13 A3.
Tel 020 7734 7700.

Cargo
89 Rivington St EC2.
Map 7 C3.
Tel 020 7749 7840.

East Village
89 Great Eastern St EC2.
Map 7 C4.
Tel 020-7739 5173.

Electric Brixton
Town Hall Parade, Brixton
Hill SW2.
Tel 020 7274 2290.

Fabric
77a Charterhouse St EC1.
Map 6 F5.
Tel 020 7336 8898.

Gate Restaurant, Bar and Club
87 Notting Hill Gate W11.
Tel 020 7727 9007.

Guanabara
Drury Lane WC2. Map 13
C1. Tel 020 7242 8600.

Heaven
Under the Arches, Villiers
St WC2. Map 13 C3.
Tel 020 7930 2020.

Madame Jojo's
8–10 Brewer St W1. Map
13 A2. Tel 020 7734 3040.

Ministry of Sound
103 Gaunt St SE1.
Tel 0870 060 0010.

Punk
14 Soho St W1. Map 13
A1. Tel 020 773 4004.

Queen of Hoxton
1 Curtain Rd EC2.
Map 7 C3.
Tel 020 7422 0958.

Tattershall Castle
Victoria Embankment,
SW1. Map 13 C3.
Tel 020 7839 6548.

The Roof Gardens
99 Kensington High St
W8. Map 10 D5.
Tel 020 7937 7994.

Sports

The range of sports offered in London is quite phenomenal. Should you feel the urge to watch a game of medieval tennis or go scuba diving downtown, you've come to the right place. More likely, you'll just want to watch a soccer or rugby match, or play a set of tennis in a park. With far more public facilities than most European capitals, London is the place to enjoy cheap, accessible sports. Wembley Stadium, the national stadium for soccer, is located in northwest London. The Olympic Stadium, Aquatics Centre, and other venues were built in Stratford for the 2012 Olympic Games. Events were also held at venues across the city.

Running

Athletes will find a good choice of running tracks, often with free admission. **Linford Christie Stadium** has good facilities; **Regent's Park** is free; try also **Parliament Hill Fields**. For a sociable jog, meet the Bow Street Runners at **Jubilee Hall** on Tuesdays at 6pm.

Cricket

Five-day test matches and one-day internationals are played in summer at **Lord's** (see p248) and the **Kia Oval**, near Vauxhall. Tickets for the first four days of tests and for one-day games are hard to get, but you may get in on the last day and see a thrilling finish. When Middlesex and Surrey play county games at these grounds, there are always seats.

Football (Soccer)

This is the most popular spectator sport in Britain, its season running from August to May, with matches on weekends and weekday evenings. It is the most common topic of conversation in pubs, where games are often shown live on TV. Premier League and FA Cup games are frequently sold out in advance. London's top clubs include **Arsenal, Chelsea, West Ham,** and **Tottenham Hotspur**.

Golf

There are no golf courses in central London, but a few are scattered around the outskirts. The most accessible public courses are **Hounslow Heath, Chessington** (nine holes, train from Waterloo) and **Richmond Park** (two courses, computerized indoor teaching room). If you didn't pack your clubs, sets can be rented at a reasonable price.

Greyhound Racing

At a night "down the dogs," you can follow the races on a screen in the bar, stand by the track, or watch from the comfort of the restaurant (book in advance) at **Romford Stadium** or **Wimbledon Stadium**.

Horse Racing

High-class flat racing in summer and steeplechasing in winter can be seen at **Ascot, Kempton Park,** and **Sandown Park**, which are all less than an hour from central London by train. Britain's most famous flat race, the Derby, is run at **Epsom** in June.

Horse-Riding

For centuries, fashionable riders have exercised their steeds in Hyde Park; **Ross Nye** will provide you with a horse so that you can follow a long tradition.

Ice Skating

Ice skaters should head for London's best-known rink, **Queens**. The most attractive ice rinks, open only in winter, are at **Somerset House** (see p119) and at the **Tower of London** (see pp156–9).

Rugby Football

Rugby union, or rugger, is a 15-a-side game, once played only by amateurs, but now a professional sport. International matches are played at **Twickenham Rugby Football Ground**. The season runs from September to April, and you can watch "friendly" weekend games at local grounds. Top London teams **Saracens** and **Rosslyn Park** can be seen at their own grounds outside the center of town.

Squash

Squash courts tend to be busy, so try to book at least two days ahead. Many sports centers have squash facilities and will rent out equipment, including **Swiss Cottage Sports Centre** and the **Oasis Sports Centre**.

Swimming

Best indoor pools include **Chelsea Sports Centre**, the **Oasis**, and **Porchester Baths**; for outdoor swimming, try **Highgate and Hampstead Ponds** (two separate ponds for men and women and one mixed) and the **Oasis**.

Tennis

There are hundreds of tennis courts in London's public parks, most of them cheap to rent and easily reserved. It can be busy in the summer, so book your court two or three days ahead. You must supply your own racquet and balls. Good public tennis courts include **Holland Park** and **Parliament Hill**.

Tickets for the Centre Court of the **All England Lawn Tennis Club** at Wimbledon are hard to get – it is possibly easier to enter the tournament as a player than to obtain tickets for Centre Court. Try waiting overnight, or line up for return tickets after lunch on the day of the match – for a bargain price, you can still enjoy a good four hours of tennis (see p59).

Traditional Sports

An old London tradition is the University Boat Race, held in March or April, when teams from Oxford and Cambridge row from Putney to Mortlake *(see p58)*; a newer tradition is the London Marathon, which is run from Greenwich to the Mall at Westminster *(see p58)* on an April Sunday. You can watch croquet at **Dulwich Croquet Club** and medieval (real) tennis at **Queen's Club**.

Water Sports

There are facilities for a wide variety of water sports at the **Docklands Sailing & Water Sports Centre**. You can choose from sports such as windsurfing, dinghy sailing, powerboating, waterskiing, and canoeing. Rowboats are also available for rental by the hour on the calmer, central London waters of the **Serpentine** in Hyde Park and **Regent's Park Lake**.

Working Out

Most sports centers have gymnasiums, workout studios, and health clubs. If you are a member of the YMCA, you'll be able to use the excellent facilities at the **Central YMCA**. **Jubilee Hall Clubs** and the **Oasis Sports Centre** both offer a variety of aerobic classes and fitness and weight training. For those who have overdone it, the **Chelsea Sports Centre** has a sports injury clinic.

DIRECTORY

All England Lawn Tennis and Croquet Club
Church Rd, Wimbledon SW19. **Tel** 020 8944 1066.

Arsenal (Emirates) Stadium
Ashburton Grove N7.
Tel 020 7619 5000.

Ascot Racecourse
Ascot, Berkshire.
Tel 0844 346 3000.

Central YMCA
112 Great Russell St WC1.
Map 13 B1.
Tel 020 7343 1844.

Chelsea Football Club
Stamford Bridge SW6.
Tel 0871 984 1955.

Chelsea Sports Centre
Chelsea Manor St SW3.
Map 19 B3.
Tel 020 7352 6985.

Chessington Golf Course
Garrison Lane, Surrey.
Tel 020 8391 0948.

Docklands Sailing & Watersports Centre
235a Westferry Rd, E14.
Tel 020 7537 2626.
w dswc.org

Dulwich Croquet Club
Giant Arches Rd, Off Burbage Rd SE24.
w dulwichcroquet.com

Epsom Racecourse
Epsom Downs, Surrey.
Tel 01372 726 311.

Hampstead and Highgate Ponds
Mixed: off East Heath Rd NW3. **Map** 1 C4. Men's and Women's: Millfield Lane N6. **Map** 2 E3.
Tel 020 7482 7073.

Holland Park Public Tennis Courts
1 Ilchester Place W8. **Map** 9 B5. **Tel** 020 7602 2226.

Hounslow Heath Golf Course
Staines Rd, Middlesex TW4.
Tel 020 8570 5271.

Jubilee Hall Clubs
30 The Piazza, Covent Garden WC2. **Map** 13 C2.
Tel 020 7836 4007.

Kempton Park
Sunbury on Thames, Middx.
Tel 01932 782 292.

Kia Oval
Kennington Oval SE11.
Map 22 D4.
Tel 0844 375 1845.

Linford Christie Stadium
Du Cane Rd W12.
Tel 07908 788 739.

Lord's Cricket Ground
St. John's Wood NW8.
Map 3 A3.
Tel 020 7616 8500.

Oasis Swimming Pool & Sports Centre
32 Endell St WC2. **Map** 13 B1. **Tel** 020 7831 1804.

Parliament Hill
Highgate Rd NW5. **Map** 2 E5. **Tel** 020 7485 4491.

Porchester Centre
Queensway W2. **Map** 10 D1. **Tel** 020 7792 2919.

Queen's Club (Real Tennis)
Palliser Rd W14. **Map** 17 A3. **Tel** 020 7385 3400.

Queens Ice Skating Club
17 Queensway W2. **Map** 10 E2. **Tel** 020 7229 0172.

Regent's Park and Lake
Regent's Park NW1.
Map 3 C3. **Tel** 0300 061 2300, 020 7724 4069 (boat rentals).

Richmond Park Golf
Roehampton Gate, Priory Lane SW15.
Tel 020 8876 3205.

Romford Stadium
London Road, Essex RM7.
Tel 01708 762 345.

Rosslyn Park Rugby
Priory Lane, Upper Richmond Rd SW15.
Tel 020 8876 1879.

Ross Nye Stables
8 Bathurst Mews W2. **Map** 11 A2. **Tel** 020 7262 3791.

Sandown Park Racecourse
Esher, Surrey.
Tel 01372 464 348.

Saracens Rugby Football Club
5 Vicarage Rd, Watford, Hertfordshire, WD1.
Tel 01727 792 800.

Serpentine
Hyde Park W2. **Map** 11 B4.
Tel 020 7262 1330 (boat rentals).

Somerset House Ice Rink
Strand WC2. **Map** 14 D2.
Tel 0844 847 1520.

Tottenham Hotspur FC
White Hart Lane, 748 High Rd N17.
Tel 0844 499 5000.

Twickenham Rugby Ground
Whitton Rd, Twickenham, Middlesex.
Tel 020 8892 8877.

West Ham United
Boleyn Ground, Green St, Upton Park E13.
Tel 0871 529 1966.

CHILDREN'S LONDON

London offers children a potential gold mine of fun, excitement, and adventure. Each year there are new attractions and sights opening up and older ones being updated.

First-time visitors may want to watch traditional ceremonies (see pp54–7) or visit famous buildings (see p39), but these are only the tip of the iceberg. While London's parks, zoos, and adventure playgrounds provide outdoor activities, there are also lots of workshops, activity centers, and museums providing quizzes, hands-on experiments, and interactive displays. A day out need not be costly: children under 11 are entitled to free Tube, bus, and DLR travel provided they are traveling with an adult who has a valid ticket or Oystercard, and most major museums are free to everyone anyway.

Practical Advice

A little planning is the key to a successful outing with children. You may want to check the opening hours of the places you plan to visit in advance, by telephone or online via the venue's website. Plan your travel carefully using the Tube map at the end of this book.

If you are traveling with very young children, remember that there are likely to be lines at the Underground stations or bus stops near popular sights. These lines are long during peak hours, so buy your tickets, Travelcard, or Oyster card in advance (see p370).

Children under 11 can travel free on buses and the Underground, and child fares apply to all children between the ages of 11 and 15. Children very often enjoy using public transportation, especially when it's a novelty, so consider using one form of travel for the outward trip and another for the return home. You can get around London easily by bus,

Punch and Judy show in the Piazza, Covent Garden

Underground, taxi, train, and riverboat (see pp370–77).

Visiting all the exhibitions and museums as a family doesn't have to be as expensive as it sounds. The majority of London's principal museums have no entry charge. For those where you do have to pay, an annual family season ticket, usually for two adults and up to four children,

is available. This often costs only marginally more than the initial visit. In some cases you can buy a family ticket that covers a group of museums. Being able to visit a sight more than once means that you won't exhaust your children and put them off museums for life by trying to see absolutely everything over one long, tiring day.

If your children want a break from sightseeing, most borough councils provide information on activities for children such as play groups, theaters, fairs, and activity centers in their area. Leaflets are usually available from libraries and leisure centers, as well as local town halls. During the long summer school vacation (July to the beginning of September) there are organized activity programs all over London.

Children and the Law

Children under 14 are not allowed into British pubs and wine bars (unless there is a special family room or garden) and only people over 18 can drink or buy any alcohol. In restaurants, the law is a little more relaxed. Those over 16 can drink wine or beer with their meal, but you still have to be over 18 to be served liquor. In general, young children are rarely welcome anywhere they might create a nuisance. Some movies are rated unsuitable for children (see p339).

If you want to take your children by car, you must use seat belts wherever they are provided. Children

Covent Garden clowns

Eating Out with Children

Restaurants are becoming more welcoming of tiny patrons. Italian eateries are often the most friendly, but even the traditional British pub, once resolutely child-free, has relented, with beer gardens and family rooms. As long as your offspring are reasonably well-behaved, most informal restaurants will be happy to serve a family. Some can also provide high chairs and booster cushions, as well as coloring mats to keep children entertained while waiting for their food to arrive. Many will also offer special children's menus with small portions, which will reduce the cost of your meal.

On weekends, some restaurants (such as **Smollensky's** and **Sticky Fingers**) provide live entertainment for children in the form of clowns, face painters, and magicians. A number accept reservations for children's parties. It is always worth trying to reserve in advance (especially for Sunday lunch), so that you don't have to hang around waiting with tired and hungry children.

Coming up for air at Smollensky's

London has a number of restaurants ideal for older children. Among these are the **Rainforest Café** and the **Hard Rock Café** on Old Park Lane.

For budget eating, try the Café in the Crypt, St. Martin-in-the-Fields (*see p104*).

Dine with the elephants at the Rainforest Cafe

Useful Addresses

Hard Rock Café
150 Old Park Lane W1. **Map** 12 E4.
Tel 020 7514 1700.

Rainforest Café
20 Shaftesbury Ave W1. **Map** 13 A2.
Tel 020 7434 3111.

Smollensky's
105 Strand WC2. **Map** 14 D2.
Tel 020 7497 2101.

Sticky Fingers
1a Phillimore Gdns, W8. **Map** 9 C5.
Tel 020 7938 5338.

---

shorter than 4 ft 5 inches (135 cm) or under 12 years need a special car seat.

Family Fun

Many London museums (*see pp42–5*) and theaters (*see pp336–8*) provide wonderful activities and workshops: craft sessions, story times, child-friendly trails around museums or historic sites, or themed events specifically designed to get children engaged in and interacting with the exhibits and information on display. Some activities are educational; others purely for the fun of it. The children's theaters are also a great way to spend a rainy afternoon. A day at the fair is always a success – try Hampstead fair on summer bank holidays. London has a great many sports centers (*see pp346–7*), which often have special clubs to occupy children of every age. For more family-friendly ideas, see DK's *Family Guide to London*.

If you want a break from your children, call **Nannies Unlimited, Sitters, Kensington Nannies**, or **Pippa Pop-Ins**, a nursery school offering child care. Babysitters are vetted by the Criminal Records Bureau.

Babysitting

Kensington Nannies
3 Hornton Place W8.
Map 10 D5.
Tel 020 7937 2333.
🆆 **kensington-nannies.com**

Nannies Unlimited
64 The Moores, Redhill, Surrey, RH1 2PE. **Tel** 01737 643918.

Pippa Pop-Ins
430 Fulham Road SW6. **Map** 18 D5.
Tel 020 7731 1445.
Also at 233 New King's Rd SW6.

Sitters
Tel 08447 367367.
🆆 **sitters.co.uk**

Airborne at the Hampstead fair

Vacation fun at Pippa Pop-Ins

Shopping

All children love a visit to **Hamleys** toy shop or Harrods toy department (see p313). **Davenport's Magic Shop** and **The Disney Store** are smaller and more specialized.

Both the **Early Learning Centre** (many branches) and **The Golden Treasury Bookshop** have good selections of books. Some shops present readings and signings by children's authors, especially during Children's Book Week, held in October.

Useful Numbers The Golden Treasury Bookshop Tel 020 8333 0167; Davenport's Magic Shop Tel 020 7836 0408; The Disney Store Tel 020 7491 9136; Early Learning Centre Tel 020 7581 5764; Hamleys Tel 0870 333 2455.

Bears at Hamleys toy shop

Museums and Galleries

London has a wealth of museums, exhibitions, and galleries; more information on those listed here is to be found on pages 42–45. Most have been updated over the last few years to incorporate some exciting modern display techniques. It's unlikely that you'll have to drag reluctant children around an assortment of lifeless, stuffy exhibits.

The V&A Museum of Childhood (p250), the children's branch of the V&A in East London, and Pollock's Toy Museum (p133) are both especially good for young children.

For older children try one of London's Brass Rubbing Centres: the great Brass Rubbing Centre in the Crypt of St. Martin-in-the-Fields (p104) or at St. James's Church on Piccadilly (p92). Madame Tussauds (p226) and Tower Bridge (p155) are firm favorites with children.

The British Museum (pp128–9) has fabulous treasures from all over the world, and the Horniman Museum (p252) has colorful displays from many different cultures. The Science Museum (pp208–209), with over 600 working exhibits, is one of London's best attractions for children – its hands-on galleries in the basement, including the much-loved Launch Pad, will help keep them amused for hours. The interactive displays in the high-tech Wellcome Wing are also entertaining. If you have the stamina, the Natural History Museum (pp204–5) next door contains hundreds of amazing objects and animals from the world of nature. Included is a Dinosaur Exhibition. Suits of armor built for knights

Shirley Temple doll at Bethnal Green Museum

and monarchs can be seen at the Tower of London (pp156–9). More up-to-date armory and weapons, including aircraft and the tools of modern warfare, can be seen at the National Army Museum (p199) and the Imperial War Museum (pp192–3).

Also worth a visit is the Guards' Museum (p82) located on Birdcage Walk. London's colorful past is brought to life at the Museum of London. The superb London Aquarium (p190), on the south bank of the Thames, offers close-up encounters with sea life from starfish to sharks.

The Great Outdoors

London is fortunate in having many parks and open spaces (see pp50–53). Most local parks contain conventional playgrounds for children, many with modern, safe equipment. Some parks also have One O'Clock Clubs (enclosed areas for children under 5 with activities supervised by play-workers) as well as adventure playgrounds, nature trails, boating ponds, and athletic tracks for older children and energetic adults.

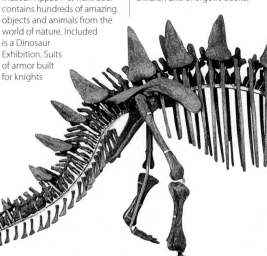

Puppets at the Little Angel Theatre, Islington

Playground at Gunnersbury Park

A delightful children's park in Bloomsbury is Coram's Fields (p131), where grassy areas, sandboxes, and playgrounds make it perfect for picnics. Kite-flying on Blackheath (p245), Hampstead Heath, or Parliament Hill can be fun, as can boating in Regent's Park. A trip to Primrose Hill (pp268–9) can be combined with a visit to the Zoo and Regent's Canal (p229). The large parks are one of London's greatest assets for parents who have energetic children.

For a good walk or cycle ride, there are parks all over London. For instance, there's Hyde Park in the central city; Hampstead Heath to the north; Wimbledon Common in southwest London; and Gunnersbury Park in west London. Cyclists should be sure to watch out for pedestrians and remember that some paths may be closed to bicycles.

Battersea Park has a children's zoo, and Crystal Palace Park (Penge SE20) has a dinosaur park. Richmond Park has a deer herd. For a relaxing trip, go and feed the ducks in St. James's Park.

Tuojiangasaurus skeleton at the Natural History Museum

Children's Theater

Introducing children to the theater can be great fun for adults too. Get involved at the **Little Angel Theatre,** or the **Puppet Theatre Barge** in Little Venice. The **Unicorn Theatre** offers the best range of children's theater and the **Polka Children's Theatre** has some good shows.

Useful Numbers

Little Angel Theatre
Tel 020 7226 1787.

Polka Children's Theatre
Tel 020 8543 4888.
W polkatheatre.com

Puppet Theatre Barge
Marionette Performers
Tel 020 7249 6876.
W puppetbarge.com

Unicorn Theatre
Tel 020 7645 0560.
W unicorntheatre.com

Deer in Richmond Park

Sightseeing

For seeing the sights of London you can't beat the top of a double-decker bus (see pp374–5). It's a cheap and easy way of entertaining children, and if they get restless you can always jump off the bus at the next stop. London's colorful ceremonies are detailed on pages 54–7. Children will also enjoy such spectacles as the summer fairs in London's

Boating lake near Winfield House in Regent's Park

parks, the fireworks displays throughout London on Guy Fawkes Night (November 5), and the Christmas decorations on Oxford Street and Regent Street and Trafalgar Square's Christmas tree.

Behind the Scenes

Older children in particular will love the opportunity to look "behind the scenes" and see how famous events or institutions are run.

If you have a brood of sports enthusiasts, you should visit Twickenham Rugby Football Ground (see p347), Lord's Cricket Ground (p248), the Wimbledon Lawn Tennis Museum (p253), and Chelsea Football Stadium (p347).

For budding theater buffs, the Royal National Theatre (p190), the Royal Opera House (p117), Sadler's Wells (p342), and the Theatre Royal Drury Lane (p117) all offer tours.

Other good buildings for children to visit include the Tower of London (pp156–9), the Old Bailey law courts (p149), and the Houses of Parliament (pp74–5).

If none of the above satisfies the children, the London Fire Brigade (020 7587 4063) offers more unusual guided tours.

SURVIVAL GUIDE

PRACTICAL INFORMATION

London has responded well to the demands of modern tourism. The range of facilities available to travelers, from ATMs and medical clinics to boutique hotels and late-night transportation, continues to expand. Whether you find London an expensive city will depend on the exchange rate between the pound and your own currency. London is known for high hotel prices, but even here there are good mid-range and budget options *(see pp280–3)*. You need not spend a lot on food, if you choose carefully and make the most of the options London has to offer; for the price of a single meal at some West End restaurants, you could eat enjoyably for several days *(see pp304–7)*. The following tips will help you make the most of your visit.

Crossing the Millennium Bridge

When to Go

London's weather is famously changeable, but in general it is chilly from November to February, and warmest from June to August *(see p61)*. It can rain at any time of year, so pack accordingly. Extremes of temperature – whether of cold in winter or heat in summer – are rare, so there is no one time of year when London closes down and everyone goes on vacation. Events and cultural programs run throughout the year. Many major concert series and exhibitions take place in winter and spring, but there are plenty of cultural events during the summer too, such as the BBC Proms season of classical concerts, and open-air theater seasons. In short, there's plenty to see all year *(see pp58–61)*.

Visas and Passports

Citizens of European Union countries may enter the UK for an unlimited period with a passport or national identity card. Visitors from the United States, Canada, Australia, and New Zealand need only a full passport for tourist and business stays of up to six months, but on arrival they must fill in an Immigration Card, which is given out on incoming flights. Citizens of some countries may require a visa; details can be found in the "Visa Services" section of the **UK Border Agency** (UKBA) website. The UK has not signed the Schengen open-borders agreement operated by most EU countries. Hence, visitors arriving from France or any other Schengen country must still pass through immigration checks when entering the UK.

The UKBA has a strict points-based visa system under which anyone from any non-EU country (including the US, Canada, Australia, and New Zealand) entering Britain for any purpose other than pure tourism or short business trips (this includes students on short study-abroad programs) must obtain a visa before traveling. The visa system is complicated and detailed, so check well in advance; details are on the UKBA website.

Signposted directions

Customs Information

EU residents may carry any amount of goods between EU countries without paying duty, as long as the goods are for their personal use. Customs officers can still question whether large amounts of any item are genuinely for your own use. Examples of amounts usually accepted are: up to 3,200 cigarettes and up to 90 liters of wine. For travelers arriving from outside the EU, stricter allowances apply – for example, 200 cigarettes. Visitors not resident in the EU can reclaim the Value Added Tax (VAT) on many goods when they leave Britain, but note that the items must have been bought from a shop operating the VAT Retail Export Scheme (which should be indicated in the shop window). Ask the retailer for the correct form, which has details on how to obtain your refund; these can also be found on the UKBA website under "Travel and Customs."

Tourist Information and Tours

Visit London is the city's central tourism service and is a key source of information. Tourist Information Centres can be found all over London (visit www.london. com has a full list). The City of London Information Centre, located by St. Paul's Cathedral, provides leaflets on attractions, tours, museums, walks and public transportation. Others can be found at major train stations. The centers sell travelcards and **London Pass** *(see p355)* discount cards, provide currency exchange, and distribute Visit London's free monthly magazine, *London Planner*.

For comprehensive listings information – including art, movies, music, theater, and nightlife – visit the websites of **LondonNet** and *Time Out London*, London's leading listings magazine.

Double-decker sightseeing boat on the Thames

Guided tours are an effective way to explore the city; a trip in an open-topped double-decker bus makes a good introduction. **Original London Sightseeing Tours** and **Big Bus Tours** are the main companies offering hop-on, hop-off services, with tickets valid for 24 or 48 hours. Other tour companies include **London Walks**, which offers over 40 different routes, and **London Duck Tours**, for tours in a World War II-era vehicle. To find a private tour guide to suit your interests, contact the **Association of Professional Tourist Guides**. For river cruises and commuter services, see page 63.

Major sights in London are often crowded, with long lines. Museums and galleries get particularly busy on weekends and late-opening nights, so try to visit midweek.

Admission Prices

Admission to the main collections of London's major public museums and galleries is free, but you will pay to see temporary exhibits. Private museums and other attractions have admission charges; they vary greatly, but for adults most are between £5 and £15. There are often reduced prices for seniors, students, and children.

If you aim to do lots of sightseeing, you can cut costs with a **London Pass**, a card that gives you free entry and fast-track admission at many attractions. Cards are valid for 1, 2, 3, or 6 days and can be combined with a bus and Underground travelcard. A London Pass can be bought in advance from www.visitlondon.com and mailed to your home or picked up from a tourist center.

Opening Hours

Opening times for individual sights are listed in the *Area by Area* section of this book. Core visiting times are 10am to 5pm or 6pm daily; last admission is usually 1 hour before closing time. Most of the big museums have at least one late-opening day each week. Opening hours are often shorter on Sundays and public holidays. Some smaller attractions are closed on Mondays.

Social Customs and Etiquette

Londoners are traditionally renowned for standing in line – whether for theater tickets, taxis, or takeouts. Things aren't quite as genteel as they used to be, but in general, anyone barging in will still encounter frosty glares.

Casual clothing is accepted in most restaurants, and only a few upscale establishments still require men to wear a jacket and tie.

The religious pattern of London reflects the city's huge ethnic diversity; all of the world's major faiths are represented here.

Smoking is forbidden in all public indoor spaces. Some hotels still designate bedrooms for smokers, but it's best to double check when booking.

Tipping

It is usual to tip in restaurants, hotels, hair salons, taxis, and minicabs, but not for bar service in pubs. Many restaurants add a service charge – usually 12.5 percent – to the bill, in which case a tip is not necessary. Be wary of places that add a service charge, then encourage you to add a "gratuity" when you pay by credit card. In taxis, tip around 10 percent; for hotel porters, £1 is usually sufficient.

Travelers with Special Needs

Access to transportation and attractions, and services for wheelchair users and others with mobility problems, are continually improving. The Visit London website has a guide to access and services. **Transport for London** (TfL) produces a *Getting around London* guide, which can be downloaded from the TfL or Visit London websites, and is available free from Underground stations. **Artsline** gives information on facilities at cultural events and venues.

Nearly all London buses have wheelchair-access ramps, and all licensed taxis and some minicabs are wheelchair-accessible. The huge task of improving access to the entire Underground network is ongoing. Underground maps show accessible stations. Most museums and theaters have access facilities, but hotels with fully adapted rooms are scarce.

Disabled drivers with a blue badge allowing free parking should note that in four London boroughs – the City, Westminster, Kensington & Chelsea, and Camden – it allows you to park only in designated blue-badge bays.

London bus with ramp for easy wheelchair access

The Natural History Museum, a great day out for the whole family

Traveling with Children

Under Transport for London's "Kids Go Free" program, travel is free on buses, the Underground, DLR, and trains within London for all children under 11 and accompanied by an adult (up to four children per adult). Children ages 11 to 15 also travel free, with or without an adult, on all buses, and for reduced prices on the Underground and DLR (see p370); also available is a Zip Oyster 11–15 Identity Card, which can be ordered online and picked up at a Tourist Information Centre on arrival in London; see the Visit London and Transport for London websites.

Most museums and attractions have reduced prices for children under 11; at several, entry is free for under-5s. Many also offer good-value family tickets. Plenty of restaurants welcome children, and a number of hotels have family rooms; the Novotel chain represents a particularly good deal for families.

London is a child-friendly city. A huge variety of entertainments and activities are put on for children, and many museums have special kids' programs. There are dozens of parks, many of them with playground facilities. The Visit London website's "Family" pages are a useful source of information. Time Out London's "Kids" pages are good for current attractions.

Senior Travelers

Older visitors enjoy fewer special benefits than younger ones, but there are reduced admission prices for over-60s at most museums and other attractions. You may be asked to show photo ID. Free travel on mass transit is only available to residents.

Gay and Lesbian Travelers

London has a huge and diverse gay scene. Its core is Soho – it even has a (non-official) **LGBT Tourist Office**, which offers advice on everything from the best gay bars to accommodations. It's hard to keep track of everything going on, but the **Pink Paper** and **Gay London** websites, as well as the gay pages of Time Out London, have up-to-date information.

Traveling on a Budget

London can be a very expensive city, but sightseeing costs can be cut with the London Pass (see p355), and remember that admission to London's largest museums is free. To get around

International Student Identity Card (ISIC)

town by public transportation, always buy a travelcard rather than single tickets; for trips out of town, coach is much cheaper than train, especially when reserved in advance. Discounted theater tickets can be bought at the **tkts** booth in Leicester Square, and many theaters have cheap-ticket nights.

London has plenty of budget restaurants and cafés, and even grand restaurants offer accessibly priced lunch menus. As well as dorm-style hostels, there are no-frills budget hotels with private rooms, some with private bathrooms, for under £50 (see p283). There's also a growing trend for spare-room rentals and "couch surfing" via **Airbnb**.

Students pay lower admission to many exhibitions, and holders of an **ISIC** (International Student Identity Card) or IYTC (International Youth Travel Card) are eligible for a range of other discounts. A **Hostelling International** card is also handy for lower rates at hostels and other discounts.

Electricity

The voltage in London is 240V AC, and plugs have three square pins. Visitors will need plug adapters for appliances, and with any older North American 110V equipment you may also need a current transformer.

Conversion Chart

Officially the metric system is used, but imperial measures are still common.

Imperial to metric
1 inch = 2.5 centimeters
1 foot = 30 centimeters
1 mile = 1.6 kilometers
1 ounce = 28 grams
1 pound = 454 grams
1 pint (1.25 US pints) = 0.6 liter
1 gallon (1.2 US gal) = 4.6 liters

Metric to imperial
1 millimeter = 0.04 inch
1 centimeter = 0.4 inch
1 meter = 3 feet 3 inches
1 kilometer = 0.6 mile
1 gram = 0.04 ounce
1 kilogram = 2.2 pounds

Time

London is on Greenwich Mean Time (GMT) during the winter months, 5 hours ahead of Eastern Standard Time and 10 hours behind Sydney. From late March to late October, clocks are set forward 1 hour to British Summer Time (equivalent to Central European Time). At any time of year you can check the correct time by dialing 123 on a BT landline to contact the 24-hour automated Speaking Clock service (note that there is a charge for this service).

Responsible tourism

London has set itself ambitious targets for improving the urban environment and reducing energy use. **Thames 21**, for example, is an environmental charity that involves the local community in programs to help keep the Thames clean and clear.

The **Green Tourism Business Scheme** awards "Green Tourism" badges to businesses in the UK that meet the highest

environmental standards. These standards ensure that each business is committed to sustainable tourism and dedicated to minimizing its damage to the environment. See the website for green accommodation details.

Recycling bins, which separate paper and plastic, are widely available and many shoppers carry reusable cloth bags to avoid using plastic bags.

Green Tourism badge

DIRECTORY

Visas and Passports

UK Border Agency
W ukba.homeoffice.gov.uk

Embassies and Consulates

Australian High Commission
Australia House,
The Strand, WC2.
Map 13 C2.
Tel 020 7379 4334.
W uk.embassy.gov.au

Canadian High Commission
1 Grosvenor Square, W1.
Map 12 D2. Tel 020 7258 6600. W unitedkingdom.gc.ca

New Zealand High Commission
80 Haymarket, SW1.
Map 13 A3.
Tel 020 7930 8422.
W nzembassy.com/united-kingdom

United States Embassy
24 Grosvenor Square, W1.
Map 12 D2.
Tel 020 7499 9000.
W usembassy.org.uk

Tourist Information

Association of Professional Tour Guides
Tel 020 7611 2545.
W guidelondon.org.uk

Big Bus Tours
Tel 020 7233 9533.
W bigbustours.com

City of London Information Centre
St. Paul's Churchyard EC4M 8BX. **Map** 15 A2.
Open Daily.

London Duck Tours
Tel 020 7928 3132.
W londonducktours.co.uk

LondonNet
W londonnet.co.uk

London Pass
W londonpass.com

London Walks
Tel 020 7624 3978.
W walks.com

Original London Sightseeing Tour
Tel 020 8877 1722.

Time Out London
W timeout.com/london

Transport for London
W tfl.gov.uk

Visit London
W visitlondon.com

Religious Services

Anglican (Episcopalian)
St. Paul's Cathedral EC4.
Map 15 A2.
Tel 020 246 8350.
W stpauls.co.uk

Catholic
Westminster Cathedral Victoria St SW1. **Map** 20 F1. **Tel** 020 7798 9055.
W westminstercathedral.org.uk

Evangelical Alliance
UK Resource Centre,
176 Copenhagen St N1.
Map 6 D1.
Tel 020 7520 3830.
W eauk.org

Jewish
Liberal Jewish Synagogue, 28 St John's Wood Rd NW8.
Map 3 A3. **Tel** 020 7286 5181. W ljs.org

United Synagogue (Orthodox)
735 High Rd, N12.
Tel 020 8343 8989.
W theus.org.uk

Muslim
Islamic Cultural Centre,
146 Park Rd NW8.
Map 3 B3.
Tel 020 7724 3363.
W iccuk.org

Travelers with Special Needs

Artsline
W artsline.org.uk

Transport for London
Tel 0843 222 1234
(24 hours).
W tfl.gov.uk

Gay & Lesbian Travelers

Diva
W divamag.co.uk

Gay London
W gaylondon.com

Gay Times
W gaytimes.co.uk

LGBT Tourist Information Office
25 Frith St, W1.
Map 13 B2.
Tel 020 7437 0003.
W gaytouristoffice.co.uk

Traveling on a Budget

Airbnb
W airbnb.com

Hostelling International
W hihostels.com

ISIC (International Student Identity Card)
W isiccard.com

tkts (Discount Theatre Tickets)
Leicester Square, WC2.
Map 13 B2. W tkts.co.uk

Responsible Tourism

Thames 21
W thames21.org.uk

Tourism Business Scheme
Tel 01738 632 162.
W greenbusiness.co.uk

Personal Security and Health

London is a large city that, like any other, has had its share of urban problems. It has also been a terrorist target, and London life is sometimes disrupted by security alerts. Nearly all of these turn out to be false alarms, but they should always still be taken seriously. Never hesitate to approach one of London's many police officers for assistance – they are trained to help the public with problems.

Mounted police

Police

If you are robbed, or are the victim of any other kind of crime, report it to the police as soon as possible. Patrolling police officers are generally fairly easy to find in central London, but if you cannot find one, call or go to the nearest police station – these are listed on the **Metropolitan Police** website; alternatively, your hotel should be able to advise. Note that the **City of London Police** is a separate force, with its own website. Police stations are also shown on the Street Finder maps toward the end of this book (pp378–415).

When you report a crime, police will take a statement from you, and you will need to list any lost or stolen items.

What to Be Aware Of

It is unlikely that your stay in London will be blighted by crime. Even in run-down parts of town, the risk of having your pocket picked or bag stolen is not particularly great. It is actually more likely to happen in the middle of heaving shopping crowds in areas like Oxford Street or Camden Lock, or perhaps on a packed Underground platform.

As in any big city, the risk of being a victim of street crime can be further reduced by following a few sensible precautions. Make sure your possessions are adequately insured before you travel.

Do not carry all your valuables around with you – take only as much cash as you need, and leave the rest in a hotel safe or a locked suitcase.

Avoid poorly lit or isolated places like back streets, parks, and unstaffed train stations at night, and don't use ATMs after dark. To be extra careful, try to travel around in a group at night.

In crowds, be aware of anyone standing especially close. Keep bags zipped up; keep a hand on your bag when walking; and never leave bags unattended in any public place – they may be stolen or considered a security threat. When you sit at a table, especially outdoors, always keep your bag within reach and in sight – preferably on your lap or on the table – and never leave it on the ground or hanging on the back of a chair.

In an Emergency

In a serious emergency you can call 999 – or the European emergency number 112 – to summon police, fire, or ambulance services. Note that this is only for genuine emergencies, so if you

have a lesser problem, it is better to contact a police station or hospital directly.

Lost and Stolen Property

Although you should report thefts, or loss of any property, to the police, be warned that it's unlikely that they will be able to recover any of it for you. However, they will give you a copy of your police statement, which you will need to make an insurance claim.

If you lose anything on buses, Underground and DLR trains, or in taxis (black cabs), it should eventually reach the **Transport for London Lost Property Office** on Baker Street. You can also inquire about lost items online, through the TfL website (under "Help & Contact" or "Useful Contacts"). It will usually take a few days for items to reach the office, so if you notice the loss the same day, try to inquire about it at the station closest to where you lost it, or at the nearest police station. Items lost on river boats or in minicabs should be held by the individual companies.

Hospitals and Pharmacies

All European Union nationals with a European Health Insurance Card (EHIC), as well as citizens of some other countries with special agreements with the UK (Australia and New Zealand among them), can obtain free treatment from the British **National Health Service (NHS)**. Visitors from other non-EU countries should have full medical cover as part of their travel insurance, and if necessary make use of an NHS or private hospital (such as **Medical Express**) on a paying basis.

Traffic police officer

Pharmacy sign

Typical London police car

London ambulance

London fire engine

In an emergency, anyone – EU or non-EU – will be treated free of charge.

If you have an accident or other problem needing medical attention, ask your hotel to recommend a doctor, or go to the nearest NHS clinic, doctor's "surgery" (office), or hospital Accident & Emergency (A&E) department. Not all hospitals have A&E departments, but those that do are listed on the NHS and Visit London websites, and in local phone books. In many cases the simplest thing may be to call **NHS Direct**, a free advice service that will give you immediate health advice and also direct you to the nearest hospital A&E department.

If you have a dental problem, you can also call NHS Direct for addresses of emergency dentists. Dental treatment through the NHS is not entirely free, so it may make more sense to arrange private treatment (again, hotels should be able to recommend a dentist) and claim the cost on your insurance policy.

Pharmacies (also known as chemists) are plentiful around London, and pharmacists are trained to dispense and advise on a wide range of medications. Some medicines are only available with a prescription. It is worth noting that prescription drugs are not free even if you are entitled to NHS treatment; if you are not, you will be charged the full price, and will need to make an insurance claim. **Boots** is the largest chain of pharmacies in the UK. Most pharmacies are closed on Sundays, but those listed in the Directory, below, have extended hours.

Travel and Health Insurance

All visitors to London should have a comprehensive travel insurance policy providing adequate cover for all eventualities including potential legal expenses, theft, lost luggage or other property, accidents, cancellations, travel delays, and medical cover. Even if you are entitled to use the NHS for medical needs, it can be a good idea to have private medical insurance included, too, as a backup, since this may allow you to get quicker treatment with fewer formalities. Your insurance company should provide you with a 24-hour emergency number in case of need.

DIRECTORY

Emergencies

Police, Fire & Ambulance services
Tel 999 or 112.
Calls are free.

Police

City of London Police
Tel 101 (non-emergencies).
W cityoflondon.
police.uk

Metropolitan Police
Tel 0300 123 1212.
W met.police.uk

West End Central Police Station
27 Saville Row, W1.
Map 12 F2.
Tel 020 7437 1212.

Lost Property

Transport for London Lost Property Office
200 Baker St, NW1.
Map 3 C5.
Tel 0343 222 1234.
Open 8.30am–4pm
Mon-Fri. W tfl.gov.uk

Health Services

Medical Express (Private)
117A Harley St, W1.
Tel 0800 9800 700.
W medicalexpress
clinic.com

NHS
W nhs.uk
To locate a hospital, look under "Find and choose services".

NHS Direct

Tel 0845 4647.
W nhsdirect.nhs.uk
(24-hr health information and nurse-led advice).

University College Hospital
Accident and Emergency,
235 Euston Road NW1.
Map 5 A4.
Tel 0845 155 5000.

Dentists

24-Hour Emergency Dental Clinic
8F Gilbert Place WC1.
Map 13 B1.
Tel 020 3199 0178.
W 24hour-london-
emergencydentist.co.uk

Late-Opening Pharmacies

Bliss Chemist
5–6 Marble Arch W1.
Map 11 C2.
Tel 020 7723 6116. Open
9am until midnight daily.

Boots the Chemist
44–46 Regent St, W1.
Map 13 A3.
Tel 020 7734 6126.
Open 8am–midnight
Mon–Fri, 9am–midnight
Sat, noon–6pm Sun.
W boots.com

Superdrug
508–520 Oxford St, W1.
Map 11 C2. Tel 020 7629
1649. Open 7am–11pm
Mon–Fri, 8am–10pm Sat,
12:30–6:30pm Sun.
W superdrug.com

Banking and Local Currency

Visitors to London will find that banks usually offer the best rates of exchange, but care should be taken to check the small print relating to commissions and other charges before completing a transaction. Privately owned bureaux de change have variable exchange rates and commissions – some, in particular, charge more for changing smaller amounts of money – but they do stay open long after the banks have closed.

ATM (cashpoint machine)

Banks and Bureax de Change

Banking hours vary. The minimum opening hours for all banks are 9:30am–3:30pm Mon–Fri, but many branches now stay open until 5 or 5:30pm, especially in central London; some also open on Saturdays from about 10am to 4pm. All banks are closed on Sundays and public holidays (see p61). The commission charged on currency exchange will vary from bank to bank.

When banks are closed, there are plenty of other facilities for changing cash and traveler's checks across the city. You will find bureaux de change at airports, main train stations, in large stores, and at many other locations. **Chequepoint, Thomas Cook,** and **Travelex** are some of the largest companies. The central London (Piccadilly) branch of **Money Corporation** is open 24 hours a day.

Credit Cards and Traveler's Checks

Major credit cards such as Visa and MasterCard, and debit cards such as Delta, Maestro, and Cirrus, are widely accepted all over London. Fewer businesses accept the American Express card because of its high commission fees.

British credit and debit cards operate on a chip-and-PIN security system; you must enter your PIN number into a card reader to validate the purchase. If you have a North American or other card that does not use chip-and-pin technology, your card will have to be swiped in the more traditional way.

It may also be useful to carry some currency n traveler's checks, in case you lose your credit or debit cards. Traveler's checks cannot be used to pay for goods directly in shops in the UK, but must be exchanged for cash at a bank or bureau de change. US dollar and euro traveler's checks are easily exchanged at all banks and change desks. Again, check the latest commission rates and conditions before cashing your checks.

ATMs

There are ATMs (also known as cashpoints), from which you can obtain cash with any of the major credit or debit cards, at all bank branches, many post offices, and many other locations such as train stations. The cards accepted by each ATM are indicated on the machine, which usually gives instructions in several languages. Given the high commission rates sometimes charged by banks and bureaux de change for exchanging traveler's checks, the most economical, as well as most convenient, way to get cash can be to withdraw it from an ATM with a debit card.

DIRECTORY

Bureaux de change

All have branches across London.

Chequepoint
Tel 1 800 528 4800.
W americanexpress.com

Money Corporation
18 Piccadilly, W1.
Map 13 A3.
Tel 08456 210 210.
Open 24 hours daily.
W moneycorp.com

Thomas Cook
Tel 0845 246 4353.
W thomascook.com/money

Travelex
Tel 0845 872 7627.
W travelex.co.uk

Lost Credit Cards

American Express
Tel 01273 696 933.

MasterCard
Tel 0800 964 767.

Visa
Tel 0800 891 725.

Major Banks

These are some of the major banks found all over London. Many also offer currency-exchange facilities, but proof of identity may be required.

Santander logo

National Westminster logo

HSBC logo

Barclays Bank logo

Lloyds TSB logo

Avoid using the independent ATMs found in some small shops, since they often add expensive extra charges. There is also a certain risk of crime at some ATMs. Avoid using any in dark streets at night, and don't use an ATM if any part of it looks damaged or as if it has been tampered with, especially the card slot. Be aware of anyone standing close to you when using an ATM, and shield the numbered keypad with your hand as you enter your PIN.

Currency

Britain's currency is the pound sterling (£), which is divided into 100 pence (p). Since there are no exchange controls in Britain, there is no limit to how much cash you may import or export. Many large stores in London accept payments in US dollars and euros, but often at a poor exchange rate.

English bank notes (bills) of all denominations always feature the Queen's head on one side

Bank Notes (Bills)

English notes used in the UK are £5, £10, £20, and £50. Scotland has its own notes, which, despite being legal tender throughout the UK, are often accepted with reluctance.

£50 note

£20 note

£10 note

£5 note

Coins of the Realm

Coins in circulation are £2, £1, 50p, 20p, 10p, 5p, 2p and 1p (they are shown here slightly smaller than actual size). They all have the Queen's head on the other side.

2 pounds (£2)

1 pound (£1)

50 pence (50p)

20 pence (20p)

10 pence (10p)

5 pence (5p)

2 pence (2p)

1 penny (1p)

Communication and Media

The telecommunications systems in Britain are efficient and inexpensive. Most landline phones and public phone booths are operated by British Telecom (BT), and there are many other cell phone operators and Internet service providers. Charges on BT lines depend on when, where, and for how long you talk. National calls are most expensive from 9am to 1pm on weekdays. A cheap rate applies before 7am or after 7pm on weekdays, and all day on weekends. Cheap times for overseas calls vary, but tend to be on weekends and in the evening.

International and Local Telephone Calls

All London landline telephone numbers have 11 digits and begin with the code 020. Phone numbers in central London continue with 7, and in outer London with 8, although some business numbers continue with 3. If you are calling from another London number, you do not need to dial the 020, only the remaining eight digits. Every other part of Britain has its own area code, beginning with 01 or 02.

British Telecom logo

If possible, avoid making calls from hotels – especially long-distance – as most add hefty surcharges; some even charge for toll-free calls. There are several special-rate numbers within the UK. Phone numbers beginning 03 are low-cost numbers used mostly by public bodies, such as the police. All 0800 or 0808 numbers are free to call from UK landlines (but not from cell phones). 0844, 0845, 0870, and 0871 numbers are reduced-rate lines that are used by many companies and organizations for information services. Numbers beginning 09 are premium-rate and thus particularly expensive.

To call Britain from abroad, dial 00 44, but then omit the initial zero from the UK area code. So to call the London number 020 7123 4567 from abroad, you would dial 00 44 20 7123 4567. To call abroad from London, dial 00 and then the usual country code (for example, Australia: 61; US and Canada: 1).

Cell Phones

All UK cell phone numbers begin with 07. Calling a cell from a landline is considerably more expensive than calling another landline.

There is a very high level of cell-phone ownership in London, and signal coverage is good all over the city. UK phones use the European standard 900 and 1900 MHz frequencies, so phones from other European countries work easily here as long as they have their roaming facility enabled. North American and Asian cell phones will not operate here unless they have a tri- or quad-band facility (which is increasingly standard on current phones). Before using a cell phone while traveling, always check with your own service provider on the current level of roaming charges, which can be high. Many companies offer "packages" of foreign calls to cut costs.

If you anticipate using the phone a great deal, it may be more economical to buy a cheap "pay-as-you-go" British phone (a basic one can cost as little as £10, or less) from one of the main local providers, such as **O2**, **EE,** or **Vodafone**, all of which have stores all over the city.

Public Telephones

You will find a **BT** phone booth on many streets in central London, and in every train station. Some are the old-style red ones, others are much more modern in appearance; but whichever type, they generally have the same technology inside. Some have multimedia terminals allowing Internet and email access. You can pay with coins, or by credit or debit card. Payphones accept 10p, 20p, 50p, £1, and £2 coins; some also accept euro coins (50c, €1, and €2). The minimum call cost is 60p for the first 30 minutes to a UK landline; and 10p for each 10 minutes after that. For a short call, use 10p or 20p pieces, as payphones only return unused coins. For credit-card calls, the minimum charge is £1.20.

Old BT phone box   Modern BT phone booth

Useful Dialing Codes

- The area code for London is 020.
- Phone numbers in central London start with 7 or 3, and in outer areas with 8. The 020 prefix must be used if dialing from outside these two areas.
- British Telecom directory assistance is 118 500.
- If you have any problems contacting a number, call the operator at 100.
- To make an international call, dial 00 followed by the country code (US and Canada: 1; Australia: 61; New Zealand: 64), the area code, and the number. The international operator number is 155 (freephone).
- A phonecard needs at least £2 credit for an international call.
- **In an emergency, dial 999 or 112. All emergency calls are free.**

Internet and Email

Internet access is very easy to find in London. Public libraries, Tourist Information Centres, and some other public buildings have free terminals. Internet cafés are common in every part of the city, and rates per hour are often very low.

Many hotels and a growing number of budget B&Bs and hostels offer Wi-Fi access. Some hotels charge, but this is increasingly rare. There are also many free Wi-Fi hotspots across London, in public libraries, arts centers, cafés, restaurants and pubs.

Postal Services

Standard mail in the UK is handled by the **Royal Mail**. There are main post offices providing all postal services in every London district, as well as many smaller sub-post offices attached to newsstands and other small shops – these can handle all normal mail. Main post offices are usually open from 9am to 5:30pm Monday to Friday, and to 12:30pm on Saturday. **Trafalgar Square Post Office** has extended hours: 8am–8pm Monday to Saturday. Post offices also exchange money and handle international money transfers.

Mail within the UK can be sent first or second class. First class costs a little more and is faster. Stamps can be bought from post offices or any shop with a "Stamps sold here" sign. Newsstands usually sell them, but may only have UK first- and second-class stamps, so for international mail you may need to find a post office. Hotels nearly always sell stamps, and larger ones may have mailboxes. Public mailboxes come in different shapes and sizes – some are sunk into walls – but are always red, and can be found throughout the city. There are several

Old-style pillar mailbox

Newsstand stocking a range of international newspapers

pick-up times each day (Mon–Sat); these times are indicated on the mailbox.

International letters and cards sent from London take about three days to reach European destinations, and four to six days to North America, Japan, or Australasia. A competitively priced Airsure service is available for express deliveries (2–4 days worldwide), as well as a much slower but cheaper surface mail option.

Newspapers and Magazines

London's main local paper is the *Evening Standard*, distributed free in the center of town from noon on weekdays. *Time Out London* magazine, published each Thursday, is London's most comprehensive listings guide.

A range of international newspapers and magazines, including *USA Today*, *International Herald Tribune*, and major European papers, is on sale at many newsstands and shops around central London. For more specialized foreign press, one of the best places to go is Old Compton Street in Soho, where newsagents regularly carry an extraordinary global variety.

TV and Radio

The UK's analog signal has been turned off; all radio and TV is digital. The publicly owned BBC operates several television stations, including BBC One,

BBC Two and BBC News. Other free-to-air channels are the independent ITV, Channel 4, and Five. Extra channels available include BBC3 (youth-oriented), BBC4 (arts-oriented), and various movie, shopping, and music channels. In addition, many hotels also have satellite systems. If you want to be able to view a wide range of US and other international channels (such as ESPN), ask whether a hotel has Sky Plus or an enhanced Freeview package.

The BBC also has a large number of radio stations, of which Radio 1 (97–99 FM) and Radio 2 (88–91 FM) focus on pop music of different kinds, Radio 3 (90.2 FM) on classical and jazz, Radio 4 (92–96 FM) on speech and drama, and Radio 5 (909/693 AM) on news and sports. BBC London (94.9 FM) is good for local issues and interests.

DIRECTORY

Telephone Services

British Telecom (BT)
Tel 150 or 0800 800 150.
W bt.com

O2
Tel 0844 202 0202.
W o2.co.uk

Orange
Tel 07973 100 150.
W orange.co.uk

T-Mobile
Tel 0800 956 2208.
W t-mobile.co.uk

Vodafone
Tel 0808 408 408.
W vodafone.co.uk

Postal Services

Royal Mail
Tel 0845 7740 740.
W royalmail.com

Trafalgar Square PO
24 William IV St, WC2.
Map 13 B3. **Tel** 020 7930 9580.

Newspapers and Magazines

Evening Standard
W thisislondon.co.uk

Time Out
W timeout.com/london

GETTING TO LONDON

London is one of Europe's central hubs for international air and rail travel. By air, travelers face a bewildering choice of carriers from Europe, North America, Australasia, East Asia, and every other part of the globe. Stiff competition on some routes, especially from major European countries and North America, means that low-fare deals can often be found, so it's always worth shopping around. Since 1995, the Channel Tunnel has provided an efficient high-speed train link – Eurostar – between France and Belgium and the UK, as well as a fast, weatherproof Channel crossing for drivers. Eurostar trains depart from St. Pancras International Station in London's King's Cross. Many European cruises sail from or finish at ports not far from London, such as Southampton, Dover, or Tilbury, and there are efficient passenger and car ferry services from Europe, using large ferries and faster jetfoils and catamarans, across the North Sea and the English Channel.

Station concourse at St. Pancras International

Arriving by Rail

Eurostar runs frequent daily trains to London from Paris, Brussels, and Lille, where the Paris and Brussels lines meet. Nonstop trains from Paris (Gare du Nord) take 2 hours 15 minutes; from Brussels, 1 hour 50 minutes. Some trains also stop at Calais before entering the Channel Tunnel on the French side, and at Ashford and Ebbsfleet on the English side. If you travel by train from any other part of Europe and want to connect with Eurostar, it's best to do so at Lille, since you change trains in the same station – faster and far easier than switching in Paris. Check-in on Eurostar is only 30 minutes before departure, so it's generally much quicker than flying.

Eurostar trains arrive in London at St. Pancras International, on the northern edge of central London, next to King's Cross Underground station. The station is an intersection of six Underground lines, so it is well connected with every part of

the city. Eurostar fares vary a good deal according to flexibility and the time of day you travel (early morning trains are often the cheapest), so check current rates on the website when booking. Information and tickets for connecting trains from other parts of Europe can be found on the **Rail Europe** website.

London has eight mainline rail stations at which trains from different parts of Britain terminate: Paddington serves the West Country, Wales, and the South Midlands; Liverpool Street serves East Anglia and Essex; King's Cross, St. Pancras, and Euston cover northern Britain; and Charing Cross, Victoria, and Waterloo cover southern England and also the main Channel ferry ports.

The current UK rail system is complicated and can be confusing. Lines are run by several different companies, but they are coordinated by **National Rail**, which operates a shared information service.

Fare structures are especially complex: tickets can be very expensive or surprisingly cheap, depending on whether you grasp how the system operates. Going to a station the same day you want to travel and buying a ticket over the counter is always the most expensive way to travel. Whenever possible, book trains in advance and check alternative fares, bearing in mind that the best fares may only be available online. The National Rail website has a useful "cheapest fare finder" feature, which then links you to the relevant company site to make the booking. Also helpful is **Trainline**, an independent booking agency that often has discounted tickets. Tickets bought online can usually be picked up at the station.

Fares on suburban rail services around London are less complex, so there is no need to book ahead. Rail lines within London accept the Oyster Card (see p370).

Rail information point at a London station, for help and advice

Cross-channel ferry heading to Calais

Arriving by Coach

International and national coach services (long-haul buses) from every part of Europe and the UK arrive in London at Victoria Coach Station on Buckingham Palace Road, about 5 minutes' walk from Victoria train and Underground stations, and with several local bus stops outside. If you're planning to travel to any UK destinations outside of the London area, it's slower but nearly always cheaper to do it by coach than by train, with fares as low as £1 on some London–Oxford services (although some train companies try to offer lower fares on the same routes).

National Express operates the most extensive UK coach network, with around 1,000 destinations covered, and is also associated with Eurolines international coach services. **Megabus** has especially low fares to many UK destinations, and also discount train offers. **Green Line** runs buses between London and the surrounding counties, and has a service to Luton Airport *(see p369)*.

Arriving by Sea and Tunnel

The **Eurotunnel** shuttle – the other train service using the Channel Tunnel – is a drive-on, drive-off service for cars between Calais and Folkestone, where the Tunnel connects with the M20 motorway to London. There are usually four shuttles per hour, with a journey time of about 35 minutes.

If you prefer to brave the elements, there are still plenty of ferry services between southeast England and Continental ports. Harwich, Essex has ferries from Esbjerg, Denmark with **DFDS Seaways**; and from Hook of Holland, Netherlands with **Stena Line**. Dover is the busiest port, with frequent services from France: from Dunkerque with **DFDS**; from Calais with **P&O Ferries** and **DFDS**; and from Boulogne with **LD Lines**. Newhaven–Dieppe ferries are operated by **LD/Transmanche**.

There are also several routes in the western Channel, which take longer but may leave you better located for western England: to Portsmouth from Caen, Cherbourg, Le Havre, and St-Malo with **Brittany Ferries**, or from Le Havre with LD Lines; to Poole from Cherbourg with Brittany Ferries; or to Poole or Weymouth from St-Malo and the Channel Islands with **Condor Ferries**.

Crossing times to Dover are around 1 hour 15 minutes; in the western Channel it takes more like 5-6 hours, although in summer, fast jetfoils and catamarans cut this to 2–3 hours.

There are also ferry services from Spain: from Santander to Plymouth or Portsmouth with Brittany Ferries; and from Bilbao to Portsmouth with P&O. Crossings take around 24 hours, on comfortable mini cruise ships.

Driving time from Dover or the Channel Tunnel to central London is usually around 2 hours; from Portsmouth, 2–2½ hours. If you bring a car to London, always try to arrange a place to stay with free parking, otherwise this can become extremely expensive.

(see p369)

DIRECTORY

Rail Services

Eurostar
London St. Pancras International.
Tel 08432 186 186.
W eurostar.com

National Rail
Tel 0845 748 4950.
W nationalrail.co.uk

Rail Europe
Tel (800) 622 8600 (USA),
0844 848 4078 (UK).
W raileurope.com

Trainline
Tel 0871 244 1545.
W thetrainline.com

Coach Services

Green Line
Tel 0844 801 7261.
W greenline.co.uk

Megabus
Tel 0900 160 0900.
W megabus.com/uk

National Express
Tel 08717 818 178.
W nationalexpress.com

Tunnel and Ferries

Brittany Ferries
Tel 0871 244 0744.
W brittany-ferries.com

Condor Ferries
Tel 01202 207 216.
W condorferries.co.uk

DFDS Seaways
W dfdsseaways.co.uk

Eurotunnel
Tel 08443-353.535.
W eurotunnel.com

LD Lines/Transmanche Ferries
Tel 0844 576 8836.
W ldlines.co.uk

P&O Ferries
Tel 0871 664 2121.
W poferries.com

Stena Line
Tel 0844 770 7070.
W stenaline.co.uk

Arriving by Air

London's two main airports, Heathrow and Gatwick, are augmented by smaller facilities at Luton, Stansted, and London City *(see pp368–9)*. Check which airport you will land at, and plan your connections from there. All the airports have train or coach (bus) links; Heathrow is also connected to central London by Underground. Because the airports are so far from each other, traveling between them is best avoided. Further details can be found online.

British Airways passenger jet at Heathrow airport

Access to the Underground in the arrivals terminal at Heathrow

Airlines and Fares

Heathrow and Gatwick have long-haul connections with every part of the world, on scores of airlines. The main United States airlines offering scheduled flights to London include **Delta, United, American Airlines,** and **US Airways,** while from Canada there are frequent services with **Air Canada. British Airways** and **Virgin Atlantic** also fly from many North American cities. The flight time from New York is about 6½ hours; from Los Angeles, about 10 hours. The choice of carriers from Australasia and Asia is enormous too: **Qantas, Air New Zealand,** and British Airways may be the obvious first choices, but operators such as **Singapore Airlines** and **Emirates** offer interesting alternatives.

All the main carrier airlines, such as British Airways, Air France, **Iberia,** and **Lufthansa,** offer frequent European connections, mostly to Heathrow or Gatwick, but they now carry less traffic than the low-cost airlines. **Ryanair** has budget flights to all of Europe, Ireland, and the UK, mostly from Stansted, while **easyJet** runs almost as extensive a European and British network from Stansted, Luton, and Gatwick.

Very few airlines now offer reduced prices for children. Low-cost flights can normally

be booked only through each airline's own website. Note that low-cost airlines regularly add "extra" charges on top of the fare – such as one for checked bags. Ryanair, in particular, charges £70 if you cannot download and print your own boarding card and need one issued by ground staff at the airport.

Security

Security is tighter than ever at London airports. Allow at least two hours to check in and get through security before your flight, especially – because of its size – at Heathrow. Allow ample time also (2 hours again) to catch low-cost flights if you are checking a bag, since in the interests of keeping costs down there are not many check-in staff and lines move slowly.

Heathrow (LHR)

Heathrow in west London is one of the world's busiest airports. It has five terminals, so it's important to know which one your flight will arrive at or depart from. Terminals 1, 2, and 3, the oldest, share an Underground station and Heathrow Central rail station; Terminal 4 has its own Underground station; Terminal 5, which opened in 2008, has Underground and rail stations. A free shuttle bus runs between the terminals. Most British Airways flights use Terminal 5; most other long-haul airlines use Terminals 3 or 4. There are shops and other facilities in every terminal.

There are several ways into London from Heathrow. The fastest rail service is the **Heathrow Express,** with trains every 15 minutes from around 5am to 11:30pm daily to Paddington station on the west side of central London. Travel time is about 15 minutes, and trains also stop at Terminal 5. To get to Terminals 1, 2, and 3, take the shuttle bus from Terminal 4. Fares are high, at around £25 one way, £39 round trip (slightly less online). **Heathrow Connect** trains run

Heathrow Terminal 5, used exclusively by British Airways

on the same lines but with several stops, and take 25–30 minutes to reach Paddington. Fares are around £9.50 one way.

The Underground (tube) offers a much cheaper way of getting into London, but is also much slower. Trains run frequently, stopping at all Heathrow terminals from around 5am to midnight Monday to Saturday, 5:50am–11:30pm Sunday. Unlike the Heathrow Express, the tube runs into the center of the city; allow about 45 minutes to get to Leicester Square. As on all London public transportation, it's cheaper with an Oyster Card (see p370); the adult fare from Heathrow into the city center is £5.50.

National Express and other companies run a number of bus routes from Heathrow to Oxford, London, other London airports, and other destinations. The main bus station is at Terminals 1, 2, and 3, but buses also stop at 4 and 5. A taxi to central London costs about £50. Driving time is from 30 minutes to 1 hour. It's worth noting that local minicab companies offer much cheaper rates (see p377).

London City Airport, within sight of the city's Docklands area

London City Airport (LCY)

London City is the closest airport to central London, in the Docklands business area just east of London's financial district (the City). Unlike the low-cost airports, it was created primarily for business travelers, so flights are quite expensive. It offers flights to many European destinations, and a luxury service to New York.

London City has its own station on the Docklands Light Railway (DLR), which connects with the Underground network at Tower Hill and Bank. An Express Shuttle Bus runs every 30 minutes to Canary Wharf, for £7 one way. A taxi to the City costs about £28 and takes 30 minutes; to the West End £40, taking around 45 minutes.

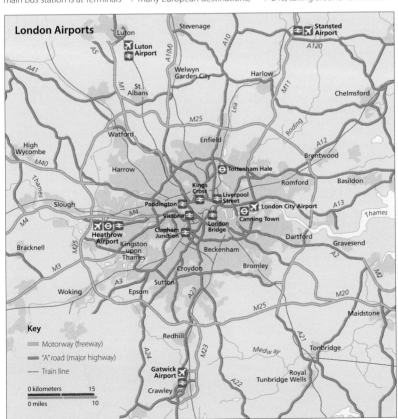

London Airports

Key

▭▭▭ Motorway (freeway)
▬▬▬ "A" road (major highway)
——— Train line

0 kilometers   15
0 miles   10

For additional map symbols *see back flap*

Gatwick (LGW)

Gatwick airport lies due south of central London, and handles long-haul, European, and low-cost flights. There are two terminals – North and South – so as at Heathrow, you need to be clear on which you need. The train station and main bus stops are at the South Terminal, from where there is a free shuttle train to the North. Allow around 20 minutes to transfer between terminals. There are banks, shops, cafés, and other facilities at both.

There is a choice of three train services from Gatwick into London, all from the same station. The **Gatwick Express** is the fastest, with trains every 15 minutes to Victoria Station. It runs from around 4:30am to midnight daily and takes about 30 minutes (a little longer on Sundays), but it isn't cheap; the fare is around £20 one way, £35 round trip. Tickets can be bought online. **First Capital Connect** runs around four trains per hour over the same period to St. Pancras International via several stops including East Croydon and London Bridge. Travel time is about an hour, and a one-way fare around £10. **Southern Railway** has several trains each hour to London Victoria, with a travel time of 30–50 minutes and a one-way fare of around £11.

Entrance to Stansted's spacious modern passenger terminal

National Express and other companies run buses from the South Terminal to Heathrow and many towns in southern England (including central London), and **easyBus** runs frequently from the North and South terminals to Earl's Court/West Brompton in London. Buses are not limited to easyJet passengers, and fares begin at £2. A taxi into central London will set you back around £90, and can take 1–2 hours. As at Heathrow, minicab companies offer better rates to Gatwick.

Stansted (STN)

Around 40 miles northeast of London, Stansted is the airport in southeast England most popular with the low-cost airlines, so it has a huge number of flights to

destinations in every part of Europe.

The rail link into London is the **Stansted Express** train, which runs every 15 minutes from around 6am to 12:30am, with variations on weekends. Trains run to Liverpool Street, on the east side of central London, with a stop at Tottenham Hale (where you can transfer to the Victoria Underground line). Trains from Liverpool Street to Stansted run from approximately 4:40am to 11:30pm daily. The trip takes 45 minutes. Adult fares to Liverpool Street are £23.40 one way, £32.80 round trip (cheaper online). **National Express East Anglia** trains also run roughly once an hour to London Stratford station in East London's Olympic Park, with several stops, taking 1 hour for a fare of about £23.50.

Several bus services run from Stansted to London. National Express runs to Victoria Coach Station (£17.50) and many other destinations around the region, but easyBus is again the cheapest, with tickets to Baker Street Underground station

Gatwick's free monorail service linking the two terminals

Airport	From central London	Average travel time	Average taxi fare
London City	6 miles (10 km)	Tube and DLR: 40 minutes	£28
Heathrow	14 miles (23 km)	Rail: 15 minutes Tube: 45 minutes	£50
Gatwick	28 miles (45 km)	Rail: 30 minutes Bus: 70 minutes	£90
Luton	32 miles (51 km)	Rail: 35 minutes Bus: 70 minutes	£60
Stansted	34 miles (55 km)	Rail: 45 minutes Bus: 75 minutes	£90

from £2. A taxi to central London can take 1 hour 30 minutes and cost £90–100.

Luton (LTN)

Luton Airport lies northwest of London near the M1 motorway, and is used almost exclusively by charter flights and low-cost airlines, especially easyJet. A shuttle bus connects the terminal with Luton Airport Parkway train station (about a 5-minute drive), from around 5am to midnight daily. First Capital Connect has about four trains each hour to London St. Pancras – a trip of around 25–40 minutes for an adult one-way fare of £14. **East Midlands Trains** operate on the same route, and are a little cheaper, at £12. Green Line buses (route 757) run every 15 minutes almost 24 hours a day between the airport and London Victoria Coach station, with adult fares around £10 (see p365); easyBus has frequent services to Victoria via Baker Street, with tickets from £2. National Express runs from Luton to Heathrow, Gatwick, Stansted, and other destinations. A taxi into London will cost around £60, and take about 45 minutes.

Airport Hotels

Given the long check-in times at the main airports, it can be a good idea – or even necessary – to stay nearby the night before departure, especially if you have an early-morning flight. There are a large number of hotels in the vicinity of Heathrow and Gatwick; many of these frequently have discount offers. All of them provide shuttle

Relaxing bar of the popular Sheraton Skyline hotel

buses to the airport terminals – in budget hotels this may cost extra. The **Premier Inn, Travelodge,** and **Holiday Inn** chains have cheap, functional rooms close to the airports. A selection of airport hotels are listed below, but there are many more to choose from.

DIRECTORY

Major Airlines

Air Canada
w aircanada.com

Air New Zealand
w airnewzealand.com

American Airlines
w aa.com

British Airways
w britishairways.com

Delta Airlines
w delta.com

easyJet
w easyjet.com

Emirates
w emirates.com

Iberia
w iberia.com

Lufthansa
w lufthansa.com

Qantas
w qantas.com.au

Ryanair
w ryanair.com

Singapore Airlines
w singaporeair.com

United Airlines
w united.com

US Airways
w usairways.com

Virgin Atlantic
w virgin-atlantic.com

Travel Websites

w bestfares.com
w cheapflights.com
w ebookers.com
w expedia.com
w flights.com
w orbitz.com
w priceline.com
w travelnow.com
w travelocity.com

Airport Information

Gatwick
Tel 0844 892 0322.
w gatwickairport.com

Heathrow
Tel 0844 335 1801.
w heathrowairport.com

London City Airport
Tel 020 7646 0088.
w londoncityairport.com

Luton
Tel 01582 405 100.
w london-luton.co.uk

Stansted
Tel 0844 335 1803.
w stanstedairport.com

Airport Transportation

easyBus
w easybus.co.uk

East Midlands Trains
Tel 08457 125 678.
w eastmidlandstrains.co.uk

First Capital Connect
Tel 0845 026 4700.
w firstcapitalconnect.co.uk

Gatwick Express
Tel 0845 850 1530.
w gatwickexpress.com

Heathrow Connect
Tel 0845 678 6975.
w heathrowconnect.com

Heathrow Express
Tel 0845 600 1515.
w heathrowexpress.com

National Express East Anglia
Tel 0845 600 7245.
w nationalexpress eastanglia.com

Southern Railway
Tel 0845 127 2920.
w southernrailway.com

Stansted Express
Tel 0845 600 7245.
w stanstedexpress.com

Hotels

Holiday Inn London Heathrow Ariel
Tel 0871 423 4901.
w ihg.com

Premier Inn Heathrow (Bath Road)
Tel 0871 527 8508.
w premierinn.com

Sofitel London Gatwick
Tel 01293 567 070.
w sofitel.com

Travelodge Gatwick Airport
Tel 0871 984 6031.
w travelodge.co.uk

GETTING AROUND LONDON

London has one of the busiest and most extensive mass transit systems in Europe; it also has all the problems of overcrowding to match. A program is underway to upgrade the Underground train system (the Tube). Within London and its suburbs, most of the public transportation – the Underground, city buses, overground rail lines, and river buses – are coordinated by Transport for London (TfL), which operates a common ticketing system centered on the pay-as-you-go Oyster Card, which commuters use to "touch in" each time they go on public transportation. Oyster Cards are rapidly replacing paper tickets.

Green Travel

Traveling around London by foot, tube, bus, train, or river bus is more energy-efficient than taking your own vehicle or a taxi. The Congestion Charge helps to discourage driving in the city center (*see p371*). London continues to invest in improved conditions for cyclists, and this can be the fastest way to get around the city – **Transport for London's** website has a cycling information page. Several "green" minicab companies, such as **Gogreencar** and **Climatecars**, use hybrid or alternative-fuel vehicles to reduce their carbon footprint.

Public Transportation

The Underground (subway) – or "Tube", as Londoners call it – is generally the fastest, most convenient way to get around the city. The Docklands business district and some other areas of east London and Greenwich are served by the Docklands Light Railway (DLR), which connects with the tube network principally at Bank, Tower Hill, Canary Wharf, and Stratford. Tube and DLR lines do not run to every part of the city, however; in particular, large parts of south London are reliant on overground rail connections. Bus routes cover every part of London. There are also several riverbus boat services (*see pp62–63*).

Avoid traveling on public transportation during morning and evening "rush hour" – 7–10am and 4–7pm Monday to Friday – if at all possible.

"Heritage" bus

For detailed information on every aspect of transportation in London, check the TfL website, which has an invaluable "Journey Planner" feature. TfL also has several Travel Information Centres. Those at Heathrow and Piccadilly Circus Underground stations and Euston, King's Cross, Liverpool Street, and Victoria train stations are particularly helpful and provide free maps and other information.

Oyster Cards and Travelcards

London's public transportation is relatively expensive compared to that of many European cities, but if you use one of the multi-trip cards available to visitors, you will cut your costs considerably. For tube, DLR, and local train fares, London is divided into six main fare zones radiating out from Zone 1 in the center (on buses, there is a flat fare for each trip, no matter how far you travel). If you aim to pack all your sightseeing into one or two days, the best ticket to get will be a one-day off-peak Travelcard, which gives unlimited travel on all systems after 9:30am on weekdays (or any time on Saturday and Sunday) within your chosen zones for a flat fee (£8.80 for an adult card for Zones 1 and 2,

A London Underground sign outside a station

which covers most of the main sights in London). If you expect to travel more, it will be better to get a pay-as-you-go Oyster Card, which you can charge up with as much credit as you wish. Whenever you use public transportation, you "touch in" with your card on a yellow Oyster Card reader, and the corresponding amount is deducted. On Underground, DLR, and overground trains, you must also remember to "touch out" at the station where you finish your journey, or you will be charged the maximum fare for the line.

Travelcards and Oyster Cards can be bought at tube and local rail stations, Travel Information Centres, and hundreds of small shops that have the TfL "Ticket Stop" sticker in the window. You can also obtain them before arriving in London, on Eurostar, Gatwick Express, or Stansted Express trains, or online, with advance delivery to 63 countries, through the Visit London and TfL websites.

Travel is free on all buses for under-16s; the Underground and DLR are free for under-11s and have reduced fares for 11–15-year-olds. A one-day Travelcard for 11–15s costs only £3.40 for fare zones 1 to 6. Details of all current fares and tickets can be found on www.tfl.gov.uk.

Pre-paid Oyster card being placed on a card reader

A pedestrian "zebra crossing"

Walking

Once you get used to traffic driving on the left, London can be enjoyably explored on foot, but be careful when crossing the road. There are two types of pedestrian crossings in London: striped "zebra" crossings, marked by beacons; and push-button crossings at traffic lights. Traffic should stop if you wait at a zebra crossing, but at push-button crossings, cars will not stop until they have a red light. Look for instructions painted on the street that tell you from which direction you can expect traffic to appear.

Driving in London

For visitors, driving is usually the worst way of getting around town. Traffic moves at an average of 11 mph (18 kmh) for much of the day, parking is scarce and expensive, and in the city center there is the added cost of the Congestion Charge – a £10-a-day fee (pay in advance) for private vehicles entering the central charging zone (roughly: the City, the West End, and Mayfair in the west; and south as far as Elephant & Castle) between 7am and 6pm Monday to Friday. If you are determined to drive, remember to drive on the left.

All the well-known car-rental firms are represented in London. Renting a car in advance through a site such as **Auto Europe**, or as an add-on with your flight, will get the best rates. To drive out of London from the center takes about an hour in any direction; if you want to tour the countryside, it can be less tiring to take a train to a city like Oxford and rent there.

Parking

Parking is prohibited at all times wherever the street is marked with red or there are double yellow lines by the kerb. If there is a single yellow line, parking is normally allowed 6:30pm–8am Monday to Saturday and all day Sunday, but exact hours vary, so always check the signs along each street. Where there is no line at all, parking is free at all times, but this is rare in central London. Note that rental car drivers are still responsible for parking tickets.

Cycling

The TfL "Cycling" page is an invaluable source of information on cycling around the city. Cycle routes – sometimes even separate cycle lanes – are signposted around the city.

Barclays Cycle Hire, London's bike rental program, has 6,000 bikes available at terminals across the city. Visit the website for details of how to access the bikes. The **London Bicycle Tour Company** delivers and picks up bikes to and from your location. With your rented bike you should be given a helmet, a lock, and other accessories.

A cycle path in one of London's parks

Traveling by Underground

The underground system, known as the "tube" to Londoners, has some 270 stations, each identified by the Underground logo. Trains run every day except Christmas Day, from about 5:30am to midnight Monday to Thursday; 5:30am to 1am on Friday and Saturday; and 6:30am to 11:30pm on Sunday. Exact times of first and last trains are posted at stations and on the Transport for London website: www.tfl.gov.uk. The Docklands Light Railway (DLR), with some 40 stations in east and southeast London, connects with the tube and also runs to London City Airport. For schedules and all other information, call 0843-222 1234 or check the TfL website.

London Underground train

Planning your Journey

There are 12 tube lines, all named and color-coded (red for Central, blue for Victoria, and so on), which intersect at various stations. Some lines, like the Jubilee, have a single branch; others, like the Northern, have more than one, so it's important to check the digital boards on the platform and the destination on the front of the train. The Circle Line is a continuous loop around central London but now extends to Hammersmith. Maps of the entire Tube system (see *inside back cover*) are posted at each station. Note that the tube map is topological, not geographical; it isn't to scale, nor can it be relied upon for directions. From it, you can work out where to change lines to travel to any station on the system. All eight of London's main train stations (see p364) have associated Tube stations. Due to the ongoing tube improvement program, normal services are sometimes suspended, usually on weekends. When this happens, replacement buses are provided. Check for line closures before traveling.

How to read the Journey Planner Maps
(see inside back cover)

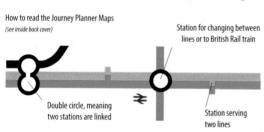

Double circle, meaning two stations are linked

Station for changing between lines or to British Rail train

Station serving two lines

Buying a Ticket

All tube and DLR stations fall within one of six main fare zones (see p370). The zones you travel through determine the cost of your journey. Unless you plan on making very few journeys by tube, it will usually be best to travel with a multi-journey Travelcard or an Oyster Card (see p370). However, you can also buy one-way or round-trip tickets from ticket offices and ticket machines. All Underground and DLR stations have touch-screen machines that give step-by-step instructions in a variety of languages. They accept coins, bills, and credit and debit cards, and you can also use them to refill your credit on an Oyster Card. To check on current fares, select the ticket type you need, choose the station you wish to travel to, and the fare will be displayed on screen.

Tube Architecture

The Underground's reputation for exciting architecture was established in the 1930s. In 1999 the Jubilee Line Extension opened to great acclaim, with six imposing and elegant stations designed by a group of top architects including Will Alsop (North Greenwich), Norman Foster (Canary Wharf), and Matthew Hopkins (Westminster). A similarly light, spacious style has been adopted in the impressive tube, DLR, bus, and mainline train hub at Stratford, which is the gateway to the Olympic Park.

Concourse at Canary Wharf Station, Jubilee Line

Taking a Trip by Underground

1 When you first enter the station, check which line, or lines, you need to take. If you have any difficulty planning your route, ask the clerk at the ticket office for help.

⊖ Journey planner

Feed your ticket into the slot at the front of the machine; retrieve it from the slot at the top.

2 Buy your ticket, Travelcard, or Oyster Card from a ticket office or ticket machine at the station. Keep your ticket; you will need it to exit at your destination. For return trips, you will usually be given one ticket that you must keep for both journeys. Oyster Cards can be refilled for later trips.

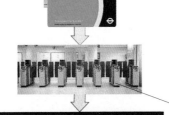
oyster

If you have an Oyster Card, just touch it on the yellow card reader.

The ticket office is near the ticket barriers in most stations.

3 The platforms are on the other side of the ticket barriers. These are easy to use if you follow the instructions above.

Central line →

Central line Westbound platform 5 →

4 Follow the directions to the line on which you need to travel. In some cases this can be a complicated route, but it will be well sign-posted.

5 You will eventually find yourself with a choice of platforms for the line you want. Look at the list of stations if you are not sure which direction to take.

6 All platforms have electronic indicators displaying the final destination of the next two or three trains and how long you will have to wait before they arrive. On lines with branches, they also indicate the route of each train.

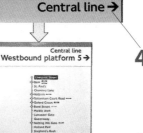
1 HAINAULT via Newbury Park
2 EPPING   5 mins

7 Once you have begun your journey, you can check on your progress using the line chart displayed in every car. On many trains, the name of the next station is announced before you arrive, and as you pull into each station you will see its name posted along the walls.

Way out →
⇌ British Rail
Hammersmith & City →
Metropolitan and Circle lines

On all DLR and some tubes, push a button to open the carriage doors.

8 After leaving the train, look for signs giving directions to exits or to platforms for any connecting lines.

Traveling by Bus and Boat

The red double-decker bus is one of London's most recognizable symbols, but the design of London buses has changed a great deal over the years. The old, classic open-backed Routemaster buses have been withdrawn (with the exception of two "heritage" routes), and in their place there are modern, square-sided double-deckers, single-deckers for less busy routes, and a modernized Routemaster bus allowing passengers to hop on and hop off. Traveling by bus is an enjoyable, easy way to see London, especially in the middle of the day, and much cheaper than going by tube or DLR if you have an Oyster Card. On the minus side, bus journeys can be slow, especially during rush hour (7–10am and 4–7pm Monday to Friday).

drivers will not stop unless they are waved down by a passenger. Destinations are displayed clearly on the front of the bus, and on many buses the next upcoming stop is indicated on electronic information boards, or announced by an automatic voice system. However, if you are unsure which stop you need, ask the driver to alert you, and stay on the lower deck.

Board buses at the front, so that you can touch in your Oyster Card on the yellow Oyster reader by the driver's cab, show your Travelcard, or buy a single ticket. In central London, single tickets cannot be bought on board the bus, but must be bought in advance from ticket machines at the bus stop, and then shown to the driver. Fares are the same for each bus trip no matter how far you travel, at £2.40 for a single ticket or £1.40 with an Oyster Card – so the Oyster saving is considerable. Inspectors often check whether passengers have valid tickets or passes.

Finding the Right Bus

Bus maps showing all the main routes are available free from Travel Information Centres, or can be downloaded from the Visit London and Transport for London websites. All London bus stops have bus route signs displaying the routes that run from that stop, with lists of their main destinations. On streets that are used by several bus routes – notably Oxford Street in the West End – routes are bunched together at different stops near each other, so make sure you find the right one. Stops also have local area maps showing which of the adjacent bus stops, identified by a letter, you need for buses to a particular area. If in doubt, check with the bus driver when boarding.

Using the London Buses

Bus stops are marked with the London bus logo. Some stops are "request" stops, where

Bus Stops

If you are boarding a bus at a yellow stop (below), you must buy a ticket at the adjacent machine before boarding. At some stops, called request stops, the driver will not stop unless asked. If you want to board, raise your arm as the bus approaches the stop; when you want to get off, ring the bell once before your stop.

Useful Bus Routes

Several of London's bus routes are particularly convenient for the capital's main sights and shops. If you arm yourself with an Oyster Card or Travelcard and are in no particular hurry, sightseeing or shopping by bus can be great fun. The cost of a trip on public transportation is far less than any of the charges levied by tour operators, although you won't have the commentary that tour companies give you as you pass sights (*see p354–5*). There are also some sights or areas in London that are either hard to get to by Underground, or can be reached much more directly by bus. Buses run regularly from the center of the city to, for instance, the Albert Hall (*see p207*) and Chelsea (*see pp194–9*).

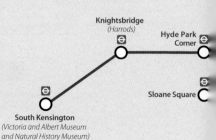

Marble Arch

Knightsbridge
(Harrods)

Hyde Park Corner

Sloane Square

South Kensington
(Victoria and Albert Museum and Natural History Museum)

BUS STOP

Parliament Square

towards
Elephant & Castle

| 12 | 53 | 159 |

| 453 | N155 | N159 |

N381

Buy tickets before
boarding on all routes

Thames Clipper boat on the river heading toward Waterloo Bridge

Night Buses

Some main bus routes run 24 hours a day. Night buses (indicated by the letter "N" added before the route number) also run on many popular routes from 11pm until 6am, generally 3–4 times per hour up to 2–3am, but often only once an hour after that. Many night bus routes originate in or pass through Trafalgar Square, then run out into the suburbs. In central areas they are often very crowded, especially on weekends, but empty out quickly as they move farther out. Plan your journey carefully;

London is so big that even if you board a bus going in the right direction, you can still be a long walk from your accommodations. As always, be aware of your personal security when traveling at night.

Riverboats

Some of London's most spectacular views can only be seen from the Thames River. River trips have also been integrated into London's mass transit system. **Thames Clippers** has a riverbus service with catamarans running every

20 minutes from 6am to 1am daily in both directions, on a route between Waterloo and Woolwich, via the London Eye, Tower Bridge, Greenwich, and other stops at the various river piers. They also operate the **Tate Boat**, a direct boat between the Tate Britain and Tate Modern museums (every 40 minutes in each direction, 10am to 5pm), as well as special services for events at the O2 Arena. Oyster Cards can be used on board, and Travelcard holders get discounted tickets. For details, check with Thames Clippers or www.tfl.gov.uk.

DIRECTORY

Riverboat Services

Tate Boat
Tel 020 7887 8888.
W tate.org.uk/tatetotate

Thames Clippers
Tel 020 7001 2222.
W thamesclippers.com

For more information on river cruises see "Cruise Highlights" on p61.

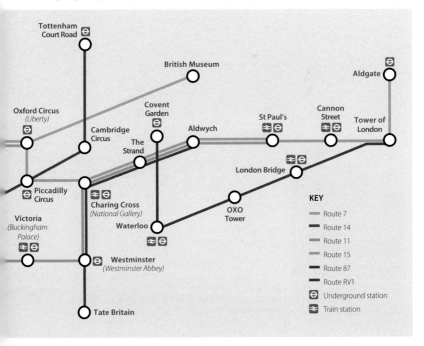

Tottenham Court Road

British Museum

Aldgate

Oxford Circus
(Liberty)

Covent Garden

St Paul's

Cannon Street

Tower of London

Cambridge Circus

Aldwych

The Strand

Piccadilly Circus

London Bridge

Charing Cross
(National Gallery)

OXO Tower

Victoria
(Buckingham Palace)

Waterloo

Westminster
(Westminster Abbey)

Tate Britain

KEY

Route 7
Route 14
Route 11
Route 15
Route 87
Route RV1
Underground station
Train station

Traveling by Train

London's local and suburban train lines (also known as the "overground") are used by hundreds of thousands of commuters every day. For visitors, train services are most useful for trips to the outskirts of London and areas of the city without nearby Underground connections (especially in south London). If you are planning to travel outside of the capital, always try to buy train tickets in advance, and check to see what alternative fares are available; for more on train tickets, see p364.

Useful Routes

Two of the most popular train lines for visitors to London are those from Charing Cross (via London Bridge) and, on weekdays, Cannon Street to Greenwich (see pp239–45); and Waterloo to Hampton Court (see pp256–9). A First Capital Connect line runs right through London, north to south, from Luton via St. Pancras International to Gatwick. The North London line makes a loop around north London all the way from the East End to Kew (see pp262–3) and Richmond.

Using the Trains

London has eight main train termini serving different parts of Britain. Each terminus is also the starting point for local and suburban lines that cover the whole of southeast England. There are over a hundred smaller London stations. Services travel overground and vary between trains that stop at every station, faster suburban trains, and express trains that run nonstop to major destinations. Some train doors will open automatically, others at the touch of a button.

Train Tickets

Travelcards and Oyster Cards are valid on nearly all overground train services that fall entirely within the London area (defined as Transport for London fare zones 1–6, plus three more suburban zones), so using one or the other will generally be much more economical, and a lot faster, than buying individual tickets. Be aware, though, that on most overground trains, peak travel times include the evening rush hour (4–7pm Monday–Friday) as well as the morning one (before 9:30am), so with an Oyster card you will be charged more during these times. Many small stations do not have staffed ticket counters, just machines.

Round-trip train tickets

Day Trips

Southern England has a lot to offer visitors besides London. By train or by bus (see p365), getting out of the city is fast and easy. For details of sights, contact Visit Britain (www.visitbritain.com; 020 8846 9000). National Rail (0845 748 4950) has details of all train services.

Boating on the Thames River at Windsor Castle

Audley End
Village with a stunning Jacobean mansion nearby.
🚆 from Liverpool Street.
40 miles (64 km); 1 hr.

Bath
Beautiful Georgian city, with Roman baths.
🚆 from Paddington.
107 miles (172 km); 1 hr 25 mins.

Brighton
Lively and attractive seaside resort. See the Royal Pavilion.
🚆 from Victoria or London Bridge.
53 miles (85 km); 1 hr.

Cambridge
University city with fine art gallery and ancient colleges.
🚆 from Liverpool Street or King's Cross.
54 miles (86 km); 1 hr.

Canterbury
Its cathedral is one of England's oldest and greatest sights.
🚆 from Victoria.
62 miles (100 km); 1 hr 25 mins.

Hatfield House
Elizabethan palace with remarkable contents.
🚆 from King's Cross or Moorgate to Hatfield station.
21 miles (33 km); 20 mins.

Oxford
Like Cambridge, famous for its ancient university.
🚆 from Paddington.
56 miles (90 km); 1 hr.

St. Albans
Cathedral and Roman theater.
🚆 from King's Cross or Moorgate.
25 miles (40 km); 30 mins.

Salisbury
Famous for its cathedral, and close to Stonehenge.
🚆 from Waterloo.
84 miles (135 km); 1 hr 40 mins.

Windsor
Riverside town with Britain's grandest royal castle.
🚆 from Paddington, change Slough.
20 miles (32 km); approx. 30 mins.

Traveling by Taxi

London's black cabs are as much of an institution as its red buses. Black cabs (some of which, it should be pointed out, are not actually black – you will often see blue, green, red, or even white cabs) are the only cabs licensed to pick up passengers who hail a taxi on the street, and their drivers have to take a stringent test on their knowledge of London and its traffic routes before they are awarded a license. Minicabs, which by law must be reserved in advance, not hailed, are a cheaper alternative for specific trips.

London taxi stand

Finding a Cab

Licensed London taxis, or "black cabs", are large, distinctive vehicles – of which there are now several models – whose yellow "Taxi" sign is lit up whenever the taxi is free. You can hail them on the street, call for them, or find them at taxi stands, especially at airports, main train stations, and major hotels. Raise your arm and wave purposefully. If a cab stops, it must take you anywhere within a radius of 6 miles (9.6 km), as long as it is in the Metropolitan

Police district, which includes most of the Greater London area and Heathrow Airport.

Taxi Fares

All black cabs have meters that start ticking at around £2.20 as soon as the driver agrees to take you. The fare then increases by the minute, or for each 340 yd (311 m) traveled. There are also three fare time bands: the cheapest is 6am–8pm Monday–Friday; the next most expensive, 8–10pm Monday–Friday and 6–10pm Saturday–Sunday; the most expensive, 10pm–6am nightly. The meter must be clearly visible in the vehicle. It is customary to tip taxi and minicab drivers. If you lose anything in a licensed taxi, contact Transport for London's lost property office (see p359). You will need the driver's cab license number, displayed in the back of the taxi.

Minicabs

Licensed minicabs are badged with a blue-and-white Transport for London sticker, usually on the back window. Do not use the unlicensed cabs that sometimes cruise for business in the street. Transport for London's Cabwise service is a good way of finding a safe cab: text "CAB" to 60835 and you will be sent phone numbers for one black cab office and two reliable minicab companies in the area. If your cell phone is international, text your location (street name and postal district) to 00-44-7797 800 000 to access the same service (international charges will apply).

DIRECTORY

Complaints (Transport for London)
Tel 0845 300 7000.
W tfl.gov.uk

Computer Cabs
Tel 020 7908 0271.
W computercab.co.uk

Dial-a-Minicab
Tel 0800 019 6768.
W dialaminicab.com

Lady Minicabs (women-only drivers)
Tel 020 7272 3300.
W ladyminicabs.co.uk

Radio Taxis
Tel 020 7272 0272.
W radiotaxis.co.uk

The light, when lit, shows the cab is available.

The meter displays your fare as it increases, plus surcharges for extra passengers, luggage, or late-night travel. Fares are the same in all licensed black cabs.

Fare   Surcharges

Licensed Taxi Cabs

London's cabs are a safe way of traveling around the city. They can carry a maximum of five passengers, are all accessible for wheelchair users, and have ample luggage space.

STREET FINDER

The map references given with all sights, hotels, restaurants, shops, and entertainment venues described in this book refer to the maps in this section only *(see* How Map References Work *opposite)*. A complete index of street names and all the places of interest marked on the maps can be found on the following pages.

The key map shows the area of London covered by the Street Finder, with the postal codes of all the various districts. The maps include the sightseeing areas (which are color-coded), as well as all of central London with all the districts important for hotels, restaurants, pubs, and entertainment venues.

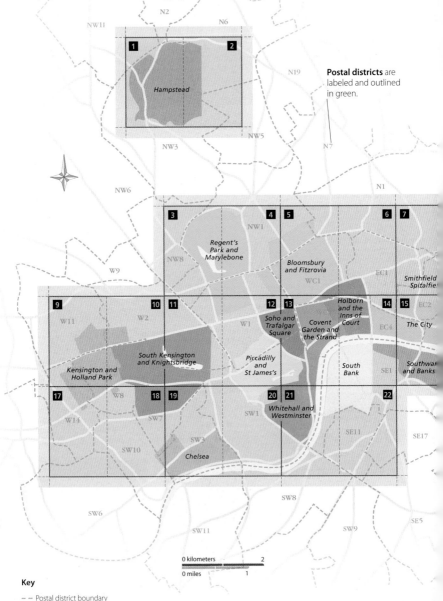

Postal districts are labeled and outlined in green.

Key

– – Postal district boundary

How the Map References Work

The first number tells you which *Street Finder* map to turn to.

❷ Wesley's Chapel–Leysian Mission

49 City Rd EC1. **Map** 7. B4.
Tel 020 7253 2262. 🚇 Old St.
House **Open** 10am–4pm Mon–Sat,
12:30–1:45pm Sun. & not house. ⛪
9:45am (not 1st Sun of month), 11am
Sun, 12:45pm Thu. 🎫 groups book
ahead. 🎥 🌐 **wesleyschapel.org**

The letter and number give
the grid reference. Letters go
across the map's top and
bottom, numbers on its sides.

The map continues
on map 15 of the
Street Finder.

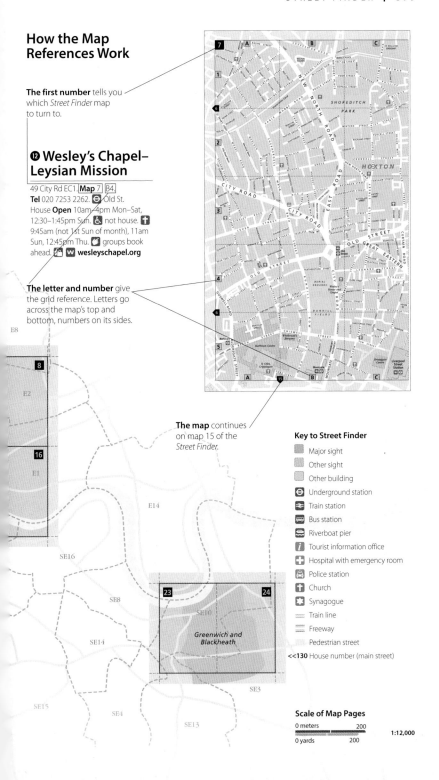

Key to Street Finder

- 🟫 Major sight
- 🟫 Other sight
- 🟫 Other building
- 🚇 Underground station
- 🚆 Train station
- 🚌 Bus station
- 🚢 Riverboat pier
- ℹ️ Tourist information office
- ➕ Hospital with emergency room
- 🏛 Police station
- ⛪ Church
- ✡️ Synagogue
- ═══ Train line
- ▬▬▬ Freeway
- ▦▦▦ Pedestrian street
- **<<130** House number (main street)

Scale of Map Pages

0 meters ——— 200
0 yards ——— 200

1:12,000

Street Finder Index

Each place name is followed by its postal district number and then by its Street Finder reference

Each place name is followed by its postal district number and then by its Street Finder reference

Each place name is followed by its postal district number and then by its Street Finder reference

Each place name is followed by its postal district number and then by its Street Finder reference

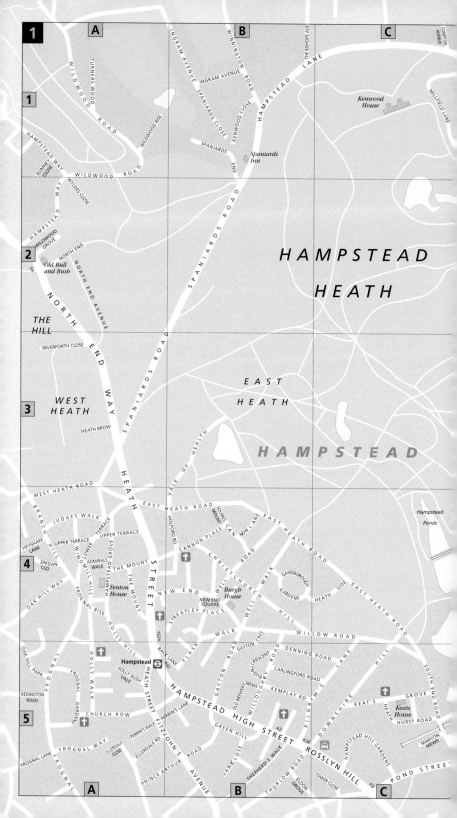

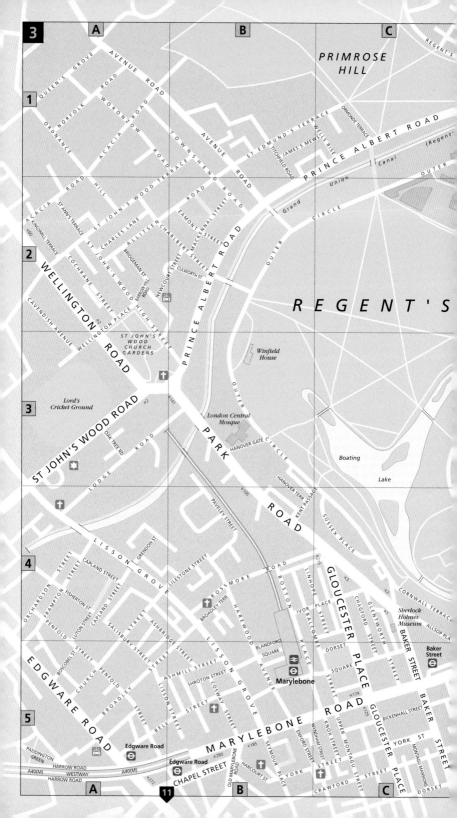

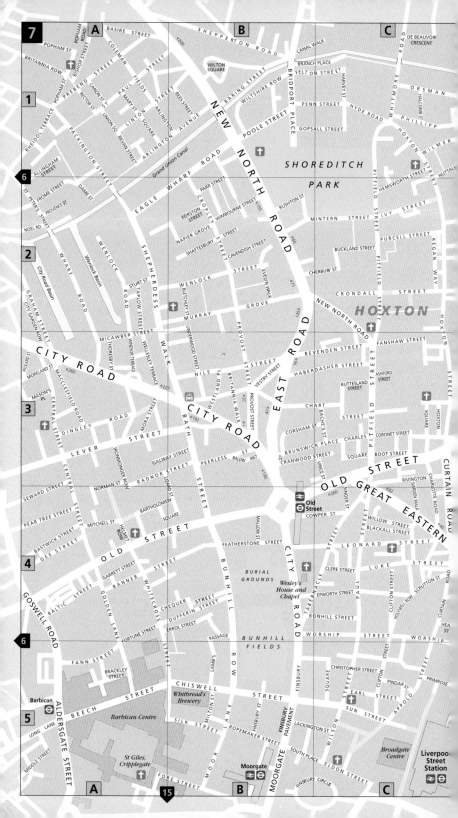

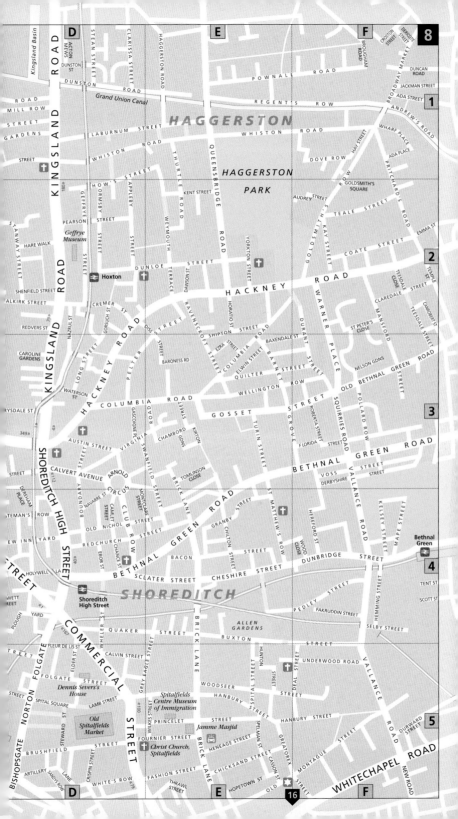

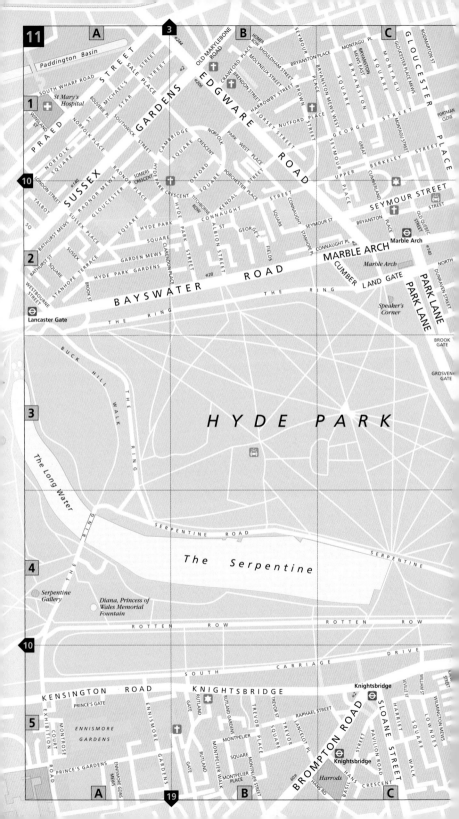

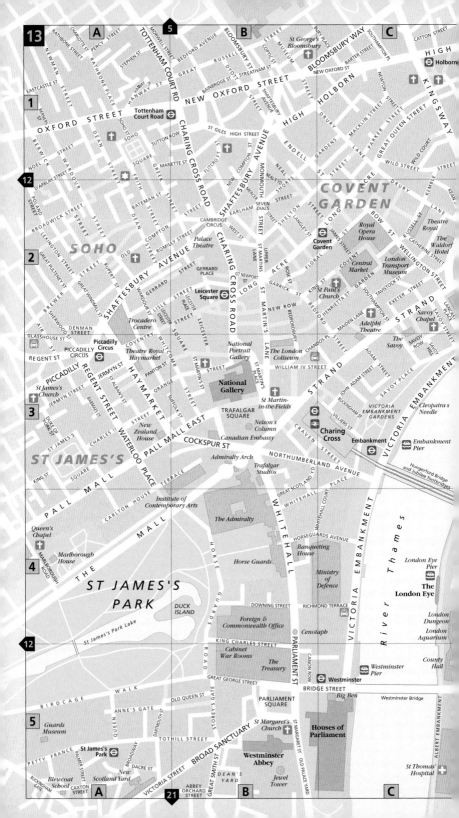

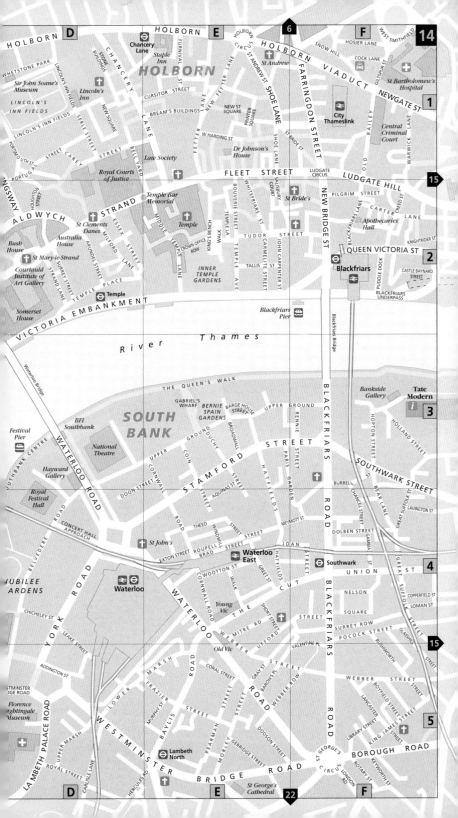

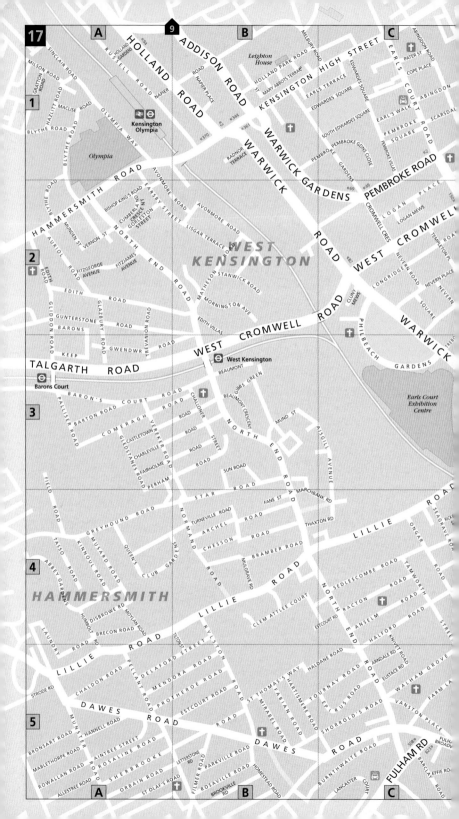

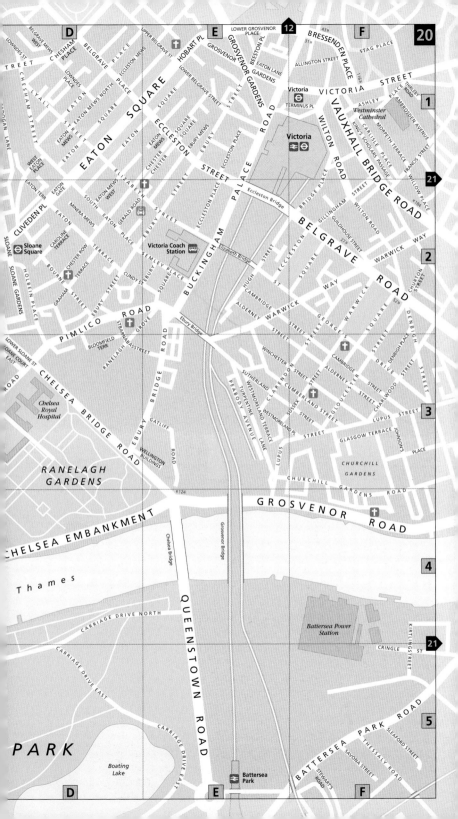

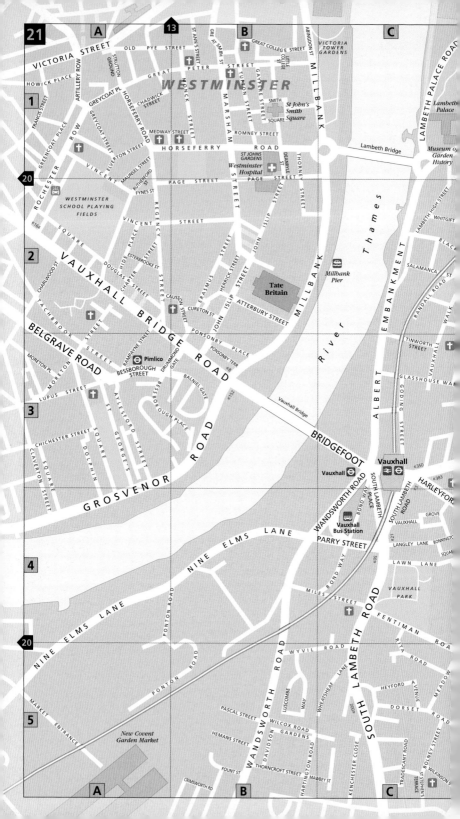

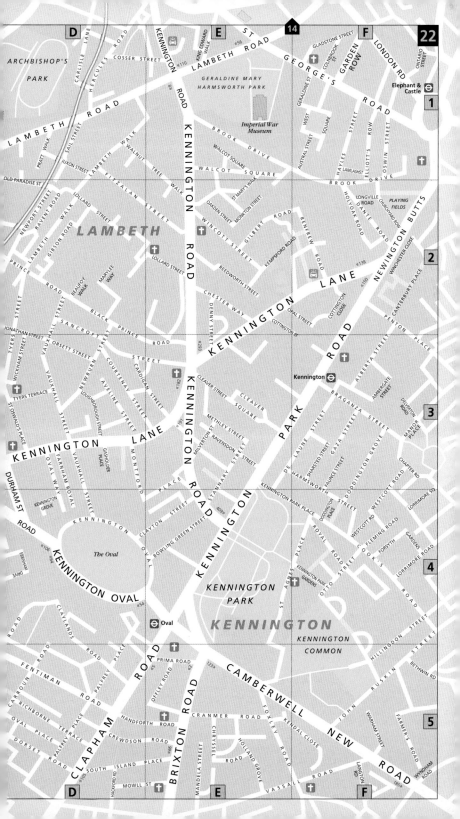

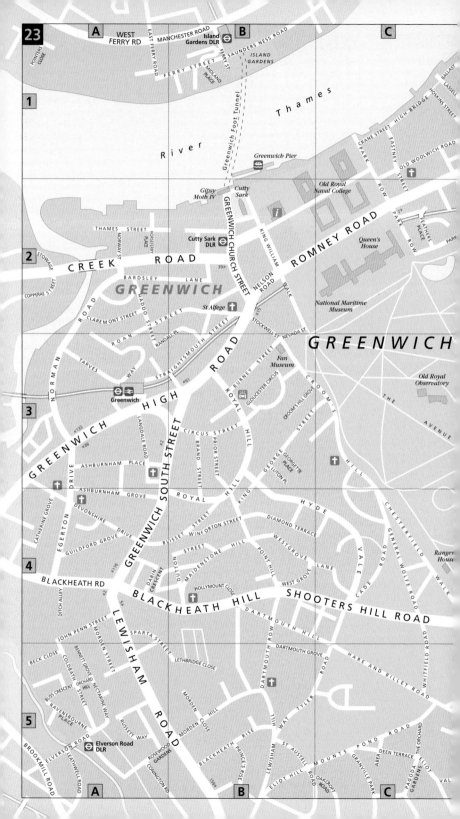

General Index

Acknowledgments

Dorling Kindersley would like to thank the following people whose help and assistance contributed to the preparation of this book.

Main Contributor

Michael Leapman was born in London in 1938 and has been a journalist since he was 20. He has worked for most British national newspapers and writes about travel and other subjects for several publications, among them *The Independent, Independent on Sunday, The Economist,* and *Country Life.* He has written ten books, including *London's River* (1991) and the award-winning *Companion Guide to New York* (1983, revised 1991). In 1989 he edited the acclaimed *Book of London.*

Contributors

James Aufenast, Yvonne Deutch, Guy Dimond, George Foster, Iain Gale, Fiona Holman, Phil Harriss, Lindsay Hunt, Christopher Middleton, Steven Parissien, Christopher Pick, Bazyli Solowij, Matthew Tanner, Mark Wareham, Jude Welton, Ian Wisniewski. Dorling Kindersley wishes to thank the following editors and researchers at Webster's International Publishers: Sandy Carr, Matthew Barrell, Siobhan Bremner, Serena Cross, Annie Galpin, Miriam Lloyd, Ava-Lee Tanner.

Additional Photography

Max Alexander, Peter Anderson, Stephen Bere, June Buck, Peter Chadwick, Michael Dent, Philip Dowell, Mike Dunning, Philip Enticknap, Andreas Einsiedel, Rhiannon Furbear, Steve Gorton, Christi Graham, Alison Harris, Peter Hayman, Stephen Hayward, Roger Hilton, Sean Hunter, Ed Ironside, Colin Keates, Dave King, Bob Langrish, Neil Lukas, Neil Mersh, Nick Nichols, Sofía Nieto, Robert O'Dea, Ian O'Leary, Vincent Oliver, John Parker, Tim Ridley, Ellen Root, Rough Guides/Viktor Borg, Rough Guides/Roger Norum, Rough Guides/ Suzanne Porter, Rough Guides/Natascha Sturny, Rough Guides/Mark Thomas, Kim Sayer, Chris Stevens, James Stevenson, James Strachan, Doug Traverso, David Ward, Mathew Ward, Steven Wooster, Nick Wright.

Additional Illustrations

Ann Child, Gary Cross, Tim Hayward, Arghya Jyoti Hore, Fiona M Macpherson, Janos Marffy, David More, Chris D Orr, Richard Phipps, Rockit Design, Michelle Ross, John Woodcock.

Cartography

Andrew Heritage, James Mills-Hicks, Chez Picthall, John Plumer (DK Cartography). Advanced Illustration (Cheshire), Contour Publishing (Derby), Euromap Ltd (Berkshire). Street Finder maps: ERA Maptec Ltd (Dublin) adapted with permission from original survey and mapping from Shobunsha (Japan).

Cartographic Research

James Anderson, Roger Bullen, Tony Chambers, Ruth Duxbury, Jason Gough, Ailsa Heritage, Jayne Parsons, Donna Rispoli, Jill Tinsley, Andrew Thompson, Iorwerth Watkins.

Design and Editorial

Managing Editor Douglas Amrine
Managing Art Editor Geoff Manders
Senior Editor Georgina Matthews
Series Design Consultant David Lamb
Art Director Anne-Marie Bulat
Production Controller Hilary Stephens
Picture Research Ellen Root, Rhiannon Furbear, Susie Peachey
DTP Editor Siri Lowe
Revisions Team Keith Addison, Emma Anacootee, Elizabeth Atherton, Sam Atkinson, Lydia Baillie, Chris Barstow, Oliver Bennett, Kate Berens, Julie Bowles, Chloe Carleton, Michelle Clark, Carey Combe, Vanessa Courtier, Lorna Damms, Hannah Dolan, Jessica Doyle, Caroline Elliker, Nicola Erdpresser, Jane Ewart, Simon Farbrother, Gadi Farfour, Fay Franklin, Leonie Glass, Simon Hall, Marcus Hardy, Kaberi Hazarika, Christine Heilman, Sasha Heseltine, Paul Hines, Phil Hunt, Stephanie Jackson, Gail Jones, Laura Jones, Nancy Jones, Bharti Karakoti, Stephen Knowlden, Priya Kukadia, Esther Labi, Maite Lantaron, Michelle de Larrabeiti, Chris Lascelles, Jude Ledger, Jeanette Leung, Carly Madden, Hayley Maher, Ferdie McDonald, Alison McGill, Caroline Mead, Jane Middleton, Rebecca Milner, Sonal Modha, Fiona Morgan, Claire Naylor, George Nimmo, Catherine Palmi, Louise Parsons, Marianne Petrou, Andrea Powell, Leigh Priest, Rada Radojicic, Mani Ramaswamy, Marisa Renzullo, Erin Richards, Nick Rider, Ellen Root, Liz Rowe, Simon Ryder, Tracy Smith, Sadie Smith, Susannah Steel, Kathryn Steve, Anna Streiffert, Rachel Symons, Andrew Szudek, Hugh Thompson, Karen Villabona, Diana Vowles, Matthew Walder, Andy Wilkinson, Sophie Wright, Karen Villabona.

Special Assistance

Christine Brandt at Kew Gardens, Sheila Brown at The Bank of England, John Cattermole at London Buses Northern, the DK picture department, especially Jenny Rayner, Pippa Grimes at the V&A, Emma Healy at the V&A Museum of Childhood, Alan Hills at the British Museum, Emma Hutton and Cooling Brown Partnership, Gavin Morgan at the Museum of London, Clare Murphy at Historic Royal Palaces, Ali Naqei at the Science Museum, Patrizio Semproni, Caroline Shaw at the Natural History Museum, Gary Smith at National Rail, Monica Thurnauer at Tate, Simon Wilson at Tate, Alastair Wardle.

Photographic Reference

The London Aerial Photo Library, and P and P F James.

Photography Permissions

Dorling Kindersley would like to thank all the museums, galleries, churches and other sights that allowed us to photograph at their establishments.

Picture Credits

a = above; b = below/bottom; c = centre; f = far; l = left; r = right; t = top.

Works of art have been reproduced with the permission of the following copyright holders:
Three Studies for Figures at the Base of the Crucifixion, (1944, detail), Francis Bacon © Estate of Francis Bacon/DACS, London 2011 84cl; *Untitled* (1964) © Larry Bell, Larry Bell Studio Annex / TAOS 233 Ranchitos Road, Taos, New Mexico, United States 183tc; *Fish* 1926, Constantin Brancusi © ADAGP, Paris and DACS, London 2008 181b; *From the Freud Museum*, (1991–96) © Susan Hiller 182cr; Bust of *Lawrence of Arabia* © The Family of Eric H. Kennington, RA 153bl; *Self-Portait with Knickers* Sarah Lucas 2000 Copyright the artist, courtesy Sadie Coles HQ, London; *Quattro Stagioni* 1993–4, © Cy Twombly 181crb.

The Publishers are grateful to the following individuals, companies and picture libraries for permission to reproduce their photographs:

123RF.com: William Perugini 265cr; **41 Hotel:** 281tr. **Alamy Images:** Mike Booth 156cla; Paul Brown 58bc; Paul Carstairs 60br; Construction Photography 222; Martyn Goddard 359tl; Scott Hortop Travel 225crb; Richard Green 125br; lynn hilton 162; Eric Nathan 138tl; 356tl; Picturebank 167br; Maurice Savage 257br; Tribaleye Images/J Marshall 180cla; SuperStock 108c; Steve Vidler 72tr; **The Albermarle Connection:** 93tr; L'ANIMA RESTAURANT: 299tr; **Arcaid:** Richard Bryant, Architect Foster and Partners 126t; Richard Bryant 251cr; **Arcblue:** Peter Durant 191clb; **The Art Archive:** 23bl, 30cla, 30bc, 31bl, 32br, 32clb, 33cra, 37tc, 37crb; British Library, London 22crb; Imperial War Museum, London 34bc; Museum of London 19b, 31br, 32bl; Science Museum, London 31crb; Stoke Museum Staffordshire Polytechnic 27bl, 29crb, 37bc; Victoria and Albert Museum, London 24clb, 25bc, 29tr; **AWL Images:** Rex Butcher 186; **Axiom:** James Morris 166tl.
Governor and Company of the Bank of England: 147tc; Bibendum Restaurant Ltd: 289br; **Bridgeman Art Library, London:** 25t; British Library, London 18, 23ca, (detail) 25br, 28cb, (detail) 36c, 36bl; © Coram in the care of the Foundling Museum 131tc; Courtesy of the Institute of Directors, London 33ca; Guildhall Library, Corporation of London 28br, 78cl; ML Holmes Jamestown – Yorktown Educational Trust, VA (detail) 21bc; Master and Fellows, Magdalene College, Cambridge (detail) 27clb; Marylebone Cricket Club, London 248c; William Morris Gallery, Walthamstow 23tl, 251bc; Museum of London 26–7; O'Shea Gallery, London (detail) 26crb; Royal Holloway & Bedford New College 159bc; Russell Cotes Art Gallery and Museum, Bournemouth 40tr; Thyssen-Bornemisza Collection, Lugano Casta 259bl; Westminster Abbey, London (detail) 36bc; White House, Bond Street, London 32c. **British Airways:** Adrian Meredith Photography: 366cla; reproduced with permission of the British Library Board: 131br; © **The British Museum:** 20ca, 21ca, 42tr, 126–7 all pics except 126t, 128–9 all pics; **Brittany Ferries:** 365tl; **BT Group plc:** 362c. **Buen Ayre Restaurant:** 301br.

Camera Press: London: Cecil Beaton 81tl; Charles Dickens Museum: 131c; **Charlotte Street Hotel:** 280bl, 284bc; **Chez Bruce:** 302bl; **The Clerkenwell Kitchen:** 298tc; **Clos Maggiore:** 292bl; **Collections:** Oliver Benn 62br; Philip Craven 262cla; Julie Hamilton 232tr; John Miller 165bl; Liz Stares 263bl; **Colorific!:** Steve Benbow 57tl; **Conran Restaurants:** 314bc; **Corbis:** 88; Bettmann 6–7; Bruce Burkhardt 291c; Sarah J Duncan 130clb; 97tc; Jason Hawkes 68–69; Angelo Hornak 63c, 185br; JAI/Alan Copson 38, 171bl, 185tl; London Aerial Photo Library 191bl, 191cla; Kim Sayer 10bl; Patrick Ward 63tl; **Courtesy of the Corporation of London:** 57c, 148tr; **Courtauld Institute, London:** 43br, 119bl; **Cutty Sark Trust:** 240cla. **Copyright Dean and Chapter of Westminster:** 80bl, 81br; **Dewynters Ltd.:** David Crosswaite 115cra; **Dr Johnson's House:** **Dorling Kindersley:** Jamie Marshall 76tl; The Science Museum, London 202bc; **Dreamstime.com:** Basphoto 261tr; Beaucroft 193tr; Lowerkase 64cla; **Courtesy of the Governors and the Directors Dulwich Picture Gallery:** 45tr, 252bl.
E&O, Ricker Restaurants: 296tc; **Francis Edwards:** 315bl; **English Heritage:** 254cr, 260b; Jonathon Bailey 243bl; **English Life Publications Ltd:** 255br; **Mary Evans Picture Library:** 20bl, 20bc, 21bl, 21br, 24bl, 26bl, 29bc, 29br, 31tl, 31ca, 31bc, 34bl, 36br, 37tl, 37clb, 37bl, 37br, 41bl, 74bc, 74clb, 92b, 114bl, 116bl, 137tl, 141tl, 161tc, 179cl, 207br, 218tr, 228br. **Courtesy of Fan Museum:** Helene Alexander Collection 245b; **Fleet River Bakery Rooms:** 287br; **Fotolia:** Balliolmin 112; **Freud Museum, London:** 248t.
Gore Hotel, London: 281bl; **The Goring Hotel, London:** 282tl; **Geffrye Museum, London:** 250tl; **Getty Images:** 35br; Gregory Bajor 246; Walter Bibikow 122; Miguel Carminati 70; Alan Copson 352–3; Flickr/Richard Newstead 2–3; Peter Macdiarmid 183br; Eric Nathan 144; SuperStock 109br; **Green Tourism Business Scheme:** 357tr; **Greenwich inc:** 240bl; **greenwichmarket.net:** 240clb. **Hakkasan Mayfair:** 295bc; **Robert Harding Picture Library:** 35cra, 44cra, 54cla, 60cr, 244tr, 335tr, 359cl, 376bl; Philip Craven 210t; Nigel Francis 368tr; Sylvain Gradadam 291tl; Brian Hawkes 25cb; Michael Jenner 25cra, 229tr; Nick Wood 65bl; **Harrods:** (printed by kind permission of Mohamed al Fayed): 312bl; **Hayes-Davidson (computer generated images):** 176clb; **Hayward Gallery:** Richard Haughton 275tl; Jonty Wilde 190tl; **Reproduced with permission of Her Majesty's Stationery Office (Crown Copyright):** 158 all pics; **John Heseltine:** 53tr, 65br, 130b; **Friends of Highgate Cemetery:** 248b; **Historic Royal Palaces (Crown Copyright):** 5ca, 5tr, 7t, 39c, 156tr, 157clb, 256–7 all except 256br and 257br, 258–9 all except 259bl; **The Hulton Getty:** 28bl, 130tl, 234tl. **The Image Bank, London:** Gio Barto 57b; Derek Berwin 35tl; Romilly Lockyer 17tl, 17br, 74cla; Leo Mason 58cr; Terry Williams 141bl; **Inamo Restaurant:** 293tr; **iStockphoto.com:** Alan Crawford 366br; peterspiro 371br. Peter Jackson Collection: 28–9; **Jewish Museum, London:** 249tl. **The Laughing Gravy:** 300br; **Leon Restaurants:** 288cla; **Leighton House:** 218bl; **Little Angel Marionette Theatre:** 351bl; **London Ambulance Service:** Tim Saunders 359cla; **London Aquarium:** 11tr, 190cr; **London Bridge**

Hotel: 281tl; London City Airport: 367tr; London Palladium: 105br; London Transport Museum: 32cla, Madame Tussauds: 224cla, 226t; Mansell Collection: 23br, 24cl, 24br, 25bl, 26cl, 26clb, 27br, 31cla; Rob Moore: 117tr; Museum of London: 17crb, 20clb, 21tc, 21crb, 22tl, 25crb, 43tc, 165crb, 168–9; Reproduced by courtesy of the Trustees, The National Gallery, London: (detail) 39tc, 106–7 all except 106t, 108tr, 108b, 109ca, 109bl; National Portrait Gallery, London: 4t, 43tl, 103cra, 104br; National Postal Museum, London: 30bl; By permission of the Keeper of the National Railway Museum, York: 32–3; National Trust Photographic Library: Wendy Aldiss 27cra; John Bethell 254tl, 255tr; Michael Boys 40br; Natural History Museum, London: 204tr, 205crb; John Downs 16clb, 205tc, 205br; Derek Adams 204b, 204cl; New Shakespeare Theatre co: 334clb; Ottolenghi: 277tc, 302tl; OXO Tower Restaurant/Harvey Nichols: 300tr.
PA Photos Ltd: 35crb; Palace Theatre Archive:110tc; Parliamentary Copyright House of Lords 2012: Photography by Chris Moyse 75crb; Pictor International, London: 62cl, 176br; Pictures Colour Library: 56br; Pippa Pop-ins Children's Nursery, London: 349br; Pitzhanger Manor Museum: 260c; Popperfoto: 33tl, 33crb, 34tl, 34tr, 34cl, 37tr, 41br; Post House Heathrow: Tim Young 369tr; La Poule au Pot: 297bl; Press Association Ltd: 33bl, 33br; Public Record Office (Crown Copyright): 22b.
Bill Rafferty: 334cb; Rainforest Cafe: 349cl; RBS Group: 360bl, 360cb; Rex Features Ltd: 55tl; Andrew Laenen 56crb; Jonathon Player 290cla; The Ritz, London: 93bl; The River Cafe: 303bl; Royal Academy of Arts, London: 92tr; The Board of Trustees of The Royal Armouries: 43tr, 159t, 159br; Trustees of the Royal Botanic Gardens, Kew: Andrew McRob 50cl, 262–3 all pics except 262cla, 263bl; The Royal Collection © 2013 Her Majesty Queen Elizabeth II: 1c, 8–9, 55bl, 95tr, 96tr, 96cla, 96ca, 97bl, 97br, 98tr, 256br; Derry Moore 97cra; Royal College of Music, London: 206c.
Image Courtesy of the Saatchi Gallery, London: Matthew Booth 289tl; St Paul's Cathedral: Sampson Lloyd 150cb, 152cla, 153tr; Salt Yard: 298br; Sam's Brasserie: 303tr; The Savoy Group: 118cr; Science Museum,

London: 208–9 all pics; Society of London Theatre/tkts: 335br; Somerset House: Peter Durant/arcblue.com 119tr; Spencer House Ltd: 90bl; Southbank Press Office: 188clb; Stephen Cummiskey 188cla; Graeme Duddridge 274cla; STA Travel Group: 356bc; Superstock: Loop Images/ Tom Hanslien 200 , /Alex Hare 174, /Ricky Leaver 230, 238; Londonstills.com 264; Nomad 194; Prisma 216; Travelshots 278-79; Syndication International: 39tr, 54clb, 55crb, 60bl, 61c; Library of Congress; 29bl.
Tate London 2001: 84–5 all pics, 86 all pics, 87br, 180–81, 182–3, 275br. Transport for London: 355bc, 370br, 372tr, 372–73 all maps and tickets, 374bl, 375tl; Travel Pictures: Stuart Black 100; Courtesy of the Board of Trustees of The Victoria and Albert Museum: 39br, 42br; 212–13 all pics; purchased with the assistance of the NACF and the Goldsmith's Company 213cra; 214–15 all pics, 350tc; View Pictures: Dennis Gilbert 372br. W Hotel London: 282br, 285tl; By kind permission of the trustees of The Wallace Collection, London: 42cla, 228cl; Philip Way Photography: 66clb, 152bl, 179br; Courtesy of the Trustees of the Wedgwood Museum, Barlaston, Stoke-on-Trent, Staffs, England: 30br; Vivienne Westwood: Patrick Fetherstonhaugh 35bl; The Wimbledon Lawn Tennis Museum: Micky White 253tr; The Wolseley: 294tl; Photo © Woodmansterne: Jeremy Marks 39tl, 151cra; Youth Hostel Association: 283tc.
Zefa: 54br, 334cl; Bob Croxford 59c; Clive Sawyer 59br.

Front Endpaper: Alamy: Construction Photography Ltr; lynn hilton Rcra; AWL Images: Rex Butcher Rbr; Corbis: Rbl; Fotolia: Balliolman Rtr; Getty Images: Walter Bibikow Rtl; Miguel Carminati Rfbl; Eric Nathan Rcrb; Superstock: age fotostock/Charles Bowman Ltc; Loop Images/Tom Hanslien Lbl, /Alex Hare Rfbr, /Ricky Leaver Ltl; Nomad Lbc; Prisma Lclb; Travel Pictures: Stuart Black Rftl.

Jacket: Front main and Spine top –
AWL Images: Alan Copson
Map Cover – AWL Images: Alan Copson
All other images © Dorling Kindersley
For further information see www.DKimages.com

Special Editions of DK Travel Guides

DK Travel Guides can be purchased in bulk quantities at discounted prices for use in promotions or as premiums. We are also able to offer special editions and personalized jackets, corporate imprints, and excerpts from all of our books, tailored specifically to meet your own needs.

To find out more, please contact:
in the United States SpecialSales@dk.com
in the UK travelspecialsales@uk.dk.com
in Canada DK Special Sales at general@tourmaline.ca
in Australia business.development@pearson.com.au

The London Underground

Legend:

- Bakerloo
- Central
- Circle
- District
- District open weekends, public holidays and some Olympia events
- Hammersmith & City
- Jubilee
- Metropolitan
- Northern
- Piccadilly
- Victoria
- Waterloo & City
- DLR
- London Overground
- Emirates Air Line

- ○ Interchange stations
- ♿ Step-free access from street to train
- ♿ Step-free access from street to platform
- ≷ National Rail
- ⛴ Riverboat services
- ▭ Tramlink
- ✈ Airport
- Emirates Air Line

MAYOR OF LONDON

tfl.gov.uk

24 hour travel information
0343 222 1234*

*Service and network charges may apply. See tfl.gov.uk/terms for details.

© Transport for London

Reg. user No. 13/2560/P

Upgrade work may affect your trip; ple